DRAWING POWER

WOMEN'S STORIES OF SEXUAL VIOLENCE, HARASSMENT, AND SURVIVAL

**A COMICS ANTHOLOGY
EDITED BY DIANE NOOMIN**

INTRODUCTION BY ROXANE GAY

ABRAMS COMICARTS • NEW YORK

CONTRIBUTOR CREDITS

All text and illustrations are copyright © their respective creators. All rights reserved.

Diane Noomin (2–3); Miss Lasko-Gross (4–7); Bridget Meyne (8–11); Ebony Flowers (12–17); Powerpaola (18–21); Marian Henley (22–23); Mary Fleener (24–28); Lenora Yerkes (29–34); Avy Jetter (35–38); Cathrin Peterslund (39–42); Sarah Allen Reed (43–46); Nicola Streeten (47); Sabba Khan (48–55); Rachel Ang (56–61); Marcela Trujillo (62–64); Joamette Gil (65–67); Lee Marrs (68–71); Trinidad Escobar (72–75); Kendra Josie Kirkpatrick (76–79); Carol Lay (80–81); Aline Kominsky-Crumb (82–83); Ajuan Mance (84–87); M. Louise Stanley (88–89); Meg O'Shea (90–93); Ariel Shrag (94–99); Liz Mayorga (100–103); Roberta Gregory (104–105); MariNaomi (106–109); Joyce Farmer (110–113); Breena Nuñez (114–116); J. Gonzalez-Blitz (117–120); Tyler Cohen (121–125); Carta Monir (126–133); Sarah Lightman (134–136); Jennifer Camper (137–140); Kelly Phillips (141–144); Nina Laden (145–147); Una (148–151); Liana Finck (152–153); Wallis Eates (154–158); Lena Merhej (159–170); Kat Fajardo (171–173); Minnie Phan (174–177); Ilana Zeffren (178–180); Claire Folkman (181–183); Zoe Belsinger (184–185); Georgiana Goodwin (186–187); Soumya Dhulekar (188–190); Katie Fricas (191–193); Kaylee Rowena (194–196); Siobhán Gallagher (197); Hila Noam (198–201); Caitlin Cass (202–205); Sarah Firth (206–211); Corinne Pearlman (212–215); Miriam Libicki (216–218); Carol Tyler (219–222); Maria Stoian (223–226); LubaDalu (227–233); Soizick Jaffre (234–236); Marguerite Dabaie (237); Noel Franklin (238–242); Emil Ferris (243–249).

Editors: Ashley Albert and Maya Bradford
Designer: Max Temescu
Managing Editor: Amy Vreeland
Production Manager: Alison Gervais

Library of Congress Control Number 2018966473

ISBN 978-1-4197-3619-3

Printed and bound in China
10 9 8 7 6 5 4 3 2 1

Abrams ComicArts books are available at special discounts when purchased in quantity for premiums and promotions as well as fundraising or educational use. Special editions can also be created to specification. For details, contact specialsales@abramsbooks.com or the address below.

Abrams ComicArts® is a registered trademark of Harry N. Abrams, Inc.

ABRAMS The Art of Books
195 Broadway, New York, NY 10007
abramsbooks.com

FOR ANITA HILL

CONTENTS

THE CONDITIONS OF OUR CULTURE

IT HAS BEEN MORE THAN A YEAR SINCE THE #METOO HASHTAG WENT VIRAL, capitalizing on the work of Tarana Burke to create a space in our cultural discourse for women and men to talk about the ways in which they have survived sexual harassment and assault. In that time, a great deal has been written about #MeToo, and though change may be slow, the arc toward justice imperceptible, we are at least talking about this epidemic of misconduct and predation, the inadequacy of the justice system, and the pain too many have endured at the hands of people who feel entitled to others' bodies without consent or consideration.

As a writer, words are everything to me. There is a real power in shaping and reshaping language to make sense of and to articulate my place in the world. I am able to say *This is what I have experienced* and *This is what I know* and, most important, *This is who I am.*

When I was twelve years old, I was gang raped by several young men. Sometimes I write around this truth. I try to temper the language I use; I try to lessen the gravity of what I went through because the truth is so ugly. The words I need to use to convey that truth are so ugly. Those young men took something from me and left me hollowed. I kept that secret for many years because the trauma stunned me into silence. For too long, I was mired in shame and guilt and a profound sense of violation. These feelings festered inside of me but, thankfully, I had words to hold on to, to help me make sense of what happened. I read anything I could get my hands on hoping I might learn the why of this terrible thing, and why I let it happen. I read to find other people who had endured similar experiences. I learned that I didn't, in fact, *let* anything happen to me and that the shame was theirs, not mine. And, eventually, I wrote, first using fiction as a thin veil for testimony, and then nonfiction. I used words to tell the truth, to add to the body of literature that made my survival possible. I wrote and I said, I, too, know what it is like to experience sexual violence and to find yourself irrevocably changed in mind and body.

I use language, more than anything, to explore power—how it is wielded, how it is abused, what it feels like to lose and gain power, what it feels like to be and feel powerful. I cannot help but think about power because, once upon a time, I was robbed of my power, and it has taken nearly three decades to gain a semblance of that power back. Now, every time I tell my story, I am powerful. Every time someone shares that my story has helped them make sense of their own experience, I am powerful. I try not to take it for granted. I try not to be the kind of person who becomes so consumed by power that I wield it irresponsibly.

There are means, beyond language, for people to make sense of and articulate their place in the world, and visual communication is one such way. Designer and brand expert Debbie Millman says that the condition of our visual communication is the condition of our culture. By that she means that the way we communicate and the way we create visual messages reflect the state of the world, the state of our society, and the state of our values.

In *Drawing Power,* more than sixty artists use visual communication to reflect, examine, and at times indict the condition of our culture. These artists grapple with this cultural moment where so many people, mostly women, are trying to reclaim power that has been taken from them. They offer testimony about the ways in which they have been violated, the ways they have searched for justice, how they have been made vulnerable and how they have found strength.

There is no looking away from the work in this anthology and what each piece says about the ways in which power is all too often taken from us. In "The Verdict," Marian Henley uses tanks as a metaphor for the experiences of rape and dealing with the justice system. Rendered in black and white, we see a woman, time and again, being put in the position of facing down something more powerful than herself. Avy Jetter draws a story about domestic violence, family, and institutions that don't believe or support women in "Hurt Not Broken." Across the panels, we see faces wrenched with pain, harsh words being spoken, and harsh truths being conveyed. "Fear is like a coat," Jetter writes. "You can get too comfortable in it."

"Got Over It," by Lee Mars, recounts her sexual assault in 1968 and how, slowly but surely, as the title suggests, she got over it. In the end, there is a haunting final caption, one that makes you wonder if indeed it is true. There are only three images in Sarah Lightman's "The Promenade," where she writes of being bitten on a public promenade in Jerusalem and of blood left behind, though we don't know if it was his or hers. In "Rage Queen," Lenora Yerkes shows a woman making sense of her rage and the complex feelings she harbors for a brother who raped her. In the end, "Only my rage felt safe now," she says.

There are no easy stories to be found here. The comics in these pages will make you think, make you feel, make you laugh, make you rage. This anthology demonstrates the importance of visual storytelling and offers depth and nuance to experiences that demand to be shared. Each of these artists wields the power of testimony, the power of using their visual voice, the power of drawing their truths. By using the power of drawing, they show us the condition of the lives they have lived, the condition of our culture, and the vital work we must do to render the need for an anthology like this obsolete.

PREFACE by Diane Noomin

I WAS JUST COMING OUT OF THE ANESTHESIA, SO EMBARRASSED WHEN I SAW the doctor's hand on my breast that I froze. Later, I was angry at myself for that all-too-common reaction. After all, I was twenty-five, a feminist, a contributor to *Wimmen's Comix*—I should have slapped him, reported him, something.

Bombarded by the recent influx of celebrities accused of sexual misconduct in the media, repressed memories of sexual assaults began to surface—not just the sleazy doctor, but the helpful friend and the guilt-inducing ex.

I became obsessed with images of the regular guy as sexual predator, walking among us unseen. Was that ordinary man stalking the ordinary woman walking in front of him? What about the oblivious teenage girl with earbuds in leaving the subway at midnight, the older woman with a cane, anyone waiting at a deserted bus stop?

So many women, so many untold stories—women who blamed themselves, women afraid to report their sexual assaults. These thoughts, my memories, and the explosive effect of the #MeToo movement on women worldwide all made me want to fight back.

I'm a cartoonist and an editor. The only logical way I could respond to this onslaught was as a cartoonist and editor.

I began asking women cartoonists to join me in making a book that would depict their own experiences of sexual assault, harassment, or rape. Out of all the women I approached, only one said she had never had such an experience. A few were too close to what had happened to them to be able to tell their stories. But most were eager to participate.

The result is an anthology with more than sixty contributors of different races, ages, nationalities, religions, and sexualities. All describe their experiences in unique and personal ways: Some use gritty realism, some use poetry or metaphor, some use humor. Some tell true accounts of rape, attempted rape, incest, and assault. Others show the poisonous daily ambush of catcalls, objectification, and harassment that so many women face when they are out in public—in the workplace, on mass transit, or just taking a walk. As the contributors relived these stories in comics form, many of them told me, "This the hardest story I have ever done."

In the time it took to get this book published, one contributor was raped, and another dropped out of the project because her accused rapist is suing her for millions. The patriarchal mindset that leads to sexual violence against women is insidious and startlingly pervasive. Nevertheless, this toxic culture of silence and complacency has been dealt a noticeable blow by the #MeToo movement.

The artists in this collection present themselves not as victims but rather as truth tellers, shining light on the dirty secrets of abusers.

I'm grateful to all the contributors in this book for their skill and courage in exposing the ugliness of sexual violence and harassment in women's lives. For years, women who reported rape were routinely disbelieved. As survivors, we offer our stories in the fight against the impunity of sexual predators.

When I titled this anthology *Drawing Power*, I intended to call upon the power of storytelling and comics art to directly confront sexual trauma. I believe that together we have done that.

ACKNOWLEDGMENTS

Thanks to Ashley Albert for being as much a perfectionist as I am.

Thanks to Maya Bradford for her energetic support and knowledge.

Thanks to Charlie Kochman for his invaluable advocacy.

Thanks also to Pamela Notarantonio and Max Temescu for their skillful design concepts.

Thanks to Georgiana Goodwin for design consultation.

Thanks to Bill Griffith for everything.

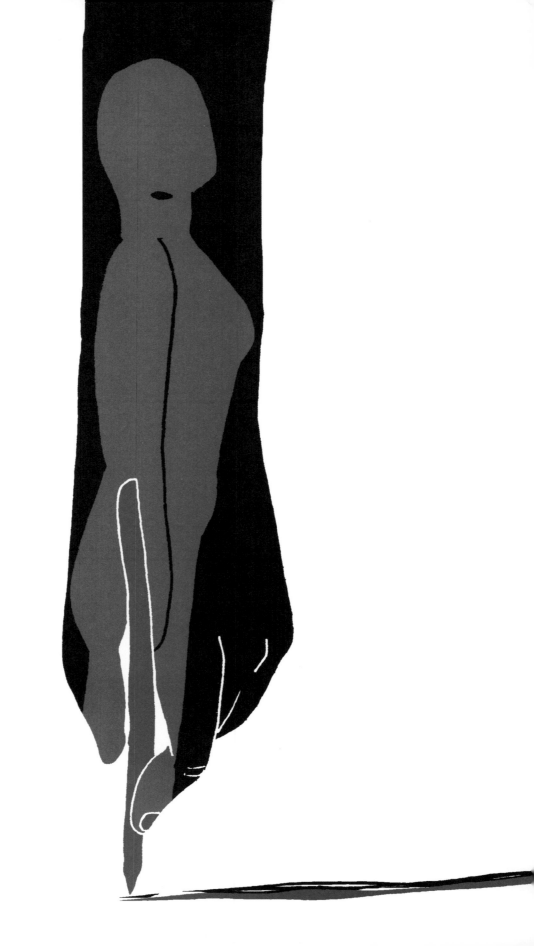

DRAWING POWER

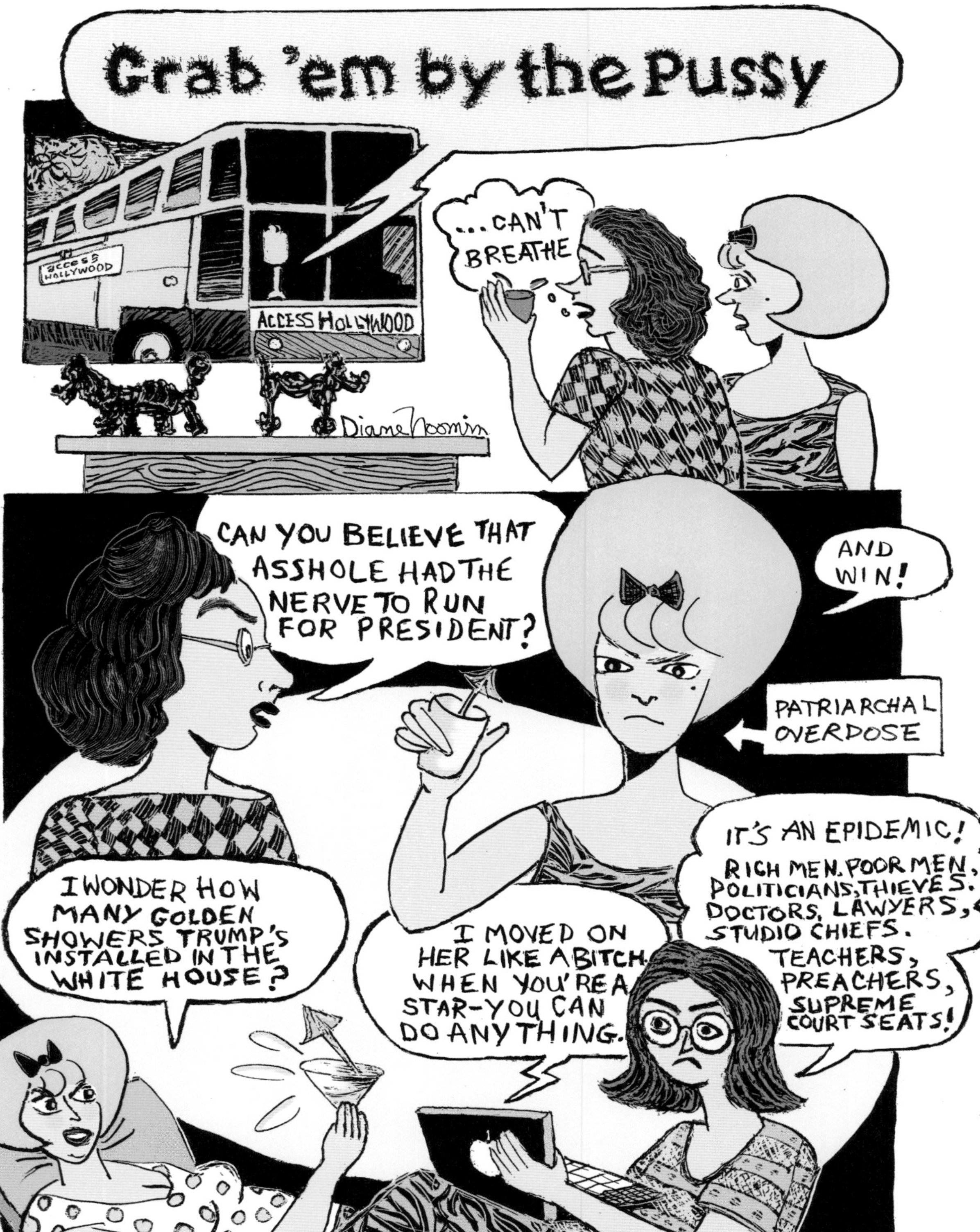
Grab 'em by the Pussy
ACCESS HOLLYWOOD
ACCESS HOLLYWOOD
...CAN'T BREATHE
Diane Noomin
CAN YOU BELIEVE THAT ASSHOLE HAD THE NERVE TO RUN FOR PRESIDENT?
AND WIN!
PATRIARCHAL OVERDOSE
I WONDER HOW MANY GOLDEN SHOWERS TRUMP'S INSTALLED IN THE WHITE HOUSE?
I MOVED ON HER LIKE A BITCH. WHEN YOU'RE A STAR-YOU CAN DO ANYTHING.
IT'S AN EPIDEMIC! RICH MEN. POOR MEN, POLITICIANS, THIEVES. DOCTORS, LAWYERS, STUDIO CHIEFS. TEACHERS, PREACHERS, SUPREME COURT SEATS!

Accusations, denials, resignations, trials...

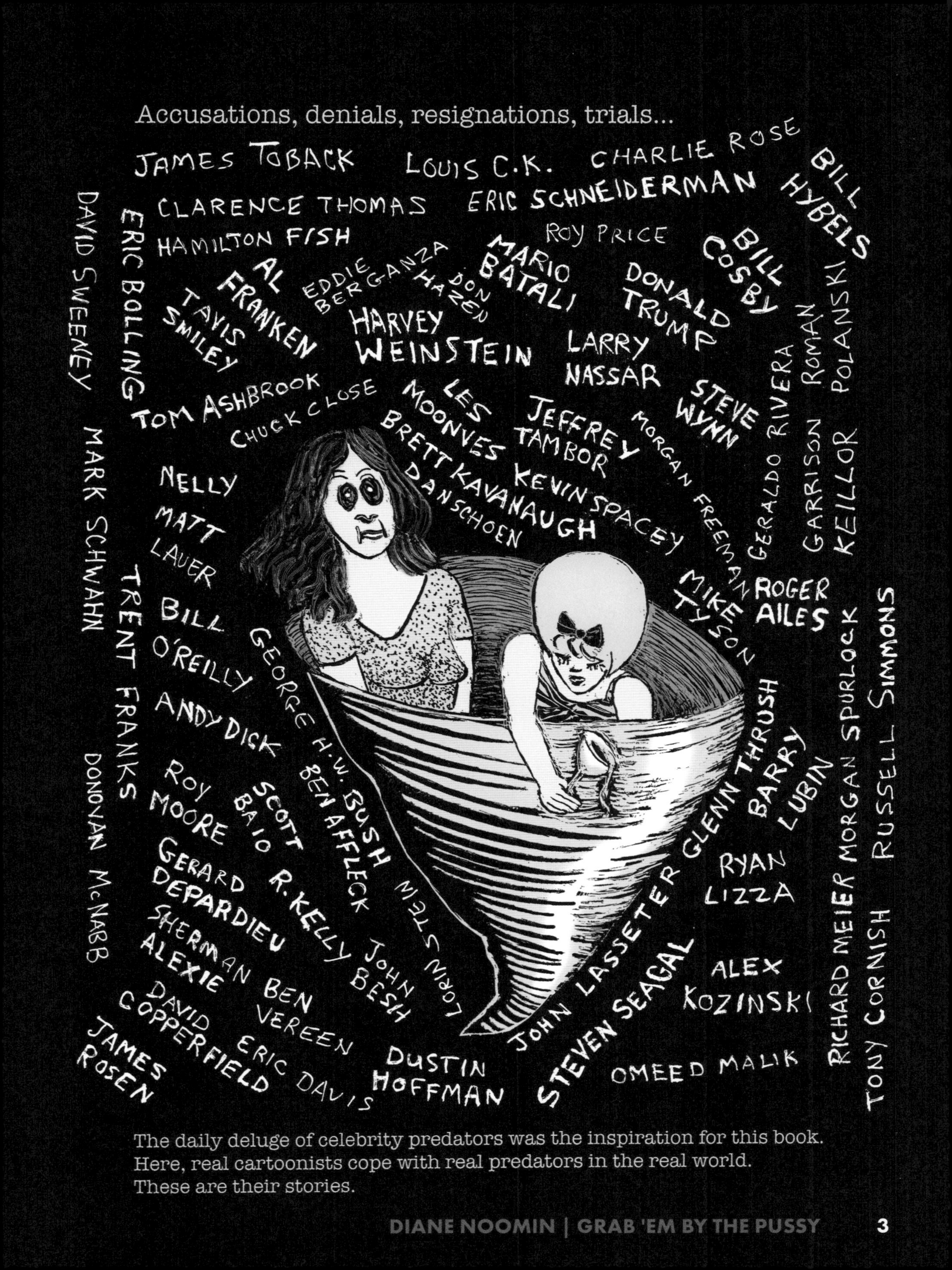
JAMES TOBACK
LOUIS C.K.
CHARLIE ROSE
BILL HYBELS
CLARENCE THOMAS
ERIC SCHNEIDERMAN
DAVID SWEENEY
ERIC BOLLING
HAMILTON FISH
ROY PRICE
BILL COSBY
AL FRANKEN
EDDIE BERGANZA
DON HAZEN
MARIO BATALI
DONALD TRUMP
TAVIS SMILEY
HARVEY WEINSTEIN
LARRY NASSAR
ROMAN POLANSKI
TOM ASHBROOK
CHUCK CLOSE
LES MOONVES
JEFFREY TAMBOR
MORGAN FREEMAN
STEVE WYNN
GERALDO RIVERA
GARRISON KEILLOR
MARK SCHWAHN
BRETT KAVANAUGH
DAN SCHOEN
KEVIN SPACEY
NELLY
MATT LAUER
TRENT FRANKS
BILL O'REILLY
MIKE TYSON
ROGER AILES
ANDY DICK
GEORGE H.W. BUSH
BEN AFFLECK
GLENN THRUSH
BARRY LUBIN
MORGAN SPURLOCK
RUSSELL SIMMONS
DONOVAN McNABB
ROY MOORE
SCOTT BAIO
GERARD DEPARDIEU
R. KELLY
LORIN STEIN
JOHN LASSETER
RYAN LIZZA
SHERMAN ALEXIE
JOHN BESH
BEN VEREEN
STEVEN SEAGAL
ALEX KOZINSKI
RICHARD MEIER
TONY CORNISH
DAVID COPPERFIELD
JAMES ROSEN
ERIC DAVIS
DUSTIN HOFFMAN
OMEED MALIK

The daily deluge of celebrity predators was the inspiration for this book.
Here, real cartoonists cope with real predators in the real world.
These are their stories.

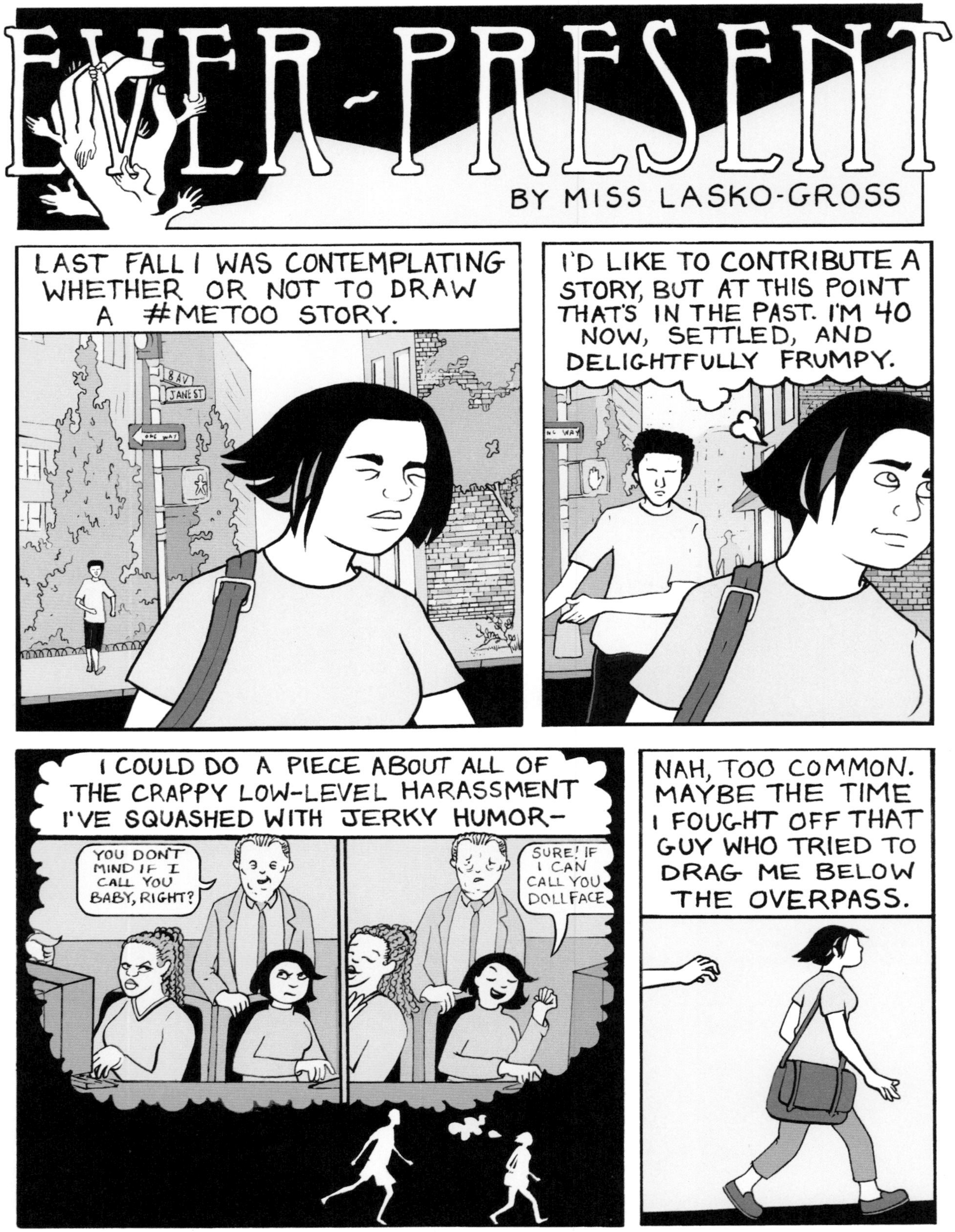
EVER-PRESENT
BY MISS LASKO-GROSS
LAST FALL I WAS CONTEMPLATING WHETHER OR NOT TO DRAW A #METOO STORY.
8 AV
JANE ST
I'D LIKE TO CONTRIBUTE A STORY, BUT AT THIS POINT THAT'S IN THE PAST. I'M 40 NOW, SETTLED, AND DELIGHTFULLY FRUMPY.
I COULD DO A PIECE ABOUT ALL OF THE CRAPPY LOW-LEVEL HARASSMENT I'VE SQUASHED WITH JERKY HUMOR–
YOU DON'T MIND IF I CALL YOU BABY, RIGHT?
SURE! IF I CAN CALL YOU DOLLFACE
NAH, TOO COMMON. MAYBE THE TIME I FOUGHT OFF THAT GUY WHO TRIED TO DRAG ME BELOW THE OVERPASS.

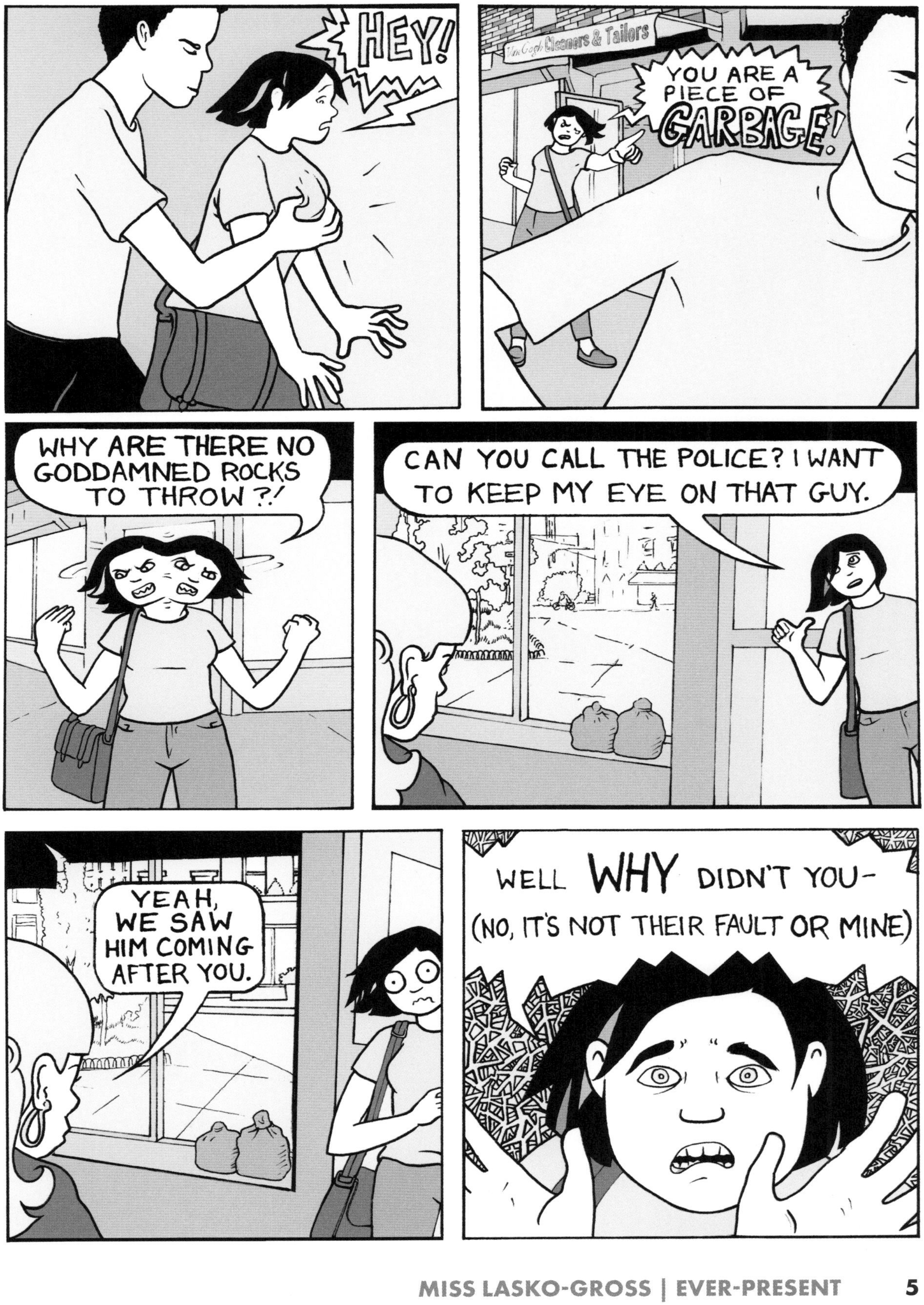
HEY!
YOU ARE A PIECE OF GARBAGE!
Van Gogh Cleaners & Tailors
WHY ARE THERE NO GODDAMNED ROCKS TO THROW?!
CAN YOU CALL THE POLICE? I WANT TO KEEP MY EYE ON THAT GUY.
YEAH, WE SAW HIM COMING AFTER YOU.
WELL WHY DIDN'T YOU-
(NO, IT'S NOT THEIR FAULT OR MINE)

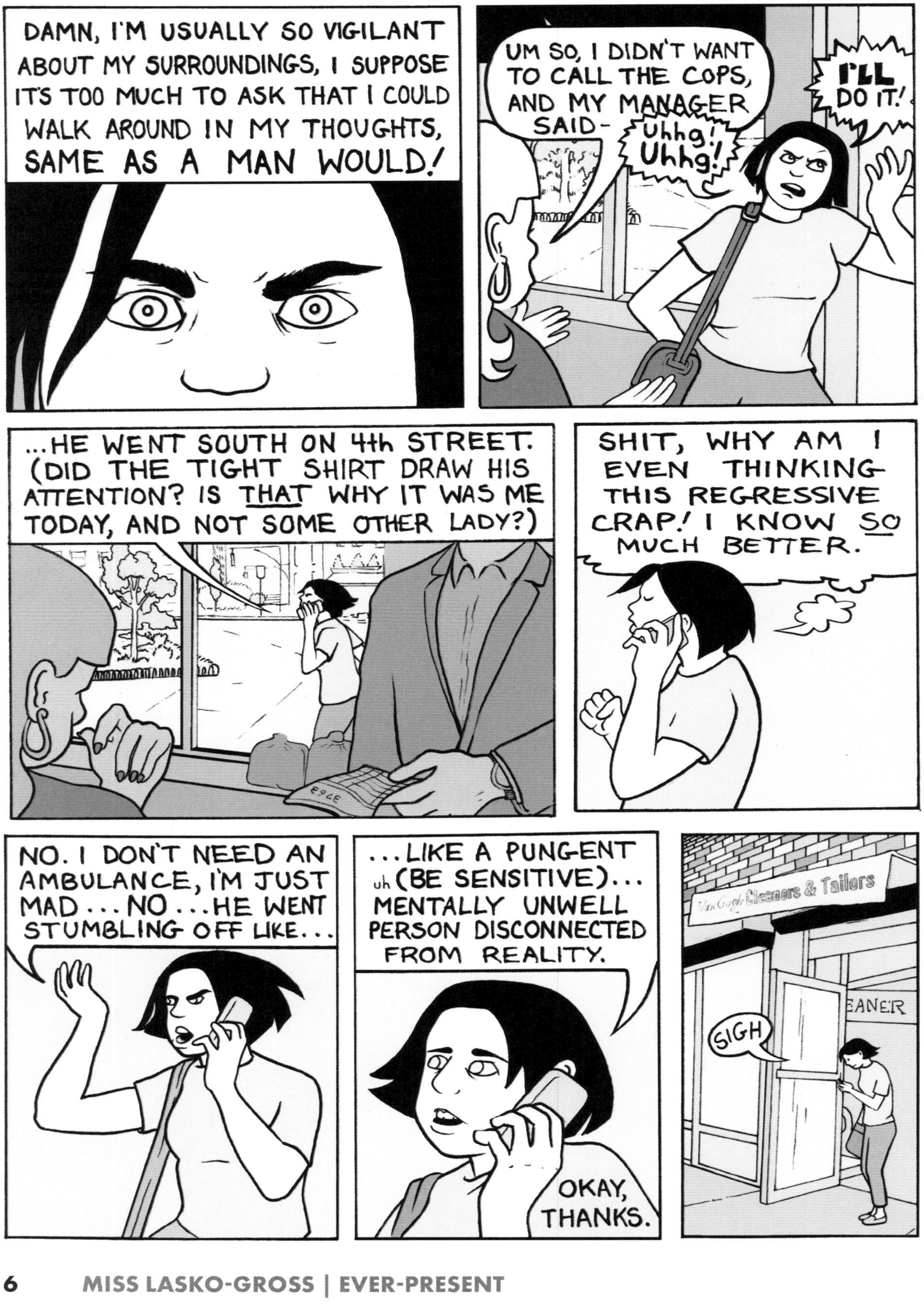

DAMN, I'M USUALLY SO VIGILANT ABOUT MY SURROUNDINGS, I SUPPOSE IT'S TOO MUCH TO ASK THAT I COULD WALK AROUND IN MY THOUGHTS, SAME AS A MAN WOULD!
UM SO, I DIDN'T WANT TO CALL THE COPS, AND MY MANAGER SAID-
Uhhg! Uhhg!
I'LL DO IT!
...HE WENT SOUTH ON 4th STREET. (DID THE TIGHT SHIRT DRAW HIS ATTENTION? IS THAT WHY IT WAS ME TODAY, AND NOT SOME OTHER LADY?)
SHIT, WHY AM I EVEN THINKING THIS REGRESSIVE CRAP! I KNOW SO MUCH BETTER.
NO. I DON'T NEED AN AMBULANCE, I'M JUST MAD ... NO ... HE WENT STUMBLING OFF LIKE...
... LIKE A PUNGENT uh (BE SENSITIVE)... MENTALLY UNWELL PERSON DISCONNECTED FROM REALITY.
OKAY, THANKS.
Van Gogh Cleaners & Tailors
EANER
SIGH

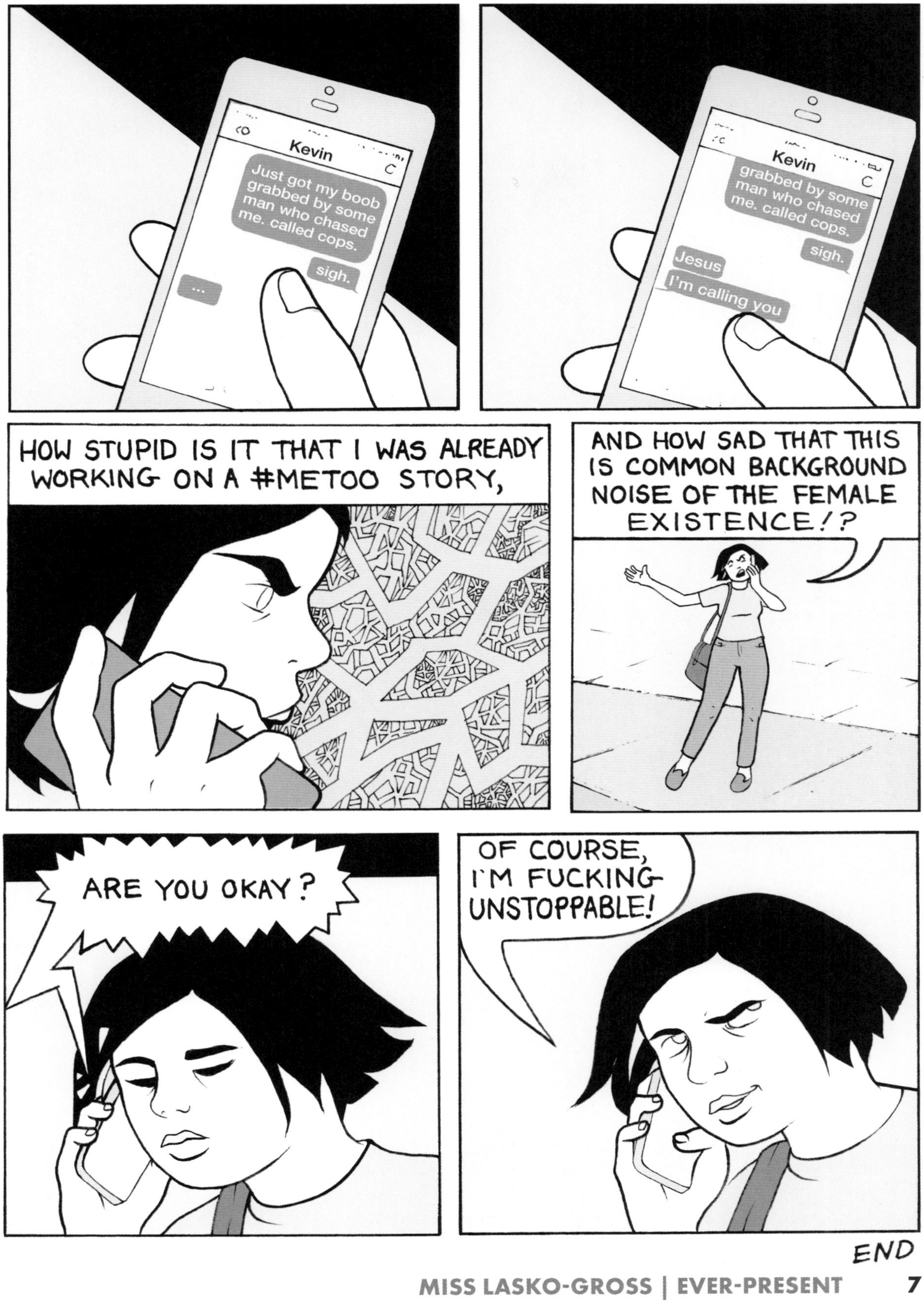
Kevin
Just got my boob grabbed by some man who chased me. called cops.
sigh.
...
Kevin
grabbed by some man who chased me. called cops.
sigh.
Jesus
I'm calling you
HOW STUPID IS IT THAT I WAS ALREADY WORKING ON A #METOO STORY,
AND HOW SAD THAT THIS IS COMMON BACKGROUND NOISE OF THE FEMALE EXISTENCE!?
ARE YOU OKAY?
OF COURSE, I'M FUCKING UNSTOPPABLE!
END

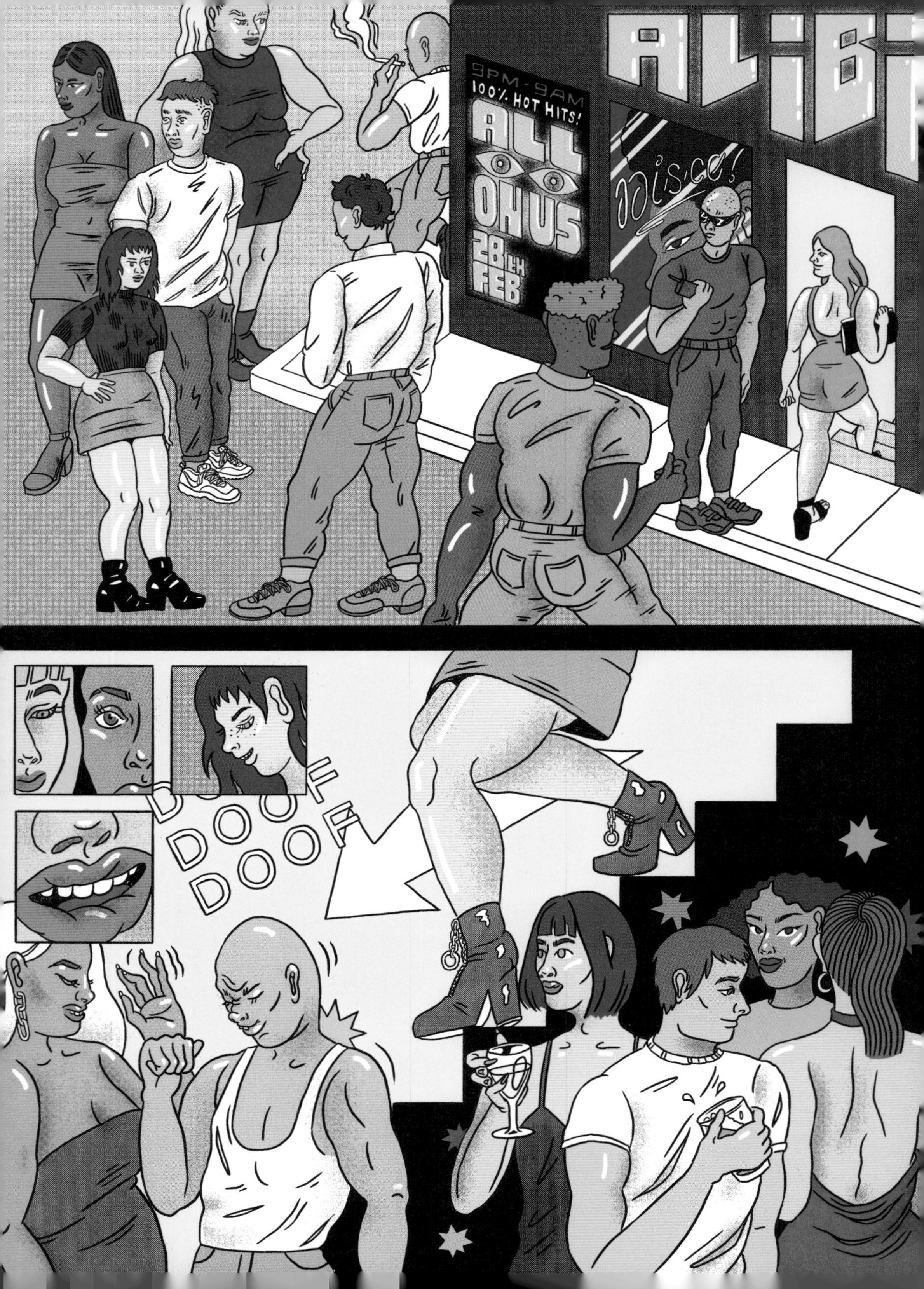
ALIBI
9PM - 9AM
100% HOT HITS!
ALL
ON US
28TH
FEB
Disco!
DOOF
DOOF
DOOF

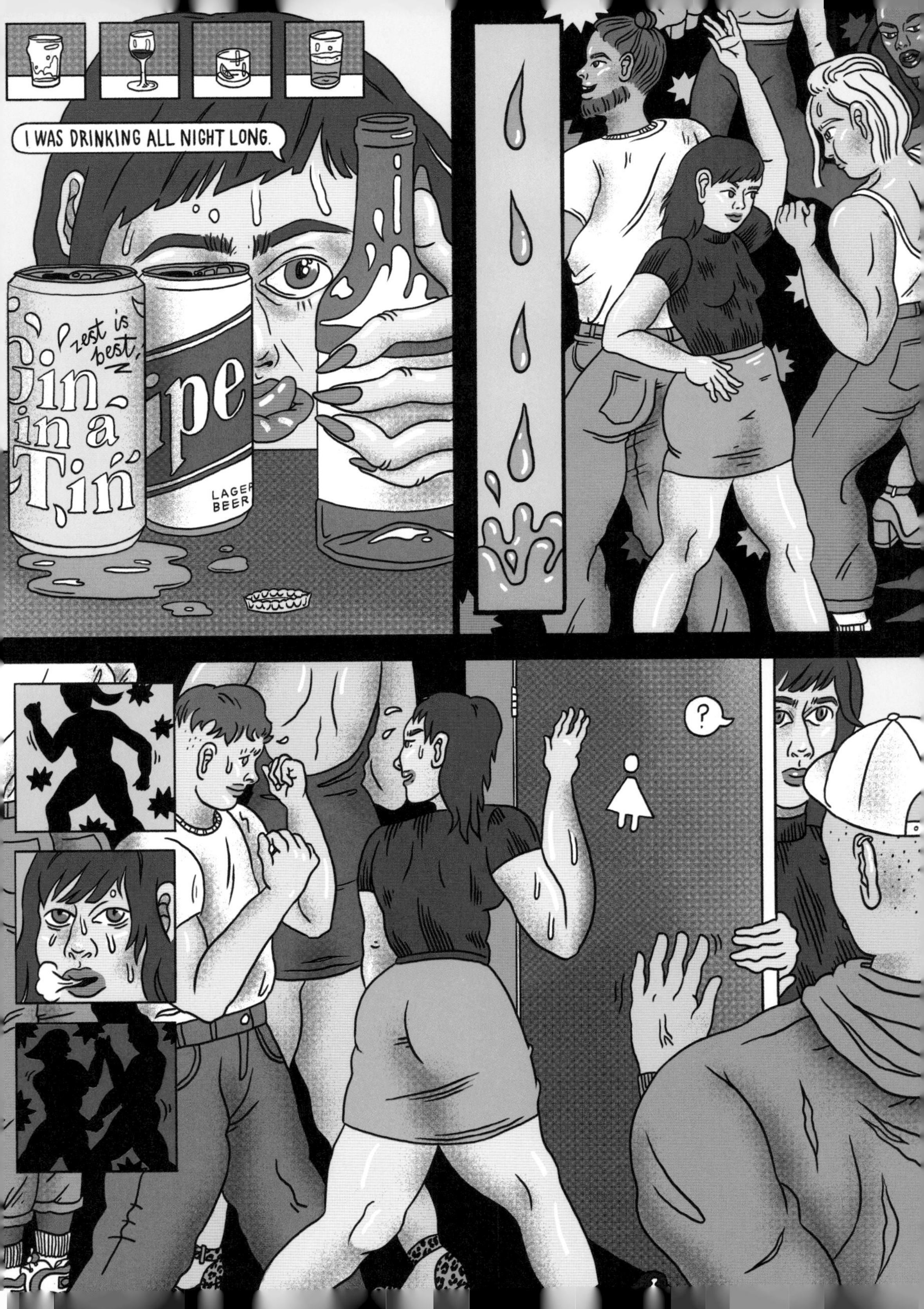
I WAS DRINKING ALL NIGHT LONG.
zest is best
Gin in a Tin
ipe
LAGER BEER
?

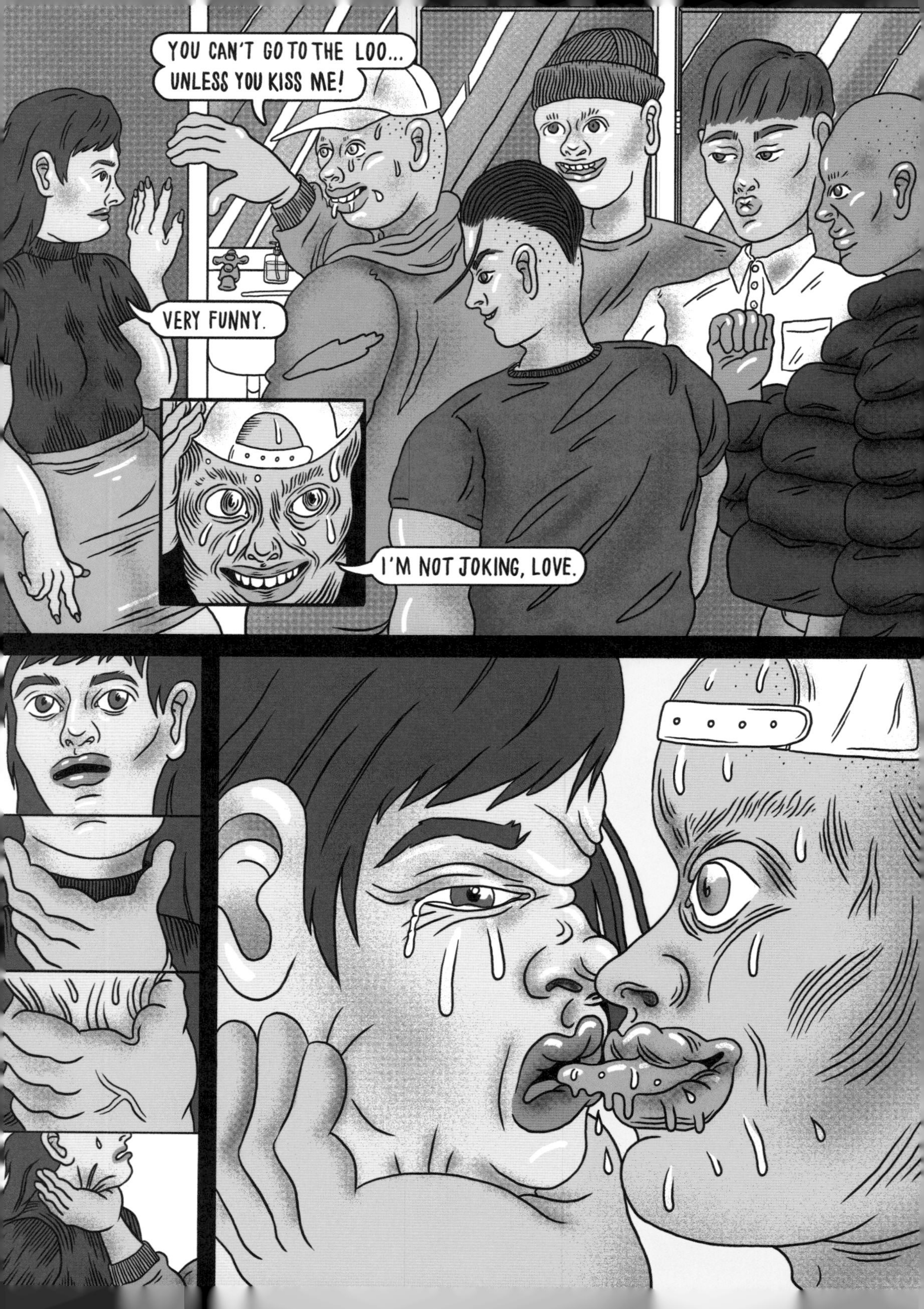
YOU CAN'T GO TO THE LOO... UNLESS YOU KISS ME!
VERY FUNNY.
I'M NOT JOKING, LOVE.

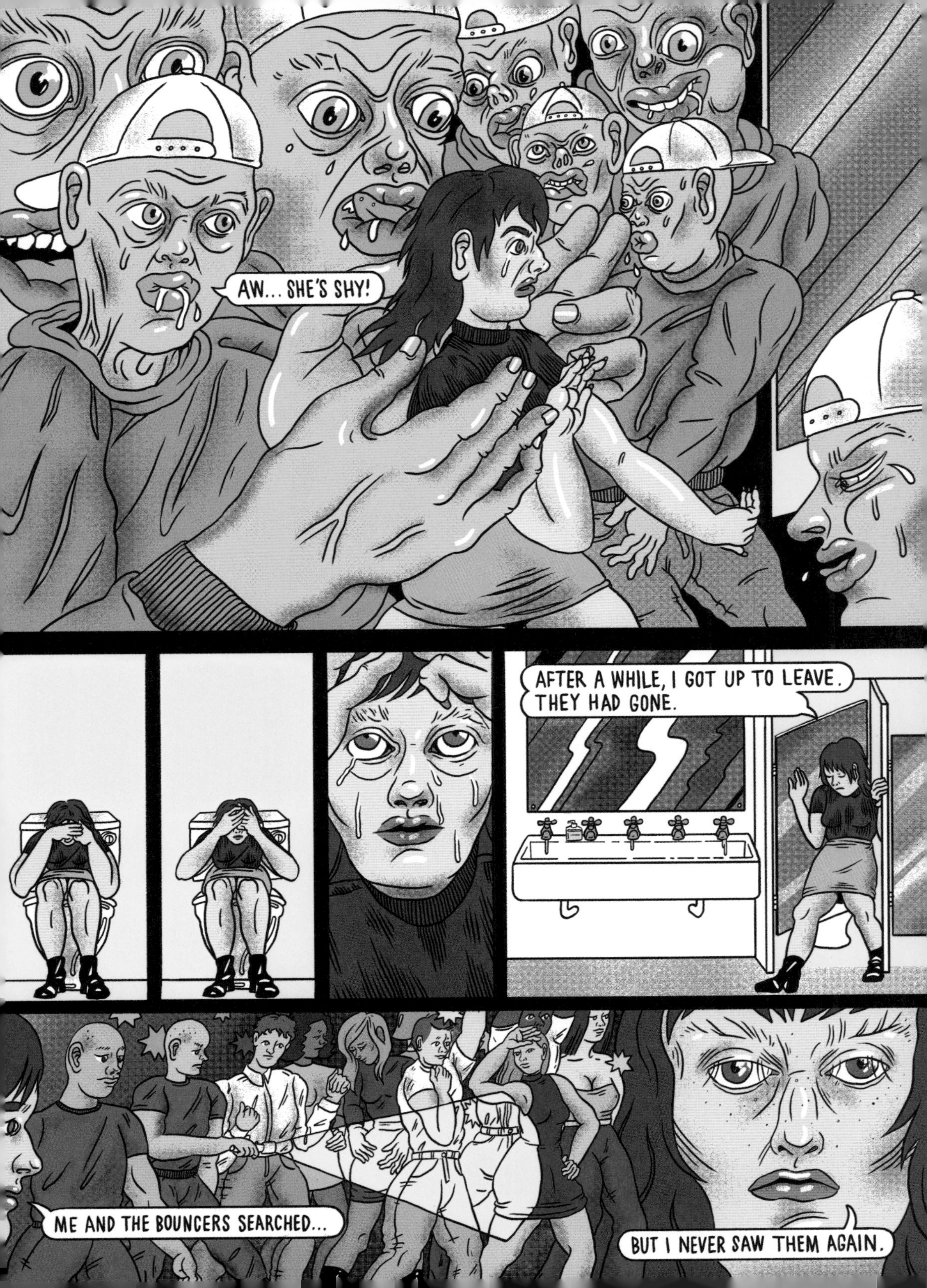
AW... SHE'S SHY!
AFTER A WHILE, I GOT UP TO LEAVE. THEY HAD GONE.
ME AND THE BOUNCERS SEARCHED...
BUT I NEVER SAW THEM AGAIN.

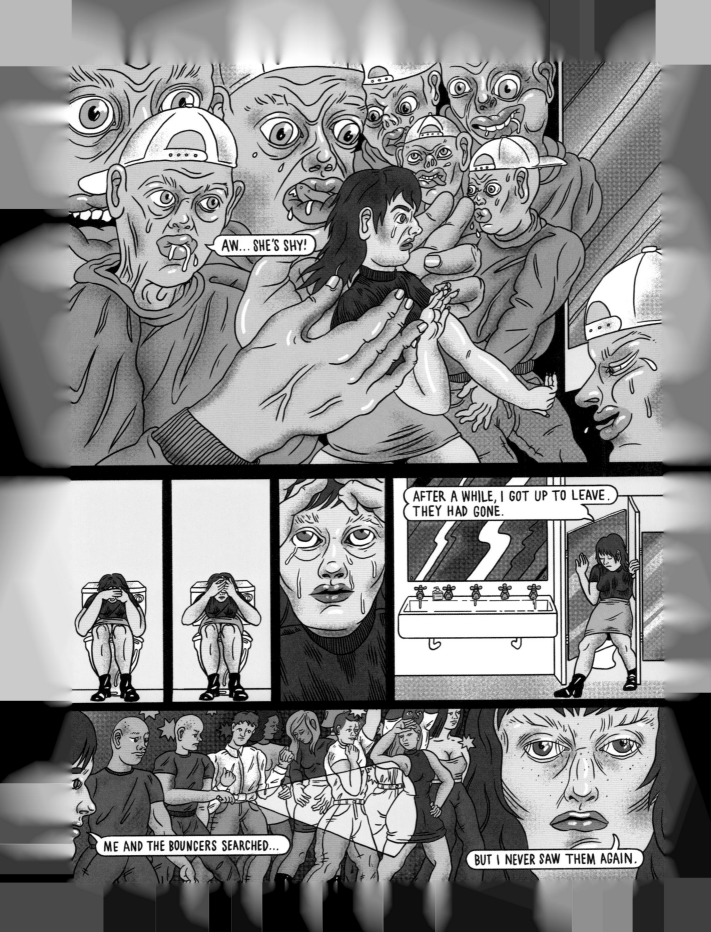

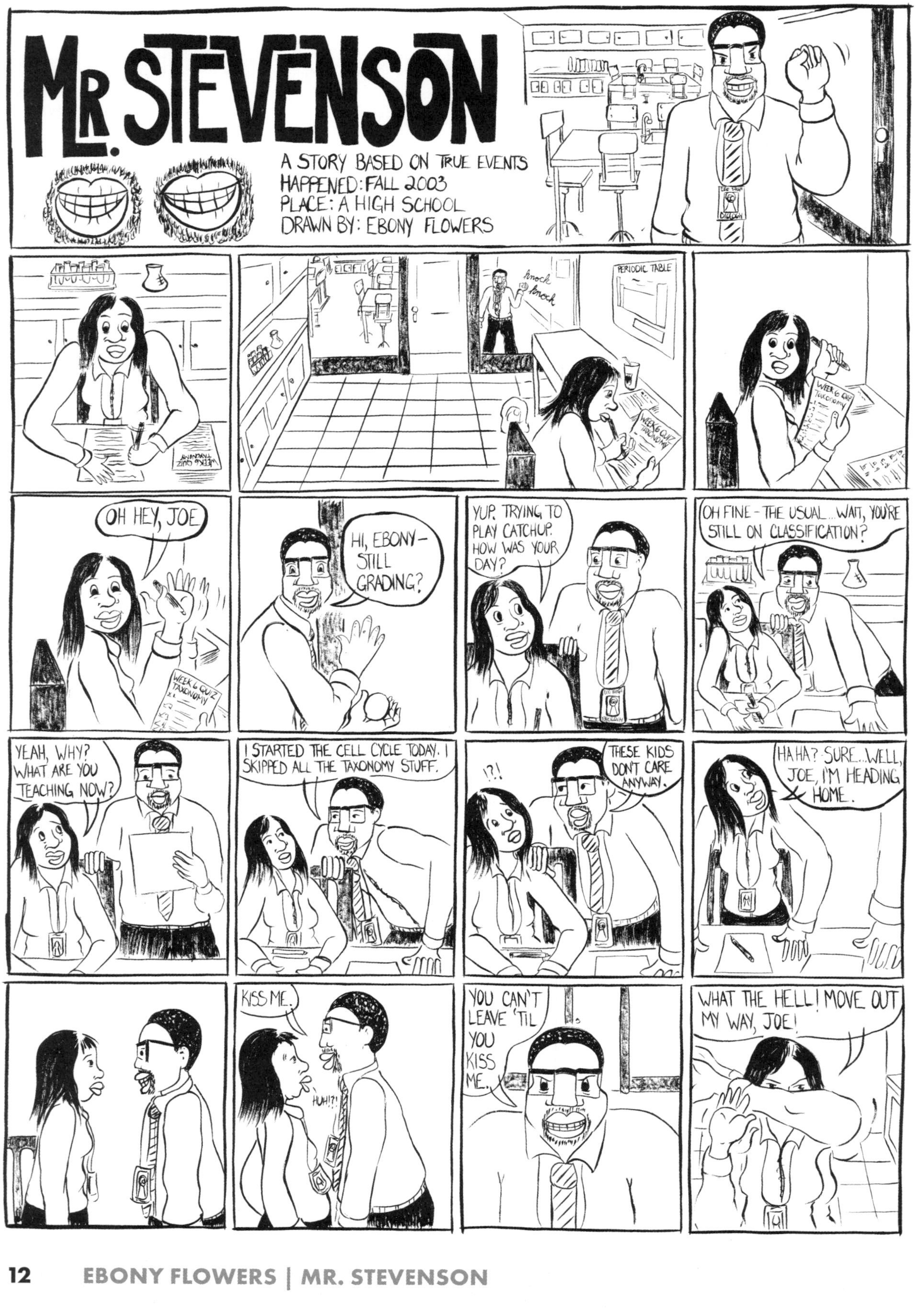
MR. STEVENSON
A STORY BASED ON TRUE EVENTS
HAPPENED: FALL 2003
PLACE: A HIGH SCHOOL
DRAWN BY: EBONY FLOWERS
WEEK 6 QUIZ TAXONOMY
knock knock
PERIODIC TABLE
WEEK 6 QUIZ TAXONOMY
WEEK 6 QUIZ Taxonomy
OH HEY, JOE
WEEK 6 QUIZ TAXONOMY
HI, EBONY- STILL GRADING?
YUP. TRYING TO PLAY CATCHUP. HOW WAS YOUR DAY?
OH FINE - THE USUAL... WAIT, YOU'RE STILL ON CLASSIFICATION?
YEAH, WHY? WHAT ARE YOU TEACHING NOW?
I STARTED THE CELL CYCLE TODAY. I SKIPPED ALL THE TAXONOMY STUFF.
!?!
THESE KIDS DON'T CARE ANYWAY.
HA HA? SURE... WELL, JOE, I'M HEADING HOME.
KISS ME.
HUH!?!
YOU CAN'T LEAVE 'TIL YOU KISS ME.
WHAT THE HELL! MOVE OUT MY WAY, JOE!

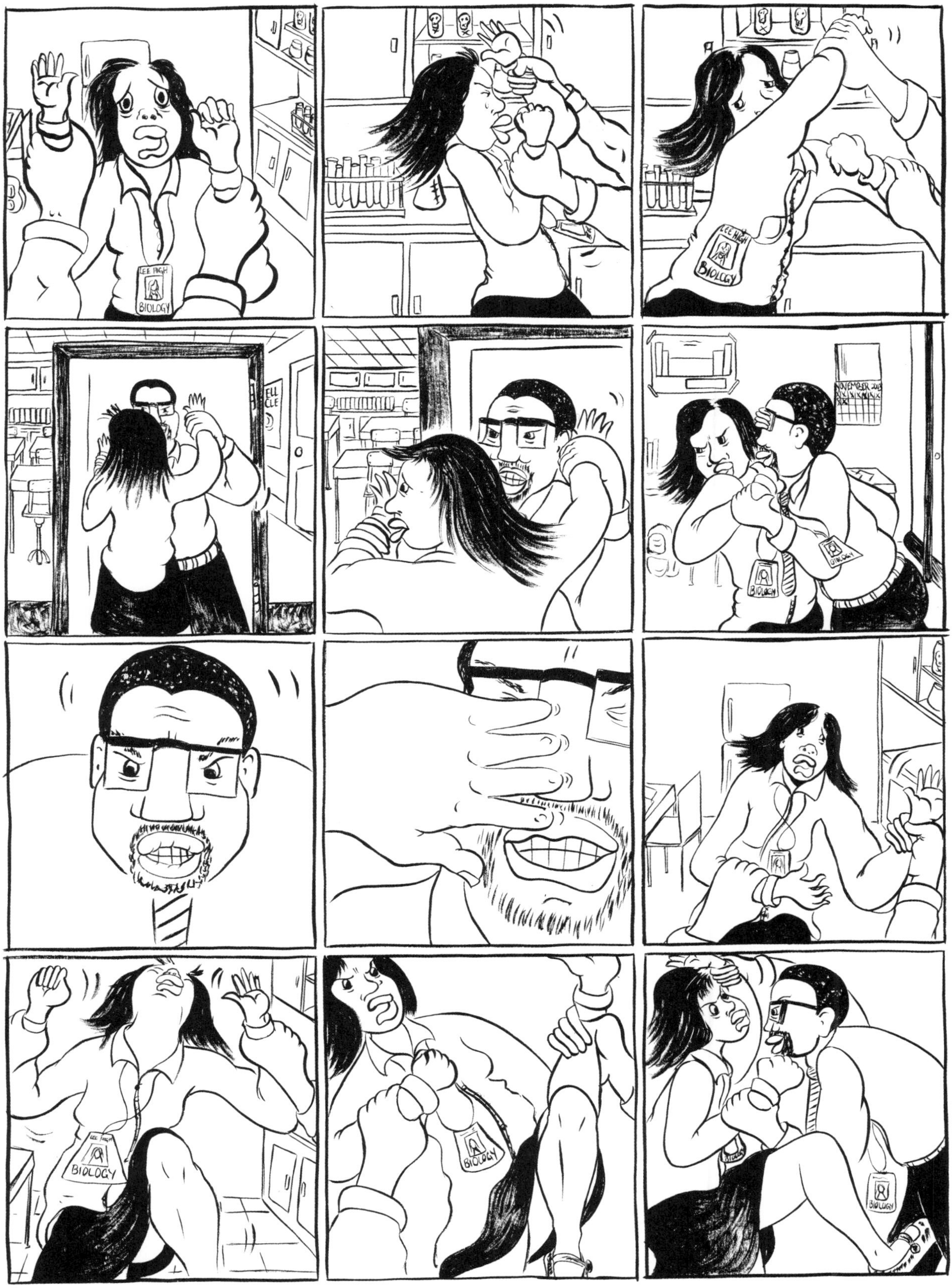
LEE HIGH
BIOLOGY
NOVEMBER 2013

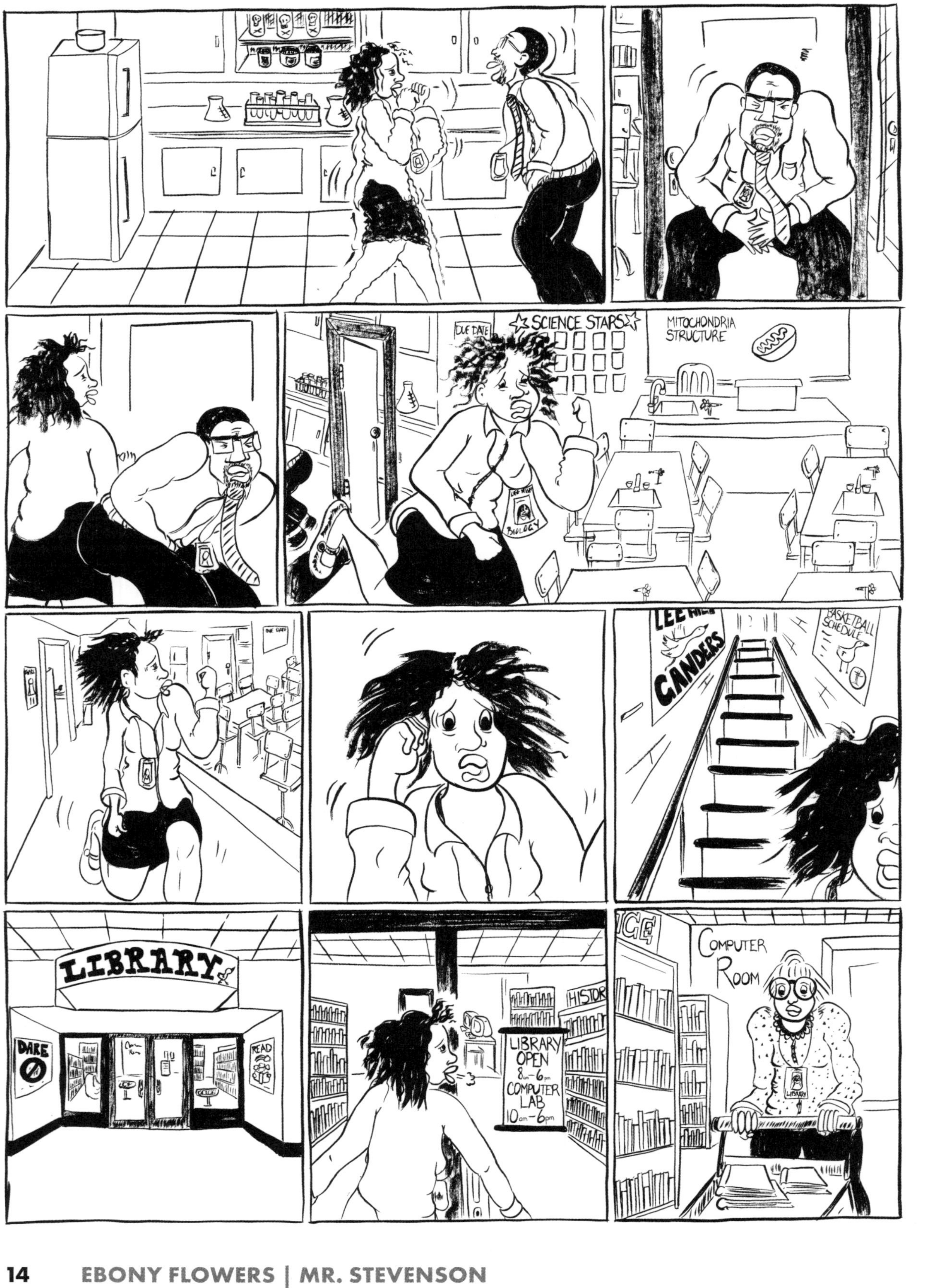
SCIENCE STARS
DUE DATE
MITOCHONDRIA STRUCTURE
BIOLOGY
GANDERS
BASKETBALL SCHEDULE
LIBRARY
DARE
READ
LIBRARY OPEN 8am–6pm COMPUTER LAB 10am–6pm
COMPUTER ROOM
LIBRARY

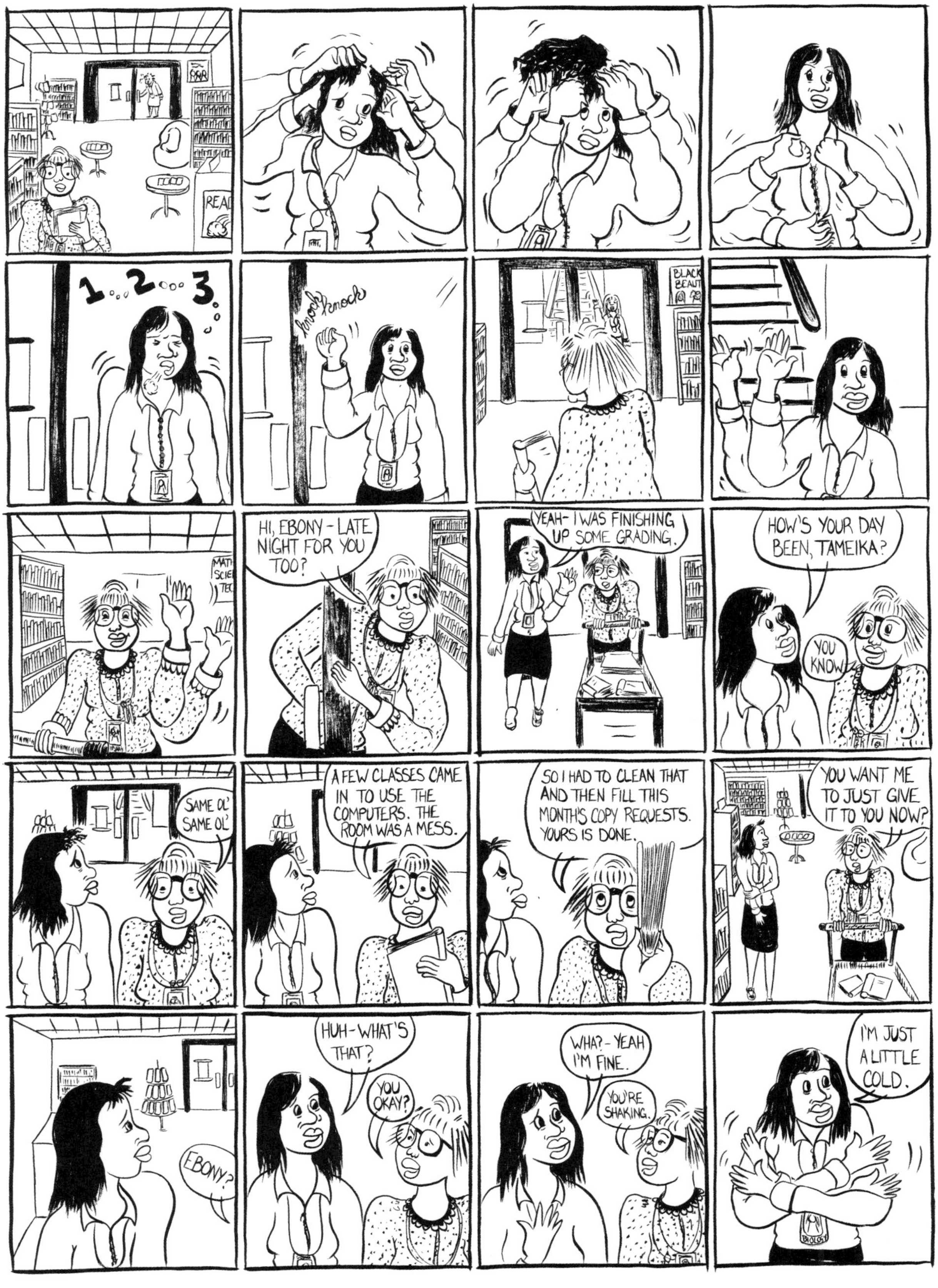

1..2...3
knock knock
HI, EBONY - LATE NIGHT FOR YOU TOO?
YEAH- I WAS FINISHING UP SOME GRADING.
HOW'S YOUR DAY BEEN, TAMEIKA?
YOU KNOW.
SAME OL' SAME OL'
A FEW CLASSES CAME IN TO USE THE COMPUTERS. THE ROOM WAS A MESS.
SO I HAD TO CLEAN THAT AND THEN FILL THIS MONTH'S COPY REQUESTS. YOURS IS DONE.
YOU WANT ME TO JUST GIVE IT TO YOU NOW?
EBONY?
HUH- WHAT'S THAT?
YOU OKAY?
WHA?- YEAH I'M FINE.
YOU'RE SHAKING.
I'M JUST A LITTLE COLD.

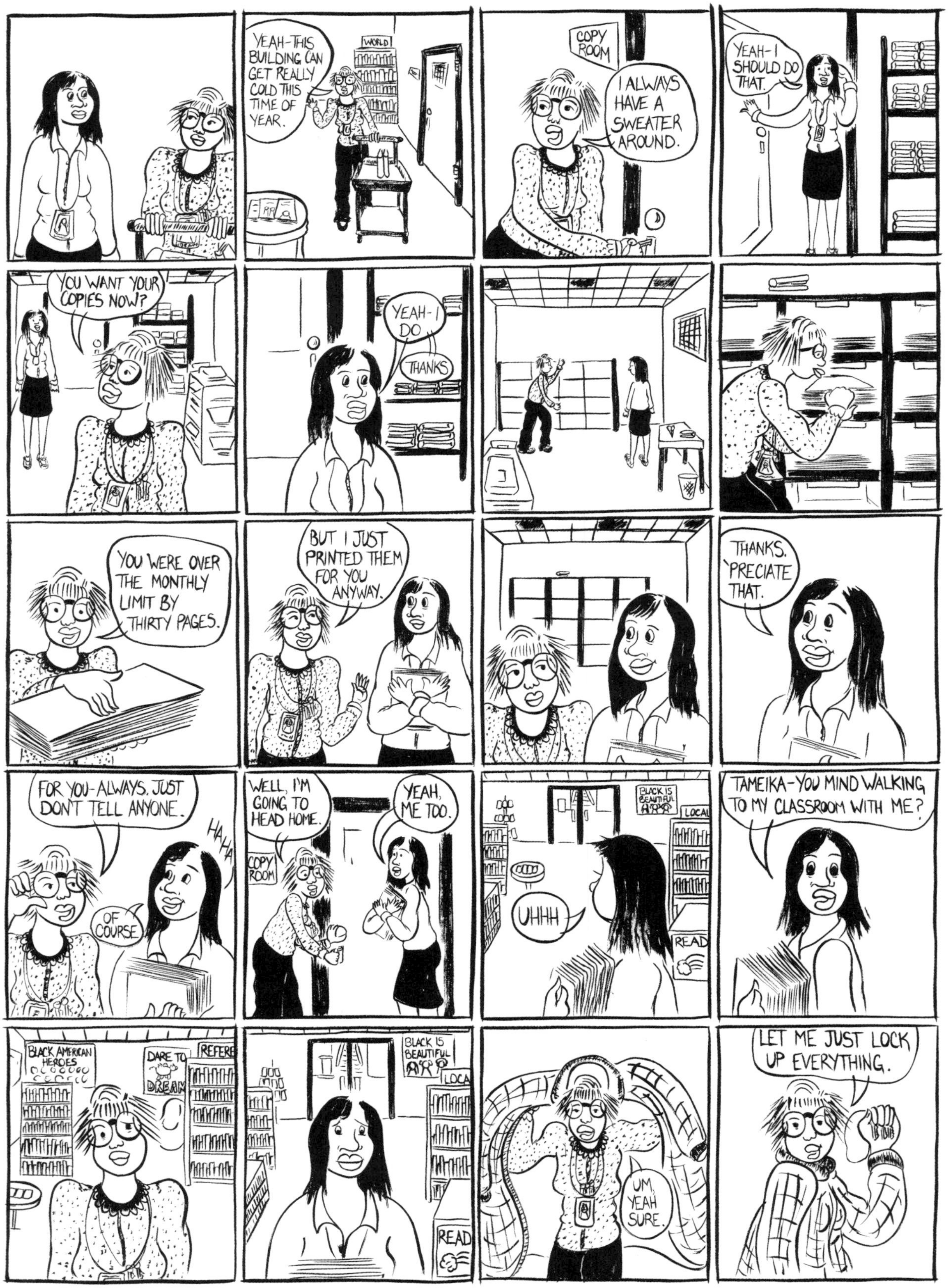
YEAH-THIS BUILDING CAN GET REALLY COLD THIS TIME OF YEAR.
WORLD
COPY ROOM
I ALWAYS HAVE A SWEATER AROUND.
YEAH-I SHOULD DO THAT.
YOU WANT YOUR COPIES NOW?
YEAH-I DO
THANKS
YOU WERE OVER THE MONTHLY LIMIT BY THIRTY PAGES.
BUT I JUST PRINTED THEM FOR YOU ANYWAY.
THANKS. 'PRECIATE THAT.
FOR YOU-ALWAYS. JUST DON'T TELL ANYONE.
HAHA
OF COURSE
WELL, I'M GOING TO HEAD HOME.
YEAH, ME TOO.
COPY ROOM
BLACK IS BEAUTIFUL
LOCAL
UHHH
READ
TAMEIKA-YOU MIND WALKING TO MY CLASSROOM WITH ME?
BLACK AMERICAN HEROES
DARE TO DREAM
REFERE
BLACK IS BEAUTIFUL
LOCA
READ
UM, YEAH SURE.
LET ME JUST LOCK UP EVERYTHING.

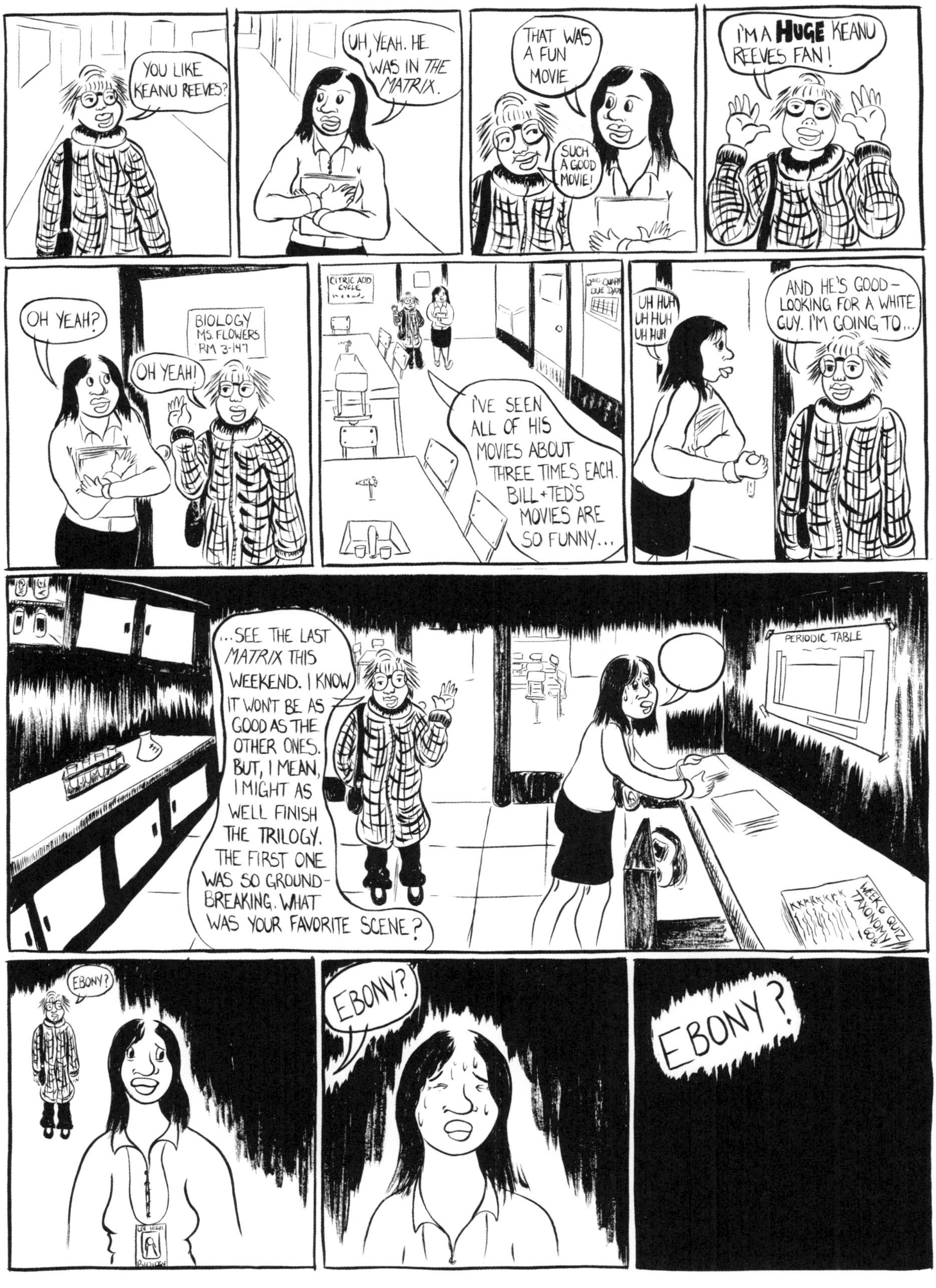
YOU LIKE KEANU REEVES?
UH, YEAH. HE WAS IN THE MATRIX.
THAT WAS A FUN MOVIE
SUCH A GOOD MOVIE!
I'M A HUGE KEANU REEVES FAN!
OH YEAH?
BIOLOGY MS. FLOWERS RM 3-147
OH YEAH!
CITRIC ACID CYCLE
2ND QUARTER DUE DATE
I'VE SEEN ALL OF HIS MOVIES ABOUT THREE TIMES EACH. BILL+TED'S MOVIES ARE SO FUNNY...
UH HUH UH HUH UH HUH
AND HE'S GOOD-LOOKING FOR A WHITE GUY. I'M GOING TO...
...SEE THE LAST MATRIX THIS WEEKEND. I KNOW IT WON'T BE AS GOOD AS THE OTHER ONES. BUT, I MEAN, I MIGHT AS WELL FINISH THE TRILOGY. THE FIRST ONE WAS SO GROUND-BREAKING. WHAT WAS YOUR FAVORITE SCENE?
PERIODIC TABLE
WEEK 6 QUIZ TAXONOMY
EBONY?
EBONY?
EBONY?

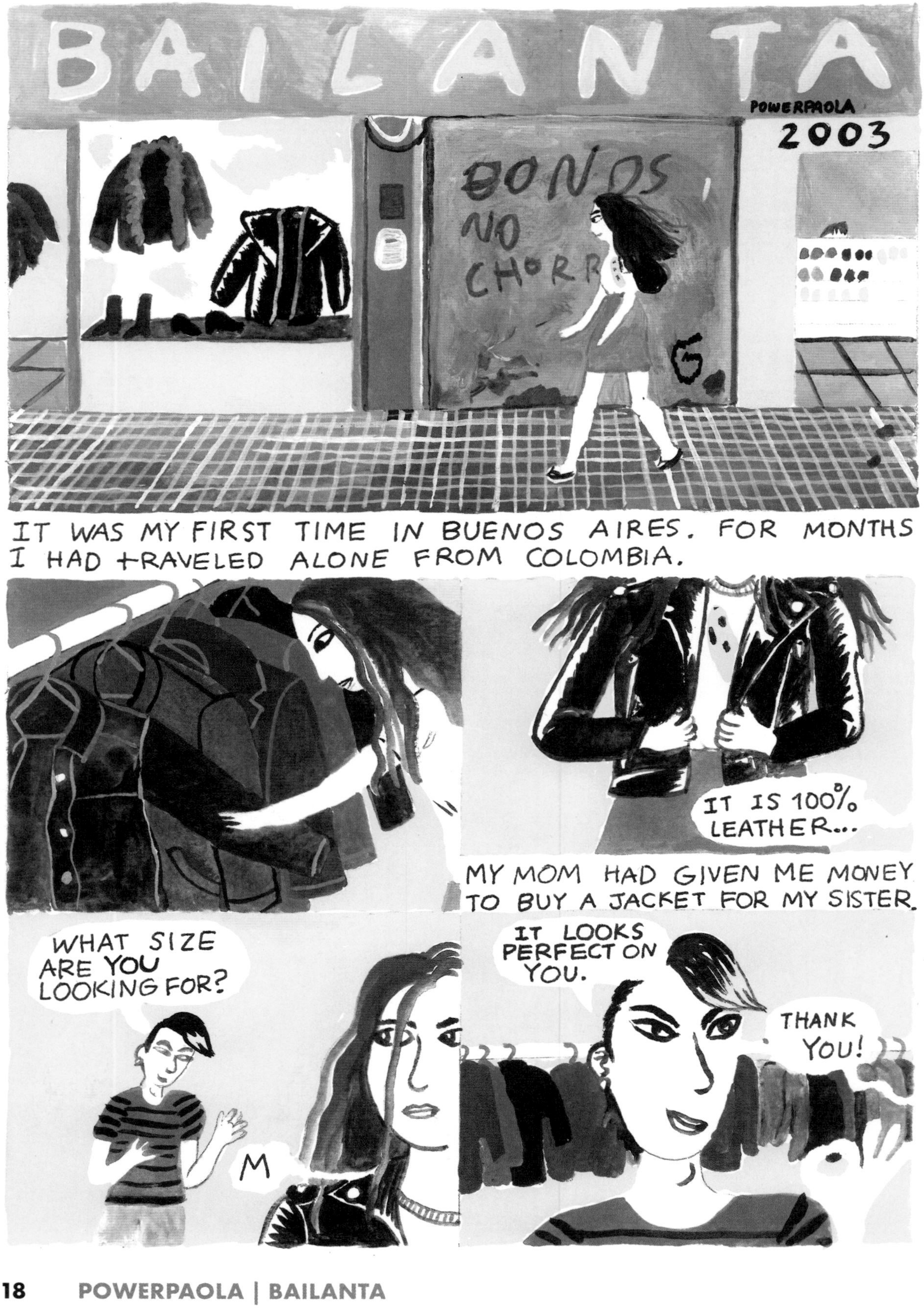
BAILANTA
POWERPAOLA
2003
IT WAS MY FIRST TIME IN BUENOS AIRES. FOR MONTHS I HAD TRAVELED ALONE FROM COLOMBIA.
IT IS 100% LEATHER...
MY MOM HAD GIVEN ME MONEY TO BUY A JACKET FOR MY SISTER.
WHAT SIZE ARE YOU LOOKING FOR?
M
IT LOOKS PERFECT ON YOU.
THANK YOU!

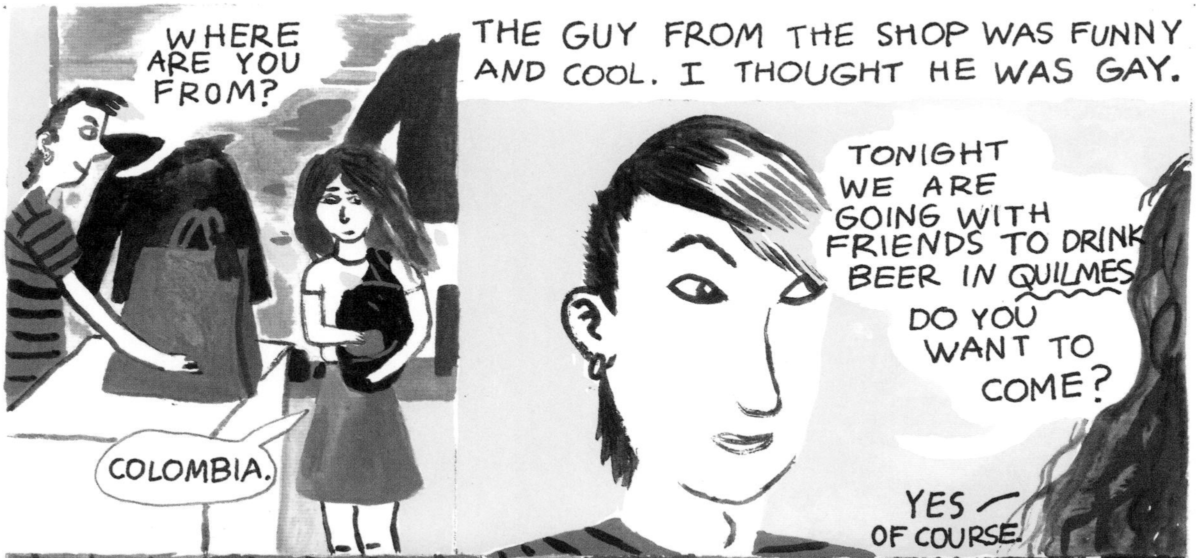
WHERE ARE YOU FROM?
COLOMBIA.
THE GUY FROM THE SHOP WAS FUNNY AND COOL. I THOUGHT HE WAS GAY.
TONIGHT WE ARE GOING WITH FRIENDS TO DRINK BEER IN QUILMES
DO YOU WANT TO COME?
YES — OF COURSE.

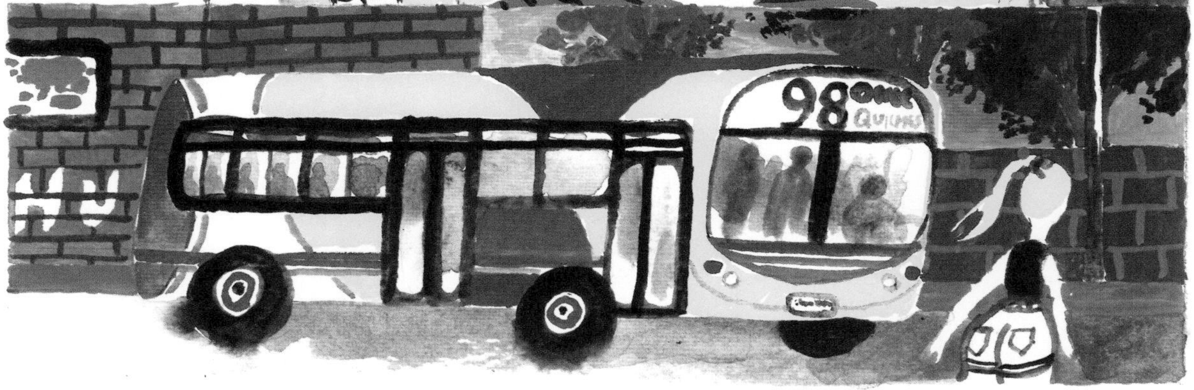
98

I ALWAYS THOUGHT THAT NOTHING WOULD EVER HAPPEN TO ME. THAT HORRIBLE THINGS HAPPEN TO OTHERS.

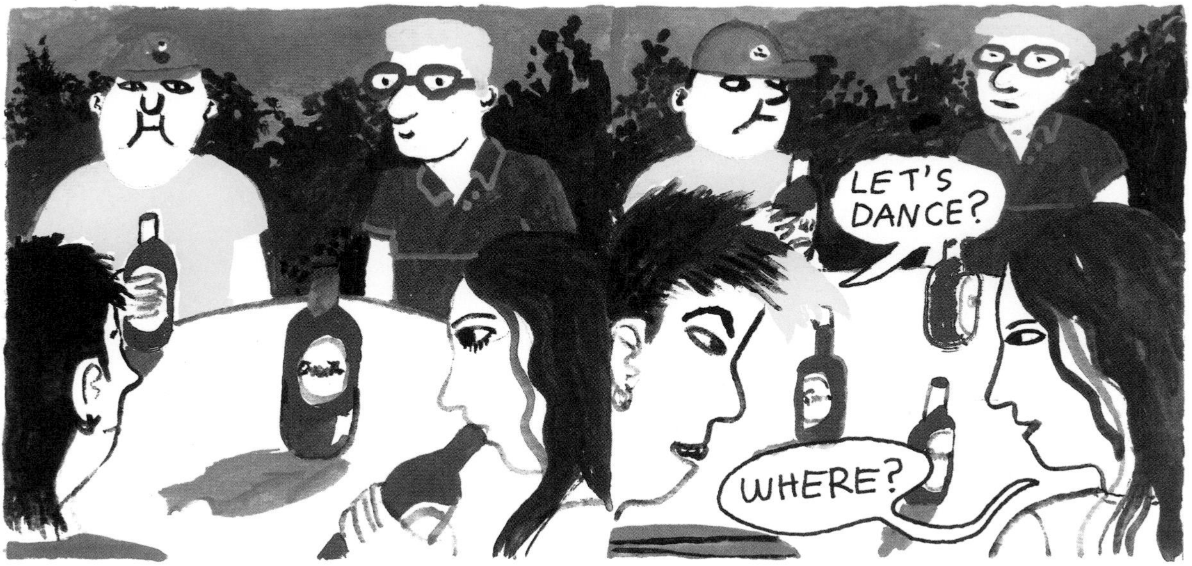
LET'S DANCE?
WHERE?

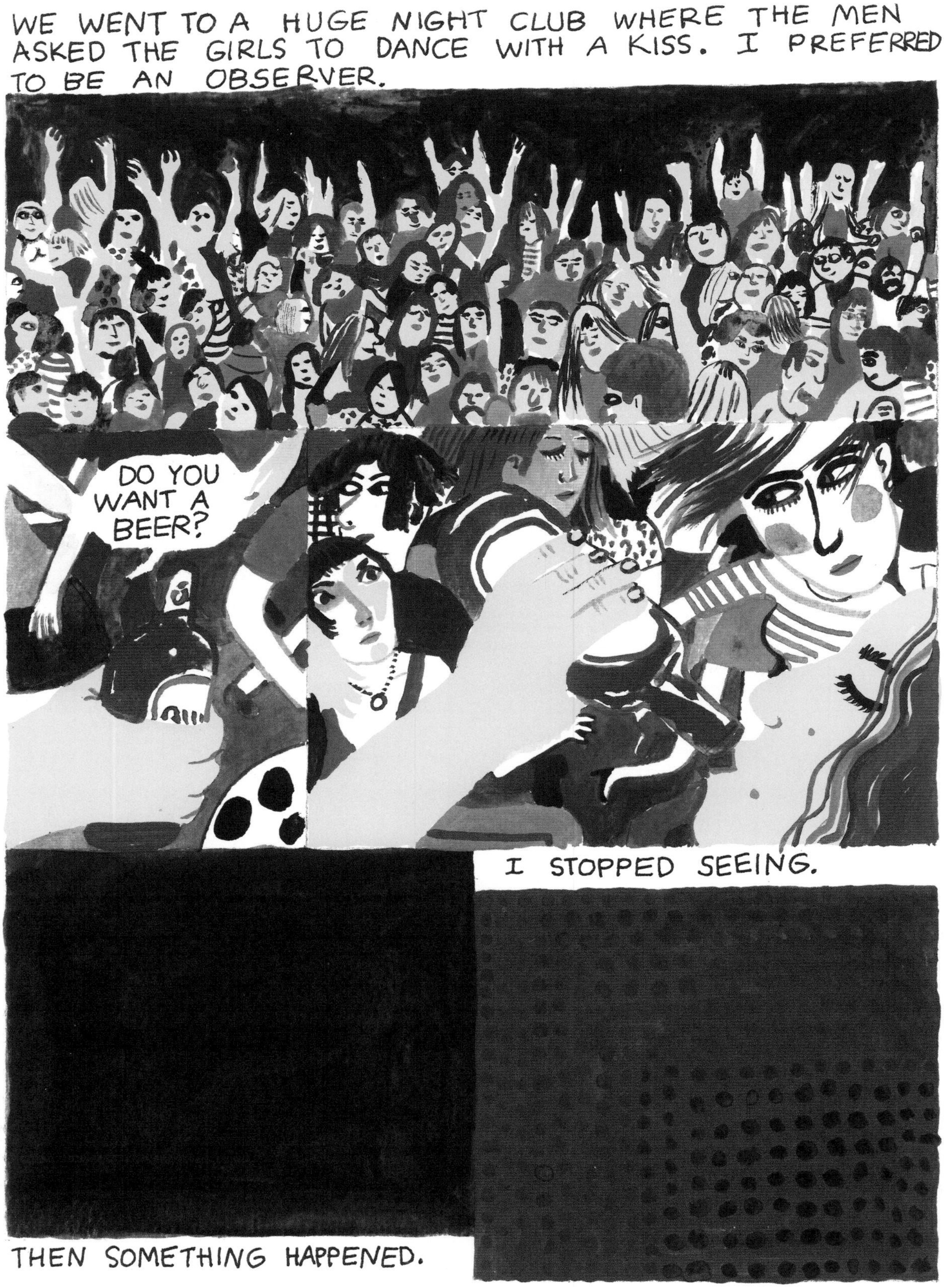
WE WENT TO A HUGE NIGHT CLUB WHERE THE MEN ASKED THE GIRLS TO DANCE WITH A KISS. I PREFERRED TO BE AN OBSERVER.
DO YOU WANT A BEER?
I STOPPED SEEING.
THEN SOMETHING HAPPENED.

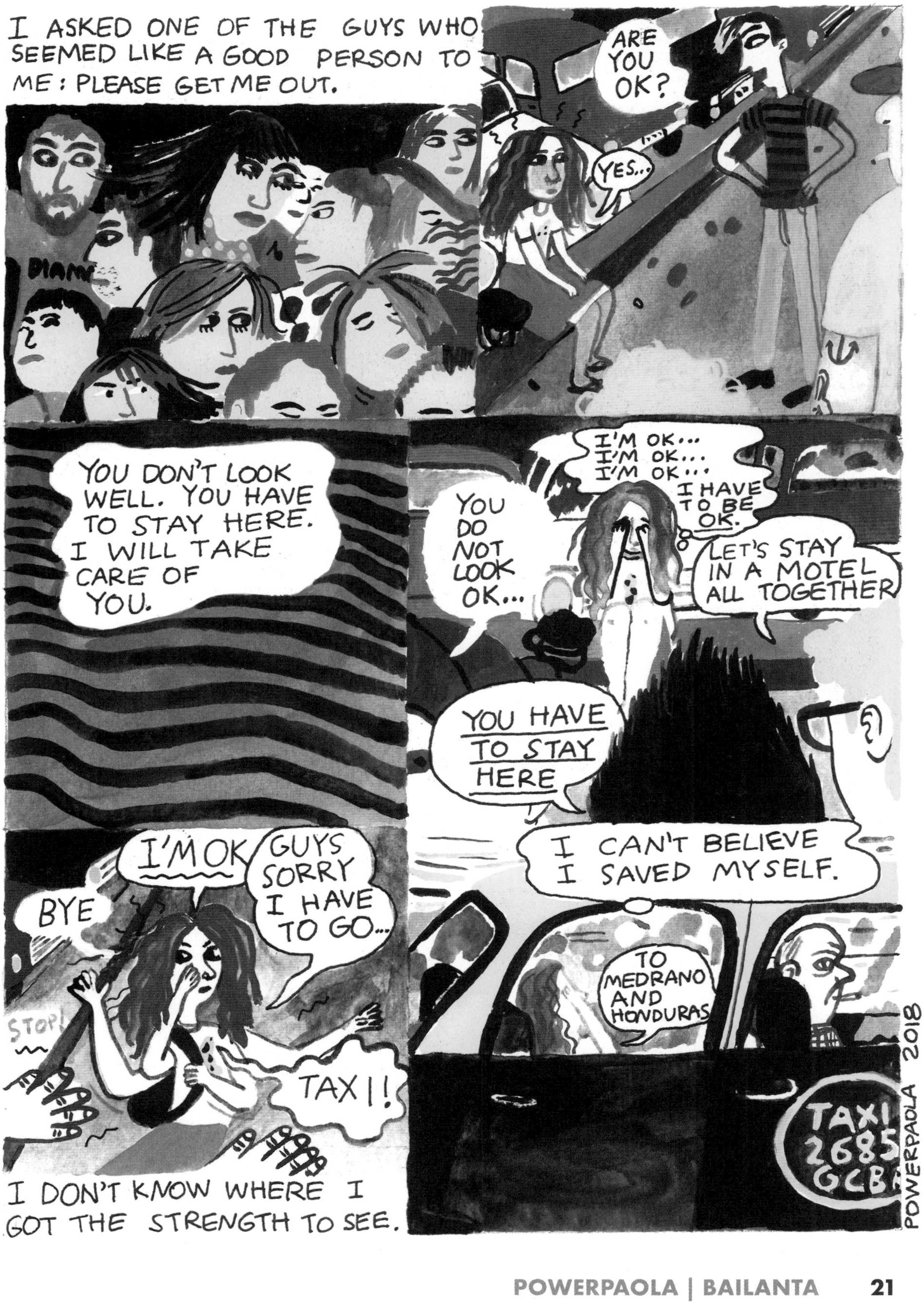
I ASKED ONE OF THE GUYS WHO SEEMED LIKE A GOOD PERSON TO ME: PLEASE GET ME OUT.
ARE YOU OK?
YES...
YOU DON'T LOOK WELL. YOU HAVE TO STAY HERE. I WILL TAKE CARE OF YOU.
I'M OK... I'M OK... I'M OK...
I HAVE TO BE OK.
YOU DO NOT LOOK OK...
LET'S STAY IN A MOTEL ALL TOGETHER
YOU HAVE TO STAY HERE
I'M OK
GUYS SORRY I HAVE TO GO...
BYE
STOP!
TAXI!
I DON'T KNOW WHERE I GOT THE STRENGTH TO SEE.
I CAN'T BELIEVE I SAVED MYSELF.
TO MEDRANO AND HONDURAS
TAXI 2685 GCB
POWERPAOLA 2018

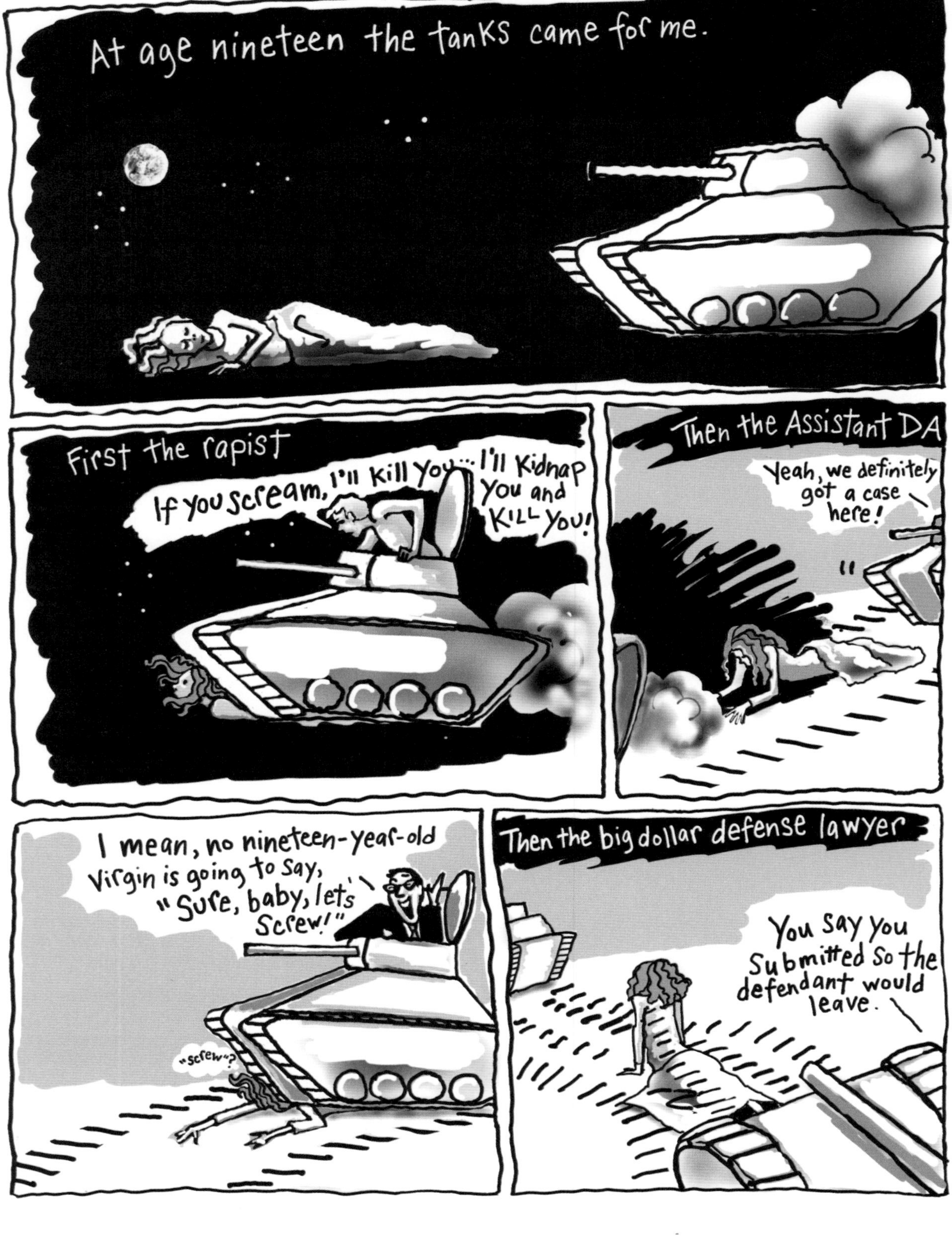
At age nineteen the tanks came for me.
First the rapist
If you scream, I'll kill you... I'll kidnap you and KILL YOU!
Then the Assistant DA
Yeah, we definitely got a case here!
I mean, no nineteen-year-old virgin is going to say, "Sure, baby, let's screw!"
"screw"?
Then the big dollar defense lawyer
You say you submitted so the defendant would leave.

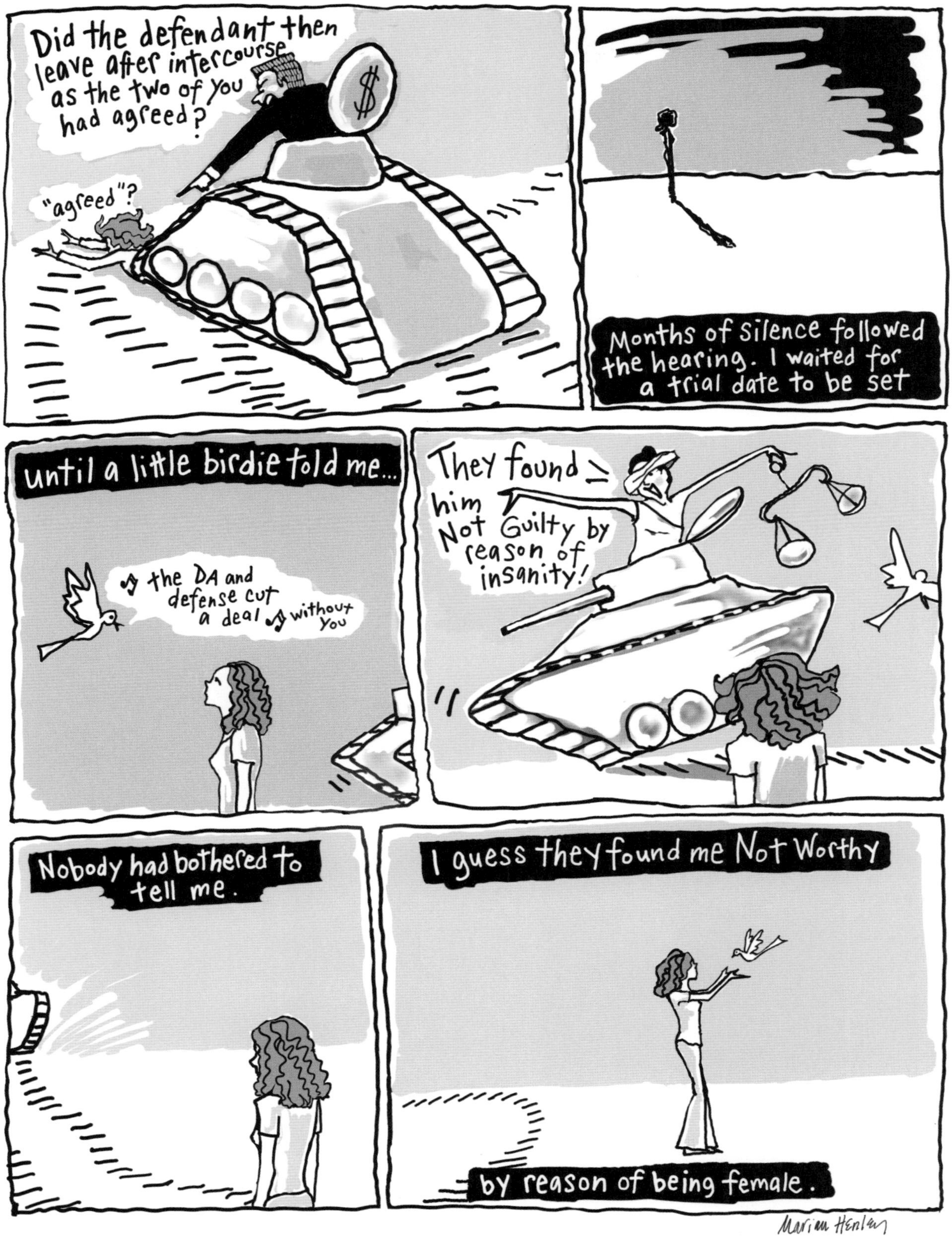

Did the defendant then leave after intercourse as the two of you had agreed?
"agreed"?
Months of silence followed the hearing. I waited for a trial date to be set
until a little birdie told me...
the DA and defense cut a deal without you
They found him Not Guilty by reason of insanity!
Nobody had bothered to tell me.
I guess they found me Not Worthy
by reason of being female.
Marian Henley

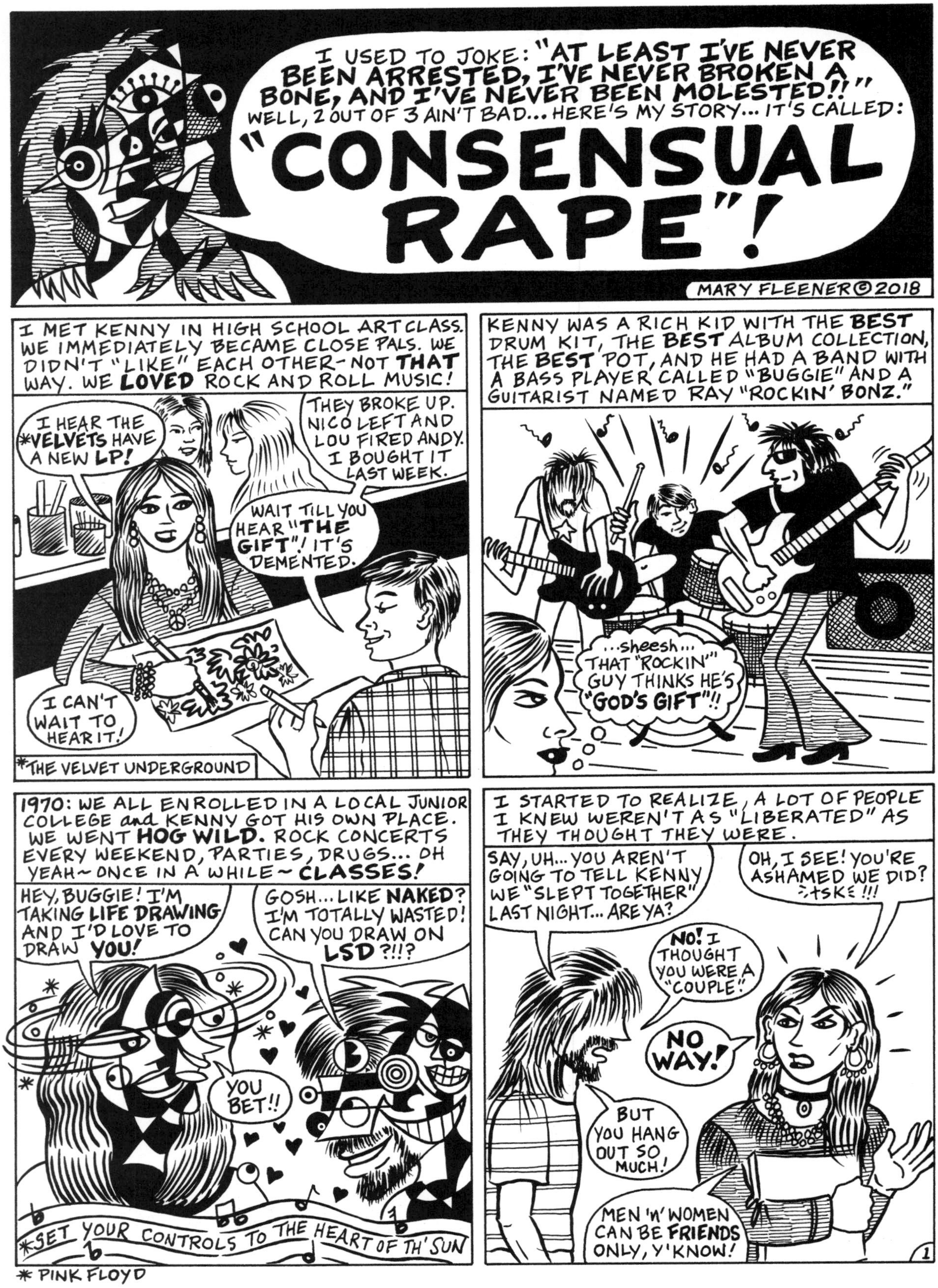
I USED TO JOKE: "AT LEAST I'VE NEVER BEEN ARRESTED, I'VE NEVER BROKEN A BONE, AND I'VE NEVER BEEN MOLESTED!!" WELL, 2 OUT OF 3 AIN'T BAD... HERE'S MY STORY... IT'S CALLED:
"CONSENSUAL RAPE"!
MARY FLEENER © 2018
I MET KENNY IN HIGH SCHOOL ART CLASS. WE IMMEDIATELY BECAME CLOSE PALS. WE DIDN'T "LIKE" EACH OTHER- NOT THAT WAY. WE LOVED ROCK AND ROLL MUSIC!
I HEAR THE *VELVETS HAVE A NEW LP!
THEY BROKE UP. NICO LEFT AND LOU FIRED ANDY. I BOUGHT IT LAST WEEK.
WAIT TILL YOU HEAR "THE GIFT"! IT'S DEMENTED.
I CAN'T WAIT TO HEAR IT!
*THE VELVET UNDERGROUND
KENNY WAS A RICH KID WITH THE BEST DRUM KIT, THE BEST ALBUM COLLECTION, THE BEST POT, AND HE HAD A BAND WITH A BASS PLAYER CALLED "BUGGIE" AND A GUITARIST NAMED RAY "ROCKIN' BONZ."
...sheesh... THAT "ROCKIN'" GUY THINKS HE'S "GOD'S GIFT"!!
1970: WE ALL ENROLLED IN A LOCAL JUNIOR COLLEGE and KENNY GOT HIS OWN PLACE. WE WENT HOG WILD. ROCK CONCERTS EVERY WEEKEND, PARTIES, DRUGS... OH YEAH ~ ONCE IN A WHILE ~ CLASSES!
HEY, BUGGIE! I'M TAKING LIFE DRAWING AND I'D LOVE TO DRAW YOU!
GOSH... LIKE NAKED? I'M TOTALLY WASTED! CAN YOU DRAW ON LSD?!!?
YOU BET!!
*SET YOUR CONTROLS TO THE HEART OF TH' SUN
I STARTED TO REALIZE, A LOT OF PEOPLE I KNEW WEREN'T AS "LIBERATED" AS THEY THOUGHT THEY WERE.
SAY, UH... YOU AREN'T GOING TO TELL KENNY WE "SLEPT TOGETHER" LAST NIGHT... ARE YA?
OH, I SEE! YOU'RE ASHAMED WE DID? TSK!!!
NO! I THOUGHT YOU WERE A "COUPLE"!
NO WAY!
BUT YOU HANG OUT SO MUCH!
MEN 'N' WOMEN CAN BE FRIENDS ONLY, Y'KNOW!
1
* PINK FLOYD

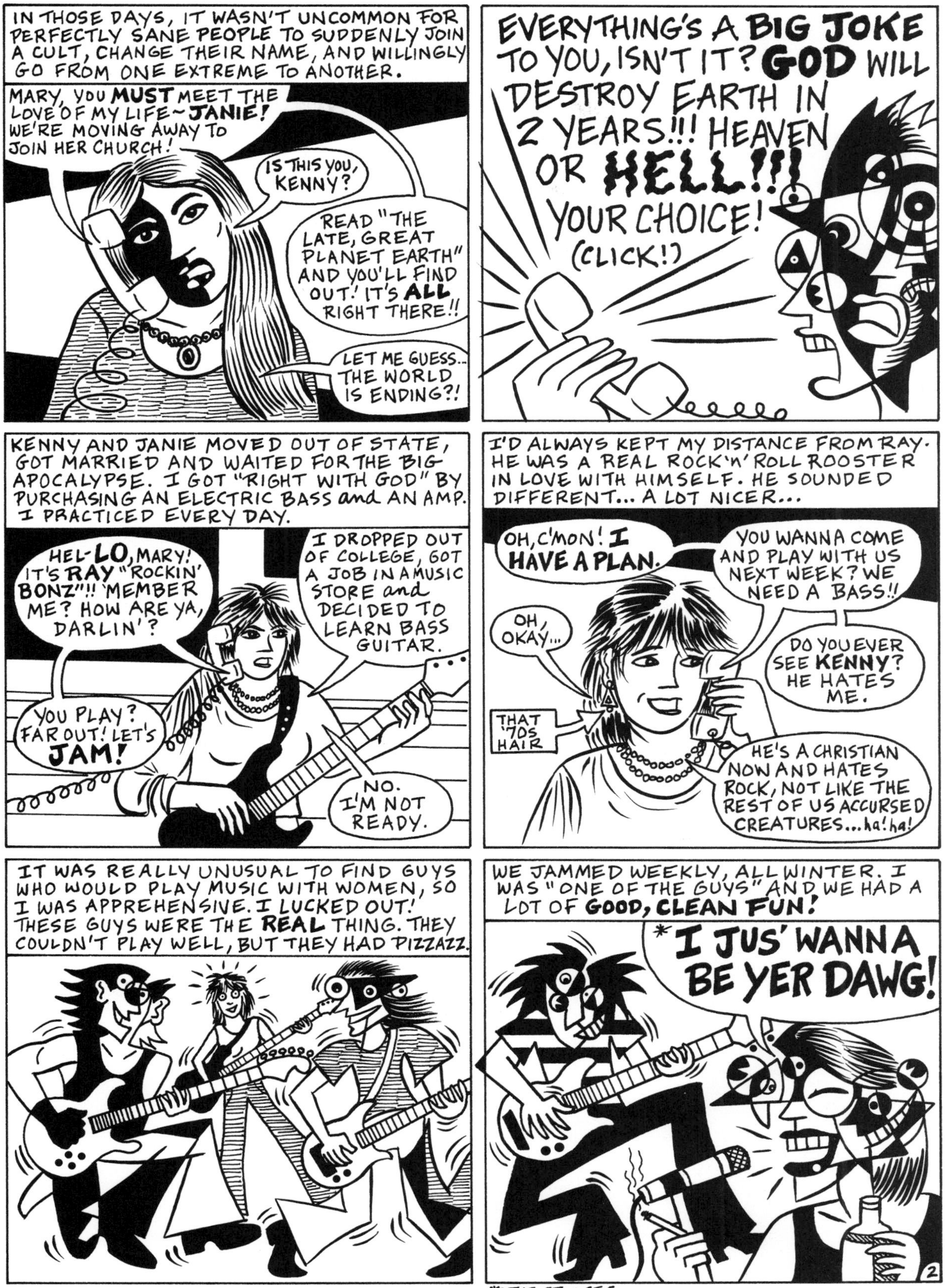

IN THOSE DAYS, IT WASN'T UNCOMMON FOR PERFECTLY SANE PEOPLE TO SUDDENLY JOIN A CULT, CHANGE THEIR NAME, AND WILLINGLY GO FROM ONE EXTREME TO ANOTHER.
MARY, YOU MUST MEET THE LOVE OF MY LIFE~JANIE! WE'RE MOVING AWAY TO JOIN HER CHURCH!
IS THIS YOU, KENNY?
READ "THE LATE, GREAT PLANET EARTH" AND YOU'LL FIND OUT! IT'S ALL RIGHT THERE!!
LET ME GUESS... THE WORLD IS ENDING?!
EVERYTHING'S A BIG JOKE TO YOU, ISN'T IT? GOD WILL DESTROY EARTH IN 2 YEARS!!! HEAVEN OR HELL!!! YOUR CHOICE!
(CLICK!)
KENNY AND JANIE MOVED OUT OF STATE, GOT MARRIED AND WAITED FOR THE BIG APOCALYPSE. I GOT "RIGHT WITH GOD" BY PURCHASING AN ELECTRIC BASS and AN AMP. I PRACTICED EVERY DAY.
HEL-LO, MARY! IT'S RAY "ROCKIN' BONZ"!! 'MEMBER ME? HOW ARE YA, DARLIN'?
I DROPPED OUT OF COLLEGE, GOT A JOB IN A MUSIC STORE and DECIDED TO LEARN BASS GUITAR.
YOU PLAY? FAR OUT! LET'S JAM!
NO. I'M NOT READY.
I'D ALWAYS KEPT MY DISTANCE FROM RAY. HE WAS A REAL ROCK'n' ROLL ROOSTER IN LOVE WITH HIMSELF. HE SOUNDED DIFFERENT... A LOT NICER...
OH, C'MON! I HAVE A PLAN.
YOU WANNA COME AND PLAY WITH US NEXT WEEK? WE NEED A BASS!!
OH, OKAY...
DO YOU EVER SEE KENNY? HE HATES ME.
THAT '70S HAIR
HE'S A CHRISTIAN NOW AND HATES ROCK, NOT LIKE THE REST OF US ACCURSED CREATURES...ha! ha!
IT WAS REALLY UNUSUAL TO FIND GUYS WHO WOULD PLAY MUSIC WITH WOMEN, SO I WAS APPREHENSIVE. I LUCKED OUT! THESE GUYS WERE THE REAL THING. THEY COULDN'T PLAY WELL, BUT THEY HAD PIZZAZZ.
WE JAMMED WEEKLY, ALL WINTER. I WAS "ONE OF THE GUYS" AND WE HAD A LOT OF GOOD, CLEAN FUN!
*I JUS' WANNA BE YER DAWG!
2

* THE STOOGES

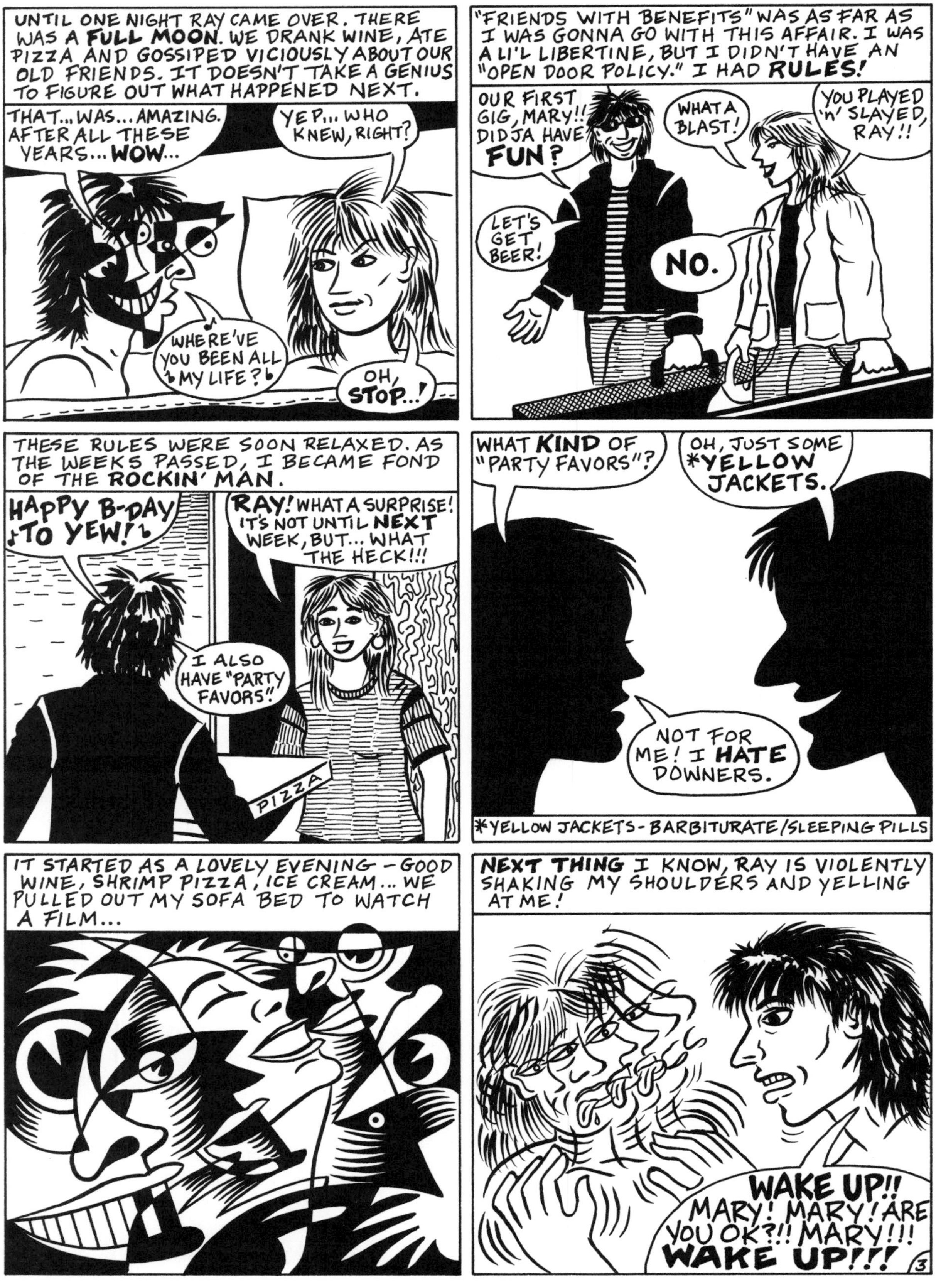

UNTIL ONE NIGHT RAY CAME OVER. THERE WAS A FULL MOON. WE DRANK WINE, ATE PIZZA AND GOSSIPED VICIOUSLY ABOUT OUR OLD FRIENDS. IT DOESN'T TAKE A GENIUS TO FIGURE OUT WHAT HAPPENED NEXT.
THAT... WAS... AMAZING. AFTER ALL THESE YEARS... WOW...
YEP... WHO KNEW, RIGHT?
WHERE'VE YOU BEEN ALL MY LIFE?
OH, STOP...!
"FRIENDS WITH BENEFITS" WAS AS FAR AS I WAS GONNA GO WITH THIS AFFAIR. I WAS A LI'L LIBERTINE, BUT I DIDN'T HAVE AN "OPEN DOOR POLICY." I HAD RULES!
OUR FIRST GIG, MARY!! DIDJA HAVE FUN?
WHAT A BLAST!
YOU PLAYED 'N' SLAYED, RAY!!
LET'S GET BEER!
NO.
THESE RULES WERE SOON RELAXED. AS THE WEEKS PASSED, I BECAME FOND OF THE ROCKIN' MAN.
HAPPY B-DAY TO YEW!
RAY! WHAT A SURPRISE! IT'S NOT UNTIL NEXT WEEK, BUT... WHAT THE HECK!!!
I ALSO HAVE "PARTY FAVORS!"
PIZZA
WHAT KIND OF "PARTY FAVORS"?
OH, JUST SOME *YELLOW JACKETS.
NOT FOR ME! I HATE DOWNERS.
*YELLOW JACKETS - BARBITURATE/SLEEPING PILLS
IT STARTED AS A LOVELY EVENING - GOOD WINE, SHRIMP PIZZA, ICE CREAM... WE PULLED OUT MY SOFA BED TO WATCH A FILM...
NEXT THING I KNOW, RAY IS VIOLENTLY SHAKING MY SHOULDERS AND YELLING AT ME!
WAKE UP!! MARY! MARY! ARE YOU OK?!! MARY!!! WAKE UP!!!
3

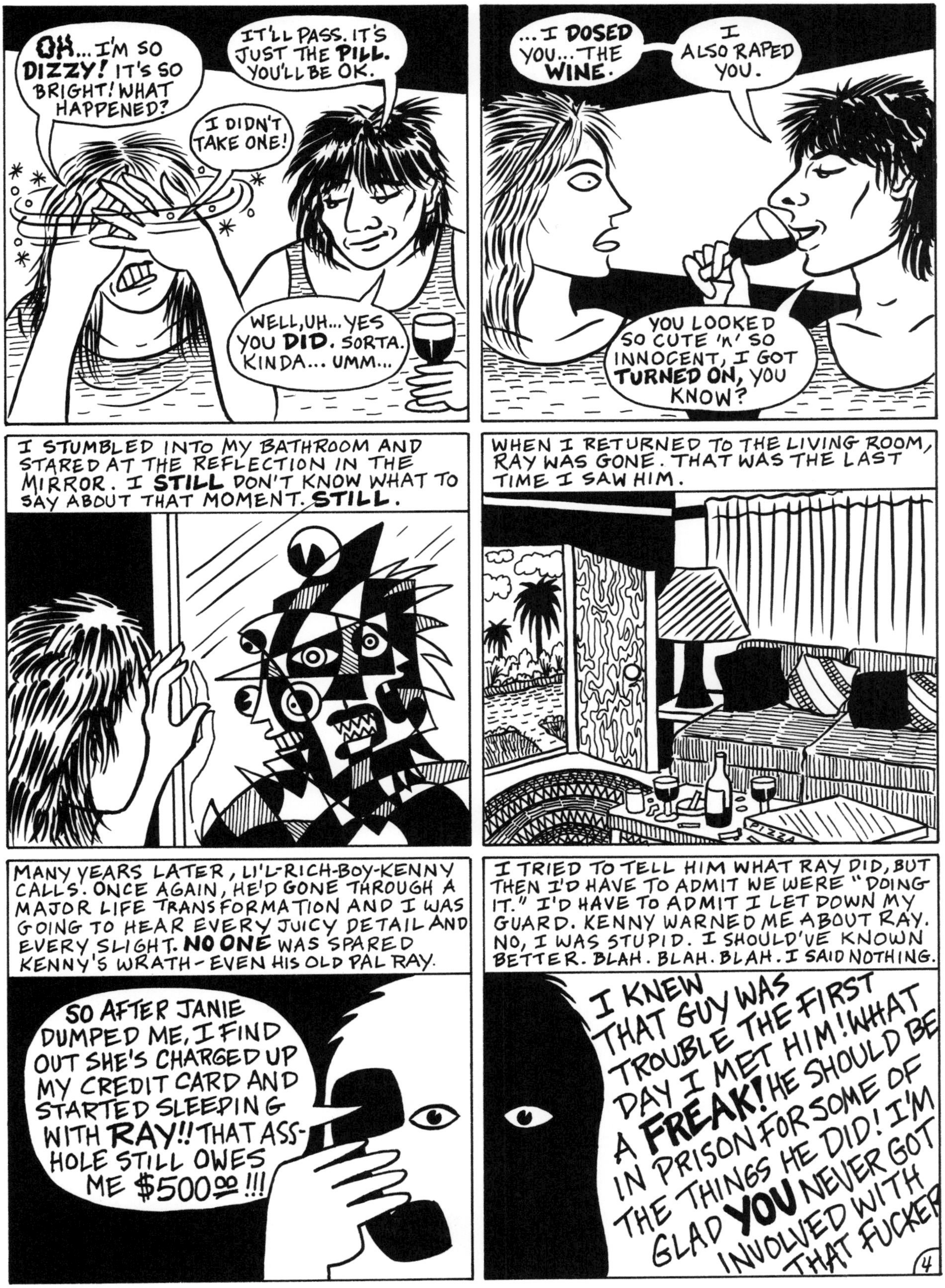
OH... I'M SO DIZZY! IT'S SO BRIGHT! WHAT HAPPENED?
IT'LL PASS. IT'S JUST THE PILL. YOU'LL BE OK.
I DIDN'T TAKE ONE!
WELL, UH... YES YOU DID. SORTA. KINDA... UMM...
...I DOSED YOU... THE WINE.
I ALSO RAPED YOU.
YOU LOOKED SO CUTE 'N' SO INNOCENT, I GOT TURNED ON, YOU KNOW?
I STUMBLED INTO MY BATHROOM AND STARED AT THE REFLECTION IN THE MIRROR. I STILL DON'T KNOW WHAT TO SAY ABOUT THAT MOMENT. STILL.
WHEN I RETURNED TO THE LIVING ROOM, RAY WAS GONE. THAT WAS THE LAST TIME I SAW HIM.
PIZZA
MANY YEARS LATER, LI'L-RICH-BOY-KENNY CALLS. ONCE AGAIN, HE'D GONE THROUGH A MAJOR LIFE TRANSFORMATION AND I WAS GOING TO HEAR EVERY JUICY DETAIL AND EVERY SLIGHT. NO ONE WAS SPARED KENNY'S WRATH - EVEN HIS OLD PAL RAY.
SO AFTER JANIE DUMPED ME, I FIND OUT SHE'S CHARGED UP MY CREDIT CARD AND STARTED SLEEPING WITH RAY!! THAT ASS-HOLE STILL OWES ME $500.00!!!
I TRIED TO TELL HIM WHAT RAY DID, BUT THEN I'D HAVE TO ADMIT WE WERE "DOING IT." I'D HAVE TO ADMIT I LET DOWN MY GUARD. KENNY WARNED ME ABOUT RAY. NO, I WAS STUPID. I SHOULD'VE KNOWN BETTER. BLAH. BLAH. BLAH. I SAID NOTHING.
I KNEW THAT GUY WAS TROUBLE THE FIRST DAY I MET HIM! WHAT A FREAK! HE SHOULD BE IN PRISON FOR SOME OF THE THINGS HE DID! I'M GLAD YOU NEVER GOT INVOLVED WITH THAT FUCKER
4

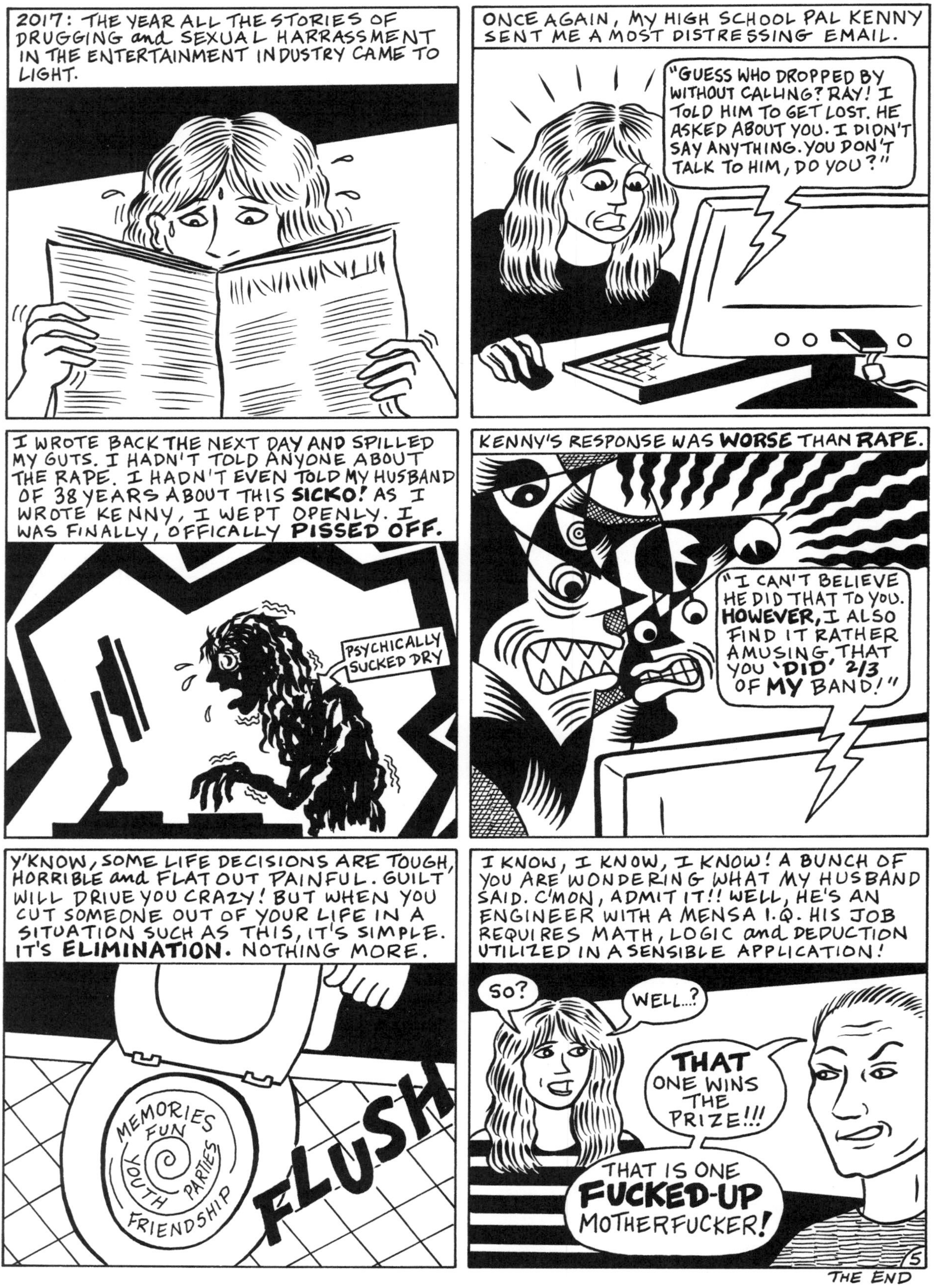
2017: THE YEAR ALL THE STORIES OF DRUGGING and SEXUAL HARRASSMENT IN THE ENTERTAINMENT INDUSTRY CAME TO LIGHT.
ONCE AGAIN, MY HIGH SCHOOL PAL KENNY SENT ME A MOST DISTRESSING EMAIL.
"GUESS WHO DROPPED BY WITHOUT CALLING? RAY! I TOLD HIM TO GET LOST. HE ASKED ABOUT YOU. I DIDN'T SAY ANYTHING. YOU DON'T TALK TO HIM, DO YOU?"
I WROTE BACK THE NEXT DAY AND SPILLED MY GUTS. I HADN'T TOLD ANYONE ABOUT THE RAPE. I HADN'T EVEN TOLD MY HUSBAND OF 38 YEARS ABOUT THIS SICKO! AS I WROTE KENNY, I WEPT OPENLY. I WAS FINALLY, OFFICALLY PISSED OFF.
PSYCHICALLY SUCKED DRY
KENNY'S RESPONSE WAS WORSE THAN RAPE.
"I CAN'T BELIEVE HE DID THAT TO YOU. HOWEVER, I ALSO FIND IT RATHER AMUSING, THAT YOU 'DID' 2/3 OF MY BAND!"
Y'KNOW, SOME LIFE DECISIONS ARE TOUGH, HORRIBLE and FLAT OUT PAINFUL. GUILT WILL DRIVE YOU CRAZY! BUT WHEN YOU CUT SOMEONE OUT OF YOUR LIFE IN A SITUATION SUCH AS THIS, IT'S SIMPLE. IT'S ELIMINATION. NOTHING MORE.
MEMORIES FUN YOUTH PARTIES FRIENDSHIP
FLUSH
I KNOW, I KNOW, I KNOW! A BUNCH OF YOU ARE WONDERING WHAT MY HUSBAND SAID. C'MON, ADMIT IT!! WELL, HE'S AN ENGINEER WITH A MENSA I.Q. HIS JOB REQUIRES MATH, LOGIC and DEDUCTION UTILIZED IN A SENSIBLE APPLICATION!
SO?
WELL...?
THAT ONE WINS THE PRIZE!!!
THAT IS ONE FUCKED-UP MOTHERFUCKER!
5
THE END

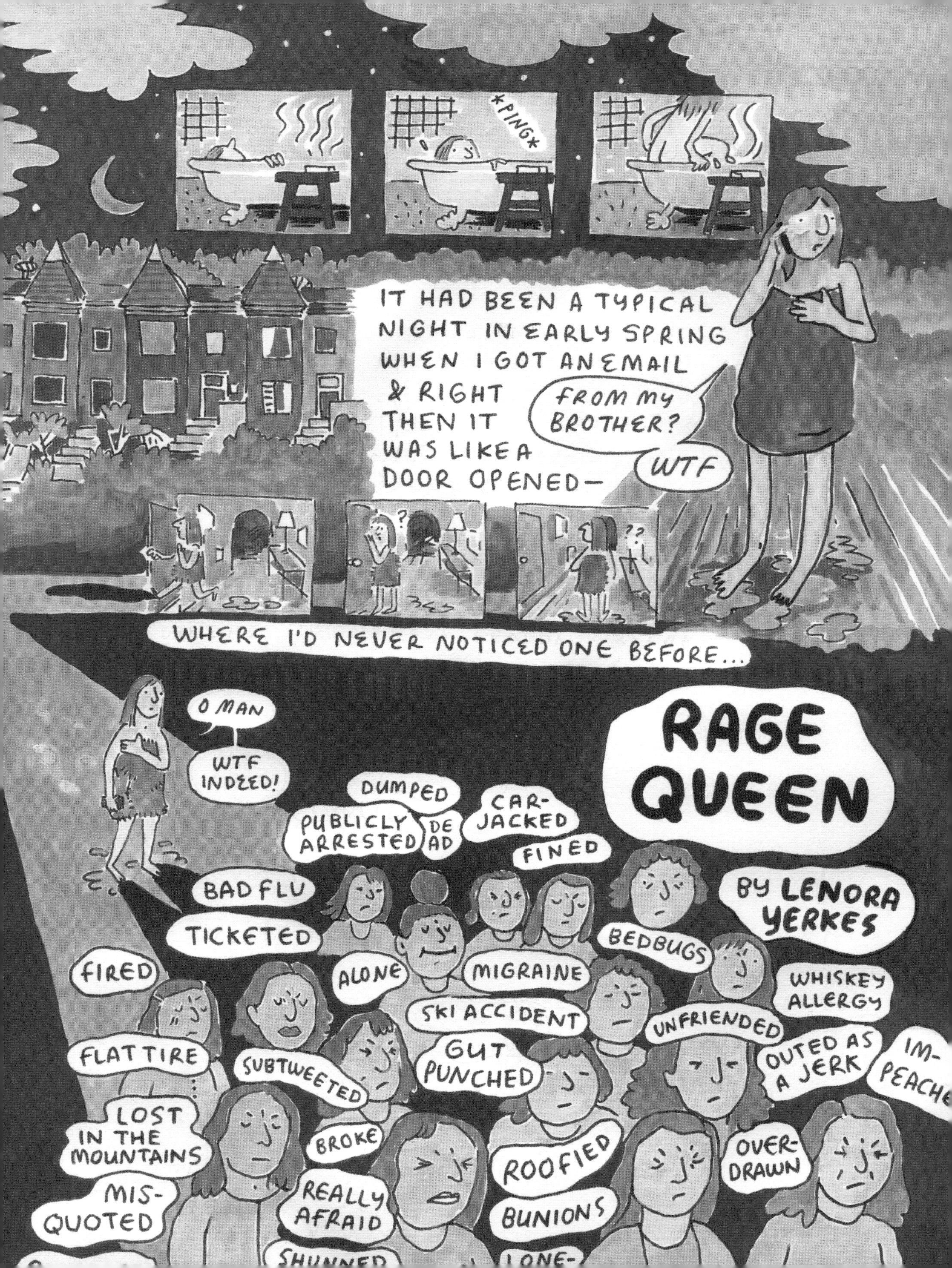
PING
IT HAD BEEN A TYPICAL NIGHT IN EARLY SPRING WHEN I GOT AN EMAIL
FROM MY BROTHER?
& RIGHT THEN IT WAS LIKE A DOOR OPENED—
WTF
?
??
WHERE I'D NEVER NOTICED ONE BEFORE...
O MAN
WTF INDEED!
RAGE QUEEN
BY LENORA YERKES
DUMPED
PUBLICLY ARRESTED
DE AD
CAR-JACKED
FINED
BAD FLU
TICKETED
BEDBUGS
FIRED
ALONE
MIGRAINE
WHISKEY ALLERGY
SKI ACCIDENT
UNFRIENDED
FLAT TIRE
SUBTWEETED
GUT PUNCHED
OUTED AS A JERK
IM-PEACHE
LOST IN THE MOUNTAINS
BROKE
ROOFIED
OVER-DRAWN
MIS-QUOTED
REALLY AFRAID
BUNIONS
SHUNNED
LONE-

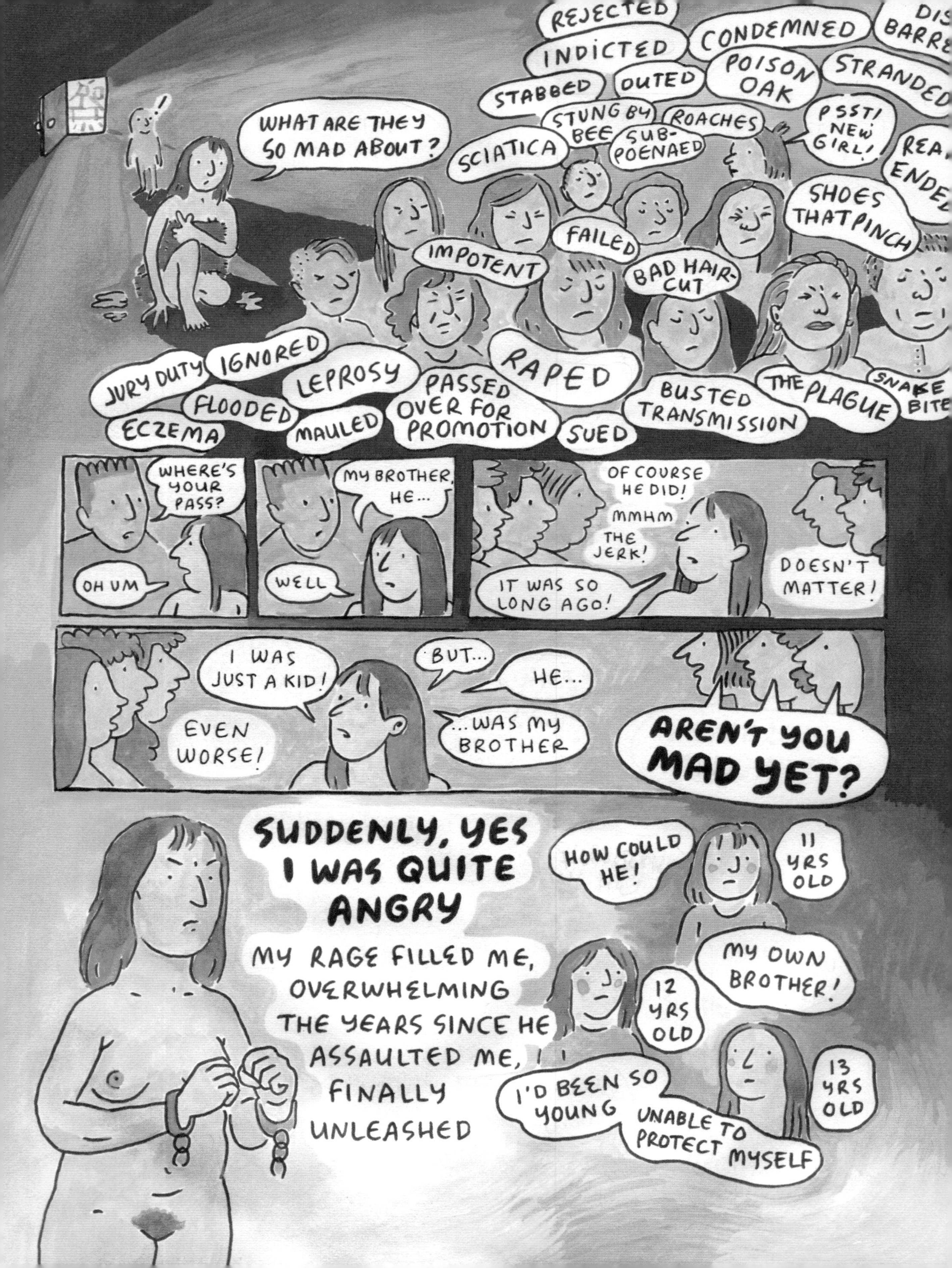
REJECTED
CONDEMNED
INDICTED
STABBED
OUTED
POISON OAK
STRANDED
STUNG BY BEE
ROACHES
SUB-POENAED
SCIATICA
PSST! NEW GIRL!
ENDED
SHOES THAT PINCH
FAILED
IMPOTENT
BAD HAIR-CUT
WHAT ARE THEY SO MAD ABOUT?
JURY DUTY
IGNORED
LEPROSY
RAPED
PASSED OVER FOR PROMOTION
FLOODED
ECZEMA
MAULED
SUED
BUSTED TRANSMISSION
THE PLAGUE
SNAKE BITE
WHERE'S YOUR PASS?
OH UM
MY BROTHER, HE...
WELL
OF COURSE HE DID!
MMHM
THE JERK!
IT WAS SO LONG AGO!
DOESN'T MATTER!
I WAS JUST A KID!
BUT...
HE...
EVEN WORSE!
...WAS MY BROTHER
AREN'T YOU MAD YET?
SUDDENLY, YES I WAS QUITE ANGRY
MY RAGE FILLED ME, OVERWHELMING THE YEARS SINCE HE ASSAULTED ME, FINALLY UNLEASHED
HOW COULD HE!
11 YRS OLD
MY OWN BROTHER!
12 YRS OLD
I'D BEEN SO YOUNG
UNABLE TO PROTECT MYSELF
13 YRS OLD

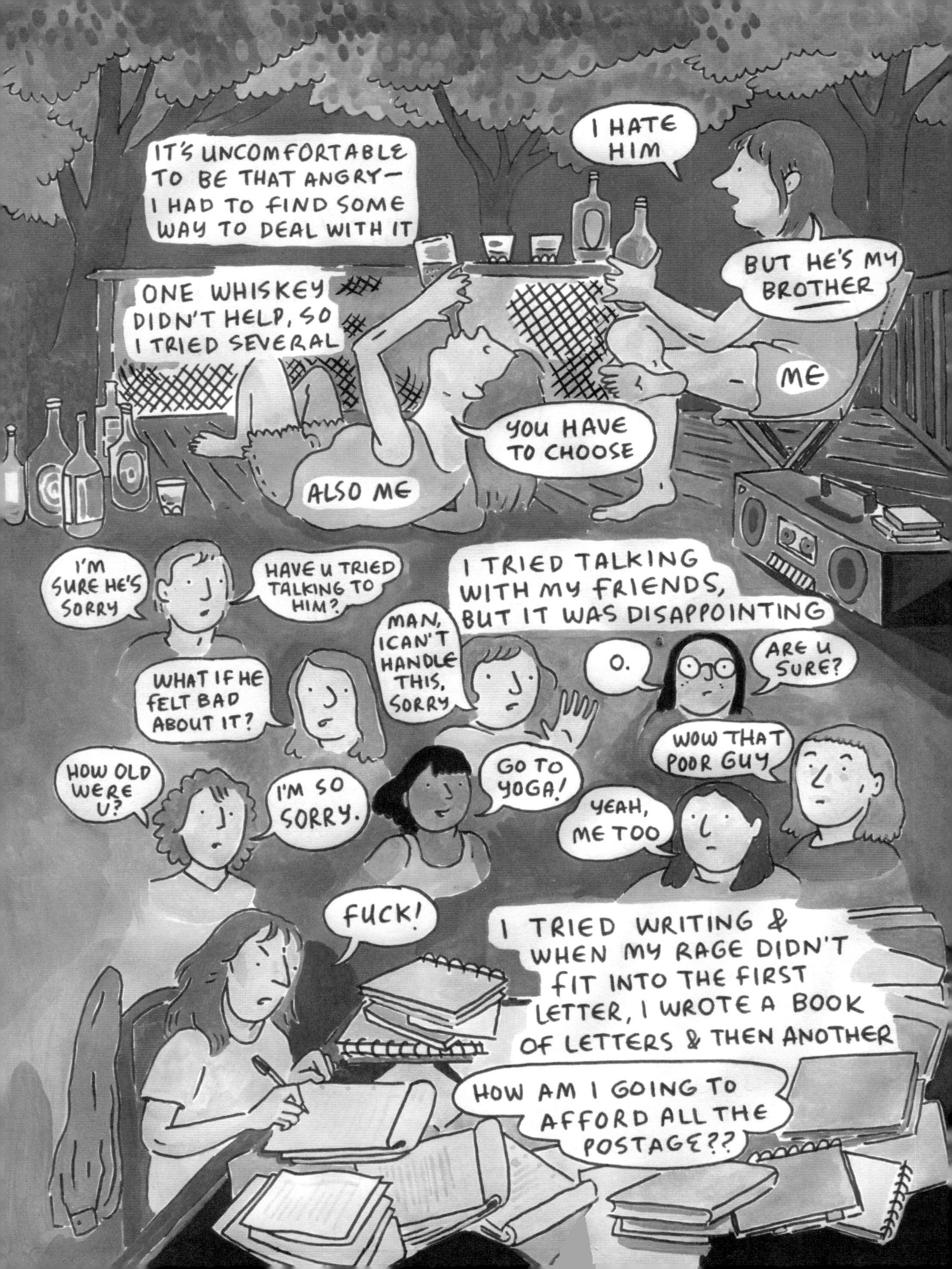

IT'S UNCOMFORTABLE TO BE THAT ANGRY— I HAD TO FIND SOME WAY TO DEAL WITH IT
I HATE HIM
BUT HE'S MY BROTHER
ONE WHISKEY DIDN'T HELP, SO I TRIED SEVERAL
ME
YOU HAVE TO CHOOSE
ALSO ME
I'M SURE HE'S SORRY
HAVE U TRIED TALKING TO HIM?
I TRIED TALKING WITH MY FRIENDS, BUT IT WAS DISAPPOINTING
MAN, I CAN'T HANDLE THIS, SORRY
WHAT IF HE FELT BAD ABOUT IT?
O.
ARE U SURE?
WOW THAT POOR GUY
HOW OLD WERE U?
I'M SO SORRY.
GO TO YOGA!
YEAH, ME TOO
FUCK!
I TRIED WRITING & WHEN MY RAGE DIDN'T FIT INTO THE FIRST LETTER, I WROTE A BOOK OF LETTERS & THEN ANOTHER
HOW AM I GOING TO AFFORD ALL THE POSTAGE??

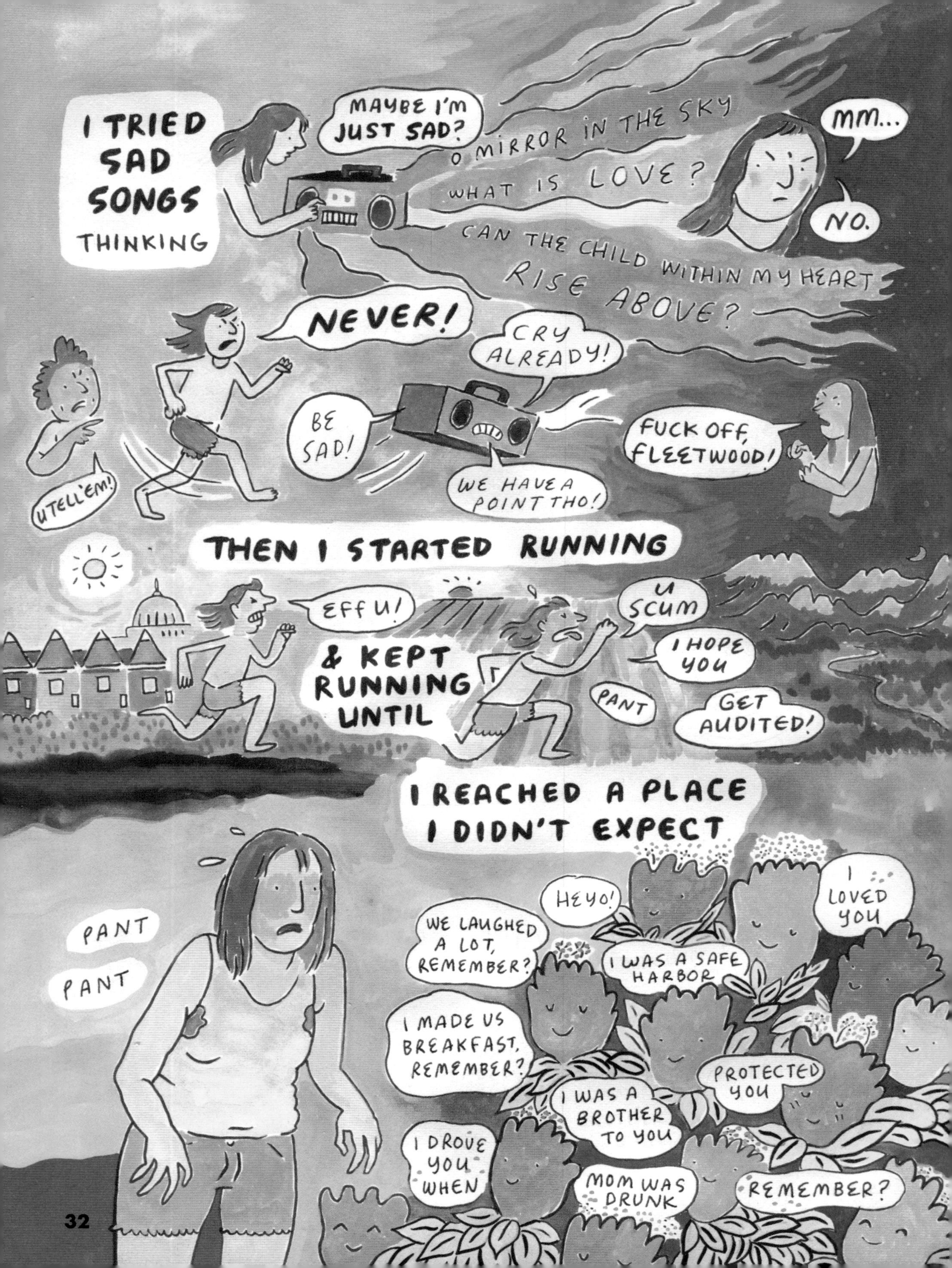
I TRIED SAD SONGS THINKING
MAYBE I'M JUST SAD?
O MIRROR IN THE SKY
WHAT IS LOVE?
MM...
NO.
CAN THE CHILD WITHIN MY HEART RISE ABOVE?
NEVER!
CRY ALREADY!
BE SAD!
WE HAVE A POINT THO!
FUCK OFF, FLEETWOOD!
UTELL'EM!
THEN I STARTED RUNNING
EFF U!
U SCUM
I HOPE YOU
PANT
GET AUDITED!
& KEPT RUNNING UNTIL
I REACHED A PLACE I DIDN'T EXPECT
PANT
PANT
HEYO!
I LOVED YOU
WE LAUGHED A LOT, REMEMBER?
I WAS A SAFE HARBOR
I MADE US BREAKFAST, REMEMBER?
PROTECTED YOU
I WAS A BROTHER TO YOU
I DROVE YOU WHEN
MOM WAS DRUNK
REMEMBER?

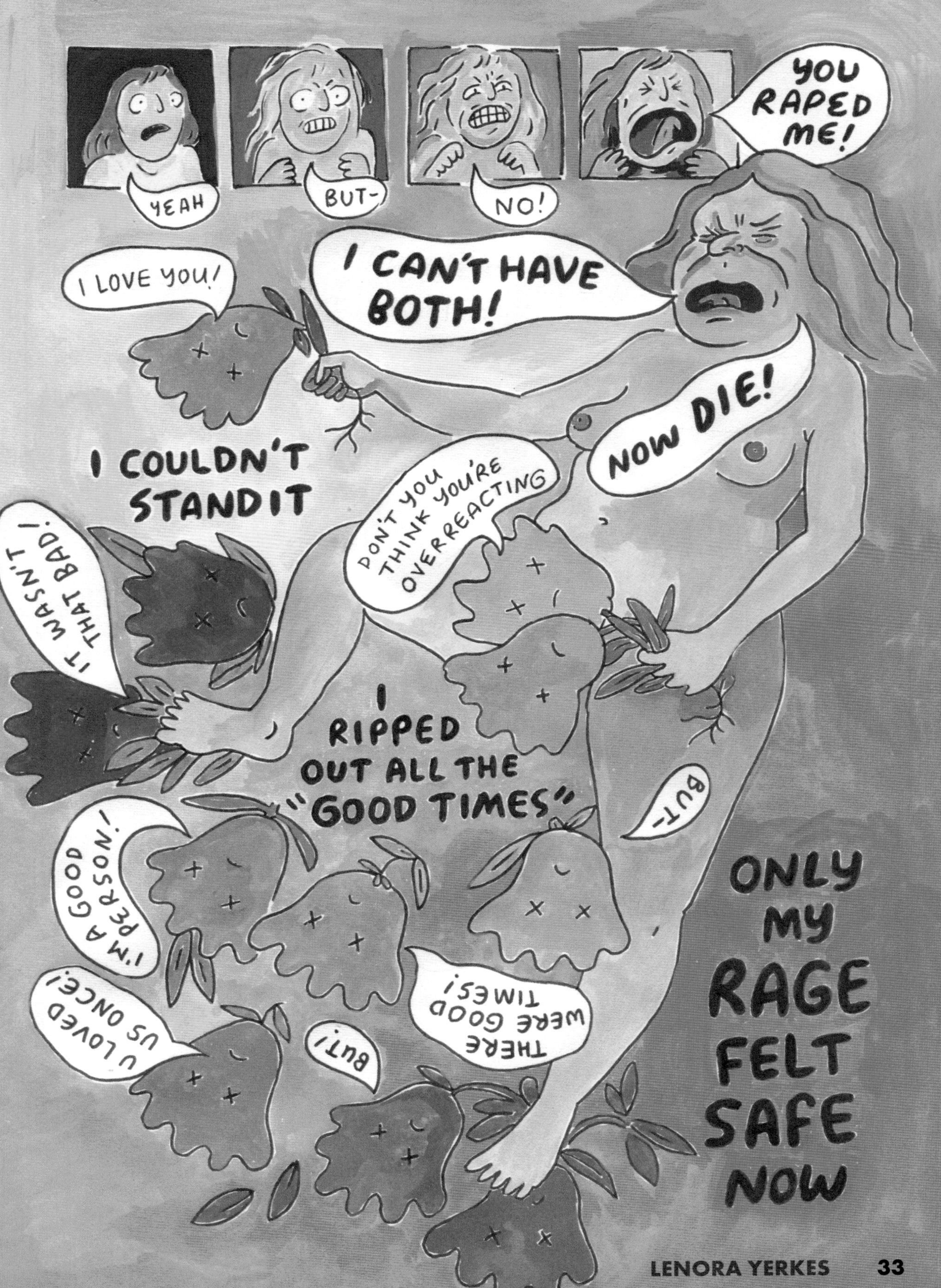
YEAH
BUT-
NO!
YOU RAPED ME!
I LOVE YOU!
I CAN'T HAVE BOTH!
NOW DIE!
I COULDN'T STAND IT
IT WASN'T THAT BAD!
DON'T YOU THINK YOU'RE OVERREACTING
I RIPPED OUT ALL THE "GOOD TIMES"
BUT-
I'M A GOOD PERSON!
THERE WERE GOOD TIMES!
U LOVED US ONCE!
BUT!
ONLY MY RAGE FELT SAFE NOW

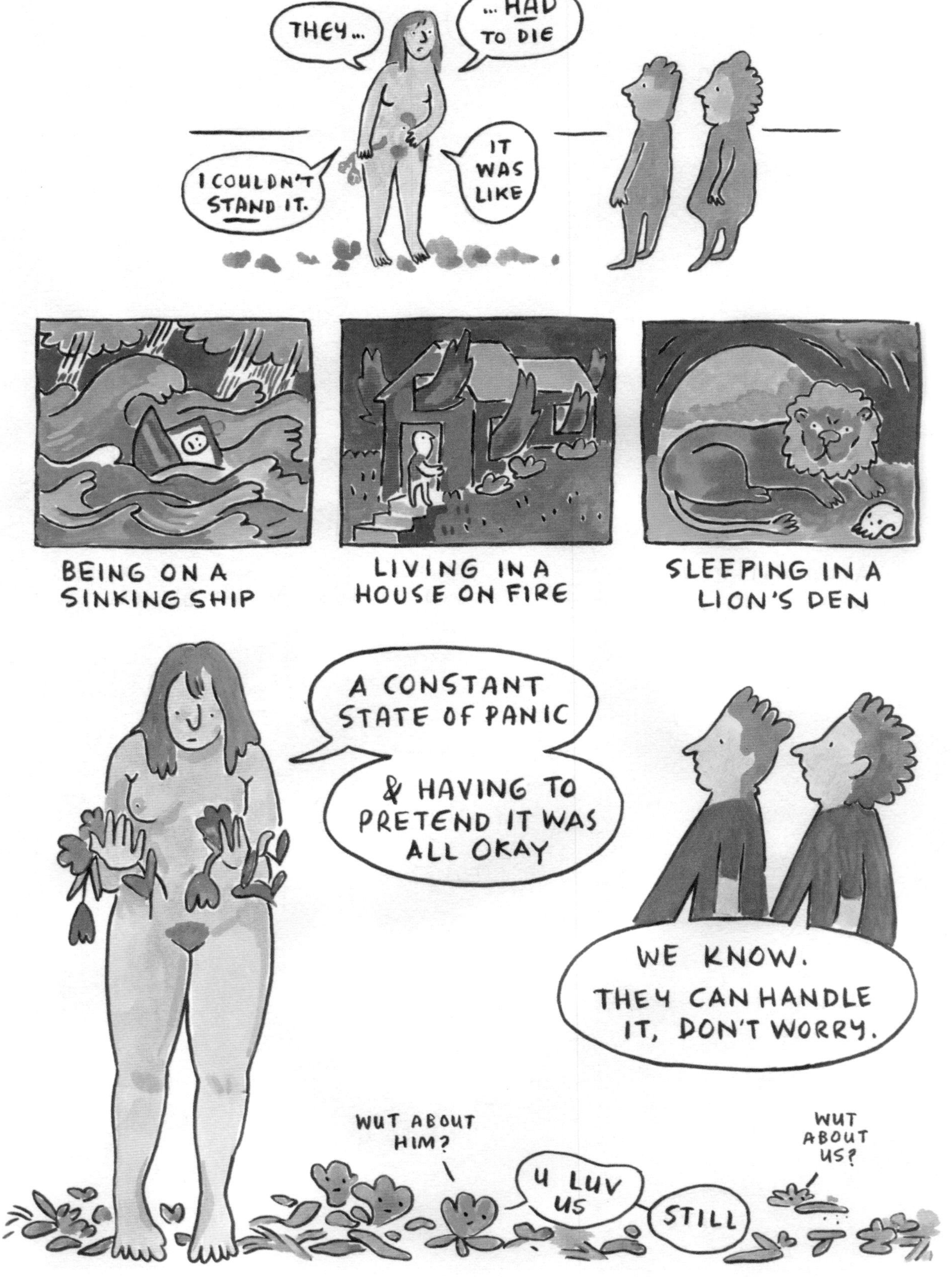
THEY...
...HAD TO DIE
I COULDN'T STAND IT.
IT WAS LIKE
BEING ON A SINKING SHIP
LIVING IN A HOUSE ON FIRE
SLEEPING IN A LION'S DEN
A CONSTANT STATE OF PANIC
& HAVING TO PRETEND IT WAS ALL OKAY
WE KNOW.
THEY CAN HANDLE IT, DON'T WORRY.
WUT ABOUT HIM?
U LUV US
STILL
WUT ABOUT US?

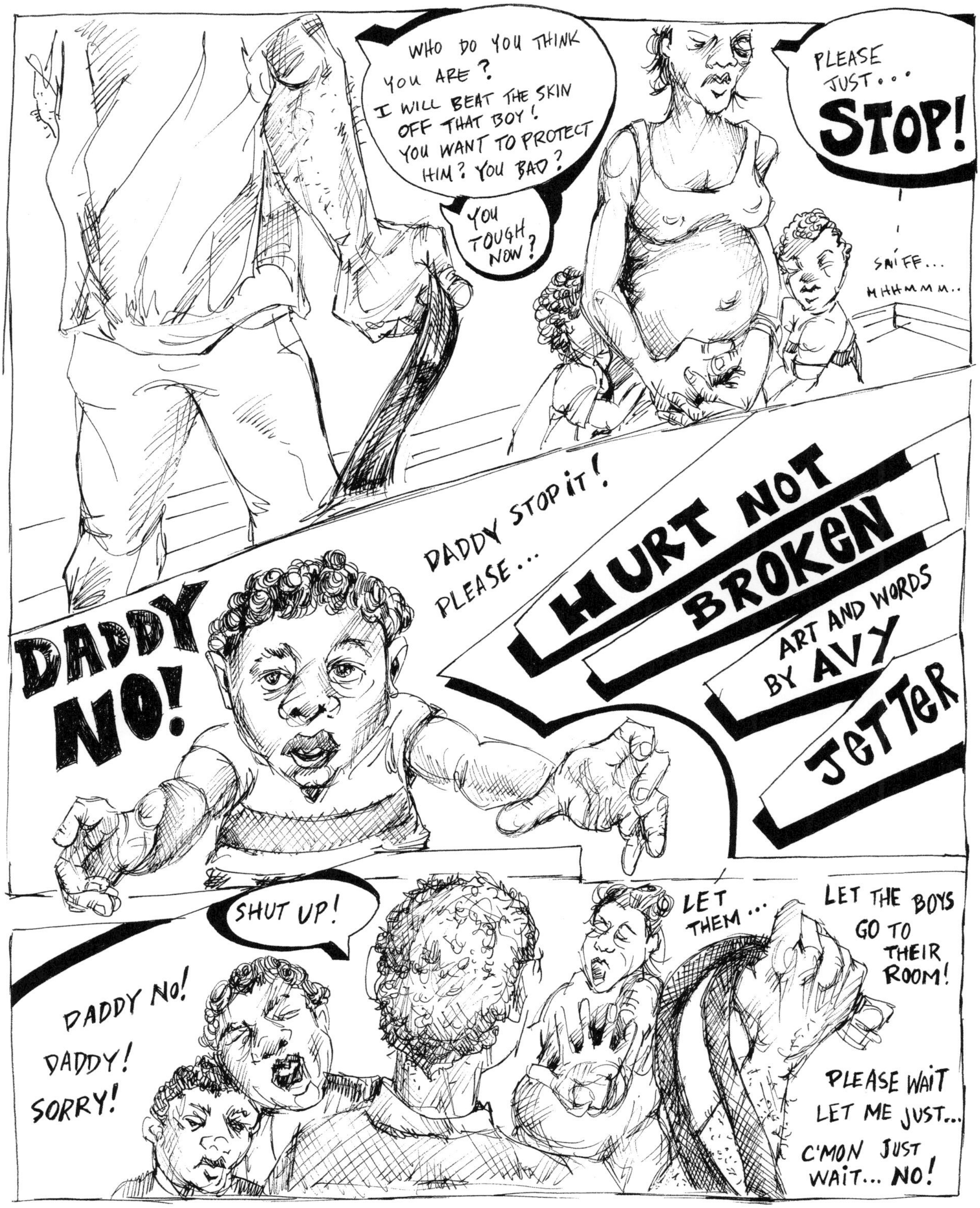
WHO DO YOU THINK YOU ARE? I WILL BEAT THE SKIN OFF THAT BOY! YOU WANT TO PROTECT HIM? YOU BAD?
YOU TOUGH NOW?
PLEASE JUST... STOP!
SNIFF... MHHMMMM...
DADDY STOP IT! PLEASE...
DADDY NO!
HURT NOT BROKEN
ART AND WORDS BY AVY JETTER
SHUT UP!
DADDY NO! DADDY! SORRY!
LET THEM...
LET THE BOYS GO TO THEIR ROOM!
PLEASE WAIT LET ME JUST...
C'MON JUST WAIT... NO!

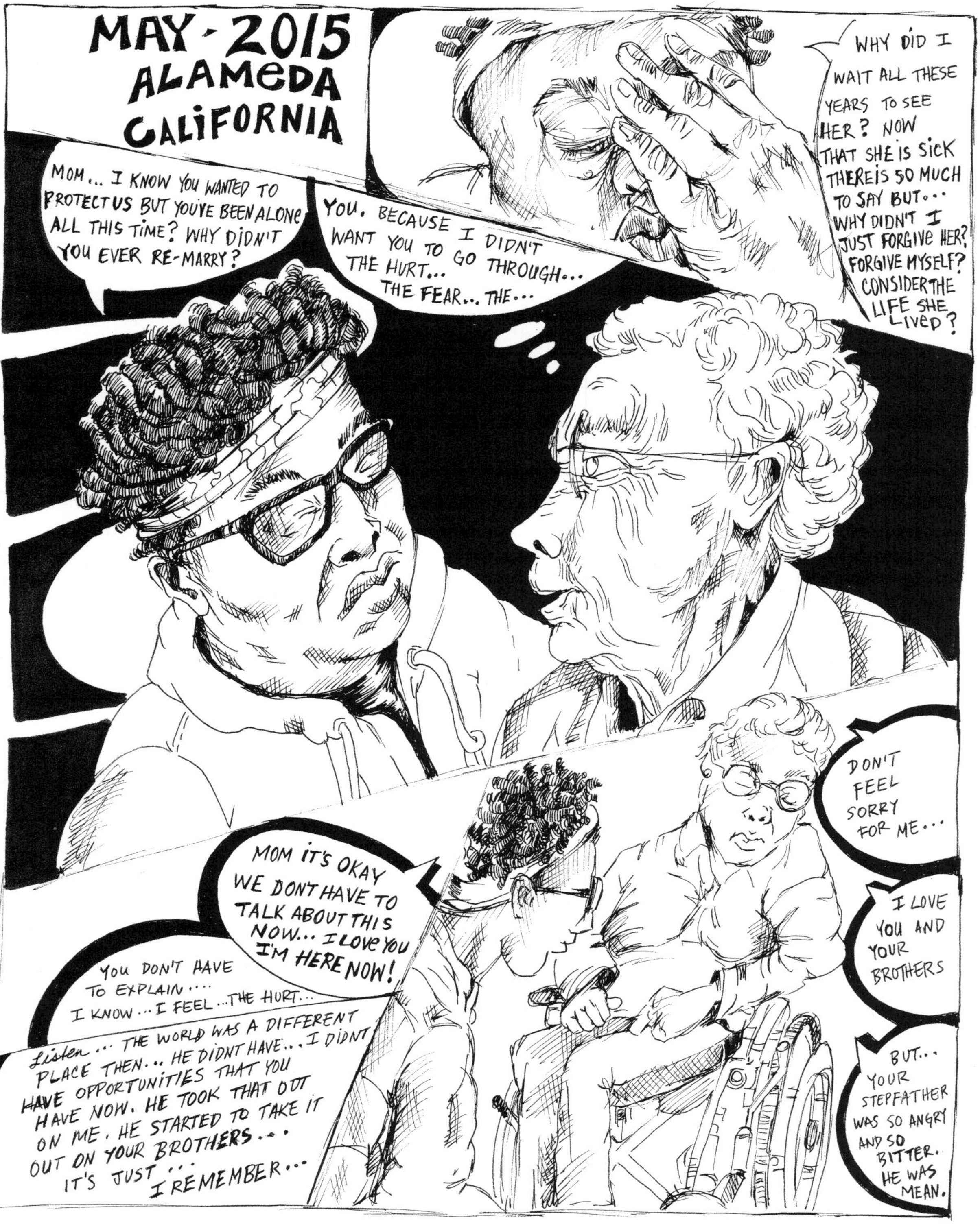
MAY - 2015 ALAMEDA CALIFORNIA
WHY DID I WAIT ALL THESE YEARS TO SEE HER? NOW THAT SHE IS SICK THERE IS SO MUCH TO SAY BUT... WHY DIDN'T I JUST FORGIVE HER? FORGIVE MYSELF? CONSIDER THE LIFE SHE LIVED?
MOM... I KNOW YOU WANTED TO PROTECT US BUT YOU'VE BEEN ALONE ALL THIS TIME? WHY DIDN'T YOU EVER RE-MARRY?
YOU. BECAUSE I DIDN'T WANT YOU TO GO THROUGH... THE HURT... THE FEAR... THE...
DON'T FEEL SORRY FOR ME...
I LOVE YOU AND YOUR BROTHERS
BUT... YOUR STEPFATHER WAS SO ANGRY AND SO BITTER. HE WAS MEAN.
MOM IT'S OKAY WE DONT HAVE TO TALK ABOUT THIS NOW... I LOVE YOU I'M HERE NOW!
YOU DON'T HAVE TO EXPLAIN.... I KNOW... I FEEL... THE HURT...
Listen... THE WORLD WAS A DIFFERENT PLACE THEN... HE DIDNT HAVE... I DIDNT HAVE OPPORTUNITIES THAT YOU HAVE NOW. HE TOOK THAT OUT ON ME. HE STARTED TO TAKE IT OUT ON YOUR BROTHERS... IT'S JUST... I REMEMBER...

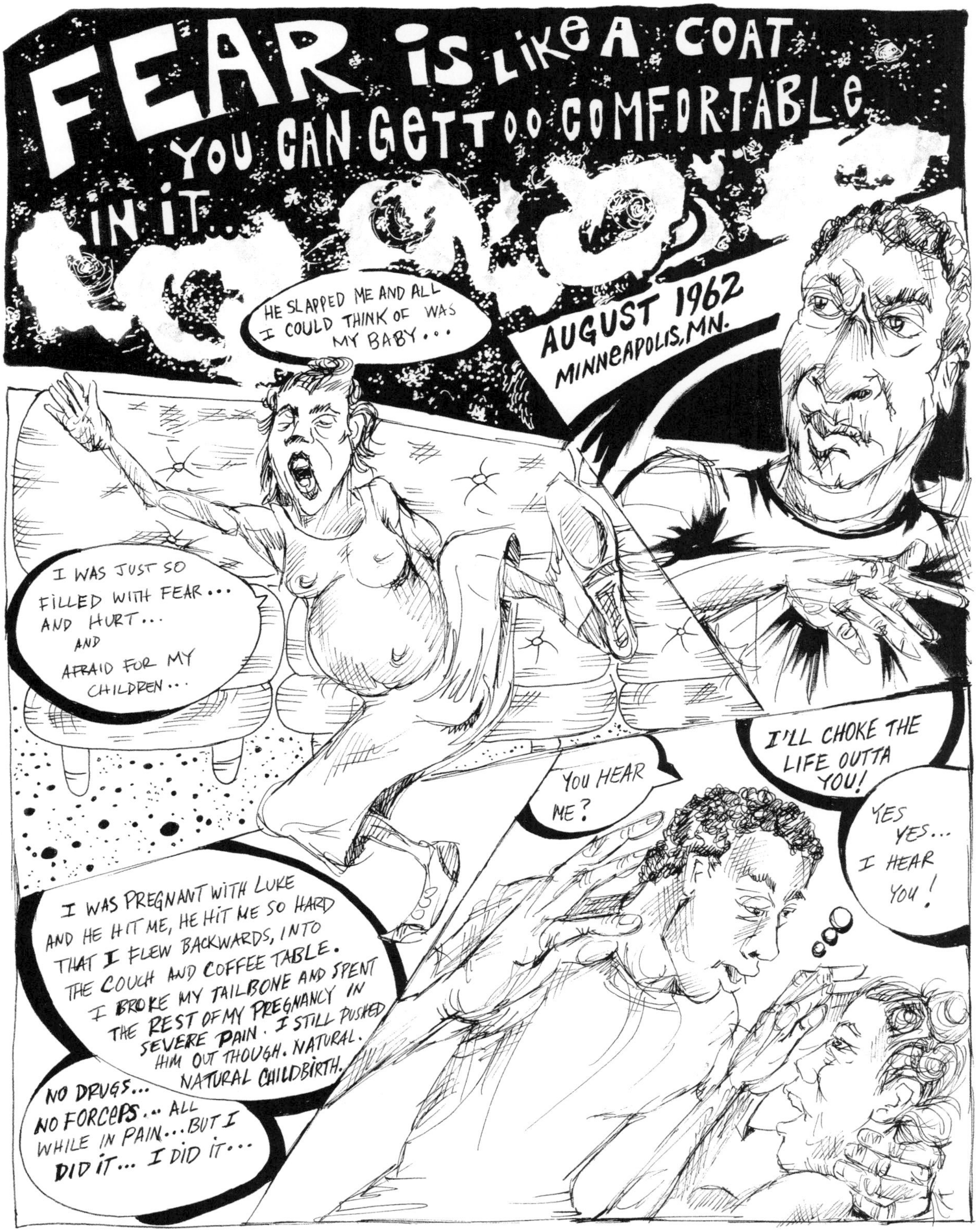
FEAR IS LIKE A COAT YOU CAN GET TOO COMFORTABLE IN IT...
HE SLAPPED ME AND ALL I COULD THINK OF WAS MY BABY...
AUGUST 1962 MINNEAPOLIS, MN.
I WAS JUST SO FILLED WITH FEAR... AND HURT... AND AFRAID FOR MY CHILDREN...
YOU HEAR ME?
I'LL CHOKE THE LIFE OUTTA YOU!
YES YES... I HEAR YOU!
I WAS PREGNANT WITH LUKE AND HE HIT ME, HE HIT ME SO HARD THAT I FLEW BACKWARDS, INTO THE COUCH AND COFFEE TABLE. I BROKE MY TAILBONE AND SPENT THE REST OF MY PREGNANCY IN SEVERE PAIN. I STILL PUSHED HIM OUT THOUGH. NATURAL. NATURAL CHILDBIRTH.
NO DRUGS... NO FORCEPS... ALL WHILE IN PAIN... BUT I DID IT... I DID IT...

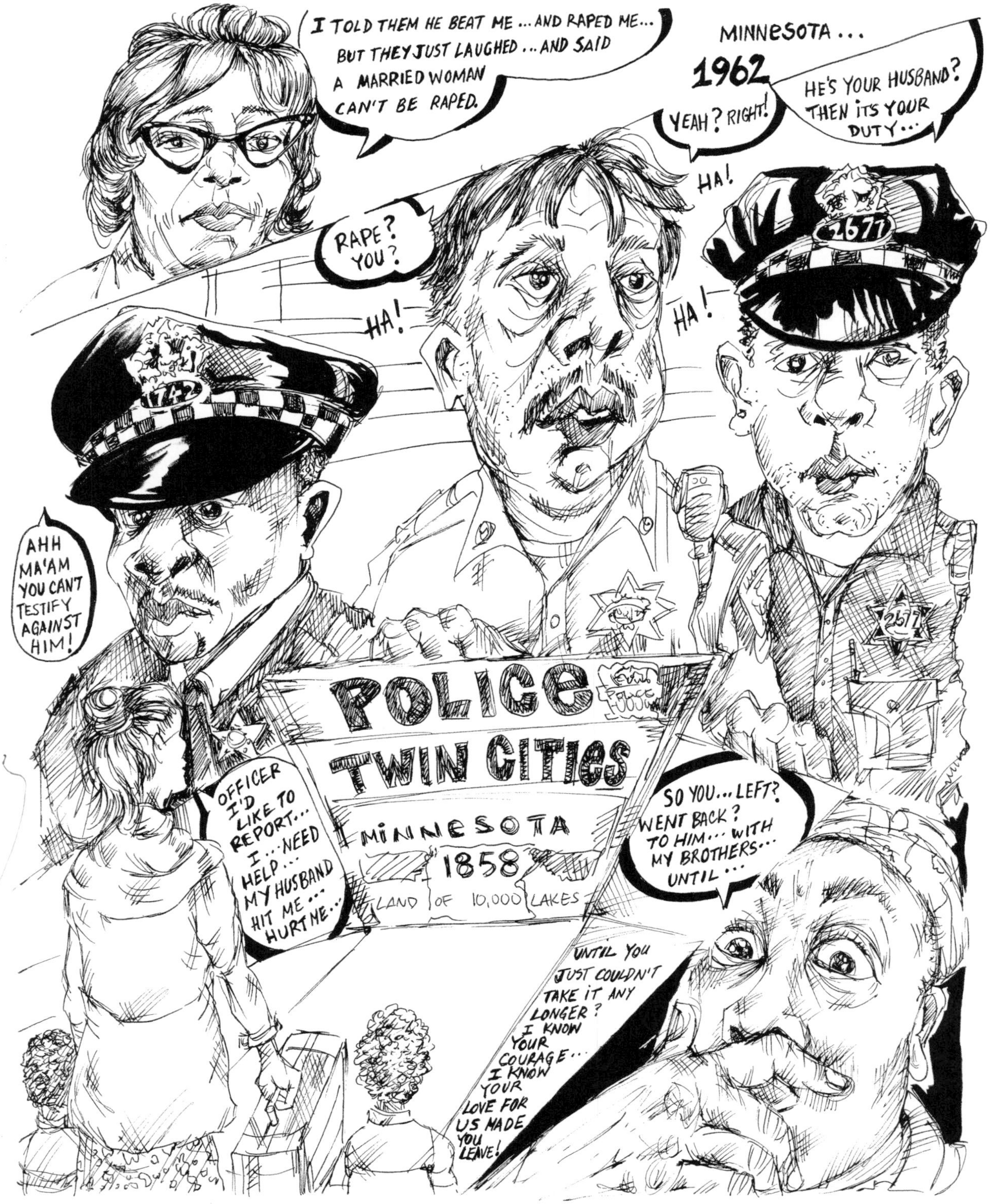
I TOLD THEM HE BEAT ME ... AND RAPED ME... BUT THEY JUST LAUGHED ... AND SAID A MARRIED WOMAN CAN'T BE RAPED.
MINNESOTA ...
1962
YEAH? RIGHT!
HE'S YOUR HUSBAND? THEN ITS YOUR DUTY...
HA!
RAPE? YOU?
HA!
HA!
AHH MA'AM YOU CAN'T TESTIFY AGAINST HIM!
POLICE
TWIN CITIES
MINNESOTA
1858
LAND OF 10,000 LAKES
OFFICER I'D LIKE TO REPORT... I...NEED HELP... MY HUSBAND HIT ME... HURT ME...
SO YOU... LEFT? WENT BACK? TO HIM... WITH MY BROTHERS... UNTIL...
UNTIL YOU JUST COULDN'T TAKE IT ANY LONGER? I KNOW YOUR COURAGE... I KNOW YOUR LOVE FOR US MADE YOU LEAVE!

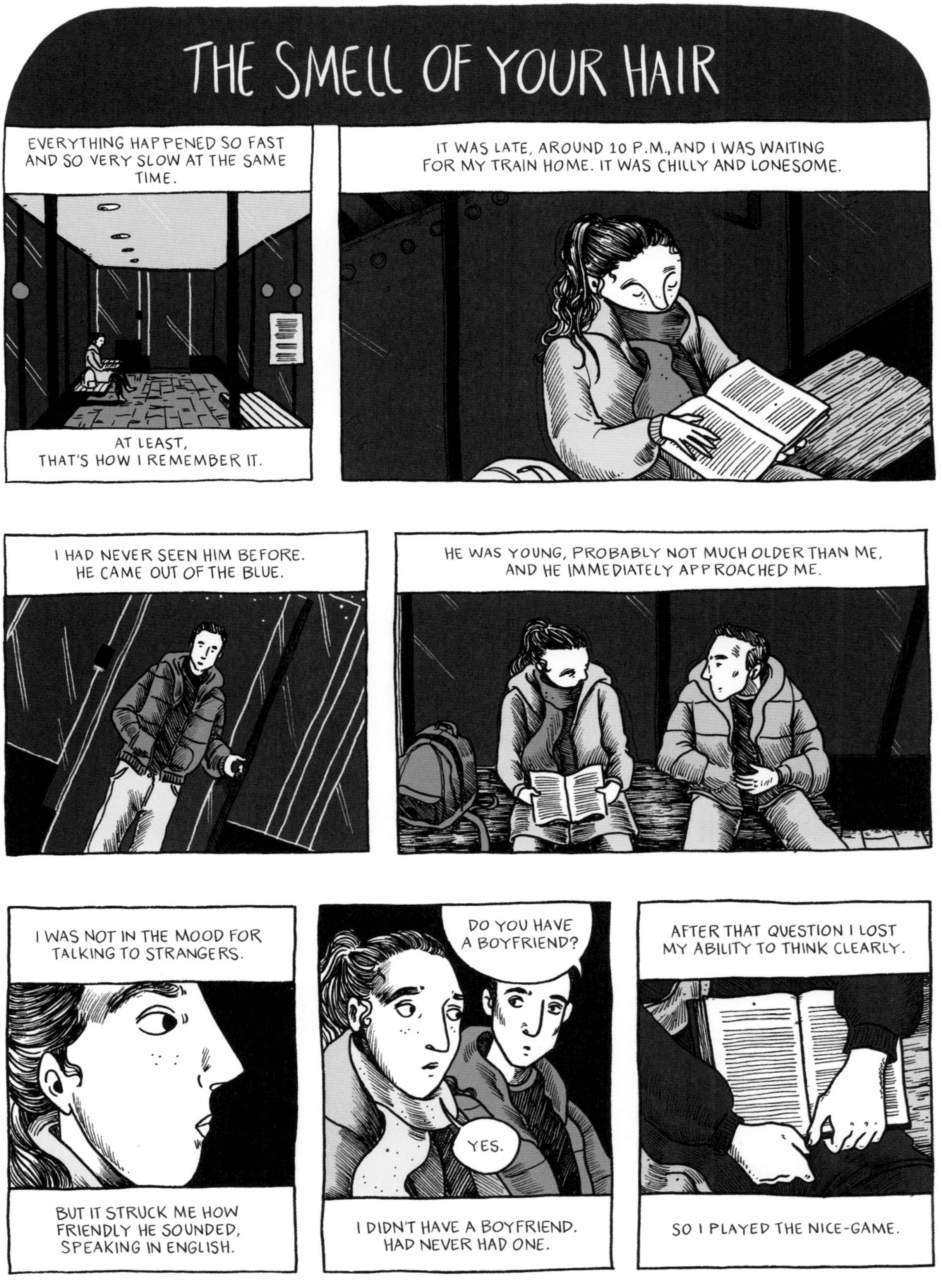
THE SMELL OF YOUR HAIR
EVERYTHING HAPPENED SO FAST AND SO VERY SLOW AT THE SAME TIME.
AT LEAST, THAT'S HOW I REMEMBER IT.
IT WAS LATE, AROUND 10 P.M., AND I WAS WAITING FOR MY TRAIN HOME. IT WAS CHILLY AND LONESOME.
I HAD NEVER SEEN HIM BEFORE. HE CAME OUT OF THE BLUE.
HE WAS YOUNG, PROBABLY NOT MUCH OLDER THAN ME, AND HE IMMEDIATELY APPROACHED ME.
I WAS NOT IN THE MOOD FOR TALKING TO STRANGERS.
BUT IT STRUCK ME HOW FRIENDLY HE SOUNDED, SPEAKING IN ENGLISH.
DO YOU HAVE A BOYFRIEND?
YES.
I DIDN'T HAVE A BOYFRIEND. HAD NEVER HAD ONE.
AFTER THAT QUESTION I LOST MY ABILITY TO THINK CLEARLY.
SO I PLAYED THE NICE-GAME.

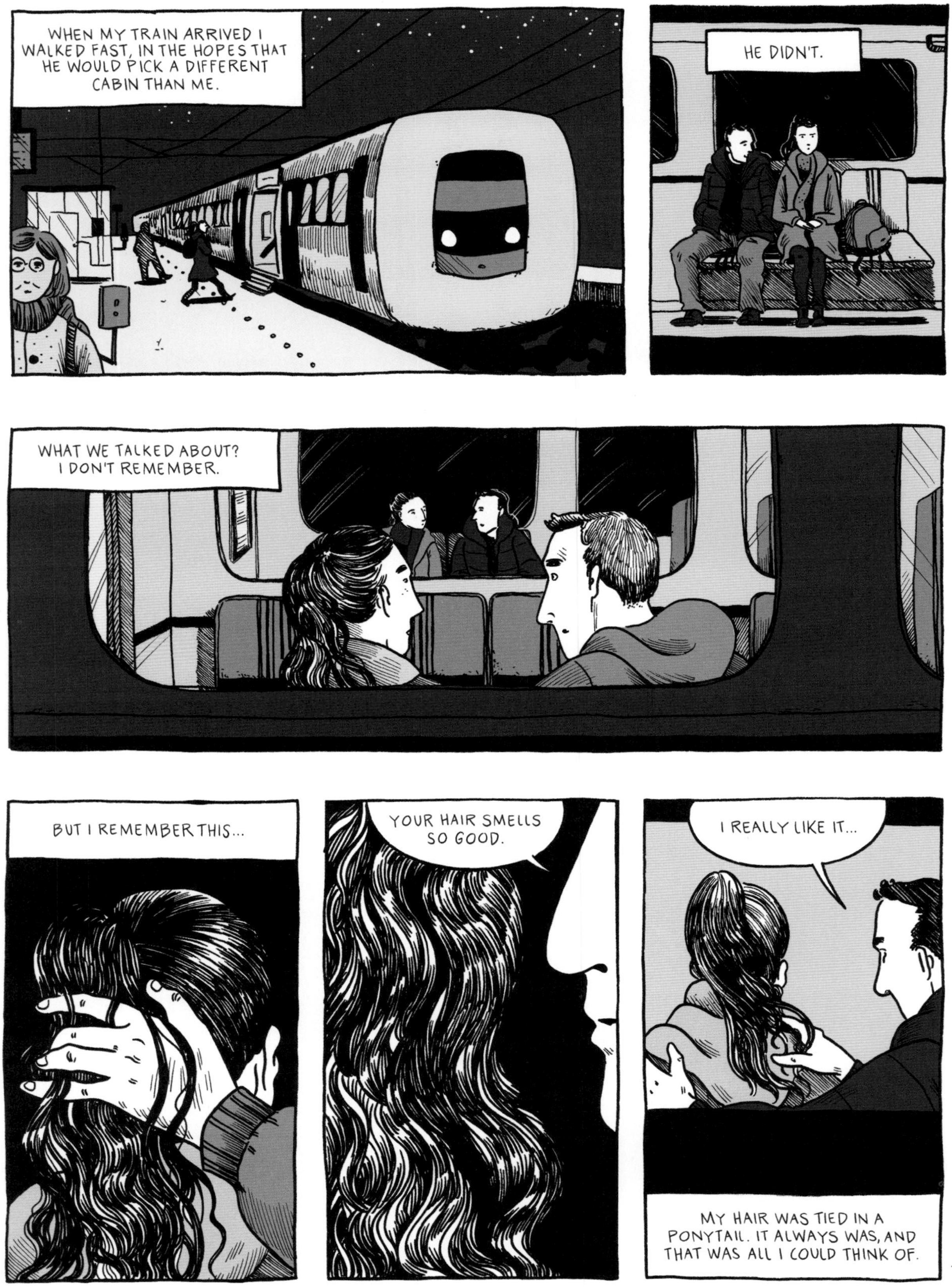

WHEN MY TRAIN ARRIVED I WALKED FAST, IN THE HOPES THAT HE WOULD PICK A DIFFERENT CABIN THAN ME.
HE DIDN'T.
WHAT WE TALKED ABOUT? I DON'T REMEMBER.
BUT I REMEMBER THIS...
YOUR HAIR SMELLS SO GOOD.
I REALLY LIKE IT...
MY HAIR WAS TIED IN A PONYTAIL. IT ALWAYS WAS, AND THAT WAS ALL I COULD THINK OF.

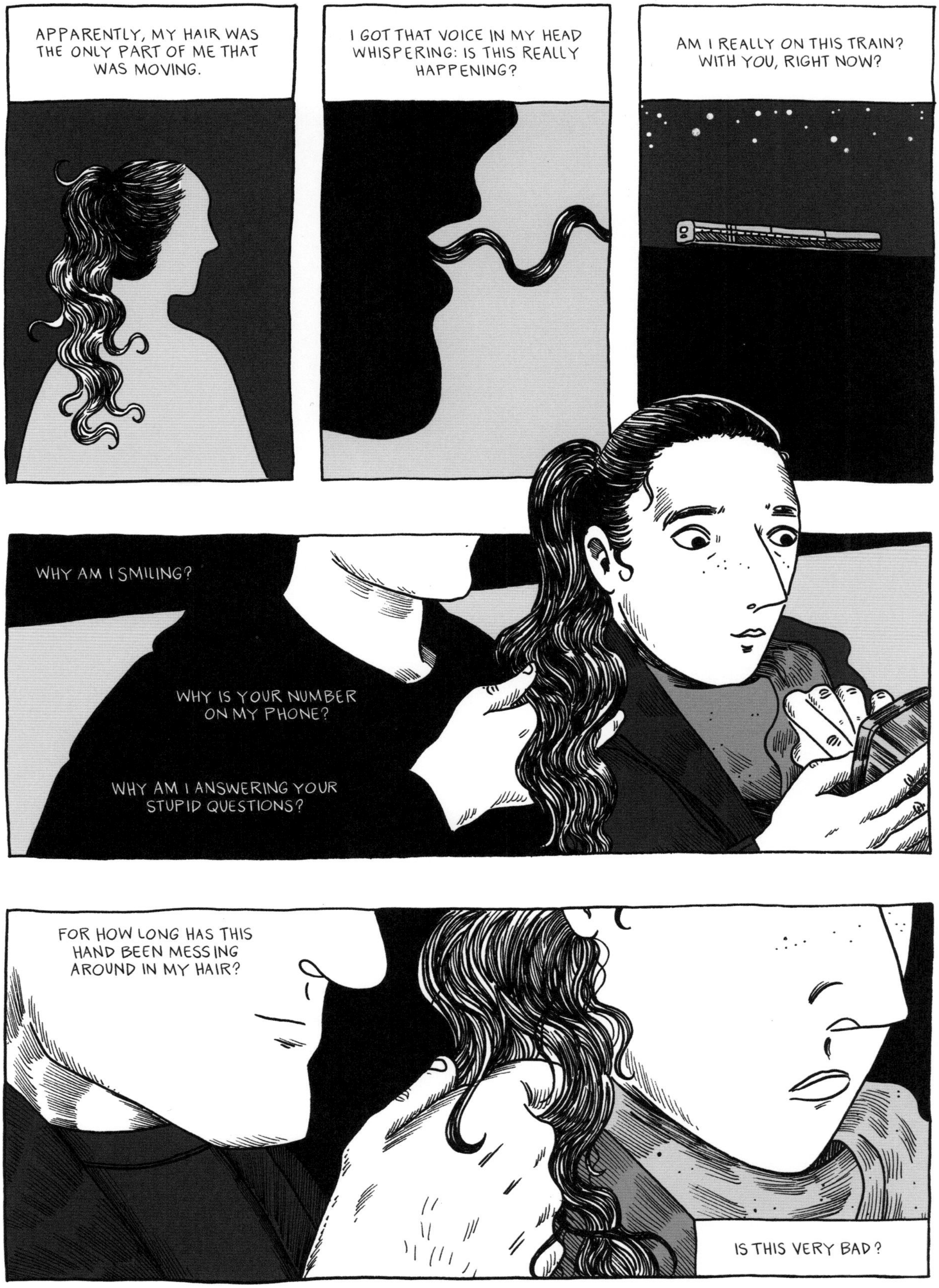
APPARENTLY, MY HAIR WAS THE ONLY PART OF ME THAT WAS MOVING.
I GOT THAT VOICE IN MY HEAD WHISPERING: IS THIS REALLY HAPPENING?
AM I REALLY ON THIS TRAIN? WITH YOU, RIGHT NOW?
WHY AM I SMILING?
WHY IS YOUR NUMBER ON MY PHONE?
WHY AM I ANSWERING YOUR STUPID QUESTIONS?
FOR HOW LONG HAS THIS HAND BEEN MESSING AROUND IN MY HAIR?
IS THIS VERY BAD?

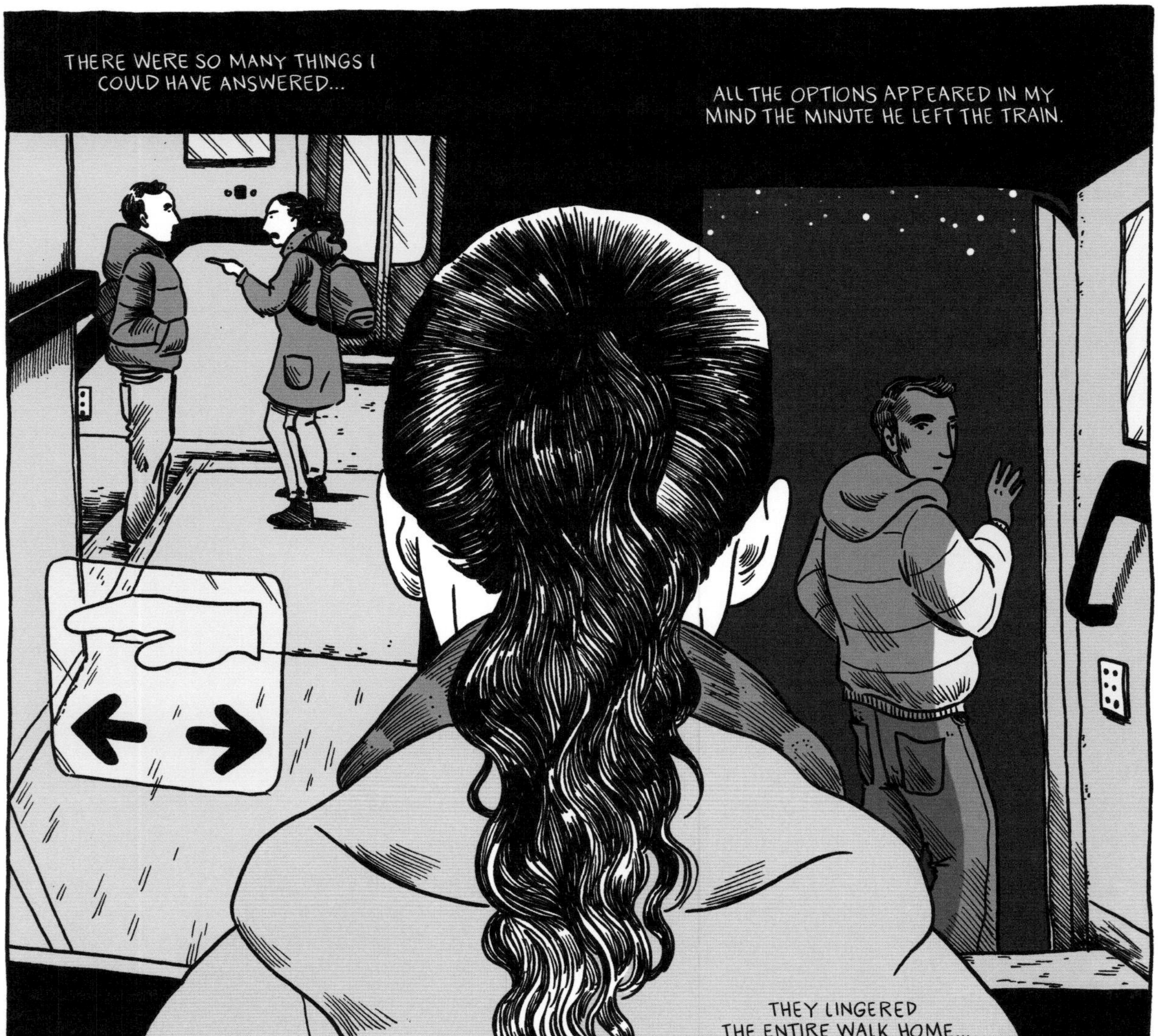
THERE WERE SO MANY THINGS I COULD HAVE ANSWERED...
ALL THE OPTIONS APPEARED IN MY MIND THE MINUTE HE LEFT THE TRAIN.
THEY LINGERED THE ENTIRE WALK HOME...

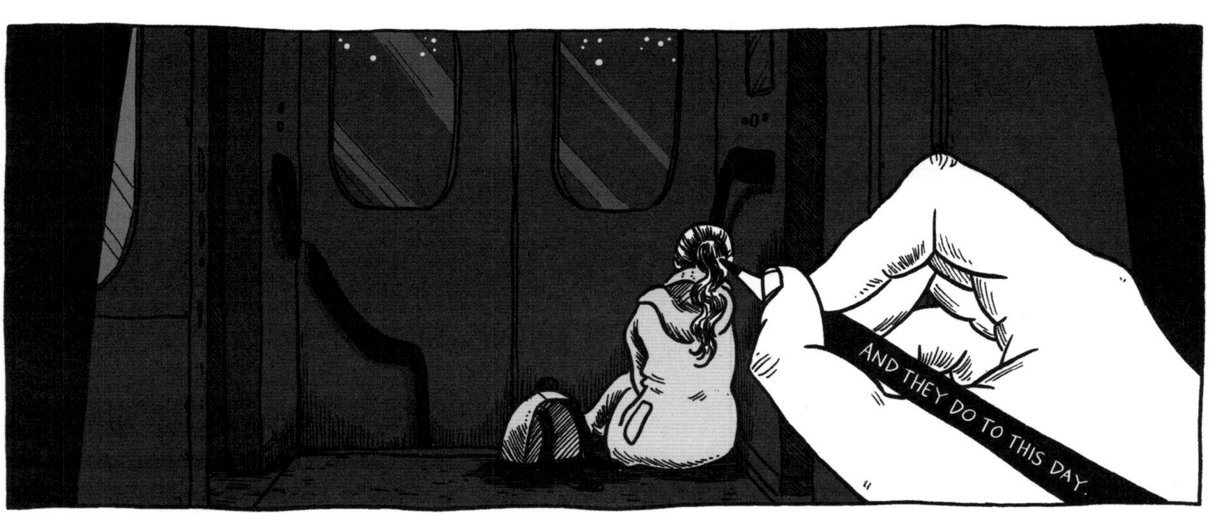
AND THEY DO TO THIS DAY.

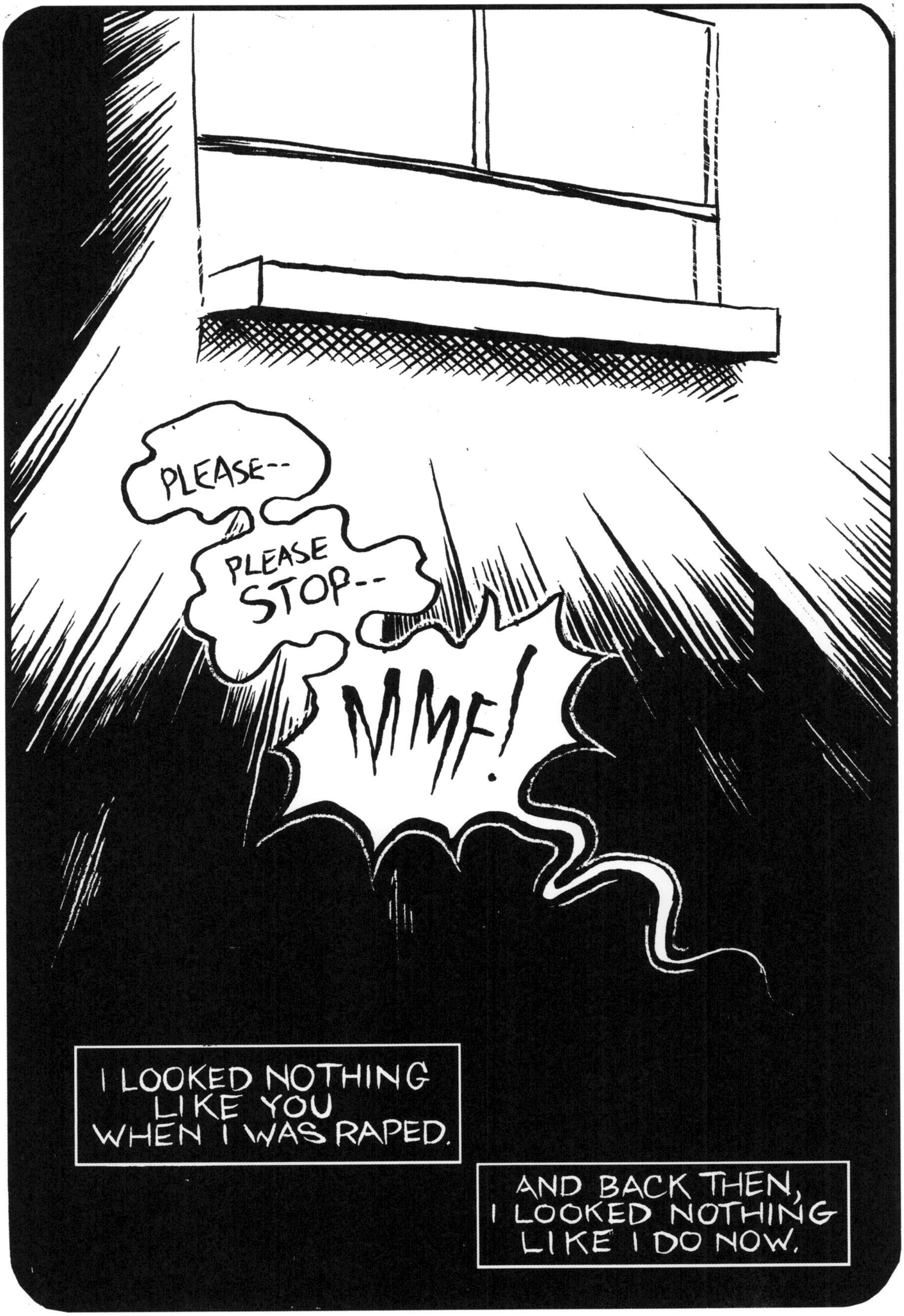
PLEASE--
PLEASE STOP--
MMF!
I LOOKED NOTHING LIKE YOU WHEN I WAS RAPED.
AND BACK THEN, I LOOKED NOTHING LIKE I DO NOW.

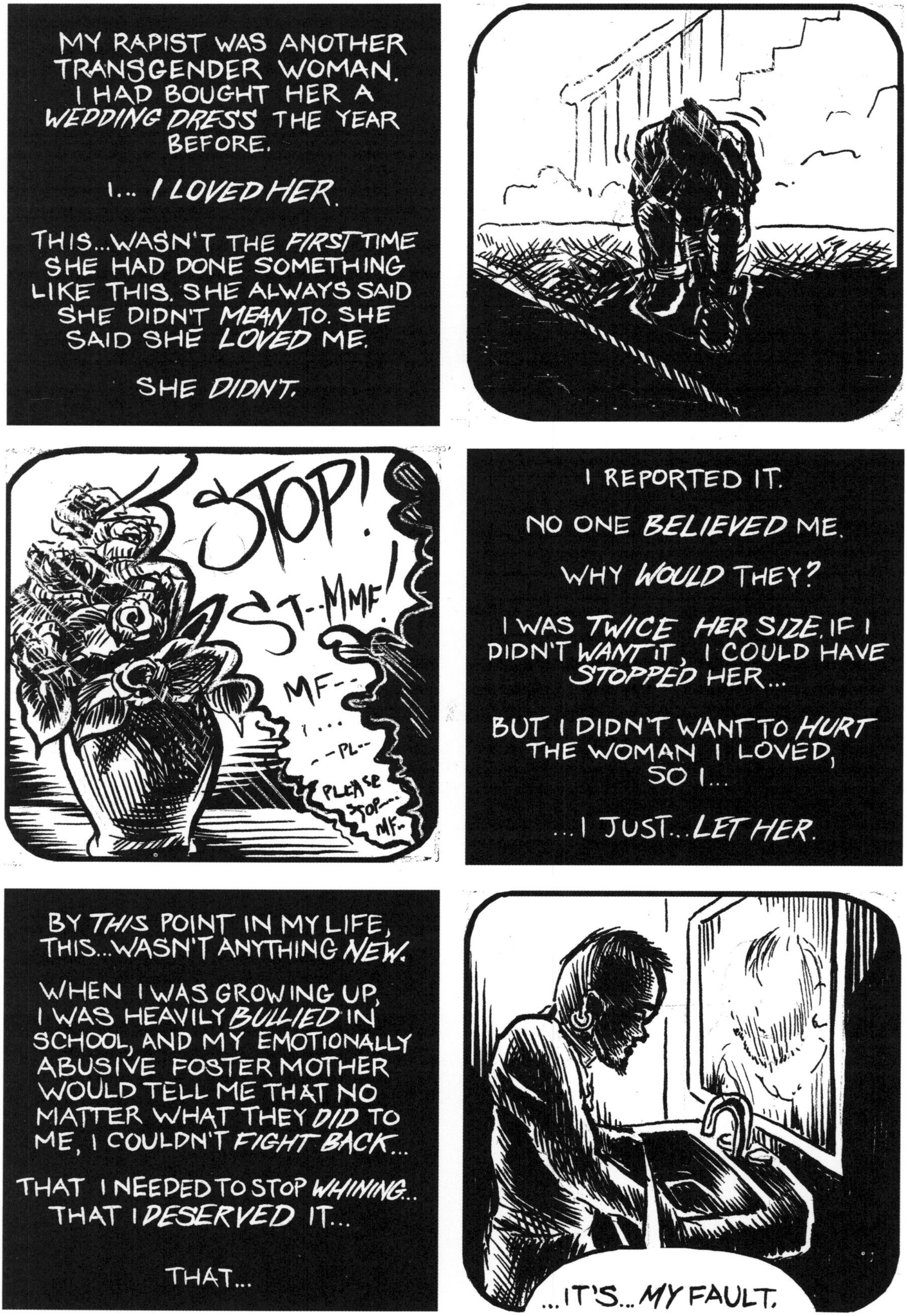
MY RAPIST WAS ANOTHER TRANSGENDER WOMAN. I HAD BOUGHT HER A *WEDDING DRESS* THE YEAR BEFORE.
I... *I LOVED HER.*
THIS...WASN'T THE *FIRST* TIME SHE HAD DONE SOMETHING LIKE THIS. SHE ALWAYS SAID SHE DIDN'T *MEAN* TO. SHE SAID SHE *LOVED* ME.
SHE *DIDN'T.*
STOP!
ST--MMF!
MF--
I...
--PL--
PLEASE STOP... MF-
I REPORTED IT.
NO ONE *BELIEVED* ME.
WHY *WOULD* THEY?
I WAS *TWICE HER SIZE.* IF I DIDN'T *WANT* IT, I COULD HAVE *STOPPED* HER...
BUT I DIDN'T WANT TO *HURT* THE WOMAN I LOVED, SO I...
...I JUST...*LET HER.*
BY *THIS* POINT IN MY LIFE, THIS...WASN'T ANYTHING *NEW.*
WHEN I WAS GROWING UP, I WAS HEAVILY *BULLIED* IN SCHOOL, AND MY EMOTIONALLY ABUSIVE FOSTER MOTHER WOULD TELL ME THAT NO MATTER WHAT THEY *DID* TO ME, I COULDN'T *FIGHT BACK*...
THAT I NEEDED TO STOP *WHINING*.. THAT I *DESERVED* IT...
THAT...
...IT'S...*MY* FAULT.

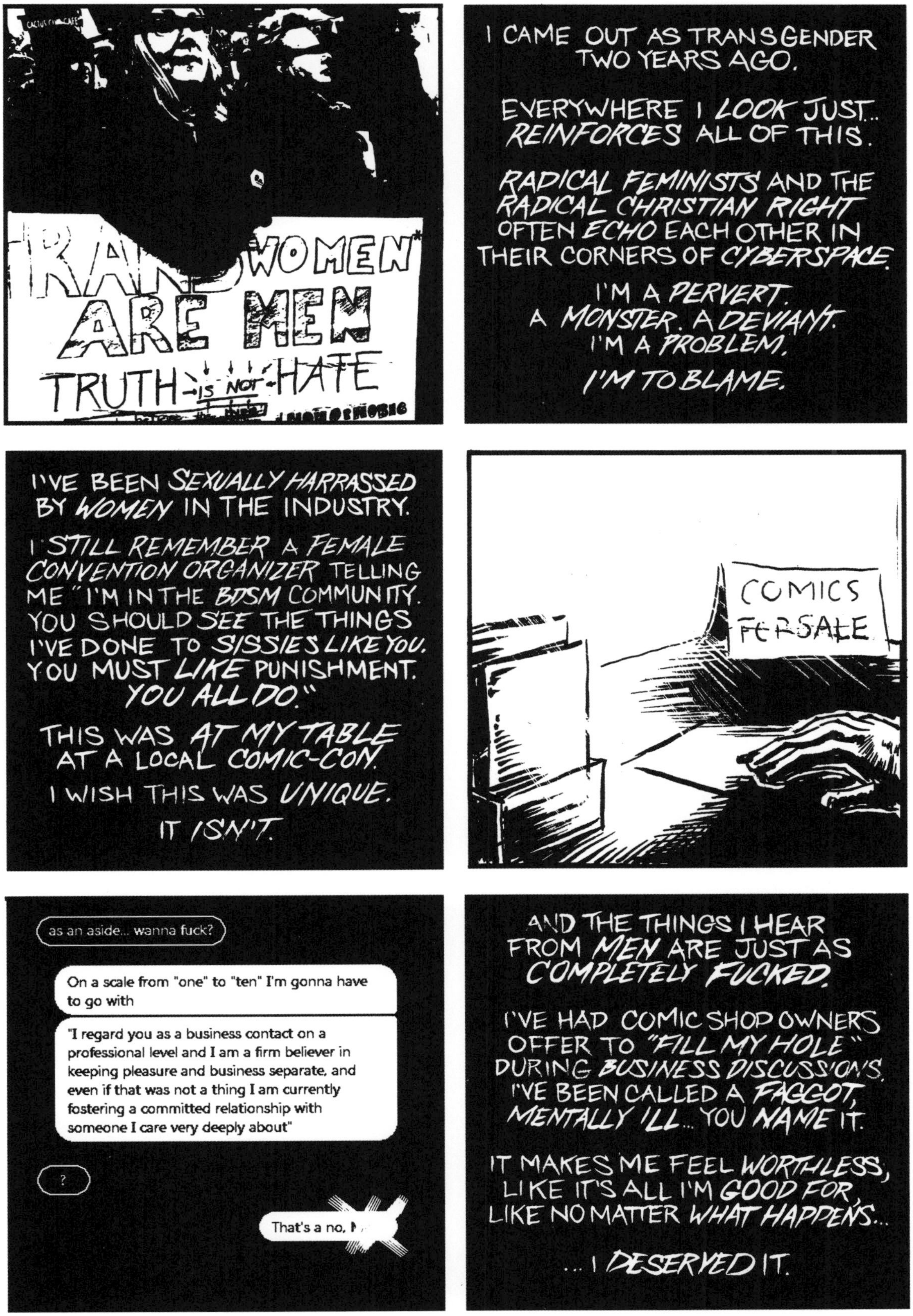
WOMEN*
ARE MEN
TRUTH IS NOT HATE
I CAME OUT AS TRANSGENDER TWO YEARS AGO.
EVERYWHERE I LOOK JUST... REINFORCES ALL OF THIS.
RADICAL FEMINISTS AND THE RADICAL CHRISTIAN RIGHT OFTEN ECHO EACH OTHER IN THEIR CORNERS OF CYBERSPACE.
I'M A PERVERT. A MONSTER. A DEVIANT. I'M A PROBLEM.
I'M TO BLAME.
I'VE BEEN SEXUALLY HARRASSED BY WOMEN IN THE INDUSTRY.
I STILL REMEMBER A FEMALE CONVENTION ORGANIZER TELLING ME "I'M IN THE BDSM COMMUNITY. YOU SHOULD SEE THE THINGS I'VE DONE TO SISSIES LIKE YOU. YOU MUST LIKE PUNISHMENT. YOU ALL DO."
THIS WAS AT MY TABLE AT A LOCAL COMIC-CON.
I WISH THIS WAS UNIQUE.
IT ISN'T.
COMICS FOR SALE
as an aside... wanna fuck?
On a scale from "one" to "ten" I'm gonna have to go with
"I regard you as a business contact on a professional level and I am a firm believer in keeping pleasure and business separate, and even if that was not a thing I am currently fostering a committed relationship with someone I care very deeply about"
?
That's a no,
AND THE THINGS I HEAR FROM MEN ARE JUST AS COMPLETELY FUCKED.
I'VE HAD COMIC SHOP OWNERS OFFER TO "FILL MY HOLE" DURING BUSINESS DISCUSSIONS. I'VE BEEN CALLED A FAGGOT, MENTALLY ILL... YOU NAME IT.
IT MAKES ME FEEL WORTHLESS, LIKE IT'S ALL I'M GOOD FOR, LIKE NO MATTER WHAT HAPPENS...
...I DESERVED IT.

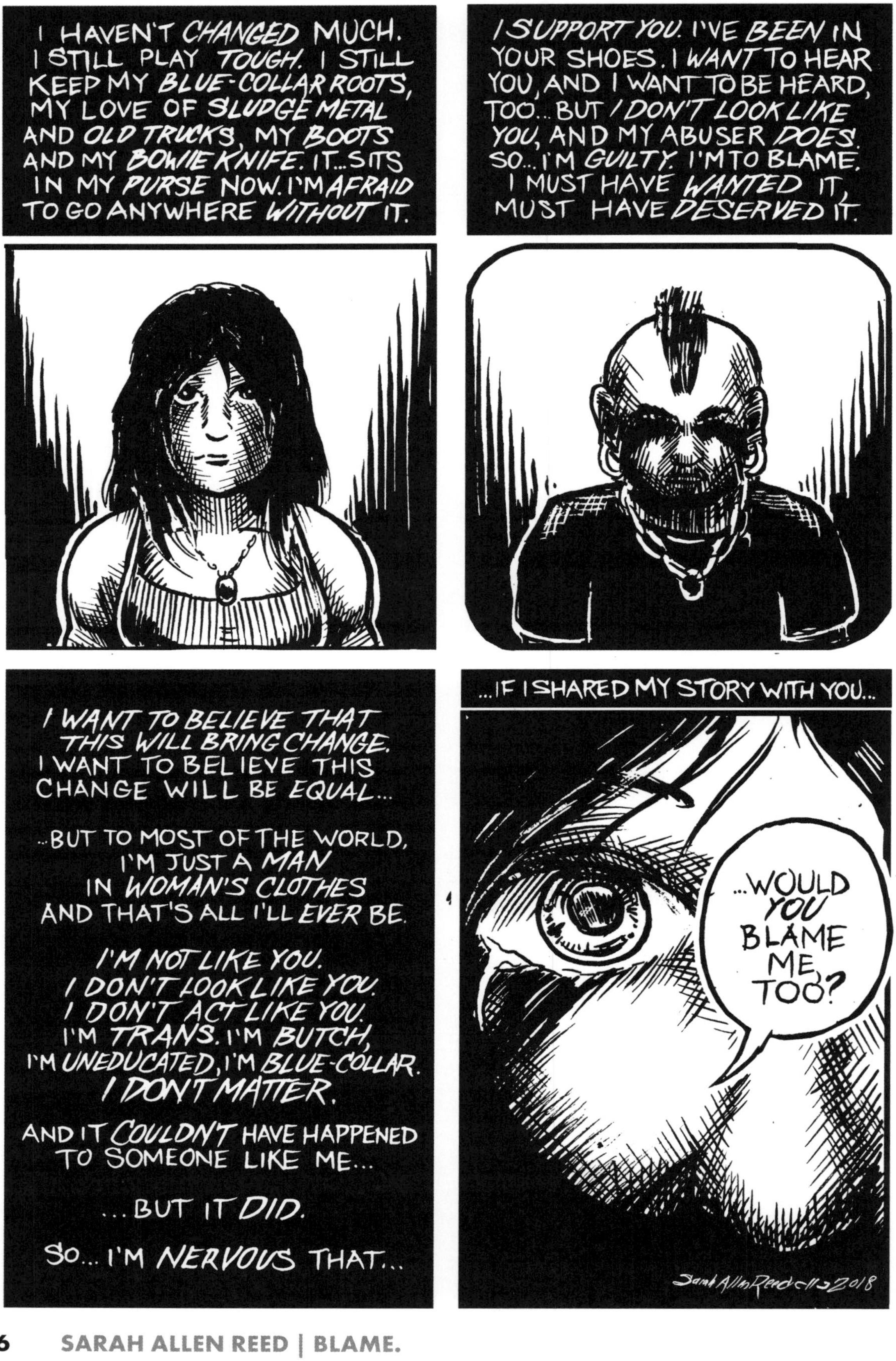
I HAVEN'T CHANGED MUCH. I STILL PLAY TOUGH. I STILL KEEP MY BLUE-COLLAR ROOTS, MY LOVE OF SLUDGE METAL AND OLD TRUCKS, MY BOOTS AND MY BOWIE KNIFE. IT...SITS IN MY PURSE NOW. I'M AFRAID TO GO ANYWHERE WITHOUT IT.
I SUPPORT YOU. I'VE BEEN IN YOUR SHOES. I WANT TO HEAR YOU, AND I WANT TO BE HEARD, TOO... BUT I DON'T LOOK LIKE YOU, AND MY ABUSER DOES. SO... I'M GUILTY. I'M TO BLAME. I MUST HAVE WANTED IT, MUST HAVE DESERVED IT.
I WANT TO BELIEVE THAT THIS WILL BRING CHANGE. I WANT TO BELIEVE THIS CHANGE WILL BE EQUAL...
...BUT TO MOST OF THE WORLD, I'M JUST A MAN IN WOMAN'S CLOTHES AND THAT'S ALL I'LL EVER BE.
I'M NOT LIKE YOU. I DON'T LOOK LIKE YOU. I DON'T ACT LIKE YOU. I'M TRANS. I'M BUTCH, I'M UNEDUCATED, I'M BLUE-COLLAR. I DON'T MATTER.
AND IT COULDN'T HAVE HAPPENED TO SOMEONE LIKE ME...
...BUT IT DID.
SO... I'M NERVOUS THAT...
...IF I SHARED MY STORY WITH YOU...
...WOULD YOU BLAME ME, TOO?
Sarah Allen Reed 2018

ALWAYS THERE by Nicola Streeten

In the 1960s when my siblings and I were little, Mum took us for picnics in a secluded part of the park

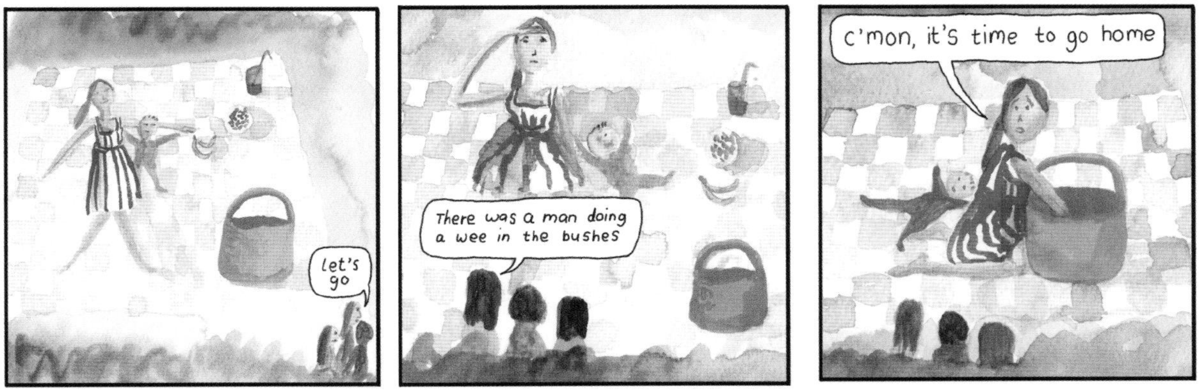
let's go
There was a man doing a wee in the bushes
c'mon, it's time to go home

In the 1970s, as a schoolgirl, I used laughter as my weapon as Hélène Cixous urged

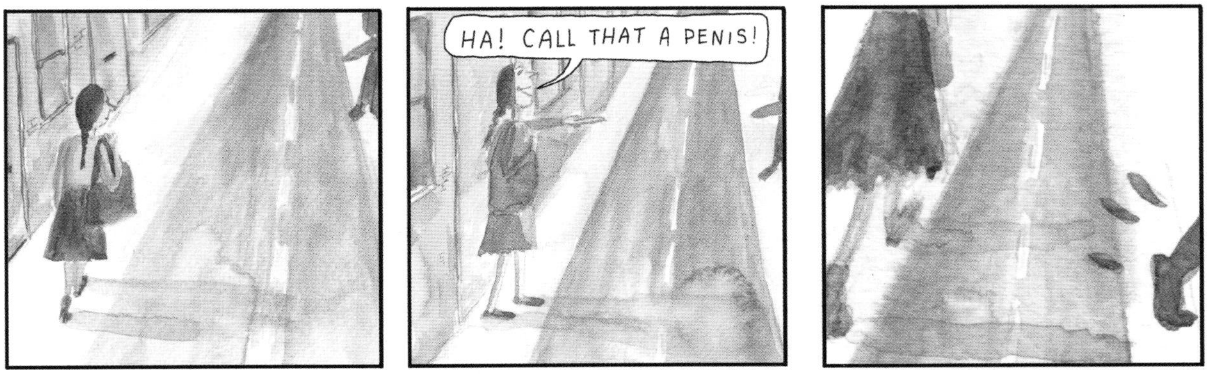
HA! CALL THAT A PENIS!

In the 1980s, my family got a big dog, designed to guard

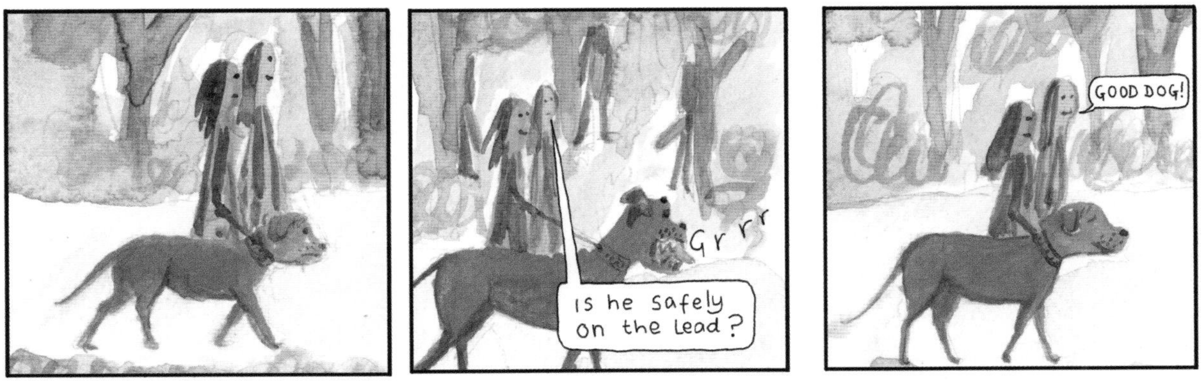
Grrr
is he safely on the lead?
GOOD DOG!

In the 21st century I worry about my daughter's safety
And I ask when will women not have to feel fear?

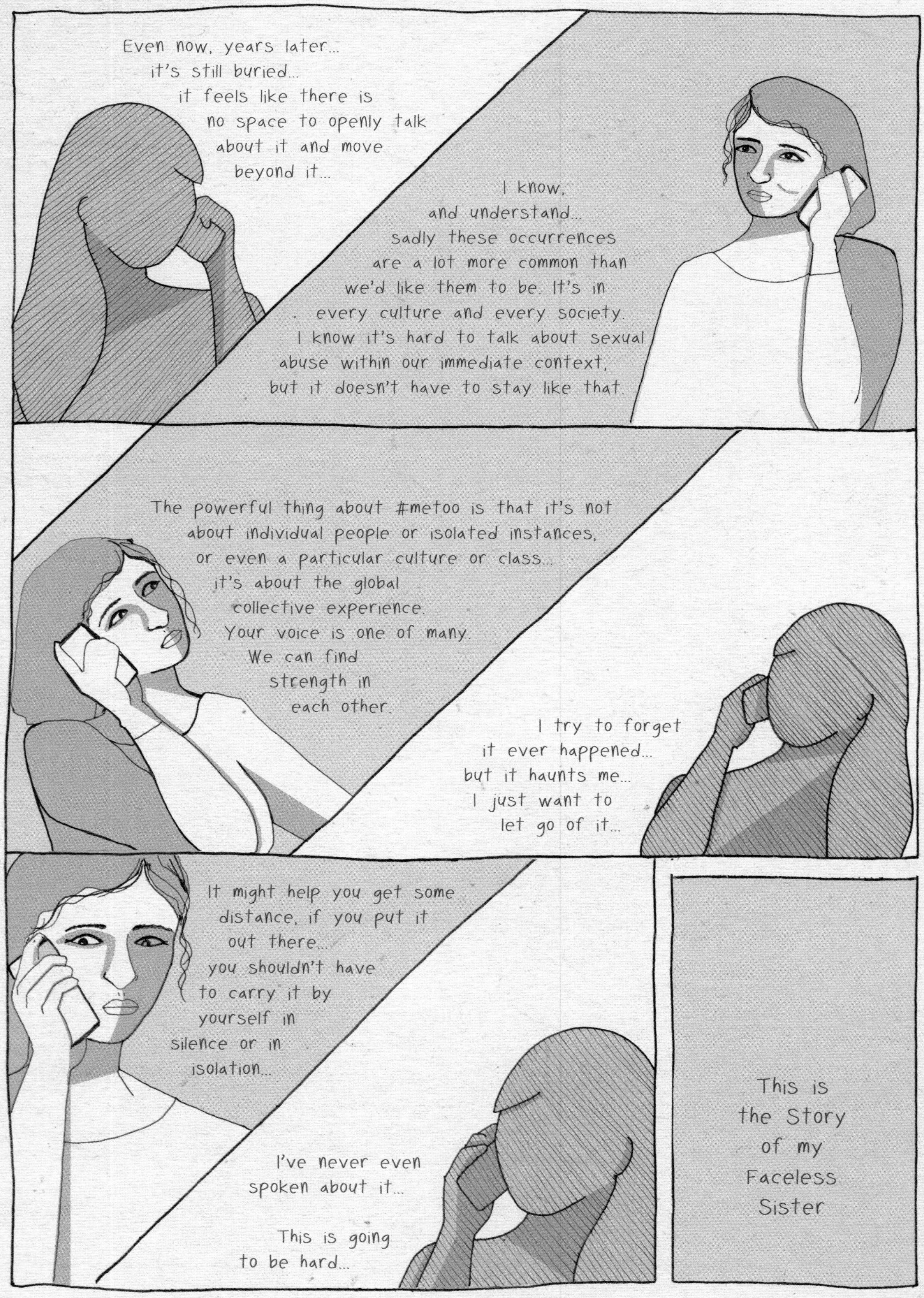
Even now, years later... it's still buried... it feels like there is no space to openly talk about it and move beyond it...
I know, and understand... sadly these occurrences are a lot more common than we'd like them to be. It's in every culture and every society. I know it's hard to talk about sexual abuse within our immediate context, but it doesn't have to stay like that.
The powerful thing about #metoo is that it's not about individual people or isolated instances, or even a particular culture or class... it's about the global collective experience. Your voice is one of many. We can find strength in each other.
I try to forget it ever happened... but it haunts me... I just want to let go of it...
It might help you get some distance, if you put it out there... you shouldn't have to carry it by yourself in silence or in isolation...
I've never even spoken about it...
This is going to be hard...
This is the Story of my Faceless Sister

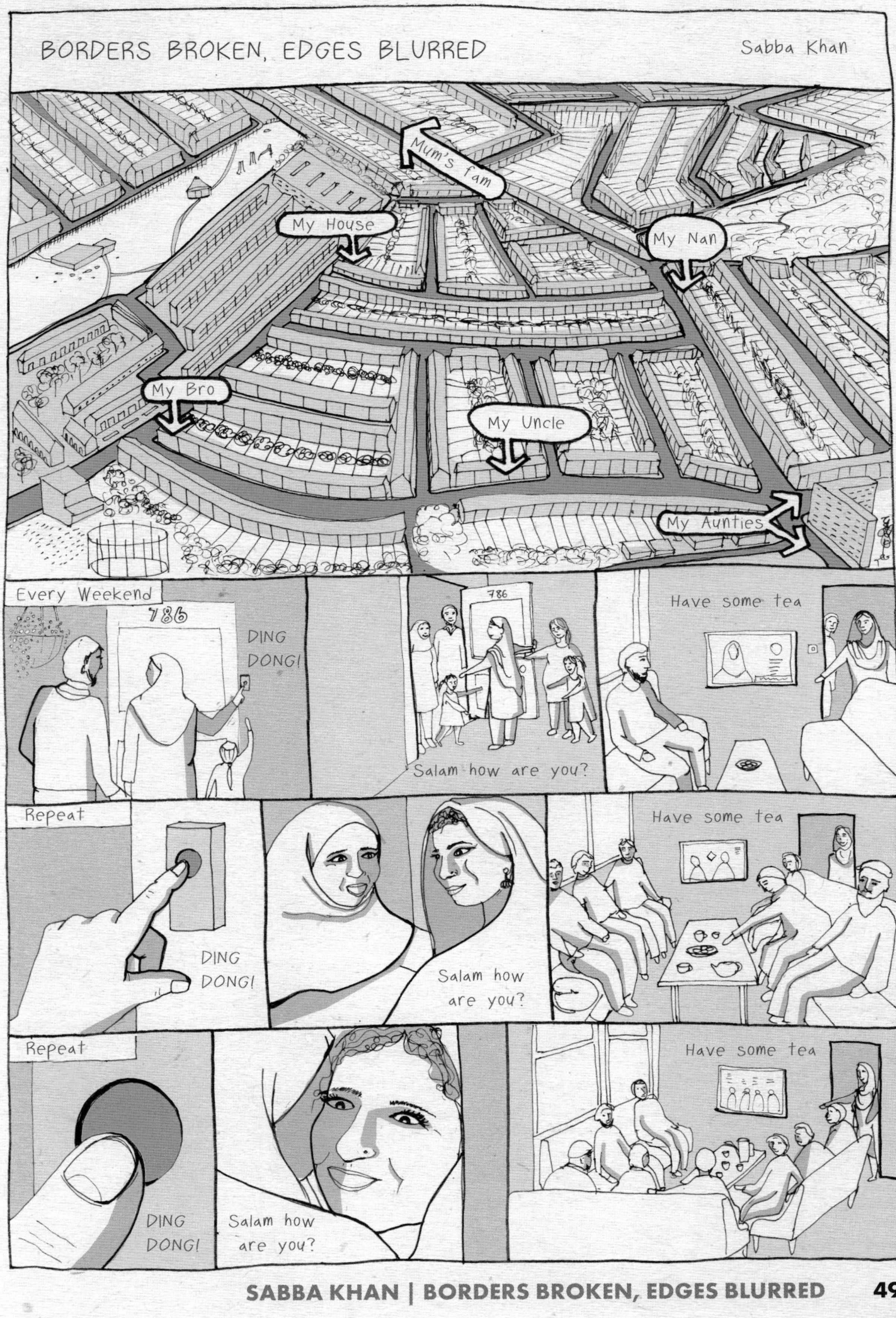
BORDERS BROKEN, EDGES BLURRED
Sabba Khan
Mum's fam
My House
My Nan
My Bro
My Uncle
My Aunties
Every Weekend
786
DING
DONG!
786
Salam how are you?
Have some tea
Repeat
DING
DONG!
Salam how
are you?
Have some tea
Repeat
DING
DONG!
Salam how
are you?
Have some tea

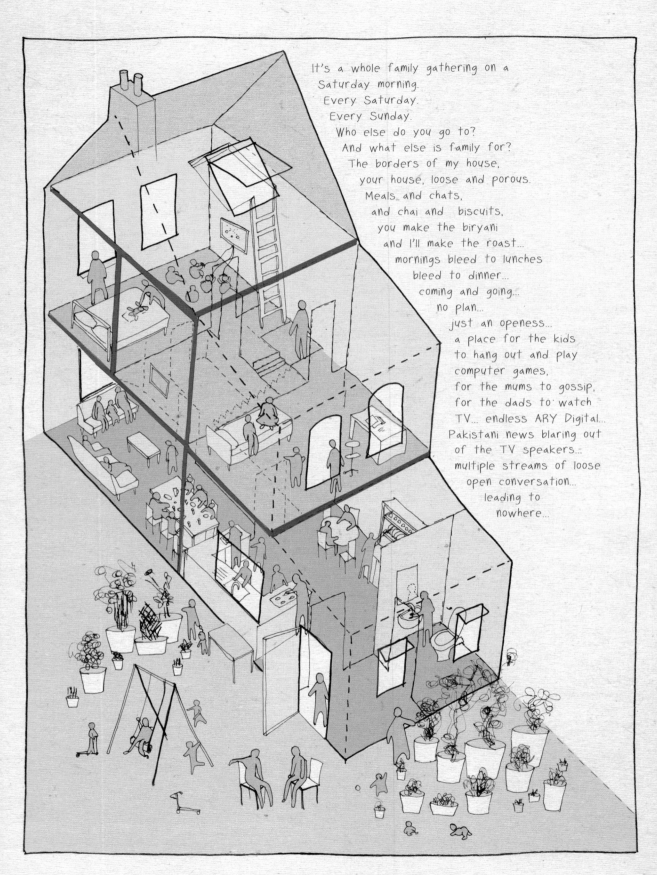

It's a whole family gathering on a
Saturday morning.
Every Saturday.
Every Sunday.
Who else do you go to?
And what else is family for?
The borders of my house,
your house, loose and porous.
Meals and chats,
and chai and biscuits,
you make the biryani
and I'll make the roast...
mornings bleed to lunches
bleed to dinner...
coming and going...
no plan...
just an openess...
a place for the kids
to hang out and play
computer games,
for the mums to gossip,
for the dads to watch
TV... endless ARY Digital...
Pakistani news blaring out
of the TV speakers...
multiple streams of loose
open conversation...
leading to
nowhere...

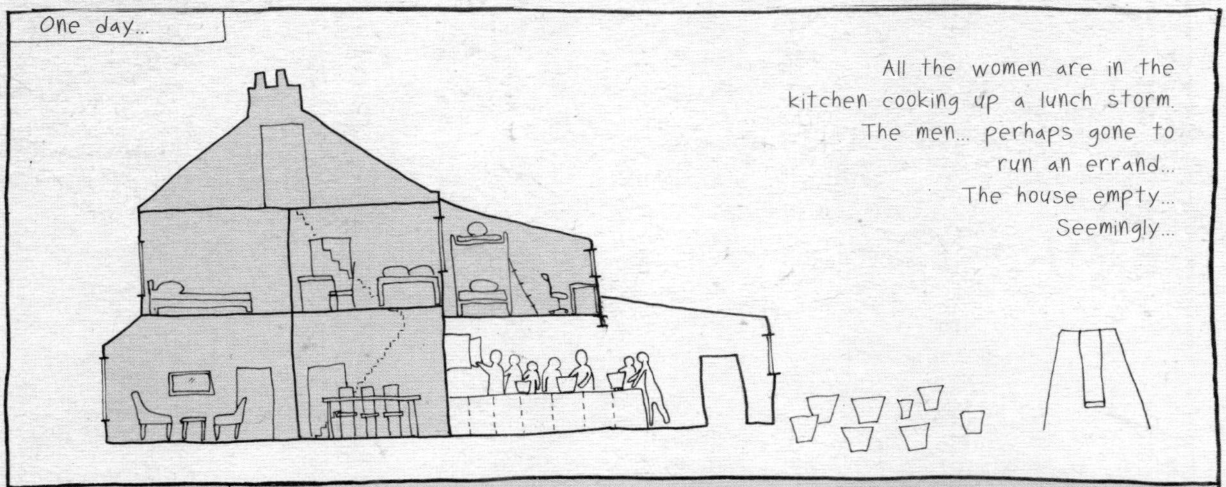
One day...
All the women are in the kitchen cooking up a lunch storm. The men... perhaps gone to run an errand... The house empty... Seemingly...

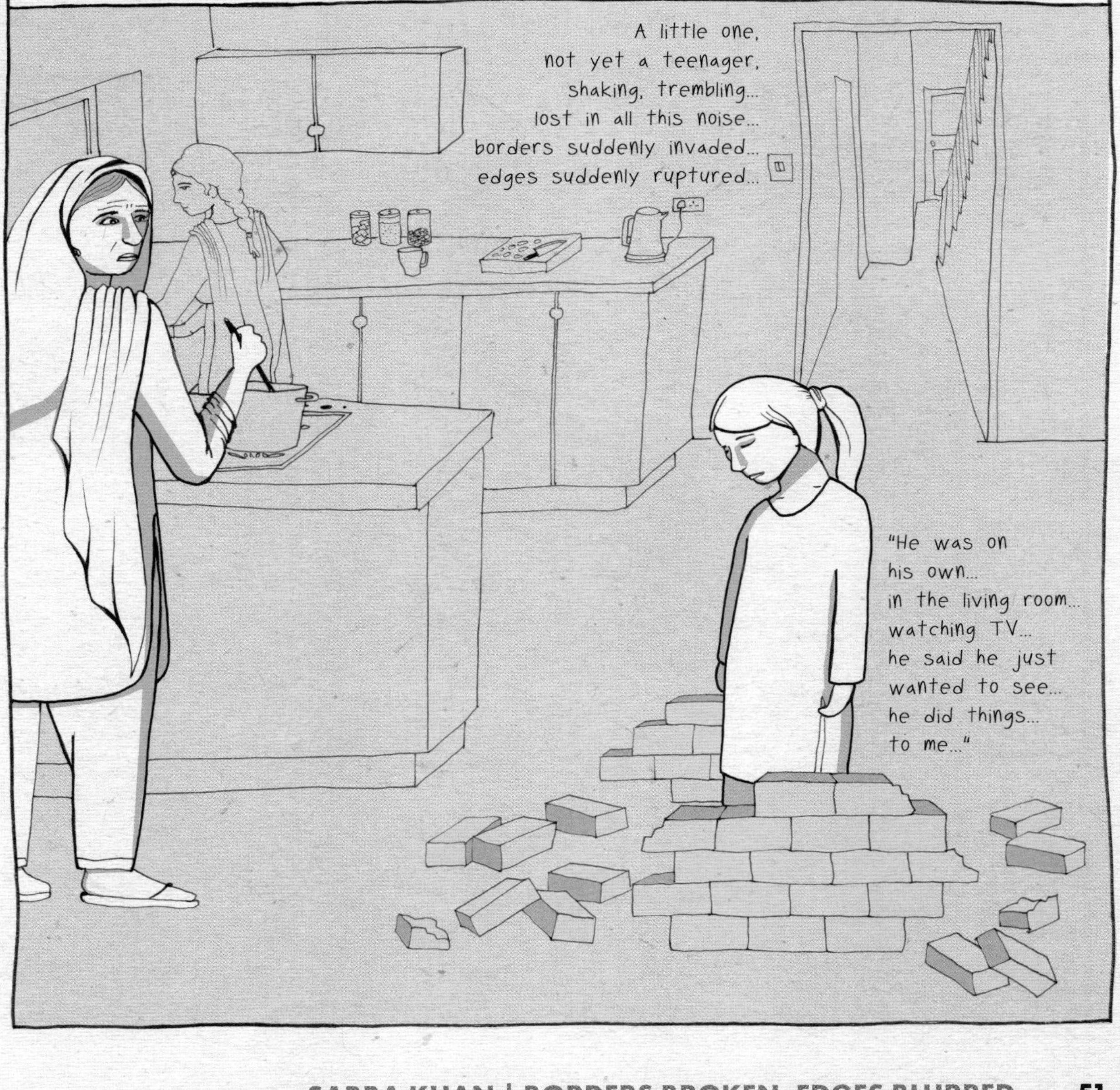
A little one, not yet a teenager, shaking, trembling... lost in all this noise... borders suddenly invaded... edges suddenly ruptured...
"He was on his own... in the living room... watching TV... he said he just wanted to see... he did things... to me..."

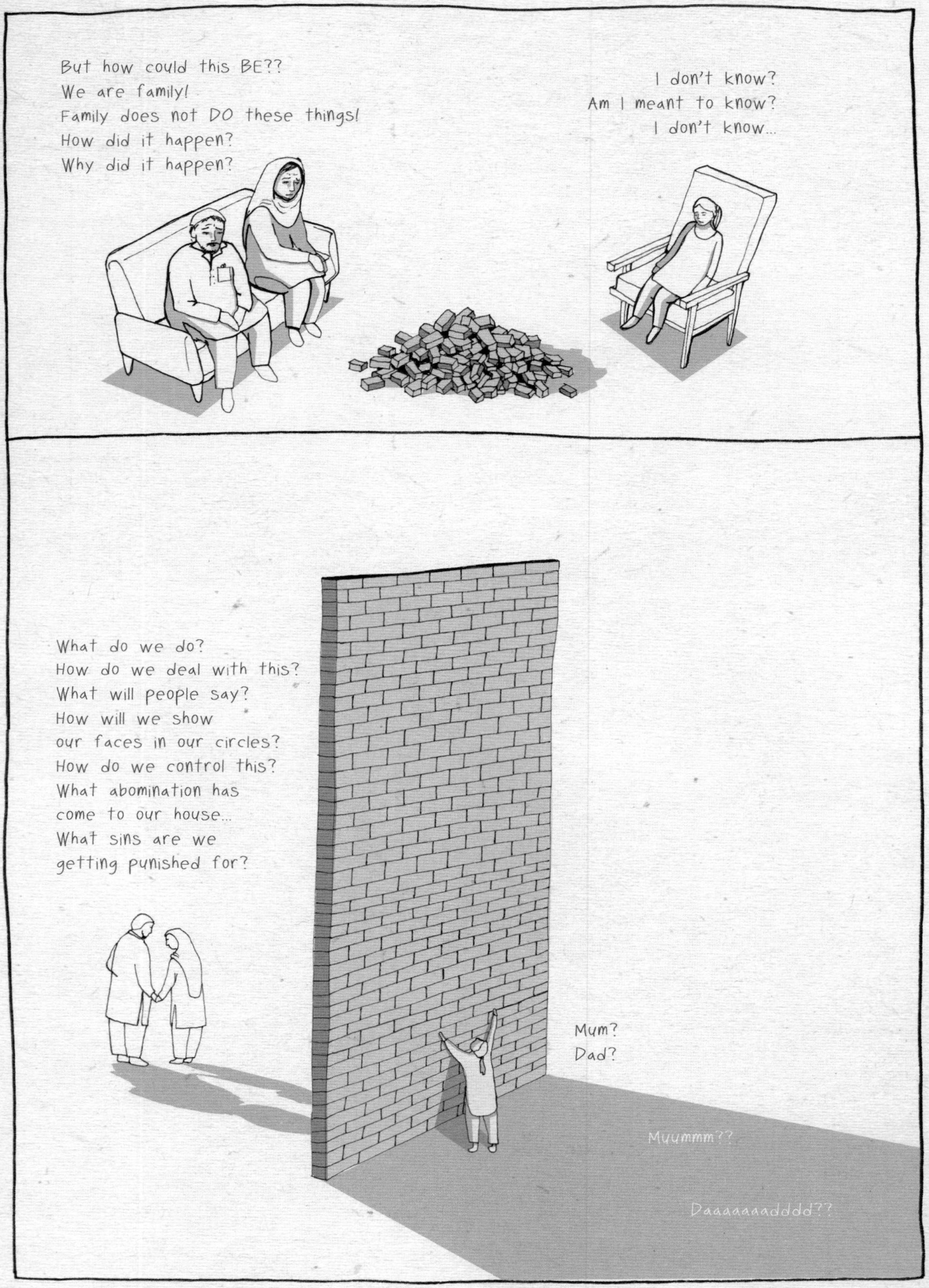
But how could this BE??
We are family!
Family does not DO these things!
How did it happen?
Why did it happen?
I don't know?
Am I meant to know?
I don't know...
What do we do?
How do we deal with this?
What will people say?
How will we show
our faces in our circles?
How do we control this?
What abomination has
come to our house...
What sins are we
getting punished for?
Mum?
Dad?
Muummm??
Daaaaaaadddd??

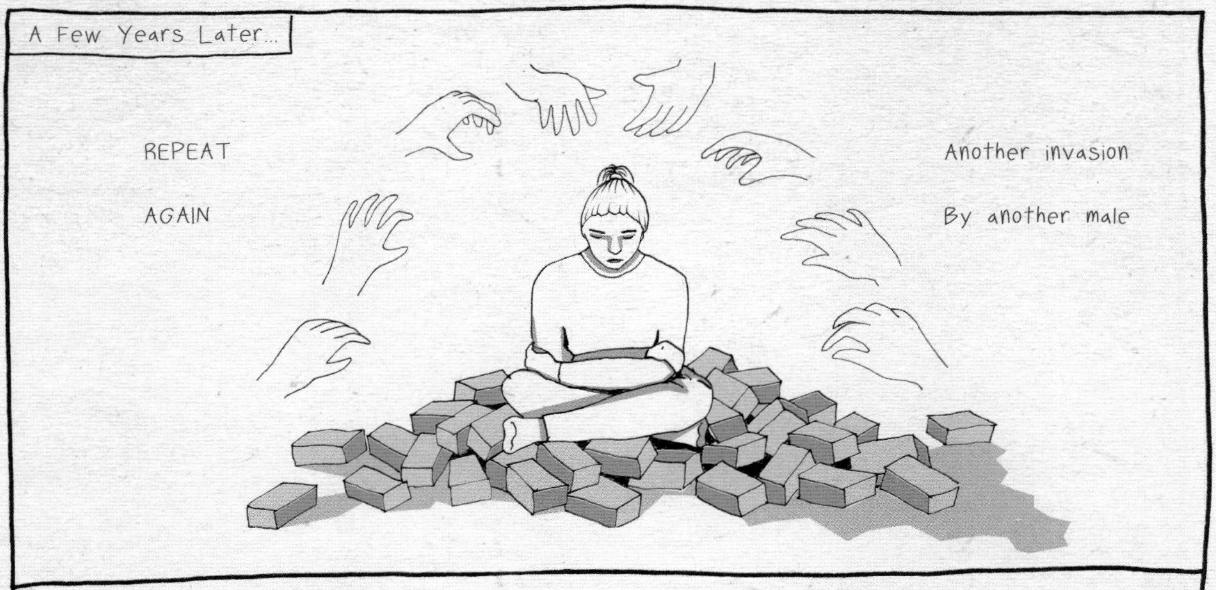
A Few Years Later...
REPEAT
AGAIN
Another invasion
By another male

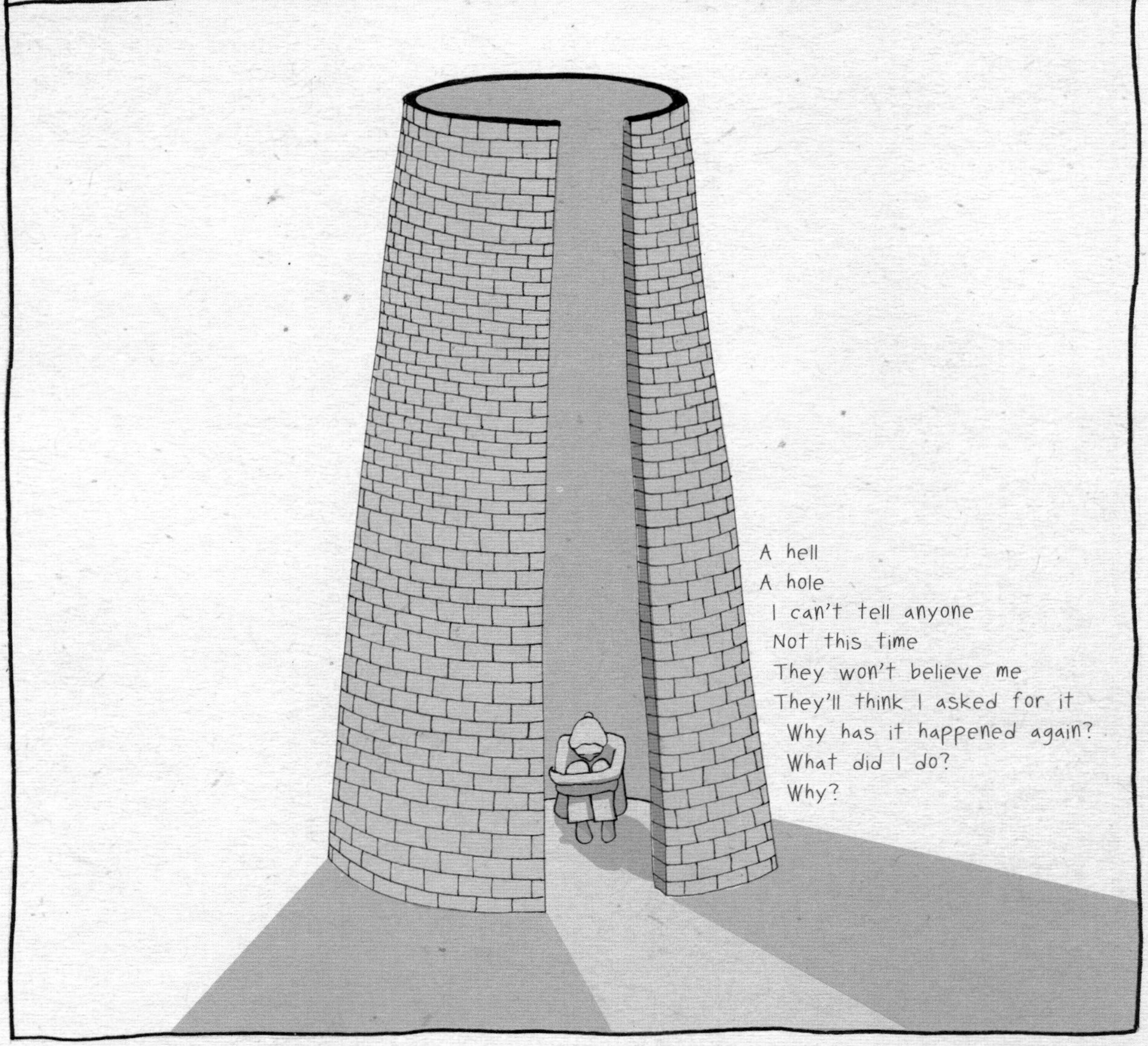
A hell
A hole
I can't tell anyone
Not this time
They won't believe me
They'll think I asked for it
Why has it happened again?
What did I do?
Why?

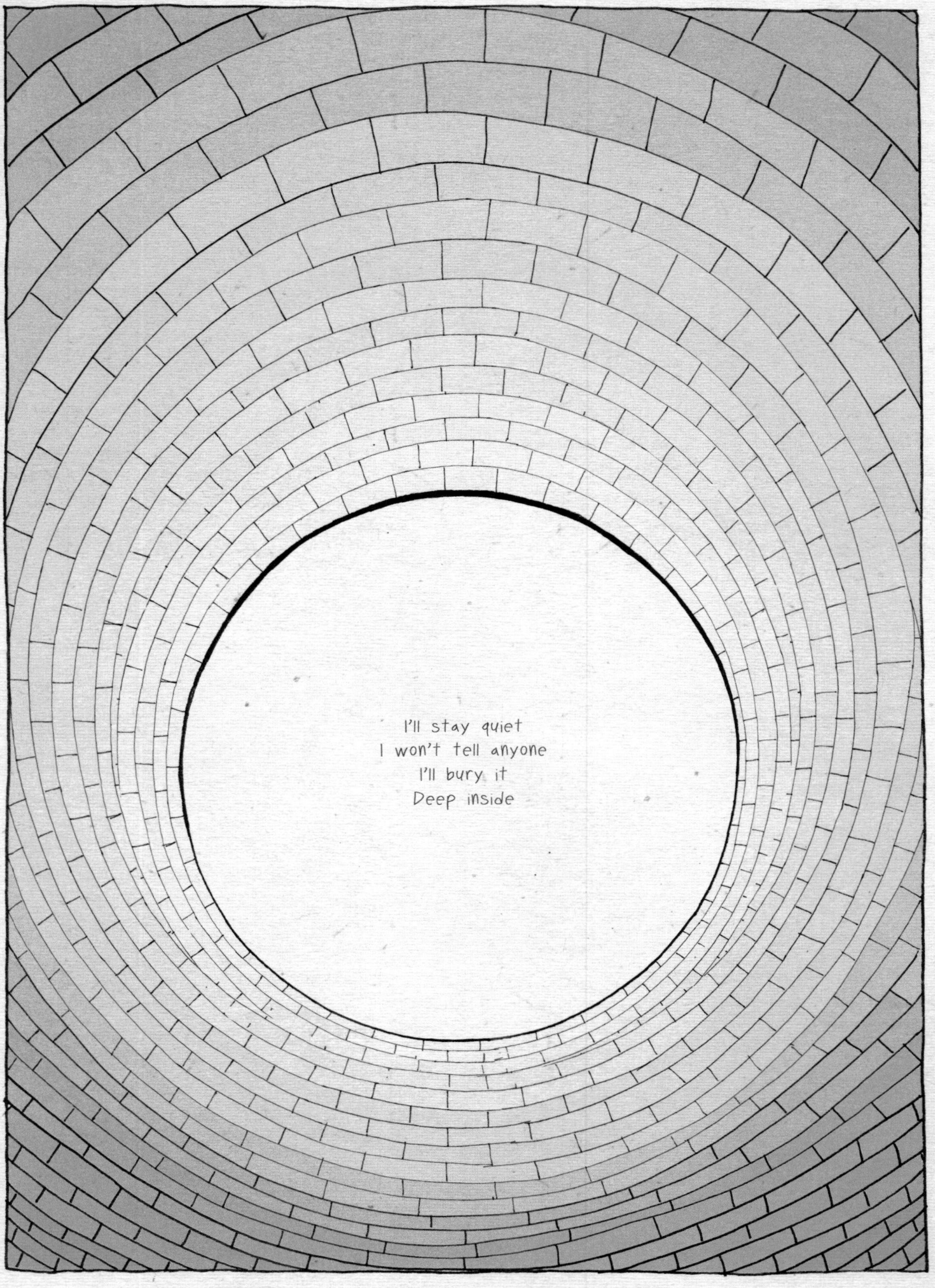
I'll stay quiet
I won't tell anyone
I'll bury it
Deep inside

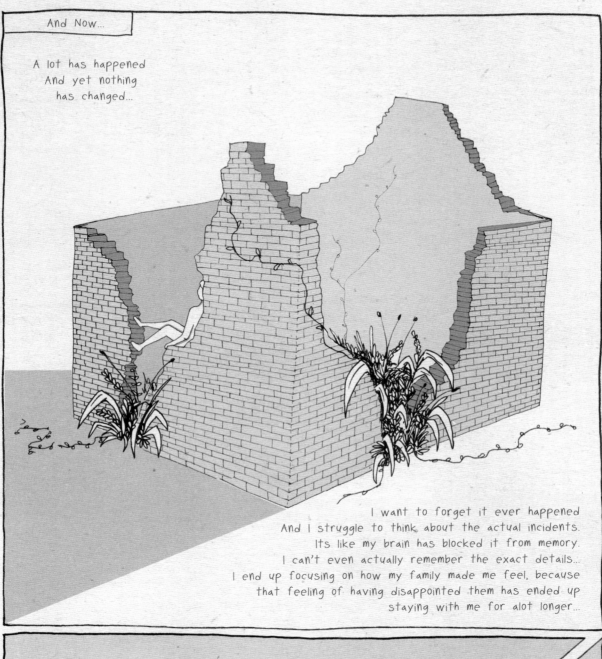

And Now...

A lot has happened
And yet nothing
has changed...

I want to forget it ever happened
And I struggle to think about the actual incidents.
Its like my brain has blocked it from memory.
I can't even actually remember the exact details...
I end up focusing on how my family made me feel, because
that feeling of having disappointed them has ended up
staying with me for alot longer...

And thats all I feel I
can say about it...

Fin

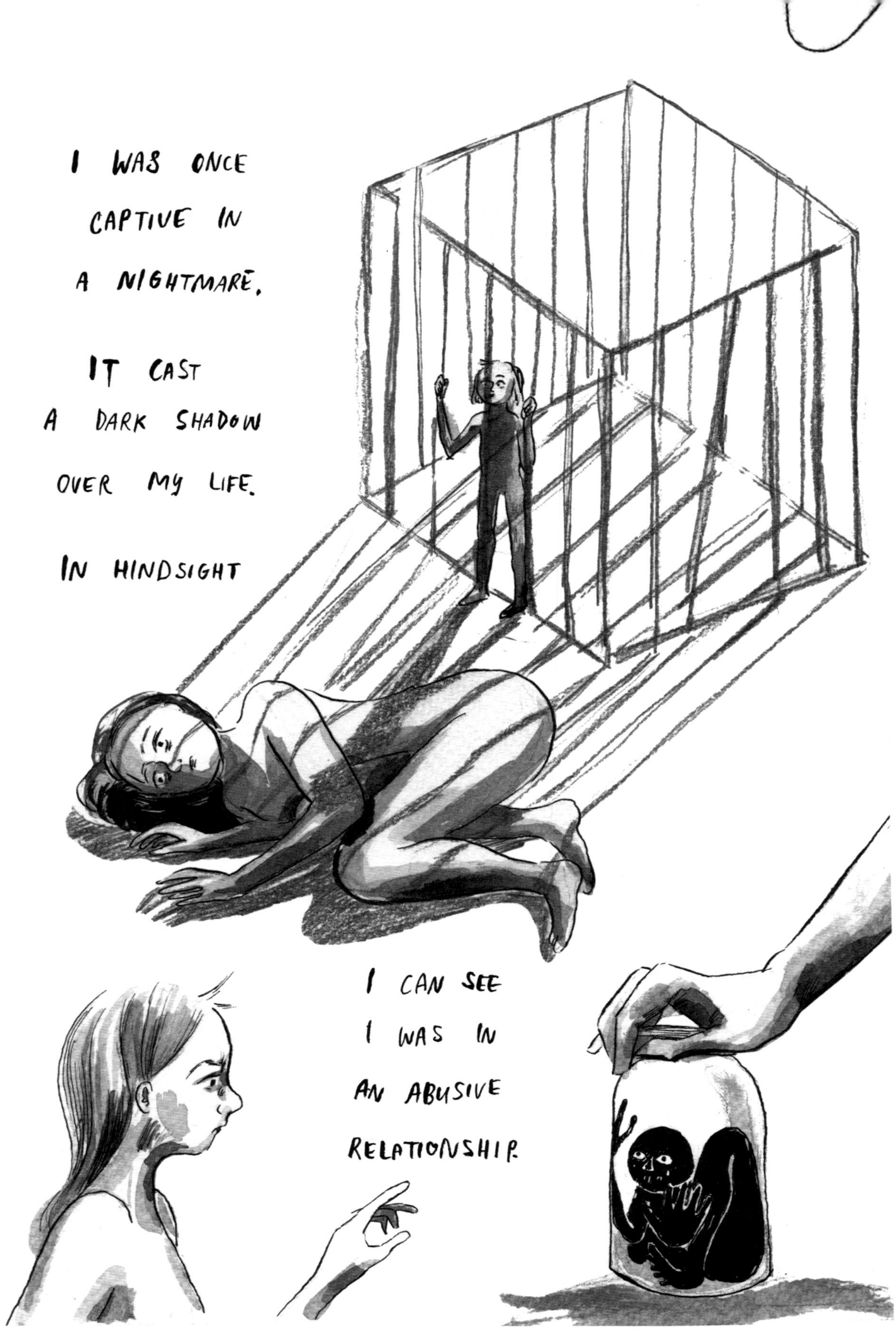
I WAS ONCE
CAPTIVE IN
A NIGHTMARE.
IT CAST
A DARK SHADOW
OVER MY LIFE.
IN HINDSIGHT
I CAN SEE
I WAS IN
AN ABUSIVE
RELATIONSHIP.

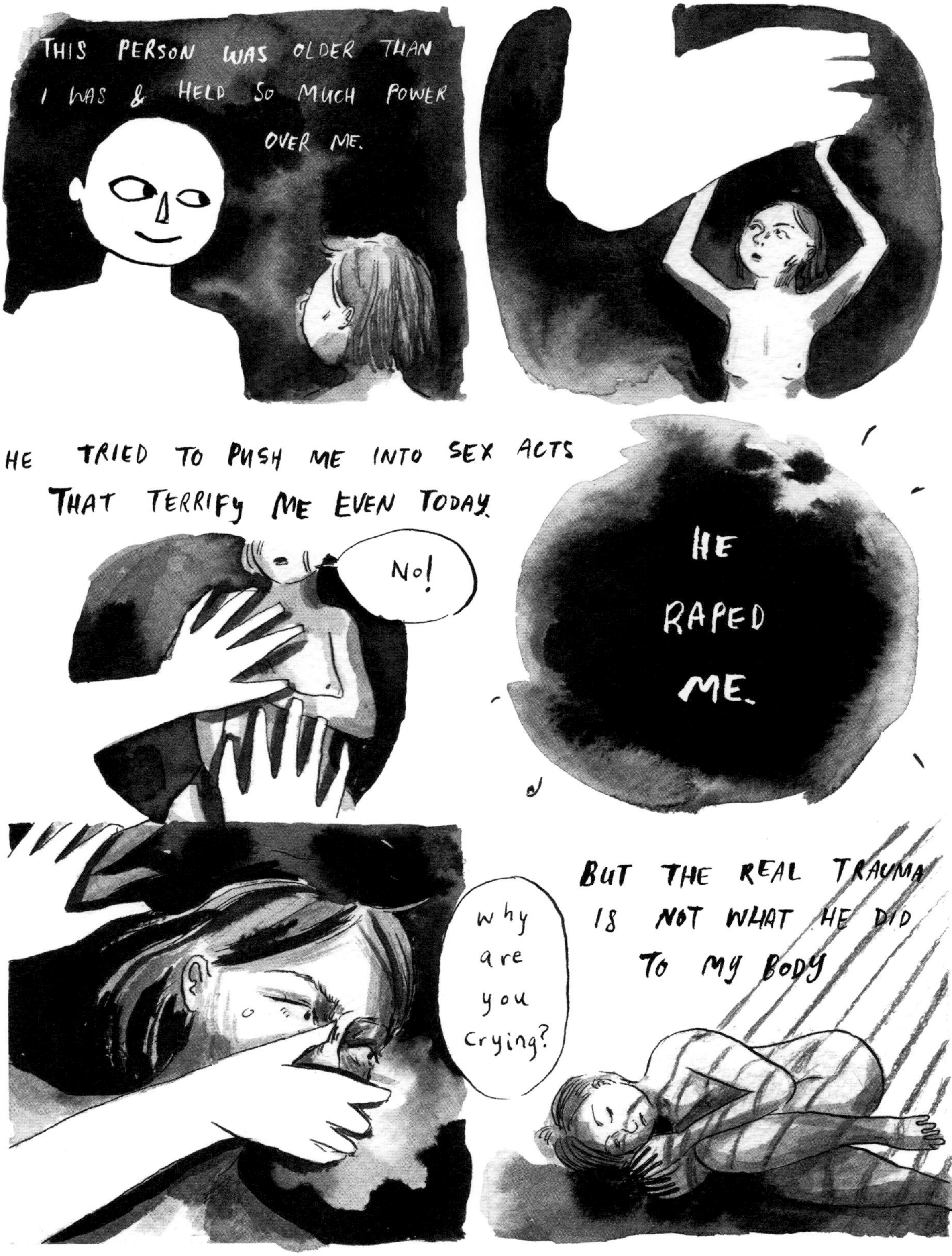
THIS PERSON WAS OLDER THAN I WAS & HELD SO MUCH POWER OVER ME.
HE TRIED TO PUSH ME INTO SEX ACTS THAT TERRIFY ME EVEN TODAY.
No!
HE RAPED ME.
why are you crying?
BUT THE REAL TRAUMA IS NOT WHAT HE DID TO MY BODY

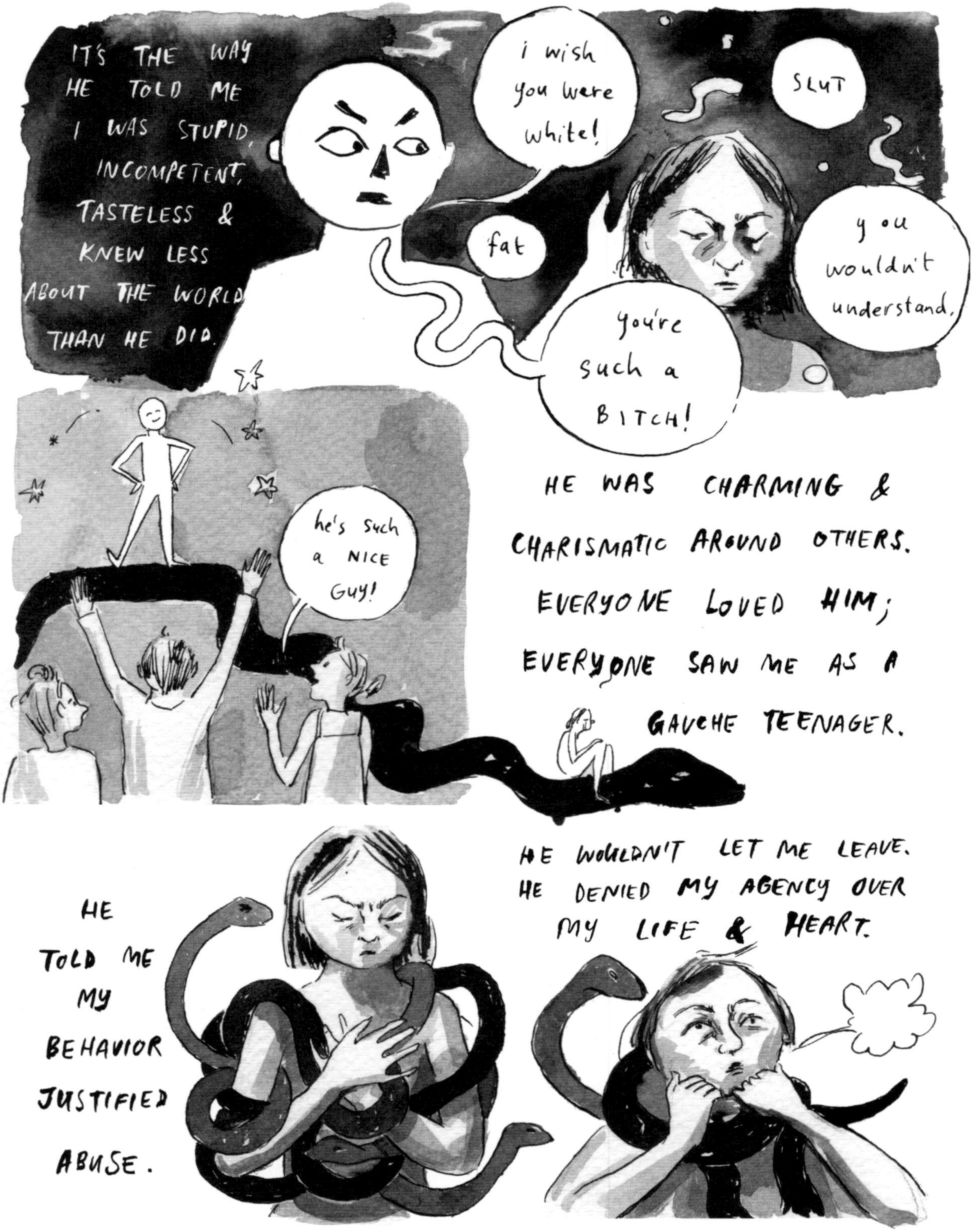
IT'S THE WAY HE TOLD ME I WAS STUPID, INCOMPETENT, TASTELESS & KNEW LESS ABOUT THE WORLD THAN HE DID.
i wish you were white!
SLUT
fat
you wouldn't understand.
you're such a BITCH!
HE WAS CHARMING & CHARISMATIC AROUND OTHERS. EVERYONE LOVED HIM; EVERYONE SAW ME AS A GAUCHE TEENAGER.
he's such a NICE GUY!
HE WOULDN'T LET ME LEAVE. HE DENIED MY AGENCY OVER MY LIFE & HEART.
HE TOLD ME MY BEHAVIOR JUSTIFIED ABUSE.

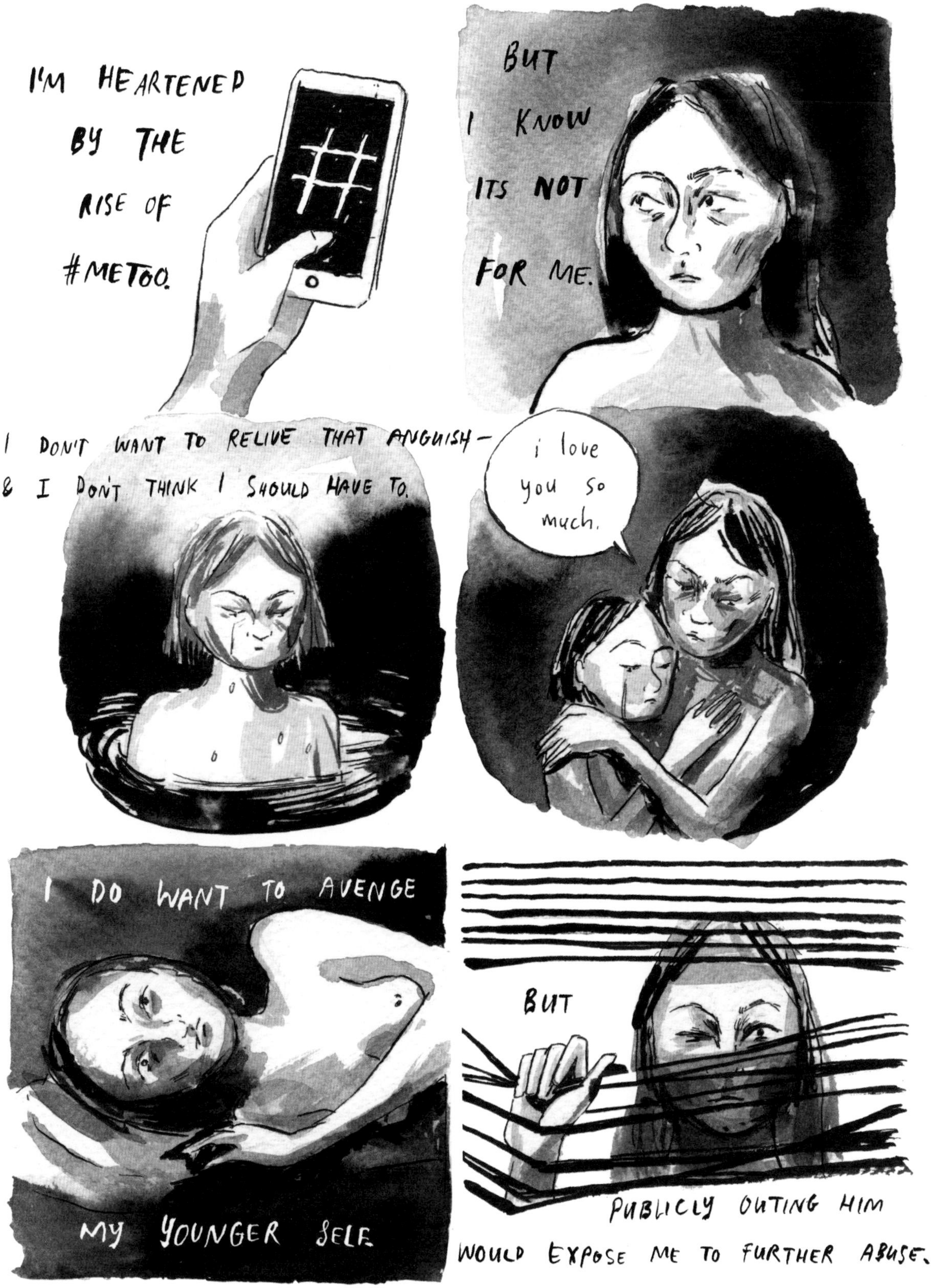
I'M HEARTENED BY THE RISE OF #METOO.
BUT I KNOW ITS NOT FOR ME.
I DON'T WANT TO RELIVE THAT ANGUISH—
& I DON'T THINK I SHOULD HAVE TO.
i love you so much.
I DO WANT TO AVENGE
MY YOUNGER SELF
BUT
PUBLICLY OUTING HIM
WOULD EXPOSE ME TO FURTHER ABUSE.

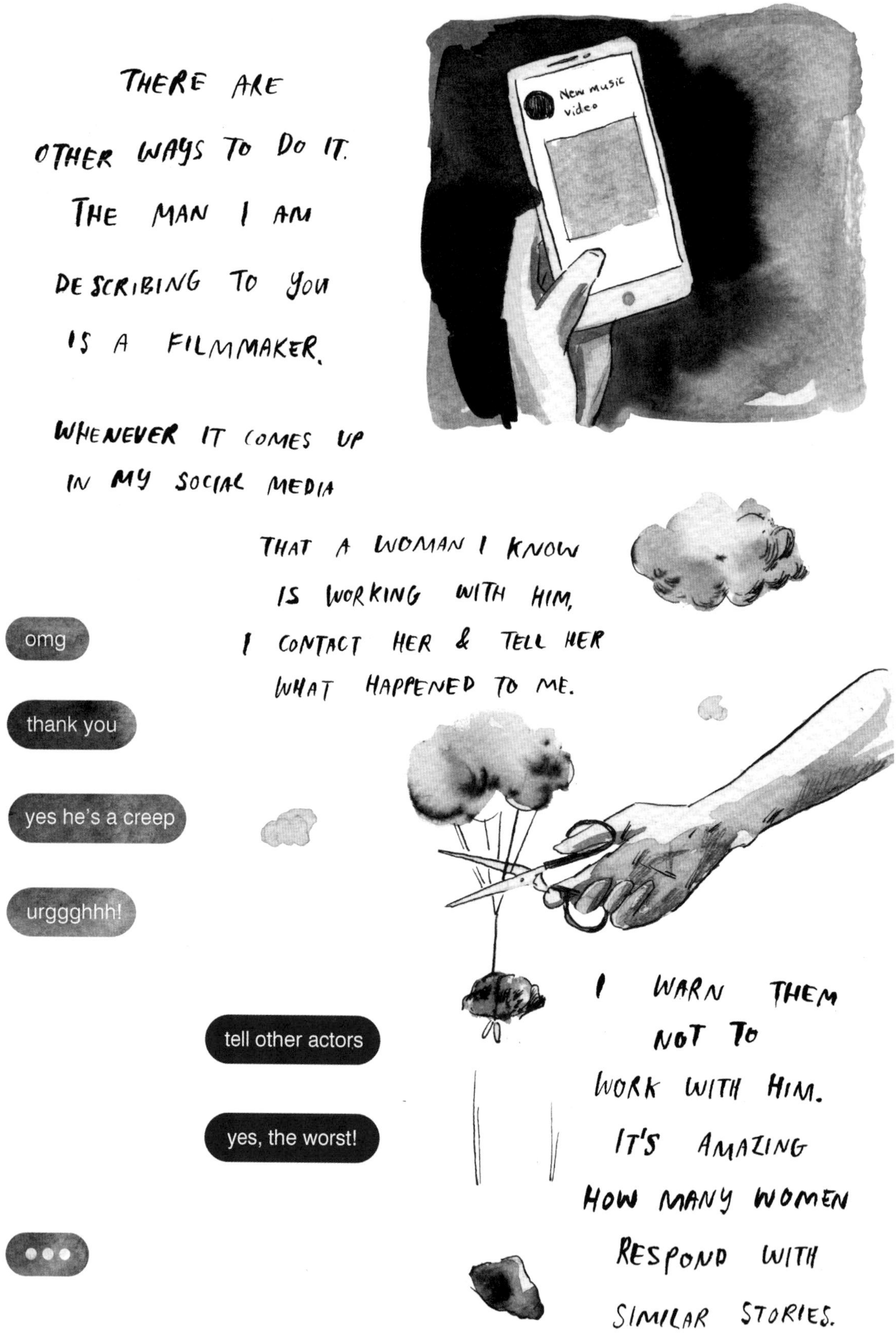
THERE ARE OTHER WAYS TO DO IT.
THE MAN I AM DESCRIBING TO YOU IS A FILMMAKER.
New music video
WHENEVER IT COMES UP IN MY SOCIAL MEDIA
THAT A WOMAN I KNOW IS WORKING WITH HIM,
I CONTACT HER & TELL HER WHAT HAPPENED TO ME.
omg
thank you
yes he's a creep
urggghhh!
I WARN THEM NOT TO WORK WITH HIM.
tell other actors
yes, the worst!
IT'S AMAZING HOW MANY WOMEN RESPOND WITH SIMILAR STORIES.

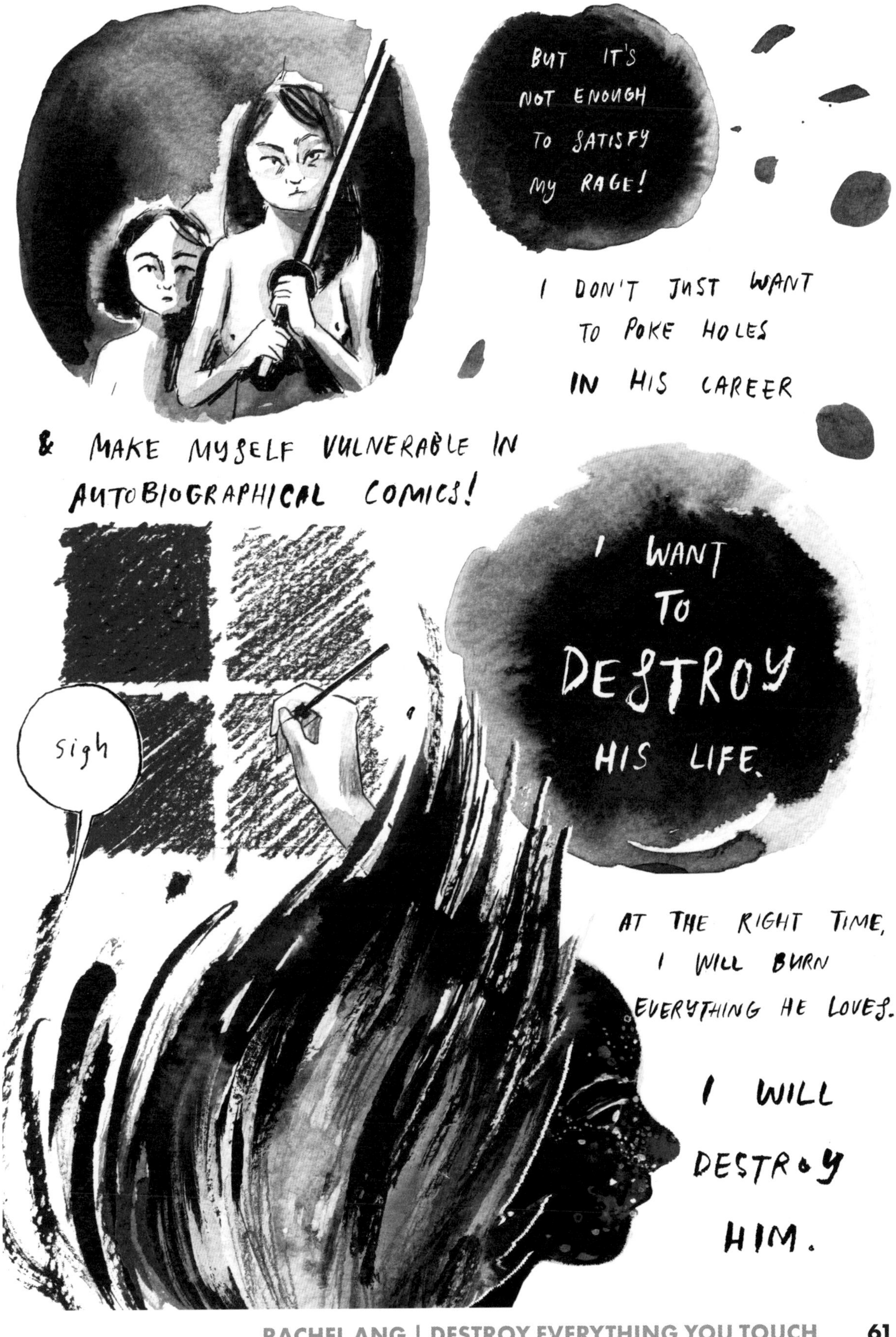
BUT IT'S NOT ENOUGH TO SATISFY MY RAGE!
I DON'T JUST WANT TO POKE HOLES IN HIS CAREER
& MAKE MYSELF VULNERABLE IN AUTOBIOGRAPHICAL COMICS!
I WANT TO DESTROY HIS LIFE.
sigh
AT THE RIGHT TIME, I WILL BURN EVERYTHING HE LOVES.
I WILL DESTROY HIM.

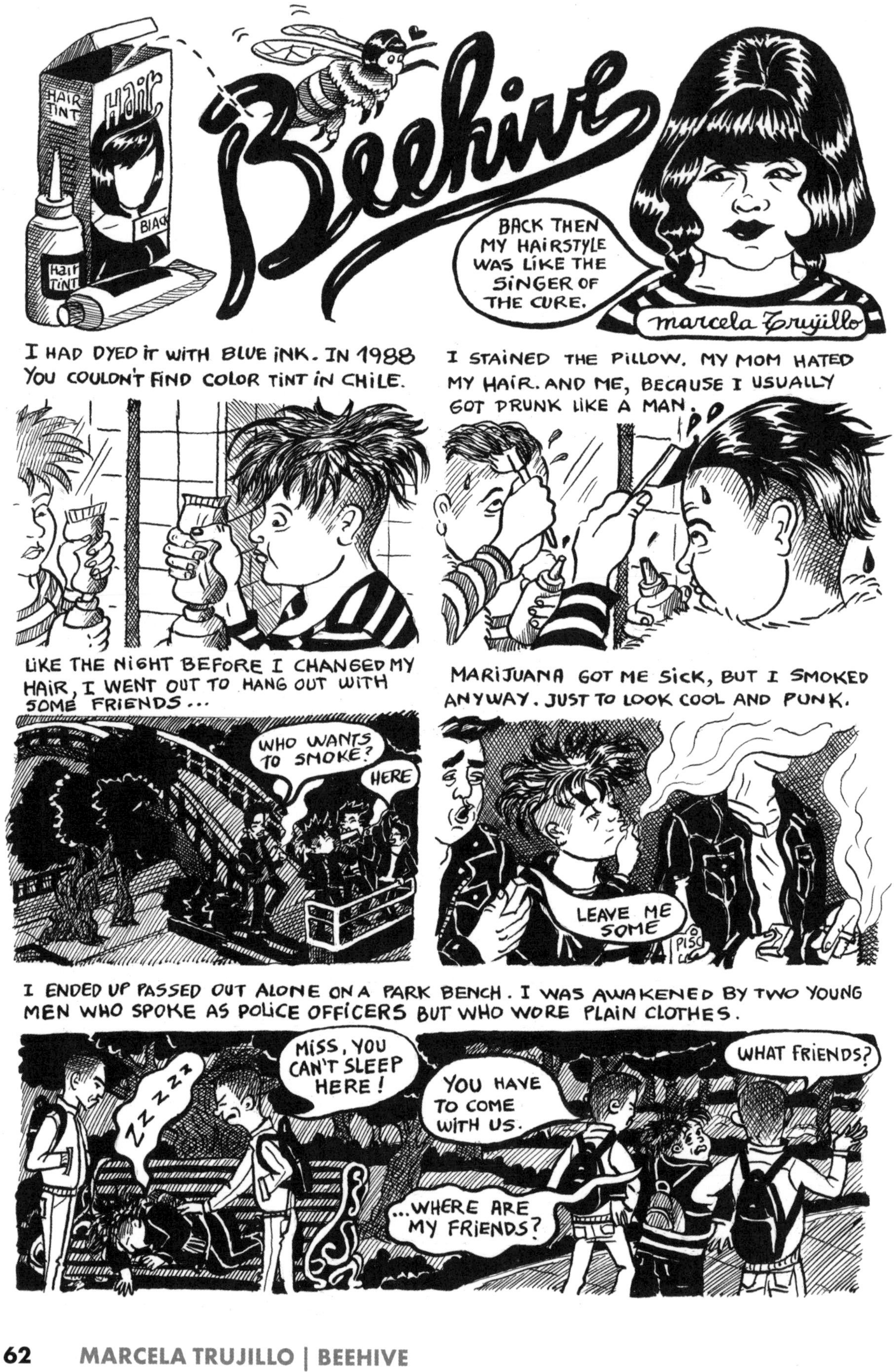
HAIR TINT
Hair
BLACK
Hair TINT
Beehive
BACK THEN MY HAIRSTYLE WAS LIKE THE SINGER OF THE CURE.
marcela Trujillo
I HAD DYED IT WITH BLUE INK. IN 1988 YOU COULDN'T FIND COLOR TINT IN CHILE.
I STAINED THE PILLOW. MY MOM HATED MY HAIR. AND ME, BECAUSE I USUALLY GOT DRUNK LIKE A MAN.
LIKE THE NIGHT BEFORE I CHANGED MY HAIR, I WENT OUT TO HANG OUT WITH SOME FRIENDS...
WHO WANTS TO SMOKE?
HERE
MARIJUANA GOT ME SICK, BUT I SMOKED ANYWAY. JUST TO LOOK COOL AND PUNK.
LEAVE ME SOME
I ENDED UP PASSED OUT ALONE ON A PARK BENCH. I WAS AWAKENED BY TWO YOUNG MEN WHO SPOKE AS POLICE OFFICERS BUT WHO WORE PLAIN CLOTHES.
ZZZZZ
MISS, YOU CAN'T SLEEP HERE!
YOU HAVE TO COME WITH US.
...WHERE ARE MY FRIENDS?
WHAT FRIENDS?

I THOUGHT I WAS BEING ARRESTED AND WE WERE GOING TO THE POLICE STATION.

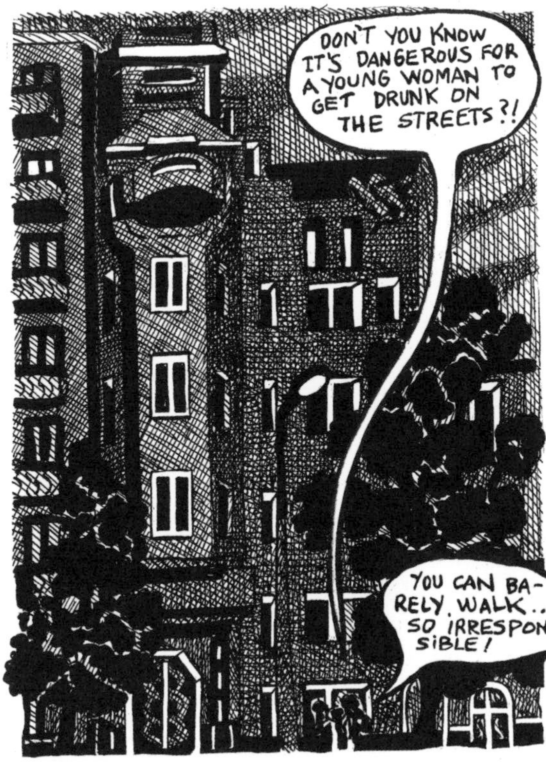
DON'T YOU KNOW IT'S DANGEROUS FOR A YOUNG WOMAN TO GET DRUNK ON THE STREETS?!
YOU CAN BARELY WALK... SO IRRESPONSIBLE!

BUT WE STOPPED AT THE DOOR OF AN OLD BUILDING AND I HEARD KEYS.

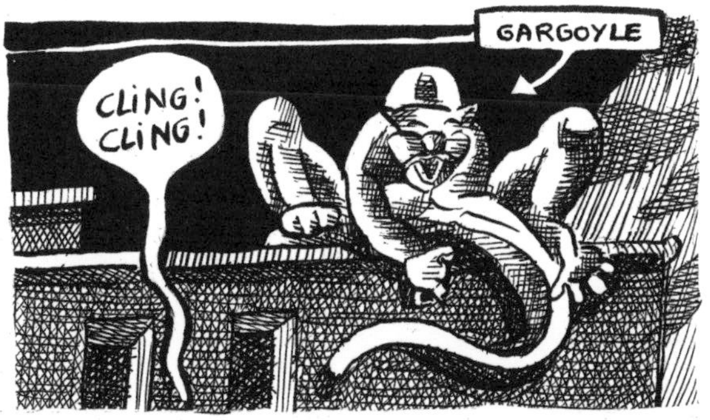
GARGOYLE
CLING! CLING!

RIGHT THERE I REALIZED WHAT WAS GOING TO HAPPEN... TO ME.

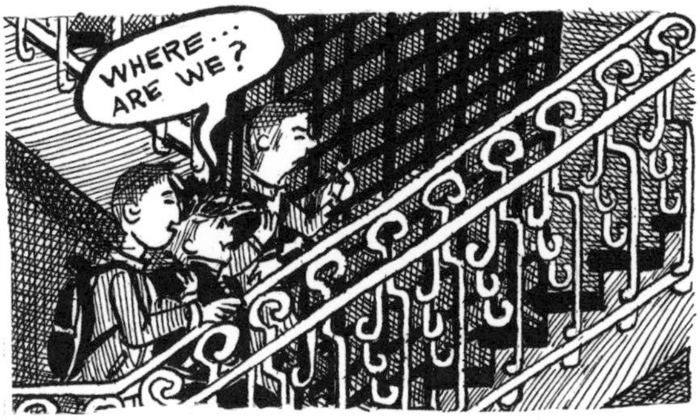
WHERE... ARE WE?

WE WERE IN A DICTATORSHIP. I COULDN'T DO ANYTHING. WE ENTERED AN EMPTY APARTMENT, THEY TOOK ME TO A ROOM, THEY LAID ME ON THE FLOOR AND CLOSED THE DOOR.

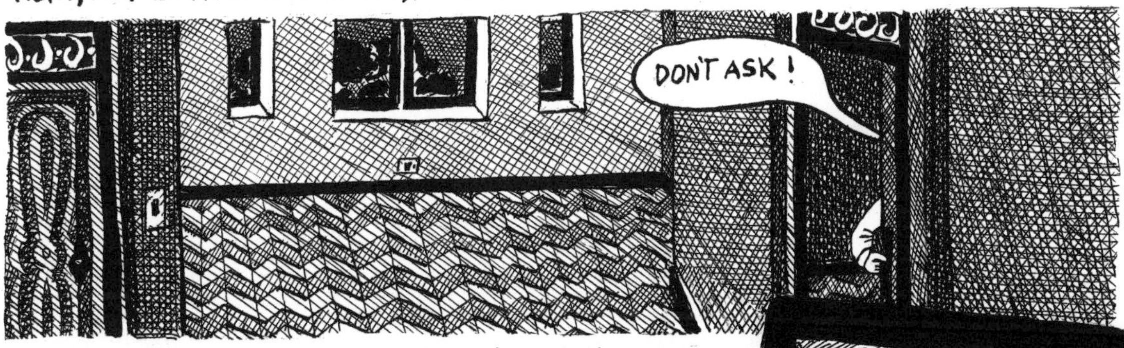
DON'T ASK!

I DIDN'T WANT TO DIE OR BE HURT. SO I DIDN'T DEFEND MYSELF, I CLOSED MY EYES AND THOUGHT OF SOMETHING NICE.

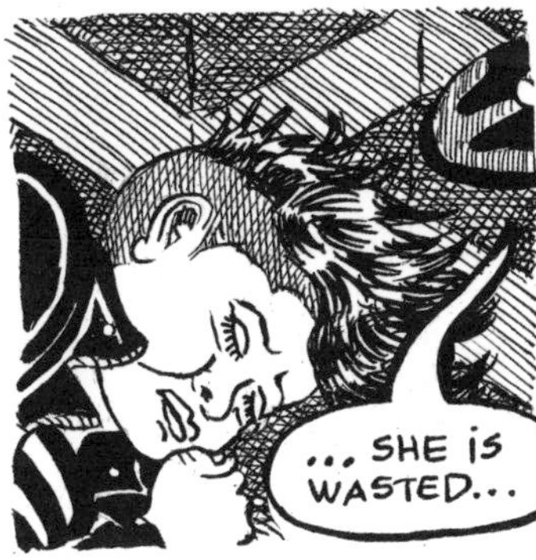
...SHE IS WASTED...

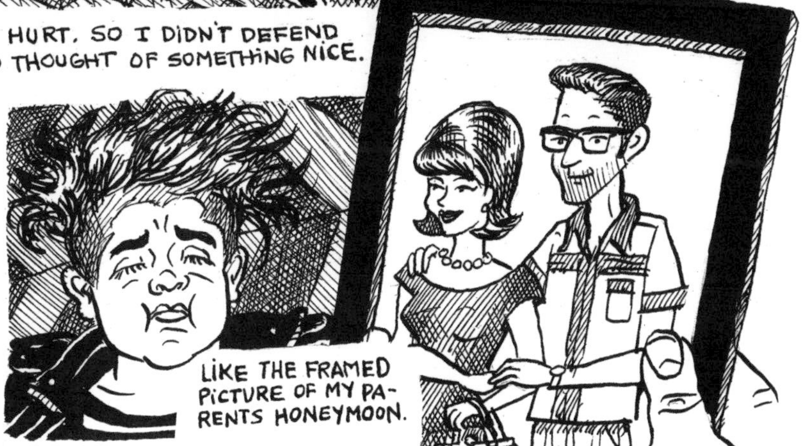
LIKE THE FRAMED PICTURE OF MY PARENTS HONEYMOON.

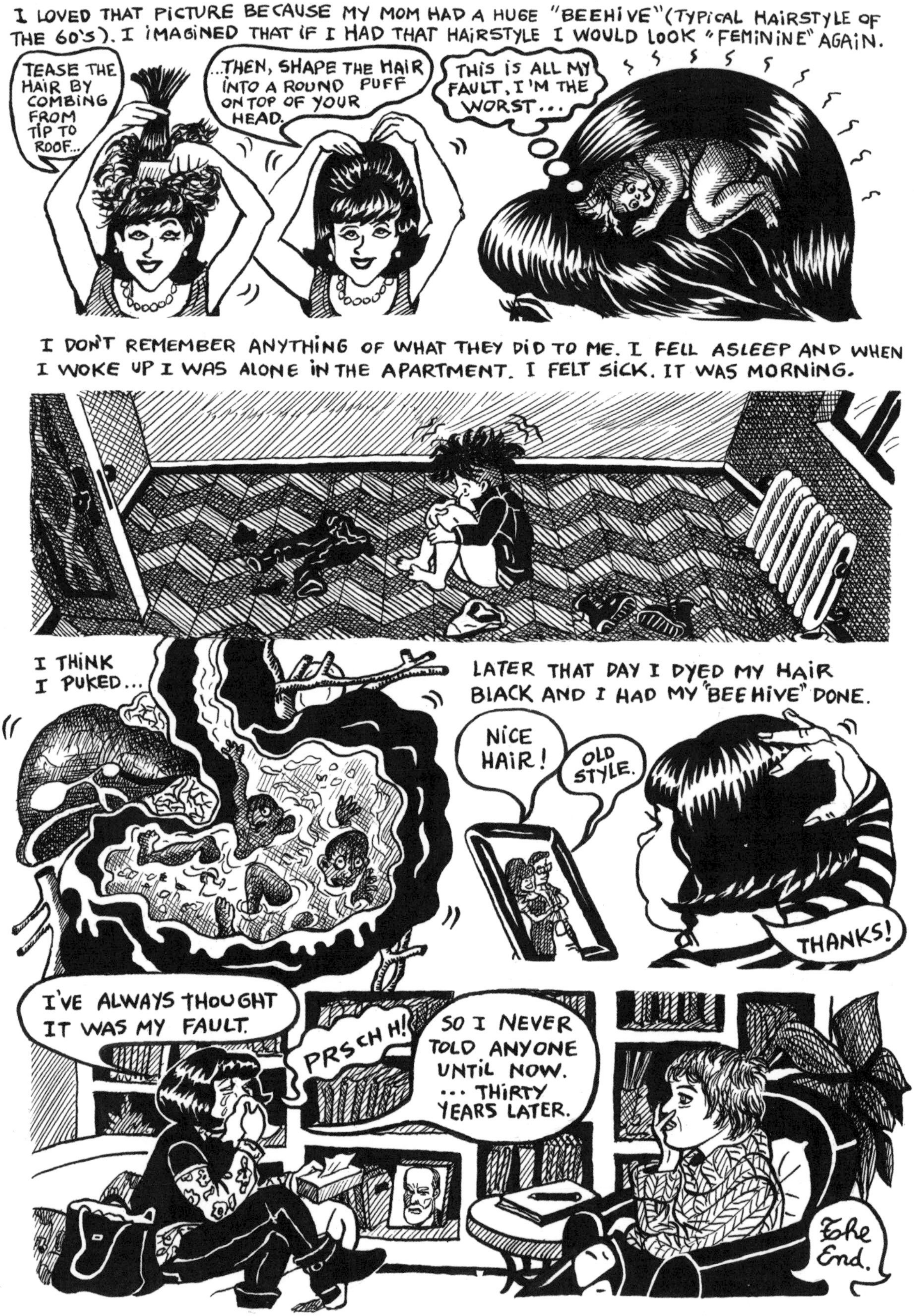
I LOVED THAT PICTURE BECAUSE MY MOM HAD A HUGE "BEEHIVE" (TYPICAL HAIRSTYLE OF THE 60'S). I IMAGINED THAT IF I HAD THAT HAIRSTYLE I WOULD LOOK "FEMININE" AGAIN.
TEASE THE HAIR BY COMBING FROM TIP TO ROOF...
...THEN, SHAPE THE HAIR INTO A ROUND PUFF ON TOP OF YOUR HEAD.
THIS IS ALL MY FAULT, I'M THE WORST...
I DON'T REMEMBER ANYTHING OF WHAT THEY DID TO ME. I FELL ASLEEP AND WHEN I WOKE UP I WAS ALONE IN THE APARTMENT. I FELT SICK. IT WAS MORNING.
I THINK I PUKED...
LATER THAT DAY I DYED MY HAIR BLACK AND I HAD MY "BEEHIVE" DONE.
NICE HAIR!
OLD STYLE.
THANKS!
I'VE ALWAYS THOUGHT IT WAS MY FAULT.
PRSCHH!
SO I NEVER TOLD ANYONE UNTIL NOW. ... THIRTY YEARS LATER.
The End.

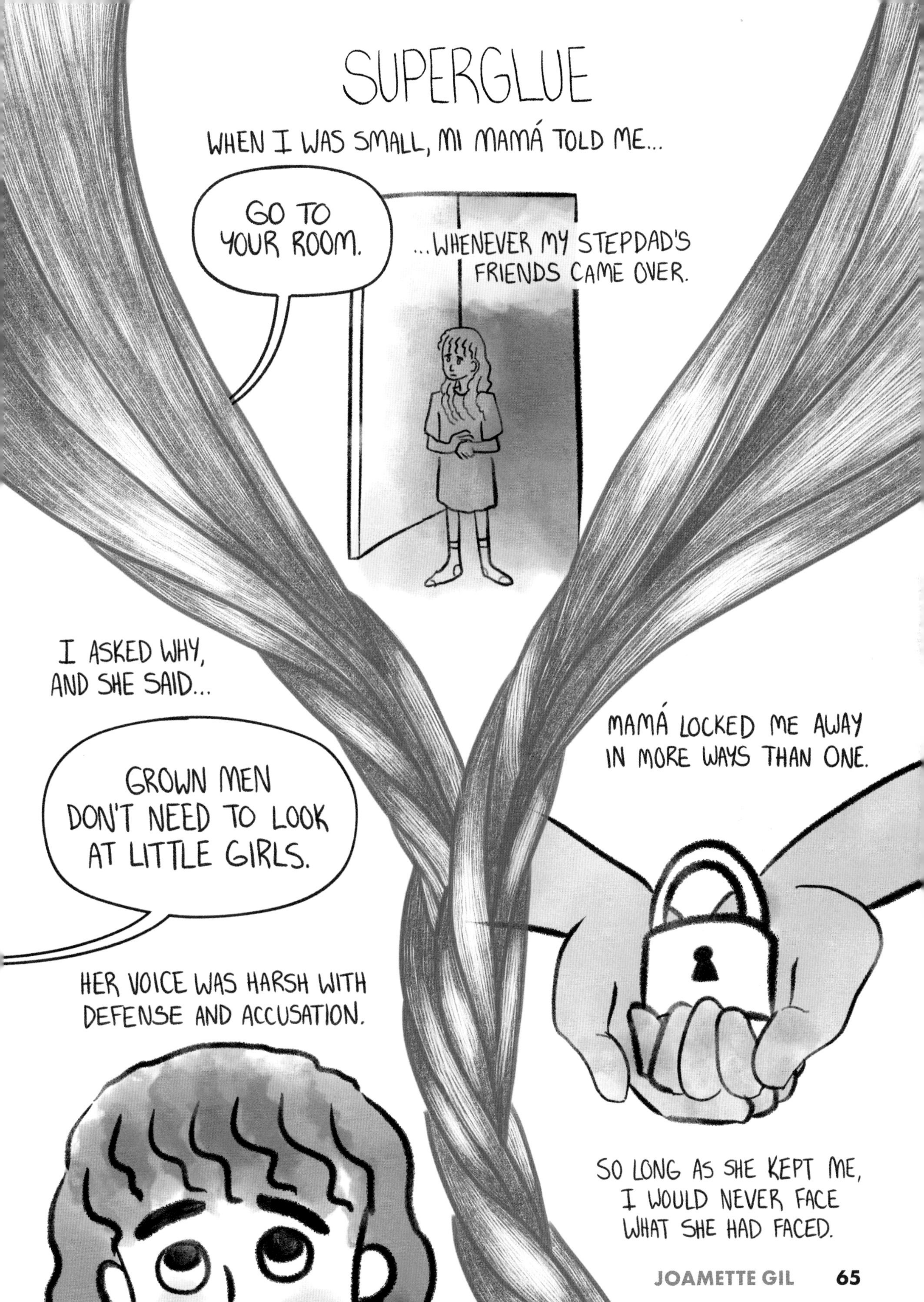
SUPERGLUE
WHEN I WAS SMALL, MI MAMÁ TOLD ME...
GO TO YOUR ROOM.
...WHENEVER MY STEPDAD'S FRIENDS CAME OVER.
I ASKED WHY, AND SHE SAID...
GROWN MEN DON'T NEED TO LOOK AT LITTLE GIRLS.
HER VOICE WAS HARSH WITH DEFENSE AND ACCUSATION.
MAMÁ LOCKED ME AWAY IN MORE WAYS THAN ONE.
SO LONG AS SHE KEPT ME, I WOULD NEVER FACE WHAT SHE HAD FACED.

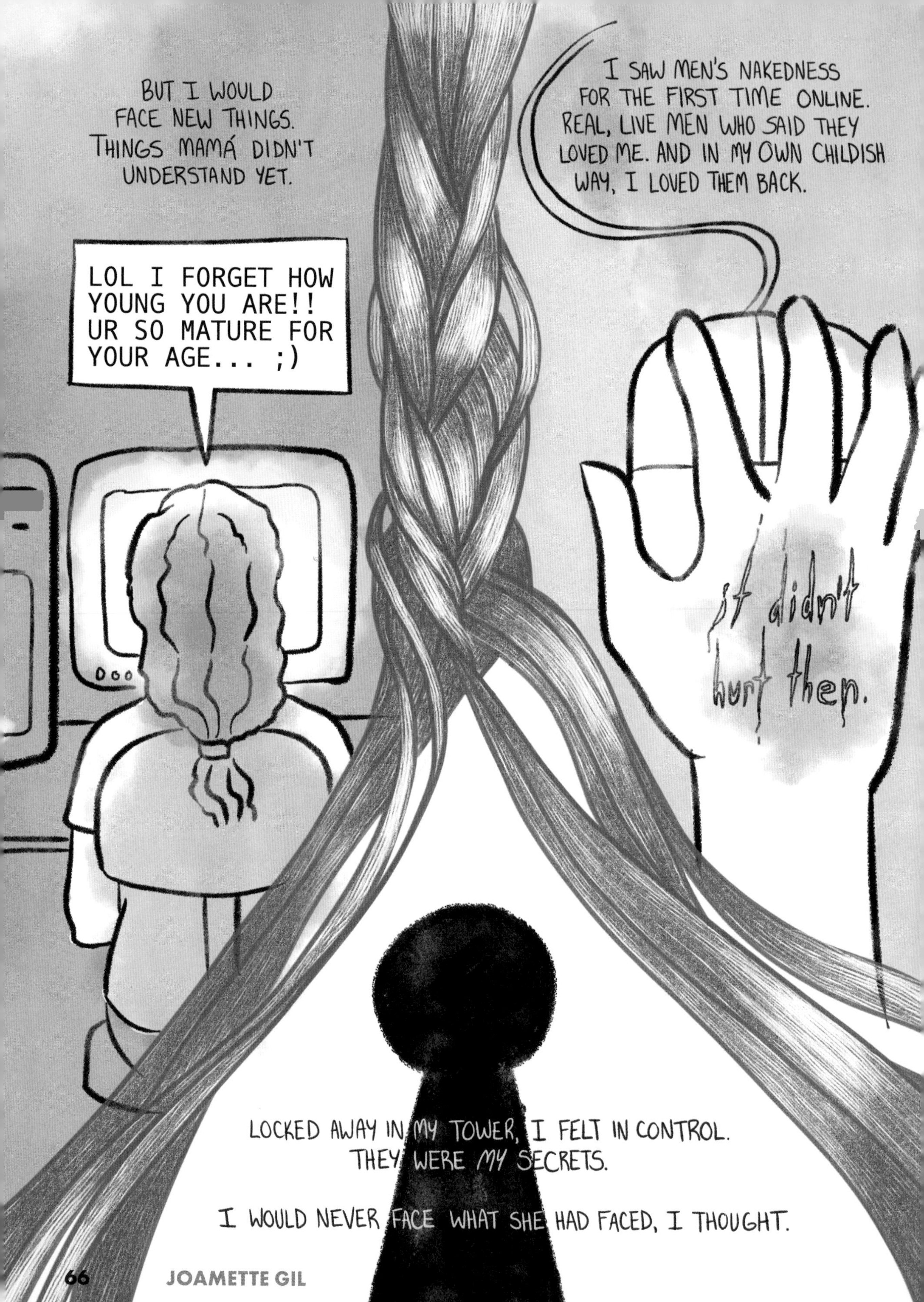
BUT I WOULD FACE NEW THINGS. THINGS MAMÁ DIDN'T UNDERSTAND YET.
I SAW MEN'S NAKEDNESS FOR THE FIRST TIME ONLINE. REAL, LIVE MEN WHO SAID THEY LOVED ME. AND IN MY OWN CHILDISH WAY, I LOVED THEM BACK.
LOL I FORGET HOW YOUNG YOU ARE!! UR SO MATURE FOR YOUR AGE... ;)
it didn't hurt then.
LOCKED AWAY IN MY TOWER, I FELT IN CONTROL. THEY WERE *MY* SECRETS.
I WOULD NEVER FACE WHAT SHE HAD FACED, I THOUGHT.

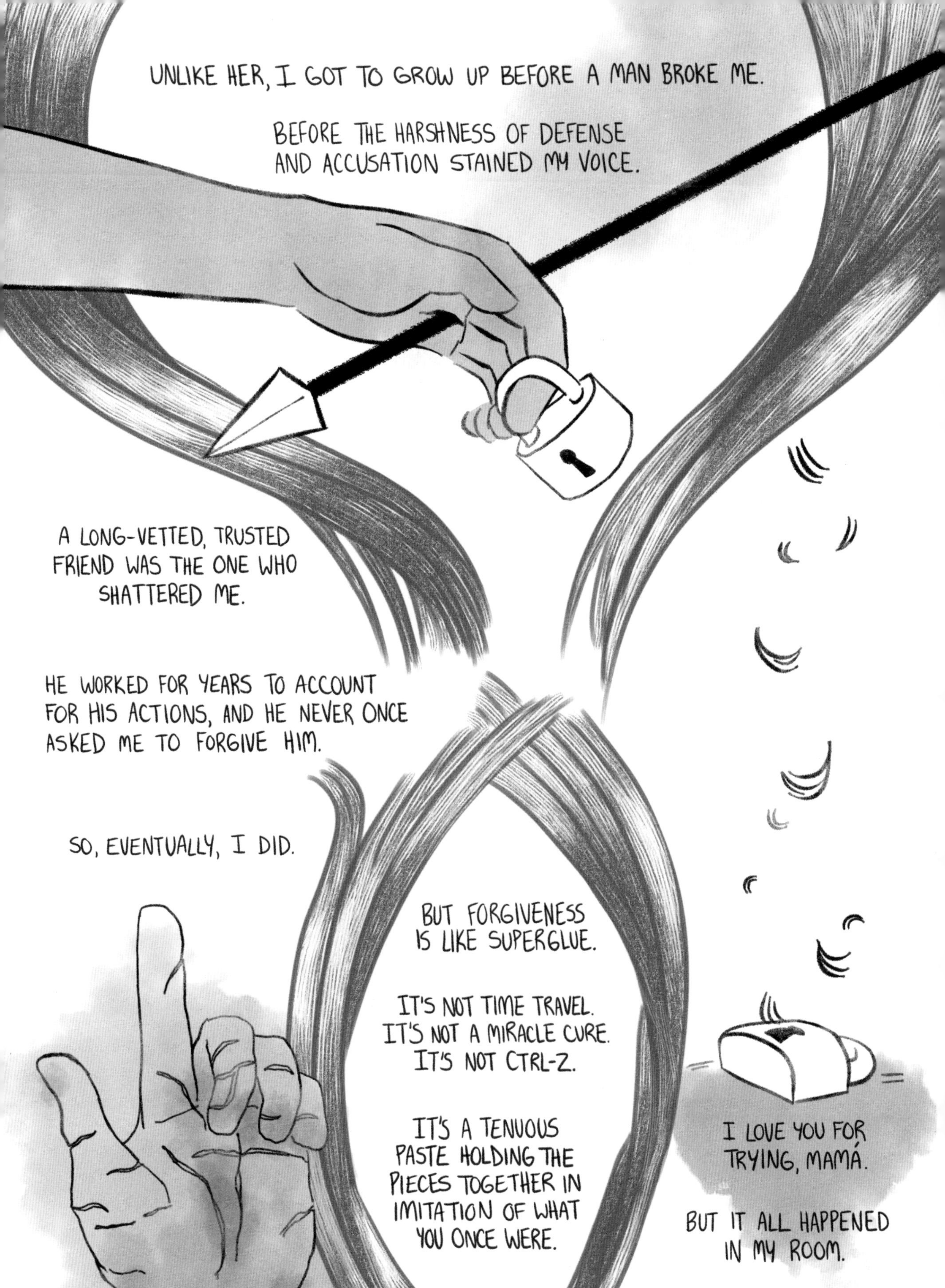
UNLIKE HER, I GOT TO GROW UP BEFORE A MAN BROKE ME.
BEFORE THE HARSHNESS OF DEFENSE AND ACCUSATION STAINED MY VOICE.
A LONG-VETTED, TRUSTED FRIEND WAS THE ONE WHO SHATTERED ME.
HE WORKED FOR YEARS TO ACCOUNT FOR HIS ACTIONS, AND HE NEVER ONCE ASKED ME TO FORGIVE HIM.
SO, EVENTUALLY, I DID.
BUT FORGIVENESS IS LIKE SUPERGLUE.
IT'S NOT TIME TRAVEL. IT'S NOT A MIRACLE CURE. IT'S NOT CTRL-Z.
IT'S A TENUOUS PASTE HOLDING THE PIECES TOGETHER IN IMITATION OF WHAT YOU ONCE WERE.
I LOVE YOU FOR TRYING, MAMÁ.
BUT IT ALL HAPPENED IN MY ROOM.

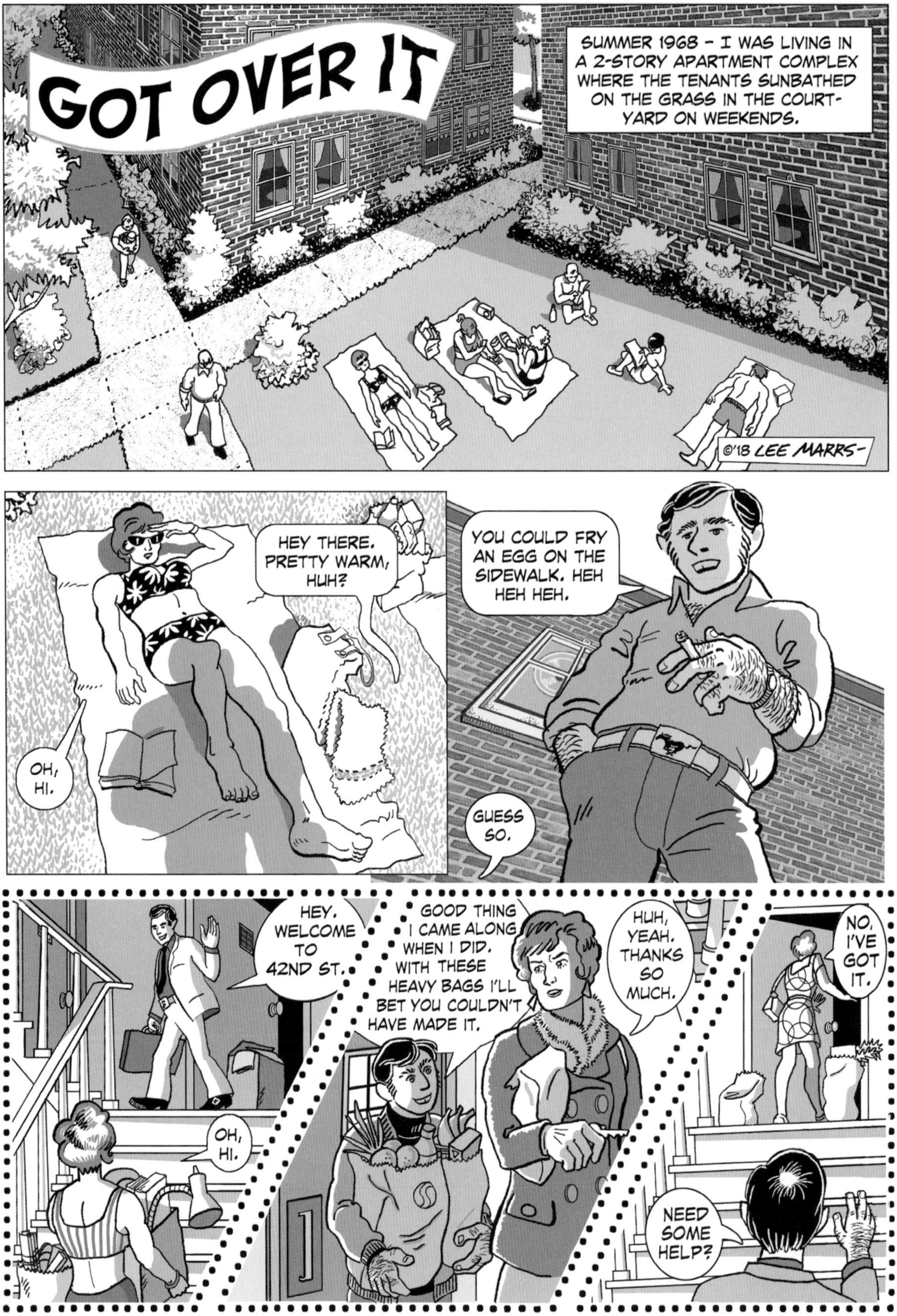
GOT OVER IT
SUMMER 1968 – I WAS LIVING IN A 2-STORY APARTMENT COMPLEX WHERE THE TENANTS SUNBATHED ON THE GRASS IN THE COURT-YARD ON WEEKENDS.
©'18 LEE MARRS-
HEY THERE. PRETTY WARM, HUH?
OH, HI.
YOU COULD FRY AN EGG ON THE SIDEWALK. HEH HEH HEH.
GUESS SO.
HEY. WELCOME TO 42ND ST.
OH, HI.
GOOD THING I CAME ALONG WHEN I DID. WITH THESE HEAVY BAGS I'LL BET YOU COULDN'T HAVE MADE IT.
HUH, YEAH. THANKS SO MUCH.
NEED SOME HELP?
NO, I'VE GOT IT.

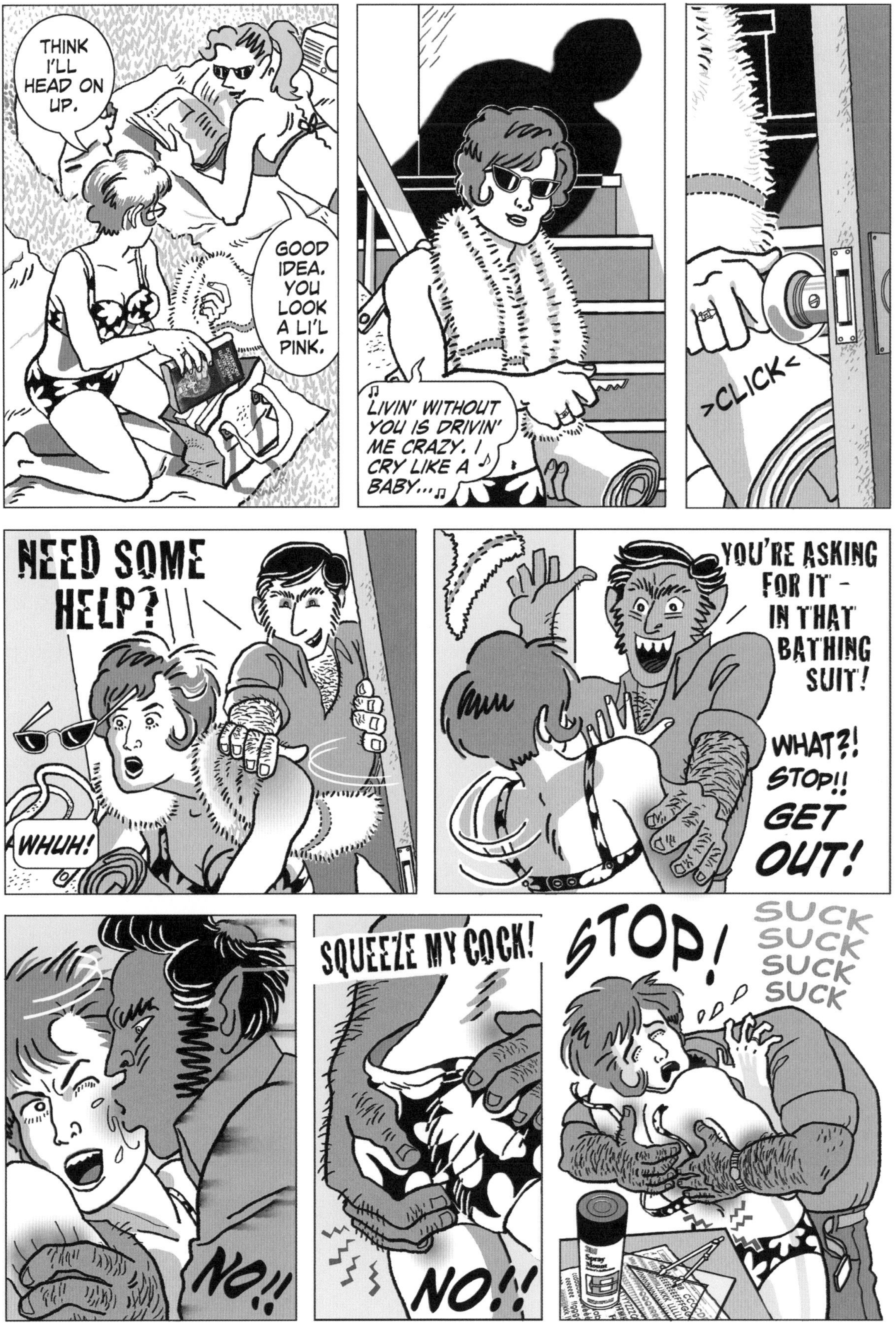
THINK I'LL HEAD ON UP.
GOOD IDEA. YOU LOOK A LI'L PINK.
♫ LIVIN' WITHOUT YOU IS DRIVIN' ME CRAZY. I CRY LIKE A ♪ BABY... ♫
>CLICK<
NEED SOME HELP?
WHUH!
YOU'RE ASKING FOR IT – IN THAT BATHING SUIT!
WHAT?! STOP!! GET OUT!
NO!!
SQUEEZE MY COCK!
NO!!
STOP!
SUCK SUCK SUCK SUCK

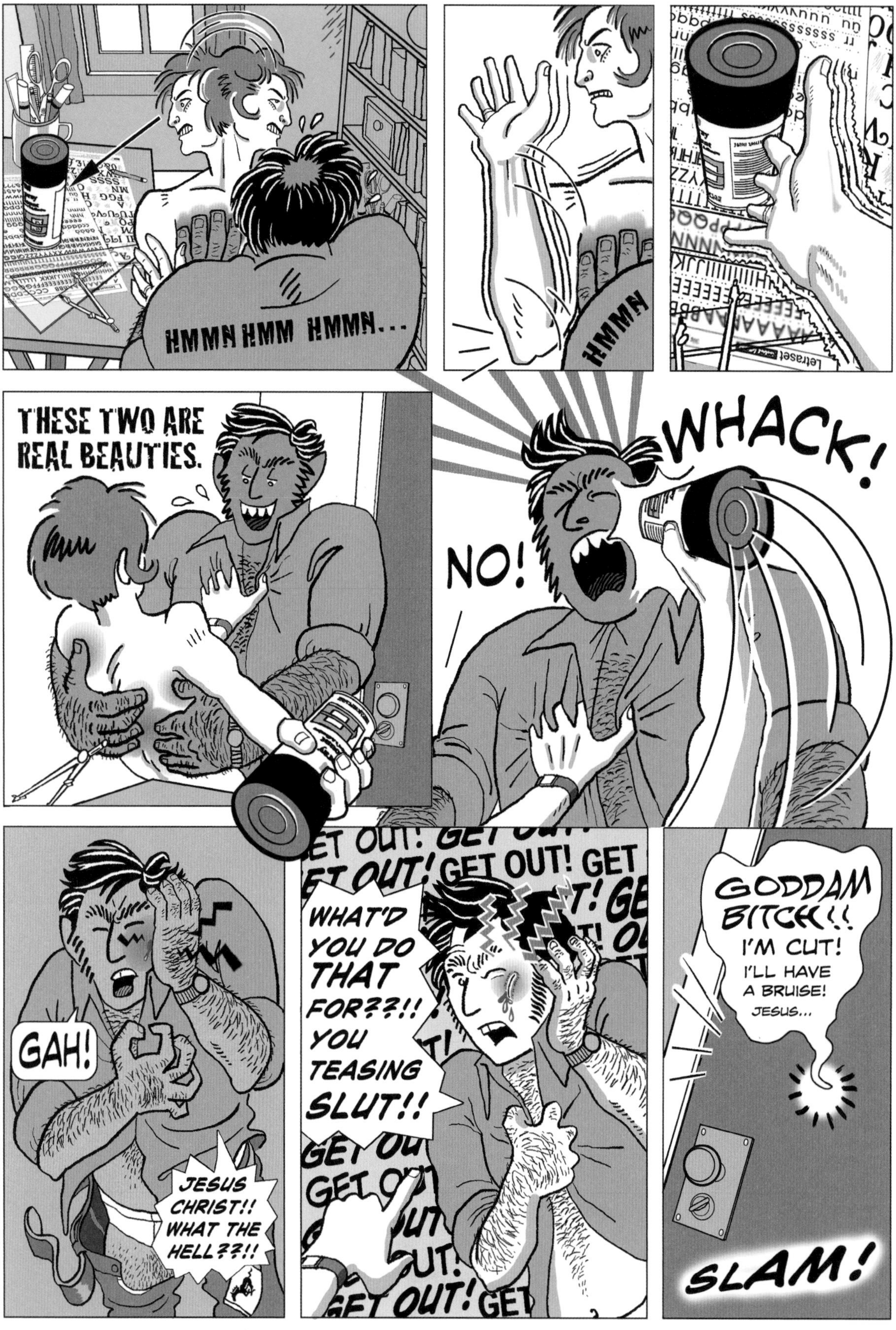
HMMN HMM HMMN...
HMMN
THESE TWO ARE REAL BEAUTIES.
WHACK!
NO!
GAH!
JESUS CHRIST!! WHAT THE HELL??!!
GET OUT! GET OUT! GET OUT! GET
WHAT'D YOU DO THAT FOR??!! YOU TEASING SLUT!!
GODDAM BITCH!! I'M CUT! I'LL HAVE A BRUISE! JESUS...
SLAM!

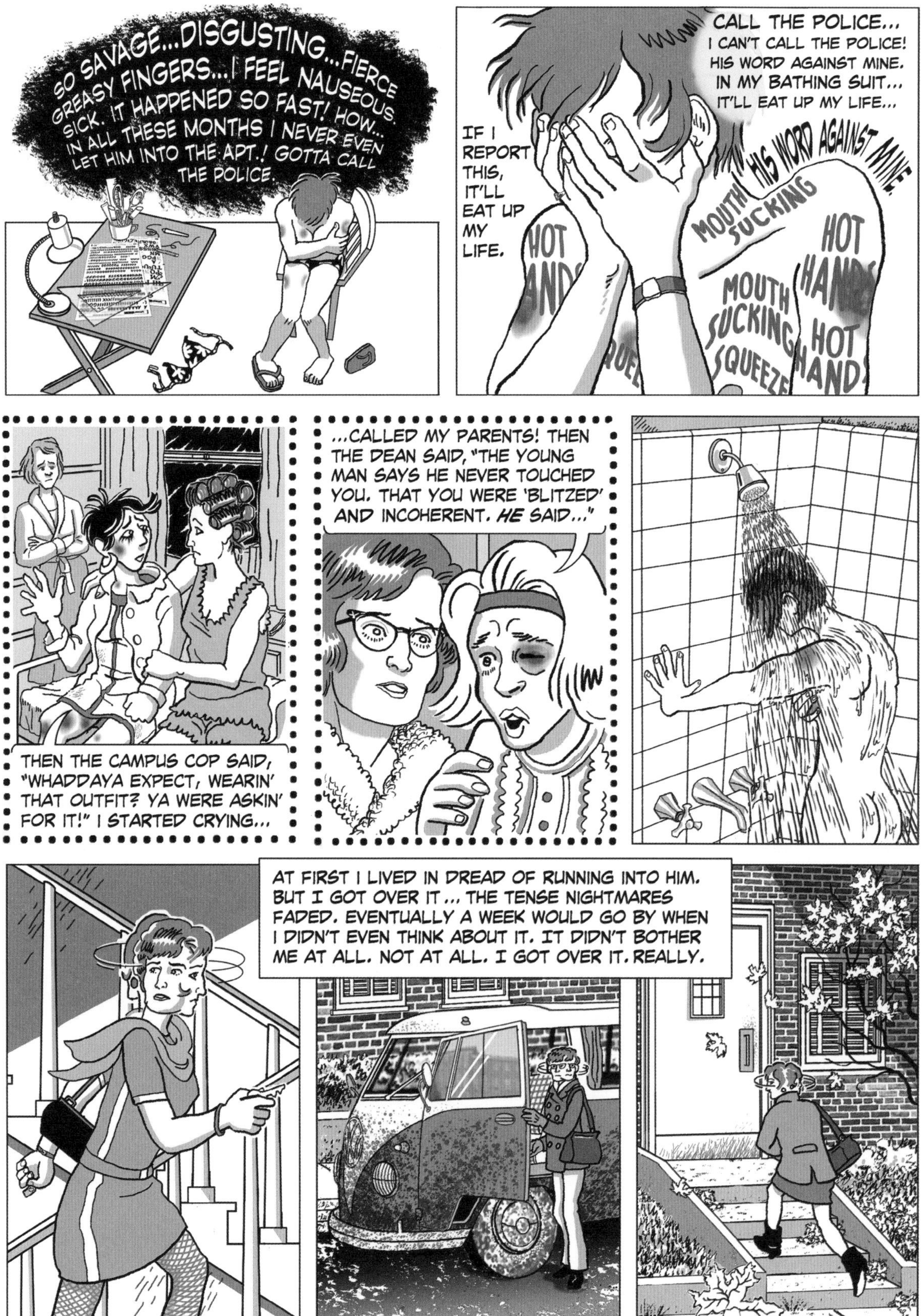
SO SAVAGE...DISGUSTING...FIERCE GREASY FINGERS...I FEEL NAUSEOUS. SICK. IT HAPPENED SO FAST! HOW... IN ALL THESE MONTHS I NEVER EVEN LET HIM INTO THE APT.! GOTTA CALL THE POLICE.
CALL THE POLICE... I CAN'T CALL THE POLICE! HIS WORD AGAINST MINE. IN MY BATHING SUIT... IT'LL EAT UP MY LIFE...
IF I REPORT THIS, IT'LL EAT UP MY LIFE.
HIS WORD AGAINST MINE.
MOUTH SUCKING
HOT HANDS
MOUTH SUCKING SQUEEZE
HOT HANDS
THEN THE CAMPUS COP SAID, "WHADDAYA EXPECT, WEARIN' THAT OUTFIT? YA WERE ASKIN' FOR IT!" I STARTED CRYING...
...CALLED MY PARENTS! THEN THE DEAN SAID, "THE YOUNG MAN SAYS HE NEVER TOUCHED YOU. THAT YOU WERE 'BLITZED' AND INCOHERENT. HE SAID..."
AT FIRST I LIVED IN DREAD OF RUNNING INTO HIM. BUT I GOT OVER IT... THE TENSE NIGHTMARES FADED. EVENTUALLY A WEEK WOULD GO BY WHEN I DIDN'T EVEN THINK ABOUT IT. IT DIDN'T BOTHER ME AT ALL. NOT AT ALL. I GOT OVER IT. REALLY.
END.
I NEVER WENT INTO THE COURTYARD AGAIN.

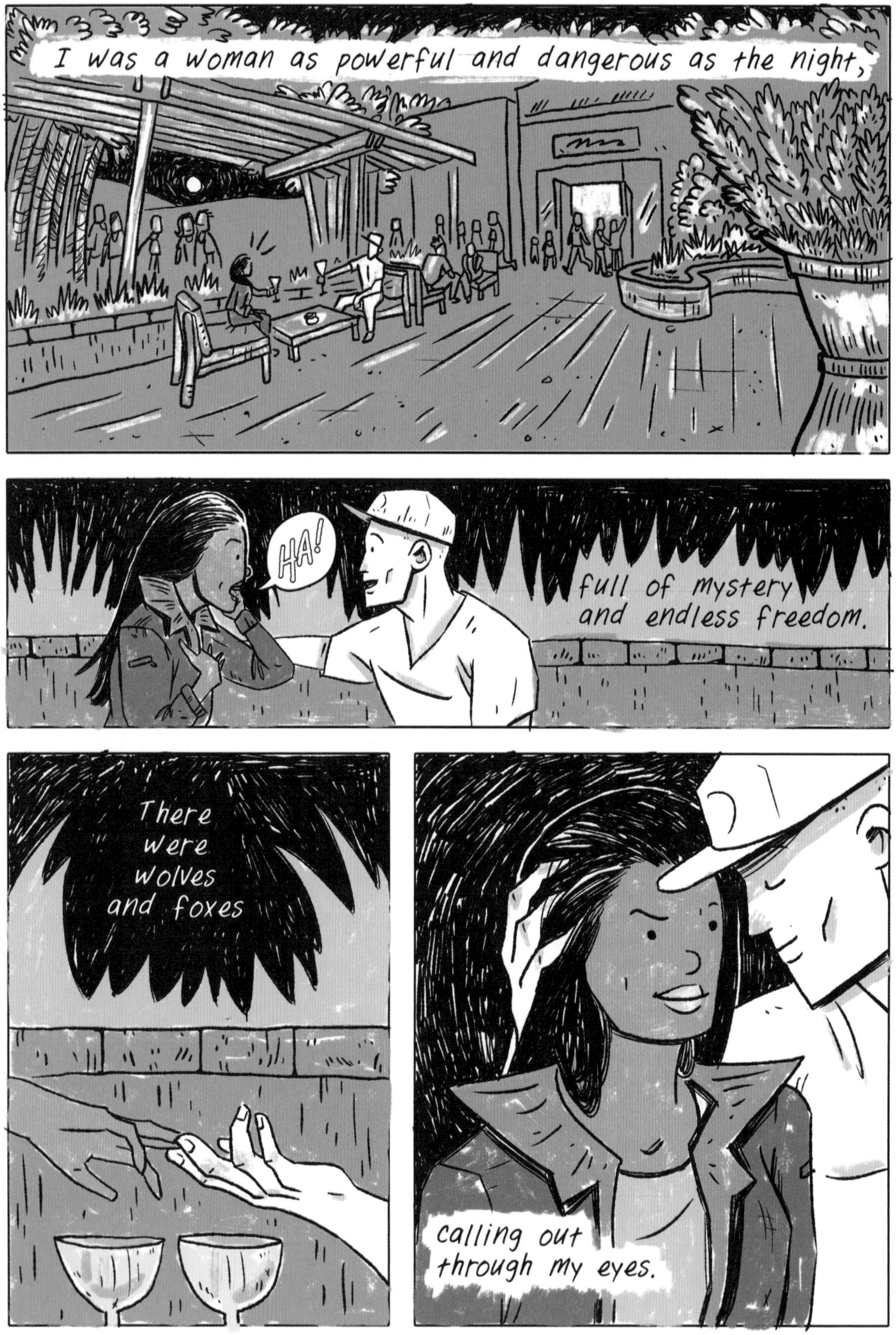
I was a woman as powerful and dangerous as the night,
HA!
full of mystery and endless freedom.
There were wolves and foxes
calling out through my eyes.

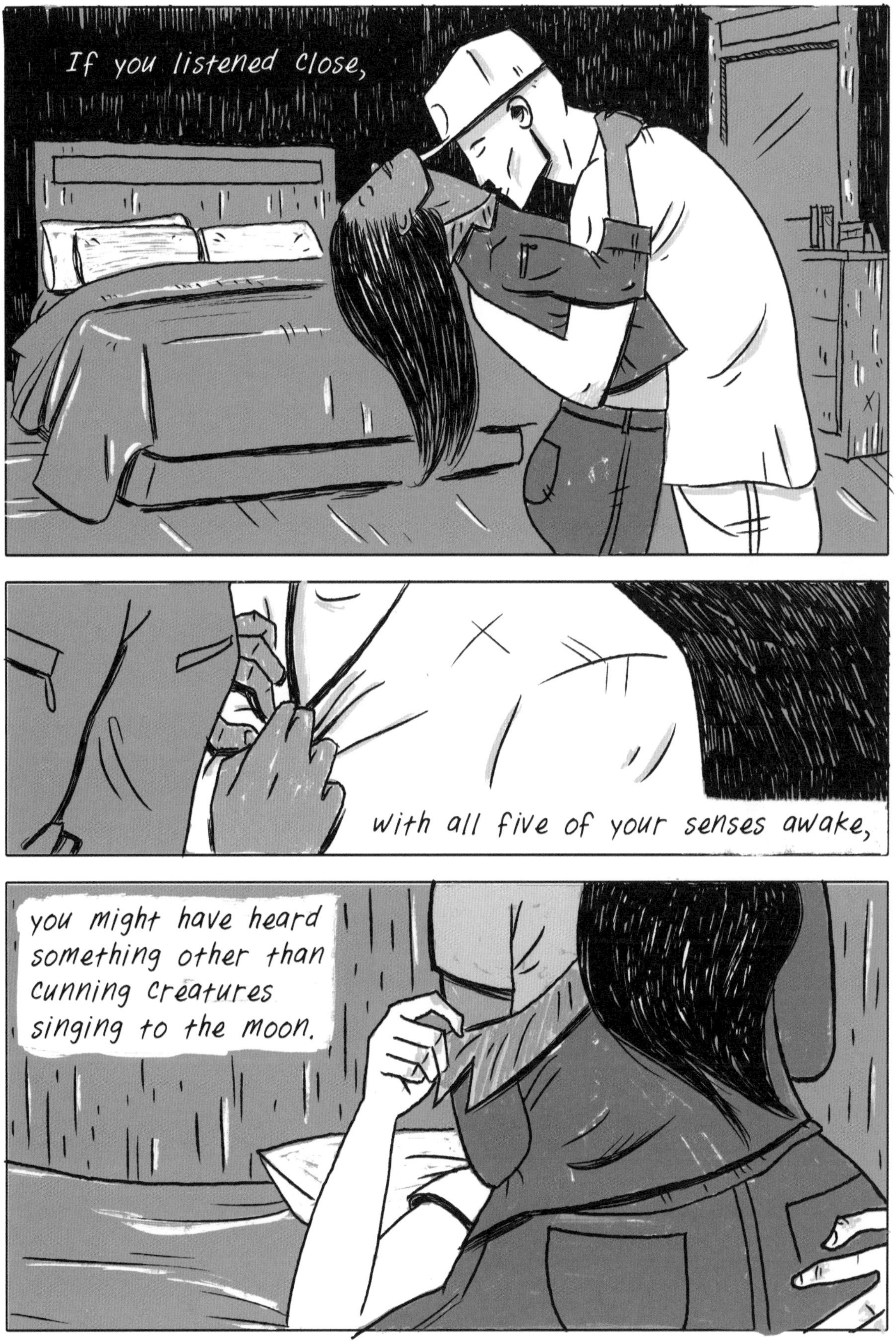
If you listened close,
with all five of your senses awake,
you might have heard something other than cunning creatures singing to the moon.

I stayed in the darkness,

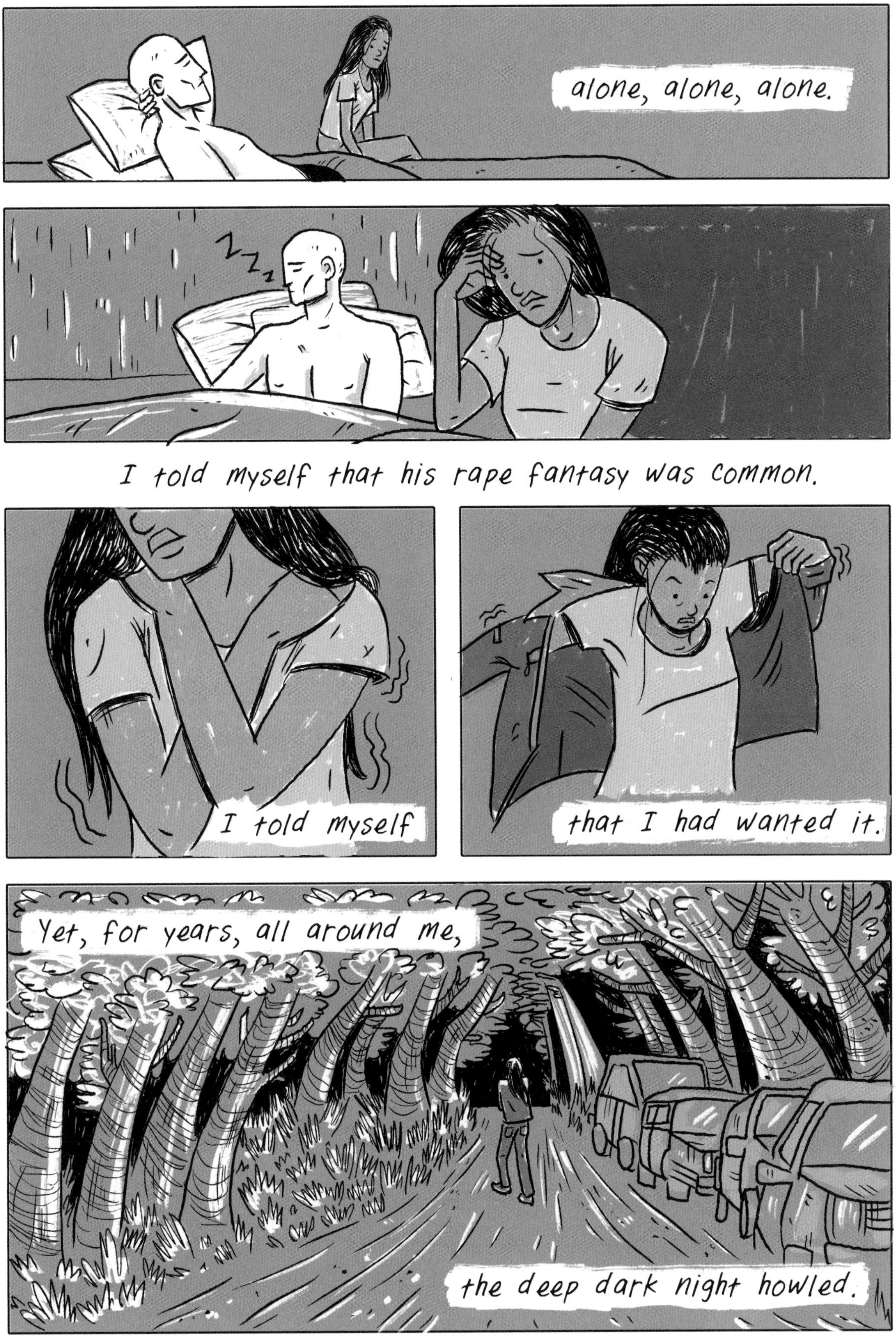
alone, alone, alone.
I told myself that his rape fantasy was common.
I told myself
that I had wanted it.
Yet, for years, all around me,
the deep dark night howled.

PLACEBO

KENDRA
JOSIE
KIRKPATRICK

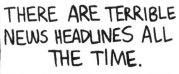

THERE ARE TERRIBLE NEWS HEADLINES ALL THE TIME.
DUGGAR SCANDAL
DUGGAR SON MOLESTED SISTERS
I DON'T NOTICE THEM ALL.
PHARMACY
NEXT IN LINE!
Rx
PEOPLE TEND TO ONLY NOTICE THE ONES THAT UPSET THEM SPECIFICALLY. THE ONES THAT I NOTICE ARE CELEBRITY SUICIDES.
HOWEVER, I'VE NEVER SEEN A HEADLINE THAT DESCRIBED WORD FOR WORD SOMETHING I EXPERIENCED.
DUGGAR SON MOLESTED SISTERS
Rx
IN 2015, A SCANDAL BROKE IN TABLOIDS THAT REVEALED JOSH DUGGAR HAD MOLESTED HIS SISTERS.
THE PARENTS KEPT THE ABUSE A SECRET FOR YEARS, CHOOSING TO HANDLE THE ISSUE "WITHIN THEIR CHURCH."
BECAUSE THE FAMILY HAD A POPULAR REALITY SHOW, OF COURSE THE STORY WAS EVERYWHERE.
IT'S COMMON KNOWLEDGE THIS WOULD CAUSE FLASH-BACKS FOR VICTIMS OF SIMILAR ABUSE.
WHAT IS NOT COMMON KNOWLEDGE IS HOW THE INDIVIDUAL SHOULD DEAL WITH THEIR TRAUMA.
Rx

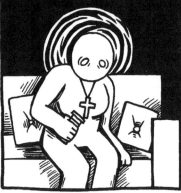

HAVING POSITIVE EXPERIENCES WITH TREATMENTS SOMETIMES MAKES YOU THINK YOU ARE AN EXPERT.

YOU NEED TO GO TO YOUR PSYCHIATRIST.

MY PSYCHIATRIST WON'T AUTOMATICALLY FIX **THIS**...

THEN GO TO **THERAPY**.

I'VE **BEEN** TO THERAPY! I'VE BEEN GOING TO THERAPY FOR THIS FOR **YEARS**...

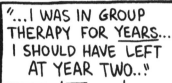

"...I WAS IN GROUP THERAPY FOR UEARS... I SHOULD HAVE LEFT AT YEAR TWO..."

"...MY INDIVIDUAL THERAPIST KEPT SAYING I HAD TO KEEP GOING TO THE GROUP THERAPY."

THAT WON'T HELP ME WITH THIS RIGHT NOW— I'M NOT SURE IT EVER HAS...

"...I NEED TO SEE MY PASTOR."

YOUR PASTOR...ARE YOU SERIOUS? THIS WHOLE DUGGAR THING HAPPENED BECAUSE OF A RELIGION.

NEVER HAVING A RELIGION WORK FOR YOU PERSONALLY ALSO MAKES YOU THINK YOU ARE AN EXPERT.

I'M GOING TO SEE MY PASTOR.

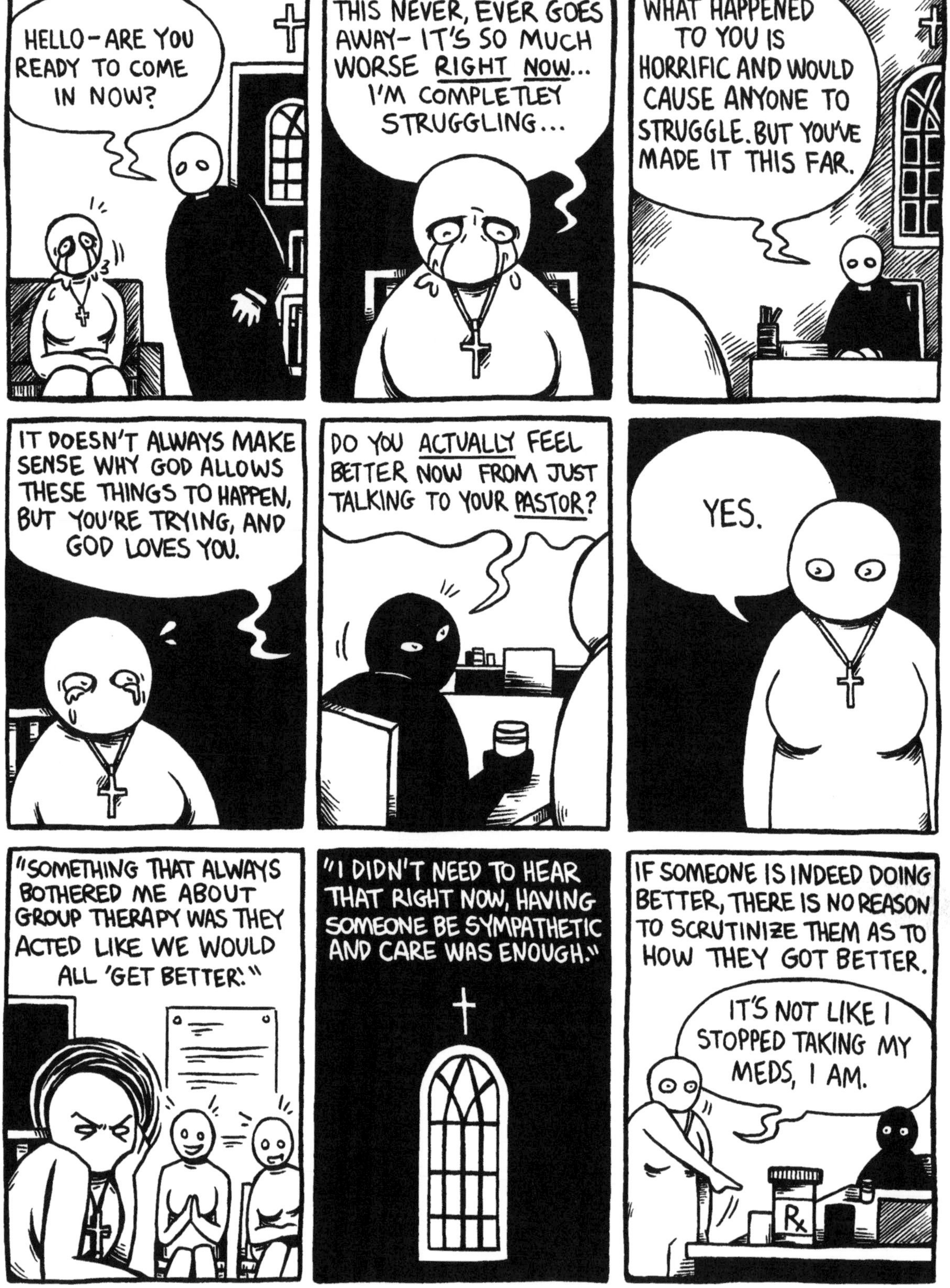
HELLO- ARE YOU READY TO COME IN NOW?
THIS NEVER, EVER GOES AWAY- IT'S SO MUCH WORSE RIGHT NOW... I'M COMPLETLEY STRUGGLING...
WHAT HAPPENED TO YOU IS HORRIFIC AND WOULD CAUSE ANYONE TO STRUGGLE. BUT YOU'VE MADE IT THIS FAR.
IT DOESN'T ALWAYS MAKE SENSE WHY GOD ALLOWS THESE THINGS TO HAPPEN, BUT YOU'RE TRYING, AND GOD LOVES YOU.
DO YOU ACTUALLY FEEL BETTER NOW FROM JUST TALKING TO YOUR PASTOR?
YES.
"SOMETHING THAT ALWAYS BOTHERED ME ABOUT GROUP THERAPY WAS THEY ACTED LIKE WE WOULD ALL 'GET BETTER.'"
"I DIDN'T NEED TO HEAR THAT RIGHT NOW, HAVING SOMEONE BE SYMPATHETIC AND CARE WAS ENOUGH."
IF SOMEONE IS INDEED DOING BETTER, THERE IS NO REASON TO SCRUTINIZE THEM AS TO HOW THEY GOT BETTER.
IT'S NOT LIKE I STOPPED TAKING MY MEDS, I AM.
Rx

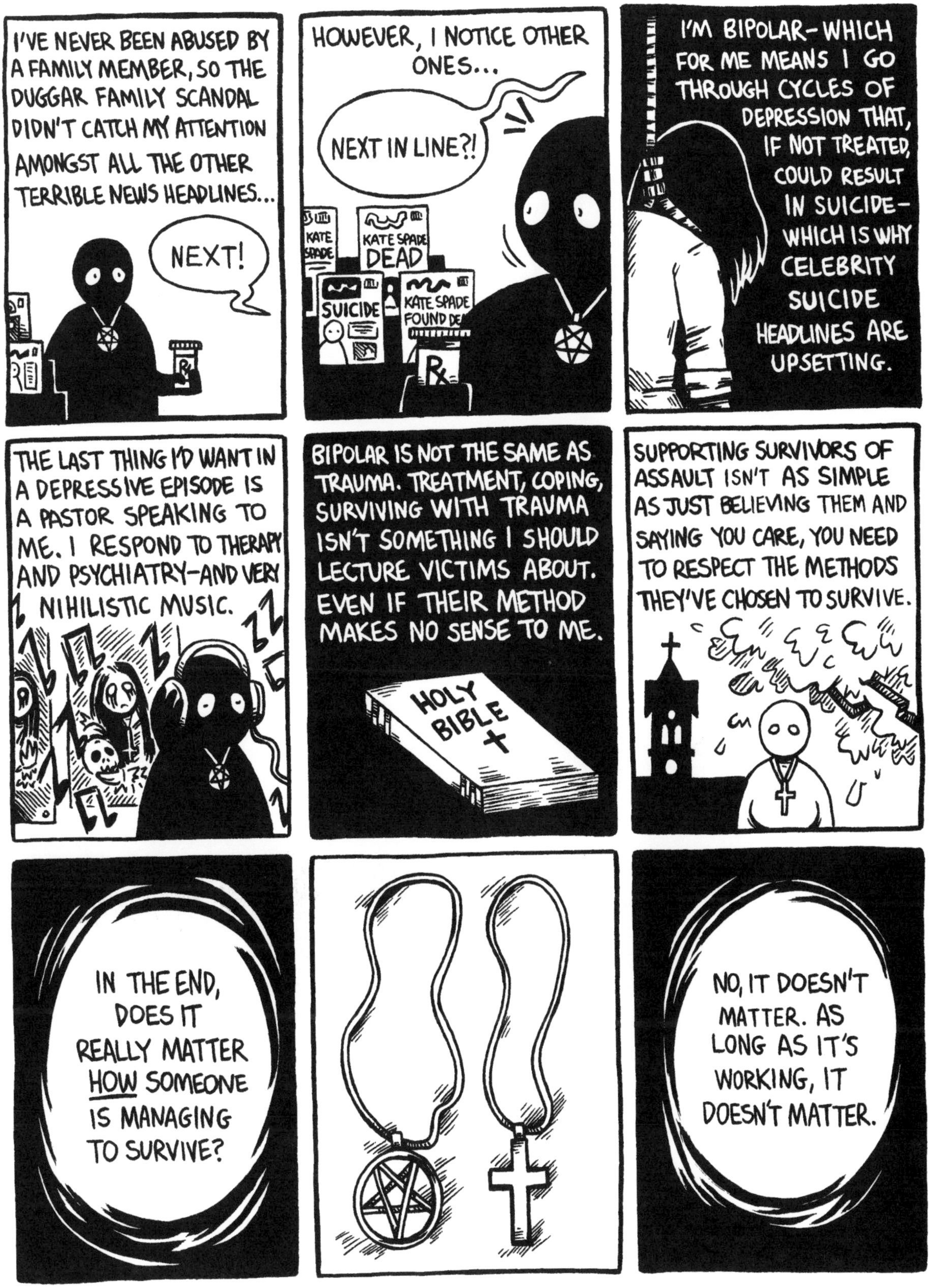
I'VE NEVER BEEN ABUSED BY A FAMILY MEMBER, SO THE DUGGAR FAMILY SCANDAL DIDN'T CATCH MY ATTENTION AMONGST ALL THE OTHER TERRIBLE NEWS HEADLINES...
NEXT!
HOWEVER, I NOTICE OTHER ONES...
NEXT IN LINE?!
KATE SPADE
KATE SPADE DEAD
SUICIDE
KATE SPADE FOUND DE
I'M BIPOLAR-WHICH FOR ME MEANS I GO THROUGH CYCLES OF DEPRESSION THAT, IF NOT TREATED, COULD RESULT IN SUICIDE-WHICH IS WHY CELEBRITY SUICIDE HEADLINES ARE UPSETTING.
THE LAST THING I'D WANT IN A DEPRESSIVE EPISODE IS A PASTOR SPEAKING TO ME. I RESPOND TO THERAPY AND PSYCHIATRY-AND VERY NIHILISTIC MUSIC.
BIPOLAR IS NOT THE SAME AS TRAUMA. TREATMENT, COPING, SURVIVING WITH TRAUMA ISN'T SOMETHING I SHOULD LECTURE VICTIMS ABOUT. EVEN IF THEIR METHOD MAKES NO SENSE TO ME.
HOLY BIBLE
SUPPORTING SURVIVORS OF ASSAULT ISN'T AS SIMPLE AS JUST BELIEVING THEM AND SAYING YOU CARE, YOU NEED TO RESPECT THE METHODS THEY'VE CHOSEN TO SURVIVE.
IN THE END, DOES IT REALLY MATTER HOW SOMEONE IS MANAGING TO SURVIVE?
NO, IT DOESN'T MATTER. AS LONG AS IT'S WORKING, IT DOESN'T MATTER.

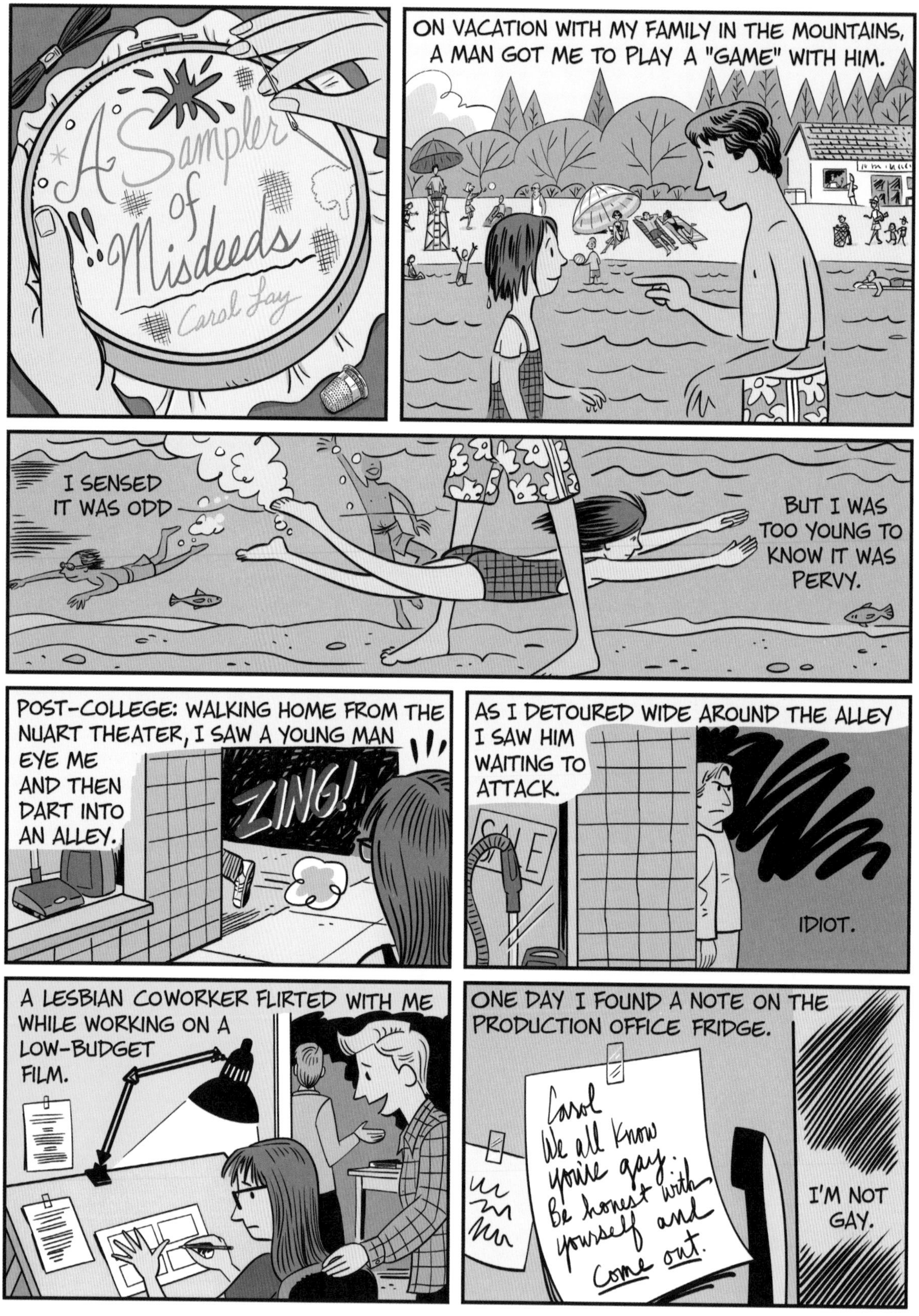
A Sampler of Misdeeds
Carol Lay
ON VACATION WITH MY FAMILY IN THE MOUNTAINS, A MAN GOT ME TO PLAY A "GAME" WITH HIM.
I SENSED IT WAS ODD
BUT I WAS TOO YOUNG TO KNOW IT WAS PERVY.
POST-COLLEGE: WALKING HOME FROM THE NUART THEATER, I SAW A YOUNG MAN EYE ME AND THEN DART INTO AN ALLEY.
ZING!
AS I DETOURED WIDE AROUND THE ALLEY I SAW HIM WAITING TO ATTACK.
SALE
IDIOT.
A LESBIAN COWORKER FLIRTED WITH ME WHILE WORKING ON A LOW-BUDGET FILM.
ONE DAY I FOUND A NOTE ON THE PRODUCTION OFFICE FRIDGE.
Carol
We all know you're gay.
Be honest with yourself and come out.
I'M NOT GAY.

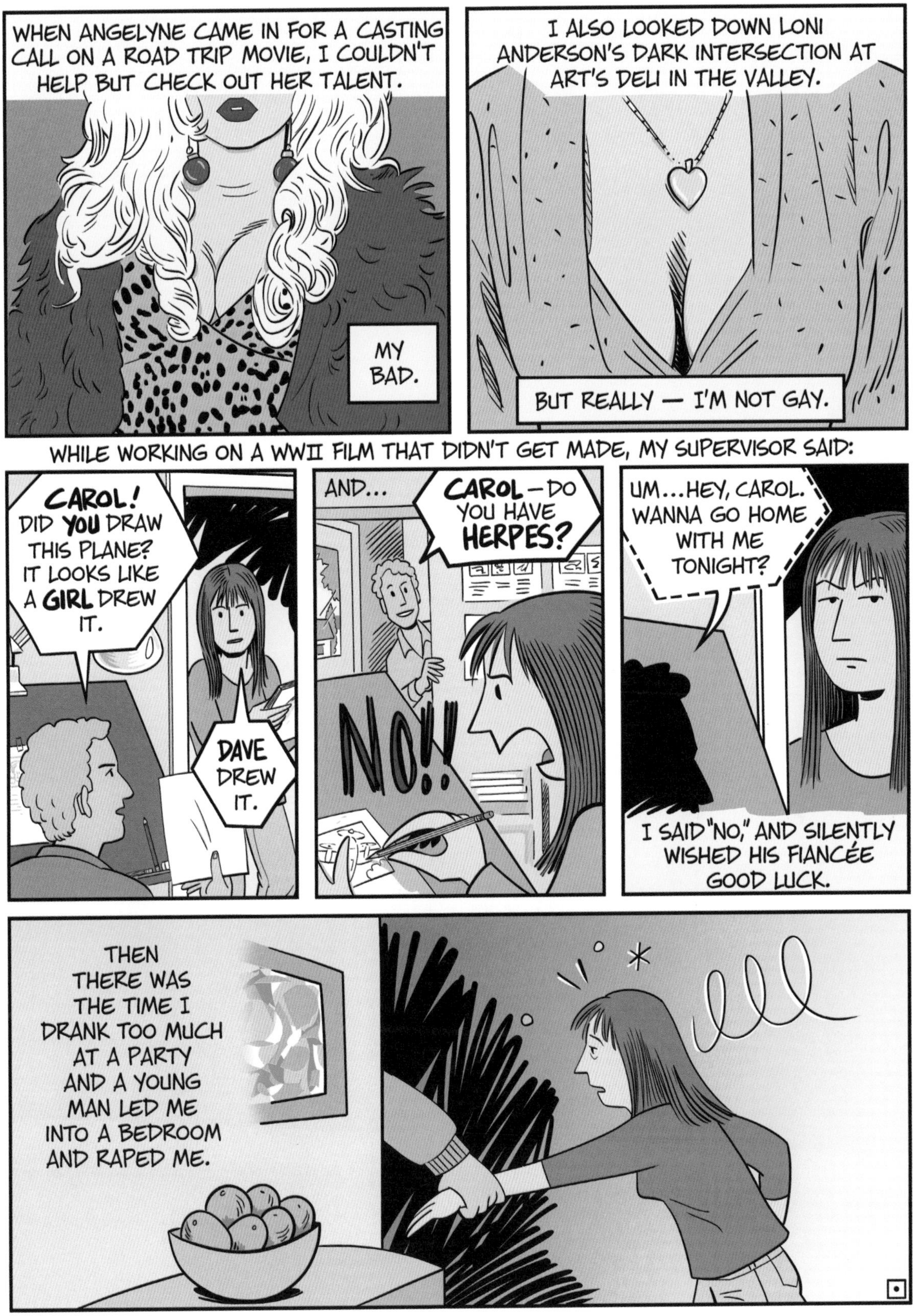
WHEN ANGELYNE CAME IN FOR A CASTING CALL ON A ROAD TRIP MOVIE, I COULDN'T HELP BUT CHECK OUT HER TALENT.
MY BAD.
I ALSO LOOKED DOWN LONI ANDERSON'S DARK INTERSECTION AT ART'S DELI IN THE VALLEY.
BUT REALLY — I'M NOT GAY.
WHILE WORKING ON A WWII FILM THAT DIDN'T GET MADE, MY SUPERVISOR SAID:
CAROL! DID YOU DRAW THIS PLANE? IT LOOKS LIKE A GIRL DREW IT.
DAVE DREW IT.
AND...
CAROL — DO YOU HAVE HERPES?
NO!!
UM...HEY, CAROL. WANNA GO HOME WITH ME TONIGHT?
I SAID "NO," AND SILENTLY WISHED HIS FIANCÉE GOOD LUCK.
THEN THERE WAS THE TIME I DRANK TOO MUCH AT A PARTY AND A YOUNG MAN LED ME INTO A BEDROOM AND RAPED ME.

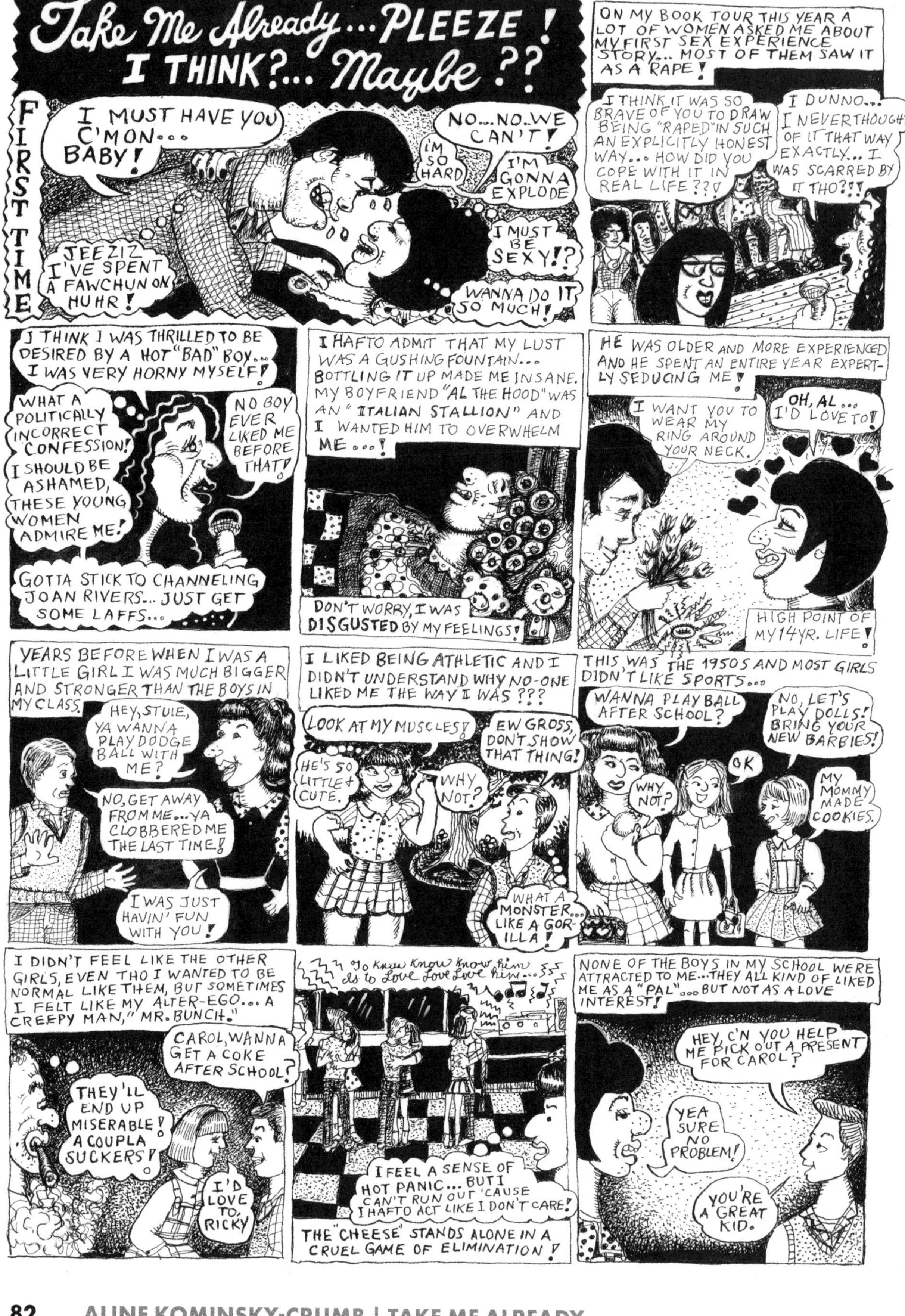
Take Me Already... PLEEZE! I THINK?... Maybe ??
FIRST TIME
I MUST HAVE YOU C'MON... BABY!
NO...NO..WE CAN'T!
I'M SO HARD
I'M GONNA EXPLODE
JEEZIZ I'VE SPENT A FAWCHUN ON HUHR!
I MUST BE SEXY!?
WANNA DO IT SO MUCH!
ON MY BOOK TOUR THIS YEAR A LOT OF WOMEN ASKED ME ABOUT MY FIRST SEX EXPERIENCE STORY... MOST OF THEM SAW IT AS A RAPE!
I THINK IT WAS SO BRAVE OF YOU TO DRAW BEING "RAPED" IN SUCH AN EXPLICITLY HONEST WAY... HOW DID YOU COPE WITH IT IN REAL LIFE???
I DUNNO... I NEVER THOUGHT OF IT THAT WAY EXACTLY... I WAS SCARRED BY IT THO?!!
I THINK I WAS THRILLED TO BE DESIRED BY A HOT "BAD" BOY... I WAS VERY HORNY MYSELF!
WHAT A POLITICALLY INCORRECT CONFESSION! I SHOULD BE ASHAMED, THESE YOUNG WOMEN ADMIRE ME!
NO BOY EVER LIKED ME BEFORE THAT!
GOTTA STICK TO CHANNELING JOAN RIVERS... JUST GET SOME LAFFS...
I HAFTO ADMIT THAT MY LUST WAS A GUSHING FOUNTAIN... BOTTLING IT UP MADE ME INSANE. MY BOYFRIEND "AL THE HOOD" WAS AN "ITALIAN STALLION" AND I WANTED HIM TO OVERWHELM ME...!
DON'T WORRY, I WAS DISGUSTED BY MY FEELINGS!
HE WAS OLDER AND MORE EXPERIENCED AND HE SPENT AN ENTIRE YEAR EXPERTLY SEDUCING ME!
I WANT YOU TO WEAR MY RING AROUND YOUR NECK.
OH, AL... I'D LOVE TO!
HIGH POINT OF MY 14 YR. LIFE!
YEARS BEFORE WHEN I WAS A LITTLE GIRL I WAS MUCH BIGGER AND STRONGER THAN THE BOYS IN MY CLASS.
HEY, STUIE, YA WANNA PLAY DODGE BALL WITH ME?
NO, GET AWAY FROM ME... YA CLOBBERED ME THE LAST TIME!
I WAS JUST HAVIN' FUN WITH YOU!
I LIKED BEING ATHLETIC AND I DIDN'T UNDERSTAND WHY NO-ONE LIKED ME THE WAY I WAS???
LOOK AT MY MUSCLES!
EW GROSS, DON'T SHOW THAT THING!
HE'S SO LITTLE + CUTE.
WHY NOT?
WHAT A MONSTER... LIKE A GORILLA!
THIS WAS THE 1950S AND MOST GIRLS DIDN'T LIKE SPORTS...
WANNA PLAY BALL AFTER SCHOOL?
NO, LET'S PLAY DOLLS! BRING YOUR NEW BARBIES!
OK
WHY NOT?
MY MOMMY MADE COOKIES.
I DIDN'T FEEL LIKE THE OTHER GIRLS, EVEN THO I WANTED TO BE NORMAL LIKE THEM, BUT SOMETIMES I FELT LIKE MY ALTER-EGO... A CREEPY MAN, "MR. BUNCH."
CAROL, WANNA GET A COKE AFTER SCHOOL?
THEY'LL END UP MISERABLE! A COUPLA SUCKERS!
I'D LOVE TO, RICKY
To Know Know Know him is to Love Love Love him...
I FEEL A SENSE OF HOT PANIC... BUT I CAN'T RUN OUT 'CAUSE I HAFTO ACT LIKE I DON'T CARE!
THE "CHEESE" STANDS ALONE IN A CRUEL GAME OF ELIMINATION!
NONE OF THE BOYS IN MY SCHOOL WERE ATTRACTED TO ME... THEY ALL KIND OF LIKED ME AS A "PAL"... BUT NOT AS A LOVE INTEREST!
HEY, C'N YOU HELP ME PICK OUT A PRESENT FOR CAROL?
YEA SURE NO PROBLEM!
YOU'RE A GREAT KID.

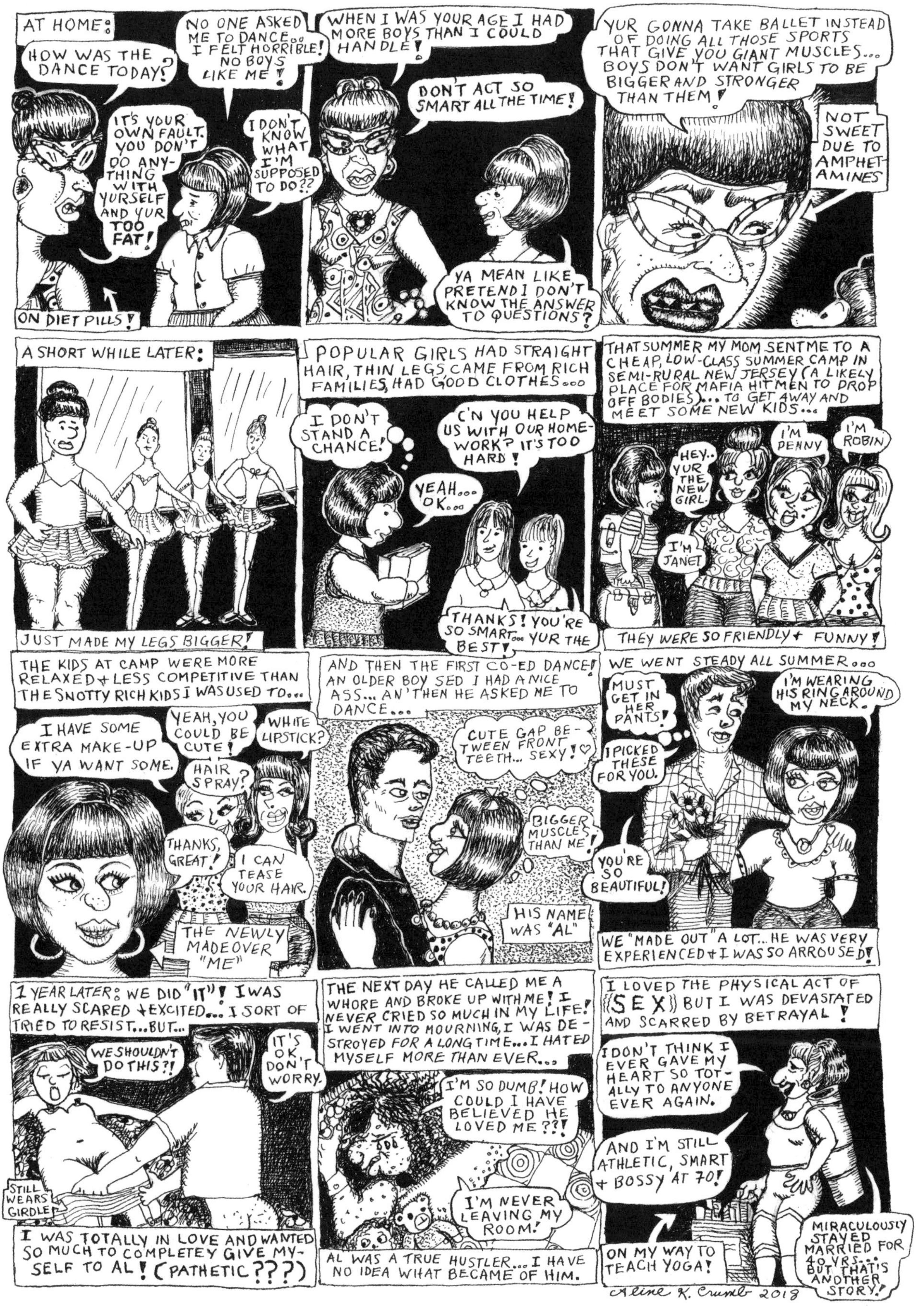
AT HOME:
HOW WAS THE DANCE TODAY?
NO ONE ASKED ME TO DANCE... I FELT HORRIBLE! NO BOYS LIKE ME!
IT'S YOUR OWN FAULT. YOU DON'T DO ANYTHING WITH YURSELF AND YUR TOO FAT!
I DON'T KNOW WHAT I'M SUPPOSED TO DO??
ON DIET PILLS!
WHEN I WAS YOUR AGE I HAD MORE BOYS THAN I COULD HANDLE!
DON'T ACT SO SMART ALL THE TIME!
YA MEAN LIKE PRETEND I DON'T KNOW THE ANSWER TO QUESTIONS?
YUR GONNA TAKE BALLET INSTEAD OF DOING ALL THOSE SPORTS THAT GIVE YOU GIANT MUSCLES... BOYS DON'T WANT GIRLS TO BE BIGGER AND STRONGER THAN THEM!
NOT SWEET DUE TO AMPHETAMINES
A SHORT WHILE LATER:
JUST MADE MY LEGS BIGGER!
POPULAR GIRLS HAD STRAIGHT HAIR, THIN LEGS CAME FROM RICH FAMILIES, HAD GOOD CLOTHES...
I DON'T STAND A CHANCE!
C'N YOU HELP US WITH OUR HOMEWORK? IT'S TOO HARD!
YEAH... OK...
THANKS! YOU'RE SO SMART... YUR THE BEST!
THAT SUMMER MY MOM SENT ME TO A CHEAP, LOW-CLASS SUMMER CAMP IN SEMI-RURAL NEW JERSEY (A LIKELY PLACE FOR MAFIA HIT MEN TO DROP OFF BODIES)... TO GET AWAY AND MEET SOME NEW KIDS...
HEY.. YUR THE NEW GIRL.
I'M PENNY
I'M ROBIN
I'M JANET
THEY WERE SO FRIENDLY + FUNNY!
THE KIDS AT CAMP WERE MORE RELAXED + LESS COMPETITIVE THAN THE SNOTTY RICH KIDS I WAS USED TO...
I HAVE SOME EXTRA MAKE-UP IF YA WANT SOME.
YEAH, YOU COULD BE CUTE!
WHITE LIPSTICK?
HAIR SPRAY?
THANKS, GREAT!
I CAN TEASE YOUR HAIR.
THE NEWLY MADE OVER "ME"
AND THEN THE FIRST CO-ED DANCE! AN OLDER BOY SED I HAD A NICE ASS... AN' THEN HE ASKED ME TO DANCE...
CUTE GAP BETWEEN FRONT TEETH... SEXY!♡
BIGGER MUSCLES THAN ME!
HIS NAME WAS "AL"
WE WENT STEADY ALL SUMMER...
MUST GET IN HER PANTS!
I'M WEARING HIS RING AROUND MY NECK.
I PICKED THESE FOR YOU.
YOU'RE SO BEAUTIFUL!
WE "MADE OUT" A LOT... HE WAS VERY EXPERIENCED + I WAS SO ARROUSED!
1 YEAR LATER: WE DID "IT"! I WAS REALLY SCARED + EXCITED... I SORT OF TRIED TO RESIST... BUT...
WE SHOULDN'T DO THIS?!
IT'S OK. DON'T WORRY.
STILL WEARS GIRDLE
I WAS TOTALLY IN LOVE AND WANTED SO MUCH TO COMPLETEY GIVE MYSELF TO AL! (PATHETIC???)
THE NEXT DAY HE CALLED ME A WHORE AND BROKE UP WITH ME! I NEVER CRIED SO MUCH IN MY LIFE! I WENT INTO MOURNING, I WAS DESTROYED FOR A LONG TIME... I HATED MYSELF MORE THAN EVER...
I'M SO DUMB! HOW COULD I HAVE BELIEVED HE LOVED ME??!
I'M NEVER LEAVING MY ROOM!
AL WAS A TRUE HUSTLER... I HAVE NO IDEA WHAT BECAME OF HIM.
I LOVED THE PHYSICAL ACT OF SEX BUT I WAS DEVASTATED AND SCARRED BY BETRAYAL!
I DON'T THINK I EVER GAVE MY HEART SO TOTALLY TO ANYONE EVER AGAIN.
AND I'M STILL ATHLETIC, SMART + BOSSY AT 70!
ON MY WAY TO TEACH YOGA!
MIRACULOUSLY STAYED MARRIED FOR 40 YRS... BUT THAT'S ANOTHER STORY!
Aline K. Crumb 2018

Delusions of Safety

By Ajuan Mance © 2018

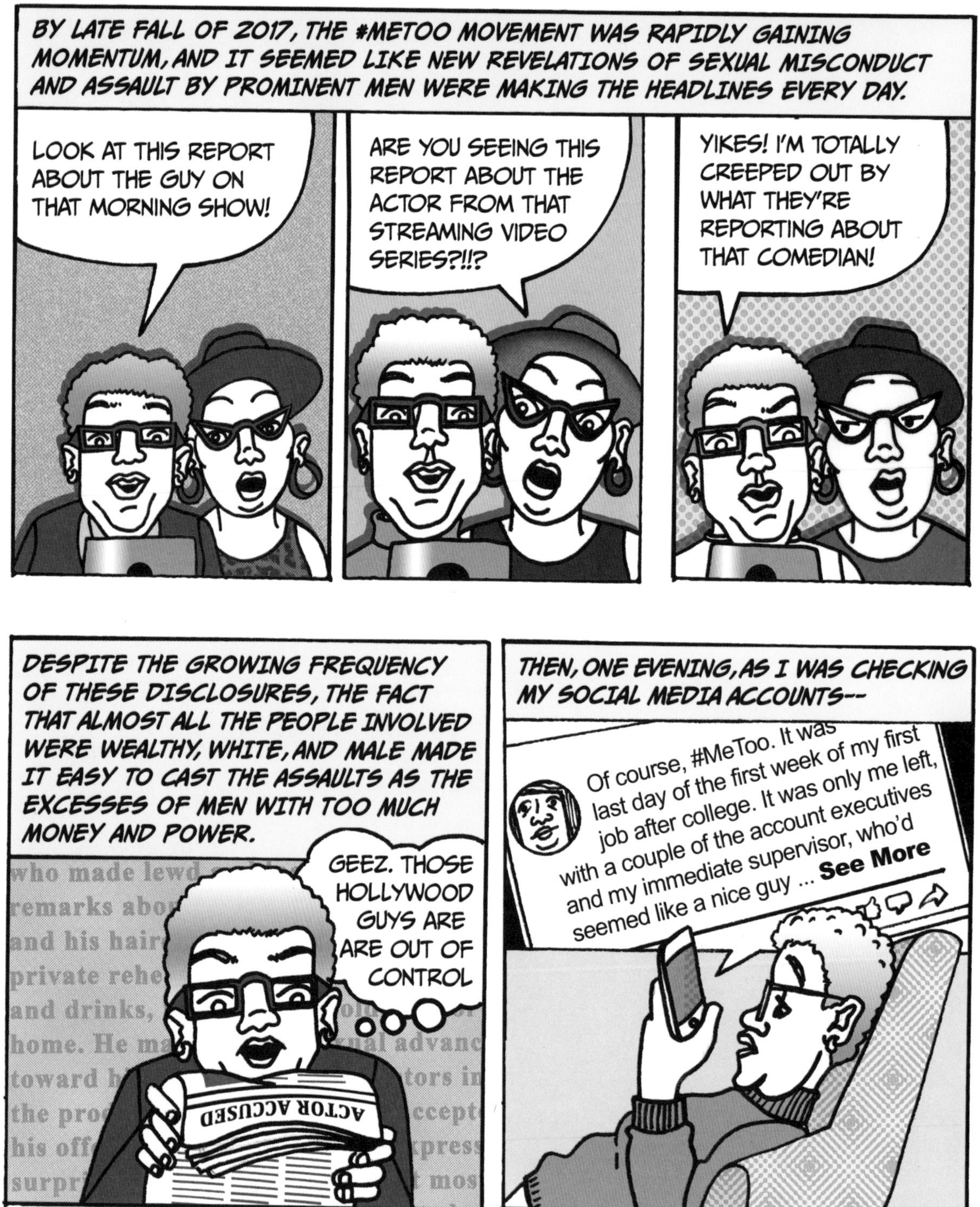
BY LATE FALL OF 2017, THE #METOO MOVEMENT WAS RAPIDLY GAINING MOMENTUM, AND IT SEEMED LIKE NEW REVELATIONS OF SEXUAL MISCONDUCT AND ASSAULT BY PROMINENT MEN WERE MAKING THE HEADLINES EVERY DAY.
LOOK AT THIS REPORT ABOUT THE GUY ON THAT MORNING SHOW!
ARE YOU SEEING THIS REPORT ABOUT THE ACTOR FROM THAT STREAMING VIDEO SERIES?!!?
YIKES! I'M TOTALLY CREEPED OUT BY WHAT THEY'RE REPORTING ABOUT THAT COMEDIAN!
DESPITE THE GROWING FREQUENCY OF THESE DISCLOSURES, THE FACT THAT ALMOST ALL THE PEOPLE INVOLVED WERE WEALTHY, WHITE, AND MALE MADE IT EASY TO CAST THE ASSAULTS AS THE EXCESSES OF MEN WITH TOO MUCH MONEY AND POWER.
GEEZ. THOSE HOLLYWOOD GUYS ARE ARE OUT OF CONTROL
ACTOR ACCUSED
THEN, ONE EVENING, AS I WAS CHECKING MY SOCIAL MEDIA ACCOUNTS--
Of course, #MeToo. It was last day of the first week of my first job after college. It was only me left, with a couple of the account executives and my immediate supervisor, who'd seemed like a nice guy ... See More

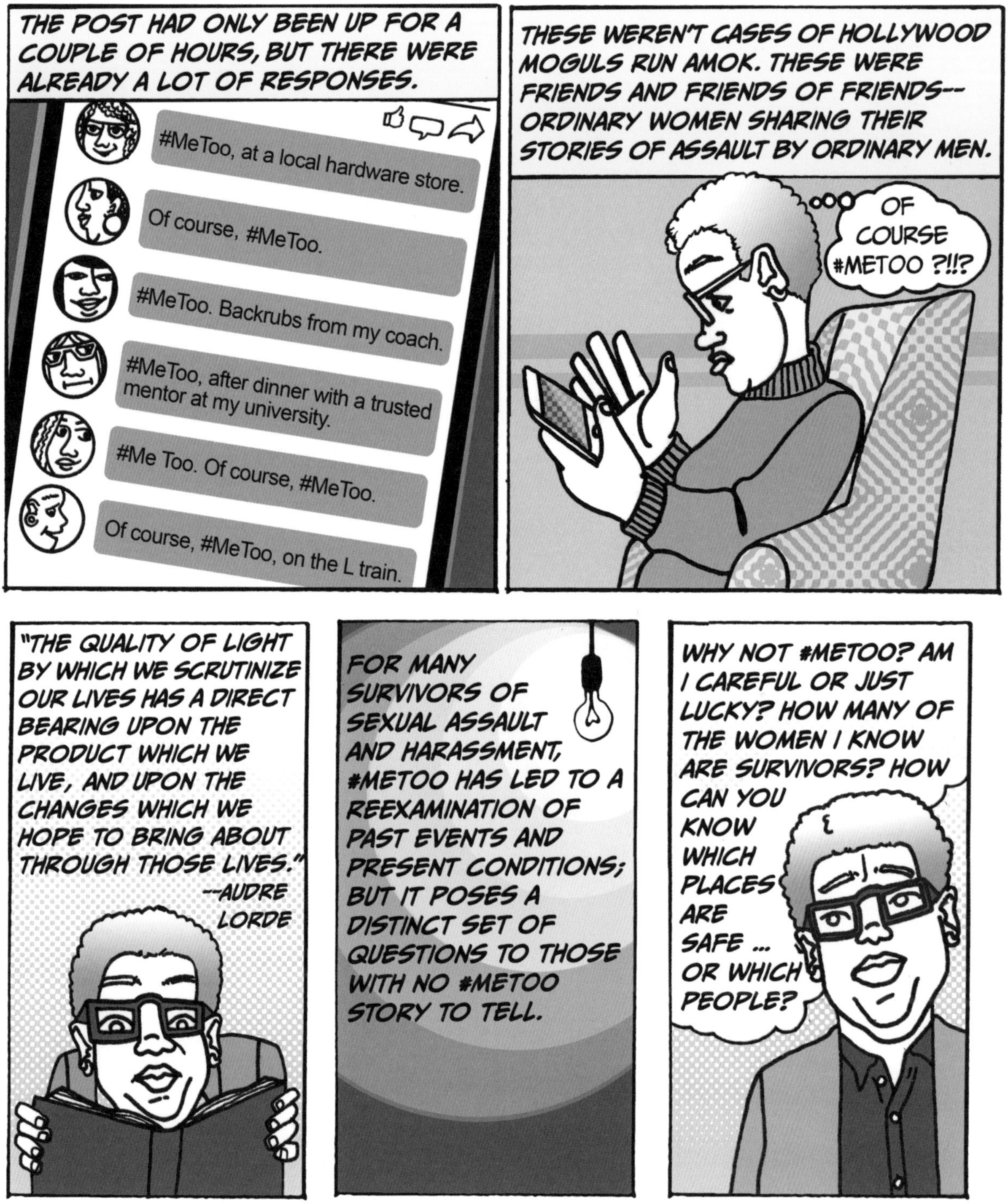

THE POST HAD ONLY BEEN UP FOR A COUPLE OF HOURS, BUT THERE WERE ALREADY A LOT OF RESPONSES.
#MeToo, at a local hardware store.
Of course, #MeToo.
#MeToo. Backrubs from my coach.
#MeToo, after dinner with a trusted mentor at my university.
#Me Too. Of course, #MeToo.
Of course, #MeToo, on the L train.
THESE WEREN'T CASES OF HOLLYWOOD MOGULS RUN AMOK. THESE WERE FRIENDS AND FRIENDS OF FRIENDS-- ORDINARY WOMEN SHARING THEIR STORIES OF ASSAULT BY ORDINARY MEN.
OF COURSE #METOO ?!!?
"THE QUALITY OF LIGHT BY WHICH WE SCRUTINIZE OUR LIVES HAS A DIRECT BEARING UPON THE PRODUCT WHICH WE LIVE, AND UPON THE CHANGES WHICH WE HOPE TO BRING ABOUT THROUGH THOSE LIVES." --AUDRE LORDE
FOR MANY SURVIVORS OF SEXUAL ASSAULT AND HARASSMENT, #METOO HAS LED TO A REEXAMINATION OF PAST EVENTS AND PRESENT CONDITIONS; BUT IT POSES A DISTINCT SET OF QUESTIONS TO THOSE WITH NO #METOO STORY TO TELL.
WHY NOT #METOO? AM I CAREFUL OR JUST LUCKY? HOW MANY OF THE WOMEN I KNOW ARE SURVIVORS? HOW CAN YOU KNOW WHICH PLACES ARE SAFE ... OR WHICH PEOPLE?

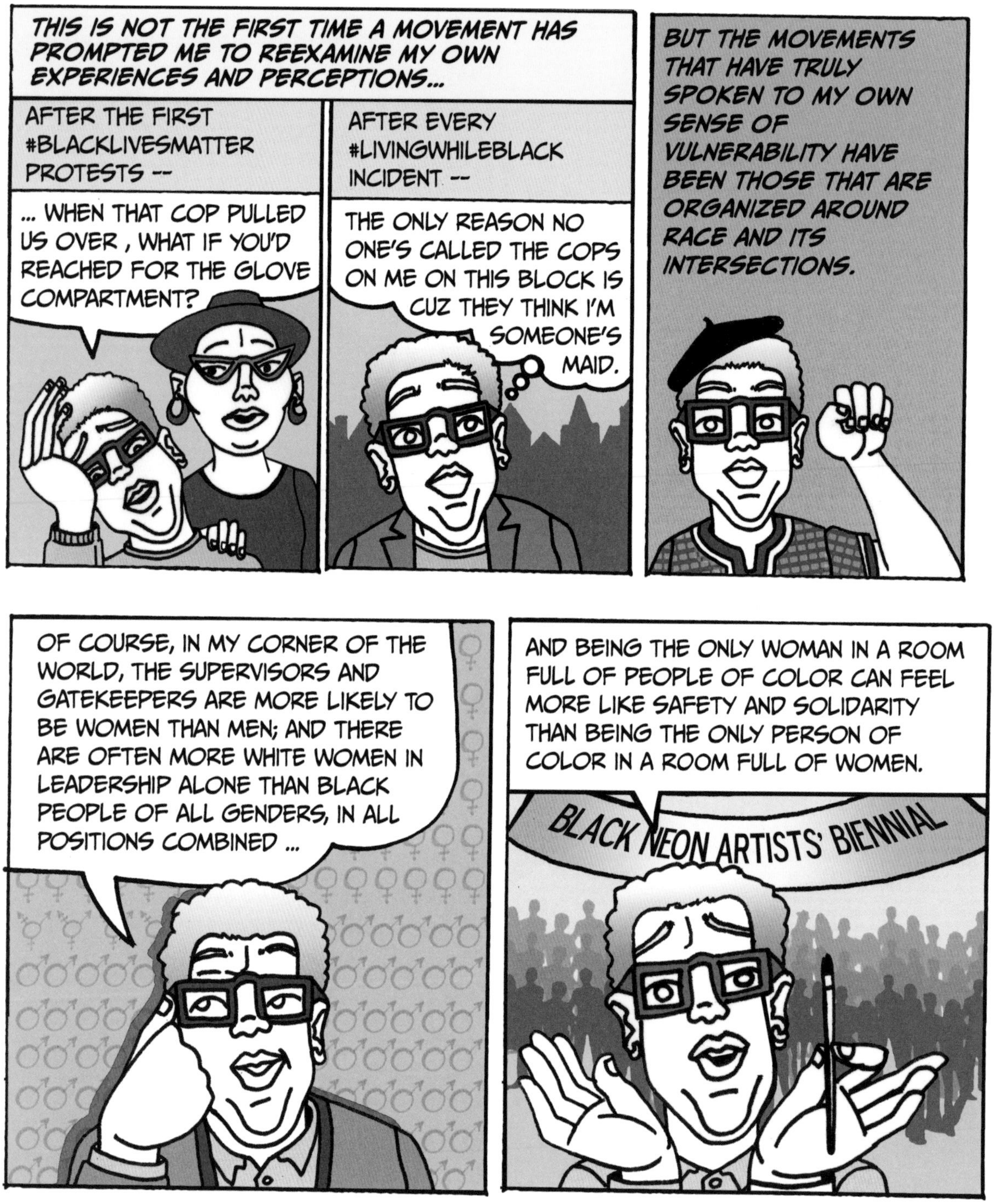
THIS IS NOT THE FIRST TIME A MOVEMENT HAS PROMPTED ME TO REEXAMINE MY OWN EXPERIENCES AND PERCEPTIONS...
AFTER THE FIRST #BLACKLIVESMATTER PROTESTS --
... WHEN THAT COP PULLED US OVER, WHAT IF YOU'D REACHED FOR THE GLOVE COMPARTMENT?
AFTER EVERY #LIVINGWHILEBLACK INCIDENT --
THE ONLY REASON NO ONE'S CALLED THE COPS ON ME ON THIS BLOCK IS CUZ THEY THINK I'M SOMEONE'S MAID.
BUT THE MOVEMENTS THAT HAVE TRULY SPOKEN TO MY OWN SENSE OF VULNERABILITY HAVE BEEN THOSE THAT ARE ORGANIZED AROUND RACE AND ITS INTERSECTIONS.
OF COURSE, IN MY CORNER OF THE WORLD, THE SUPERVISORS AND GATEKEEPERS ARE MORE LIKELY TO BE WOMEN THAN MEN; AND THERE ARE OFTEN MORE WHITE WOMEN IN LEADERSHIP ALONE THAN BLACK PEOPLE OF ALL GENDERS, IN ALL POSITIONS COMBINED ...
AND BEING THE ONLY WOMAN IN A ROOM FULL OF PEOPLE OF COLOR CAN FEEL MORE LIKE SAFETY AND SOLIDARITY THAN BEING THE ONLY PERSON OF COLOR IN A ROOM FULL OF WOMEN.
BLACK NEON ARTISTS' BIENNIAL

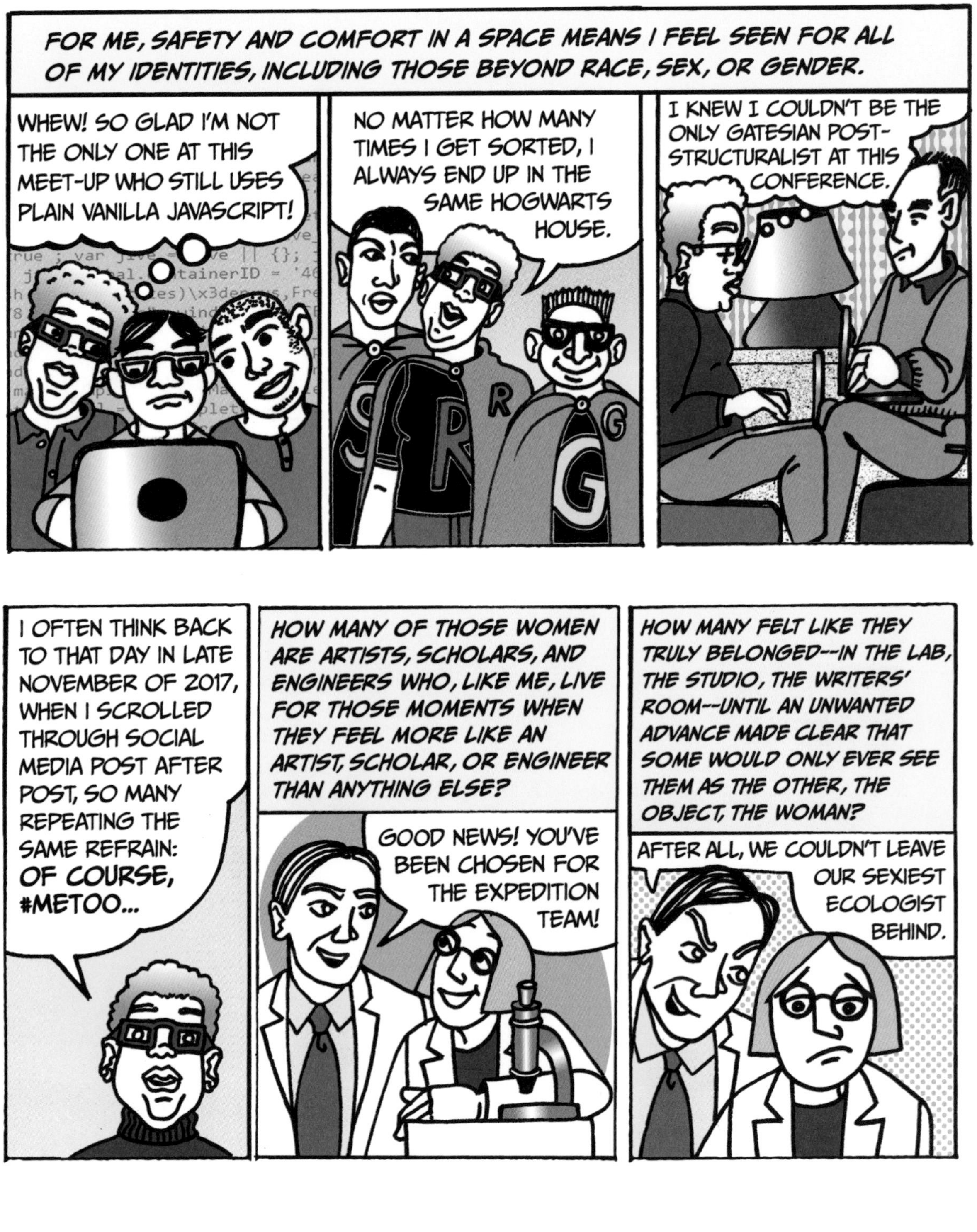
FOR ME, SAFETY AND COMFORT IN A SPACE MEANS I FEEL SEEN FOR ALL OF MY IDENTITIES, INCLUDING THOSE BEYOND RACE, SEX, OR GENDER.
WHEW! SO GLAD I'M NOT THE ONLY ONE AT THIS MEET-UP WHO STILL USES PLAIN VANILLA JAVASCRIPT!
NO MATTER HOW MANY TIMES I GET SORTED, I ALWAYS END UP IN THE SAME HOGWARTS HOUSE.
I KNEW I COULDN'T BE THE ONLY GATESIAN POST-STRUCTURALIST AT THIS CONFERENCE.
I OFTEN THINK BACK TO THAT DAY IN LATE NOVEMBER OF 2017, WHEN I SCROLLED THROUGH SOCIAL MEDIA POST AFTER POST, SO MANY REPEATING THE SAME REFRAIN: OF COURSE, #METOO...
HOW MANY OF THOSE WOMEN ARE ARTISTS, SCHOLARS, AND ENGINEERS WHO, LIKE ME, LIVE FOR THOSE MOMENTS WHEN THEY FEEL MORE LIKE AN ARTIST, SCHOLAR, OR ENGINEER THAN ANYTHING ELSE?
GOOD NEWS! YOU'VE BEEN CHOSEN FOR THE EXPEDITION TEAM!
HOW MANY FELT LIKE THEY TRULY BELONGED--IN THE LAB, THE STUDIO, THE WRITERS' ROOM--UNTIL AN UNWANTED ADVANCE MADE CLEAR THAT SOME WOULD ONLY EVER SEE THEM AS THE OTHER, THE OBJECT, THE WOMAN?
AFTER ALL, WE COULDN'T LEAVE OUR SEXIEST ECOLOGIST BEHIND.

DEAR SUSIE,   Sept. 28, 1968

I'LL HAVE TO GET IT OVER WITH AND TELL YOU WHAT HAPPENED TO ME NIGHT BEFORE LAST. I WAS WALKING HOME FROM STUDIO I AT 11 PM AND THIS GUY CAME FROM ACROSS THE STREET AND STARTED TALKING TO ME. JUST AS WE GOT TO THE BUSHES NEXT TO TESTICAL HIGH SCHOOL. HE GOT A HAMMER-LOCK ON MY NECK. I SCREAMED AND SCREAMED BUT NOBODY CAME. I REMEM-BERED WATCHING MYSELF STRUGGLE FROM ACROSS THE STREET AND THE CARS ON BROADWAY GOING

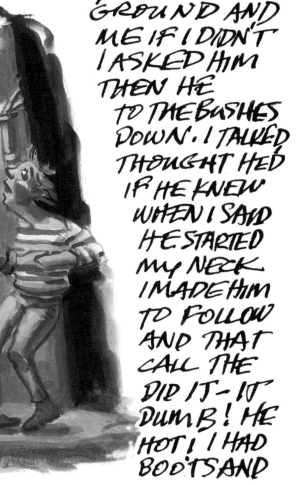

ME ON THE
SAID HE'D STAB
STOP SCREAMING.
NOT TO KILL ME.
DRAGGED ME
AND WE SAT
AND TALKED.
LET ME GO
ME BETTER.
THIS IS STUPID,
GRABBING
AGAIN.
PROMISE NOT
ME AFTER
I WOULD NOT
POLICE, WE
WAS SORT OF
WASN'T TOO
MY HIKING

BY. HE THREW
GROUND AND
ME IF I DIDN'T
I ASKED HIM
THEN HE
TO THE BUSHES
DOWN. I TALKED
THOUGHT HE'D
IF HE KNEW
WHEN I SAID
HE STARTED
MY NECK
I MADE HIM
TO FOLLOW
AND THAT
CALL THE
DID IT - IT
DUMB! HE
HOT, I HAD
BOOTS AND

JEANS, SWEATER, AND JACKET - ICK! IT WAS AWFUL. I HAD TO TAKE EVERYTHING OFF - GOT ALL MUDDY 'CAUSE THE GROUND WAS WET DIRT. AFTER, I KEPT TALKING. SAID IF HE WENT TO A COUNSELOR TO FIND A JOB HE COULD GET A NICE GIRLFRIEND. HE WOULDN'T HAVE TO RAPE. I JUST KEPT TALKING TILL I GOT DRESSED AND MADE HIM PROMISE NOT TO FOLLOW ME. AS I CROSSED THE STREET I PASSED A GUY FROM SCHOOL WHO SAID, "IT'S NOT SAFE FOR YOU TO BE WALKING HOME IN THE DARK."

MY NECK IS REALLY SORE FROM BEING GAGGED. I BIT MY TONGUE AND MY PUBIC BONE IS BRUISED. WOW, IT IS REALLY WEIRD TO BE IN DANGER LIKE THAT. YUK! IT WAS JUST LIKE IN THE MOVIES, BUT WITHOUT THE MUSIC. WELL, SO MUCH FOR THAT. SORRY FOR SUCH A GORY LETTER. THOUGHT I'D TELL YOU NOW - GET IT OVER WITH.

LOVE, LULU (YOUR TAINTED SISTER).

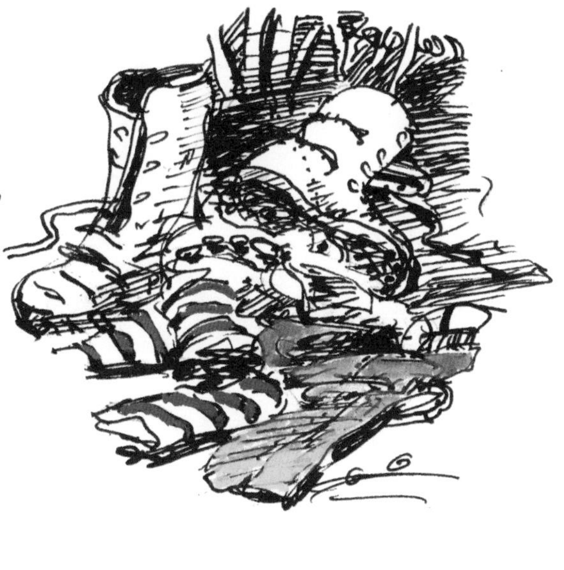

P.S. I SAW HIM IN BERKELEY THE NEXT DAY!

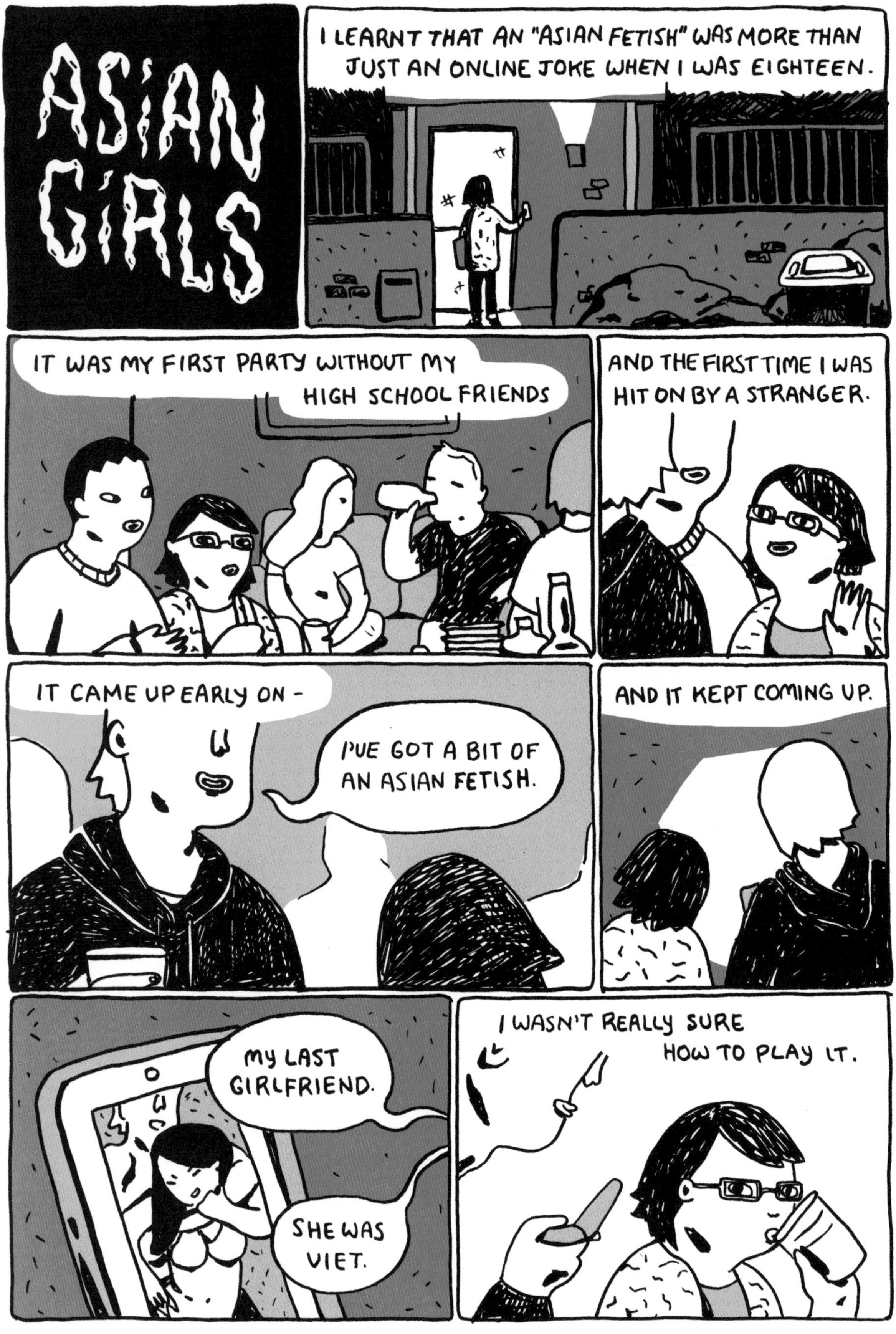
ASIAN GIRLS
I LEARNT THAT AN "ASIAN FETISH" WAS MORE THAN JUST AN ONLINE JOKE WHEN I WAS EIGHTEEN.
IT WAS MY FIRST PARTY WITHOUT MY HIGH SCHOOL FRIENDS
AND THE FIRST TIME I WAS HIT ON BY A STRANGER.
IT CAME UP EARLY ON -
I'VE GOT A BIT OF AN ASIAN FETISH.
AND IT KEPT COMING UP.
MY LAST GIRLFRIEND.
SHE WAS VIET.
I WASN'T REALLY SURE HOW TO PLAY IT.

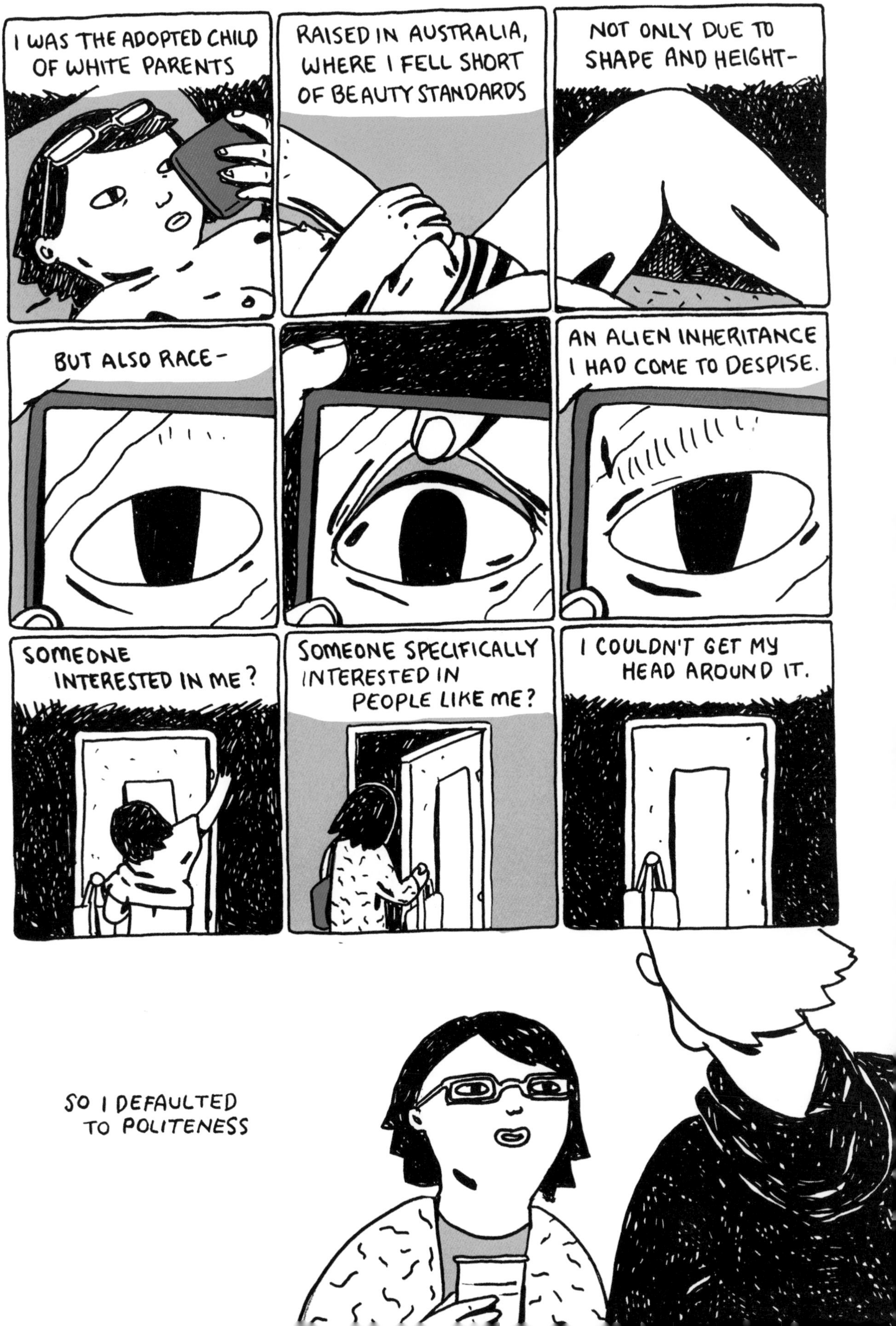
I WAS THE ADOPTED CHILD OF WHITE PARENTS
RAISED IN AUSTRALIA, WHERE I FELL SHORT OF BEAUTY STANDARDS
NOT ONLY DUE TO SHAPE AND HEIGHT-
BUT ALSO RACE-
AN ALIEN INHERITANCE I HAD COME TO DESPISE.
SOMEONE INTERESTED IN ME?
SOMEONE SPECIFICALLY INTERESTED IN PEOPLE LIKE ME?
I COULDN'T GET MY HEAD AROUND IT.
SO I DEFAULTED TO POLITENESS

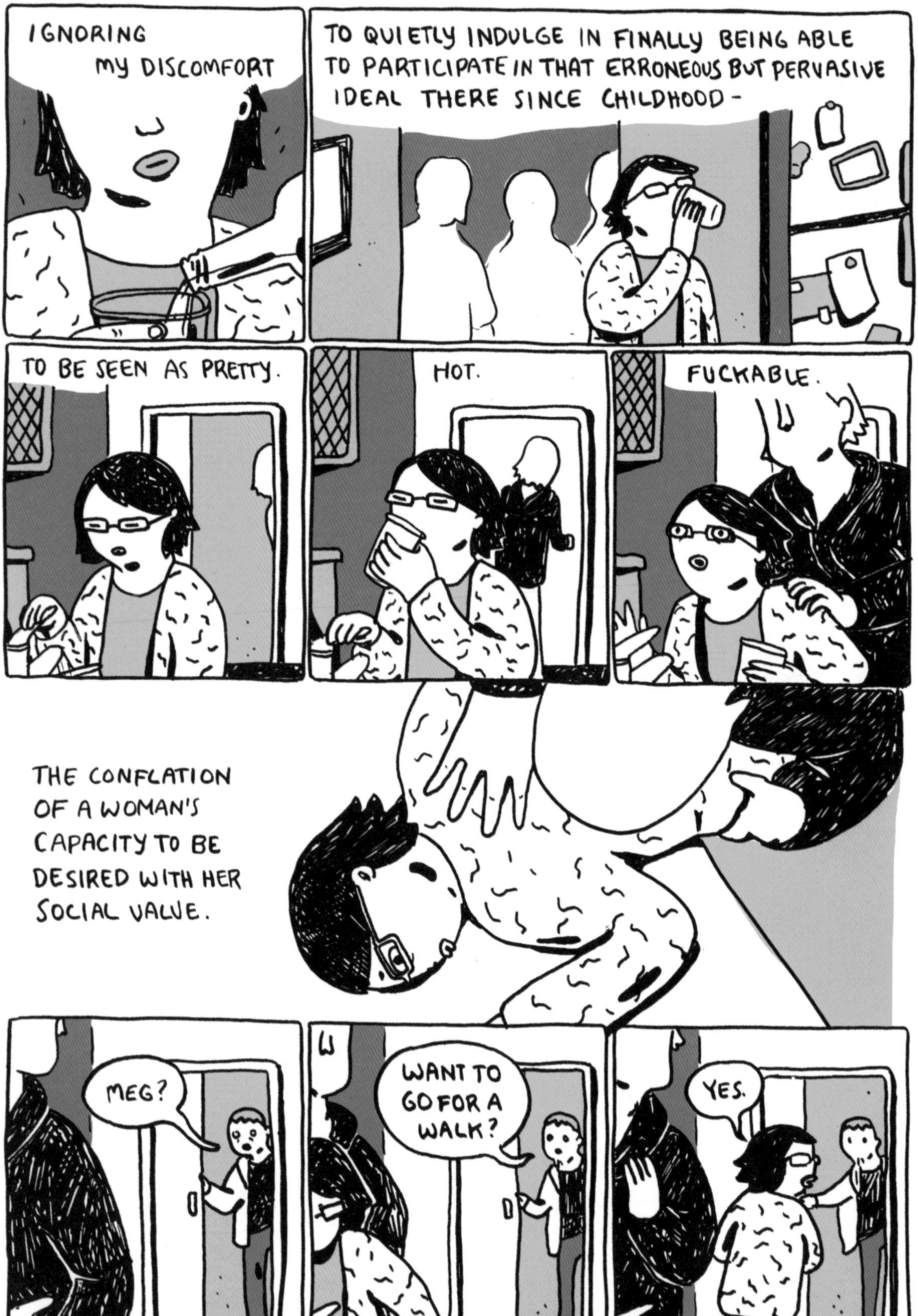
IGNORING
MY DISCOMFORT
TO QUIETLY INDULGE IN FINALLY BEING ABLE TO PARTICIPATE IN THAT ERRONEOUS BUT PERVASIVE IDEAL THERE SINCE CHILDHOOD -
TO BE SEEN AS PRETTY.
HOT.
FUCKABLE.
THE CONFLATION OF A WOMAN'S CAPACITY TO BE DESIRED WITH HER SOCIAL VALUE.
MEG?
WANT TO GO FOR A WALK?
YES.

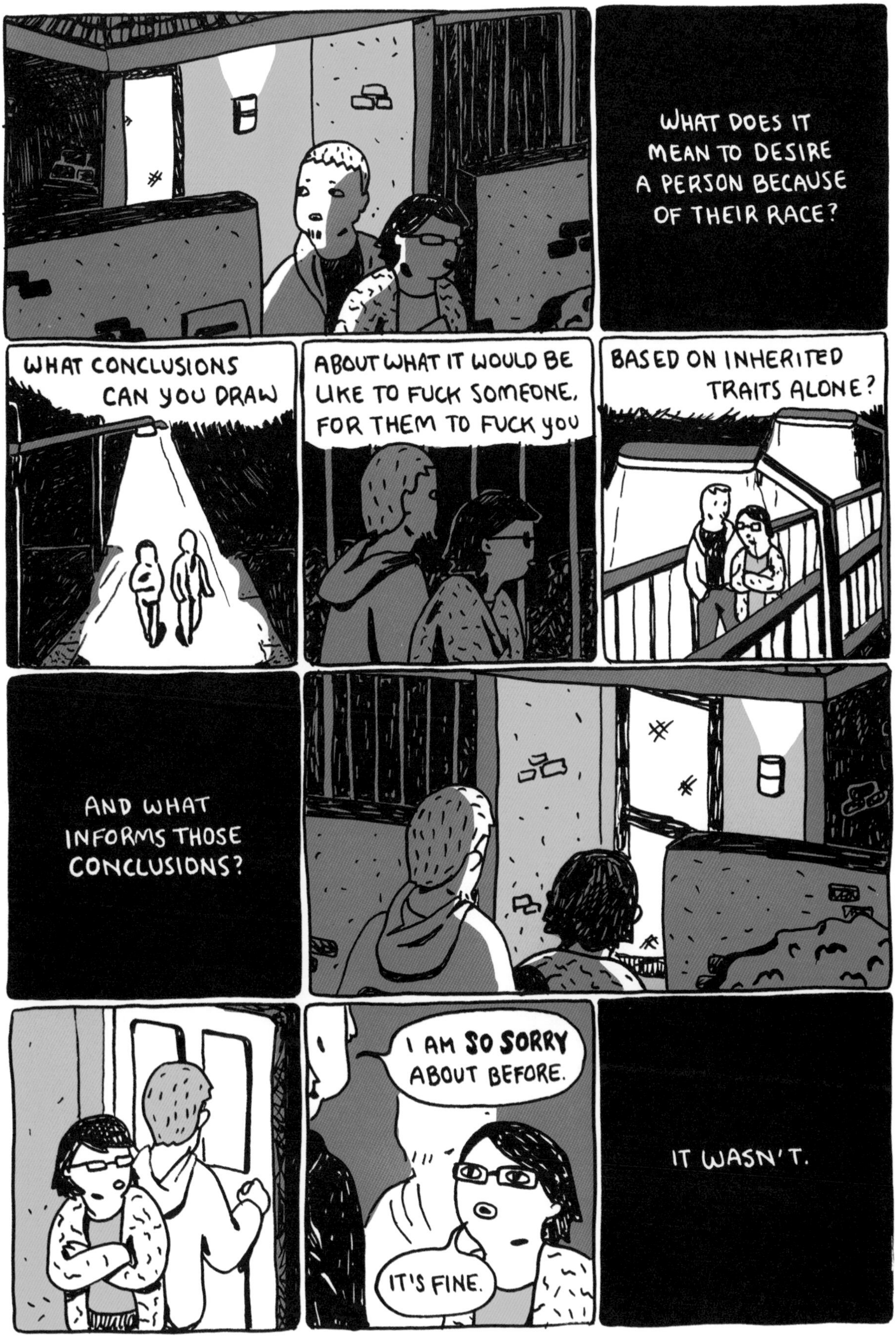
WHAT DOES IT MEAN TO DESIRE A PERSON BECAUSE OF THEIR RACE?
WHAT CONCLUSIONS CAN YOU DRAW
ABOUT WHAT IT WOULD BE LIKE TO FUCK SOMEONE, FOR THEM TO FUCK YOU
BASED ON INHERITED TRAITS ALONE?
AND WHAT INFORMS THOSE CONCLUSIONS?
I AM **SO SORRY** ABOUT BEFORE.
IT'S FINE.
IT WASN'T.

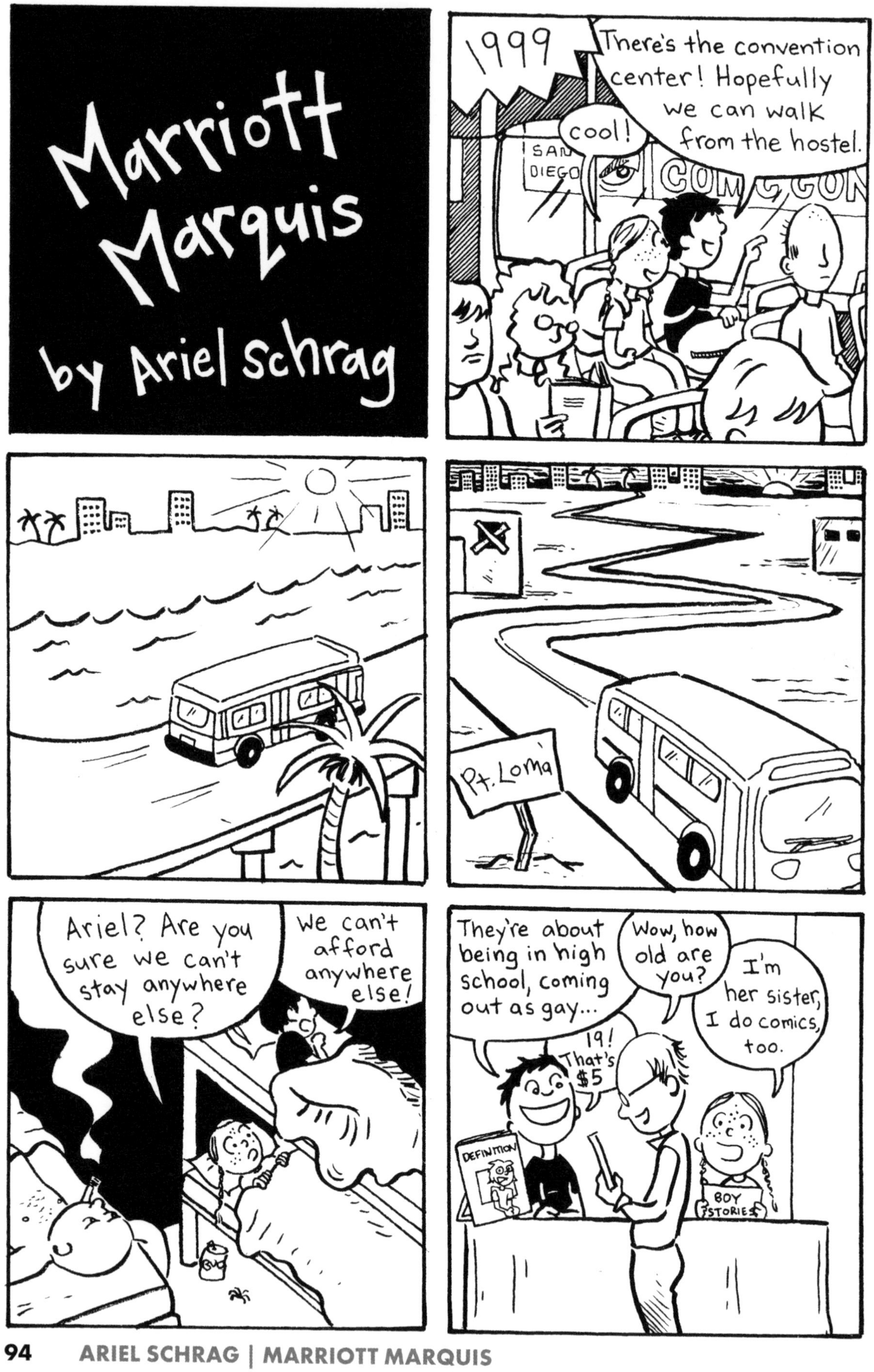
Marriott Marquis
by Ariel Schrag
1999
There's the convention center! Hopefully we can walk from the hostel.
cool!
SAN DIEGO
COMIC CON
Pt. Loma
Ariel? Are you sure we can't stay anywhere else?
We can't afford anywhere else!
They're about being in high school, coming out as gay...
Wow, how old are you?
19! That's $5
I'm her sister, I do comics, too.
DEFINITION
BOY STORIES

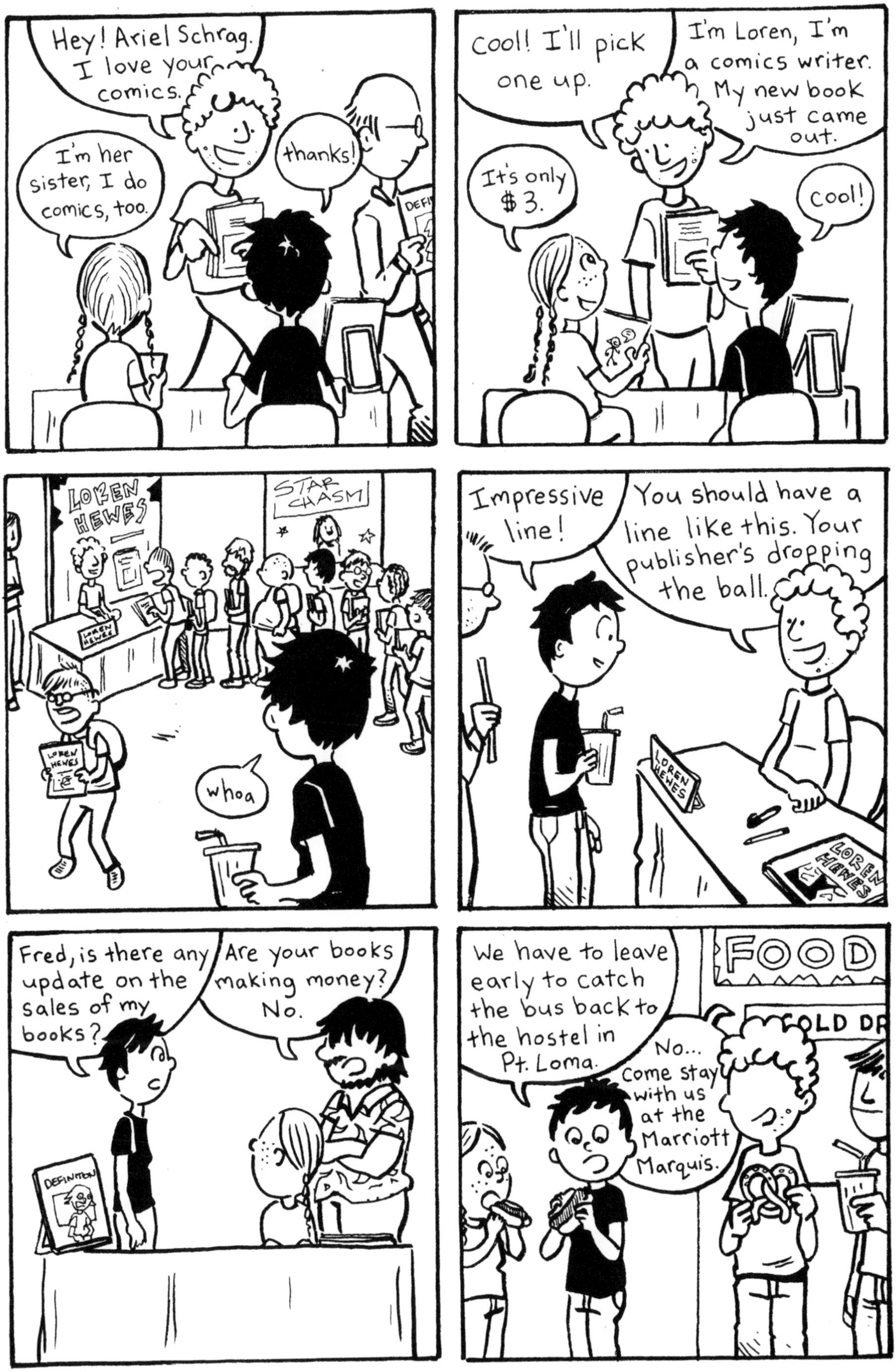
Hey! Ariel Schrag. I love your comics.
I'm her sister, I do comics, too.
thanks!
DEFI
Cool! I'll pick one up.
I'm Loren, I'm a comics writer. My new book just came out.
It's only $3.
Cool!
LOREN HEWES
STAR CHASM
LOREN HEWES
LOREN HEWES
whoa
Impressive line!
You should have a line like this. Your publisher's dropping the ball.
LOREN HEWES
LOREN HEWES
Fred, is there any update on the sales of my books?
Are your books making money? No.
DEFINITION
We have to leave early to catch the bus back to the hostel in Pt. Loma.
No... Come stay with us at the Marriott Marquis.
FOOD

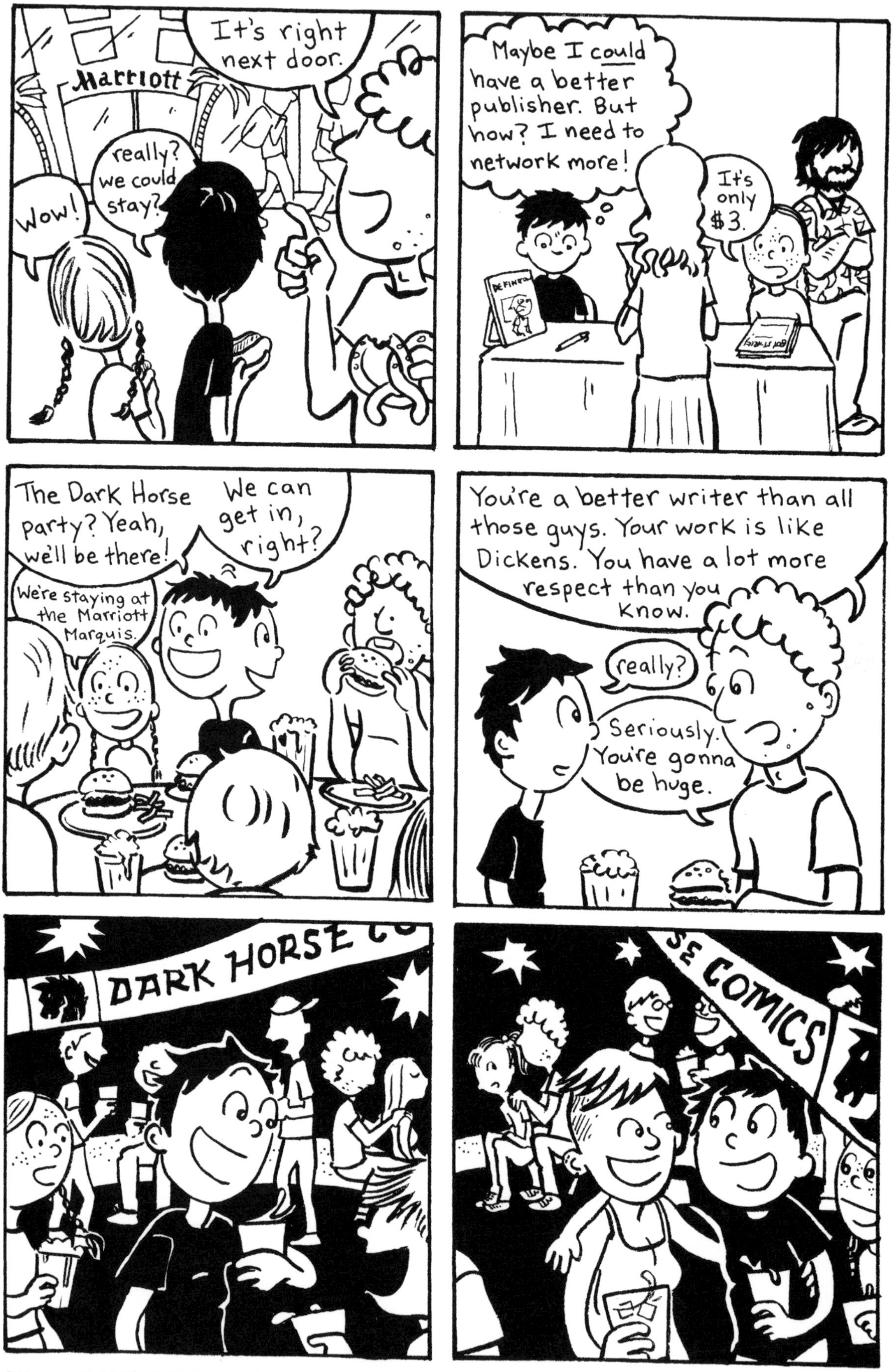
Marriott
It's right next door.
really? we could stay?
Wow!
Maybe I could have a better publisher. But how? I need to network more!
It's only $3.
The Dark Horse party? Yeah, we'll be there!
We can get in, right?
We're staying at the Marriott Marquis.
You're a better writer than all those guys. Your work is like Dickens. You have a lot more respect than you know.
really?
Seriously. You're gonna be huge.
DARK HORSE CO
SE COMICS

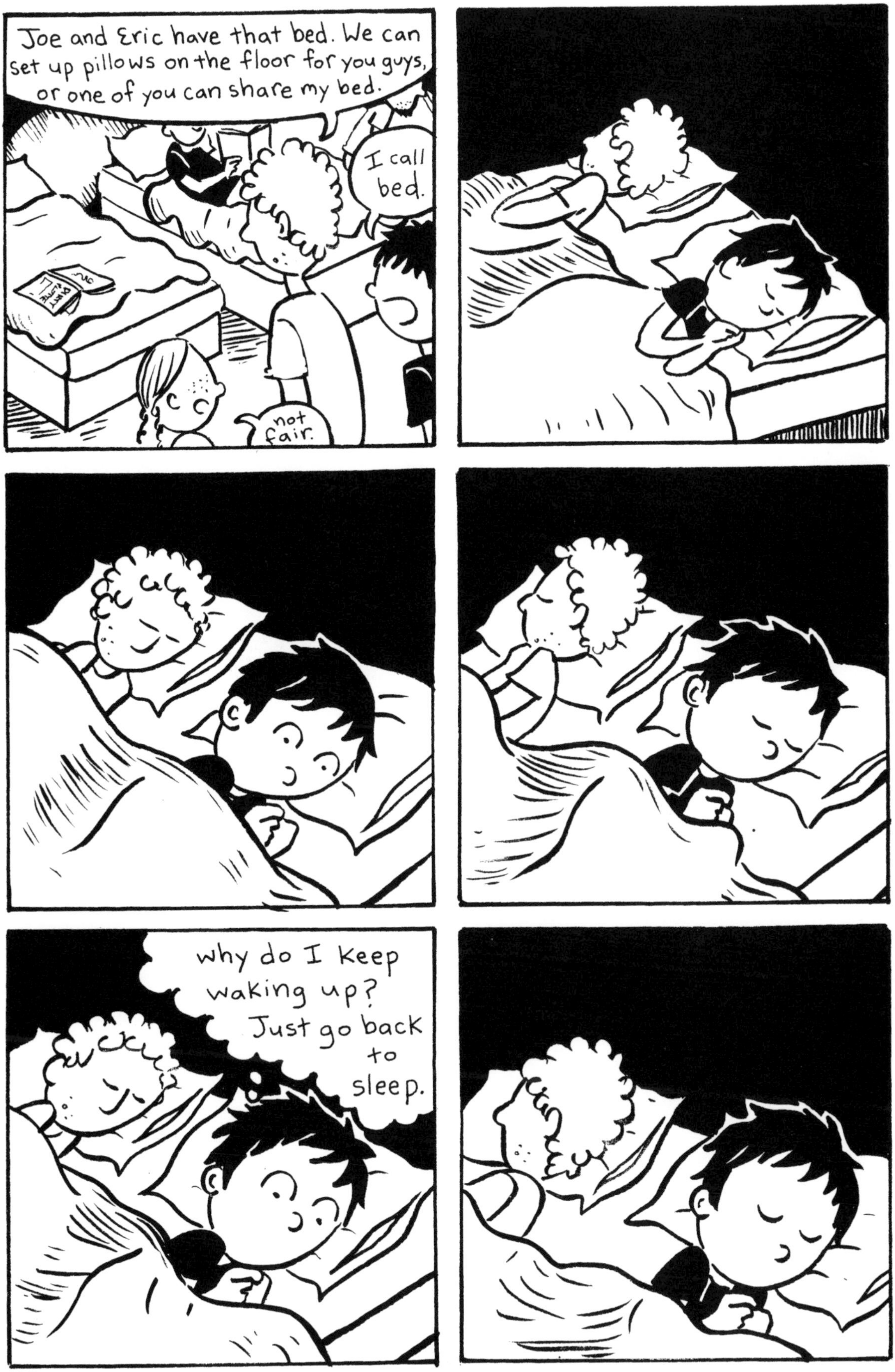
Joe and Eric have that bed. We can set up pillows on the floor for you guys, or one of you can share my bed.
I call bed.
not fair.
why do I keep waking up? Just go back to sleep.

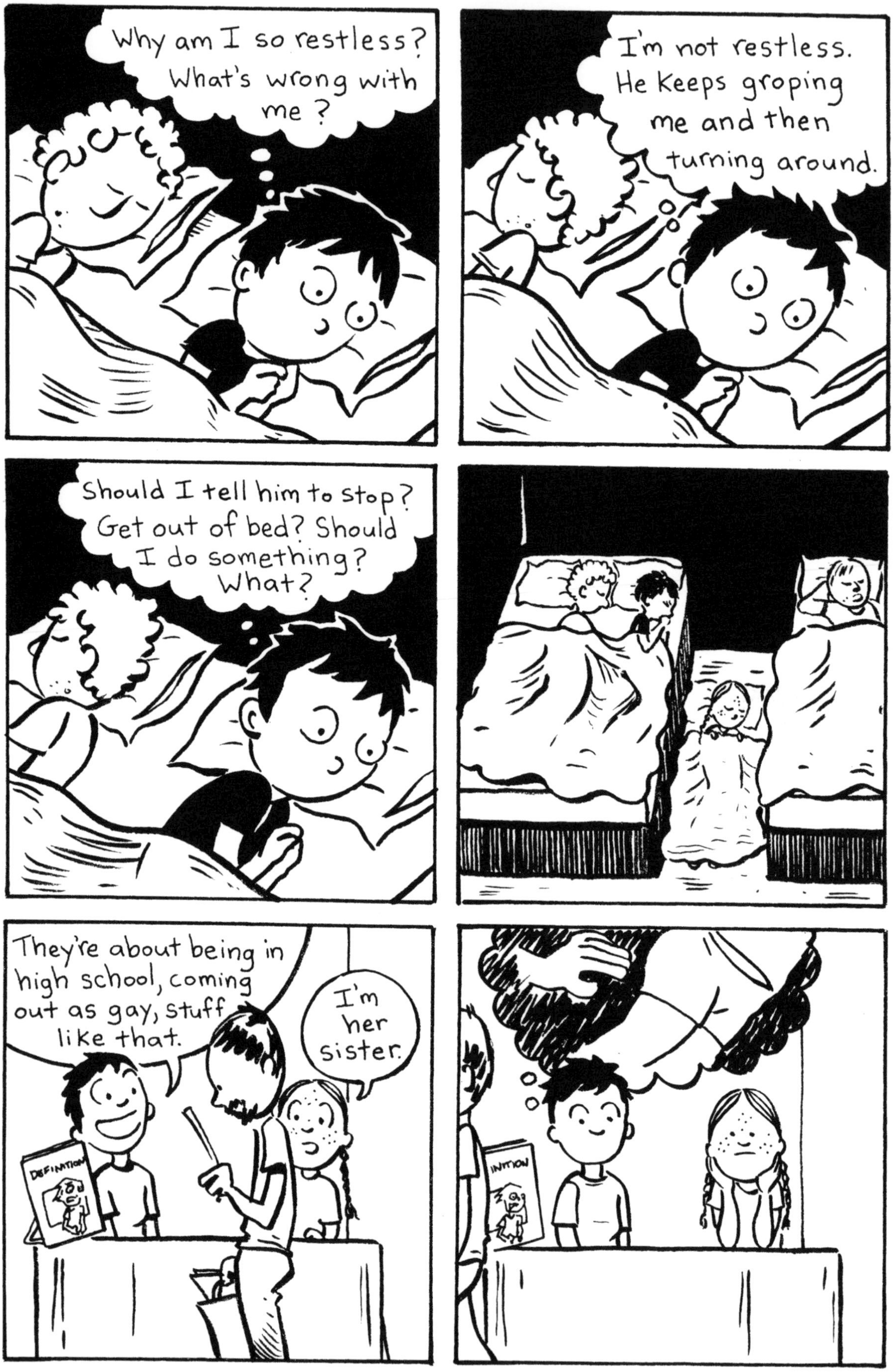
Why am I so restless? What's wrong with me?
I'm not restless. He keeps groping me and then turning around.
Should I tell him to stop? Get out of bed? Should I do something? What?
They're about being in high school, coming out as gay, stuff like that.
I'm her sister.
DEFINITION
INITION

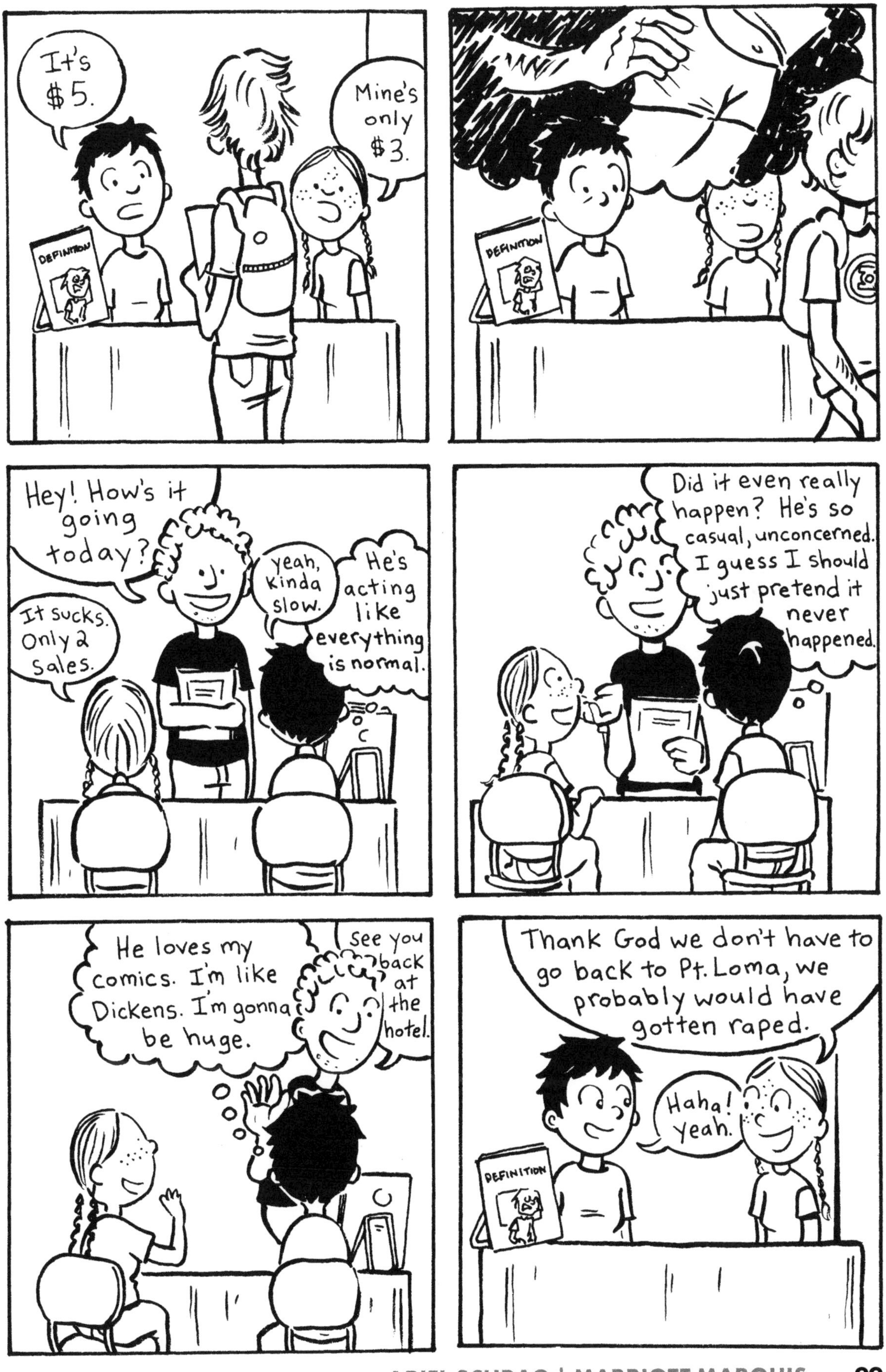
It's $5.
Mine's only $3.
DEFINITION
DEFINITION
Hey! How's it going today?
It sucks. Only 2 sales.
Yeah, kinda slow.
He's acting like everything is normal.
Did it even really happen? He's so casual, unconcerned. I guess I should just pretend it never happened.
He loves my comics. I'm like Dickens. I'm gonna be huge.
See you back at the hotel.
Thank God we don't have to go back to Pt. Loma, we probably would have gotten raped.
Haha! Yeah.
DEFINITION

SLEEPING FURY

by: Liz Mayorga '18

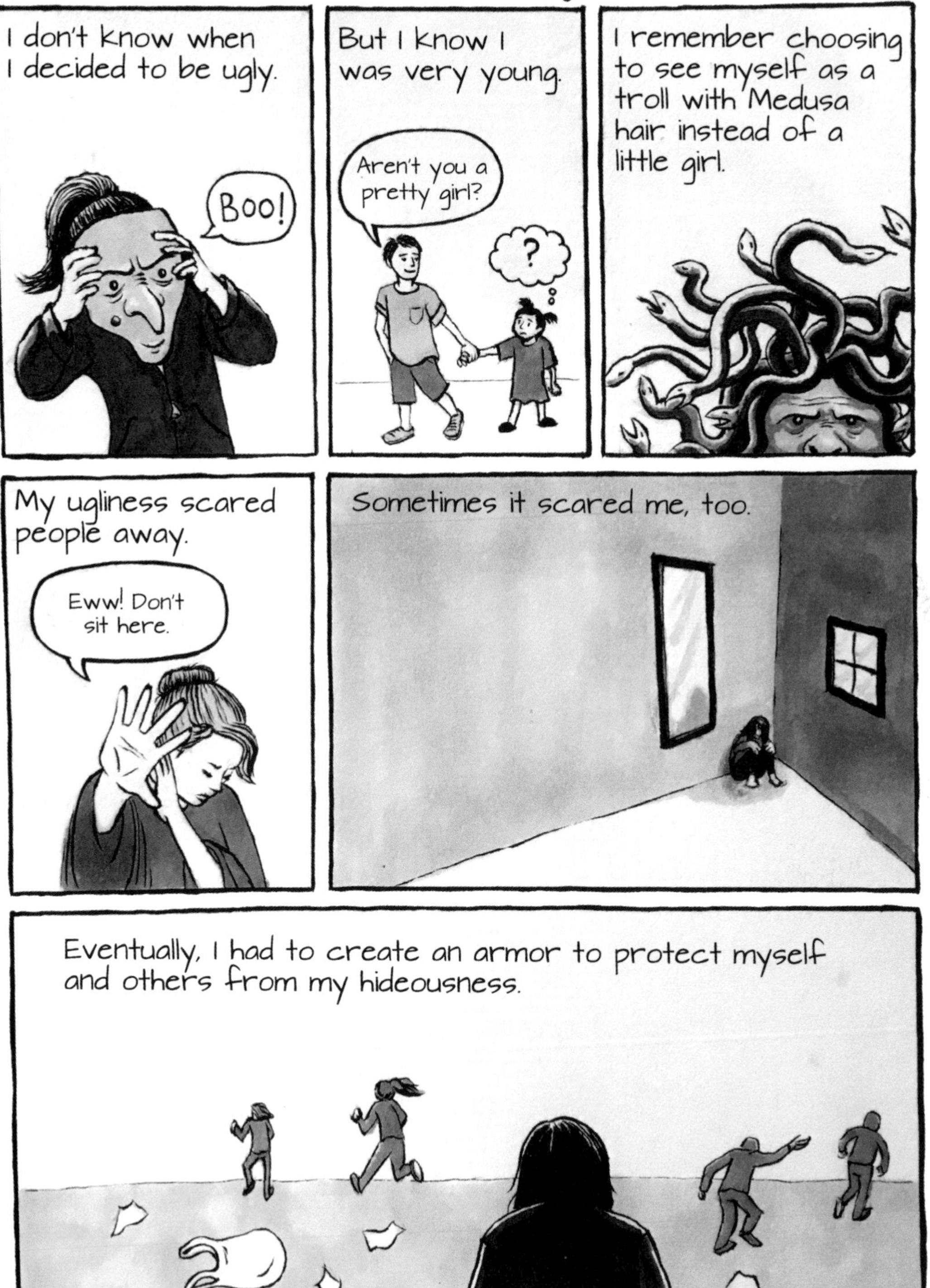
I don't know when I decided to be ugly.
Boo!
But I know I was very young.
Aren't you a pretty girl?
?
I remember choosing to see myself as a troll with Medusa hair instead of a little girl.
My ugliness scared people away.
Eww! Don't sit here.
Sometimes it scared me, too.
Eventually, I had to create an armor to protect myself and others from my hideousness.

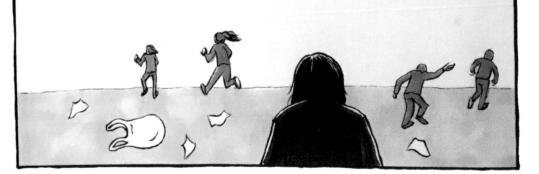

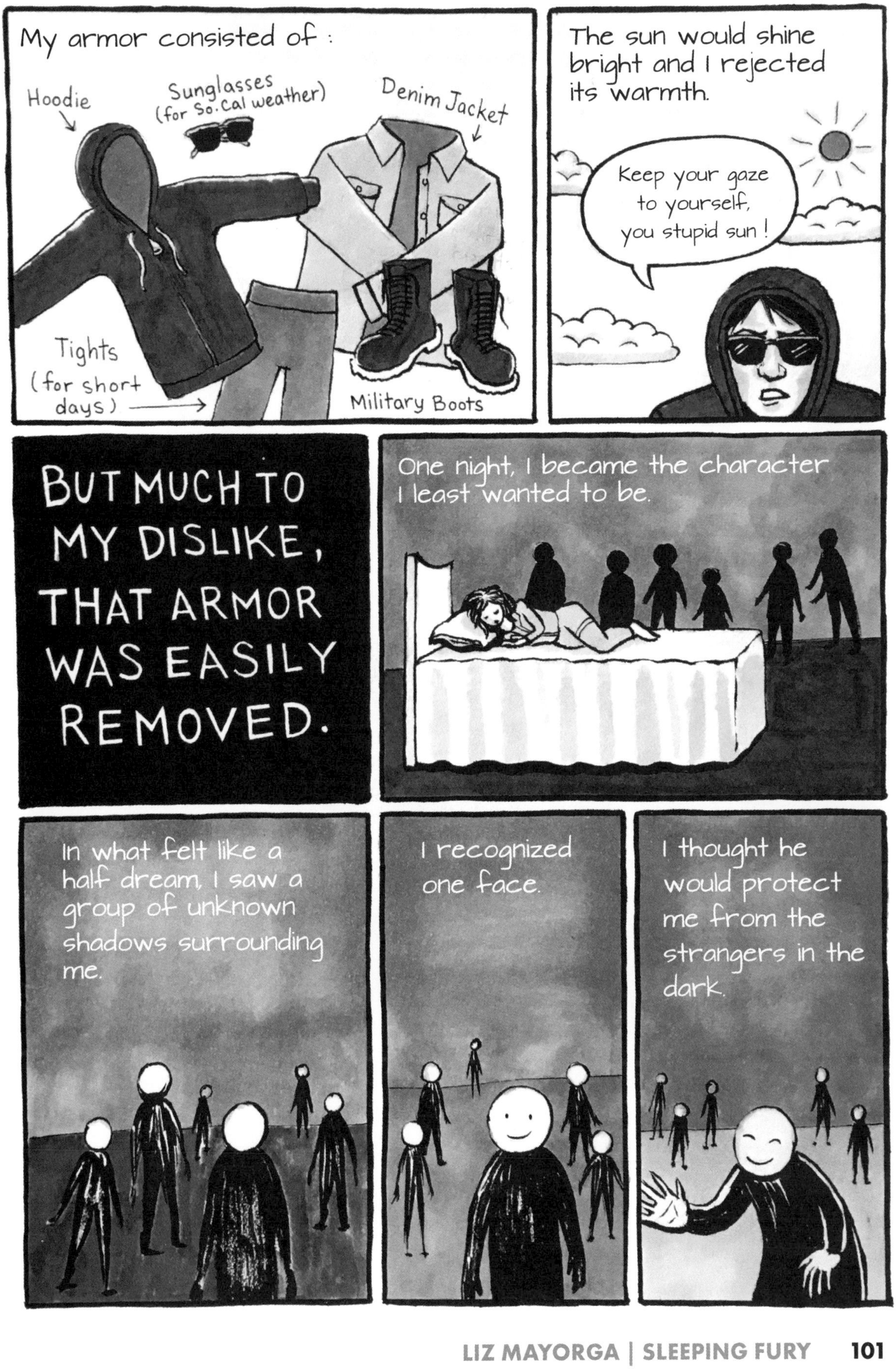
My armor consisted of :
Hoodie
Sunglasses (for So. Cal weather)
Denim Jacket
Tights (for short days)
Military Boots
The sun would shine bright and I rejected its warmth.
Keep your gaze to yourself, you stupid sun !
BUT MUCH TO MY DISLIKE, THAT ARMOR WAS EASILY REMOVED.
One night, I became the character I least wanted to be.
In what felt like a half dream, I saw a group of unknown shadows surrounding me.
I recognized one face.
I thought he would protect me from the strangers in the dark.

But he was there for a kiss.
You're so cute!
And everyone else was there to watch as they waited their turn.
That kiss woke me into a living nightmare.
Kiss me back, beauty!
Just one kiss and I'll leave you alone.
Muah
In that moment, I wanted to be more than a troll. I wanted to turn into a raging beast.
Muah
Smack
Smack
Muah
Smack
And I think I did.
But my body would not move, so my beastly powers were useless.
Luckily, a knock on the door made everyone go away.

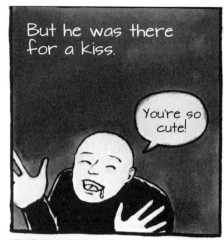

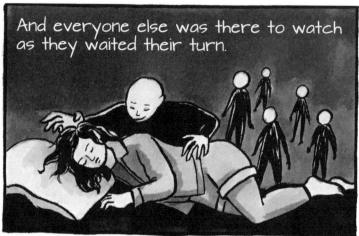

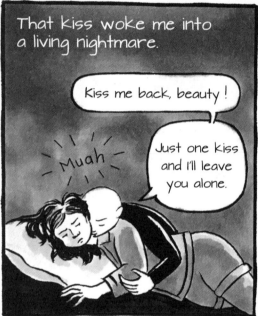

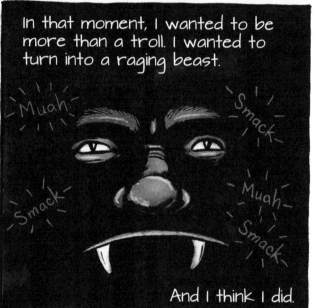

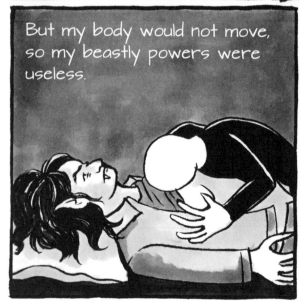

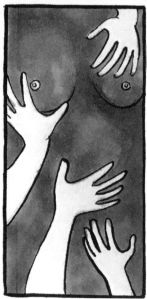

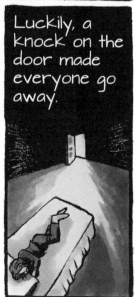

But that nightmare hasn't ended.

I feel the shame and rage when I look in the mirror.

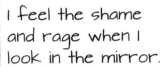

Mirror, mirror, on the wall, who is the ugliest of them all?

I wish it would say, "You."

But it doesn't. Not really.

Instead it shows me this :

Defensive Posture

Messy hair

Dark Eyes

Breasts

Pubes

Strong Arms

Lots of Tattoos

Soft Stomach

Strong Legs

And I stare.

And stare.

And stare.

Searching for beauty in my scars.

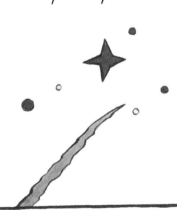

Fighting to see myself for myself.

Reclaiming my beauty through my own gaze, and accepting the beast within.

RAWR!

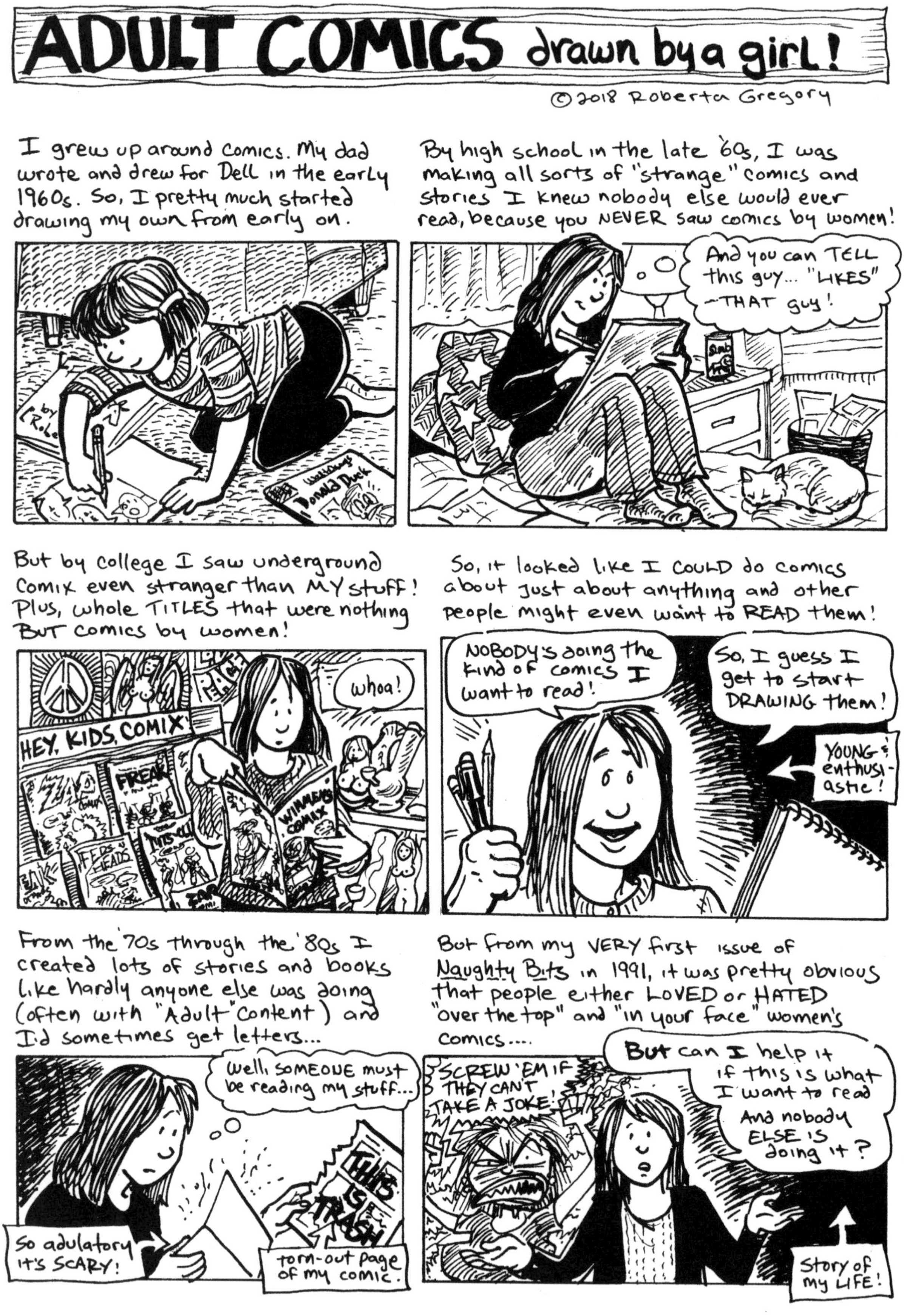
ADULT COMICS drawn by a girl!
©2018 Roberta Gregory
I grew up around comics. My dad wrote and drew for Dell in the early 1960s. So, I pretty much started drawing my own from early on.
by Robe
Walt Disney's Donald Duck
By high school in the late '60s, I was making all sorts of "strange" comics and stories I knew nobody else would ever read, because you NEVER saw comics by women!
And you can TELL this guy... "LIKES" —THAT guy!
But by college I saw underground comix even stranger than MY stuff! Plus, whole TITLES that were nothing BUT comics by women!
HEY, KIDS, COMIX
whoa!
FREAK
FEDS 'N HEADS
WIMMEN'S COMIX
ZAP
So, it looked like I COULD do comics about just about anything and other people might even want to READ them!
NOBODY's doing the kind of comics I want to read!
So, I guess I get to start DRAWING them!
YOUNG & enthusiastic!
From the '70s through the '80s I created lots of stories and books like hardly anyone else was doing (often with "Adult" content) and I'd sometimes get letters...
Well, SOMEONE must be reading my stuff...
THIS IS TRASH
So adulatory it's SCARY!
torn-out page of my comic.
But from my VERY first issue of Naughty Bits in 1991, it was pretty obvious that people either LOVED or HATED "over the top" and "in your face" women's comics....
SCREW 'EM IF THEY CAN'T TAKE A JOKE!
But can I help it if this is what I want to read And nobody ELSE is doing it?
Story of my LIFE!

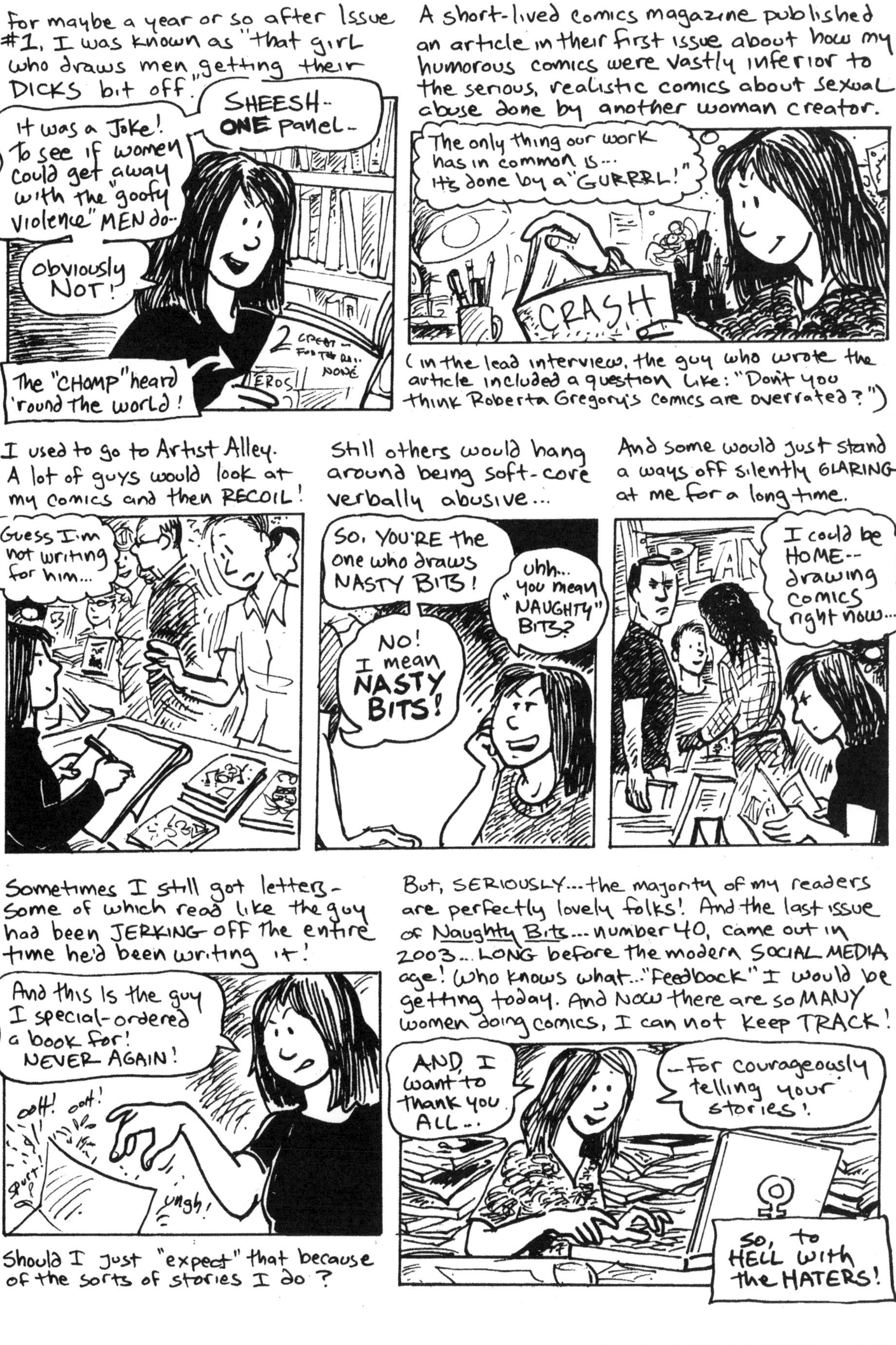
for maybe a year or so after Issue #1, I was known as "that girl who draws men getting their DICKS bit off"
It was a Joke! To see if women could get away with the "goofy violence" MEN do..
SHEESH-- ONE panel--
obviously NOT!
The "CHOMP" heard 'round the world!
EROS
A short-lived comics magazine published an article in their first issue about how my humorous comics were vastly inferior to the serious, realistic comics about sexual abuse done by another woman creator.
The only thing our work has in common is... it's done by a "GURRRL!"
CRASH
(in the lead interview, the guy who wrote the article included a question like: "Don't you think Roberta Gregory's comics are overrated?")
I used to go to Artist Alley. A lot of guys would look at my comics and then RECOIL!
Guess I'm not writing for him...
Still others would hang around being soft-core verbally abusive...
So, YOU'RE the one who draws NASTY BITS!
uhh... you mean "NAUGHTY" BITS?
NO! I mean NASTY BITS!
And some would just stand a ways off silently GLARING at me for a long time.
I could be HOME-- drawing comics right now...
Sometimes I still got letters-- some of which read like the guy had been JERKING OFF the entire time he'd been writing it!
And this is the guy I special-ordered a book for! NEVER AGAIN!
ooh! ooh!
spurt!
ungh!
Should I just "expect" that because of the sorts of stories I do?
But, SERIOUSLY... the majority of my readers are perfectly lovely folks! And the last issue of Naughty Bits... number 40, came out in 2003... LONG before the modern SOCIAL MEDIA age! Who knows what... "Feedback" I would be getting today. And NOW there are so MANY women doing comics, I can not keep TRACK!
AND, I want to thank you ALL..
--For courageously telling your stories!
So, to HELL with the HATERS!

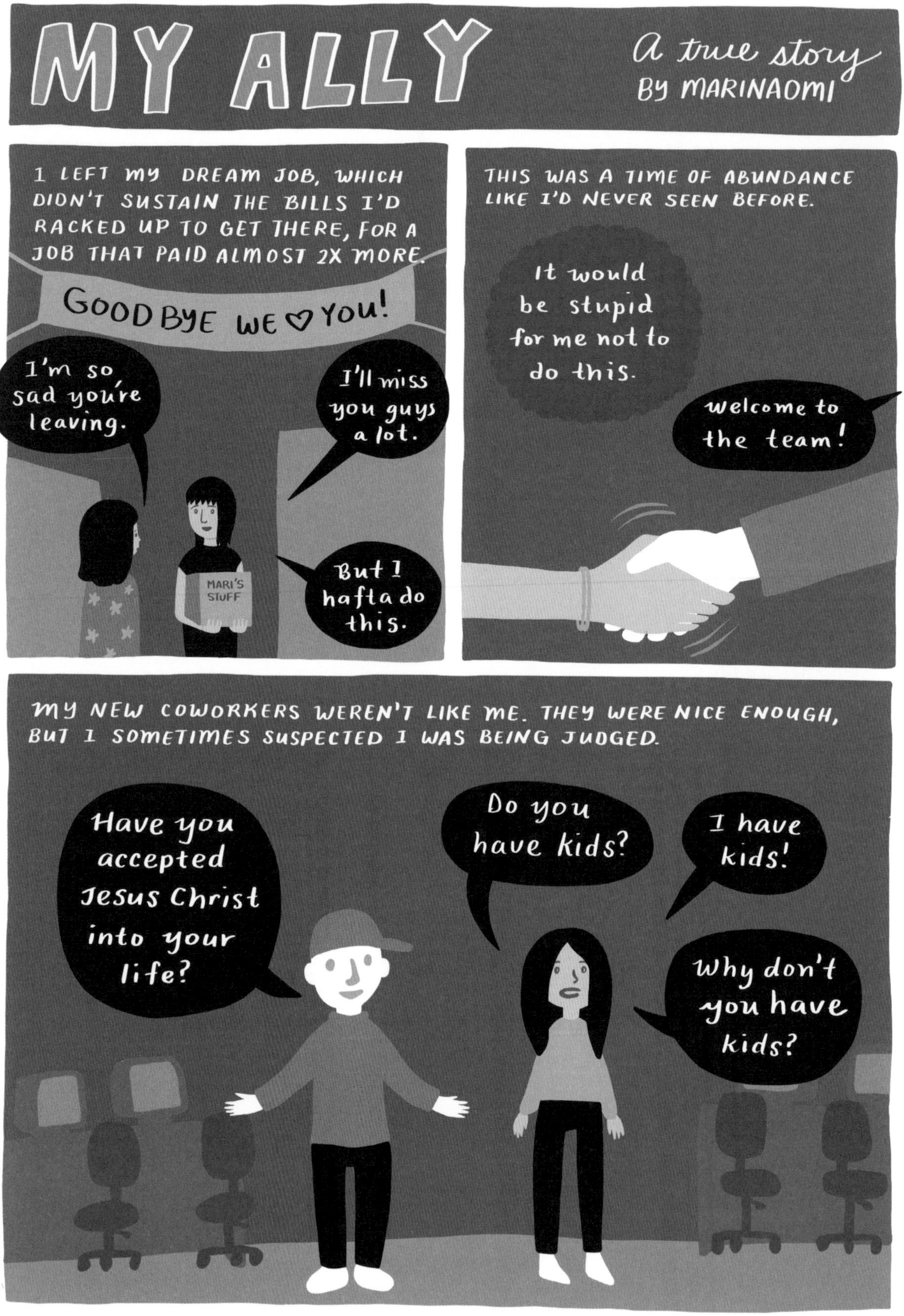
MY ALLY
A true story
BY MARINAOMI
I LEFT MY DREAM JOB, WHICH DIDN'T SUSTAIN THE BILLS I'D RACKED UP TO GET THERE, FOR A JOB THAT PAID ALMOST 2X MORE.
GOODBYE WE ♡ YOU!
I'm so sad you're leaving.
I'll miss you guys a lot.
MARI'S STUFF
But I hafta do this.
THIS WAS A TIME OF ABUNDANCE LIKE I'D NEVER SEEN BEFORE.
It would be stupid for me not to do this.
welcome to the team!
MY NEW COWORKERS WEREN'T LIKE ME. THEY WERE NICE ENOUGH, BUT I SOMETIMES SUSPECTED I WAS BEING JUDGED.
Have you accepted Jesus Christ into your life?
Do you have kids?
I have kids!
Why don't you have kids?

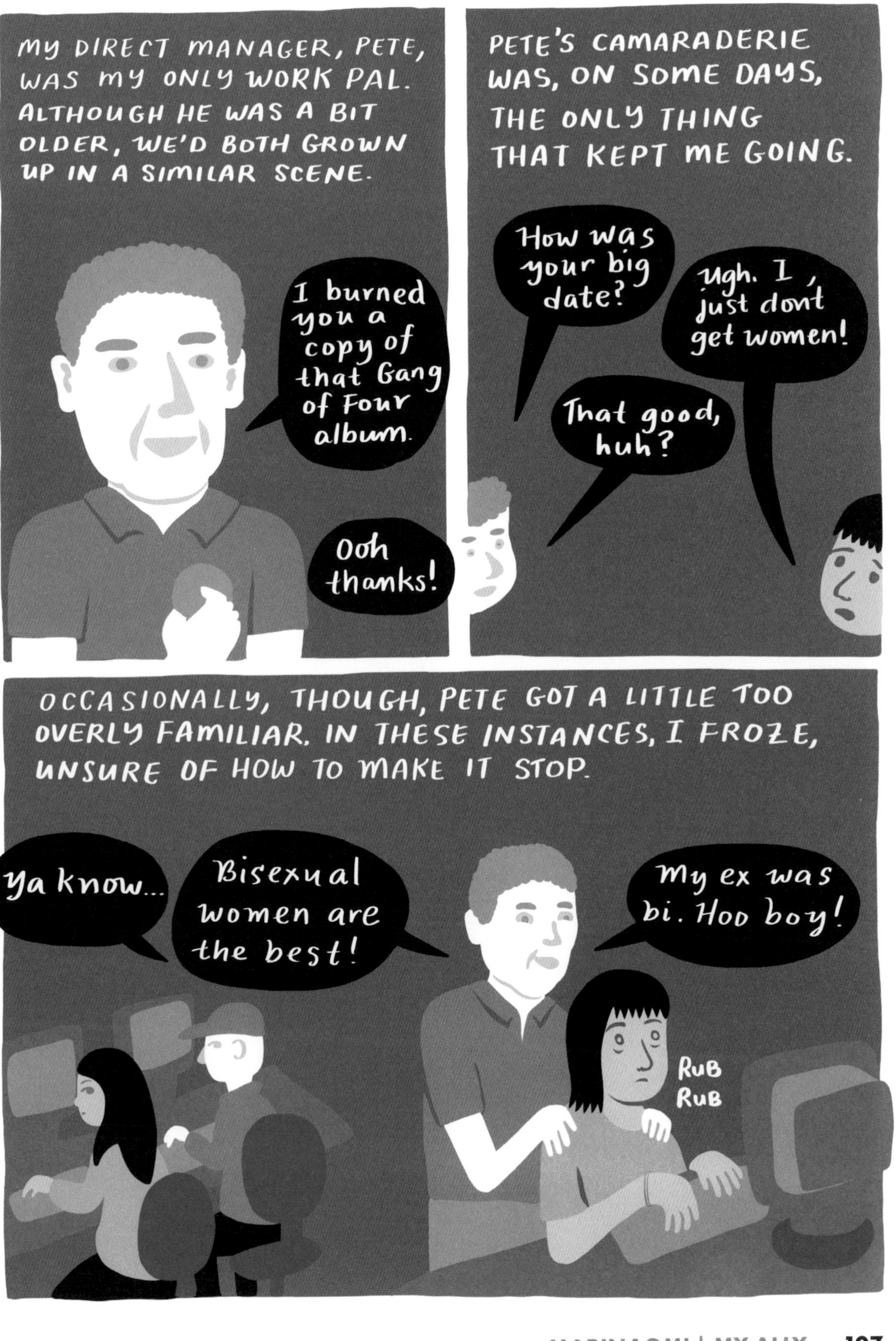
MY DIRECT MANAGER, PETE, WAS MY ONLY WORK PAL. ALTHOUGH HE WAS A BIT OLDER, WE'D BOTH GROWN UP IN A SIMILAR SCENE.
I burned you a copy of that Gang of Four album.
Ooh thanks!
PETE'S CAMARADERIE WAS, ON SOME DAYS, THE ONLY THING THAT KEPT ME GOING.
How was your big date?
Ugh. I just don't get women!
That good, huh?
OCCASIONALLY, THOUGH, PETE GOT A LITTLE TOO OVERLY FAMILIAR. IN THESE INSTANCES, I FROZE, UNSURE OF HOW TO MAKE IT STOP.
Ya know...
Bisexual women are the best!
My ex was bi. Hoo boy!
RUB
RUB

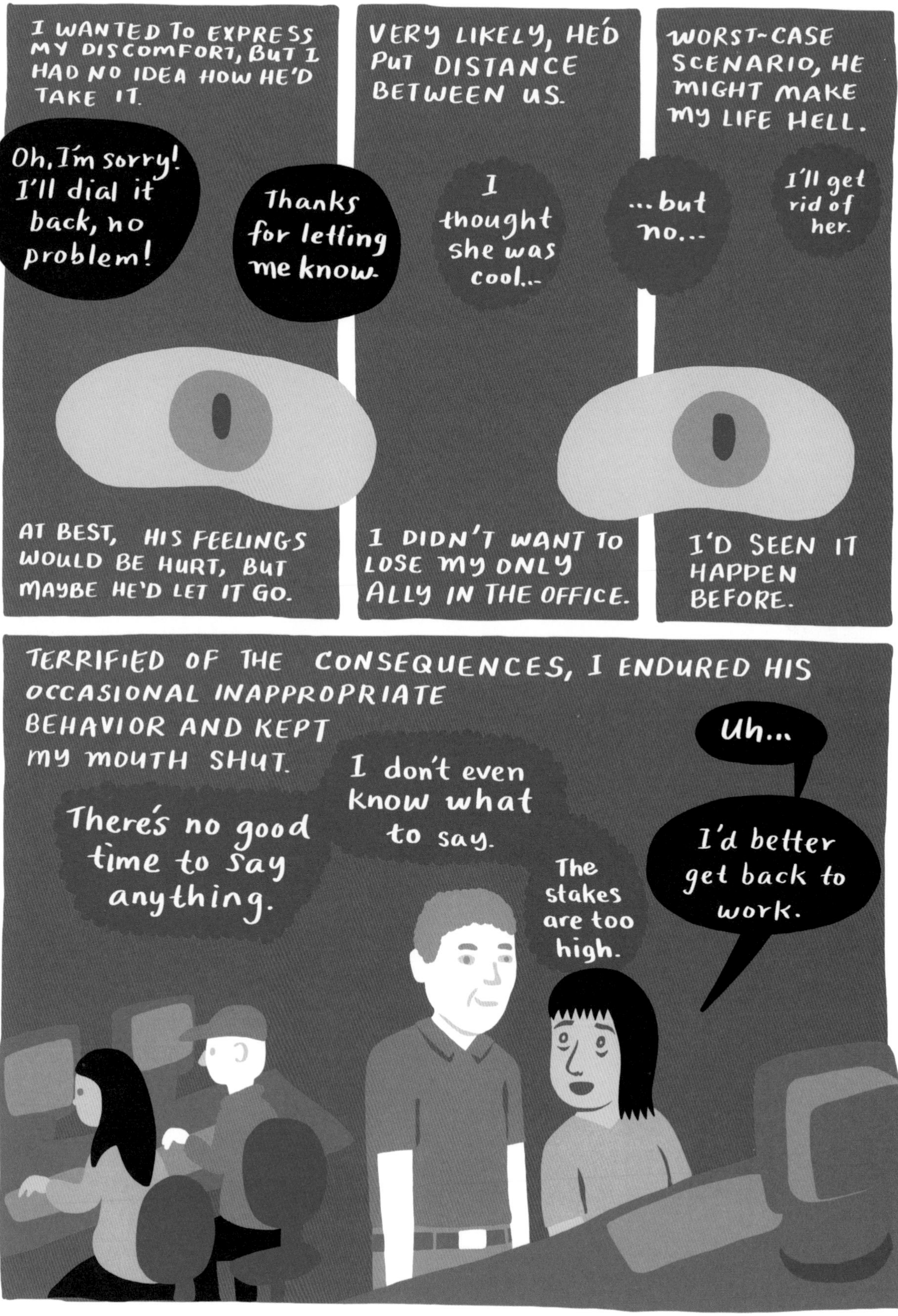
I WANTED TO EXPRESS MY DISCOMFORT, BUT I HAD NO IDEA HOW HE'D TAKE IT.
Oh, I'm sorry! I'll dial it back, no problem!
Thanks for letting me know.
AT BEST, HIS FEELINGS WOULD BE HURT, BUT MAYBE HE'D LET IT GO.
VERY LIKELY, HE'D PUT DISTANCE BETWEEN US.
I thought she was cool...
I DIDN'T WANT TO LOSE MY ONLY ALLY IN THE OFFICE.
WORST-CASE SCENARIO, HE MIGHT MAKE MY LIFE HELL.
...but no...
I'll get rid of her.
I'D SEEN IT HAPPEN BEFORE.
TERRIFIED OF THE CONSEQUENCES, I ENDURED HIS OCCASIONAL INAPPROPRIATE BEHAVIOR AND KEPT MY MOUTH SHUT.
There's no good time to say anything.
I don't even know what to say.
The stakes are too high.
Uh...
I'd better get back to work.

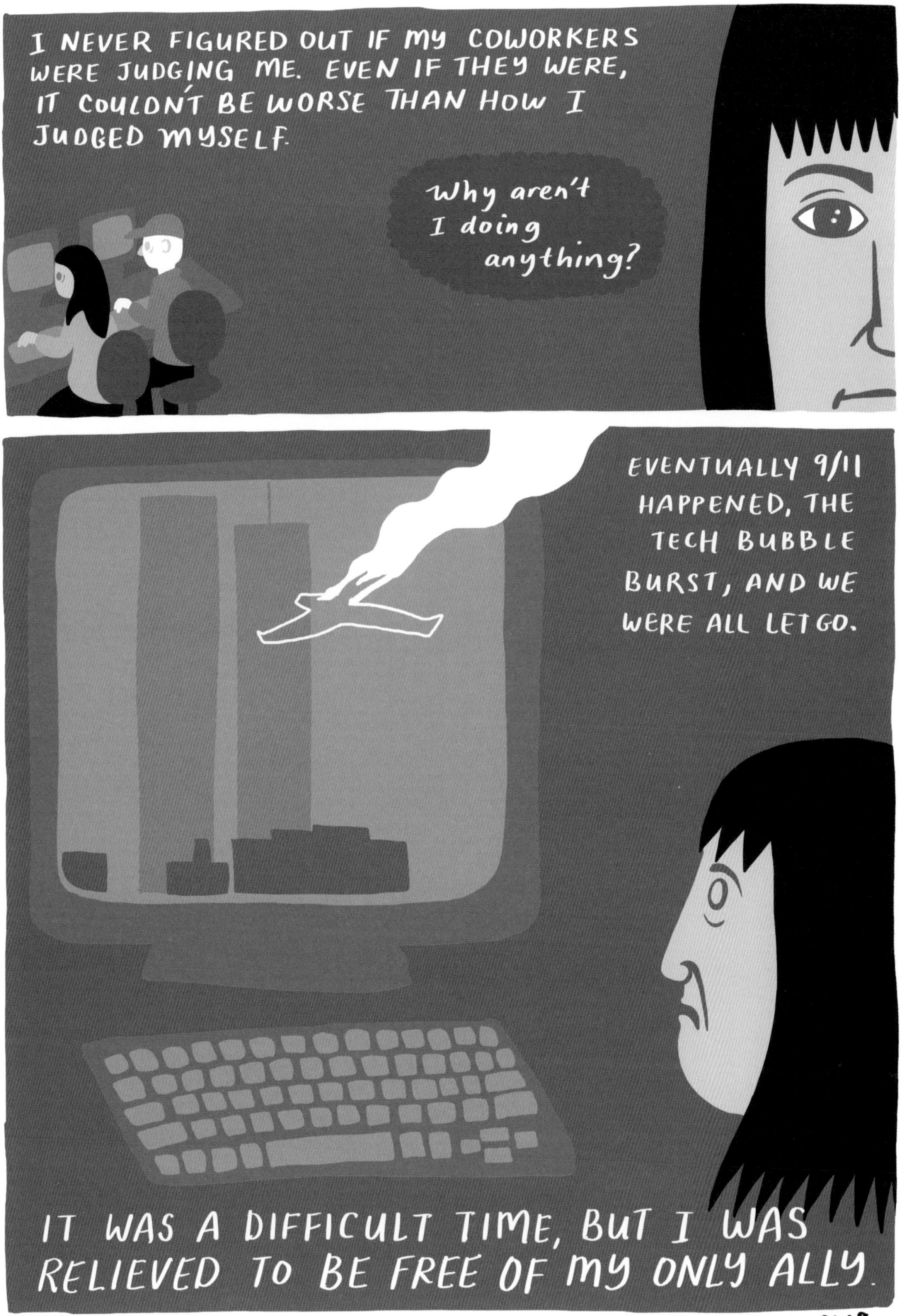
I NEVER FIGURED OUT IF MY COWORKERS WERE JUDGING ME. EVEN IF THEY WERE, IT COULDN'T BE WORSE THAN HOW I JUDGED MYSELF.
Why aren't I doing anything?
EVENTUALLY 9/11 HAPPENED, THE TECH BUBBLE BURST, AND WE WERE ALL LET GO.
IT WAS A DIFFICULT TIME, BUT I WAS RELIEVED TO BE FREE OF MY ONLY ALLY.
MARINAOMI 2018

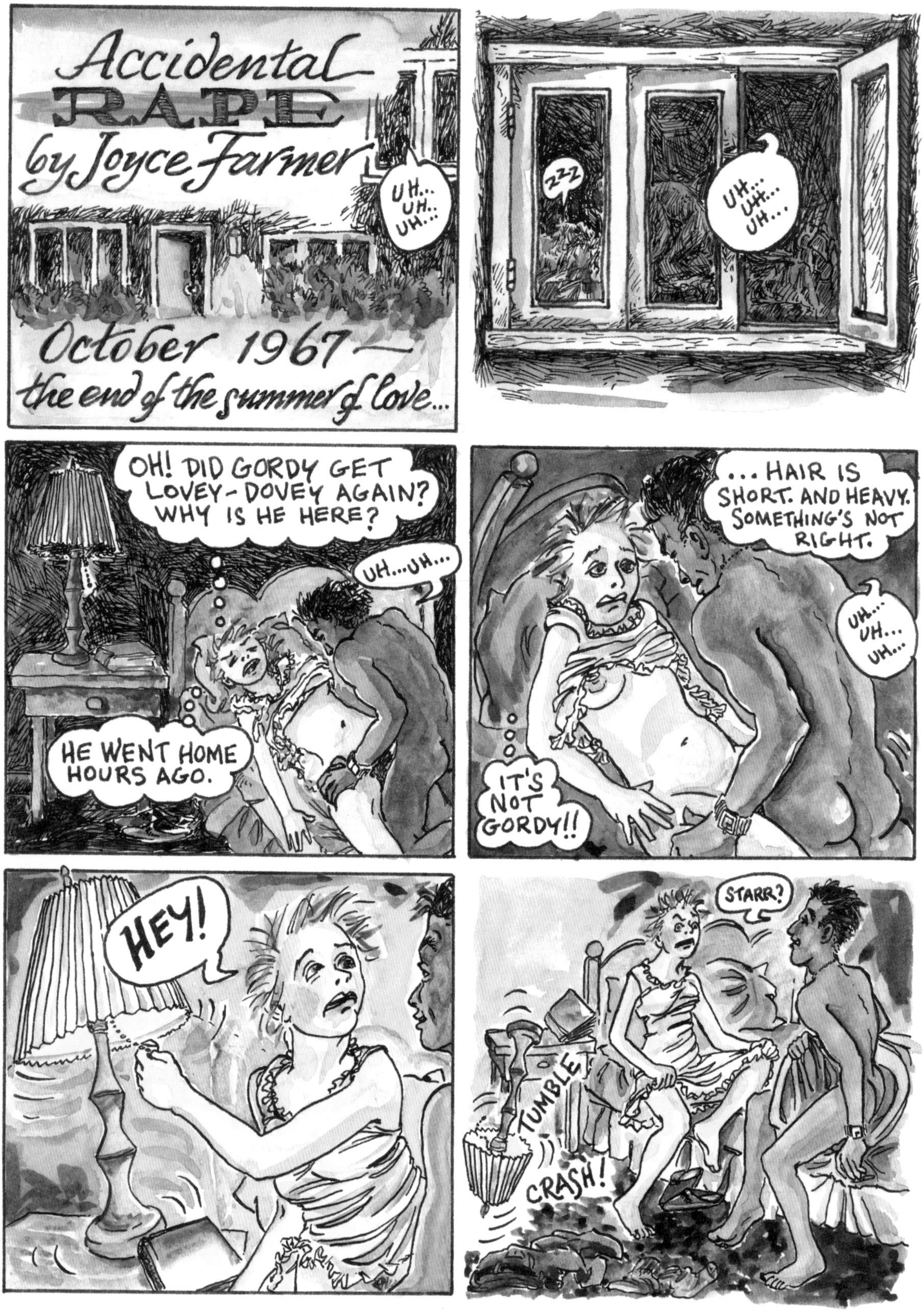
Accidental
RAPE
by Joyce Farmer
UH... UH... UH...
October 1967 —
the end of the summer of love...
ZZZ
UH... UH... UH...
OH! DID GORDY GET LOVEY-DOVEY AGAIN? WHY IS HE HERE?
UH...UH...
HE WENT HOME HOURS AGO.
... HAIR IS SHORT. AND HEAVY. SOMETHING'S NOT RIGHT.
UH... UH... UH...
IT'S NOT GORDY!!
HEY!
STARR?
TUMBLE
CRASH!

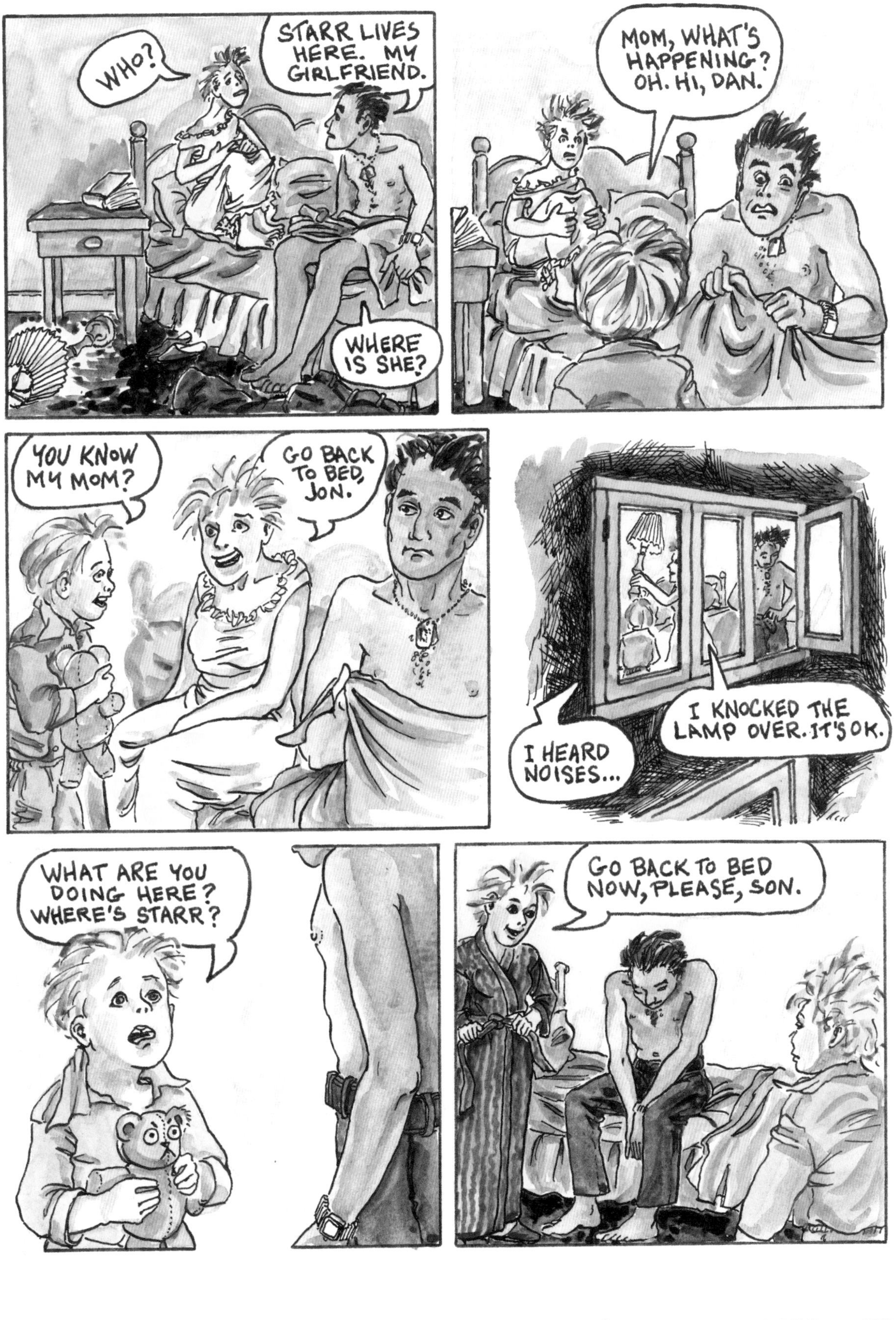
WHO?
STARR LIVES HERE. MY GIRLFRIEND.
WHERE IS SHE?
MOM, WHAT'S HAPPENING? OH. HI, DAN.
YOU KNOW MY MOM?
GO BACK TO BED, JON.
I HEARD NOISES...
I KNOCKED THE LAMP OVER. IT'S OK.
WHAT ARE YOU DOING HERE? WHERE'S STARR?
GO BACK TO BED NOW, PLEASE, SON.

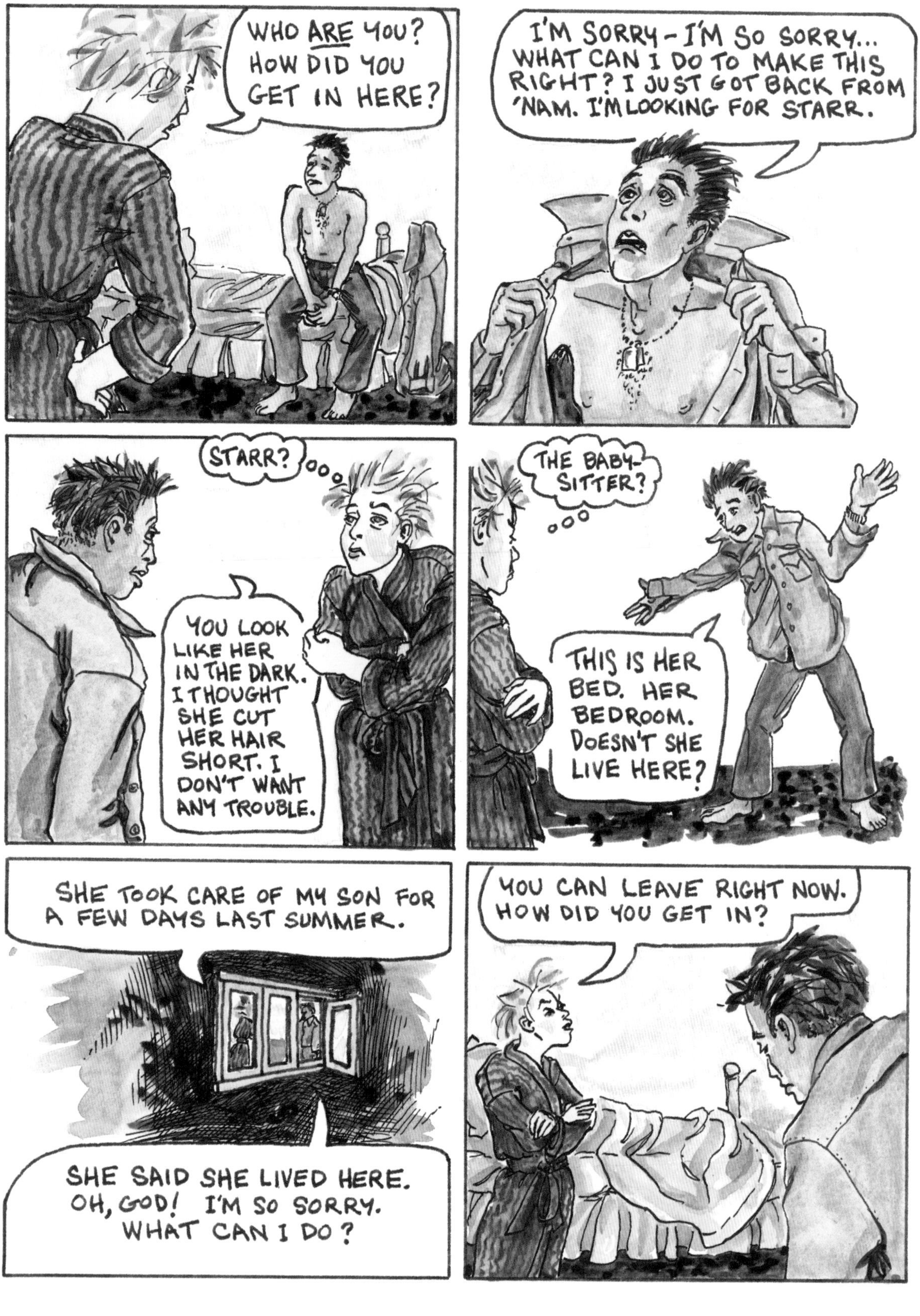
WHO ARE YOU? HOW DID YOU GET IN HERE?
I'M SORRY - I'M SO SORRY... WHAT CAN I DO TO MAKE THIS RIGHT? I JUST GOT BACK FROM 'NAM. I'M LOOKING FOR STARR.
STARR?
YOU LOOK LIKE HER IN THE DARK. I THOUGHT SHE CUT HER HAIR SHORT. I DON'T WANT ANY TROUBLE.
THE BABY-SITTER?
THIS IS HER BED. HER BEDROOM. DOESN'T SHE LIVE HERE?
SHE TOOK CARE OF MY SON FOR A FEW DAYS LAST SUMMER.
SHE SAID SHE LIVED HERE. OH, GOD! I'M SO SORRY. WHAT CAN I DO?
YOU CAN LEAVE RIGHT NOW. HOW DID YOU GET IN?

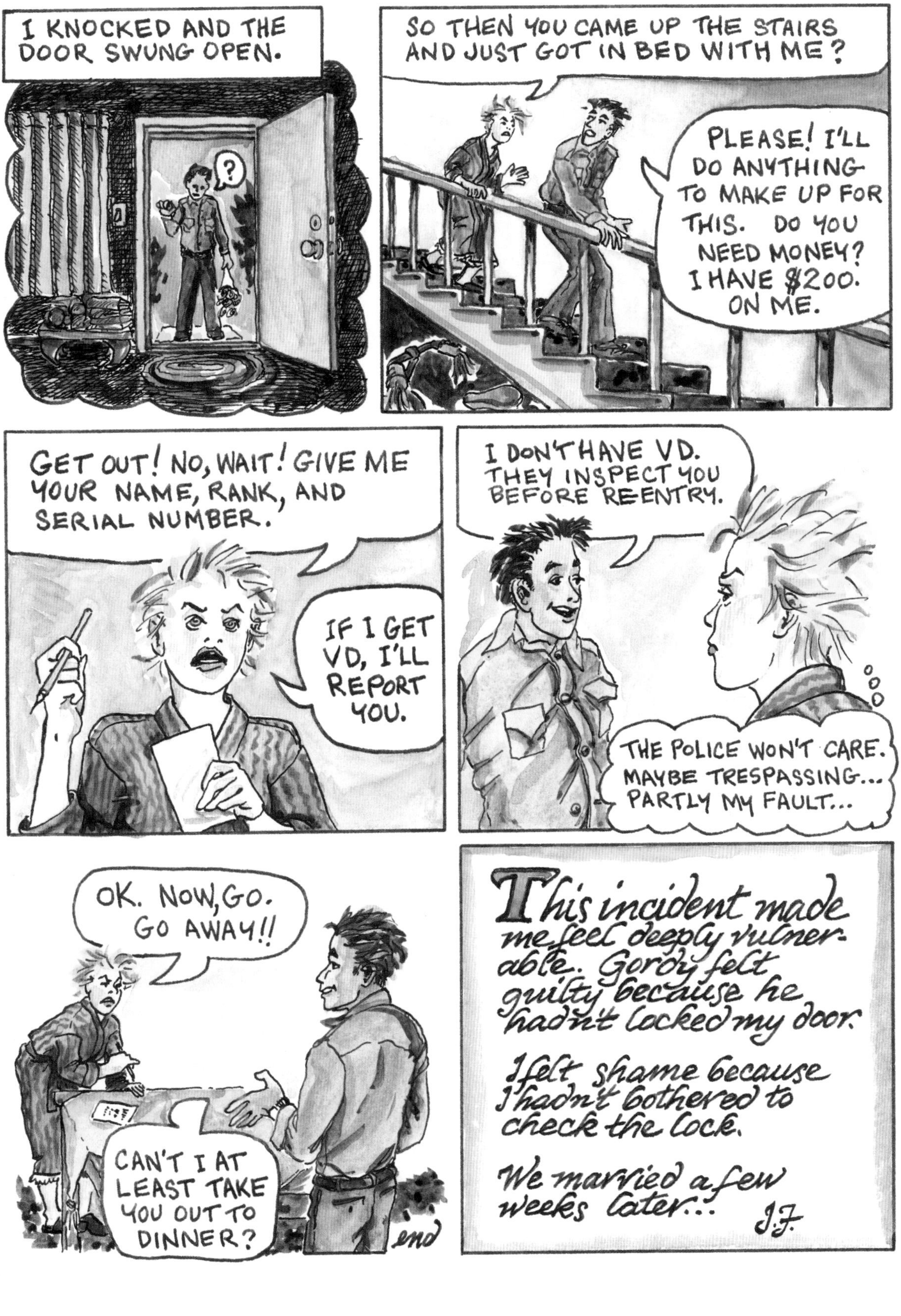
I KNOCKED AND THE DOOR SWUNG OPEN.
?
SO THEN YOU CAME UP THE STAIRS AND JUST GOT IN BED WITH ME?
PLEASE! I'LL DO ANYTHING TO MAKE UP FOR THIS. DO YOU NEED MONEY? I HAVE $200. ON ME.
GET OUT! NO, WAIT! GIVE ME YOUR NAME, RANK, AND SERIAL NUMBER.
IF I GET VD, I'LL REPORT YOU.
I DON'T HAVE VD. THEY INSPECT YOU BEFORE RE-ENTRY.
THE POLICE WON'T CARE. MAYBE TRESPASSING... PARTLY MY FAULT...
OK. NOW, GO. GO AWAY!!
CAN'T I AT LEAST TAKE YOU OUT TO DINNER?
end
This incident made me feel deeply vulnerable. Gordy felt guilty because he hadn't locked my door.
I felt shame because I hadn't bothered to check the lock.
We married a few weeks later...
J.F.

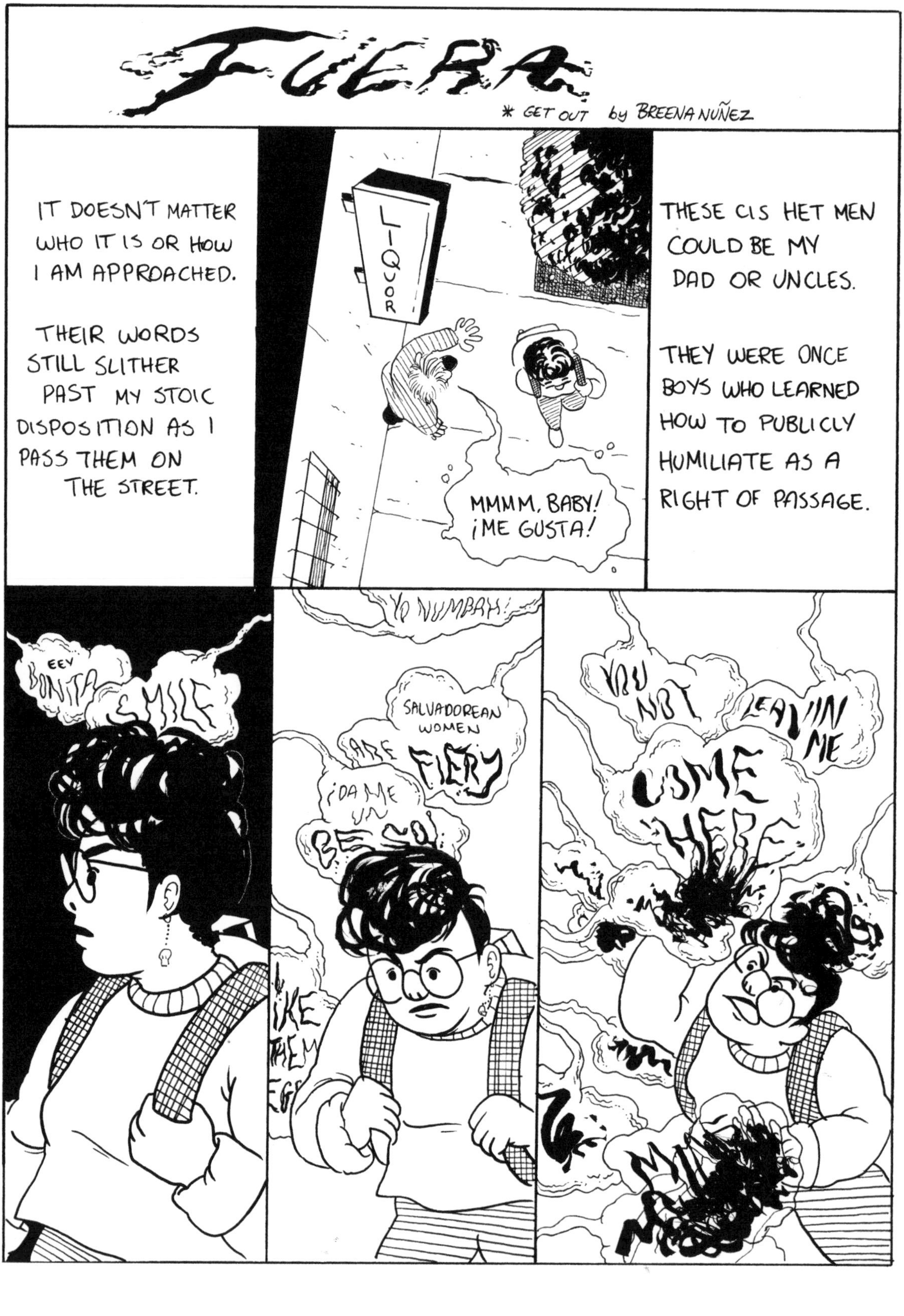
FUERA
* GET OUT by BREENA NUÑEZ
IT DOESN'T MATTER WHO IT IS OR HOW I AM APPROACHED.
THEIR WORDS STILL SLITHER PAST MY STOIC DISPOSITION AS I PASS THEM ON THE STREET.
LIQUOR
MMMM, BABY! ¡ME GUSTA!
THESE CIS HET MEN COULD BE MY DAD OR UNCLES.
THEY WERE ONCE BOYS WHO LEARNED HOW TO PUBLICLY HUMILIATE AS A RIGHT OF PASSAGE.
EEY BONITA
SMILE
YO NUMBAH!
SALVADOREAN WOMEN ARE FIERY
¡DAME UN BESO!
YOU NOT LEAVIN ME
COME HERE

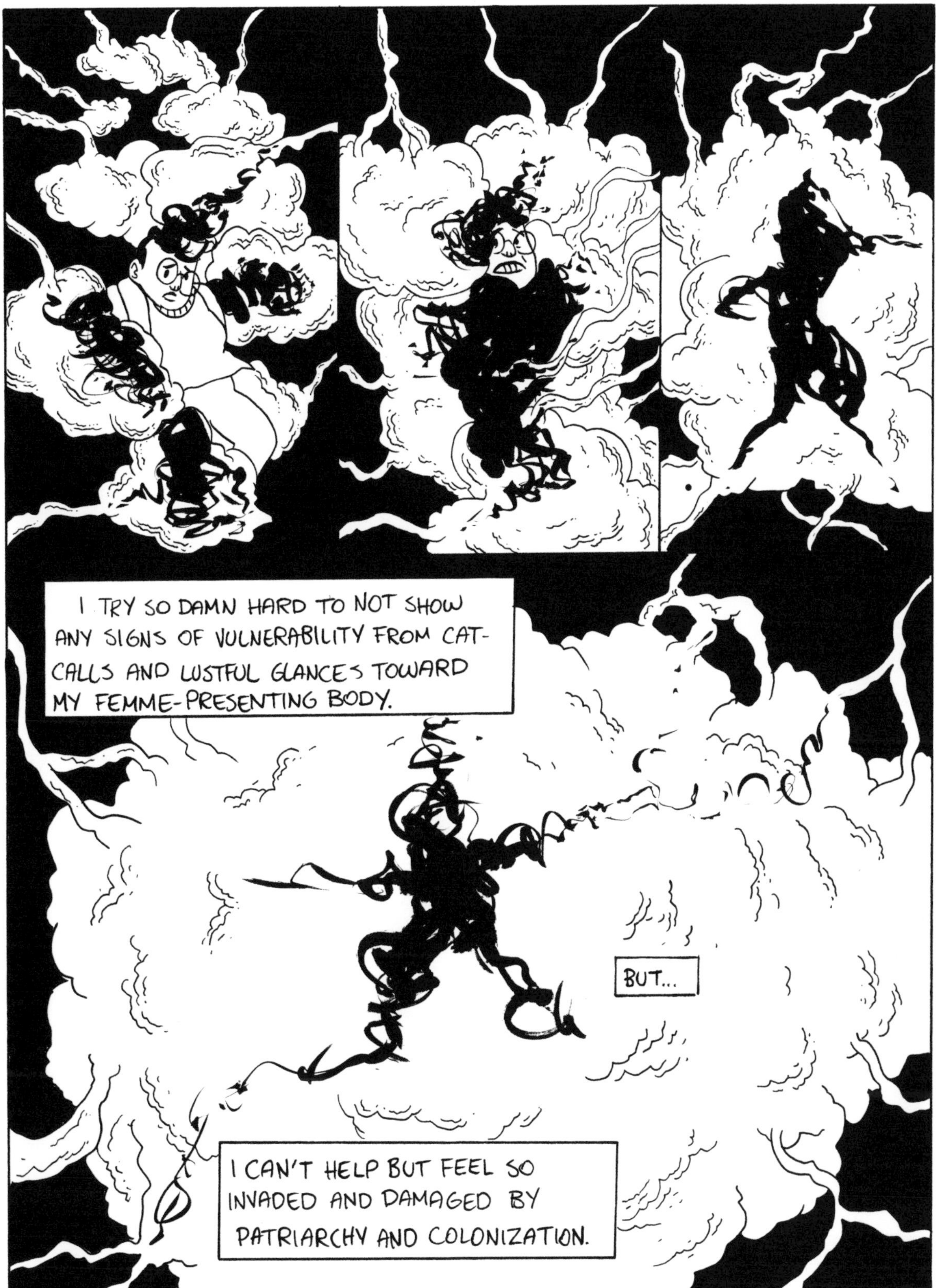
I TRY SO DAMN HARD TO NOT SHOW ANY SIGNS OF VULNERABILITY FROM CAT-CALLS AND LUSTFUL GLANCES TOWARD MY FEMME-PRESENTING BODY.
BUT...
I CAN'T HELP BUT FEEL SO INVADED AND DAMAGED BY PATRIARCHY AND COLONIZATION.

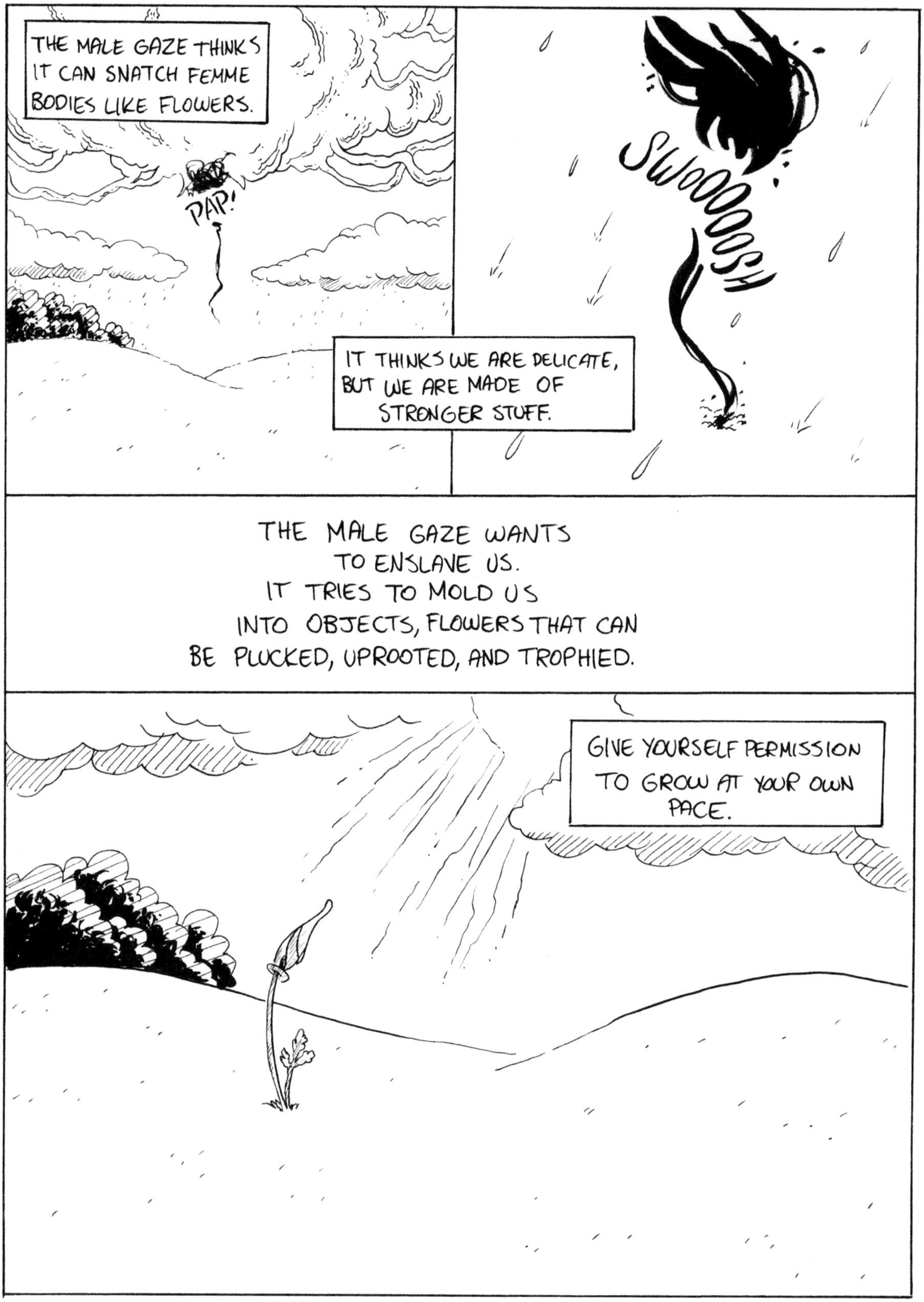
THE MALE GAZE THINKS IT CAN SNATCH FEMME BODIES LIKE FLOWERS.
PAP!
IT THINKS WE ARE DELICATE, BUT WE ARE MADE OF STRONGER STUFF.
SWOOOOOOSH
THE MALE GAZE WANTS TO ENSLAVE US.
IT TRIES TO MOLD US INTO OBJECTS, FLOWERS THAT CAN BE PLUCKED, UPROOTED, AND TROPHIED.
GIVE YOURSELF PERMISSION TO GROW AT YOUR OWN PACE.

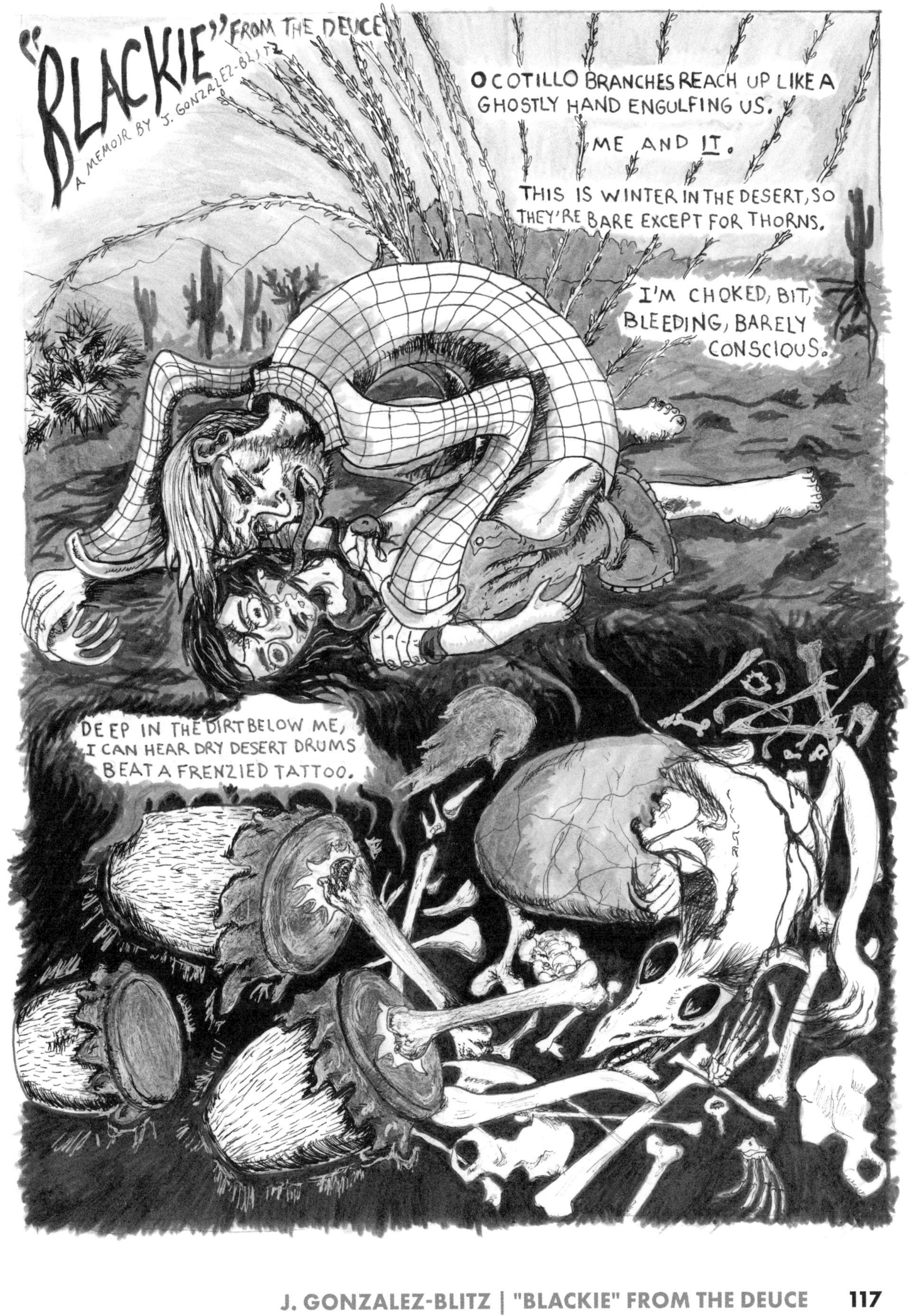
"BLACKIE" FROM THE DEUCE
A MEMOIR BY J. GONZALEZ-BLITZ
OCOTILLO BRANCHES REACH UP LIKE A GHOSTLY HAND ENGULFING US.
ME AND IT.
THIS IS WINTER IN THE DESERT, SO THEY'RE BARE EXCEPT FOR THORNS.
I'M CHOKED, BIT, BLEEDING, BARELY CONSCIOUS.
DEEP IN THE DIRT BELOW ME, I CAN HEAR DRY DESERT DRUMS BEAT A FRENZIED TATTOO.

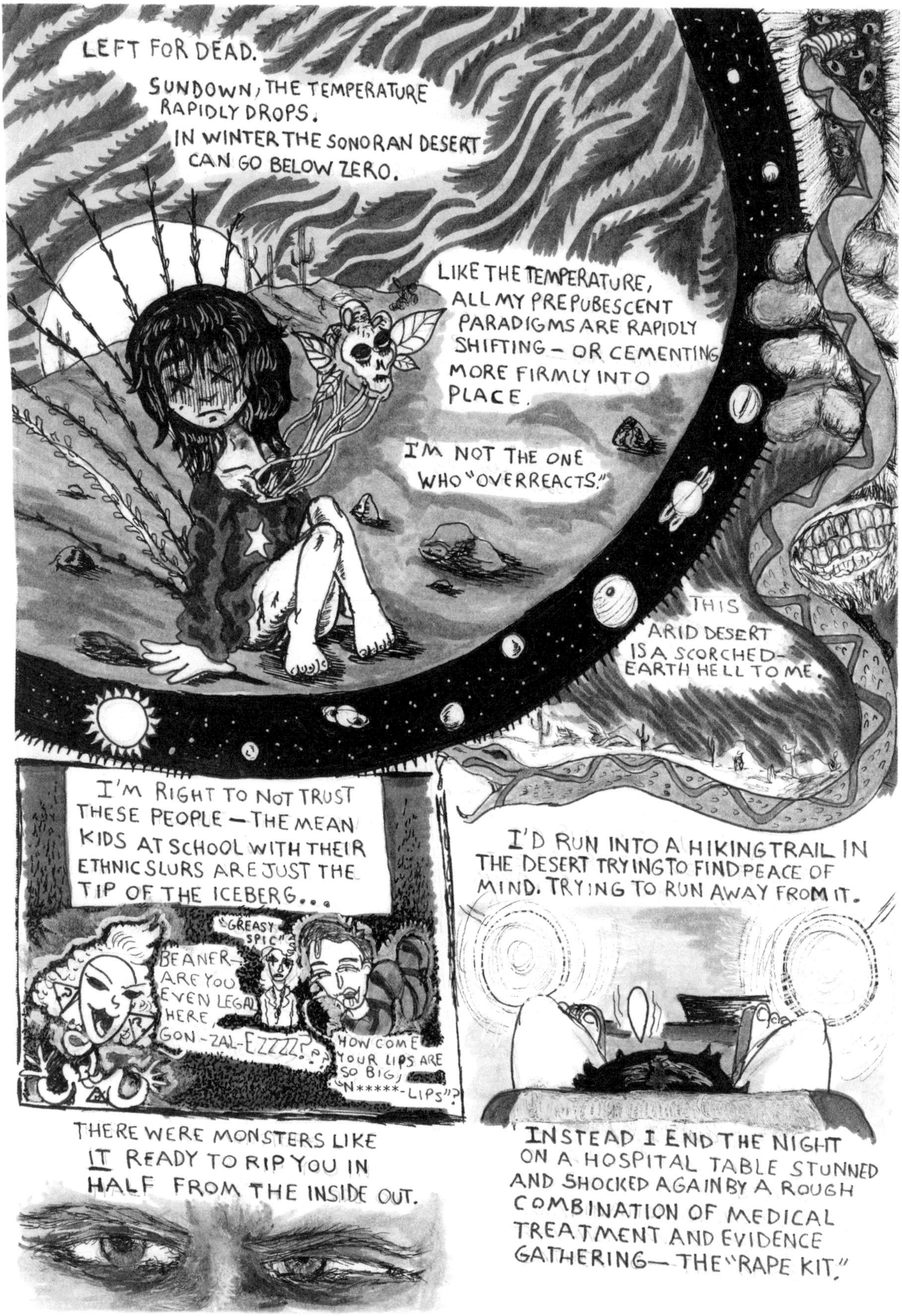

LEFT FOR DEAD.
SUNDOWN, THE TEMPERATURE RAPIDLY DROPS.
IN WINTER THE SONORAN DESERT CAN GO BELOW ZERO.
LIKE THE TEMPERATURE, ALL MY PREPUBESCENT PARADIGMS ARE RAPIDLY SHIFTING – OR CEMENTING MORE FIRMLY INTO PLACE.
I'M NOT THE ONE WHO "OVERREACTS."
THIS ARID DESERT IS A SCORCHED-EARTH HELL TO ME.
I'M RIGHT TO NOT TRUST THESE PEOPLE – THE MEAN KIDS AT SCHOOL WITH THEIR ETHNIC SLURS ARE JUST THE TIP OF THE ICEBERG...
"GREASY SPIC"
BEANER – ARE YOU EVEN LEGAL HERE, GON-ZAL-EZZZZ?
HOW COME YOUR LIPS ARE SO BIG, "N*****-LIPS"?
THERE WERE MONSTERS LIKE IT READY TO RIP YOU IN HALF FROM THE INSIDE OUT.
I'D RUN INTO A HIKING TRAIL IN THE DESERT TRYING TO FIND PEACE OF MIND. TRYING TO RUN AWAY FROM IT.
INSTEAD I END THE NIGHT ON A HOSPITAL TABLE STUNNED AND SHOCKED AGAIN BY A ROUGH COMBINATION OF MEDICAL TREATMENT AND EVIDENCE GATHERING— THE "RAPE KIT."

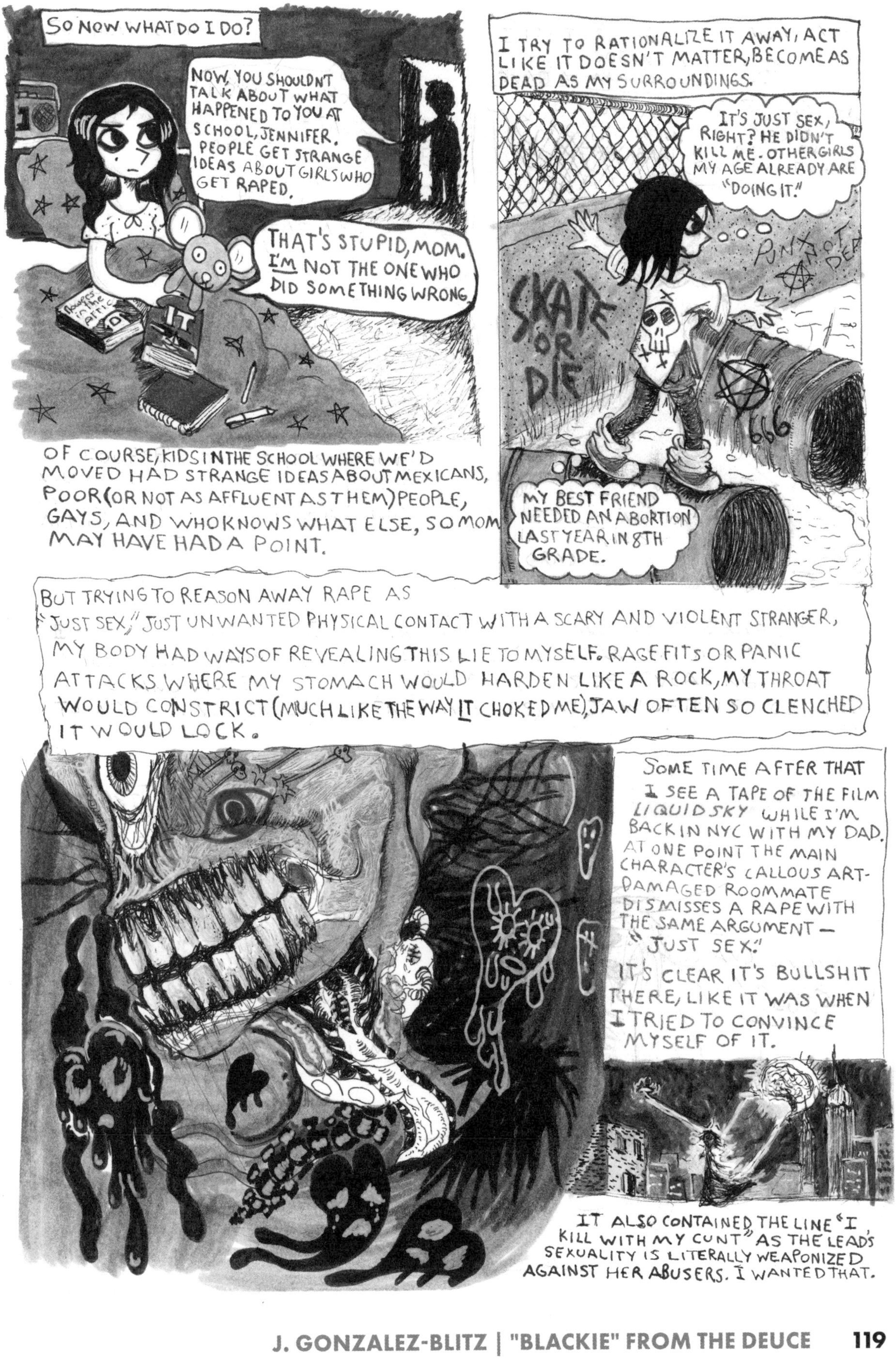
SO NOW WHAT DO I DO?
NOW, YOU SHOULDN'T TALK ABOUT WHAT HAPPENED TO YOU AT SCHOOL, JENNIFER. PEOPLE GET STRANGE IDEAS ABOUT GIRLS WHO GET RAPED.
THAT'S STUPID, MOM. I'M NOT THE ONE WHO DID SOMETHING WRONG.
IT
OF COURSE, KIDS IN THE SCHOOL WHERE WE'D MOVED HAD STRANGE IDEAS ABOUT MEXICANS, POOR (OR NOT AS AFFLUENT AS THEM) PEOPLE, GAYS, AND WHO KNOWS WHAT ELSE, SO MOM MAY HAVE HAD A POINT.
I TRY TO RATIONALIZE IT AWAY, ACT LIKE IT DOESN'T MATTER, BECOME AS DEAD AS MY SURROUNDINGS.
IT'S JUST SEX, RIGHT? HE DIDN'T KILL ME. OTHER GIRLS MY AGE ALREADY ARE "DOING IT."
SKATE OR DIE
666
MY BEST FRIEND NEEDED AN ABORTION LAST YEAR IN 8TH GRADE.
BUT TRYING TO REASON AWAY RAPE AS "JUST SEX," JUST UNWANTED PHYSICAL CONTACT WITH A SCARY AND VIOLENT STRANGER, MY BODY HAD WAYS OF REVEALING THIS LIE TO MYSELF. RAGE FITS OR PANIC ATTACKS WHERE MY STOMACH WOULD HARDEN LIKE A ROCK, MY THROAT WOULD CONSTRICT (MUCH LIKE THE WAY IT CHOKED ME), JAW OFTEN SO CLENCHED IT WOULD LOCK.
SOME TIME AFTER THAT I SEE A TAPE OF THE FILM LIQUID SKY WHILE I'M BACK IN NYC WITH MY DAD. AT ONE POINT THE MAIN CHARACTER'S CALLOUS ART-DAMAGED ROOMMATE DISMISSES A RAPE WITH THE SAME ARGUMENT — "JUST SEX."
IT'S CLEAR IT'S BULLSHIT THERE, LIKE IT WAS WHEN I TRIED TO CONVINCE MYSELF OF IT.
IT ALSO CONTAINED THE LINE "I KILL WITH MY CUNT" AS THE LEAD'S SEXUALITY IS LITERALLY WEAPONIZED AGAINST HER ABUSERS. I WANTED THAT.

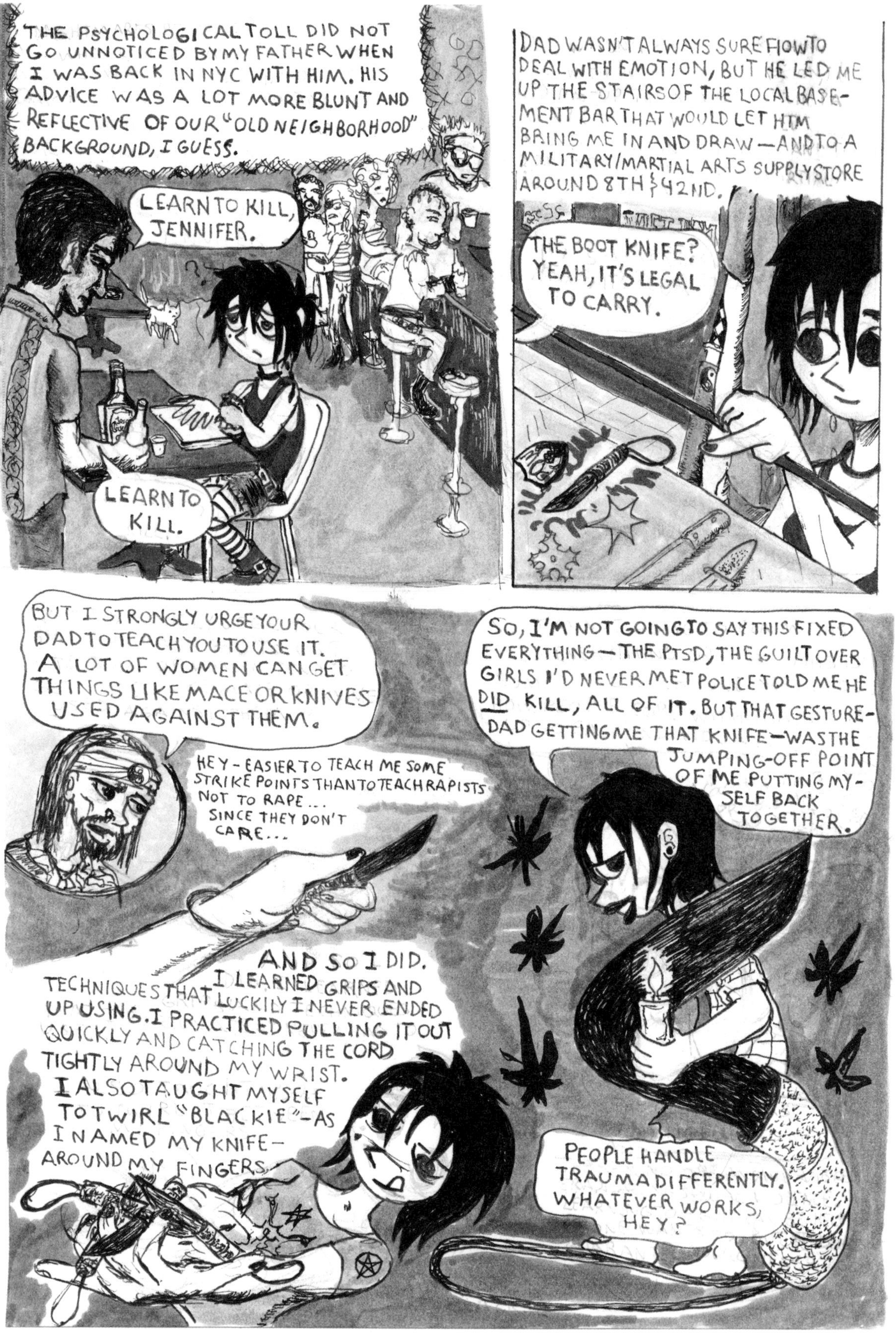
THE PSYCHOLOGICAL TOLL DID NOT GO UNNOTICED BY MY FATHER WHEN I WAS BACK IN NYC WITH HIM. HIS ADVICE WAS A LOT MORE BLUNT AND REFLECTIVE OF OUR "OLD NEIGHBORHOOD" BACKGROUND, I GUESS.
LEARN TO KILL, JENNIFER.
LEARN TO KILL.
DAD WASN'T ALWAYS SURE HOW TO DEAL WITH EMOTION, BUT HE LED ME UP THE STAIRS OF THE LOCAL BASEMENT BAR THAT WOULD LET HIM BRING ME IN AND DRAW—AND TO A MILITARY/MARTIAL ARTS SUPPLY STORE AROUND 8TH & 42ND.
THE BOOT KNIFE? YEAH, IT'S LEGAL TO CARRY.
BUT I STRONGLY URGE YOUR DAD TO TEACH YOU TO USE IT. A LOT OF WOMEN CAN GET THINGS LIKE MACE OR KNIVES USED AGAINST THEM.
HEY - EASIER TO TEACH ME SOME STRIKE POINTS THAN TO TEACH RAPISTS NOT TO RAPE... SINCE THEY DON'T CARE...
SO, I'M NOT GOING TO SAY THIS FIXED EVERYTHING—THE PTSD, THE GUILT OVER GIRLS I'D NEVER MET POLICE TOLD ME HE DID KILL, ALL OF IT. BUT THAT GESTURE-DAD GETTING ME THAT KNIFE—WAS THE JUMPING-OFF POINT OF ME PUTTING MYSELF BACK TOGETHER.
AND SO I DID. I LEARNED GRIPS AND TECHNIQUES THAT LUCKILY I NEVER ENDED UP USING. I PRACTICED PULLING IT OUT QUICKLY AND CATCHING THE CORD TIGHTLY AROUND MY WRIST. I ALSO TAUGHT MYSELF TO TWIRL "BLACKIE"-AS I NAMED MY KNIFE- AROUND MY FINGERS.
PEOPLE HANDLE TRAUMA DIFFERENTLY. WHATEVER WORKS, HEY?

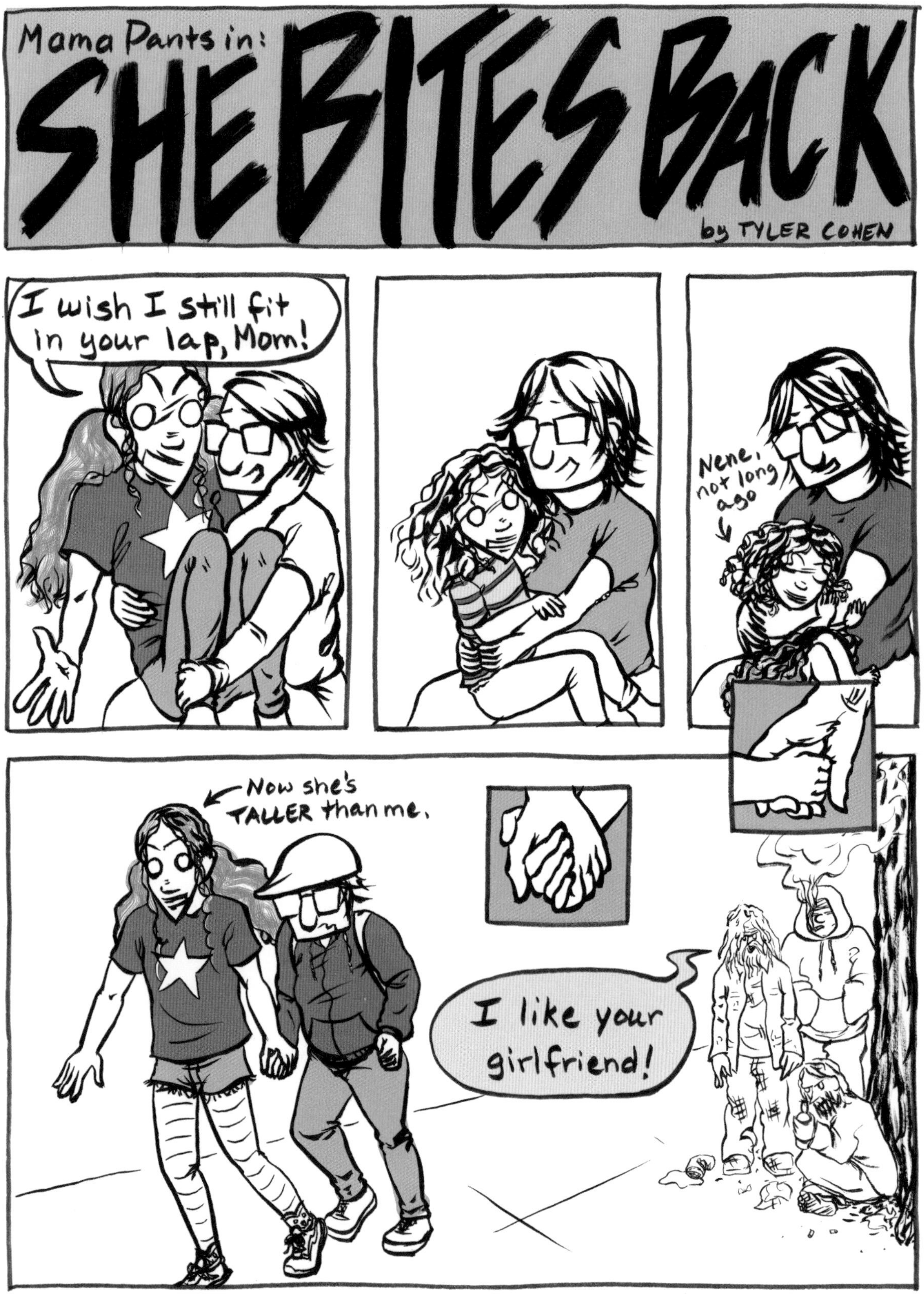
Mama Pants in:
SHE BITES BACK
by TYLER COHEN
I wish I still fit in your lap, Mom!
Nene, not long ago
Now she's TALLER than me.
I like your girlfriend!

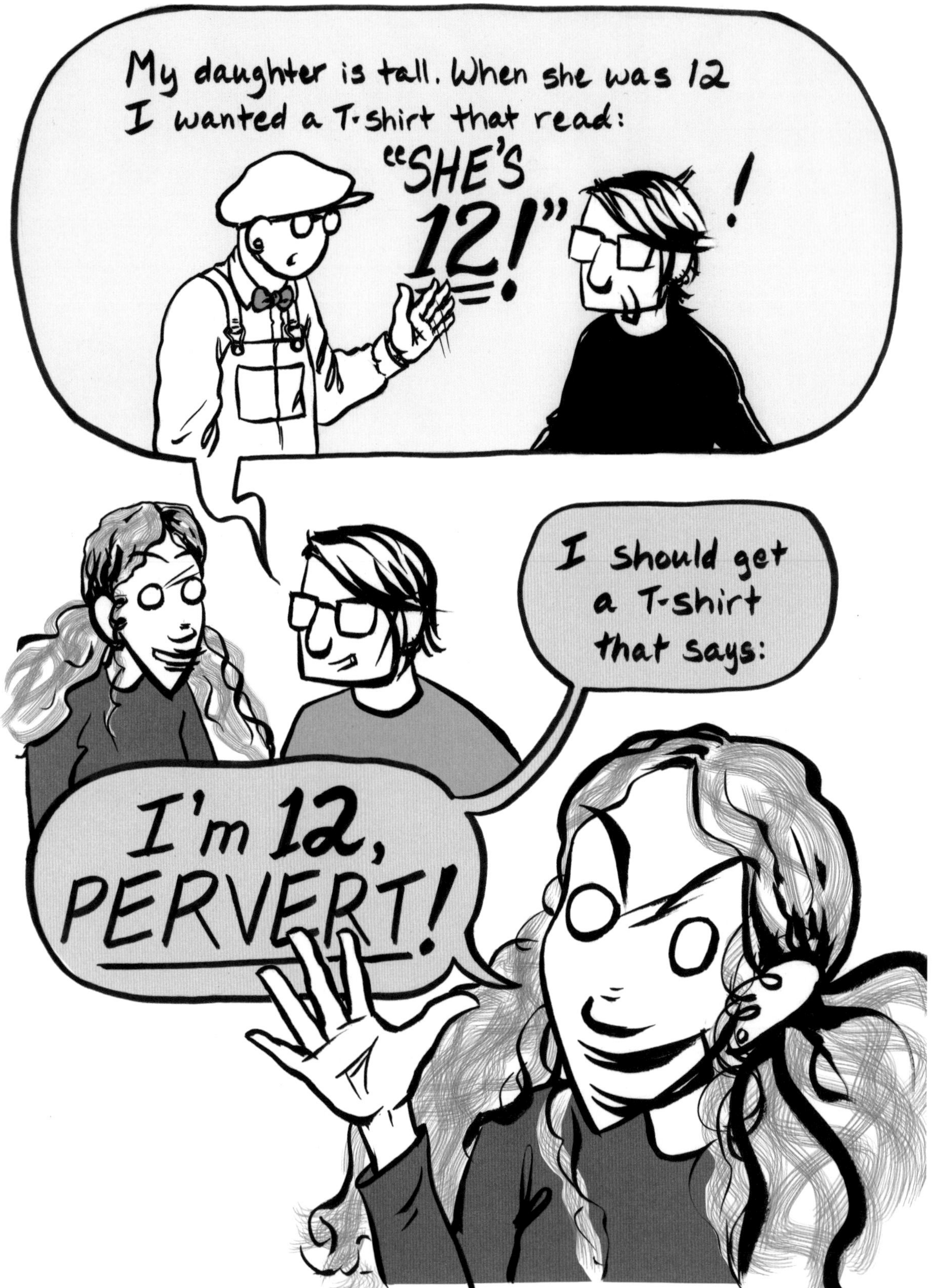
My daughter is tall. When she was 12 I wanted a T-shirt that read:
"SHE'S 12!"
!
I should get a T-shirt that says:
I'm 12, PERVERT!

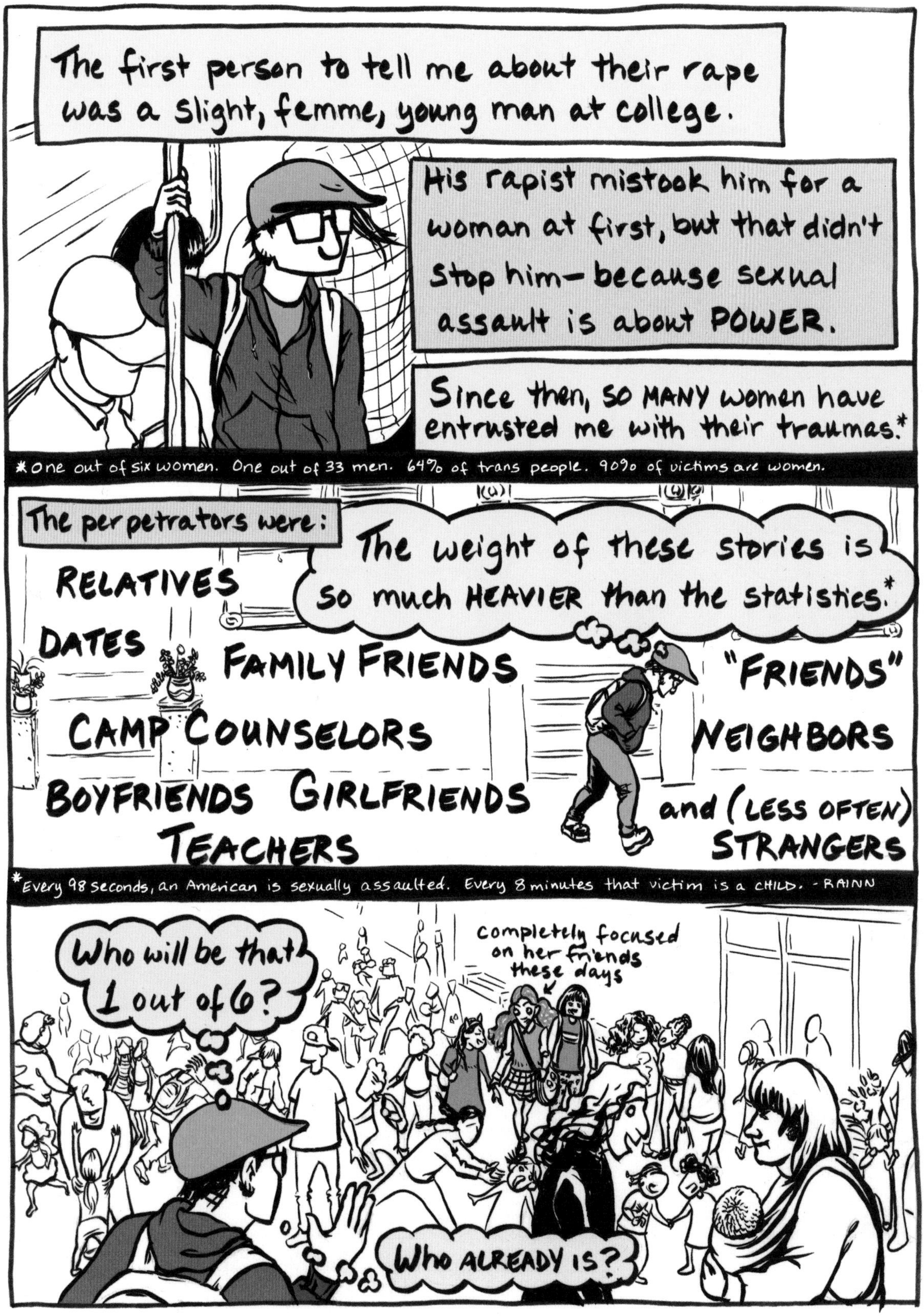

The first person to tell me about their rape was a slight, femme, young man at college.
His rapist mistook him for a woman at first, but that didn't stop him— because sexual assault is about POWER.
Since then, SO MANY women have entrusted me with their traumas.*
*One out of six women. One out of 33 men. 64% of trans people. 90% of victims are women.
The perpetrators were:
The weight of these stories is so much HEAVIER than the statistics.*
RELATIVES
DATES
FAMILY FRIENDS
"FRIENDS"
CAMP COUNSELORS
NEIGHBORS
BOYFRIENDS GIRLFRIENDS
TEACHERS
and (LESS OFTEN) STRANGERS
*Every 98 seconds, an American is sexually assaulted. Every 8 minutes that victim is a CHILD. -RAINN
Who will be that 1 out of 6?
completely focused on her friends these days
Who ALREADY is?

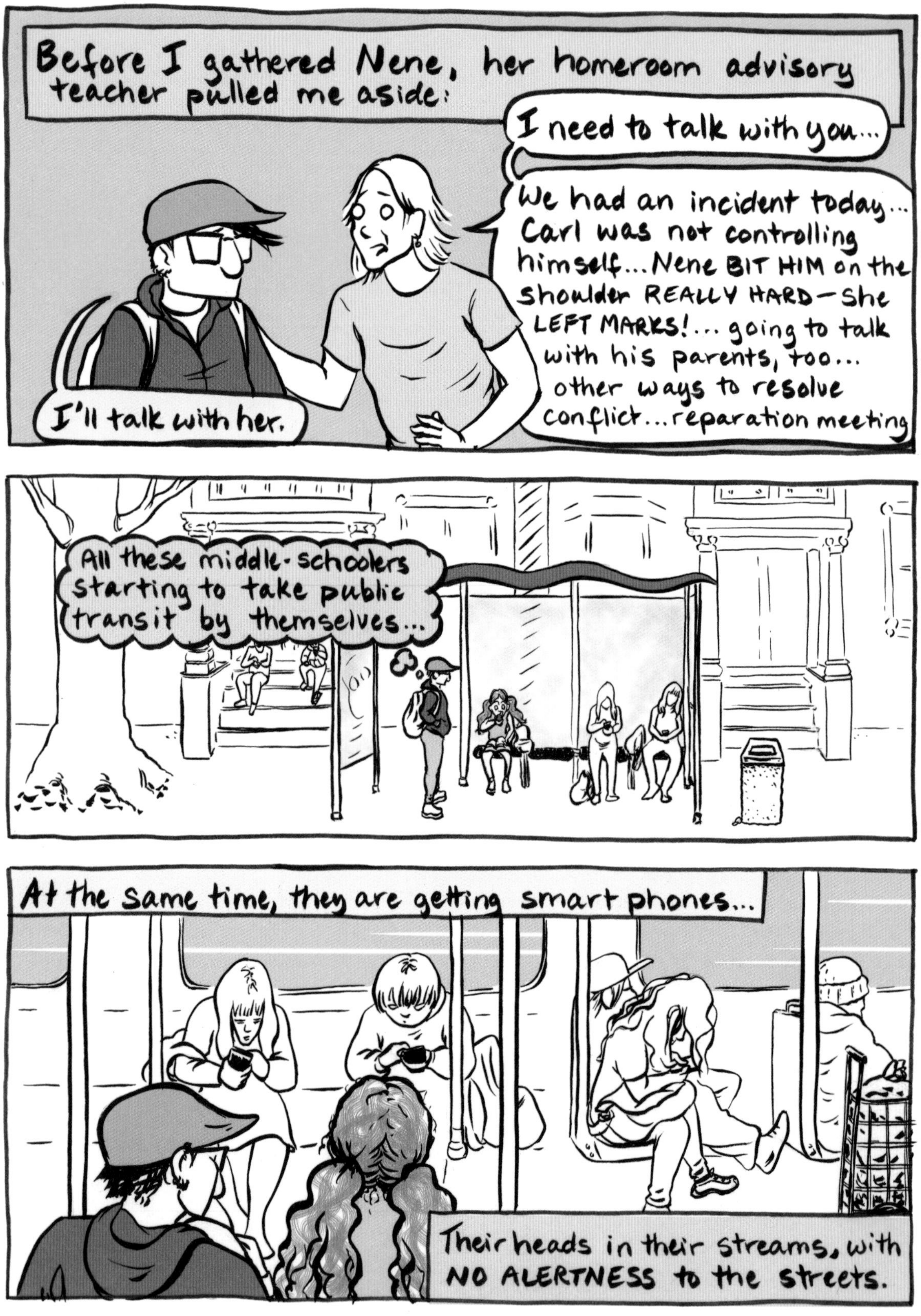
Before I gathered Nene, her homeroom advisory teacher pulled me aside:
I need to talk with you...
We had an incident today... Carl was not controlling himself... Nene BIT HIM on the shoulder REALLY HARD—She LEFT MARKS!... going to talk with his parents, too... other ways to resolve conflict... reparation meeting
I'll talk with her.
All these middle-schoolers starting to take public transit by themselves...
At the same time, they are getting smart phones...
Their heads in their streams, with NO ALERTNESS to the streets.

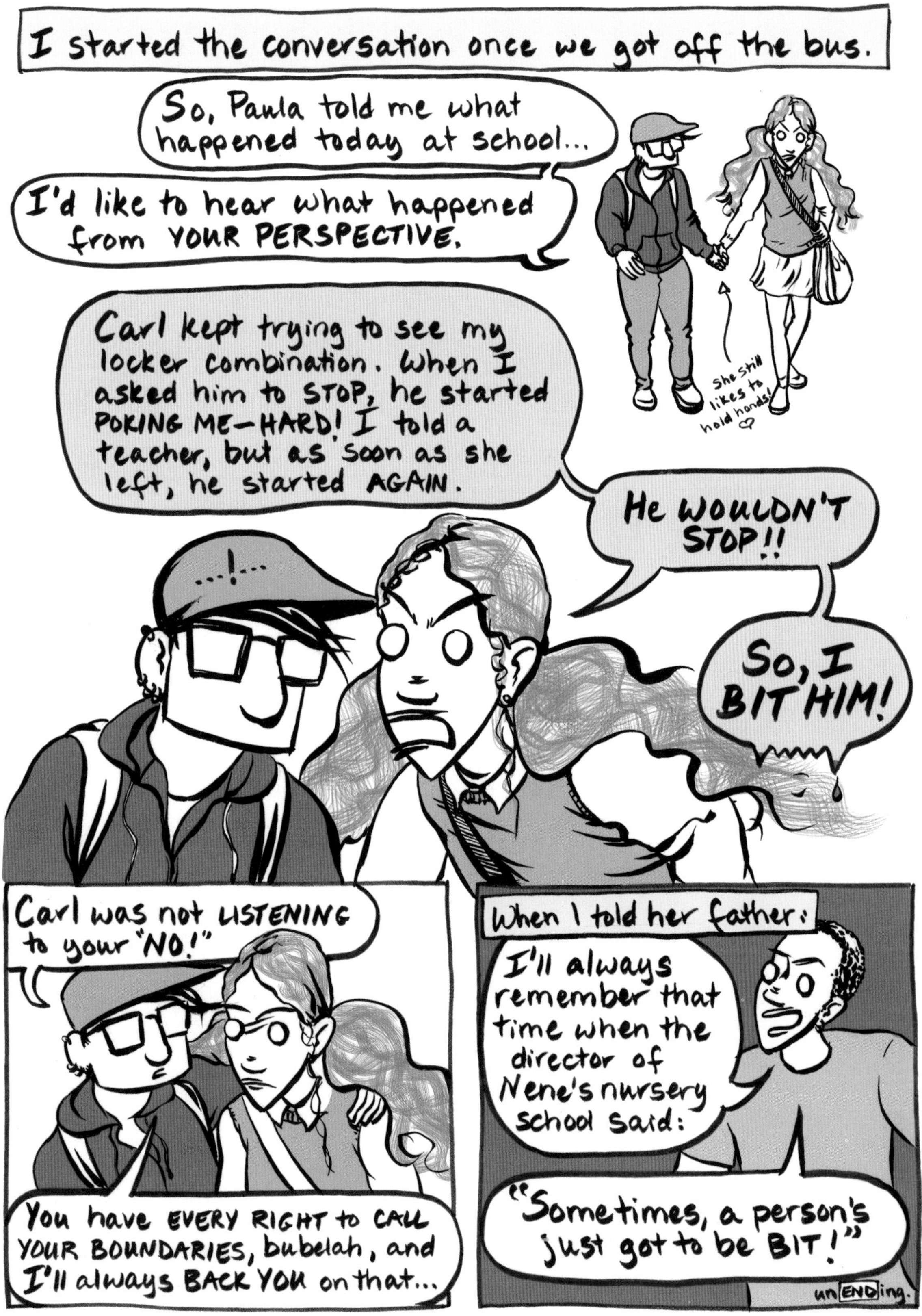
I started the conversation once we got off the bus.
So, Paula told me what happened today at school...
I'd like to hear what happened from YOUR PERSPECTIVE.
She still likes to hold hands!
Carl kept trying to see my locker combination. When I asked him to STOP, he started POKING ME—HARD! I told a teacher, but as soon as she left, he started AGAIN.
He WOULDN'T STOP!!
So, I BIT HIM!
Carl was not LISTENING to your "NO!"
You have EVERY RIGHT to CALL YOUR BOUNDARIES, bubelah, and I'll always BACK YOU on that...
When I told her father:
I'll always remember that time when the director of Nene's nursery school said:
"Sometimes, a person's just got to be BIT!"
unENDing.

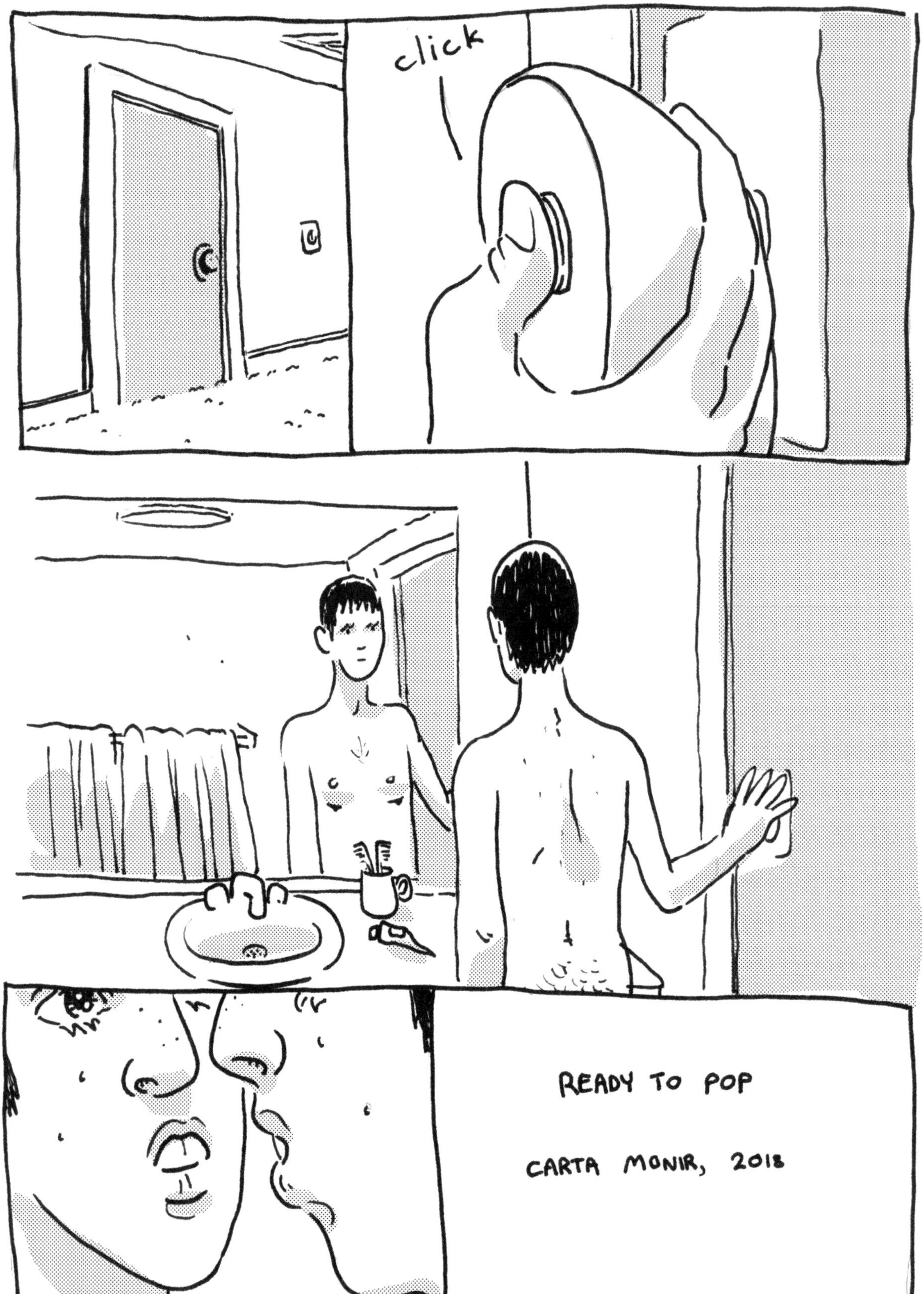
click
READY TO POP
CARTA MONIR, 2018

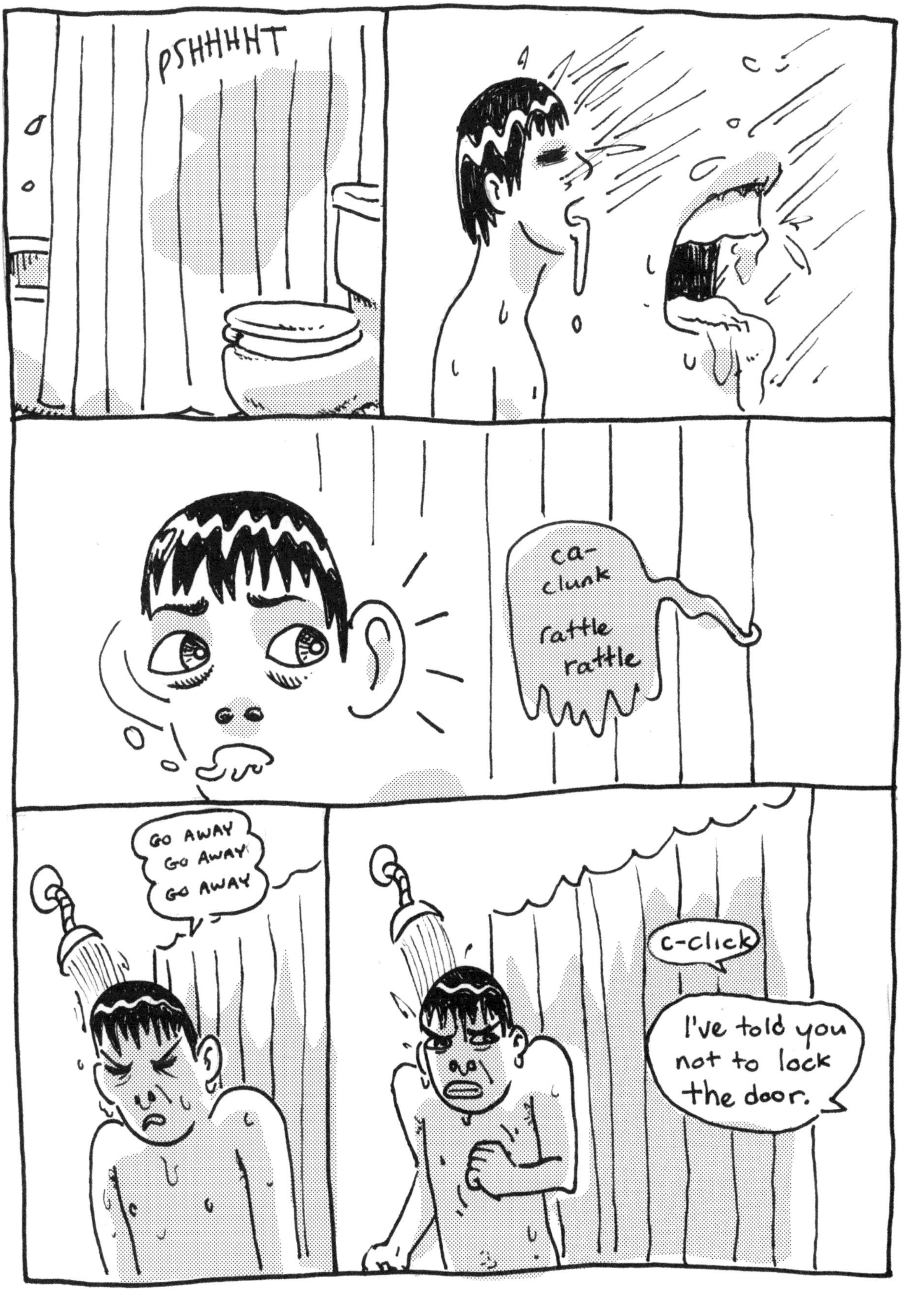
PSHHHHT
ca-
clunk
rattle
rattle
GO AWAY
GO AWAY
GO AWAY
c-click
I've told you not to lock the door.

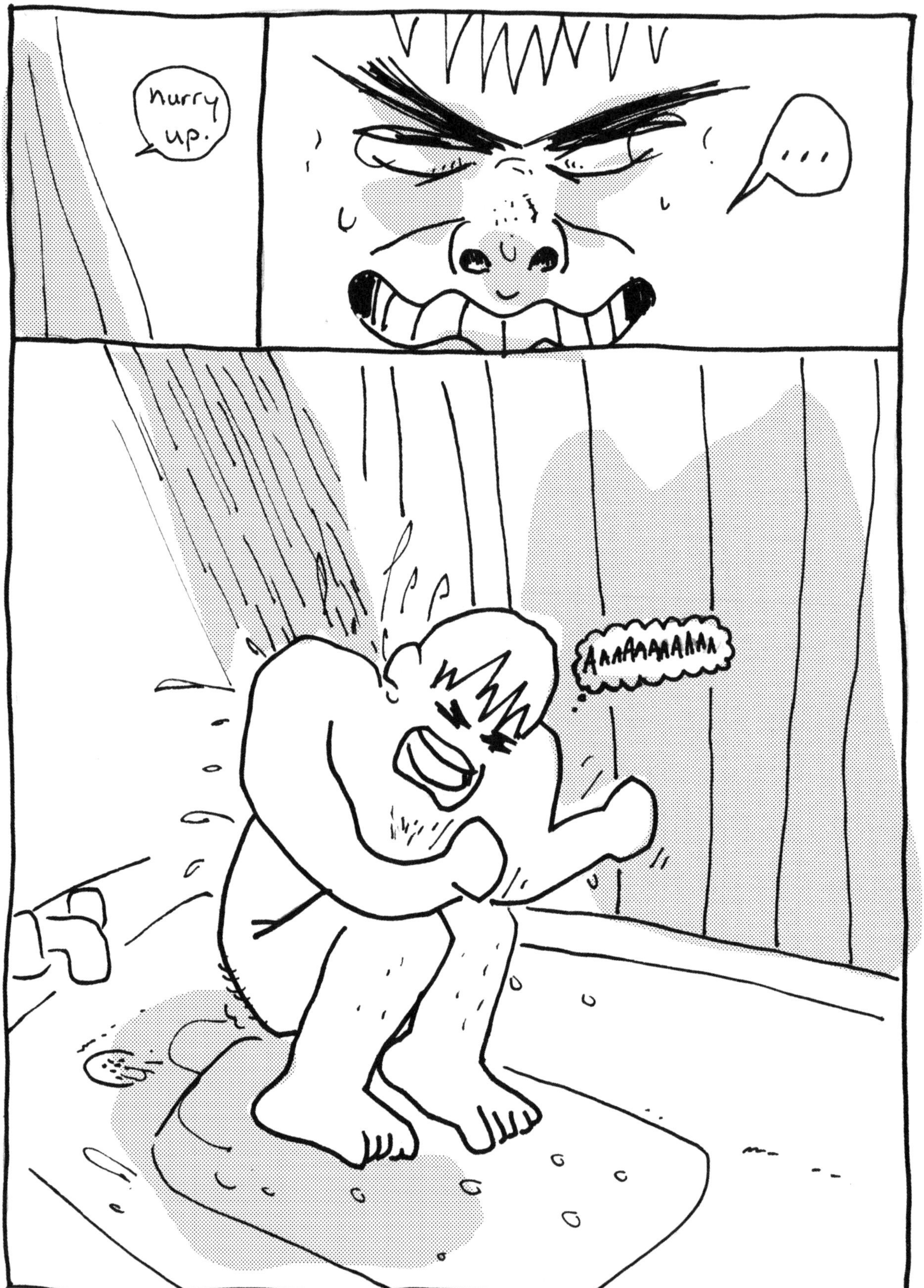
hurry up.
...
AAAAAAAAAA

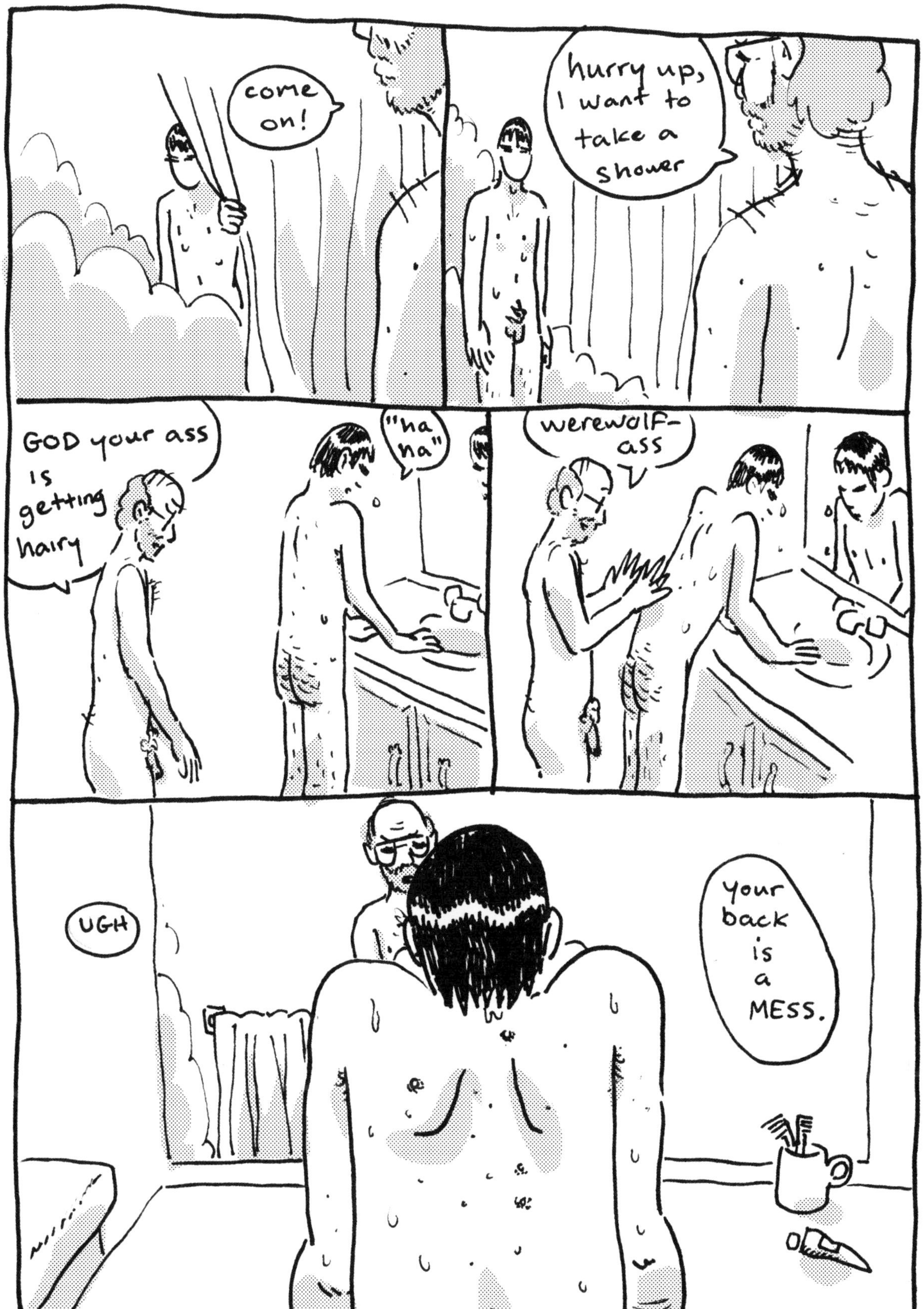
come on!
hurry up, I want to take a shower
GOD your ass is getting hairy
"ha ha"
werewolf-ass
UGH
your back is a MESS.

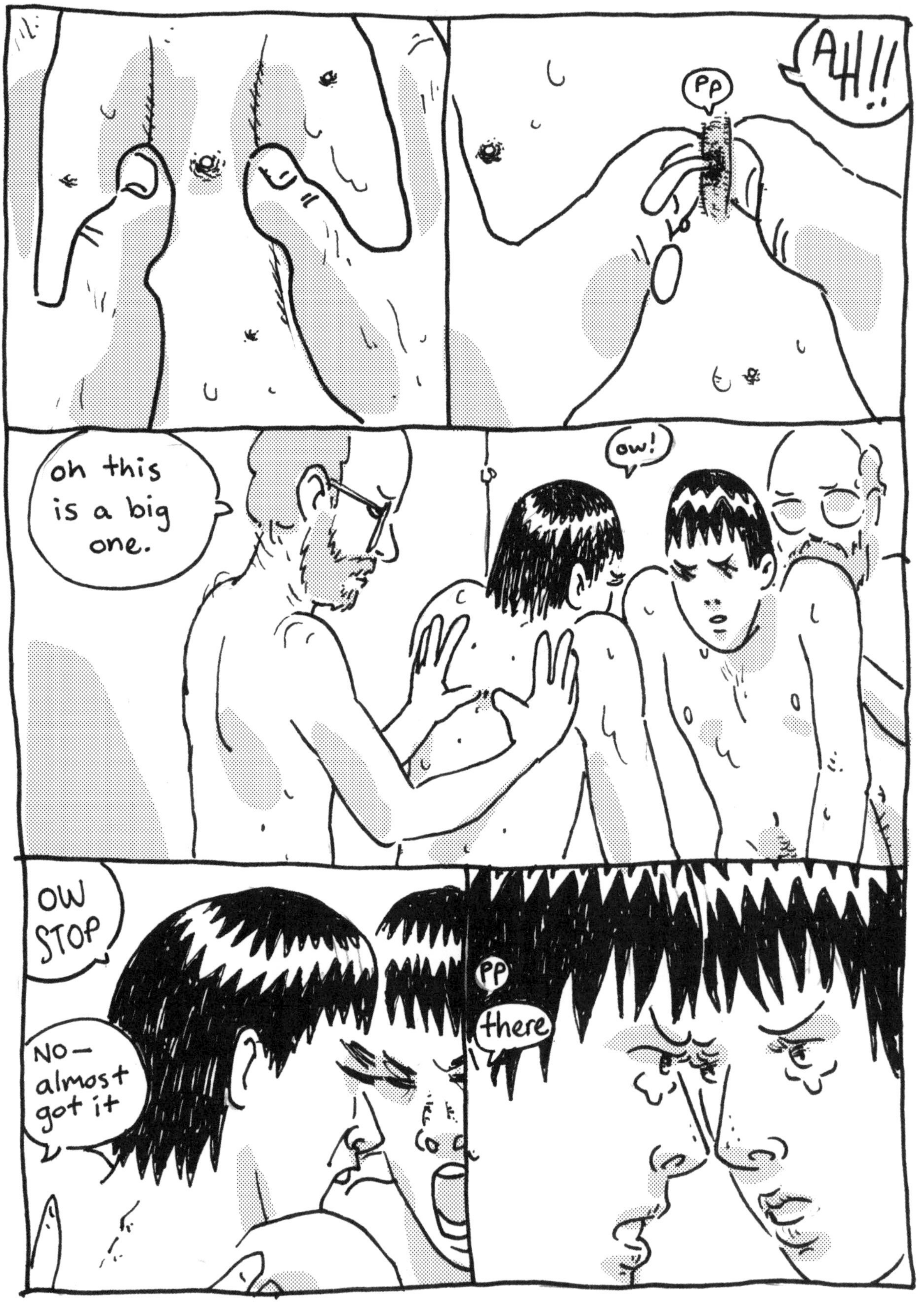
PP
AH!!
oh this is a big one.
ow!
OW STOP
No— almost got it
PP
there

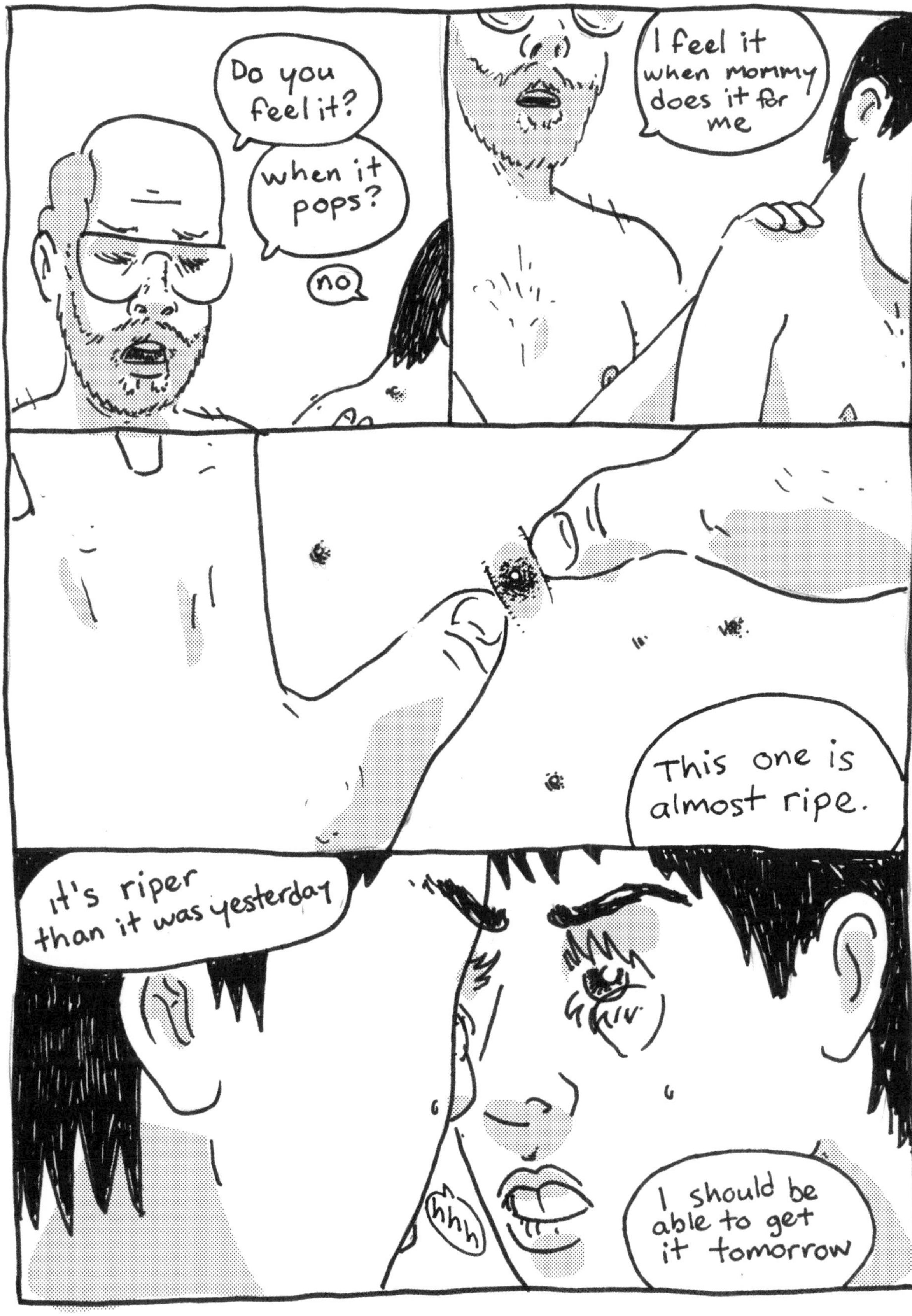
Do you feel it?
when it pops?
no
I feel it when mommy does it for me
This one is almost ripe.
it's riper than it was yesterday
hhh
I should be able to get it tomorrow

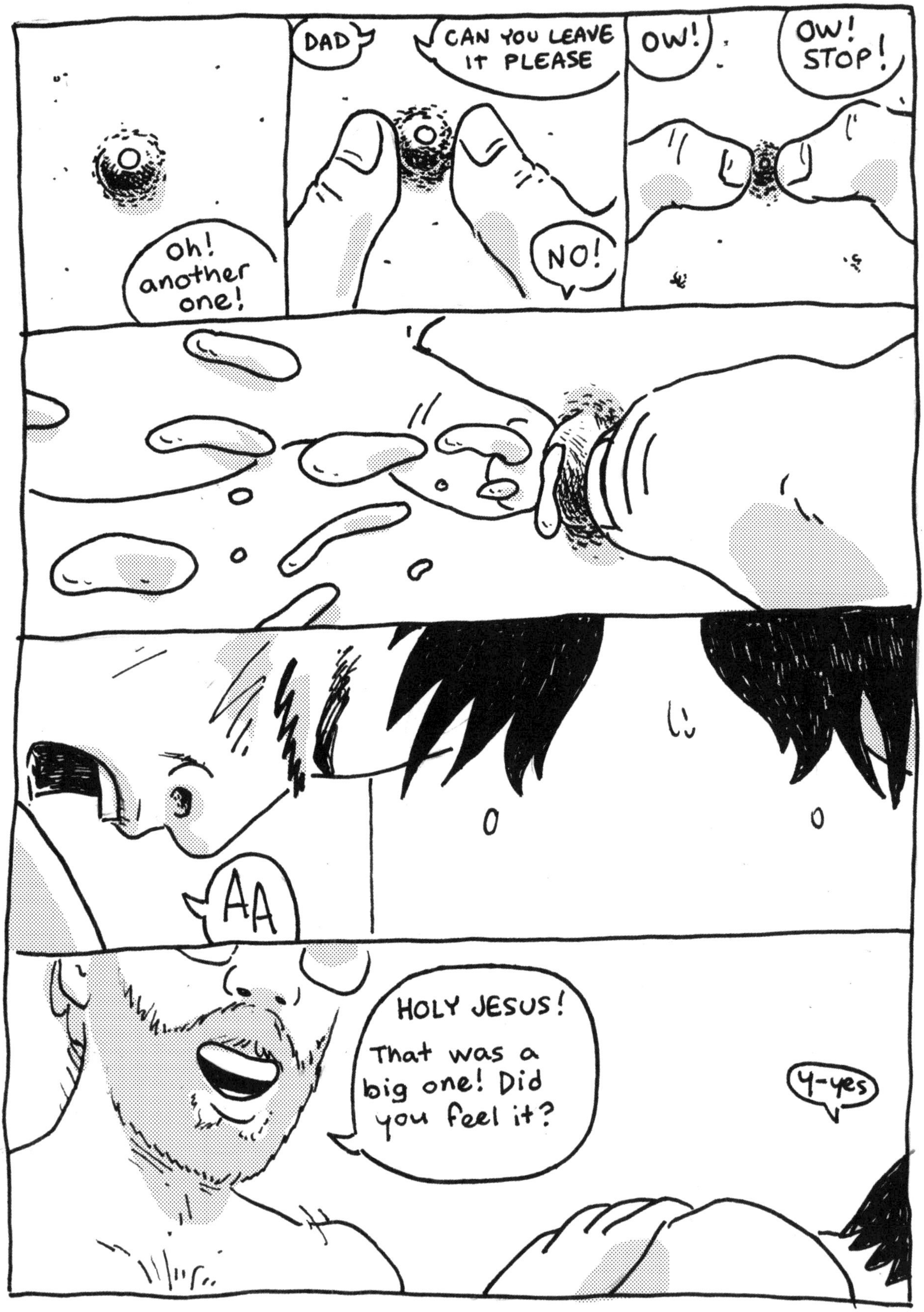
Oh! another one!
DAD
CAN YOU LEAVE IT PLEASE
NO!
OW!
OW! STOP!
AA
HOLY JESUS!
That was a big one! Did you feel it?
y-yes

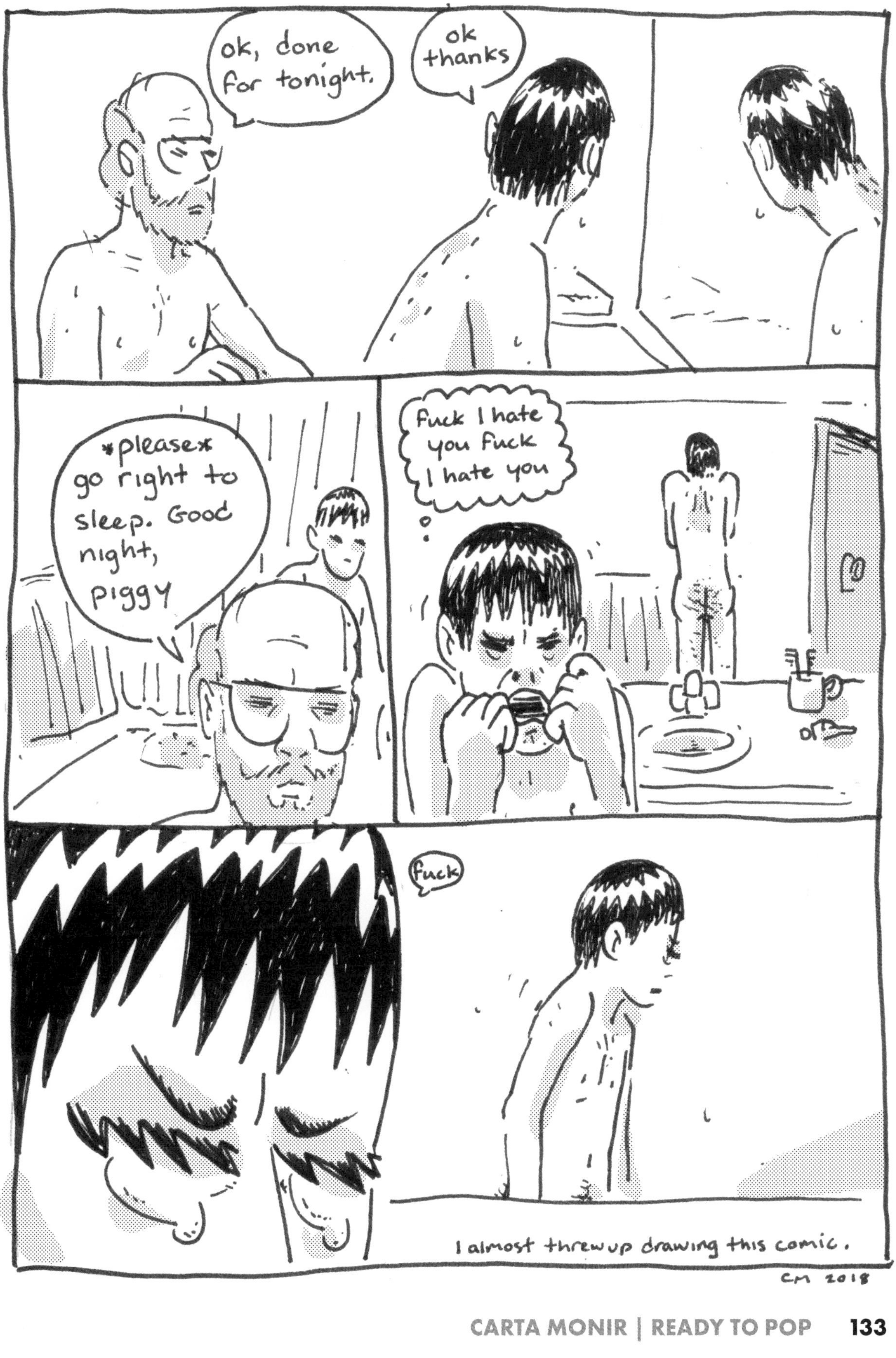
ok, done for tonight.
ok thanks
please go right to sleep. Good night, piggy
fuck I hate you fuck I hate you
fuck
I almost threw up drawing this comic.
CM 2018

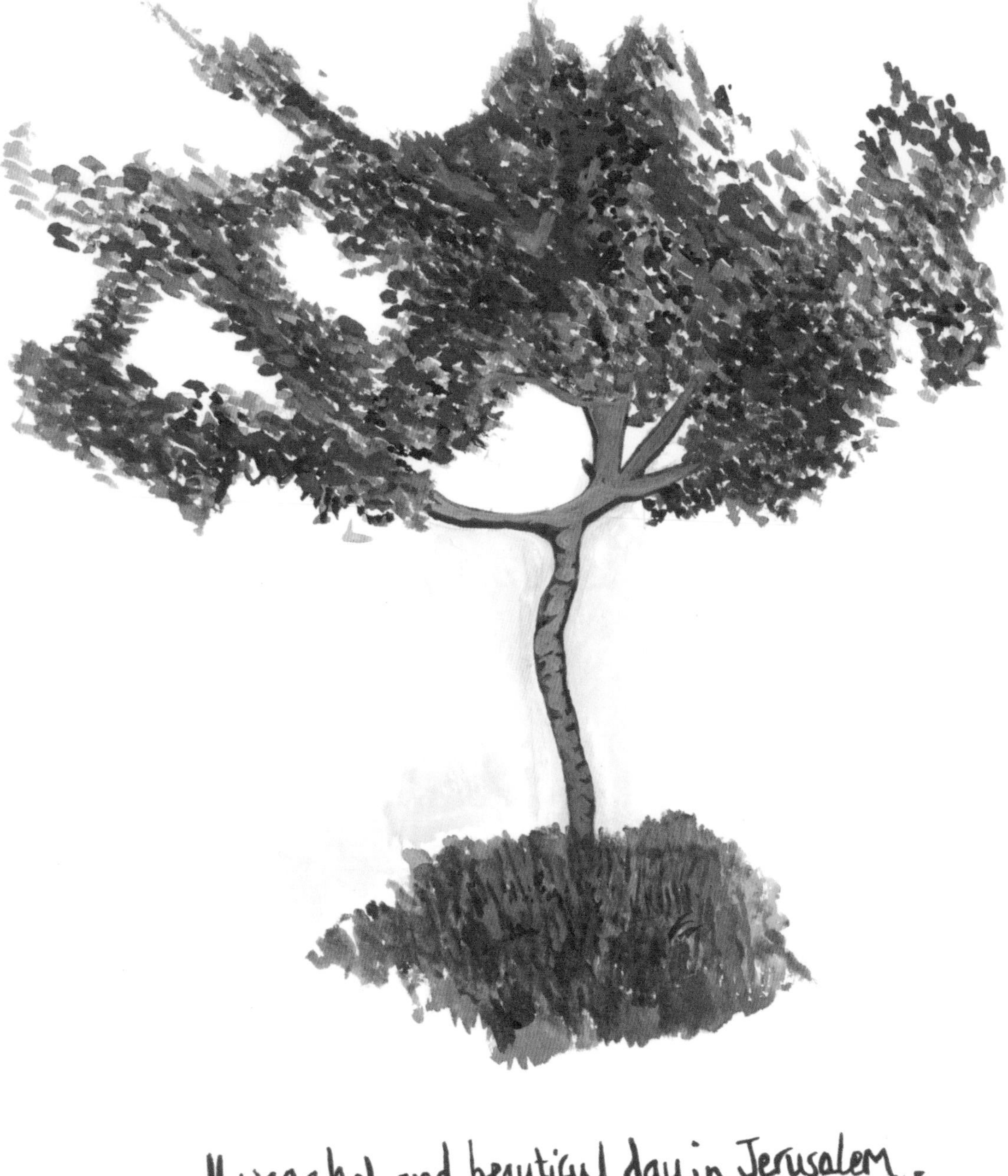

It was a hot and beautiful day in Jerusalem.

I went for a walk along the Talpiot Promenade.

I recall seeing the man from a distance. And then I was drowning in the grass. I screamed and shouted. I pulled at his face. He bit me.

When people came, he ran away. They took me to a police station.
The police officer took away my skirt. There was blood on it.
His? or mine?

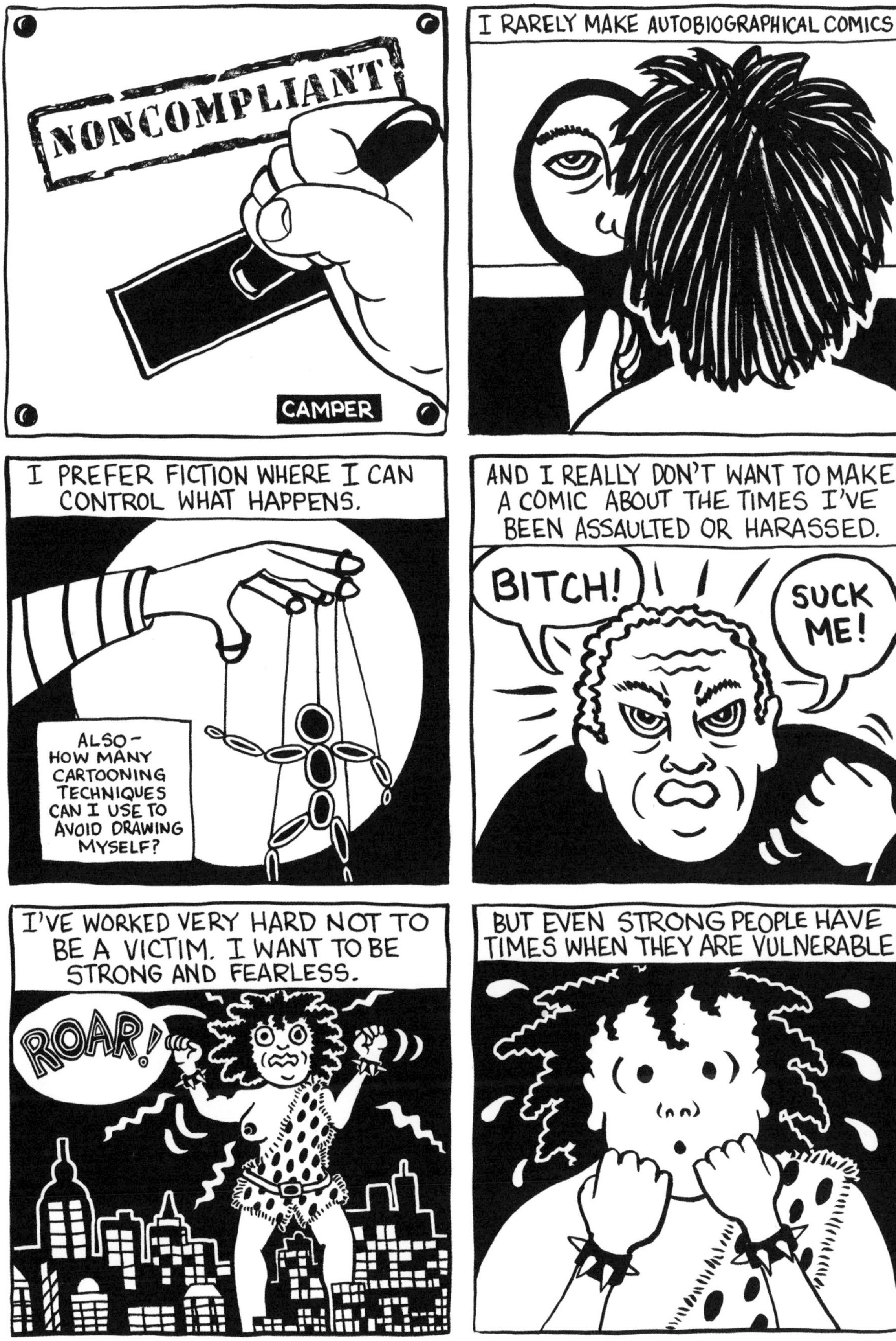
NONCOMPLIANT
CAMPER
I RARELY MAKE AUTOBIOGRAPHICAL COMICS.
I PREFER FICTION WHERE I CAN CONTROL WHAT HAPPENS.
ALSO- HOW MANY CARTOONING TECHNIQUES CAN I USE TO AVOID DRAWING MYSELF?
AND I REALLY DON'T WANT TO MAKE A COMIC ABOUT THE TIMES I'VE BEEN ASSAULTED OR HARASSED.
BITCH!
SUCK ME!
I'VE WORKED VERY HARD NOT TO BE A VICTIM. I WANT TO BE STRONG AND FEARLESS.
ROAR!
BUT EVEN STRONG PEOPLE HAVE TIMES WHEN THEY ARE VULNERABLE.

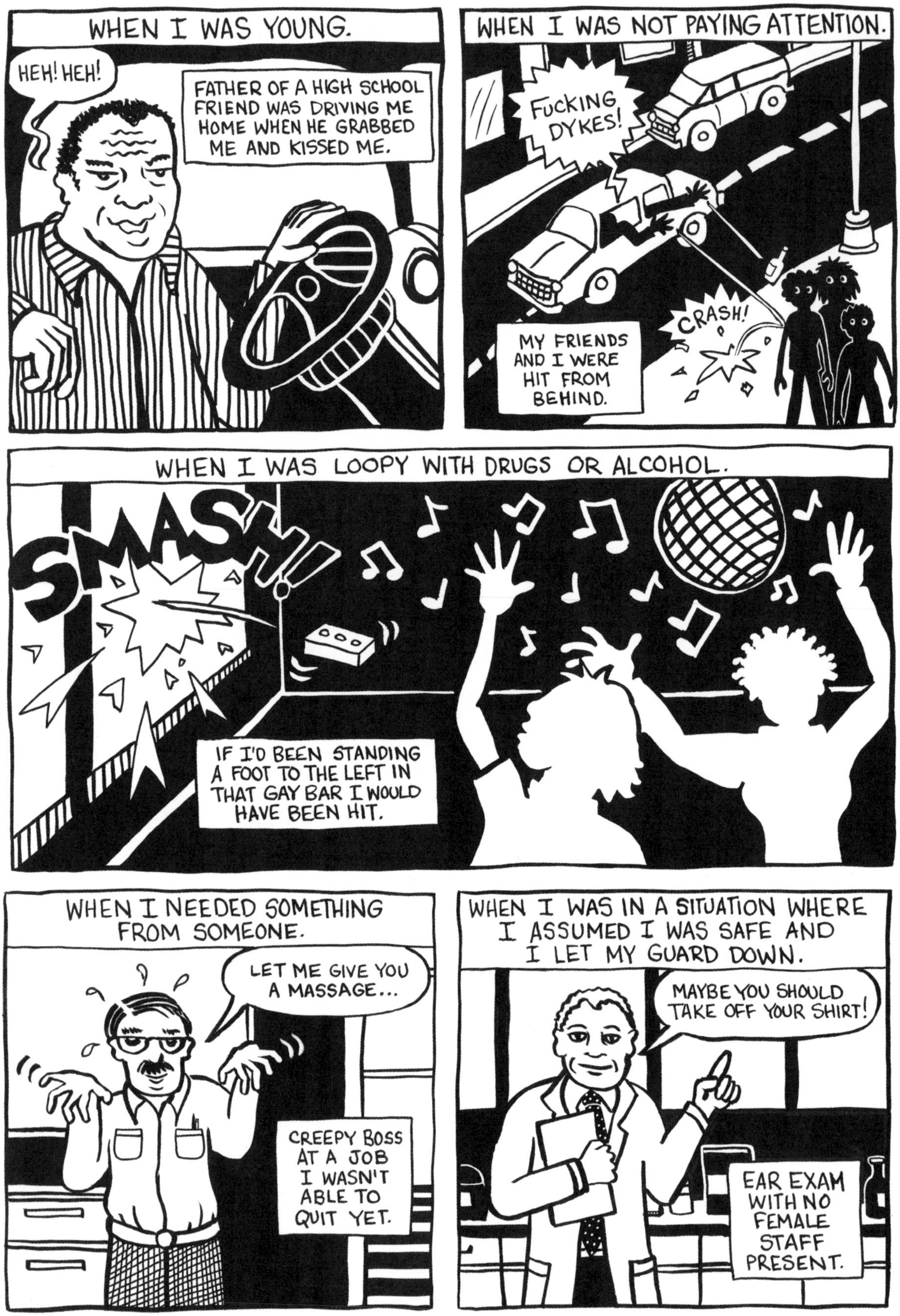
WHEN I WAS YOUNG.
HEH! HEH!
FATHER OF A HIGH SCHOOL FRIEND WAS DRIVING ME HOME WHEN HE GRABBED ME AND KISSED ME.
WHEN I WAS NOT PAYING ATTENTION.
FUCKING DYKES!
CRASH!
MY FRIENDS AND I WERE HIT FROM BEHIND.
WHEN I WAS LOOPY WITH DRUGS OR ALCOHOL.
SMASH!
IF I'D BEEN STANDING A FOOT TO THE LEFT IN THAT GAY BAR I WOULD HAVE BEEN HIT.
WHEN I NEEDED SOMETHING FROM SOMEONE.
LET ME GIVE YOU A MASSAGE...
CREEPY BOSS AT A JOB I WASN'T ABLE TO QUIT YET.
WHEN I WAS IN A SITUATION WHERE I ASSUMED I WAS SAFE AND I LET MY GUARD DOWN.
MAYBE YOU SHOULD TAKE OFF YOUR SHIRT!
EAR EXAM WITH NO FEMALE STAFF PRESENT.

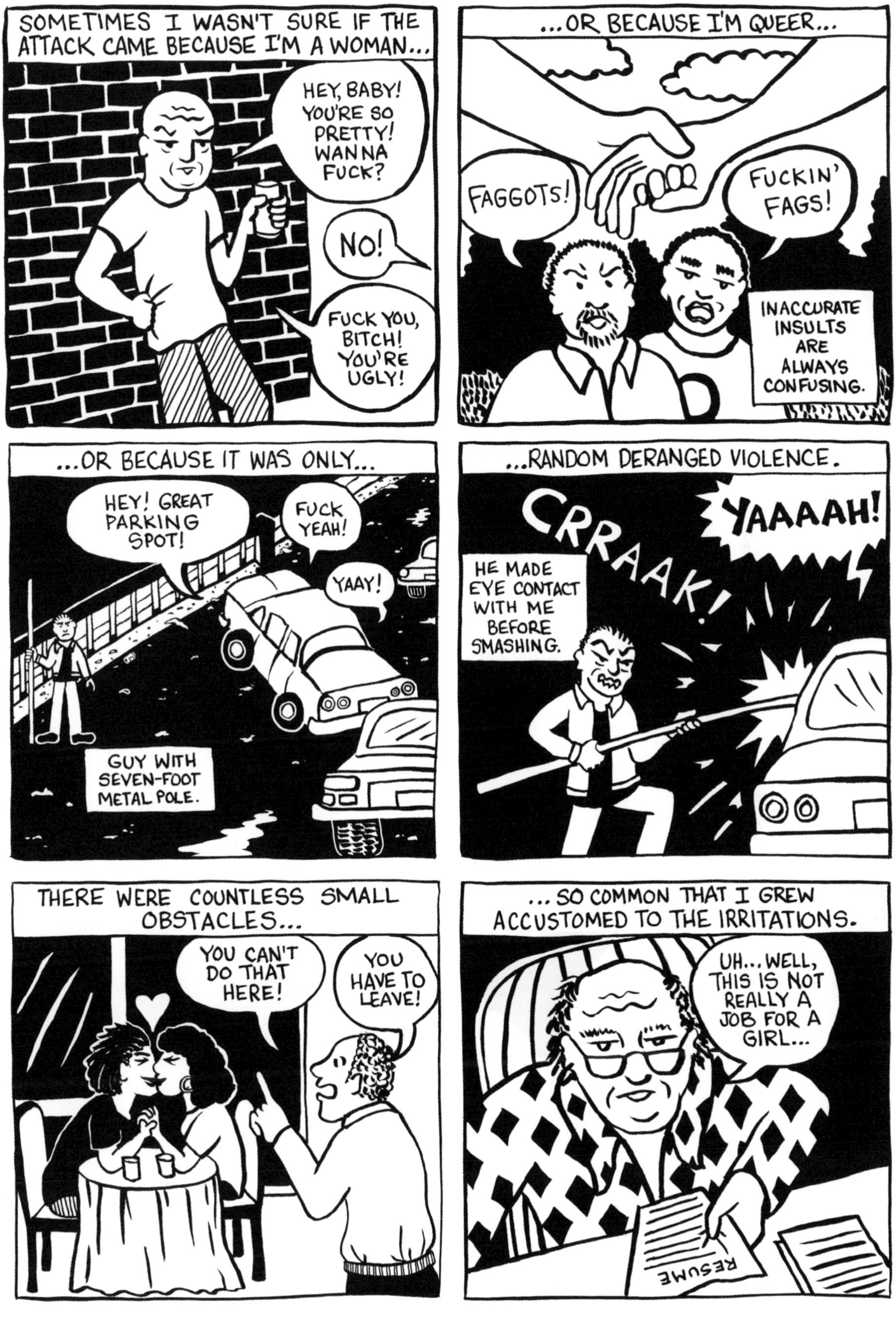
SOMETIMES I WASN'T SURE IF THE ATTACK CAME BECAUSE I'M A WOMAN...
HEY, BABY! YOU'RE SO PRETTY! WANNA FUCK?
NO!
FUCK YOU, BITCH! YOU'RE UGLY!
...OR BECAUSE I'M QUEER...
FAGGOTS!
FUCKIN' FAGS!
INACCURATE INSULTS ARE ALWAYS CONFUSING.
...OR BECAUSE IT WAS ONLY...
HEY! GREAT PARKING SPOT!
FUCK YEAH!
YAAY!
GUY WITH SEVEN-FOOT METAL POLE.
...RANDOM DERANGED VIOLENCE.
CRRAAK!
YAAAAH!
HE MADE EYE CONTACT WITH ME BEFORE SMASHING.
THERE WERE COUNTLESS SMALL OBSTACLES...
YOU CAN'T DO THAT HERE!
YOU HAVE TO LEAVE!
...SO COMMON THAT I GREW ACCUSTOMED TO THE IRRITATIONS.
UH... WELL, THIS IS NOT REALLY A JOB FOR A GIRL...
RESUME

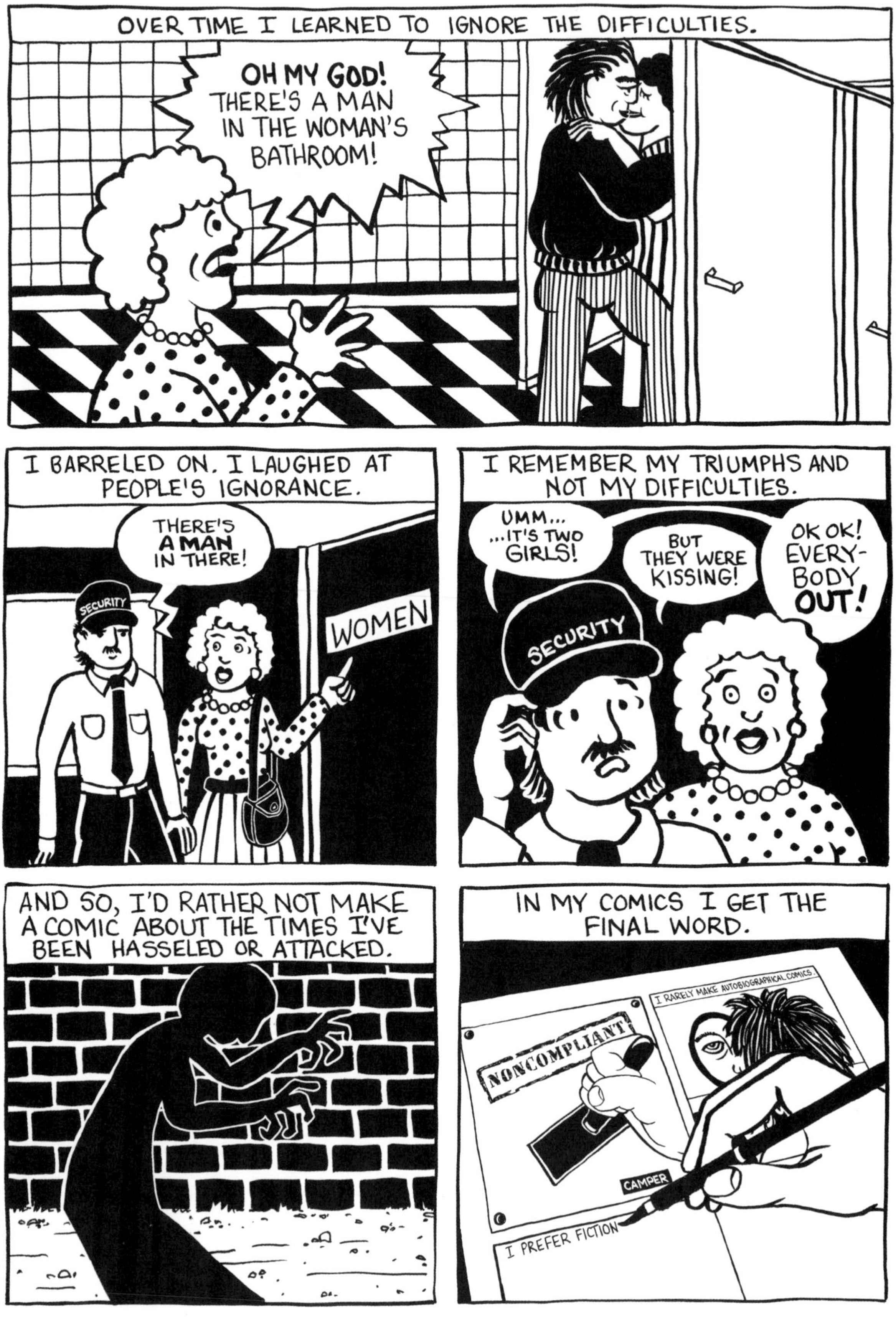
OVER TIME I LEARNED TO IGNORE THE DIFFICULTIES.
OH MY GOD! THERE'S A MAN IN THE WOMAN'S BATHROOM!
I BARRELED ON. I LAUGHED AT PEOPLE'S IGNORANCE.
THERE'S A MAN IN THERE!
SECURITY
WOMEN
I REMEMBER MY TRIUMPHS AND NOT MY DIFFICULTIES.
UMM... ...IT'S TWO GIRLS!
BUT THEY WERE KISSING!
OK OK! EVERYBODY OUT!
SECURITY
AND SO, I'D RATHER NOT MAKE A COMIC ABOUT THE TIMES I'VE BEEN HASSELED OR ATTACKED.
IN MY COMICS I GET THE FINAL WORD.
I RARELY MAKE AUTOBIOGRAPHICAL COMICS.
NONCOMPLIANT
NONCOMPLIANT
CAMPER
I PREFER FICTION

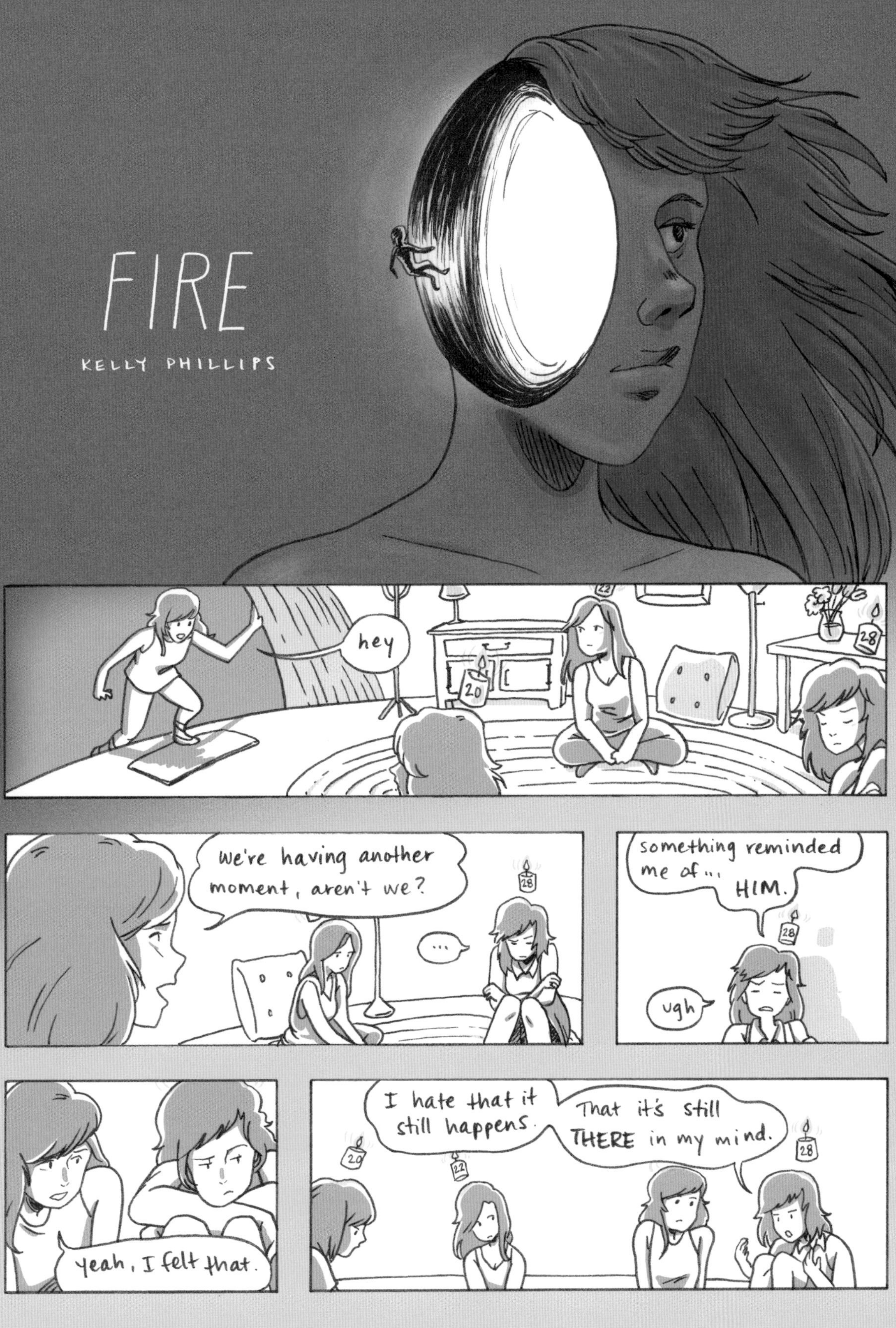
FIRE
KELLY PHILLIPS
hey
We're having another moment, aren't we?
...
something reminded me of... HIM.
ugh
Yeah, I felt that.
I hate that it still happens.
That it's still THERE in my mind.

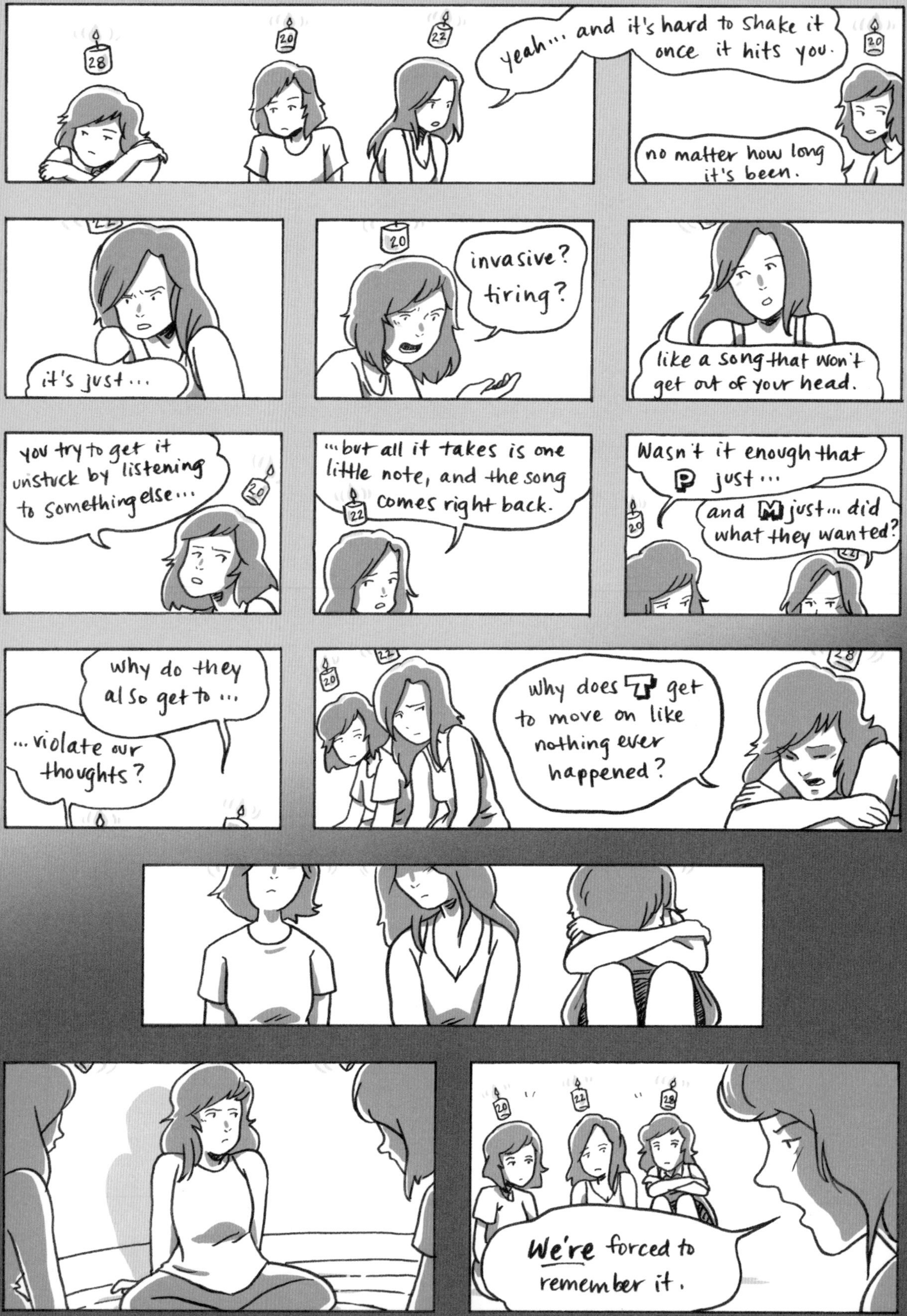

28
20
22
yeah... and it's hard to shake it once it hits you.
20
no matter how long it's been.
it's just...
20
invasive? tiring?
like a song that won't get out of your head.
you try to get it unstuck by listening to something else...
20
...but all it takes is one little note, and the song comes right back.
22
Wasn't it enough that P just...
20
and M just... did what they wanted?
why do they also get to...
...violate our thoughts?
20
why does T get to move on like nothing ever happened?
28
20
22
28
We're forced to remember it.

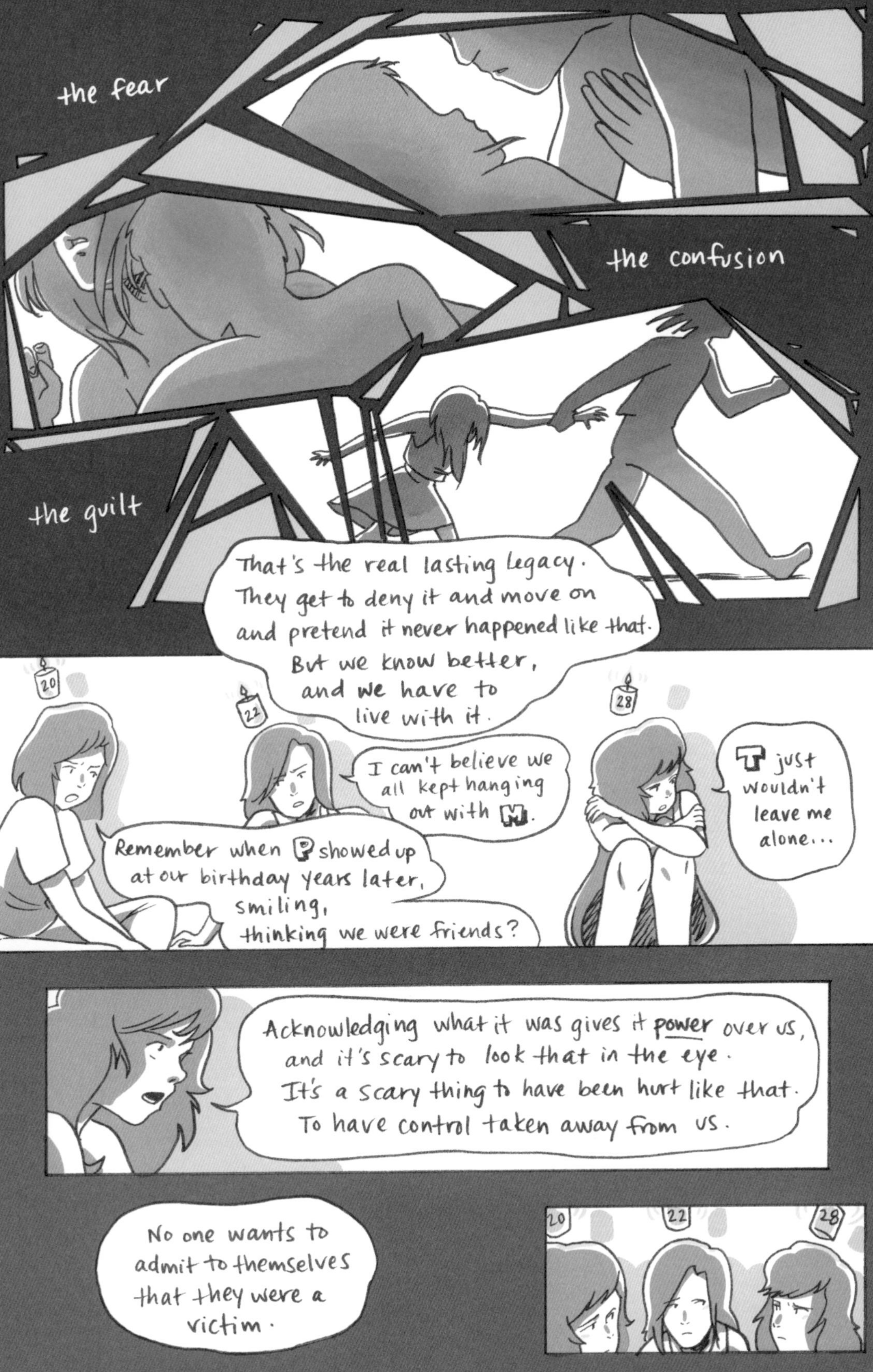
the fear
the confusion
the guilt
That's the real lasting legacy. They get to deny it and move on and pretend it never happened like that. But we know better, and we have to live with it.
20
22
28
I can't believe we all kept hanging out with M.
Remember when P showed up at our birthday years later, smiling, thinking we were friends?
T just wouldn't leave me alone...
Acknowledging what it was gives it power over us, and it's scary to look that in the eye. It's a scary thing to have been hurt like that. To have control taken away from us.
No one wants to admit to themselves that they were a victim.
20
22
28

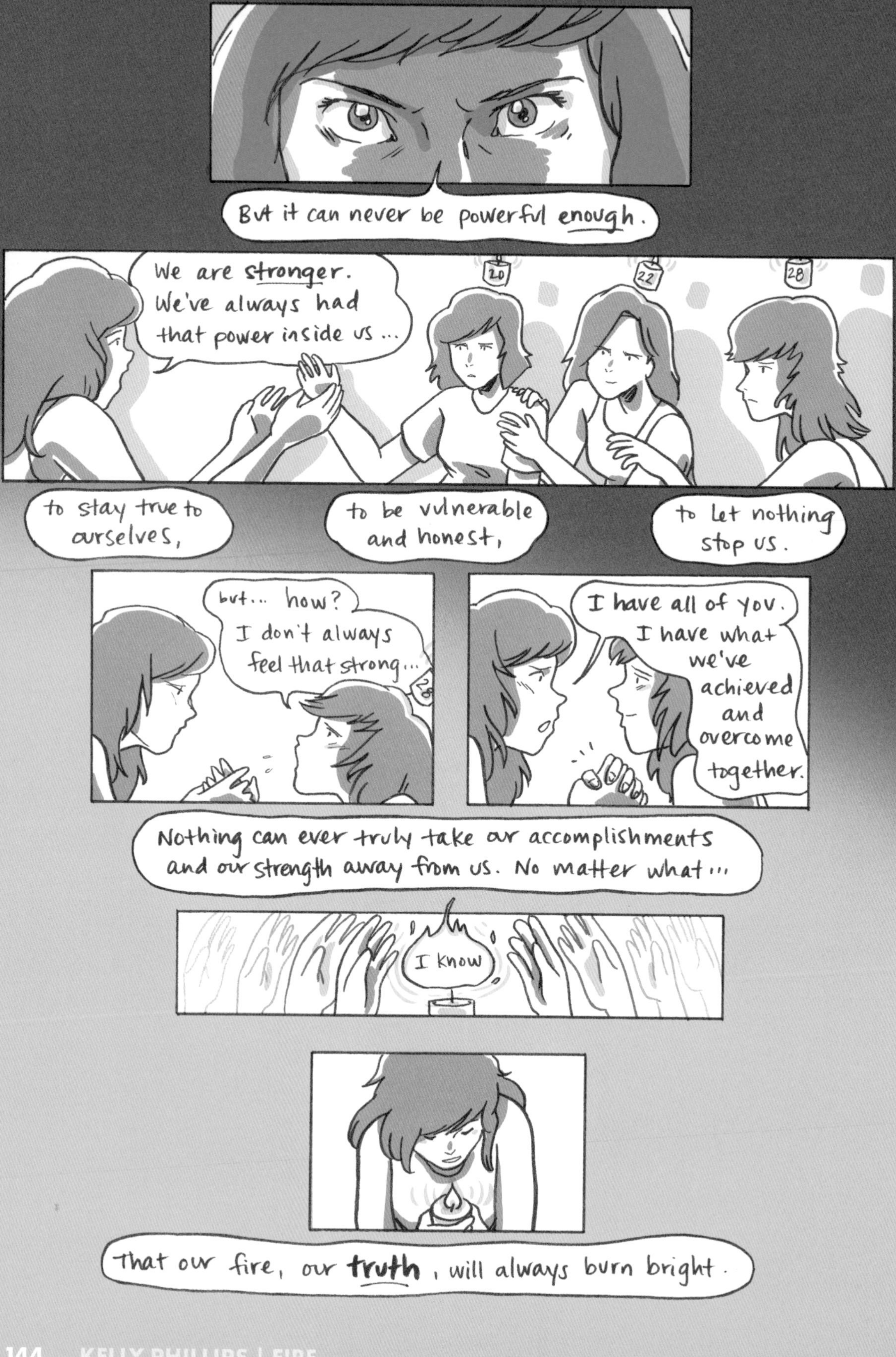
But it can never be powerful enough.
We are stronger. We've always had that power inside us ...
20
22
28
to stay true to ourselves,
to be vulnerable and honest,
to let nothing stop us.
but... how? I don't always feel that strong...
28
I have all of you. I have what we've achieved and overcome together.
Nothing can ever truly take our accomplishments and our strength away from us. No matter what...
I know
That our fire, our truth, will always burn bright.

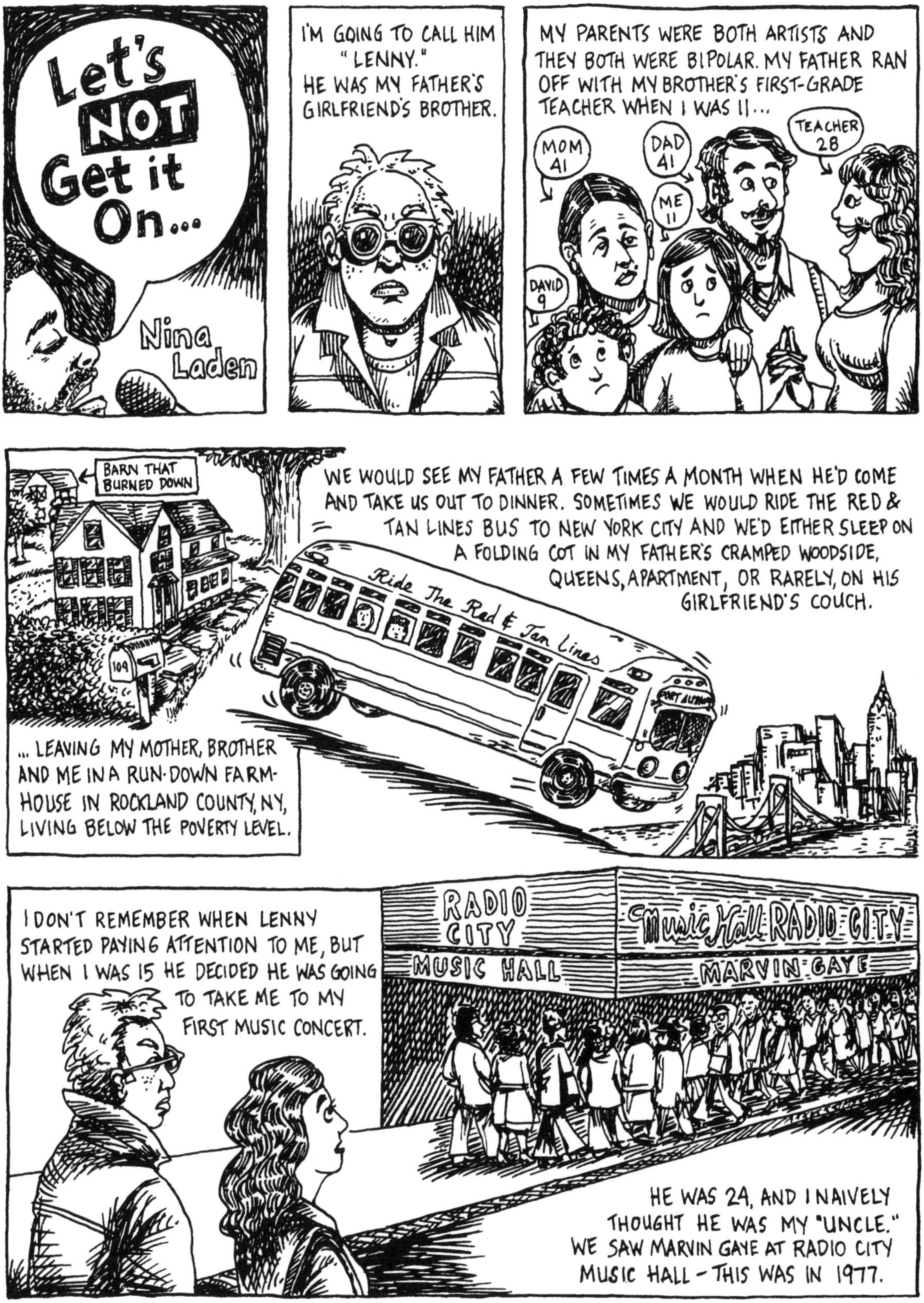
Let's NOT Get it On...
Nina Laden
I'M GOING TO CALL HIM "LENNY." HE WAS MY FATHER'S GIRLFRIEND'S BROTHER.
MY PARENTS WERE BOTH ARTISTS AND THEY BOTH WERE BIPOLAR. MY FATHER RAN OFF WITH MY BROTHER'S FIRST-GRADE TEACHER WHEN I WAS 11...
MOM 41
DAD 41
TEACHER 28
ME 11
DAVID 9
BARN THAT BURNED DOWN
WE WOULD SEE MY FATHER A FEW TIMES A MONTH WHEN HE'D COME AND TAKE US OUT TO DINNER. SOMETIMES WE WOULD RIDE THE RED & TAN LINES BUS TO NEW YORK CITY AND WE'D EITHER SLEEP ON A FOLDING COT IN MY FATHER'S CRAMPED WOODSIDE, QUEENS, APARTMENT, OR RARELY, ON HIS GIRLFRIEND'S COUCH.
109
Ride The Red & Tan Lines
... LEAVING MY MOTHER, BROTHER AND ME IN A RUN-DOWN FARMHOUSE IN ROCKLAND COUNTY, NY, LIVING BELOW THE POVERTY LEVEL.
I DON'T REMEMBER WHEN LENNY STARTED PAYING ATTENTION TO ME, BUT WHEN I WAS 15 HE DECIDED HE WAS GOING TO TAKE ME TO MY FIRST MUSIC CONCERT.
RADIO CITY MUSIC HALL
Music Hall RADIO CITY
MARVIN GAYE
HE WAS 24, AND I NAIVELY THOUGHT HE WAS MY "UNCLE." WE SAW MARVIN GAYE AT RADIO CITY MUSIC HALL – THIS WAS IN 1977.

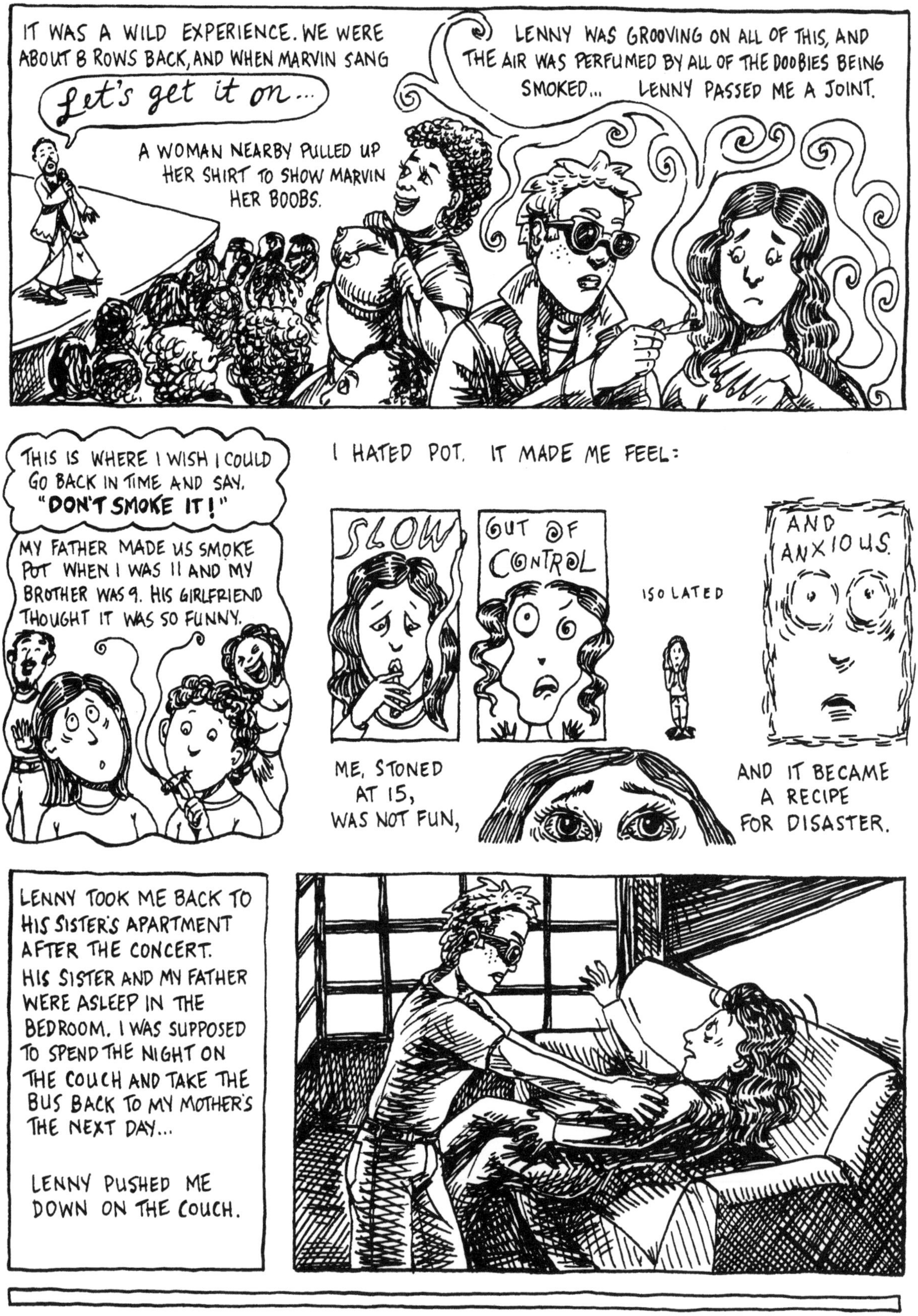
IT WAS A WILD EXPERIENCE. WE WERE ABOUT 8 ROWS BACK, AND WHEN MARVIN SANG
Let's get it on...
A WOMAN NEARBY PULLED UP HER SHIRT TO SHOW MARVIN HER BOOBS.
LENNY WAS GROOVING ON ALL OF THIS, AND THE AIR WAS PERFUMED BY ALL OF THE DOOBIES BEING SMOKED... LENNY PASSED ME A JOINT.
THIS IS WHERE I WISH I COULD GO BACK IN TIME AND SAY, "DON'T SMOKE IT!"
MY FATHER MADE US SMOKE POT WHEN I WAS 11 AND MY BROTHER WAS 9. HIS GIRLFRIEND THOUGHT IT WAS SO FUNNY.
I HATED POT. IT MADE ME FEEL:
SLOW
OUT OF CONTROL
ISOLATED
AND ANXIOUS.
ME, STONED AT 15, WAS NOT FUN,
AND IT BECAME A RECIPE FOR DISASTER.
LENNY TOOK ME BACK TO HIS SISTER'S APARTMENT AFTER THE CONCERT. HIS SISTER AND MY FATHER WERE ASLEEP IN THE BEDROOM. I WAS SUPPOSED TO SPEND THE NIGHT ON THE COUCH AND TAKE THE BUS BACK TO MY MOTHER'S THE NEXT DAY...
LENNY PUSHED ME DOWN ON THE COUCH.

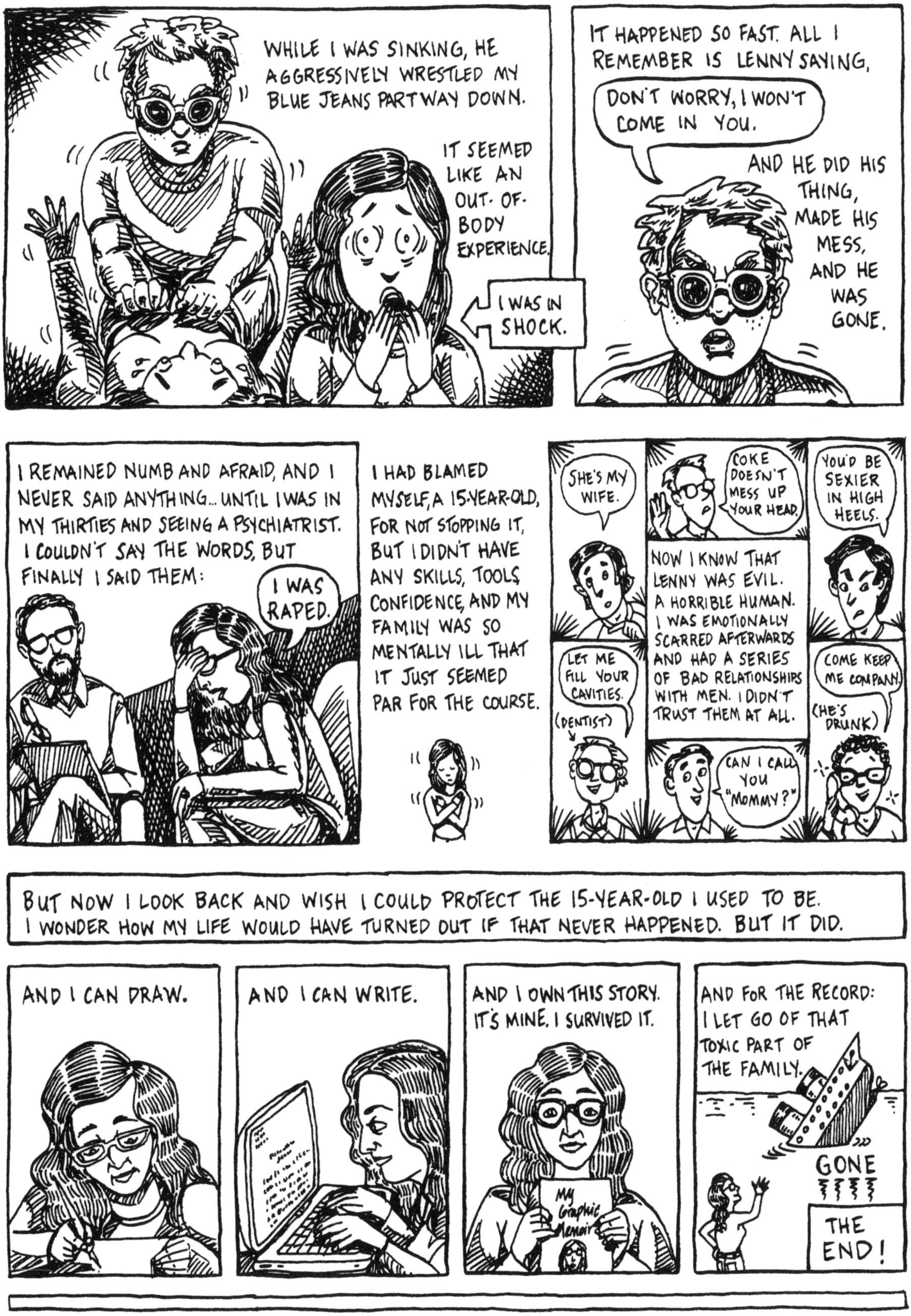

WHILE I WAS SINKING, HE AGGRESSIVELY WRESTLED MY BLUE JEANS PARTWAY DOWN.
IT SEEMED LIKE AN OUT-OF-BODY EXPERIENCE.
I WAS IN SHOCK.
IT HAPPENED SO FAST. ALL I REMEMBER IS LENNY SAYING,
DON'T WORRY, I WON'T COME IN YOU.
AND HE DID HIS THING, MADE HIS MESS, AND HE WAS GONE.
I REMAINED NUMB AND AFRAID, AND I NEVER SAID ANYTHING... UNTIL I WAS IN MY THIRTIES AND SEEING A PSYCHIATRIST. I COULDN'T SAY THE WORDS, BUT FINALLY I SAID THEM:
I WAS RAPED.
I HAD BLAMED MYSELF, A 15-YEAR-OLD, FOR NOT STOPPING IT, BUT I DIDN'T HAVE ANY SKILLS, TOOLS, CONFIDENCE, AND MY FAMILY WAS SO MENTALLY ILL THAT IT JUST SEEMED PAR FOR THE COURSE.
SHE'S MY WIFE.
COKE DOESN'T MESS UP YOUR HEAD.
YOU'D BE SEXIER IN HIGH HEELS.
NOW I KNOW THAT LENNY WAS EVIL. A HORRIBLE HUMAN. I WAS EMOTIONALLY SCARRED AFTERWARDS AND HAD A SERIES OF BAD RELATIONSHIPS WITH MEN. I DIDN'T TRUST THEM AT ALL.
LET ME FILL YOUR CAVITIES.
(DENTIST)
COME KEEP ME COMPANY.
(HE'S DRUNK)
CAN I CALL YOU "MOMMY?"
BUT NOW I LOOK BACK AND WISH I COULD PROTECT THE 15-YEAR-OLD I USED TO BE. I WONDER HOW MY LIFE WOULD HAVE TURNED OUT IF THAT NEVER HAPPENED. BUT IT DID.
AND I CAN DRAW.
AND I CAN WRITE.
AND I OWN THIS STORY. IT'S MINE. I SURVIVED IT.
My Graphic Memoir
AND FOR THE RECORD: I LET GO OF THAT TOXIC PART OF THE FAMILY.
GONE
THE END!

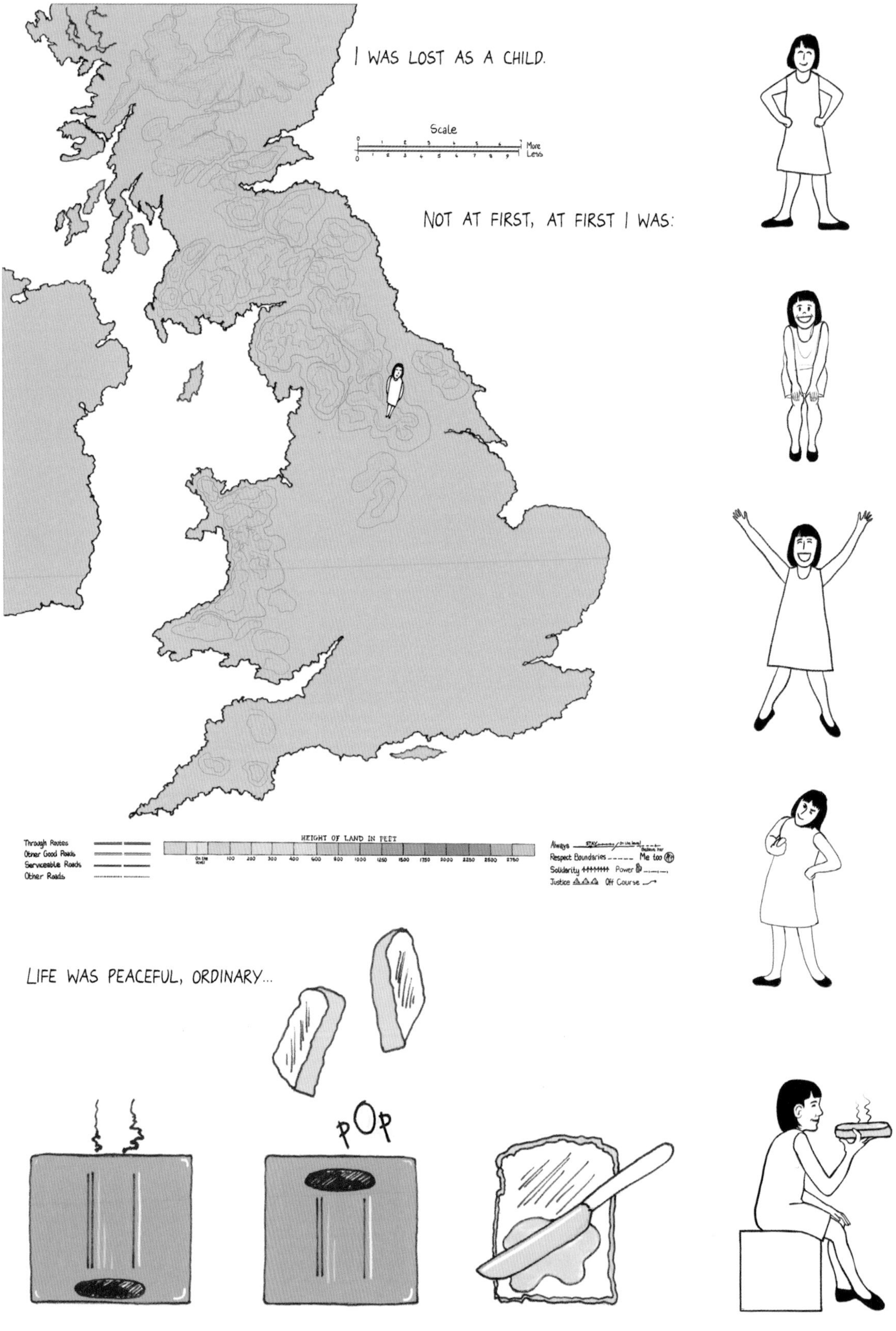
I WAS LOST AS A CHILD.
Scale
More
Less
NOT AT FIRST, AT FIRST I WAS:
Through Routes
Other Good Roads
Serviceable Roads
Other Roads
HEIGHT OF LAND IN FEET
On the level
100 200 300 400 600 800 1000 1250 1500 1750 2000 2250 2500 2750
Always STAY On the level Believe her
Respect Boundaries
Me too
Solidarity
Power
Justice
Off Course
LIFE WAS PEACEFUL, ORDINARY...
pOp

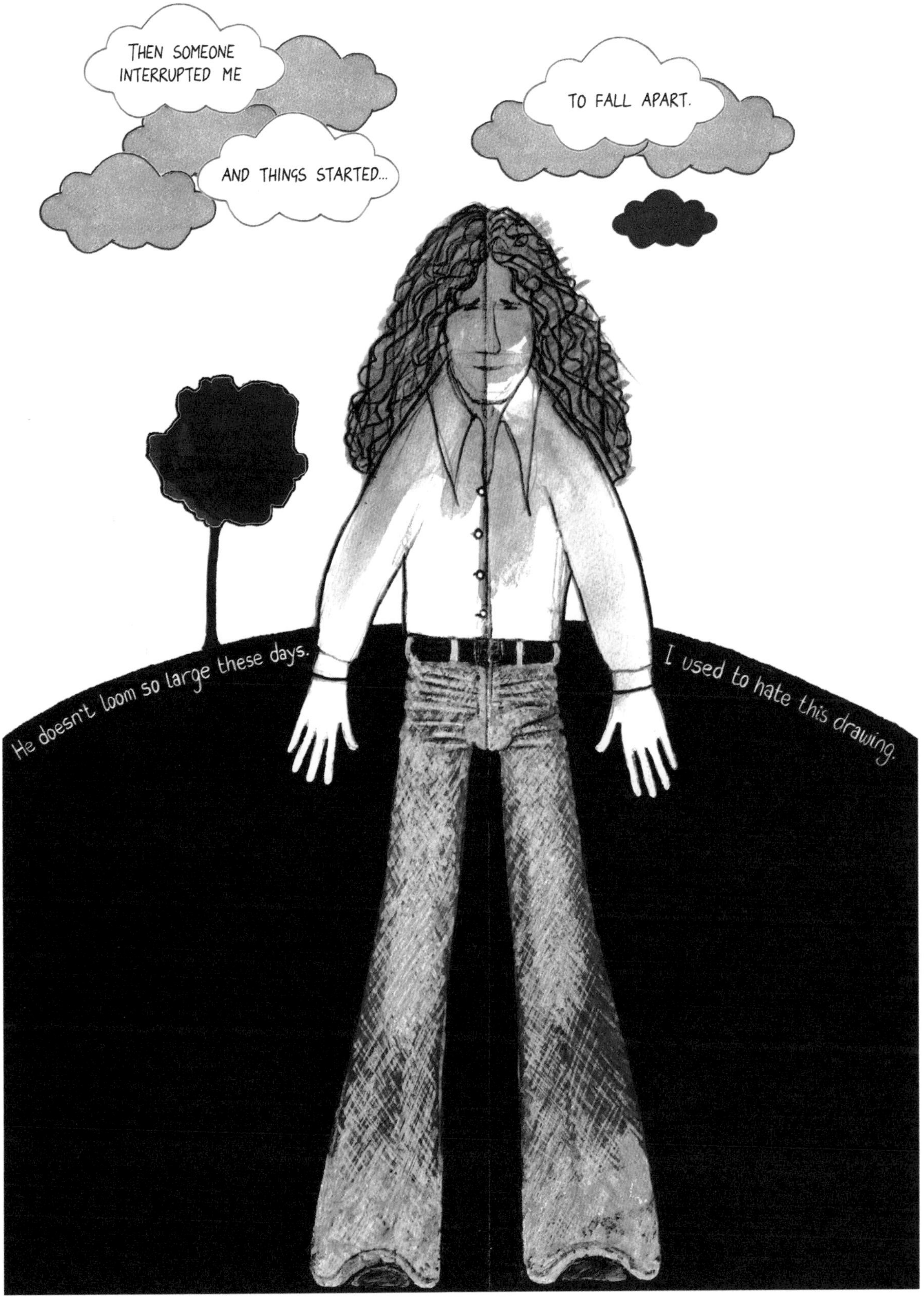
THEN SOMEONE INTERRUPTED ME
AND THINGS STARTED...
TO FALL APART.
He doesn't loom so large these days.
I used to hate this drawing.

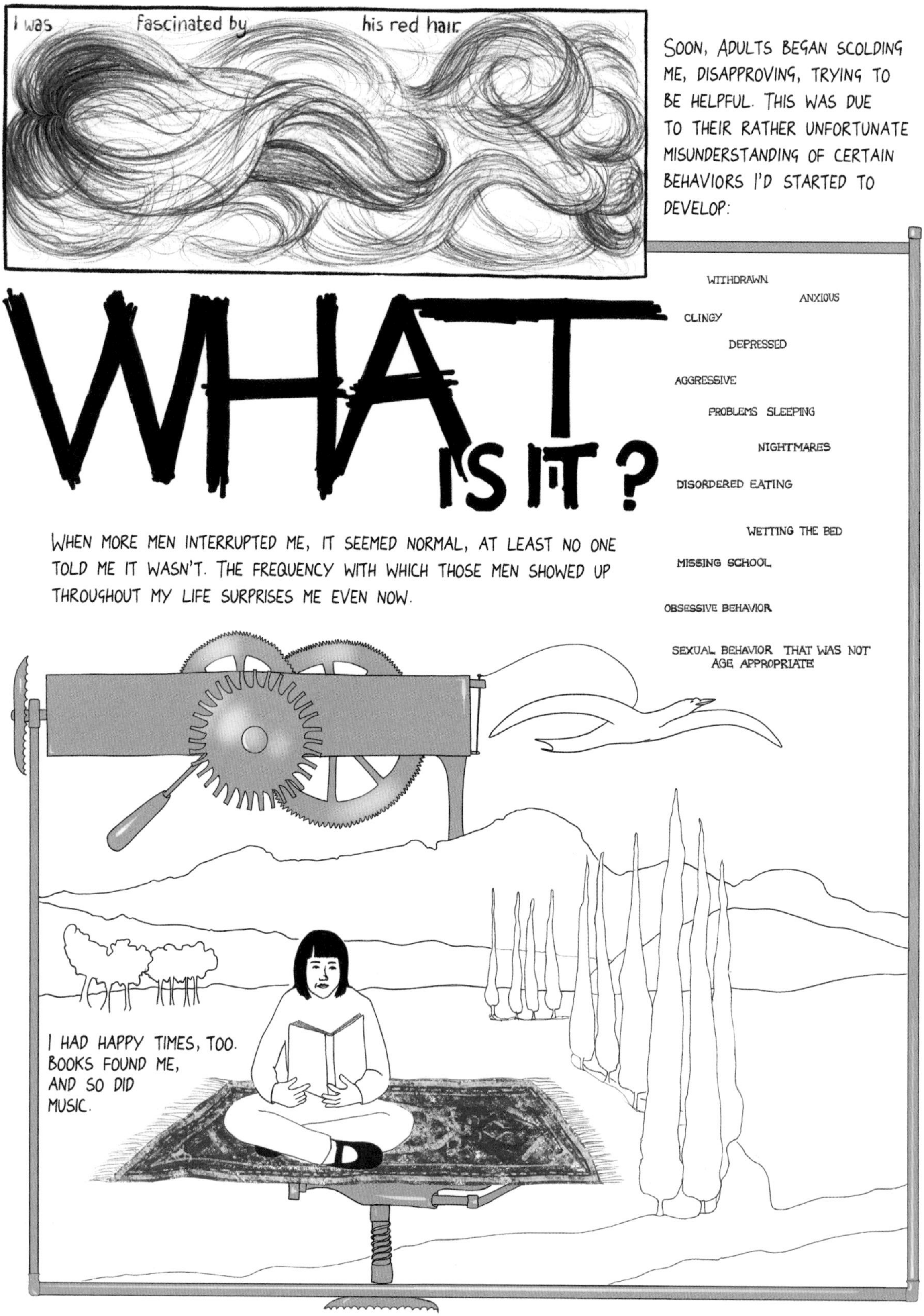
I was fascinated by his red hair.
SOON, ADULTS BEGAN SCOLDING ME, DISAPPROVING, TRYING TO BE HELPFUL. THIS WAS DUE TO THEIR RATHER UNFORTUNATE MISUNDERSTANDING OF CERTAIN BEHAVIORS I'D STARTED TO DEVELOP:
WHAT IS IT?
WITHDRAWN
ANXIOUS
CLINGY
DEPRESSED
AGGRESSIVE
PROBLEMS SLEEPING
NIGHTMARES
DISORDERED EATING
WETTING THE BED
MISSING SCHOOL
OBSESSIVE BEHAVIOR
SEXUAL BEHAVIOR THAT WAS NOT AGE APPROPRIATE
WHEN MORE MEN INTERRUPTED ME, IT SEEMED NORMAL, AT LEAST NO ONE TOLD ME IT WASN'T. THE FREQUENCY WITH WHICH THOSE MEN SHOWED UP THROUGHOUT MY LIFE SURPRISES ME EVEN NOW.
I HAD HAPPY TIMES, TOO. BOOKS FOUND ME, AND SO DID MUSIC.

ONE DAY (THE WORST DAY) WHEN I WAS 15 YEARS OLD, I FELL AND KEPT FALLING, LIKE ALICE, DOWN, DOWN, DOWN. I DIDN'T HIT THE BOTTOM WITH A BUMP TILL I WAS 30.

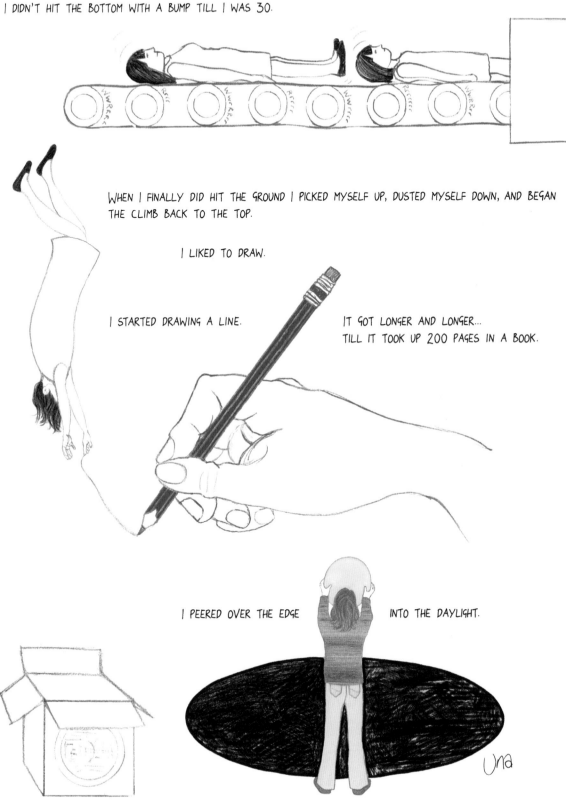

WHEN I FINALLY DID HIT THE GROUND I PICKED MYSELF UP, DUSTED MYSELF DOWN, AND BEGAN THE CLIMB BACK TO THE TOP.

I LIKED TO DRAW.

I STARTED DRAWING A LINE.

IT GOT LONGER AND LONGER...
TILL IT TOOK UP 200 PAGES IN A BOOK.

I PEERED OVER THE EDGE   INTO THE DAYLIGHT.

DRAWINGS

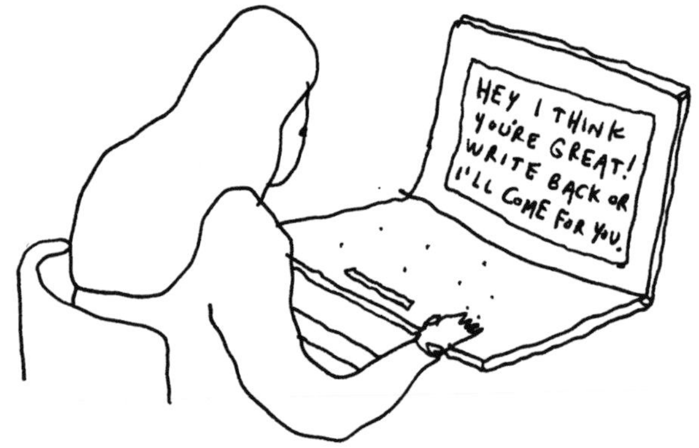
HEY I THINK YOU'RE GREAT! WRITE BACK OR I'LL COME FOR YOU.

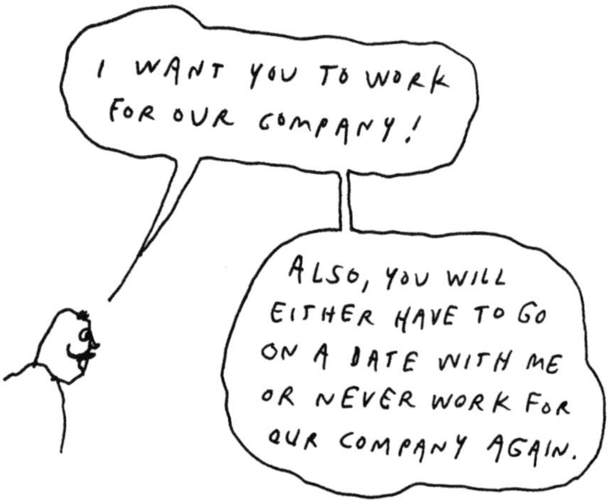
I WANT YOU TO WORK FOR OUR COMPANY!
ALSO, YOU WILL EITHER HAVE TO GO ON A DATE WITH ME OR NEVER WORK FOR OUR COMPANY AGAIN.

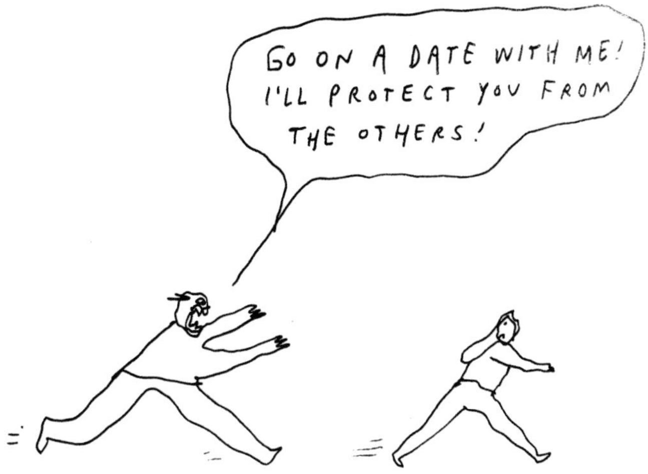
GO ON A DATE WITH ME! I'LL PROTECT YOU FROM THE OTHERS!

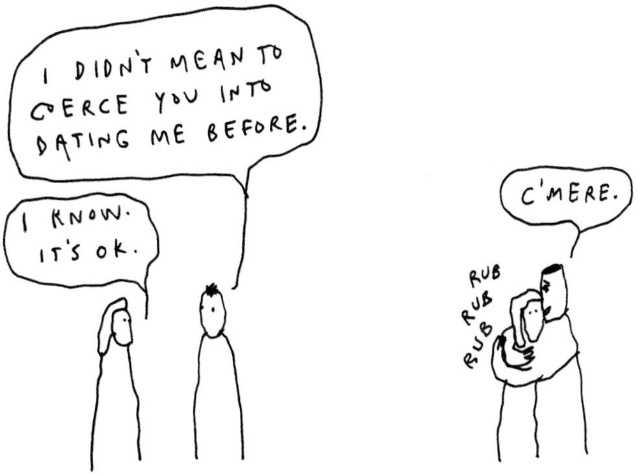
I DIDN'T MEAN TO COERCE YOU INTO DATING ME BEFORE.
I KNOW. IT'S OK.
C'MERE.
RUB RUB RUB

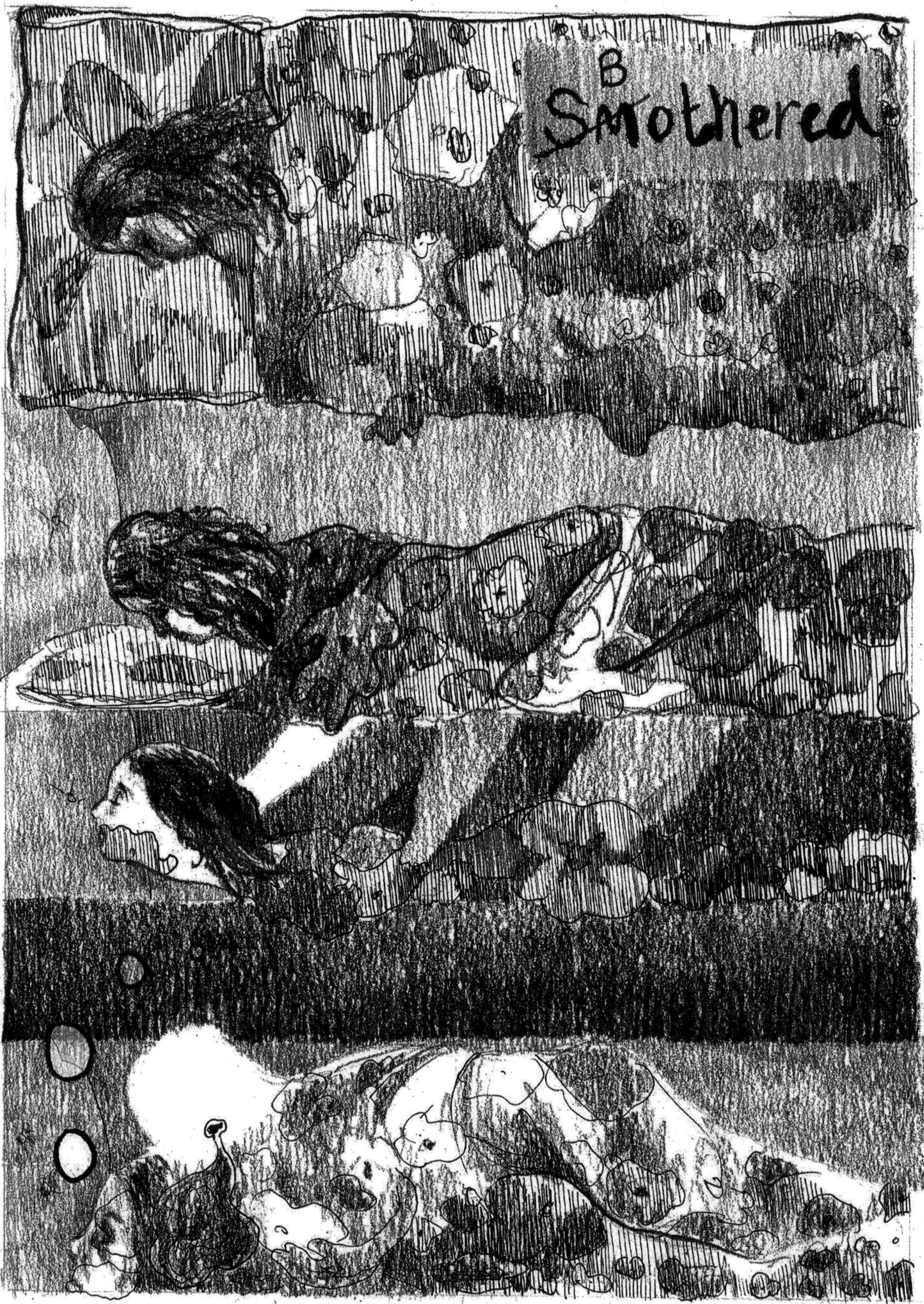
B
~~Sm~~othered

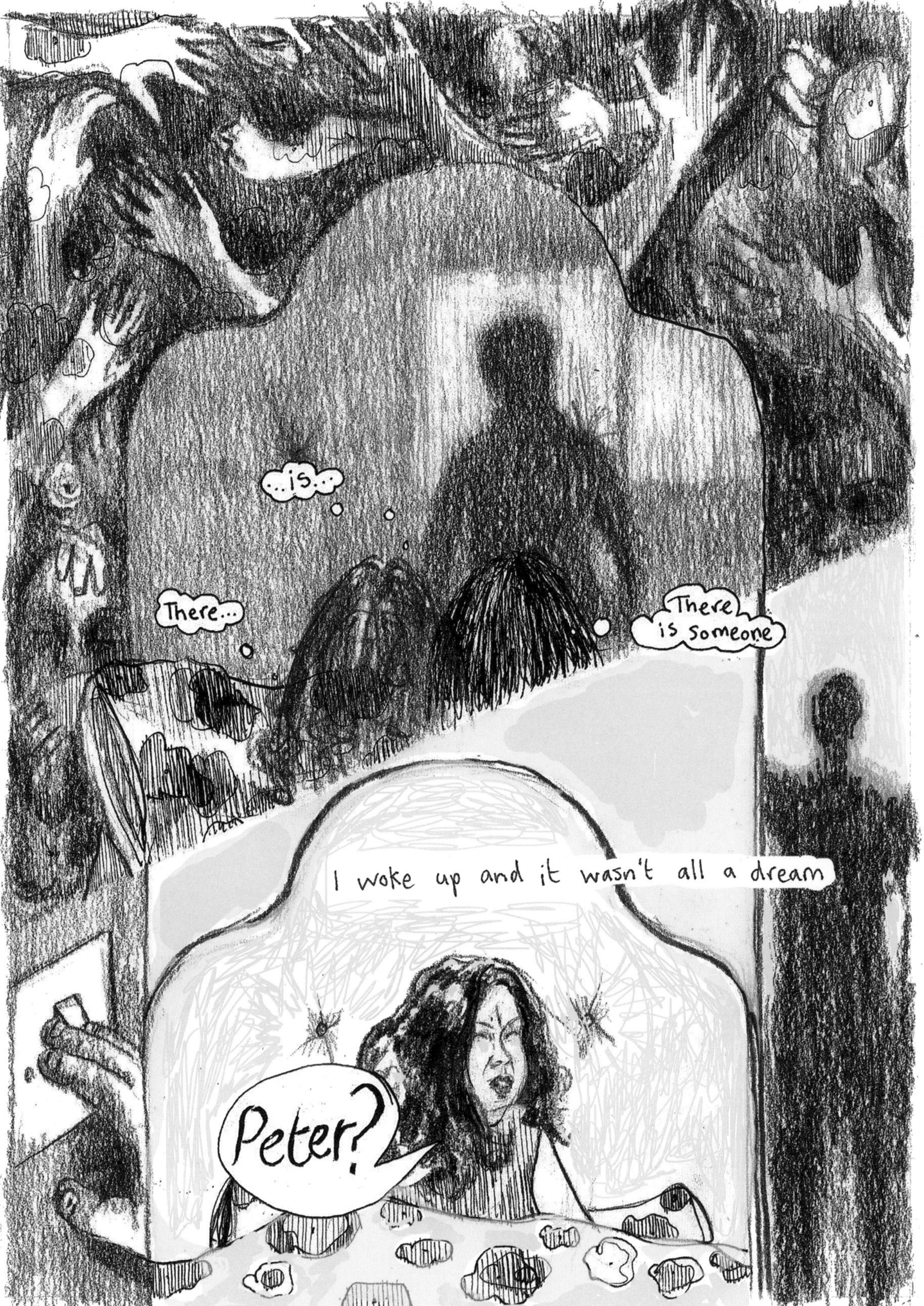

There...
...is...
There is someone
I woke up and it wasn't all a dream
Peter?

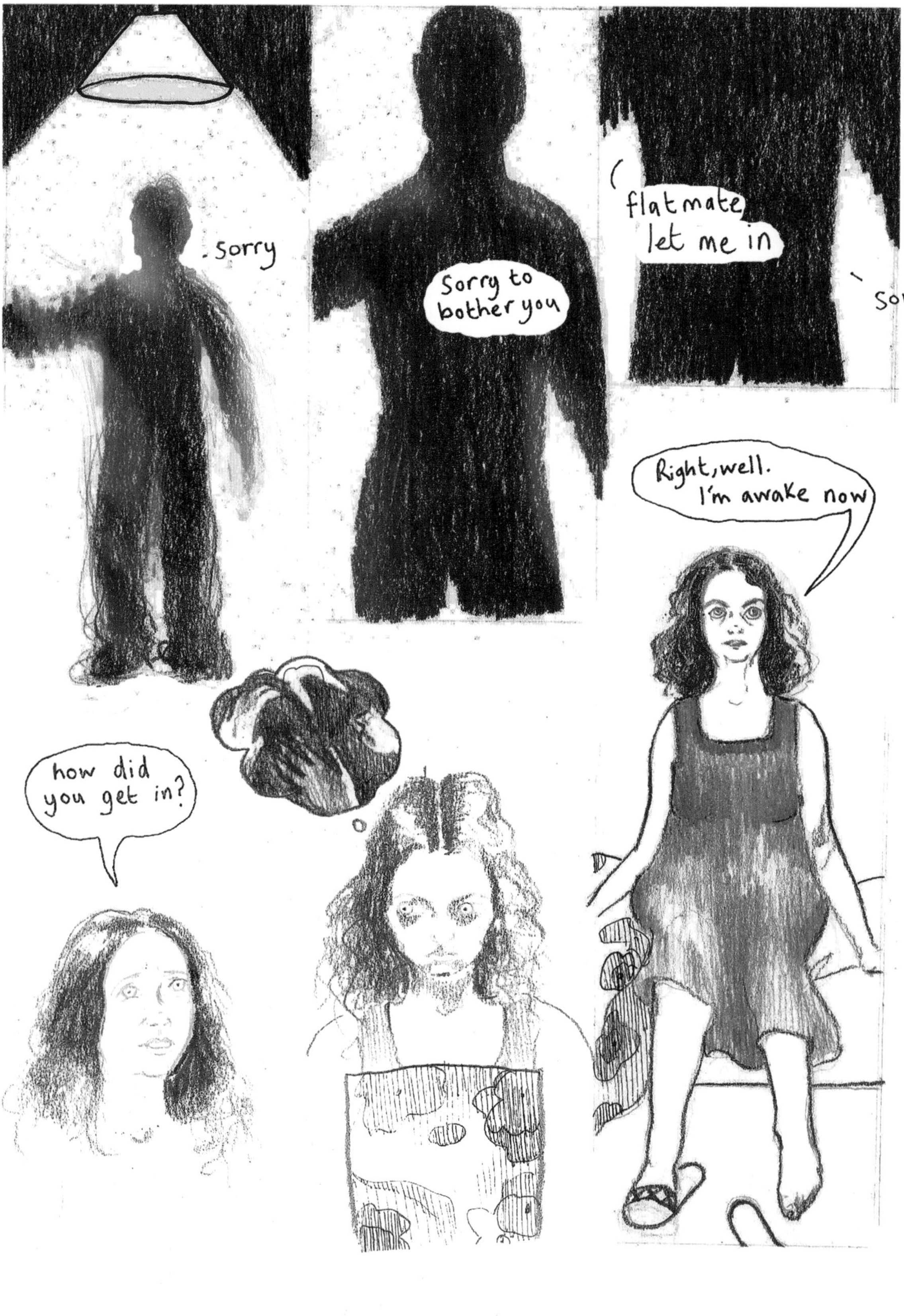
sorry
Sorry to bother you
flatmate let me in
sorry
Right, well. I'm awake now
how did you get in?

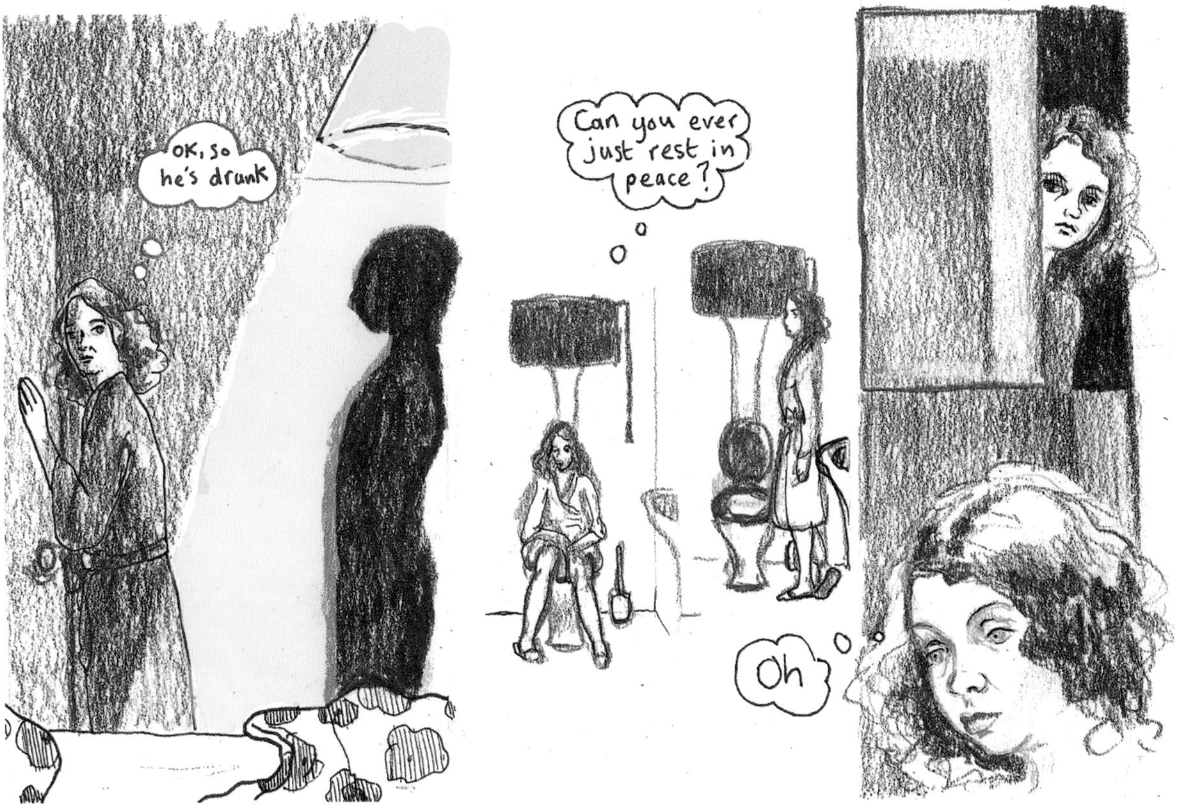
OK, so he's drunk
Can you ever just rest in peace?
Oh

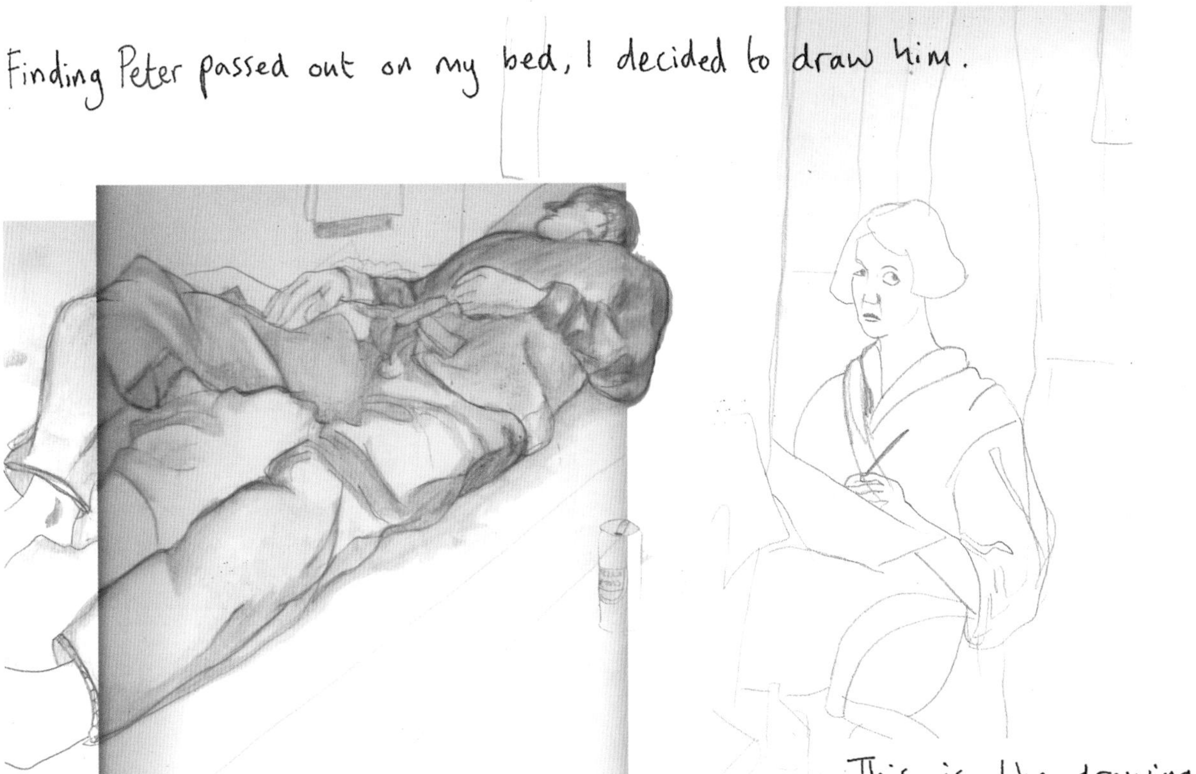
Finding Peter passed out on my bed, I decided to draw him.
This is the drawing.

Peter committed suicide nearly twenty years later. He was a complicated person and certainly not somebody I think was all bad. But this comic isn't about his complexities, it's about the reality of what happened. Of being smothered physically in my sleep, and then smothered psychologically, when Peter apologized for merely "bothering" me.

The feeling of terror that I experienced when I was being attacked by a stranger in my sleep, in my home, was suddenly accompanied by a sense of relief the moment I realized this person was someone I knew. Relief, and anger that I felt relief.

Anger at being asked to forgive his actions.

Did he get off of me because I was starting to wake up? What if I hadn't?

As drunk as he was, it seems clear that he knew what he was doing was wrong. As disturbed as I was, I didn't confront him about it. There is a silencing effect that occurs after a threat; a strange apology like his is an invitation to mutually deny what really happened, and implies the possibility of further violence.

I'm glad I put myself in the picture when I drew him lying on my bed. We must put ourselves in the picture. We need to have direct conversations about our encounters, and to educate ourselves about these issues. Did I even know how to define sexual assault back then? I don't think so. The things we do not say become toxic for us all. Maybe that's why Peter is now dead. Who knows? Let's not all die of words unsaid.

HERE LIED
THE
UNINVITED

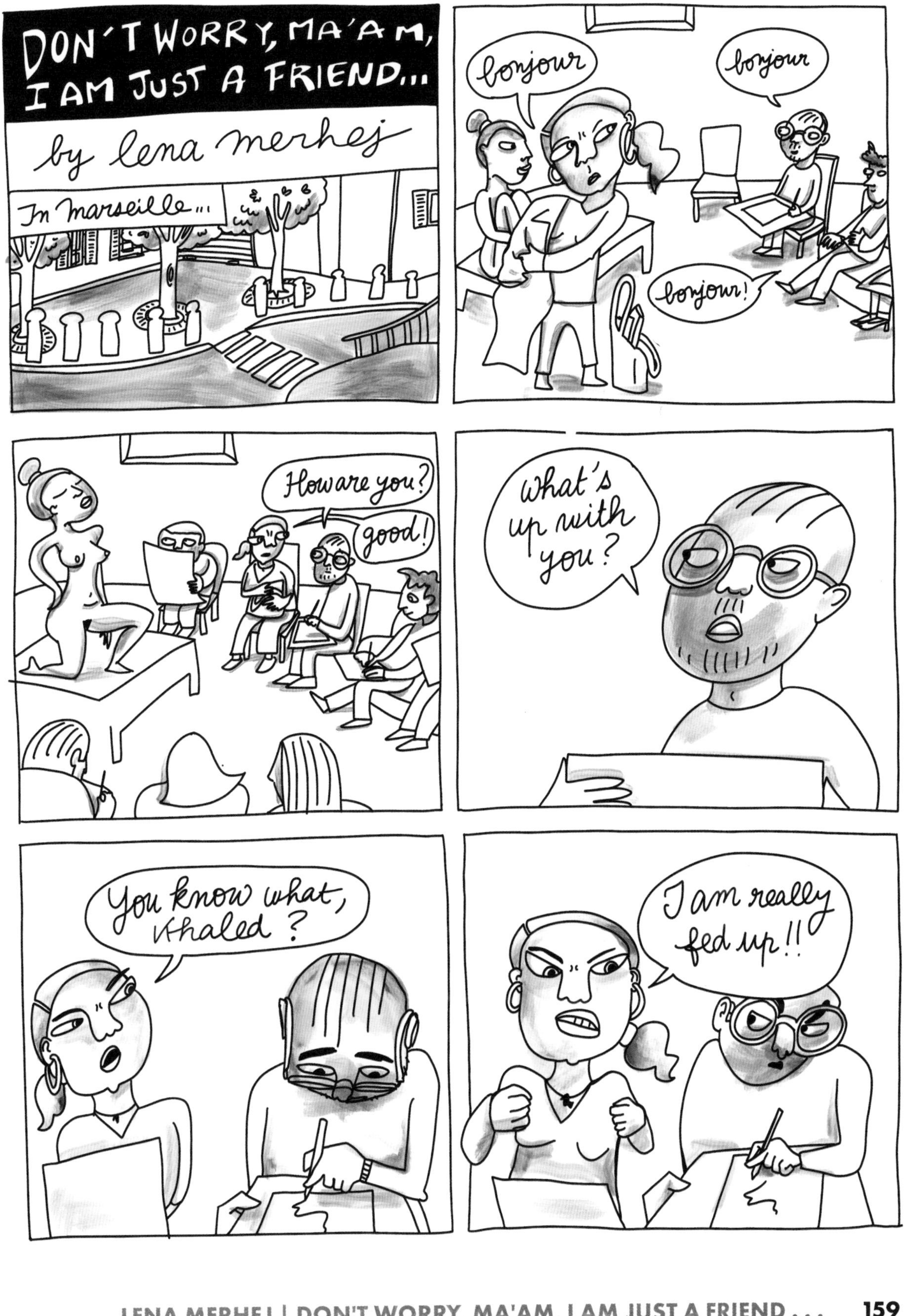
DON'T WORRY, MA'AM, I AM JUST A FRIEND...
by lena merhej
In marseille...
bonjour
bonjour
bonjour!
How are you?
good!
What's up with you?
You know what, Khaled?
I am really fed up!!

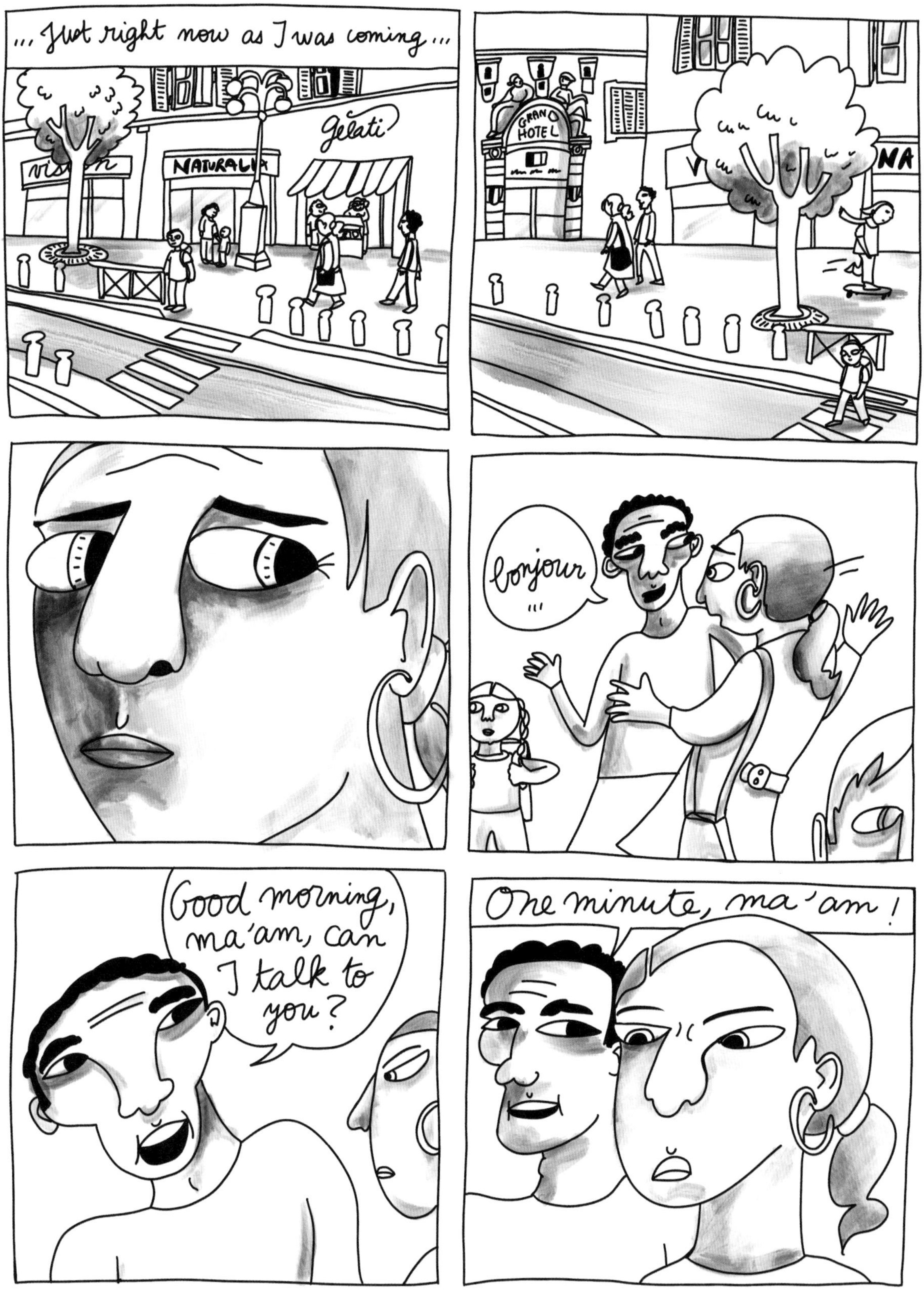
... Just right now as I was coming ...
Gelati
GRAND HOTEL
bonjour ...
Good morning, ma'am, can I talk to you?
One minute, ma'am!

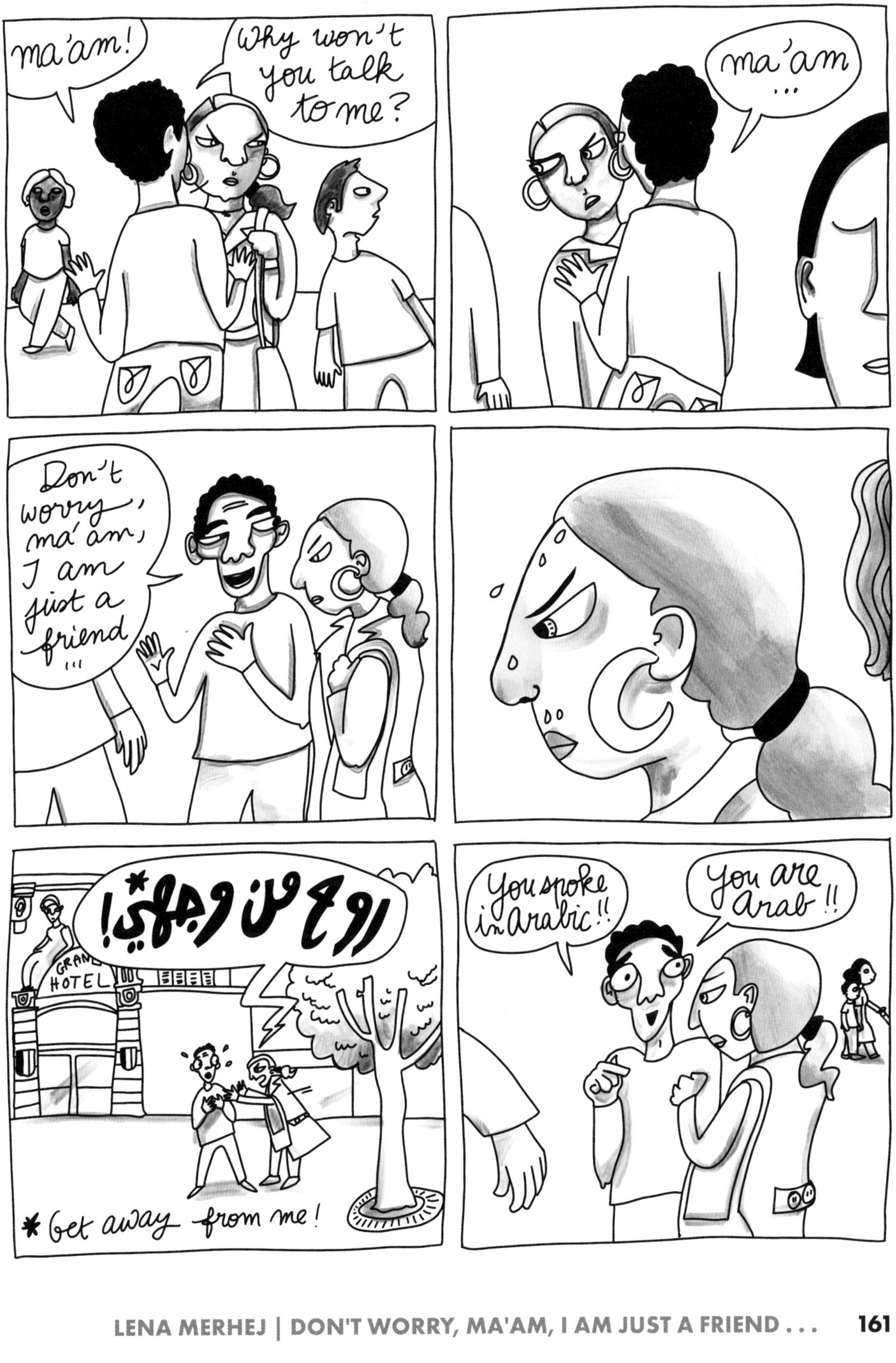
ma'am!
Why won't you talk to me?
ma'am ...
Don't worry, ma'am, I am just a friend ...
روح من وجهي!*
GRAND HOTEL
* Get away from me!
You spoke in Arabic!!
You are Arab!!

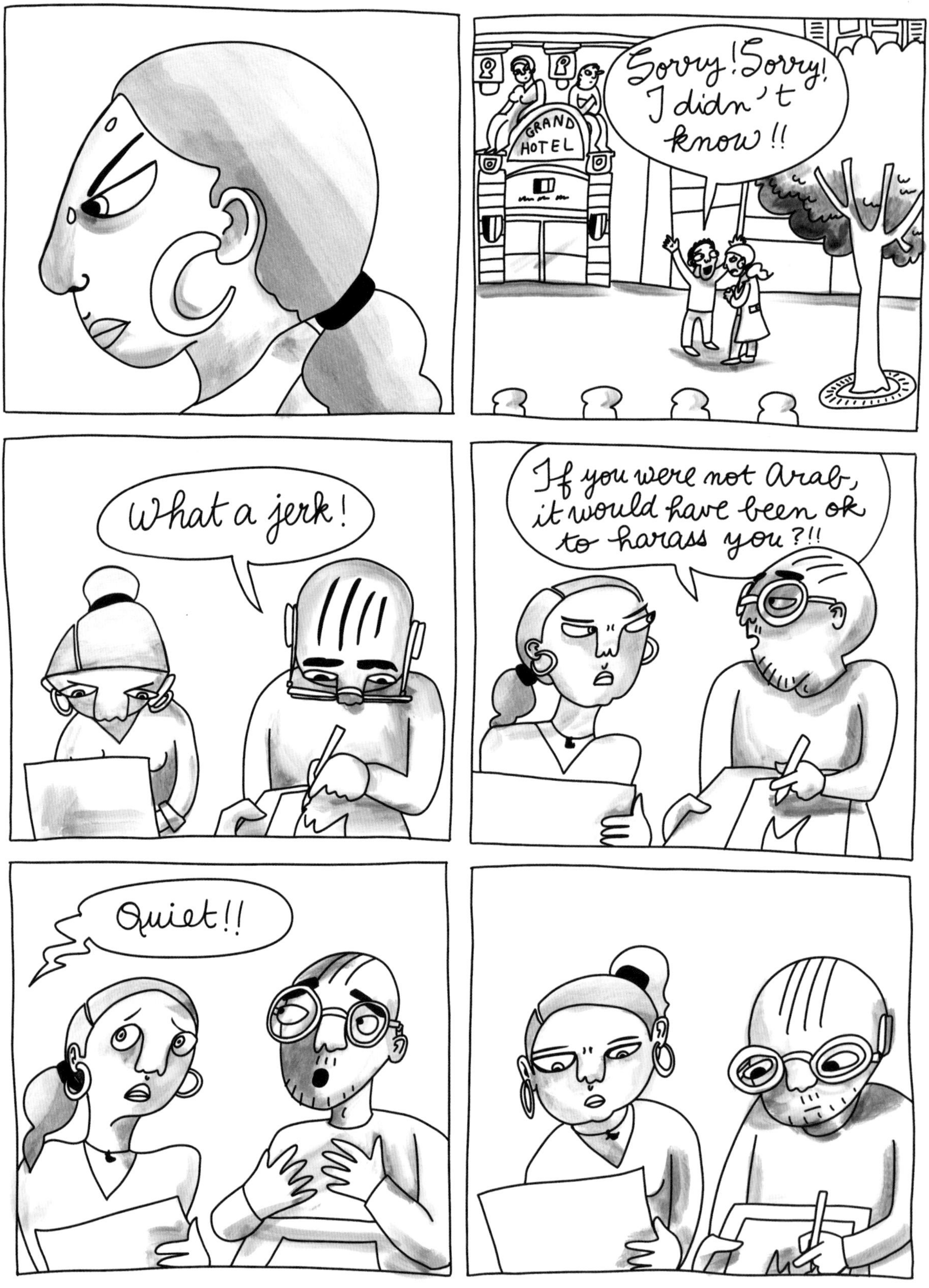
Sorry! Sorry! I didn't know!!
What a jerk!
If you were not Arab, it would have been ok to harass you?!!
Quiet!!

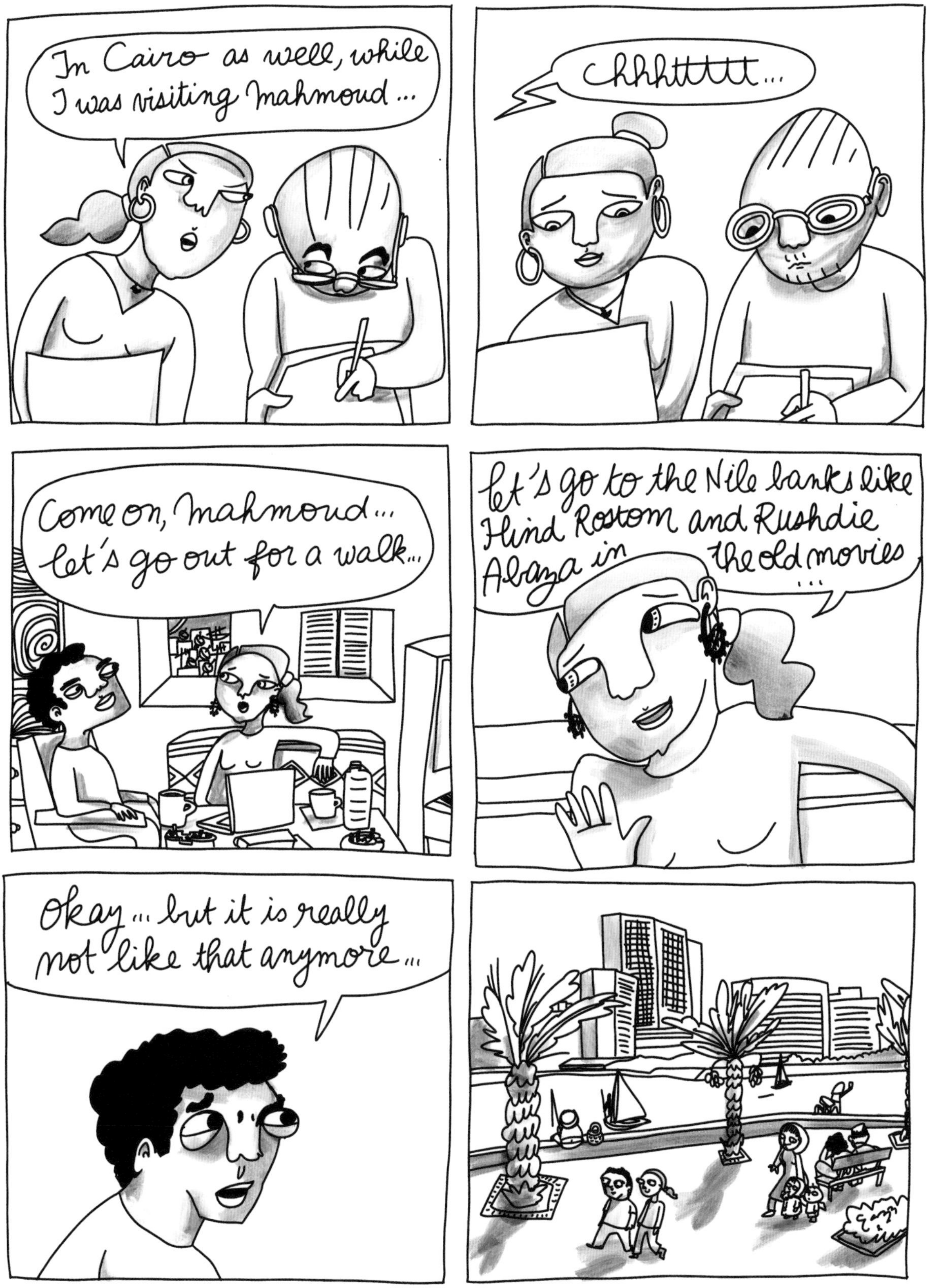
In Cairo as well, while I was visiting Mahmoud...
Chhhttttt...
Come on, Mahmoud... let's go out for a walk...
Let's go to the Nile banks like Hind Rostom and Rushdie Abaza in the old movies...
Okay... but it is really not like that anymore...

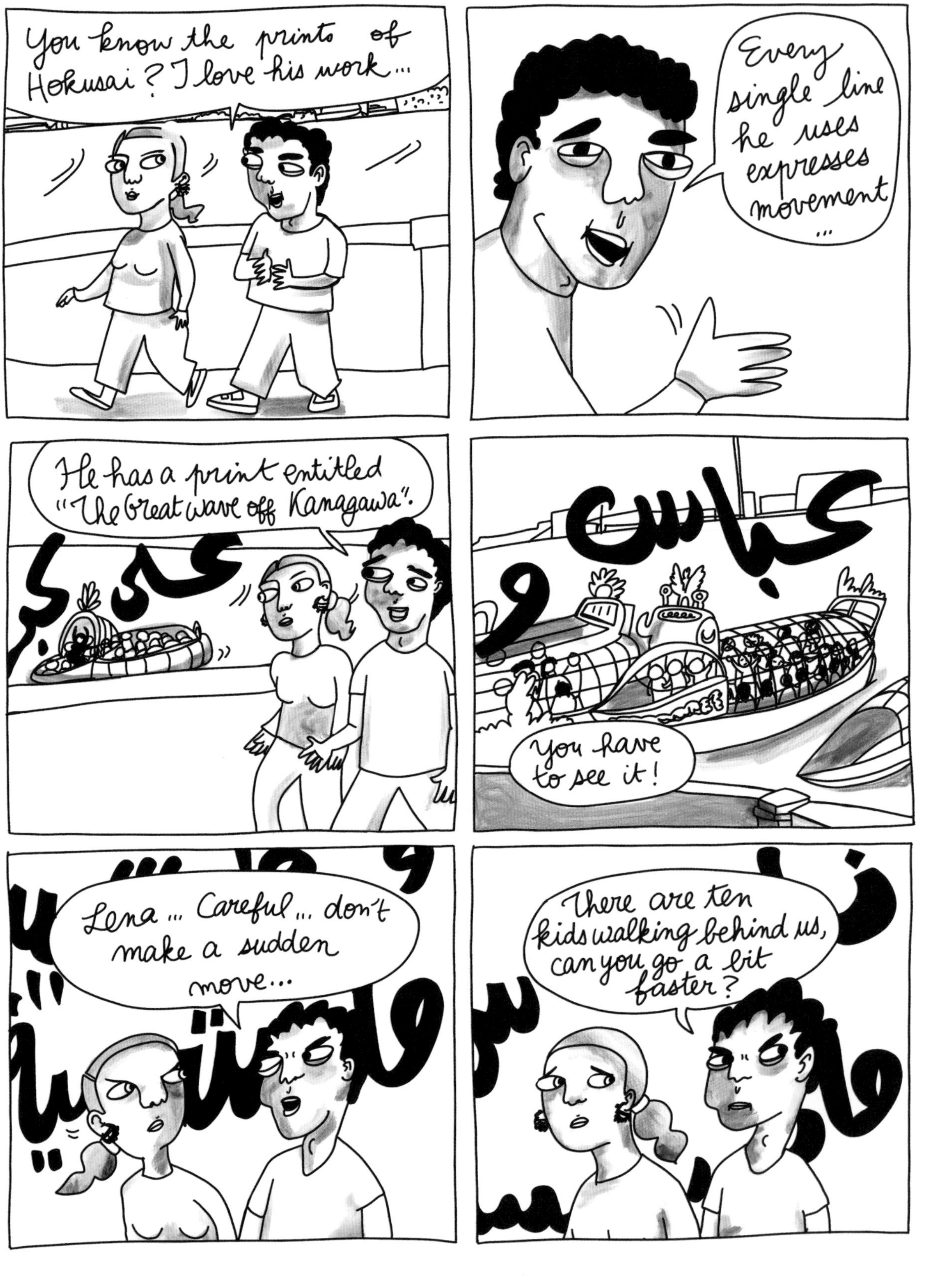
You know the prints of Hokusai? I love his work...
Every single line he uses expresses movement...
He has a print entitled "The Great wave off Kanagawa".
عباس
You have to see it!
Lena... Careful... don't make a sudden move...
There are ten kids walking behind us, can you go a bit faster?

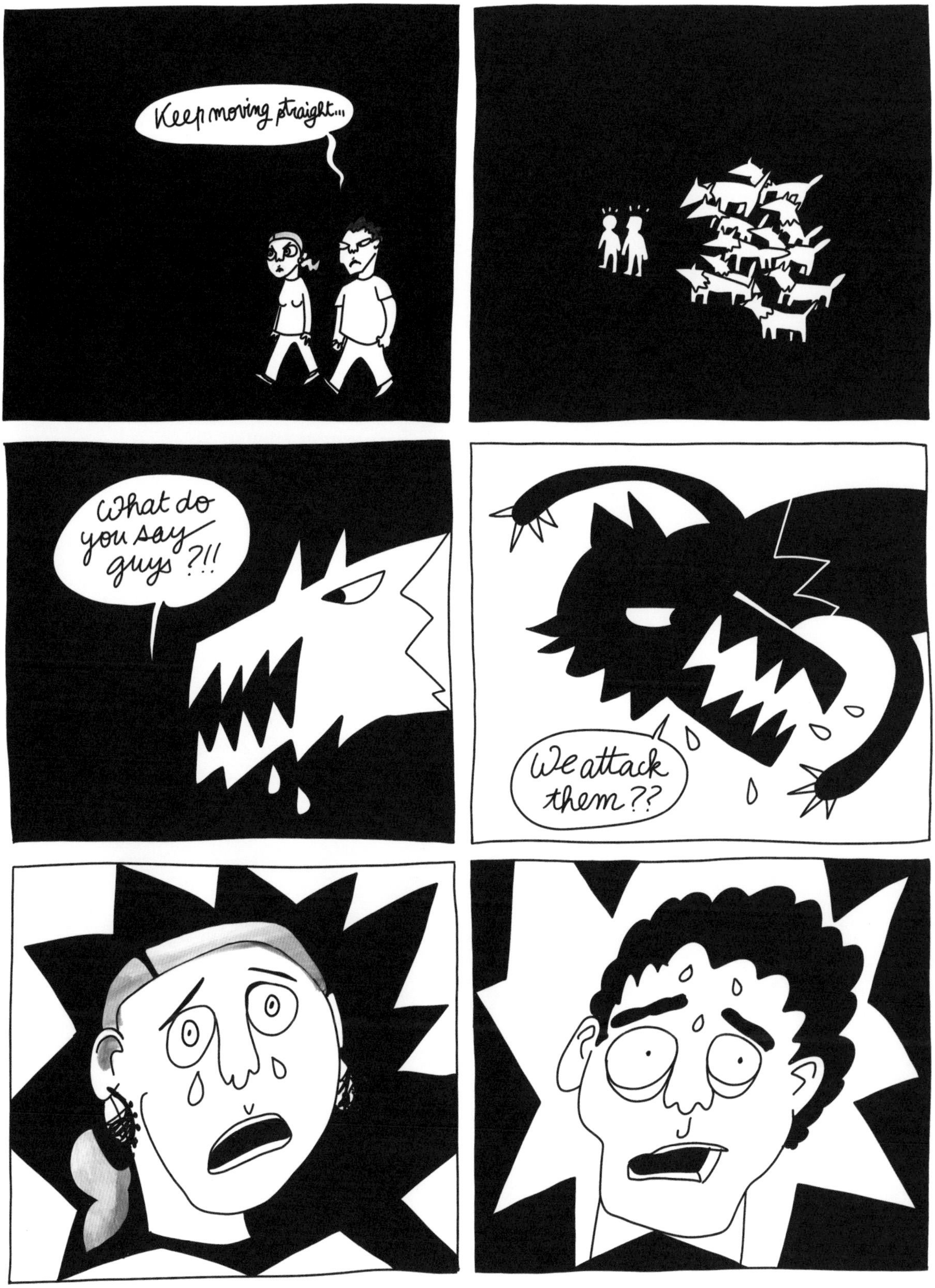
Keep moving straight...
What do you say guys ?!!
We attack them ??

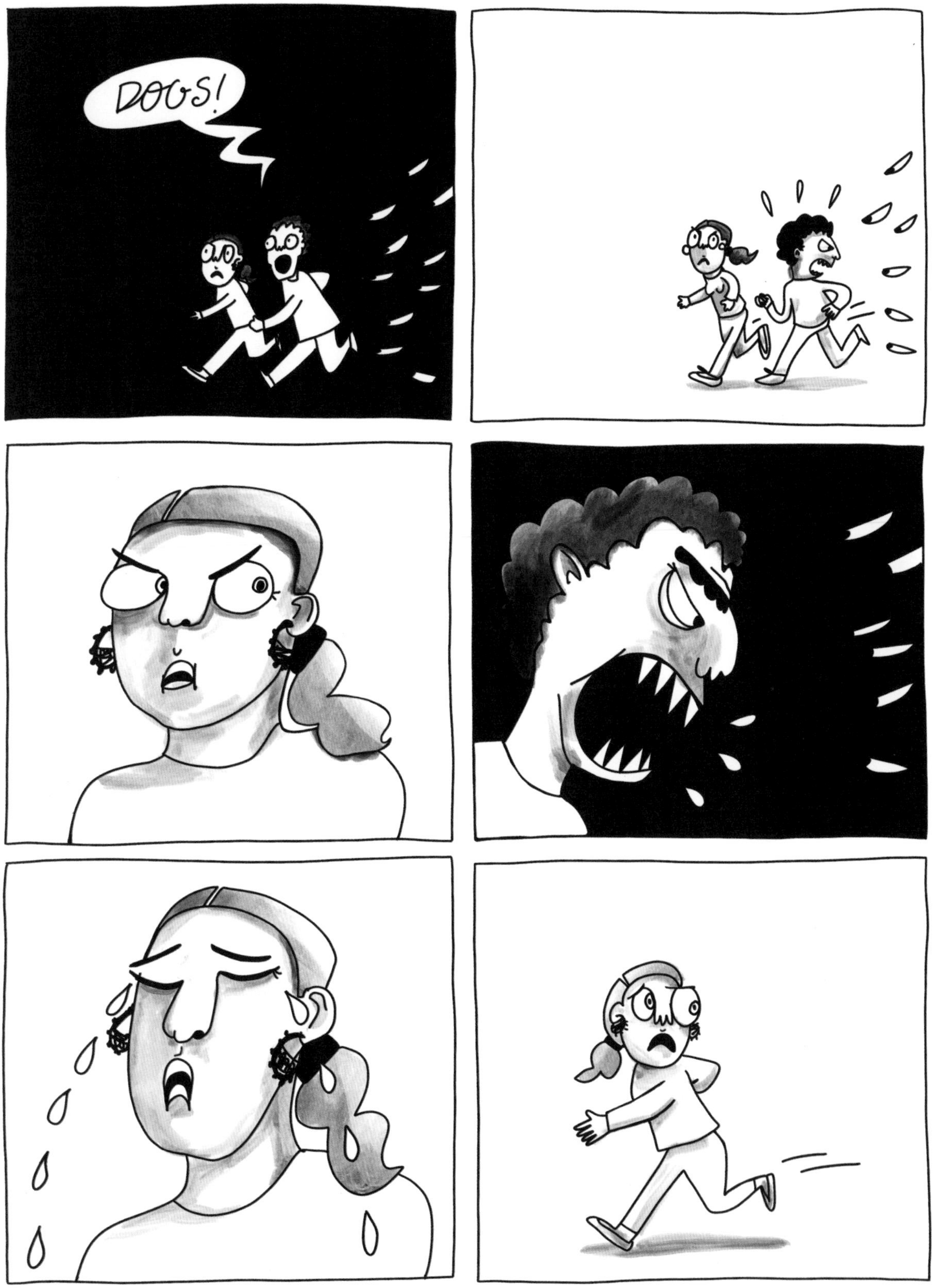
DOGS!

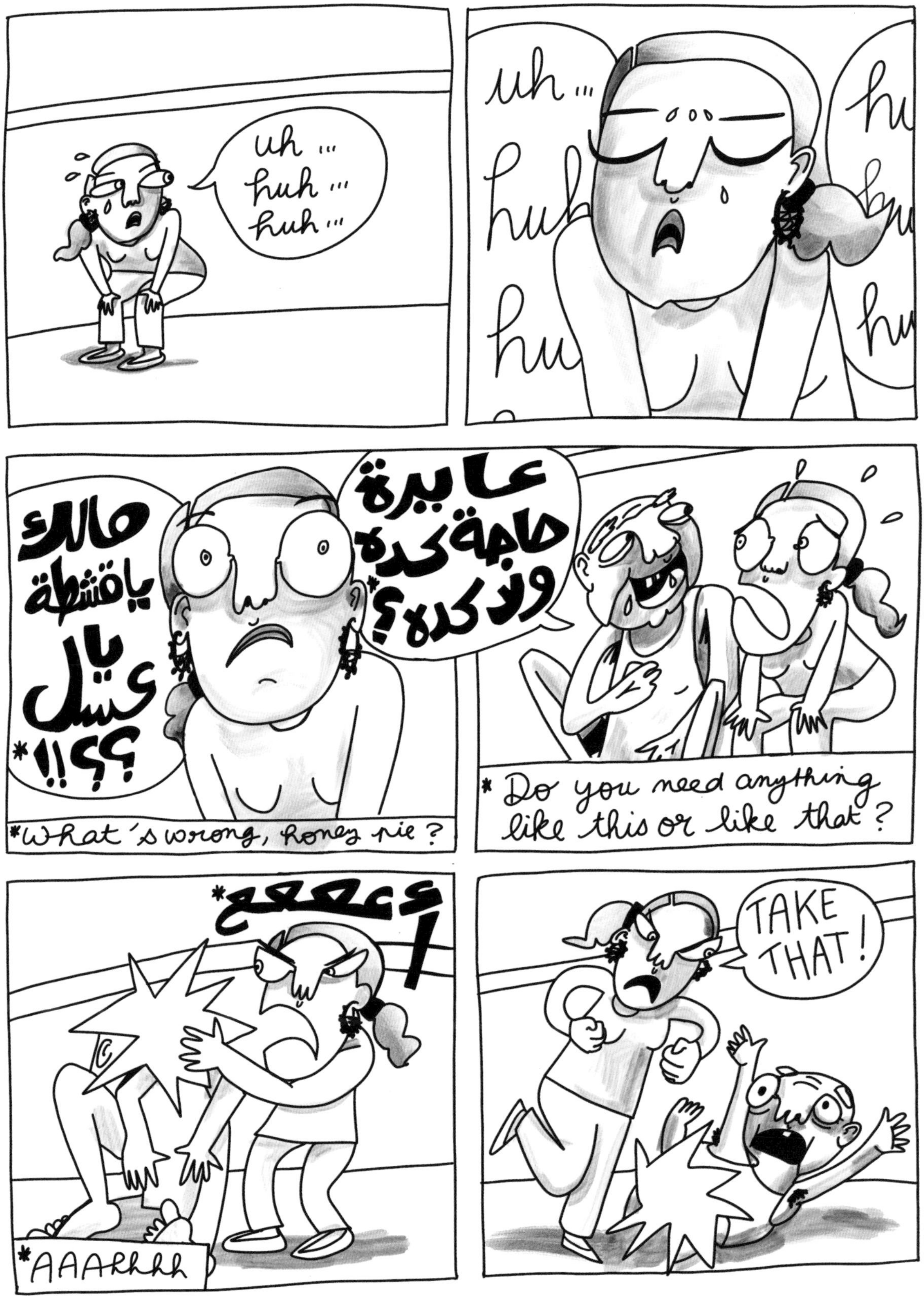
uh ... huh ... huh ...
uh ...
huh
مالك ياقشطة يا عسل ؟؟!!*
عايزة حاجة كده ولا كده ؟*
*What's wrong, honey pie?
* Do you need anything like this or like that?
أععععع !*
*AAARhhh
TAKE THAT!

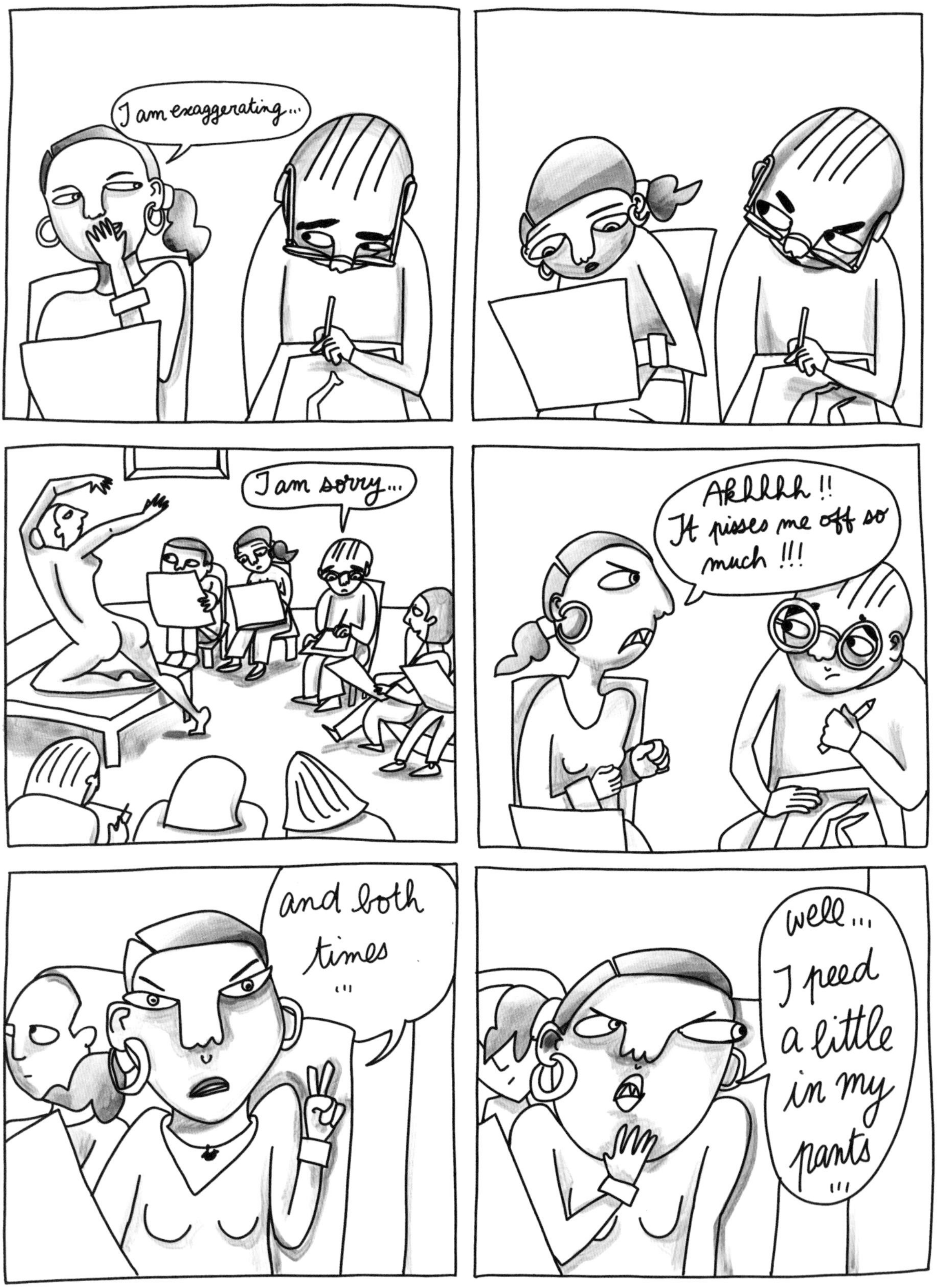
I am exaggerating...
I am sorry...
Akhhhh!! It pisses me off so much!!!
and both times ...
well... I peed a little in my pants ...

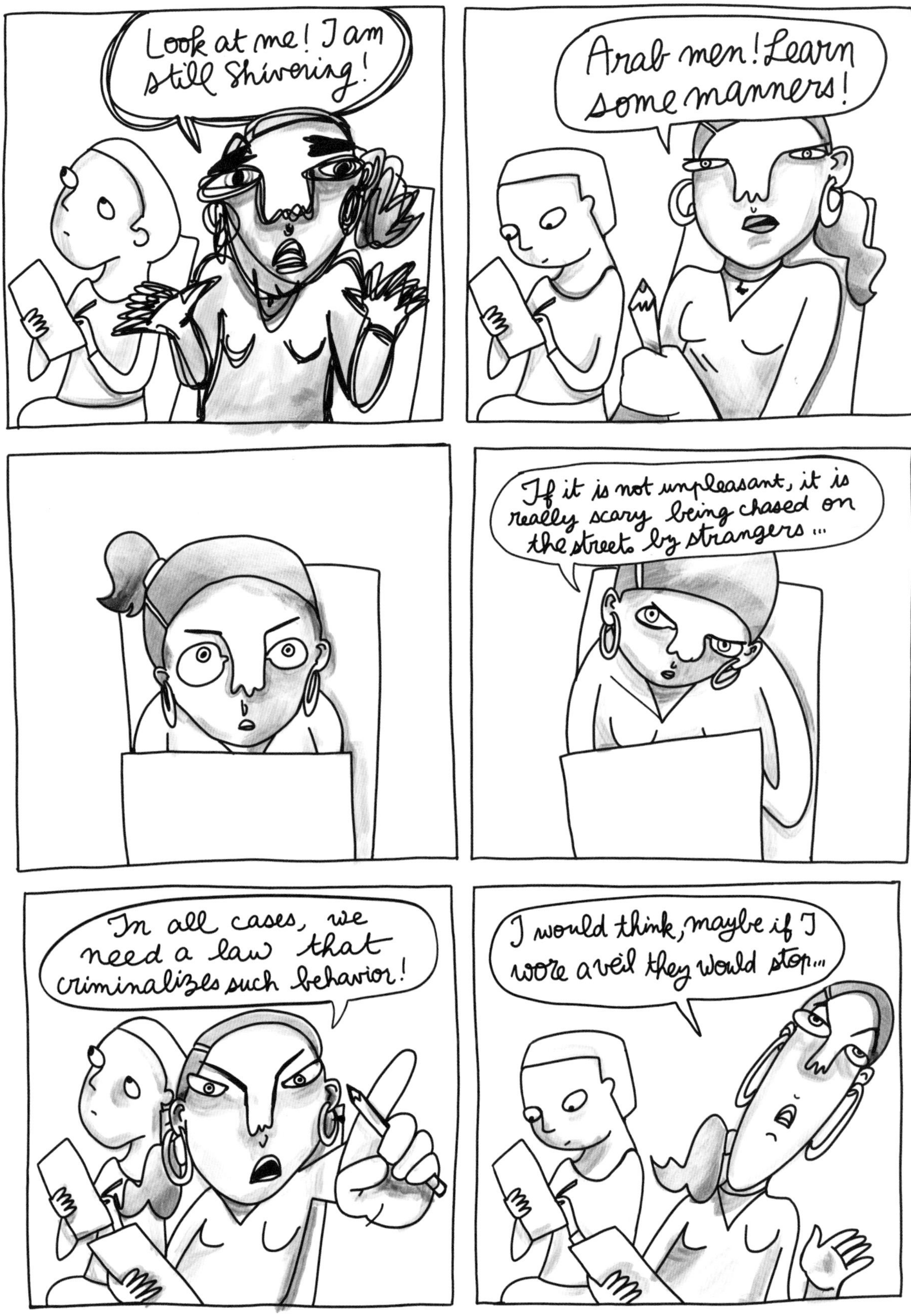
Look at me! I am still shivering!
Arab men! Learn some manners!
If it is not unpleasant, it is really scary being chased on the streets by strangers...
In all cases, we need a law that criminalizes such behavior!
I would think, maybe if I wore a veil they would stop...

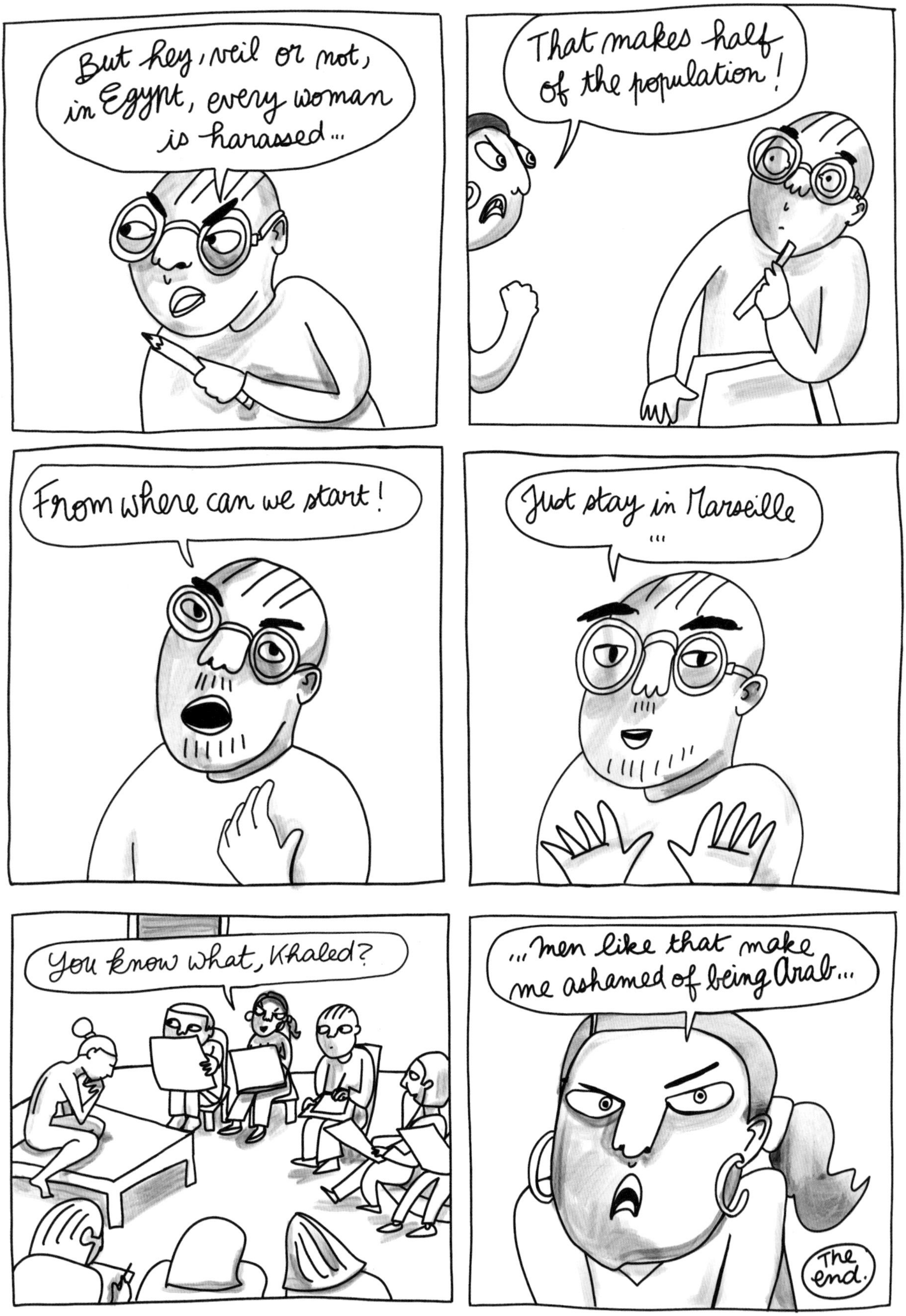
But hey, veil or not, in Egypt, every woman is harassed...
That makes half of the population!
From where can we start!
Just stay in Marseille ...
You know what, Khaled?
... men like that make me ashamed of being Arab...
The end.

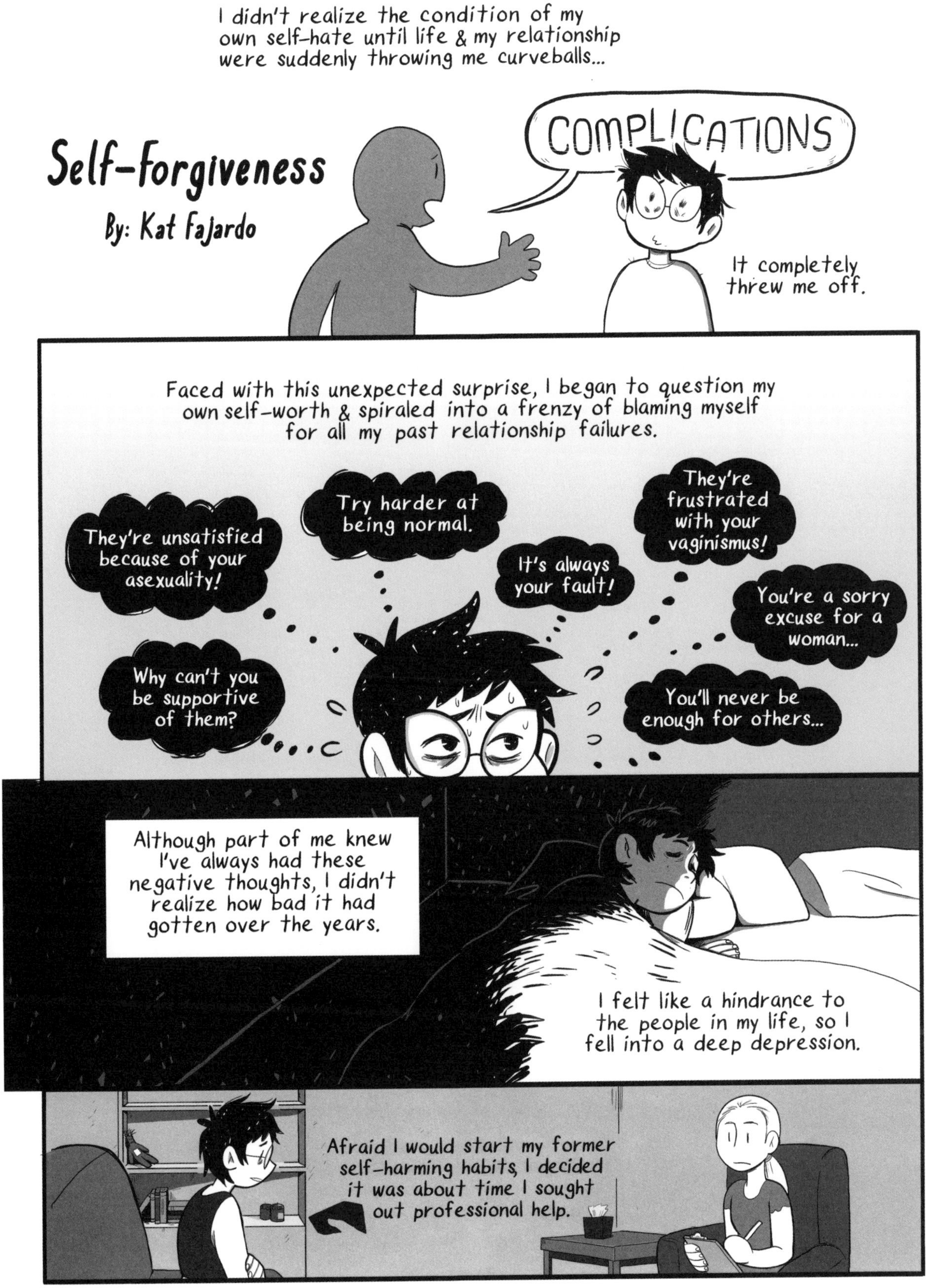
I didn't realize the condition of my own self-hate until life & my relationship were suddenly throwing me curveballs...
Self-Forgiveness
By: Kat Fajardo
COMPLICATIONS
It completely threw me off.
Faced with this unexpected surprise, I began to question my own self-worth & spiraled into a frenzy of blaming myself for all my past relationship failures.
They're unsatisfied because of your asexuality!
Try harder at being normal.
It's always your fault!
They're frustrated with your vaginismus!
You're a sorry excuse for a woman...
Why can't you be supportive of them?
You'll never be enough for others...
Although part of me knew I've always had these negative thoughts, I didn't realize how bad it had gotten over the years.
I felt like a hindrance to the people in my life, so I fell into a deep depression.
Afraid I would start my former self-harming habits, I decided it was about time I sought out professional help.

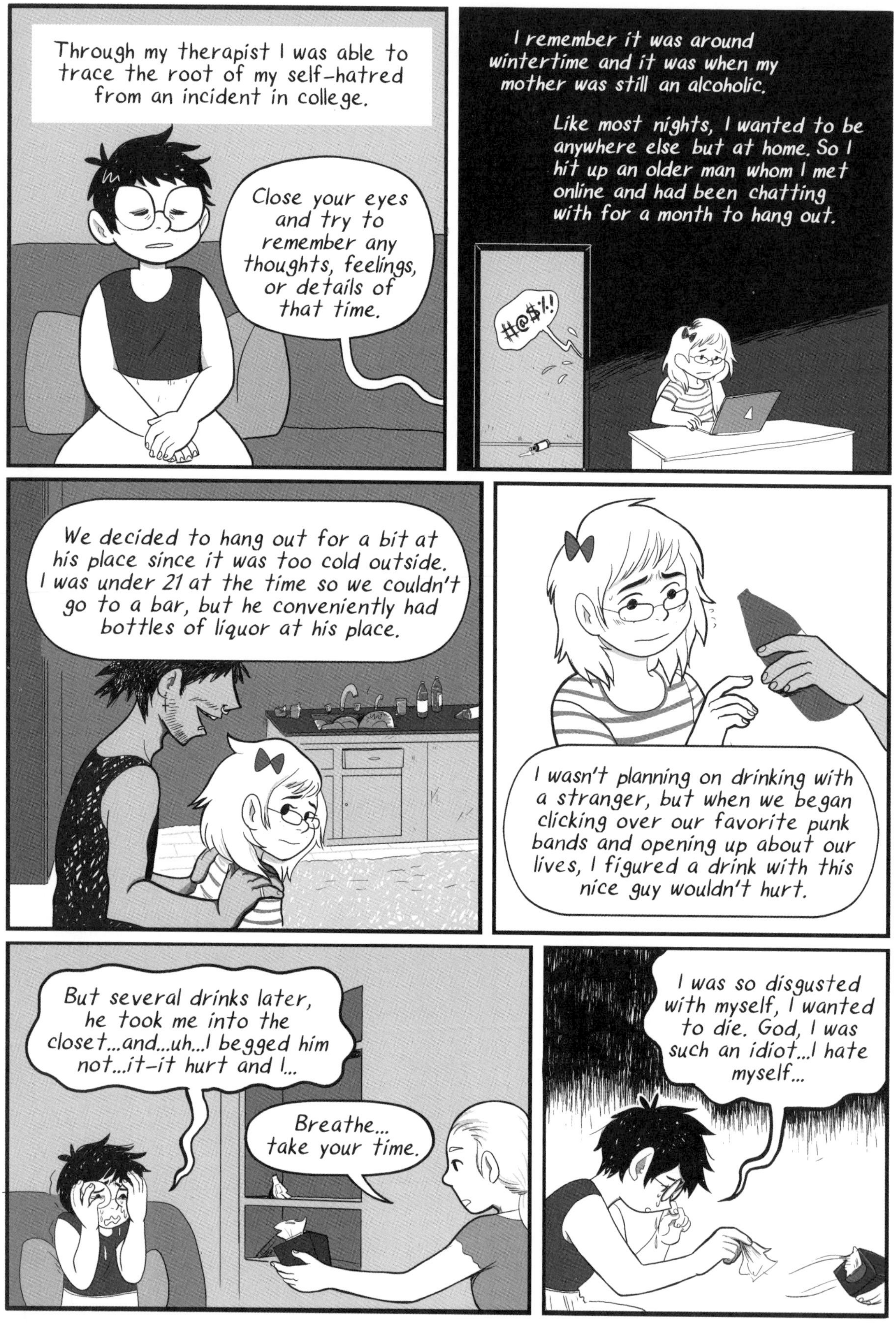

Through my therapist I was able to trace the root of my self-hatred from an incident in college.
Close your eyes and try to remember any thoughts, feelings, or details of that time.
I remember it was around wintertime and it was when my mother was still an alcoholic.
Like most nights, I wanted to be anywhere else but at home. So I hit up an older man whom I met online and had been chatting with for a month to hang out.
#@$%!
We decided to hang out for a bit at his place since it was too cold outside. I was under 21 at the time so we couldn't go to a bar, but he conveniently had bottles of liquor at his place.
I wasn't planning on drinking with a stranger, but when we began clicking over our favorite punk bands and opening up about our lives, I figured a drink with this nice guy wouldn't hurt.
But several drinks later, he took me into the closet...and...uh...I begged him not...it-it hurt and I...
Breathe... take your time.
I was so disgusted with myself, I wanted to die. God, I was such an idiot...I hate myself...

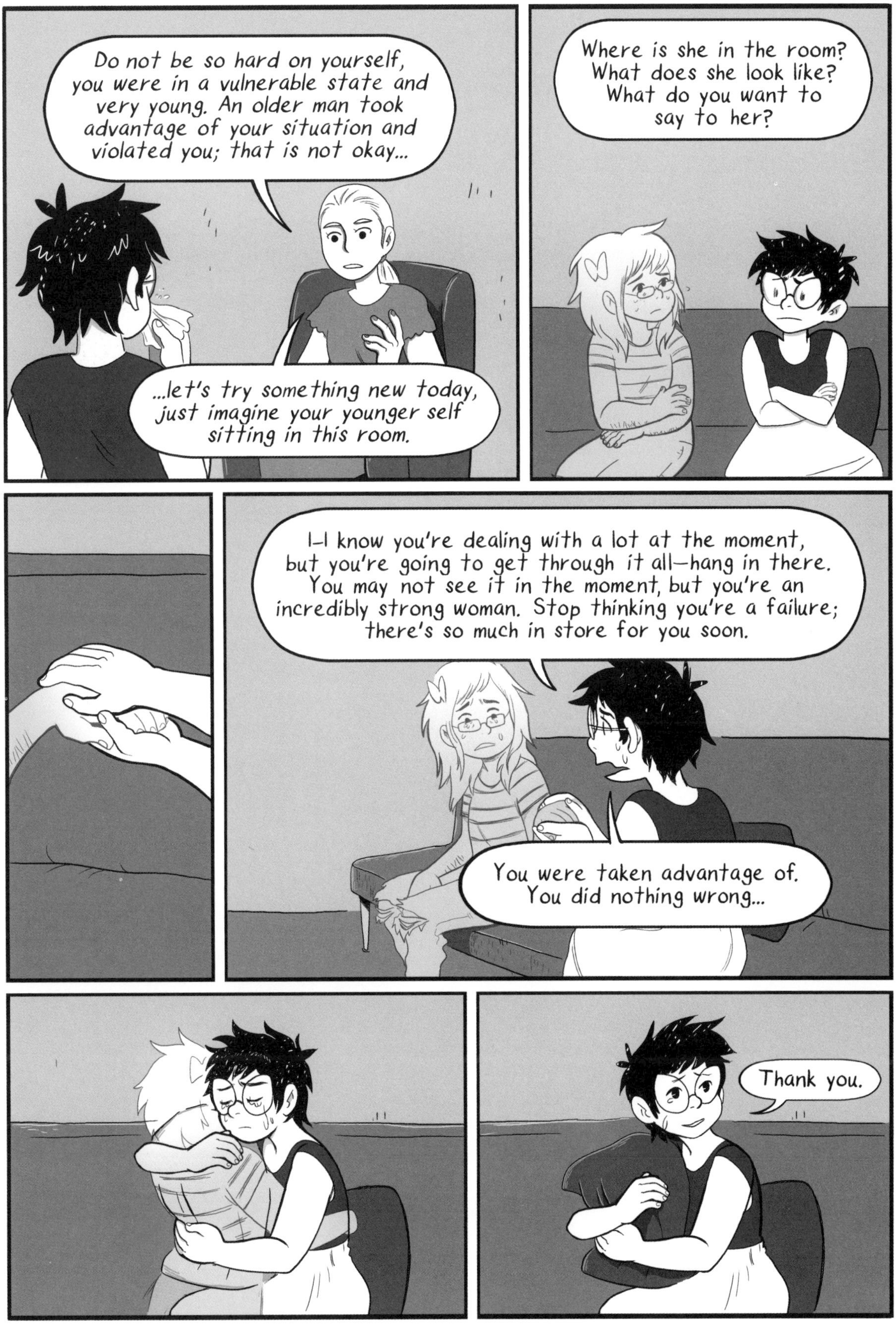
Do not be so hard on yourself, you were in a vulnerable state and very young. An older man took advantage of your situation and violated you; that is not okay...
...let's try something new today, just imagine your younger self sitting in this room.
Where is she in the room? What does she look like? What do you want to say to her?
I-I know you're dealing with a lot at the moment, but you're going to get through it all—hang in there. You may not see it in the moment, but you're an incredibly strong woman. Stop thinking you're a failure; there's so much in store for you soon.
You were taken advantage of. You did nothing wrong...
Thank you.

TWO WORDS

By Minnie Phan

I was **terrified** to type those two words. What would my friends say? How would my family feel?

Who would **know**? Me Too wasn't just a status update.

It was a confession

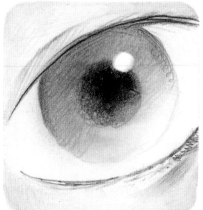

A SCREAM

A magnifying glass on the monster that nested inside me when I was five years old and burned scars deep within me.

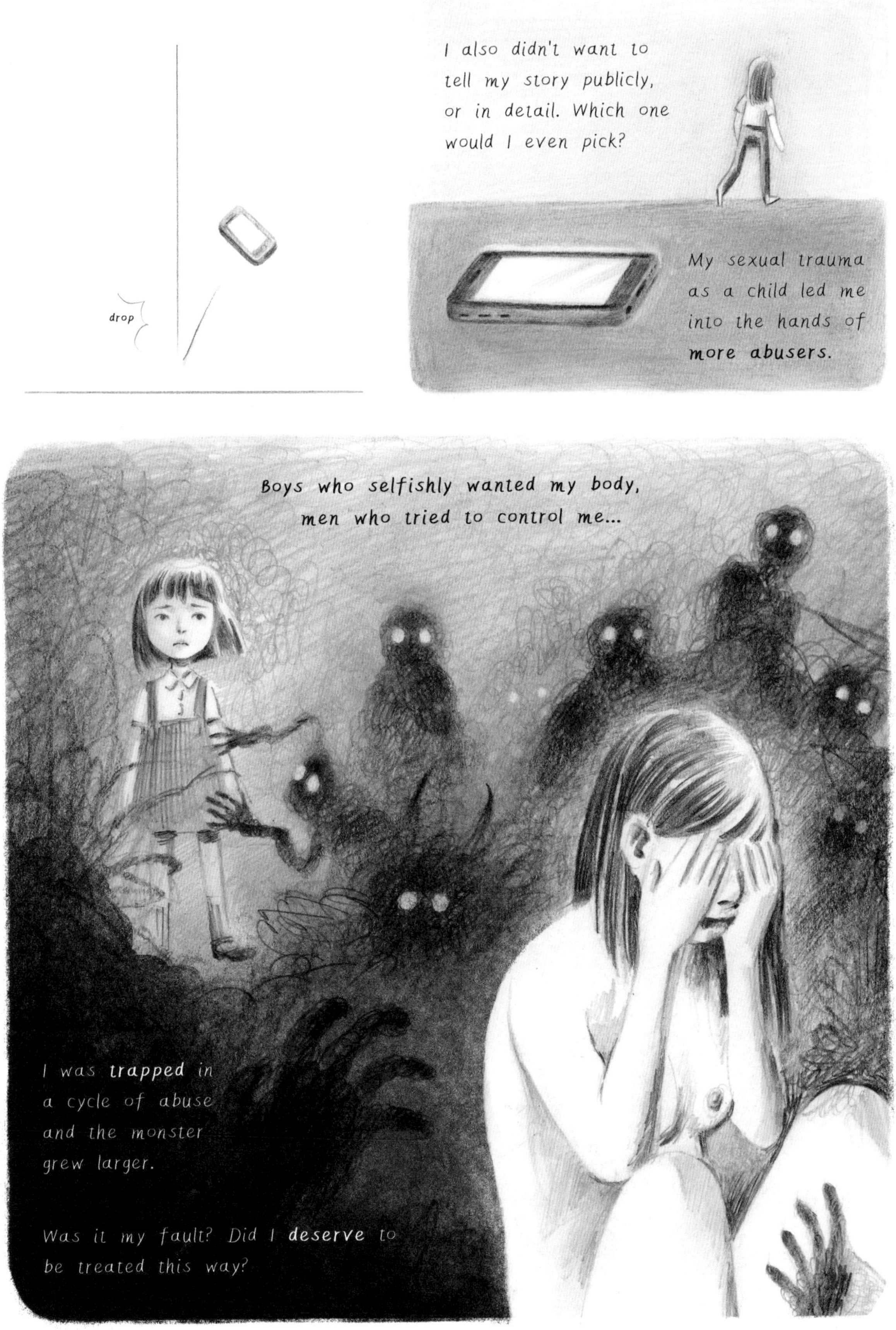
drop
I also didn't want to tell my story publicly, or in detail. Which one would I even pick?
My sexual trauma as a child led me into the hands of more abusers.
Boys who selfishly wanted my body, men who tried to control me...
I was trapped in a cycle of abuse and the monster grew larger.
Was it my fault? Did I deserve to be treated this way?

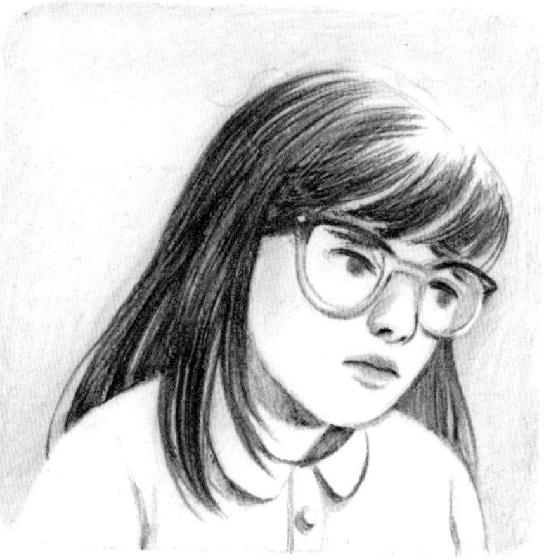

It took years to even acknowledge the trauma I've endured and the rippling effect it had all throughout my girlhood and adolescence.

I had a habit of tearing up tissues every day in therapy.

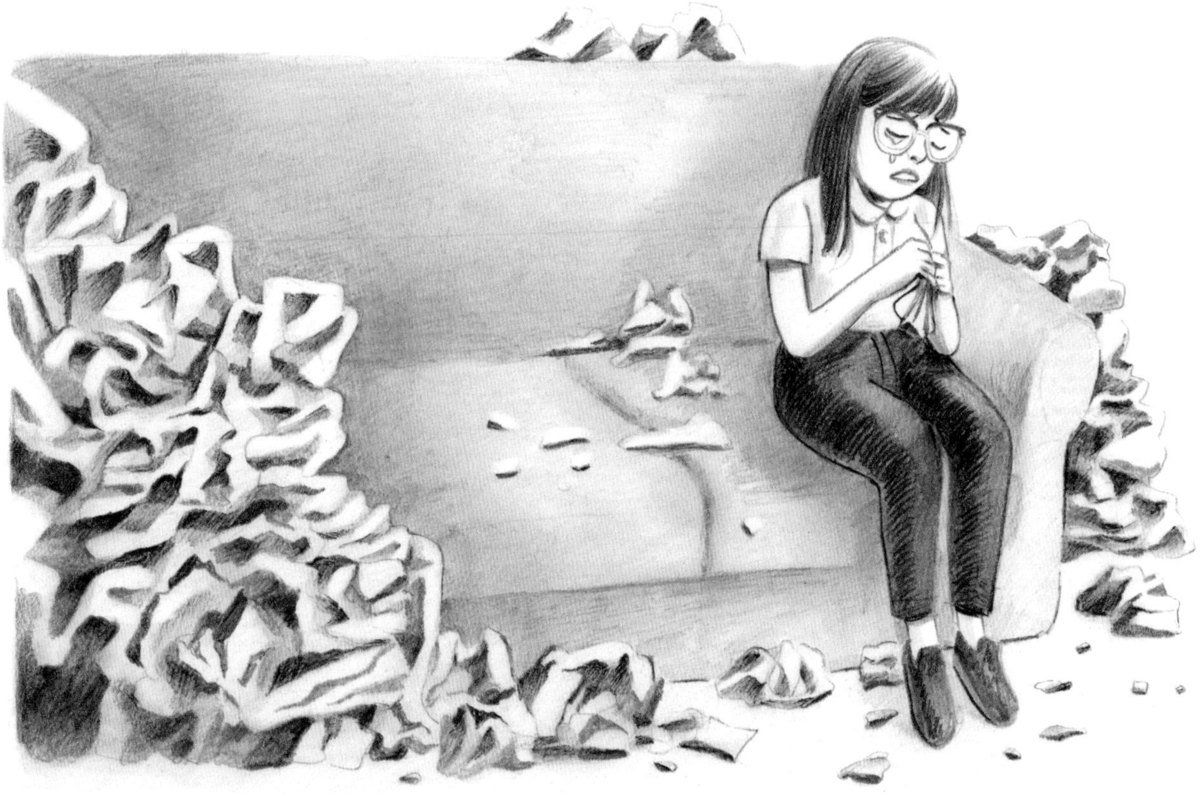

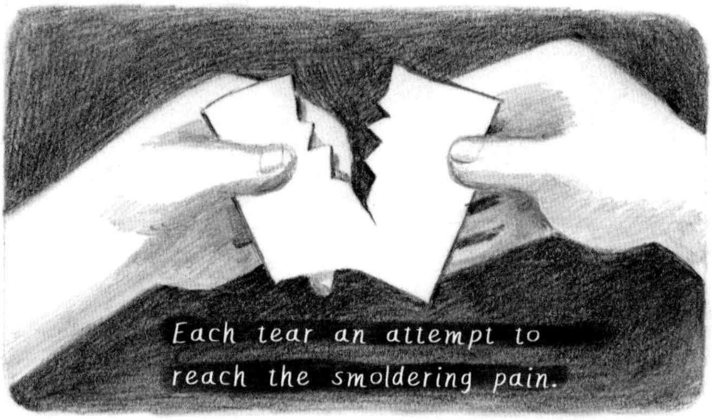
Each tear an attempt to
reach the smoldering pain.

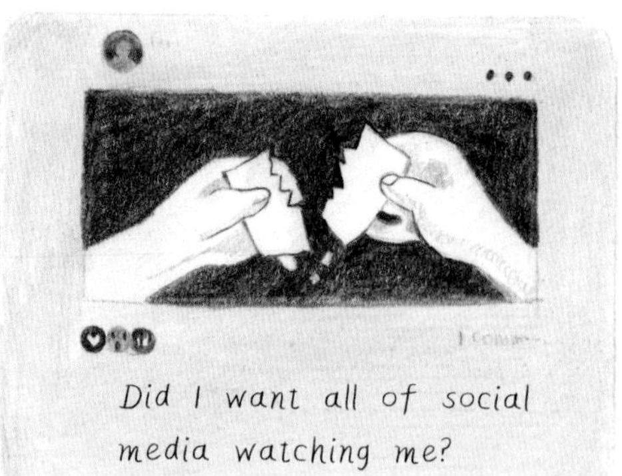
Did I want all of social
media watching me?

Still, I clicked "Post." It just felt important for me to raise my hand.

And find the reservoir of healing I hadn't known existed.

I read stories that felt familiar, and even apology letters from strangers who penned words I yearned to hear from my own abusers.

Me Too was not just a condemnation.

It was RESISTANCE. SOLIDARITY.

Strength.

And a chance to start over.

Top Secret

By Ilana Zeffren

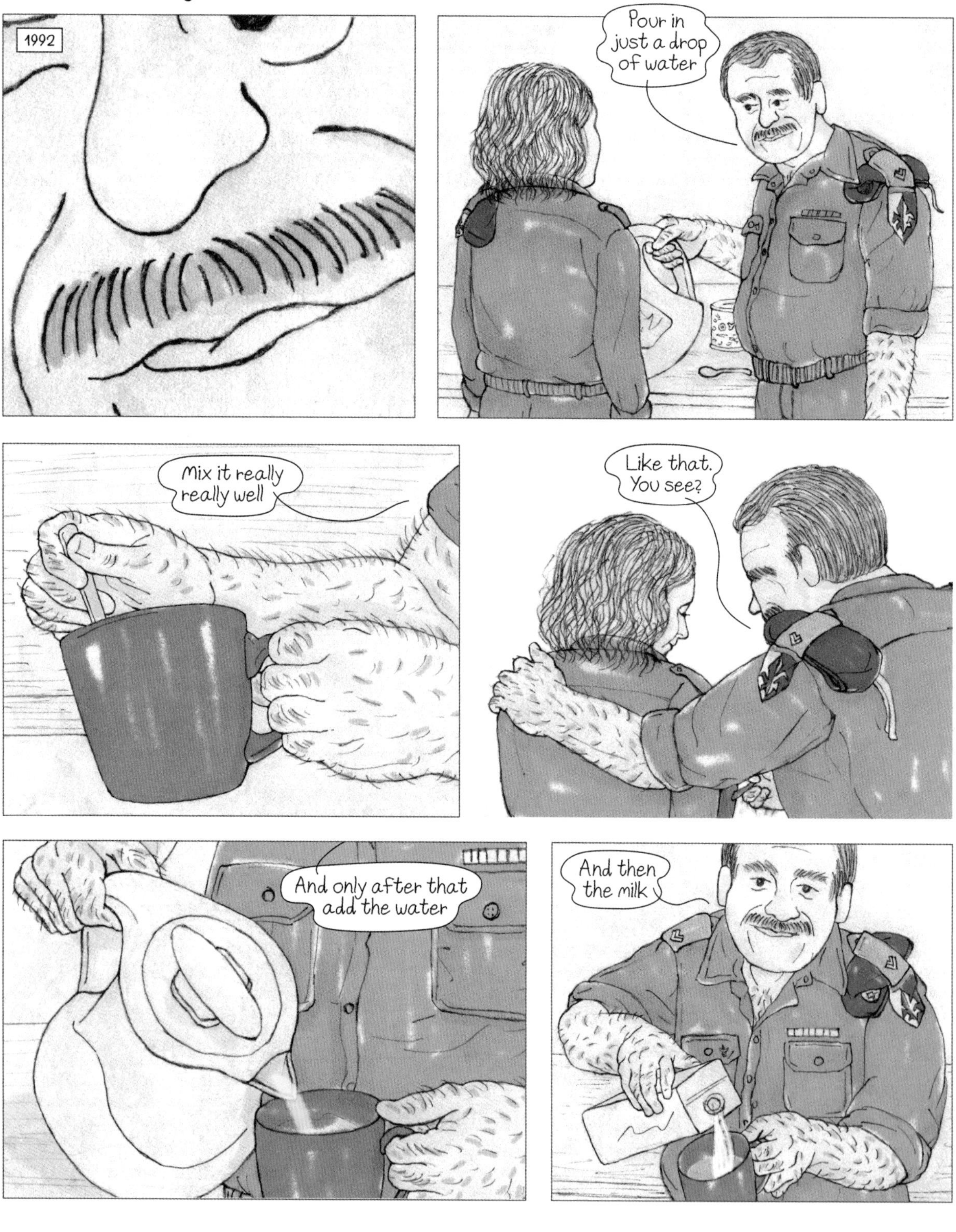
1992
Pour in just a drop of water
Mix it really really well
Like that. You see?
And only after that add the water
And then the milk

We arrived at the army base two days before, after taking part in a three-month study course at another base, ready to do a meaningful job.

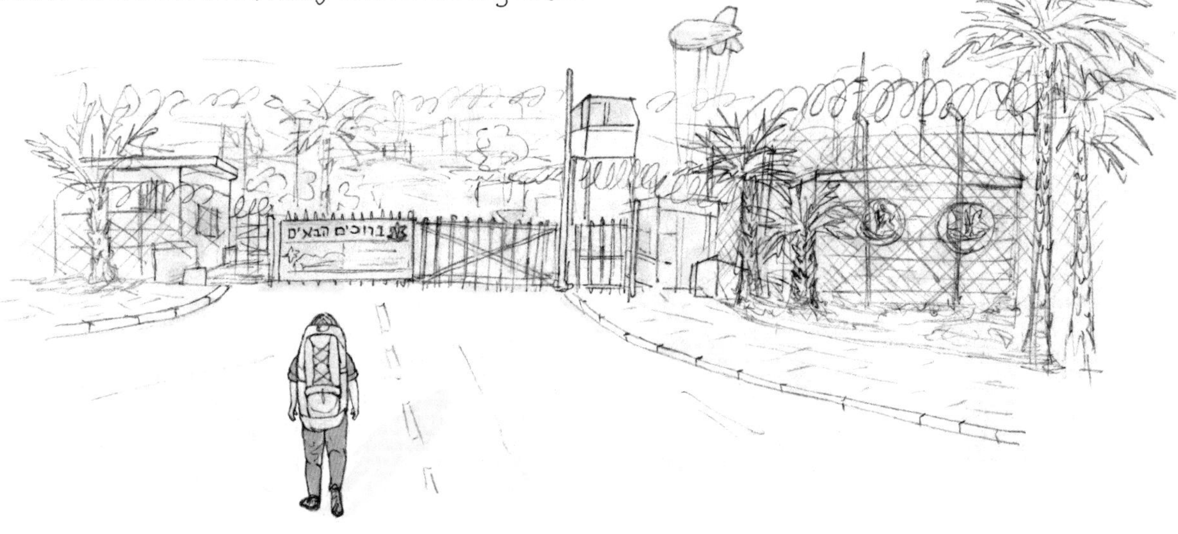
ברוכים הבאים

We were chosen carefully for that course. We were trained to listen in on the Egyptian army communication, and goverment officials' phone calls.

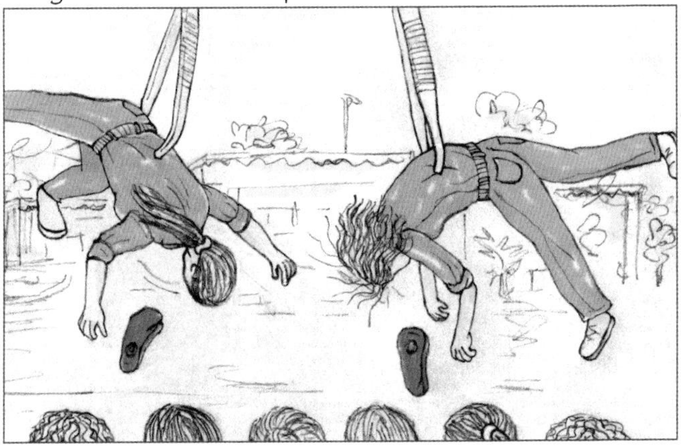

The listening in took place in a bunker divided into units.

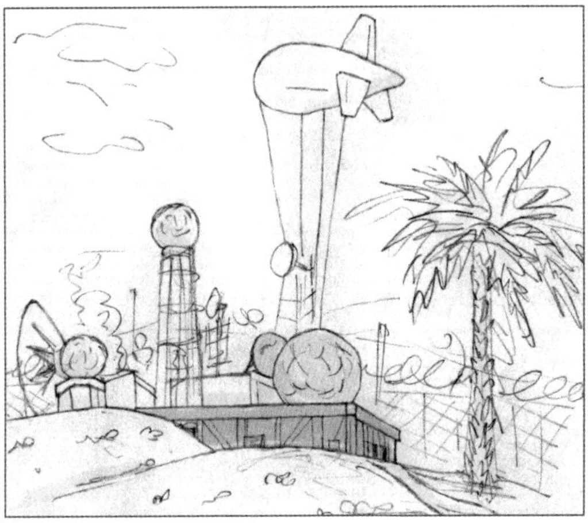

My course mates were all assigned to one unit, but me and four other girls were chosen (again carefully) to serve in another unit.

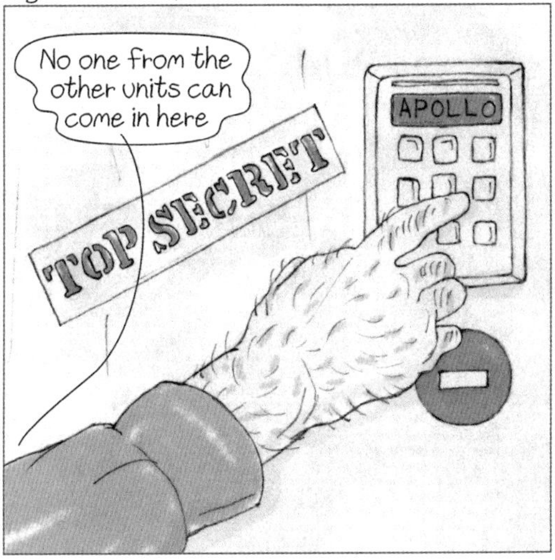
No one from the other units can come in here
APOLLO
TOP SECRET

Apollo's mission was to listen in on encrypted calls. We had to break the code that the Egyptians were using on their devices before listening in. We were eager to learn how to do that, but the first thing our deputy commander taught us was how to make instant coffee with cream.

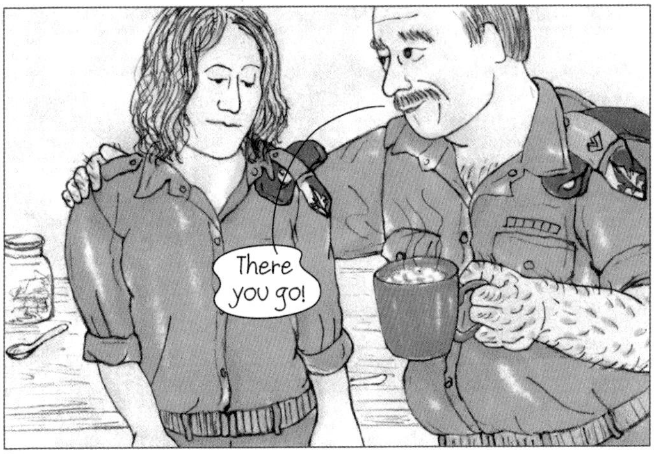
There you go!

Our training took a few days. The deputy commander and the commander taught us everything we needed to know. At the end of the day they went home to their wives and kids.

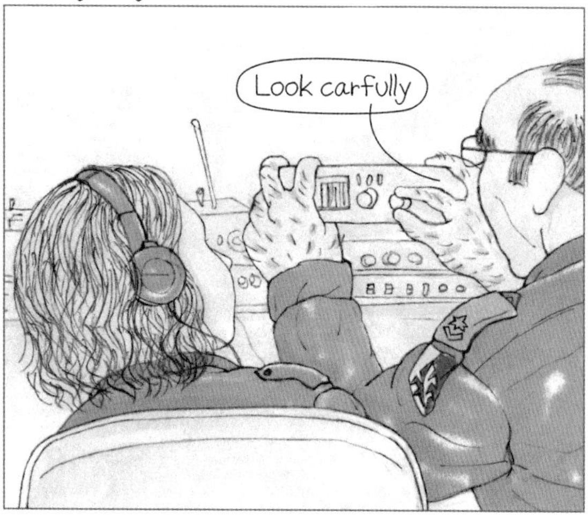
Look carfully

After that we started doing shifts. We already knew how to make coffee with cream and all the secrets of the job, but the deputy commander insisted that we keep making coffee together, his face in our face every time, and he insisted on being there while we were listening in.

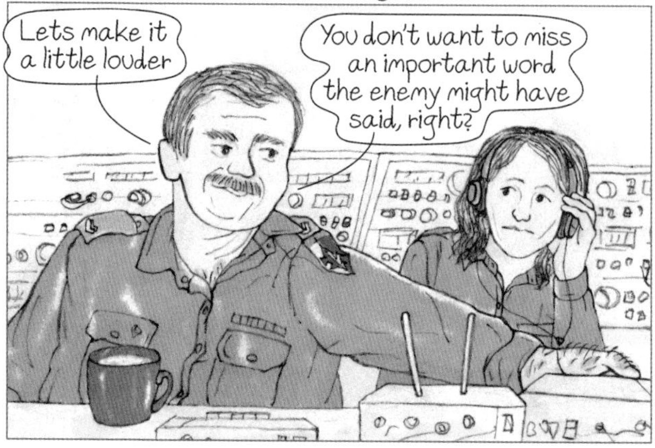
Lets make it a little louder
You don't want to miss an important word the enemy might have said, right?

The commander also kept interest in our work.

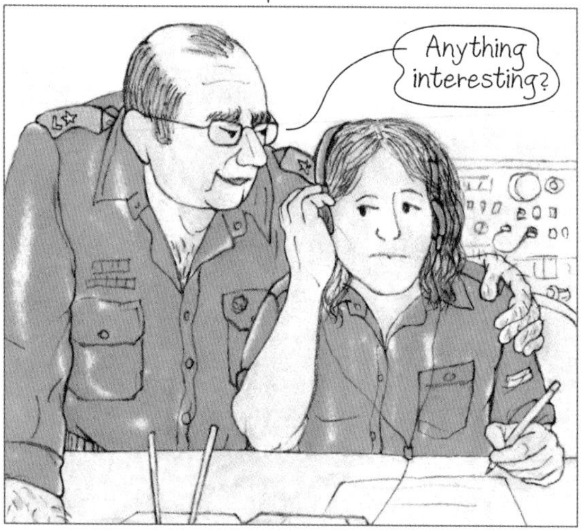
Anything interesting?

This was our daily routine for two years behind that coded door. We never said a word and we never gave it a name. We were kids that just finished high school a minute ago, thinking they're doing something important.

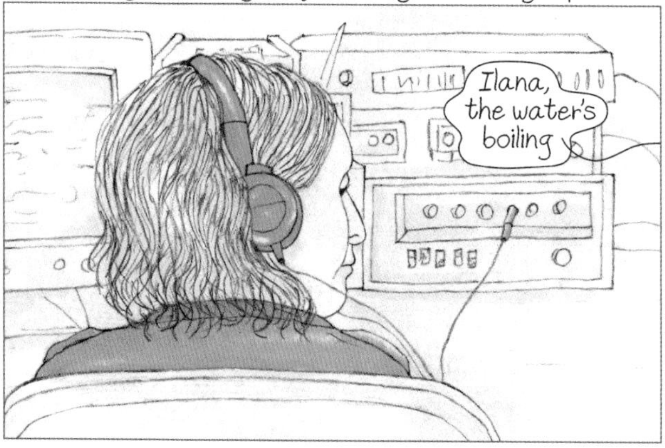
Ilana, the water's boiling

Many years have passed since then. I don't remember how to break codes anymore, I don't remember anything the Egyptians said, I forgot a lot of my Arabic, and I barely remember my course mates.

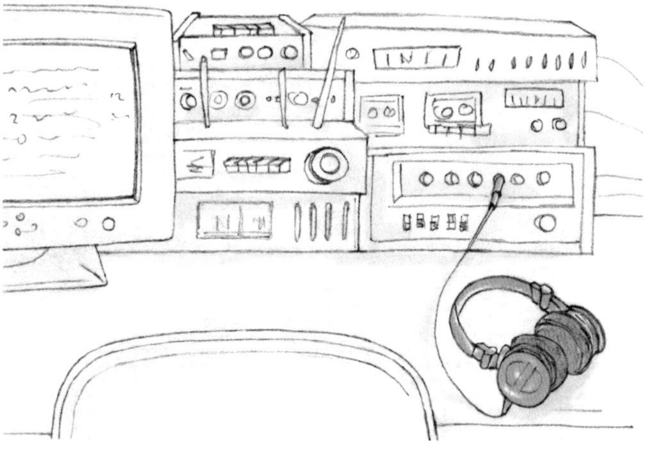

But I still remember very clearly how to make instant coffee with cream.

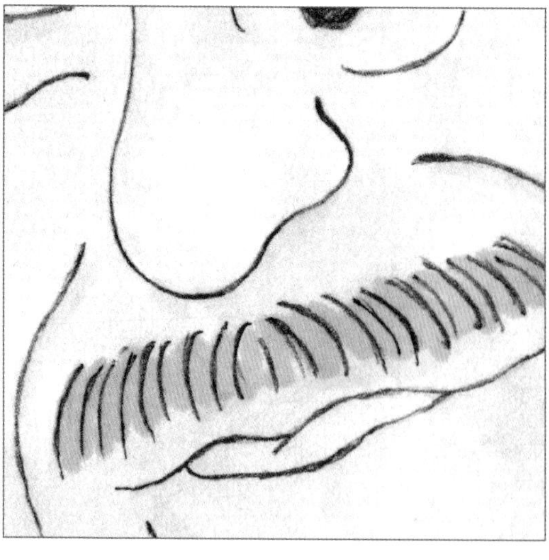

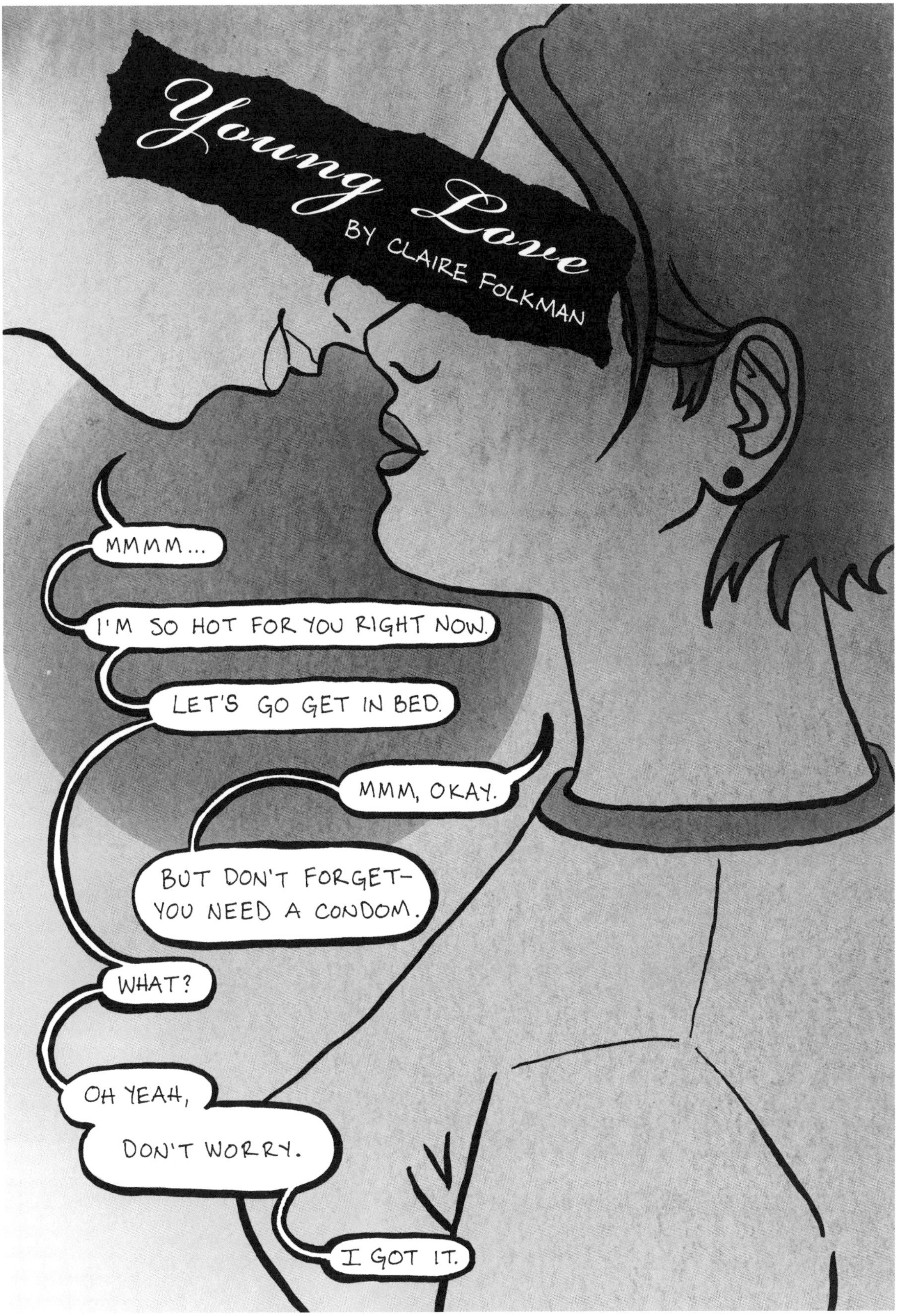
Young Love
BY CLAIRE FOLKMAN
MMMM...
I'M SO HOT FOR YOU RIGHT NOW.
LET'S GO GET IN BED.
MMM, OKAY.
BUT DON'T FORGET-
YOU NEED A CONDOM.
WHAT?
OH YEAH,
DON'T WORRY.
I GOT IT.

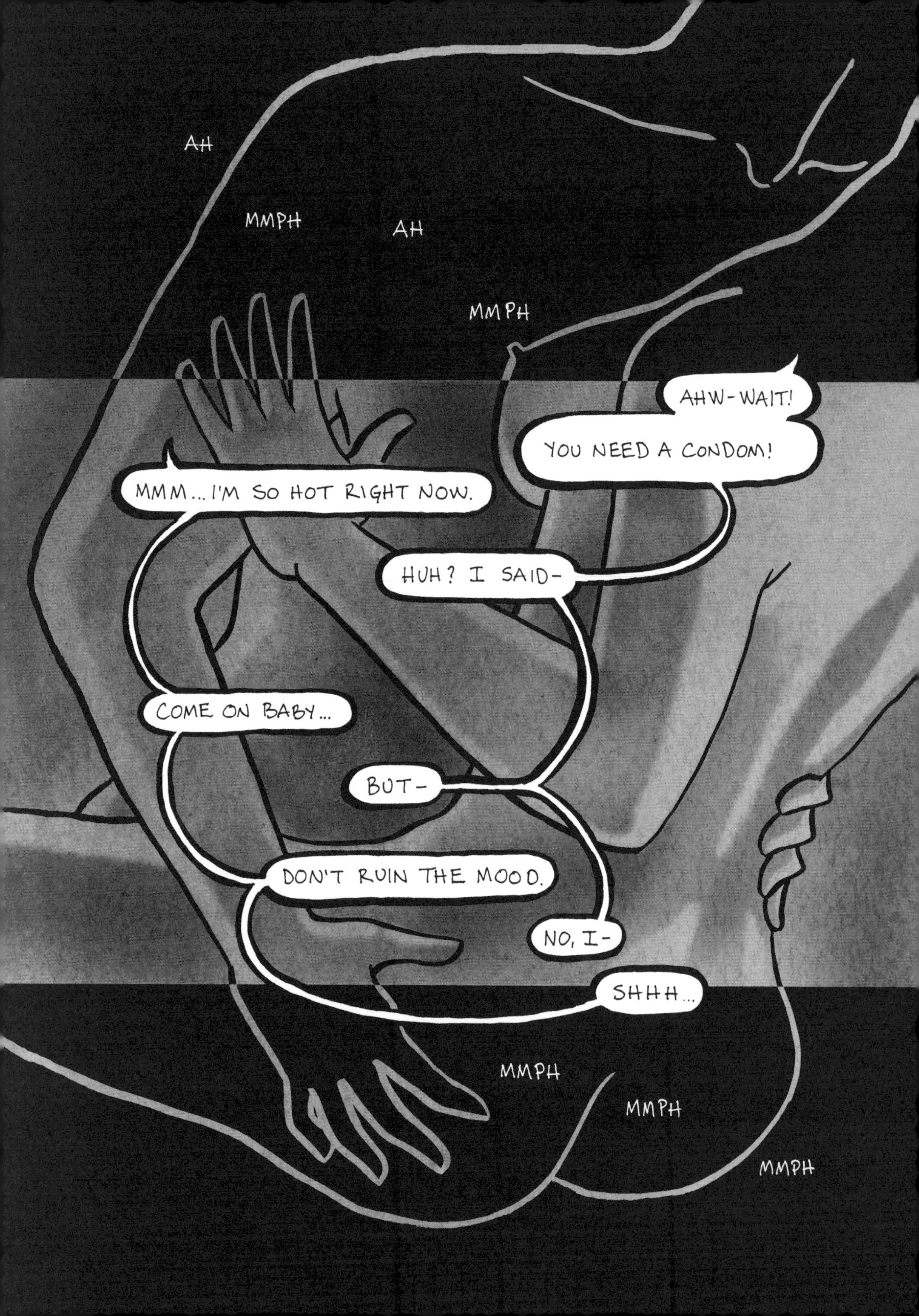
AH
MMPH
AH
MMPH
AHW-WAIT!
YOU NEED A CONDOM!
MMM... I'M SO HOT RIGHT NOW.
HUH? I SAID-
COME ON BABY...
BUT-
DON'T RUIN THE MOOD.
NO, I-
SHHH...
MMPH
MMPH
MMPH

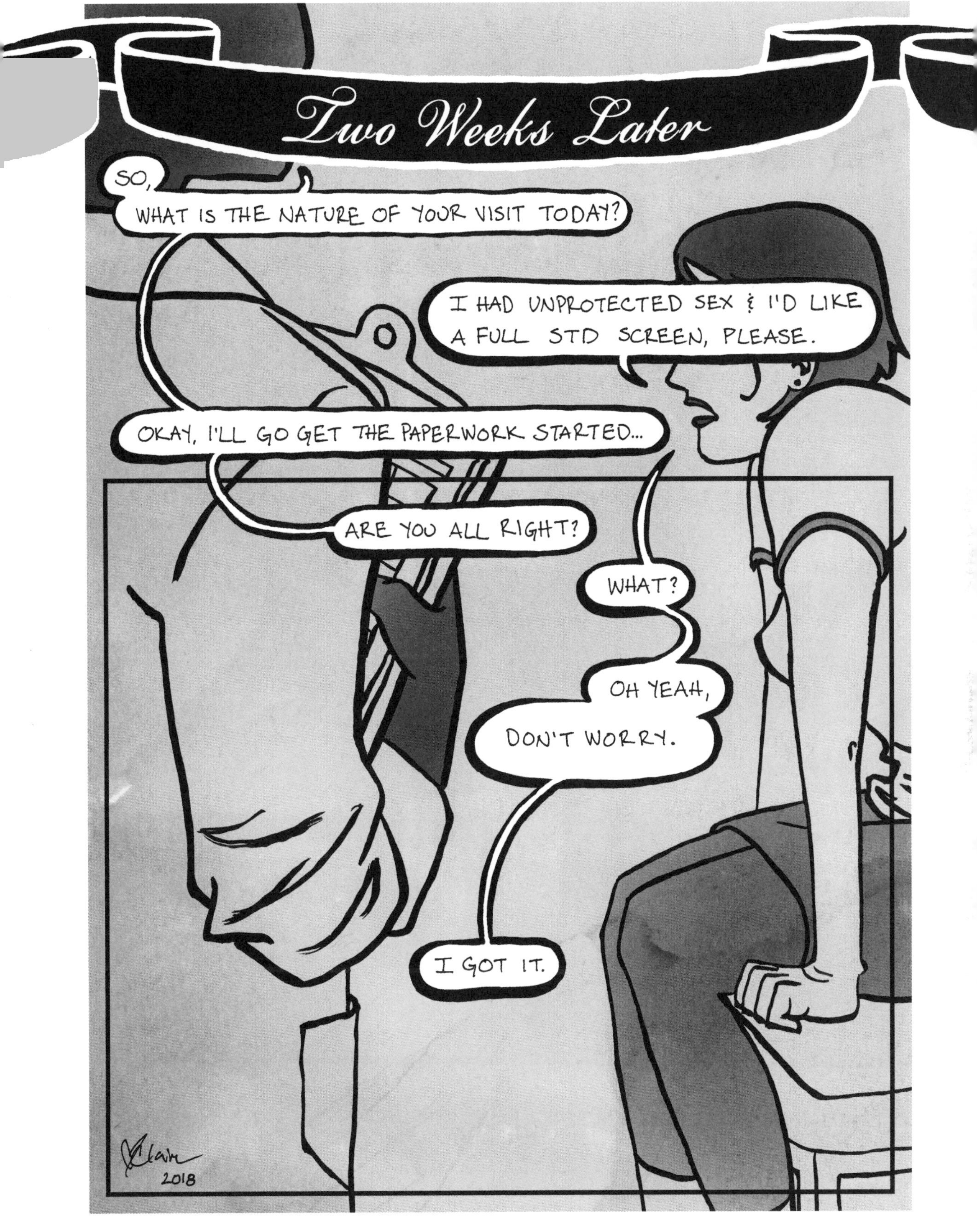
Two Weeks Later
SO,
WHAT IS THE NATURE OF YOUR VISIT TODAY?
I HAD UNPROTECTED SEX & I'D LIKE A FULL STD SCREEN, PLEASE.
OKAY, I'LL GO GET THE PAPERWORK STARTED...
ARE YOU ALL RIGHT?
WHAT?
OH YEAH,
DON'T WORRY.
I GOT IT.
Claire
2018

LIGHTWEIGHT.

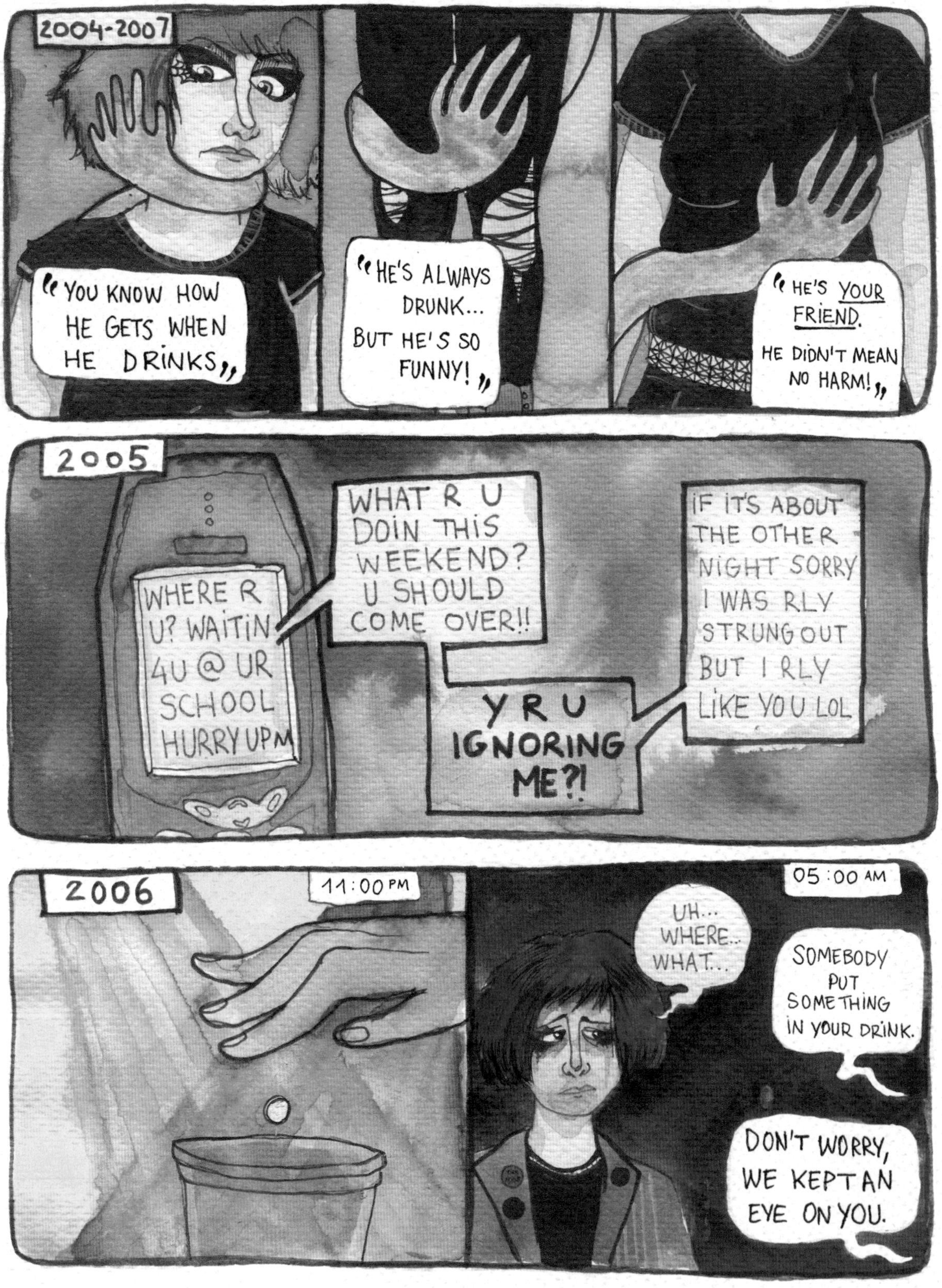
2004-2007
"YOU KNOW HOW HE GETS WHEN HE DRINKS"
"HE'S ALWAYS DRUNK... BUT HE'S SO FUNNY!"
"HE'S YOUR FRIEND. HE DIDN'T MEAN NO HARM!"
2005
WHERE R U? WAITIN 4U @ UR SCHOOL HURRY UP
WHAT R U DOIN THIS WEEKEND? U SHOULD COME OVER!!
Y R U IGNORING ME?!
IF IT'S ABOUT THE OTHER NIGHT SORRY I WAS RLY STRUNG OUT BUT I RLY LIKE YOU LOL
2006
11:00 PM
05:00 AM
UH... WHERE.. WHAT...
SOMEBODY PUT SOMETHING IN YOUR DRINK.
DON'T WORRY, WE KEPT AN EYE ON YOU.

DEADWEIGHT.

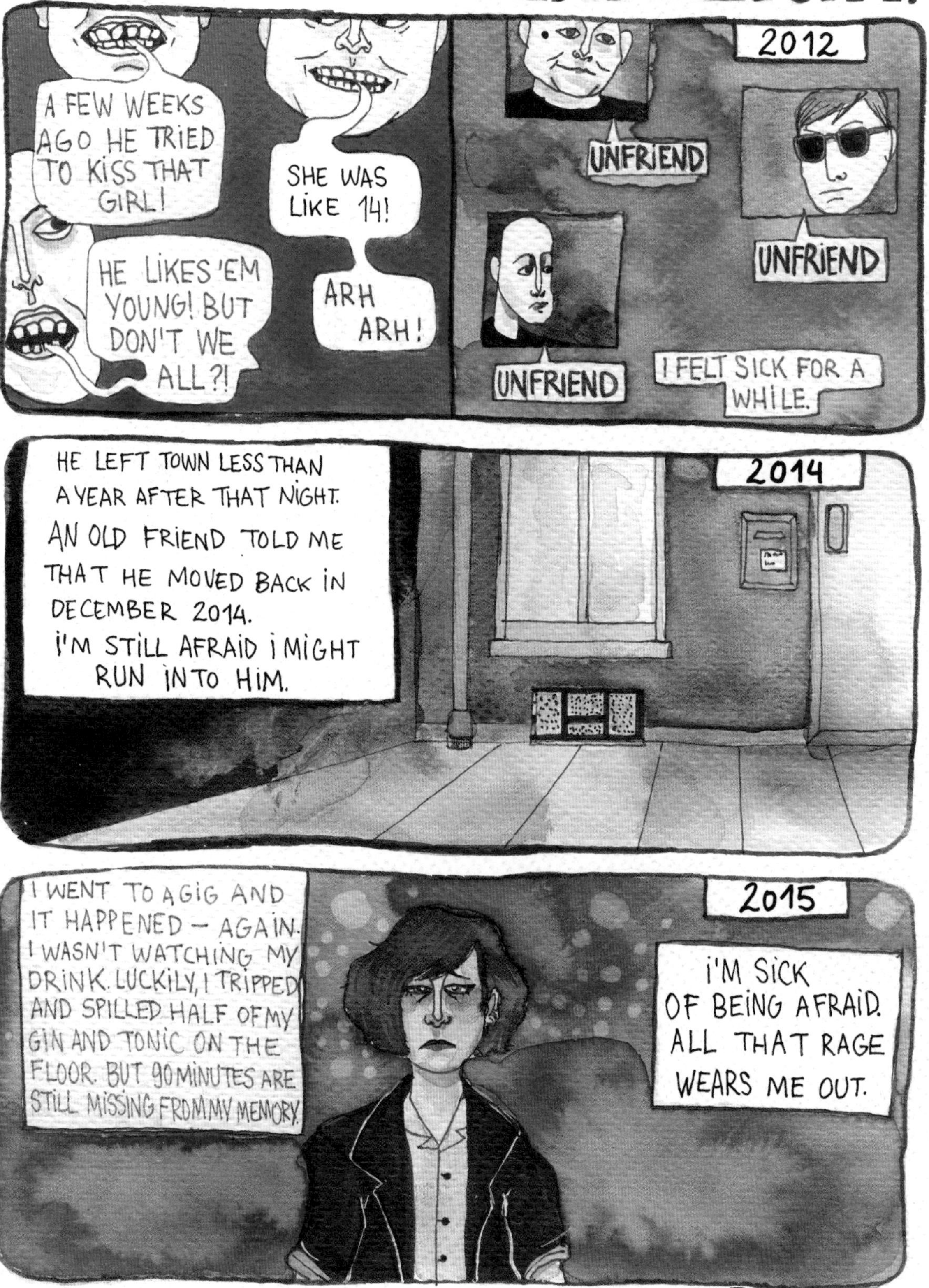

A FEW WEEKS AGO HE TRIED TO KISS THAT GIRL!
SHE WAS LIKE 14!
HE LIKES 'EM YOUNG! BUT DON'T WE ALL?!
ARH ARH!
2012
UNFRIEND
UNFRIEND
UNFRIEND
I FELT SICK FOR A WHILE.
HE LEFT TOWN LESS THAN A YEAR AFTER THAT NIGHT. AN OLD FRIEND TOLD ME THAT HE MOVED BACK IN DECEMBER 2014. I'M STILL AFRAID I MIGHT RUN INTO HIM.
2014
I WENT TO A GIG AND IT HAPPENED – AGAIN. I WASN'T WATCHING MY DRINK. LUCKILY, I TRIPPED AND SPILLED HALF OF MY GIN AND TONIC ON THE FLOOR. BUT 90 MINUTES ARE STILL MISSING FROM MY MEMORY.
2015
I'M SICK OF BEING AFRAID. ALL THAT RAGE WEARS ME OUT.

ZOE BELSINGER

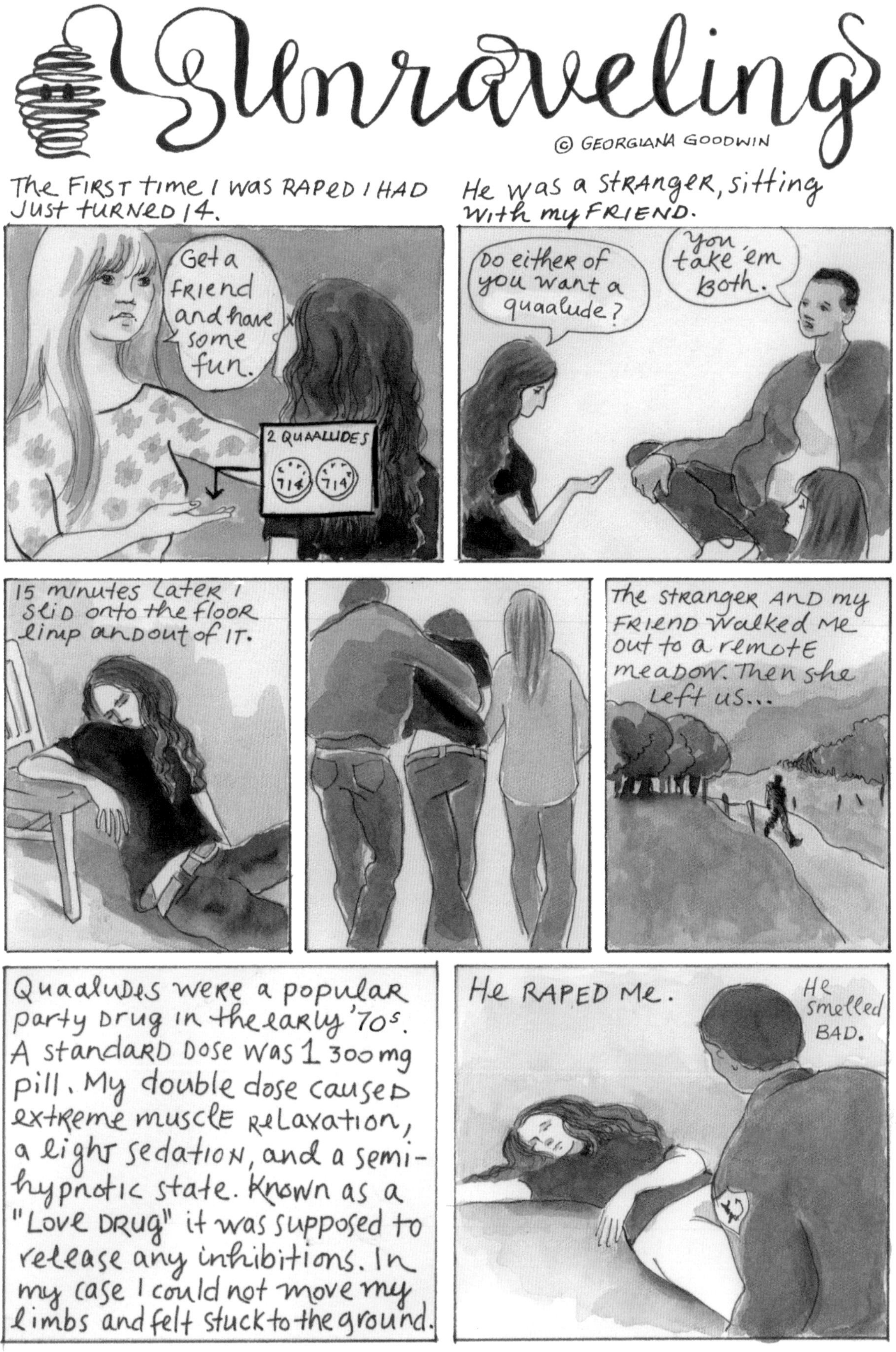
Unraveling
© GEORGIANA GOODWIN
The FIRST time I was RAPED I HAD JUST turned 14.
Get a friend and have some fun.
2 QUAALUDES
He was a STRANGER, sitting with my FRIEND.
Do either of you want a quaalude?
You take 'em Both.
15 minutes later I slid onto the floor limp and out of IT.
The stranger AND my FRIEND walked me out to a remote meadow. Then she left us...
Quaaludes were a popular party drug in the early '70s. A standard dose was 1 300mg pill. My double dose caused extreme muscle relaxation, a light sedation, and a semi-hypnotic state. Known as a "Love Drug" it was supposed to release any inhibitions. In my case I could not move my limbs and felt stuck to the ground.
He RAPED me.
He smelled BAD.

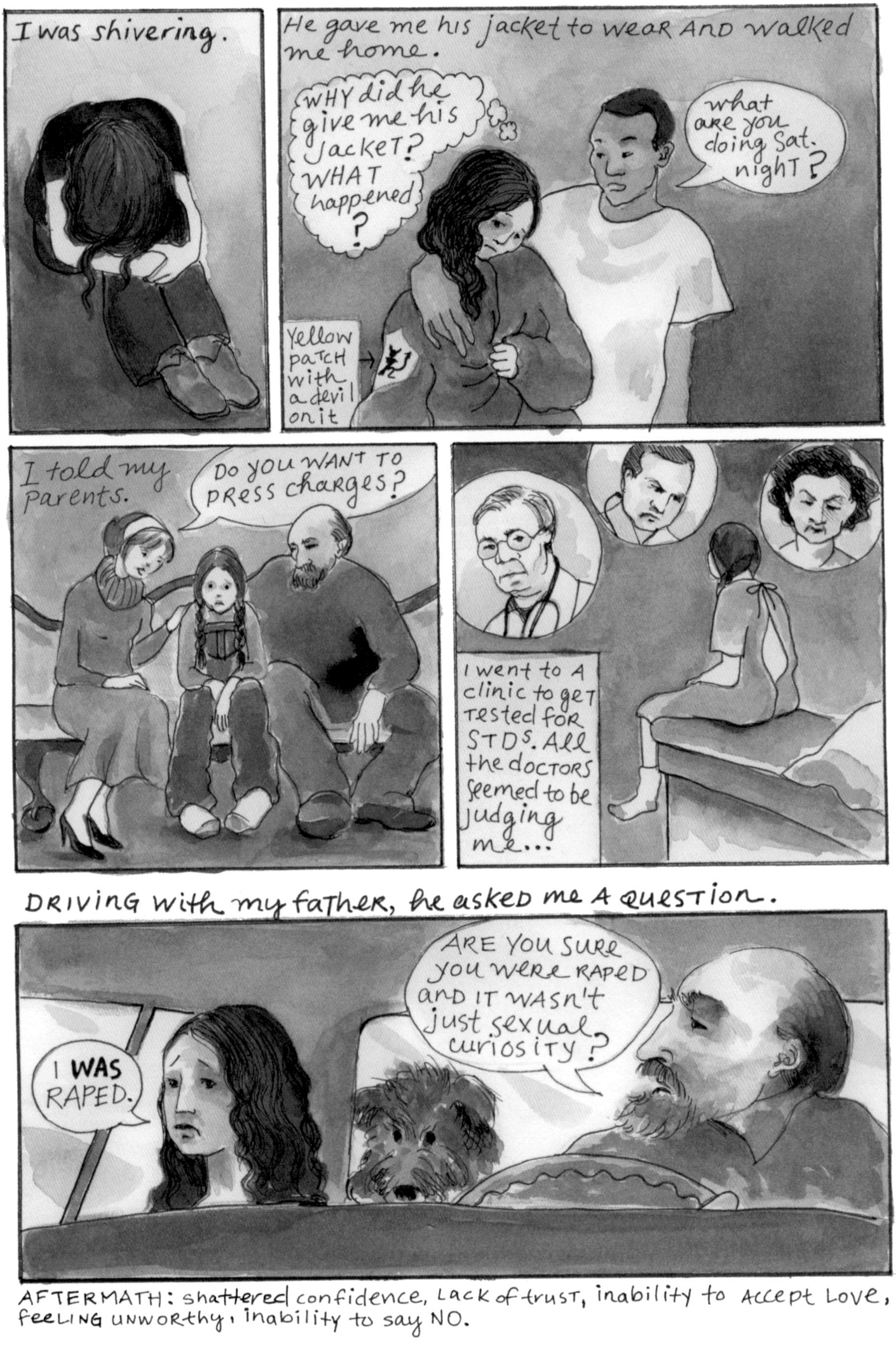
I was shivering.
He gave me his jacket to wear and walked me home.
WHY did he give me his JACKET? WHAT happened?
what are you doing Sat. night?
Yellow patch with a devil on it
I told my parents.
Do you WANT TO PRESS charges?
I went to A clinic to get tested for STDs. All the doctors seemed to be judging me...
DRIVING with my father, he asked me A question.
ARE YOU SURE you were raped and it wasn't just sexual curiosity?
I WAS RAPED.

AFTERMATH: shattered confidence, lack of trust, inability to accept love, feeling unworthy, inability to say NO.

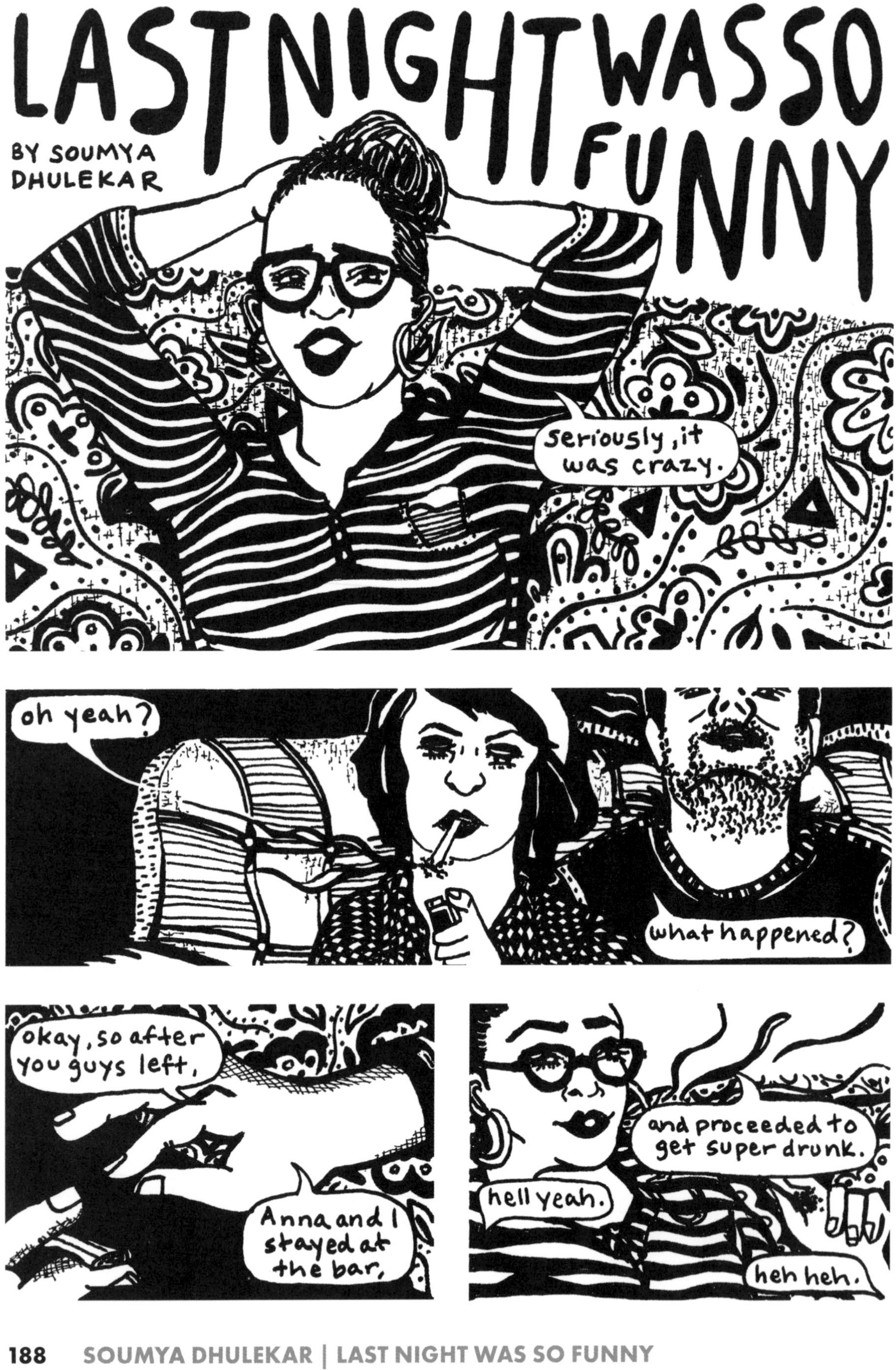
LAST NIGHT WAS SO FUNNY
BY SOUMYA DHULEKAR
seriously, it was crazy.
oh yeah?
what happened?
okay, so after you guys left,
Anna and I stayed at the bar,
and proceeded to get super drunk.
hell yeah.
heh heh.

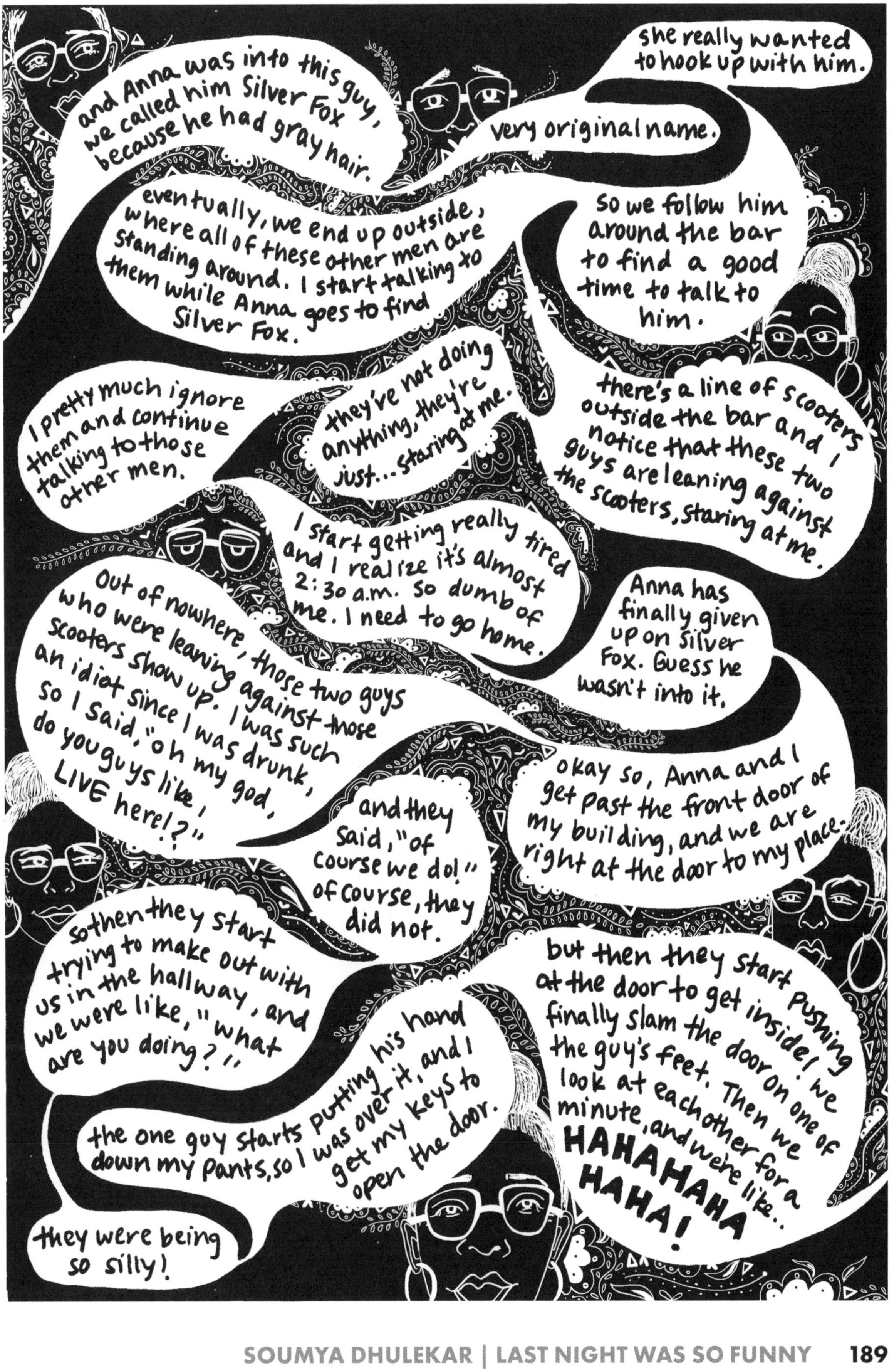
and Anna was into this guy, we called him Silver Fox because he had gray hair.
she really wanted to hook up with him.
very original name.
eventually, we end up outside, where all of these other men are standing around. I start talking to them while Anna goes to find Silver Fox.
so we follow him around the bar to find a good time to talk to him.
I pretty much ignore them and continue talking to those other men.
they're not doing anything, they're just... staring at me.
there's a line of scooters outside the bar and I notice that these two guys are leaning against the scooters, staring at me.
I start getting really tired and I realize it's almost 2:30 a.m. So dumb of me. I need to go home.
Anna has finally given up on Silver Fox. Guess he wasn't into it.
Out of nowhere, those two guys who were leaning against those scooters show up. I was such an idiot since I was drunk, so I said, "oh my god, do you guys like, LIVE here!?"
okay so, Anna and I get past the front door of my building, and we are right at the door to my place.
and they said, "of course we do!" of course, they did not.
so then they start trying to make out with us in the hallway, and we were like, "what are you doing?!"
but then they start pushing at the door to get inside! we finally slam the door on one of the guy's feet. Then we look at eachother for a minute, and we're like.. HAHAHAHAHA HAHA!
the one guy starts putting his hand down my pants, so I was over it, and I get my keys to open the door.
they were being so silly!

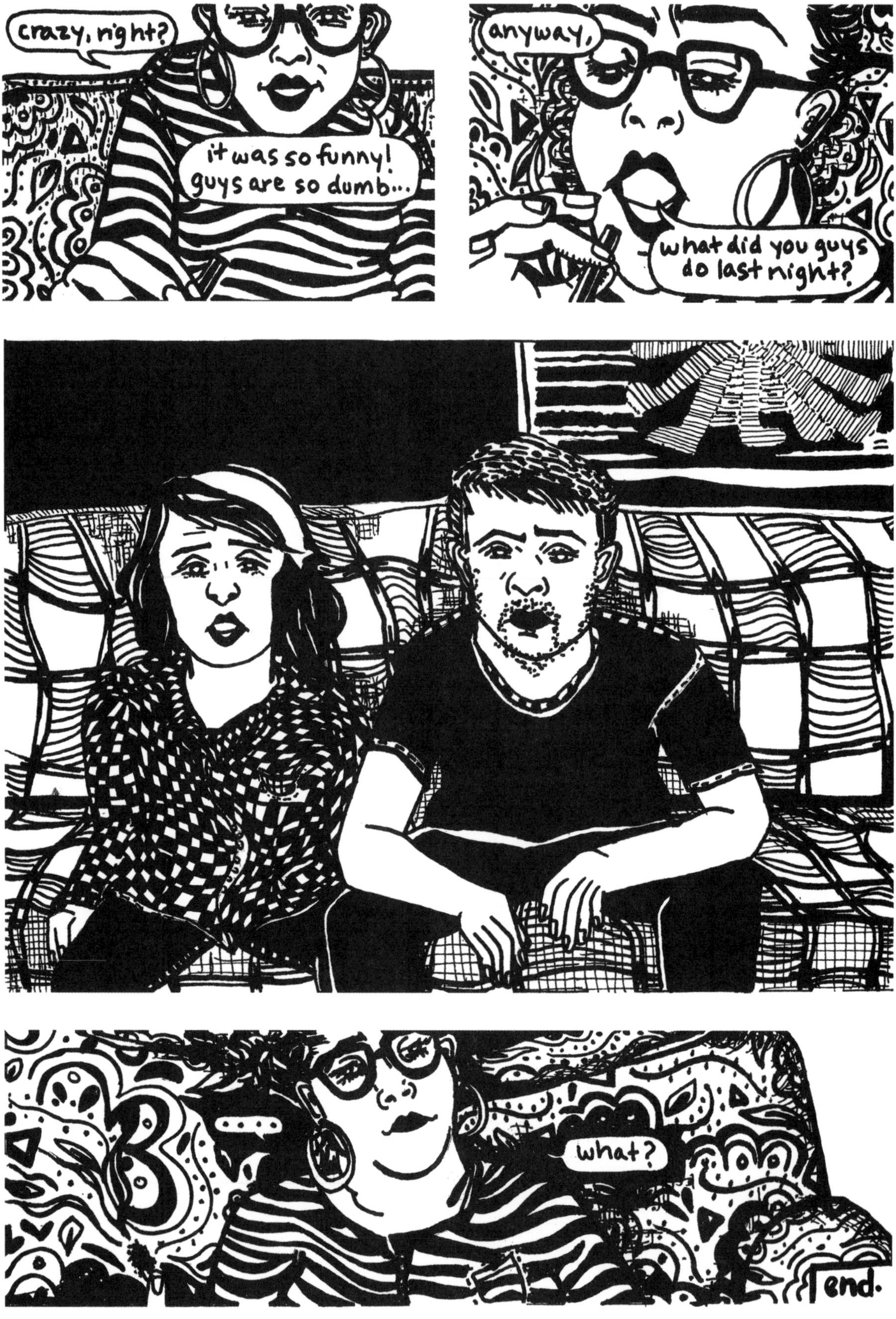
crazy, right?
it was so funny! guys are so dumb...
anyway,
what did you guys do last night?
...
what?
end.

...LET ME COUNT THE WAYS

KATIE FRICAS

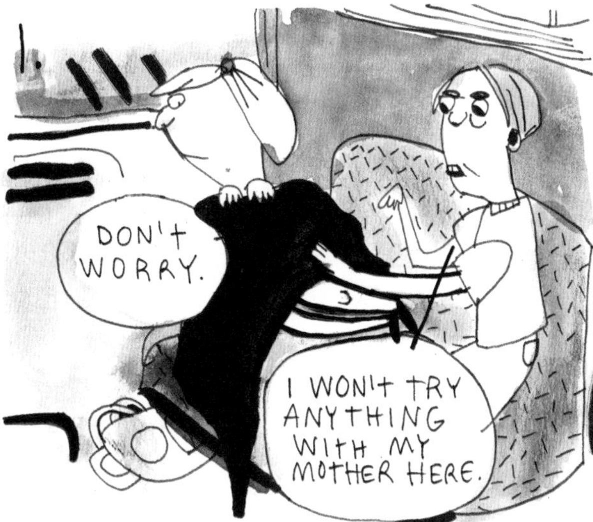
1.
DON'T WORRY.
I WON'T TRY ANYTHING WITH MY MOTHER HERE.

ON AN OVERNIGHT TRAIN BETWEEN SALZBURG AND PRAGUE, A YOUNG MAN TRAVELING WITH HIS MOM, ASLEEP ACROSS THE AISLE, PEEPS BENEATH MY BLANKET.

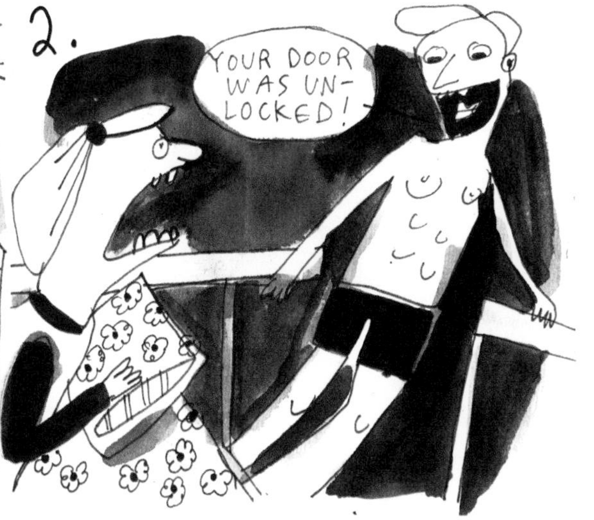
2.
YOUR DOOR WAS UN-LOCKED!

ON THE TOP BUNK OF A NEW, DARK DORM ROOM, MY FIRST WEEK OF COLLEGE, A YOUNG MAN CLIMBS INTO MY BED.

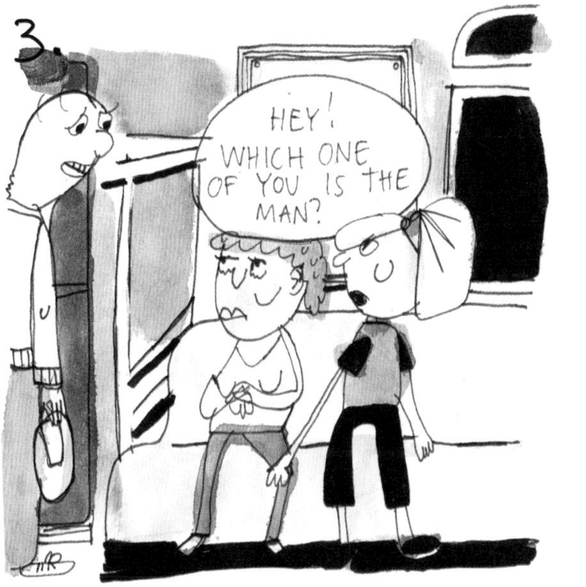
3.
HEY! WHICH ONE OF YOU IS THE MAN?

ON THE SUBWAY IN NEW YORK CITY, A CONCERNED PASSENGER INQUIRES.

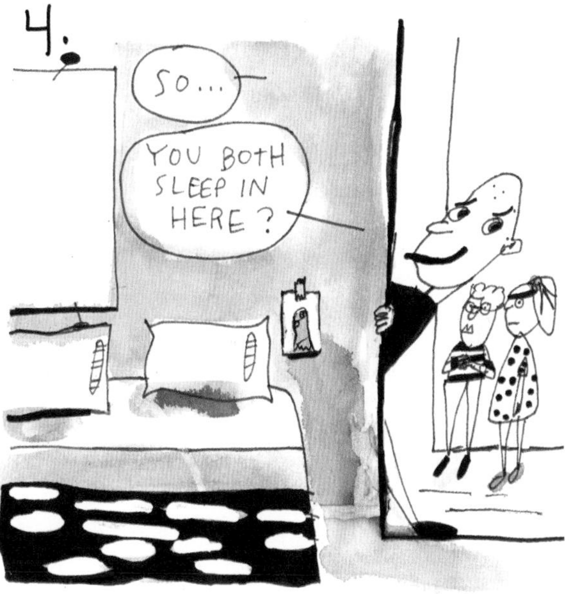
4.
SO...
YOU BOTH SLEEP IN HERE?

AT HOME, A CONCERNED LANDLORD CHECKS ON HIS TENANTS.

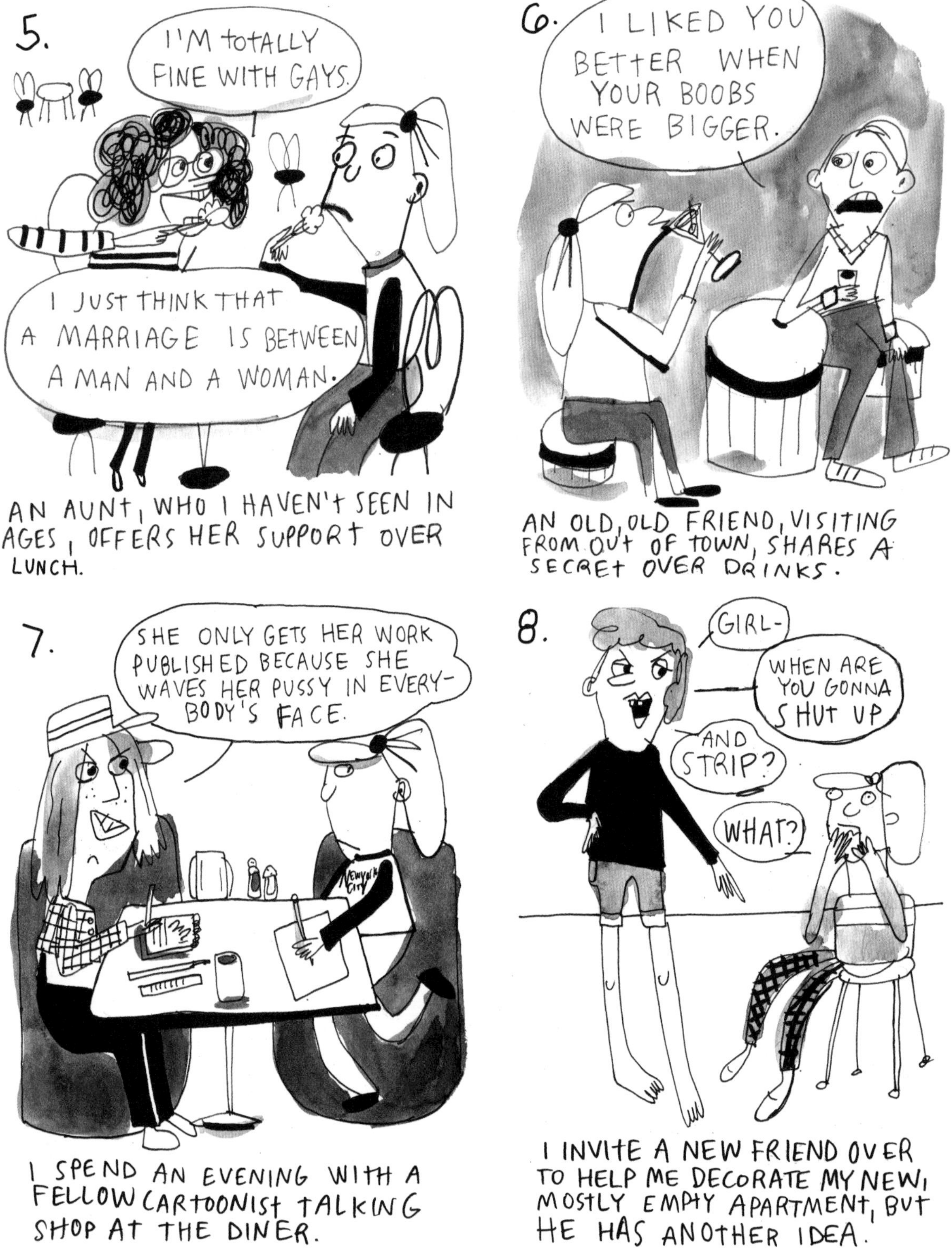
5.
I'M TOTALLY FINE WITH GAYS.
I JUST THINK THAT A MARRIAGE IS BETWEEN A MAN AND A WOMAN.
AN AUNT, WHO I HAVEN'T SEEN IN AGES, OFFERS HER SUPPORT OVER LUNCH.
6.
I LIKED YOU BETTER WHEN YOUR BOOBS WERE BIGGER.
AN OLD, OLD FRIEND, VISITING FROM OUT OF TOWN, SHARES A SECRET OVER DRINKS.
7.
SHE ONLY GETS HER WORK PUBLISHED BECAUSE SHE WAVES HER PUSSY IN EVERYBODY'S FACE.
I SPEND AN EVENING WITH A FELLOW CARTOONIST TALKING SHOP AT THE DINER.
8.
GIRL-
WHEN ARE YOU GONNA SHUT UP
AND STRIP?
WHAT?
I INVITE A NEW FRIEND OVER TO HELP ME DECORATE MY NEW, MOSTLY EMPTY APARTMENT, BUT HE HAS ANOTHER IDEA.

I TAKE A CALL AT WORK FROM A CHATTY CUSTOMER.

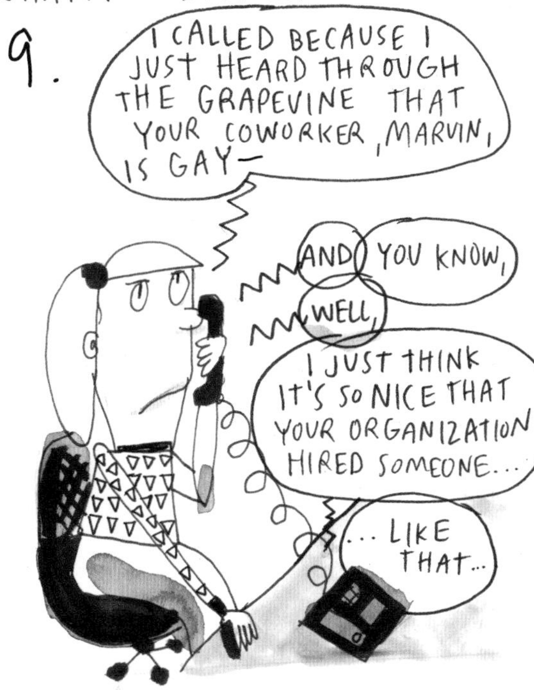
9.
I CALLED BECAUSE I JUST HEARD THROUGH THE GRAPEVINE THAT YOUR COWORKER, MARVIN, IS GAY—
AND
YOU KNOW,
WELL,
I JUST THINK IT'S SO NICE THAT YOUR ORGANIZATION HIRED SOMEONE...
...LIKE THAT...

A RUN-IN WITH A STRANGER CROSSING THE STREET YIELDS SOME BEAUTY ADVICE.

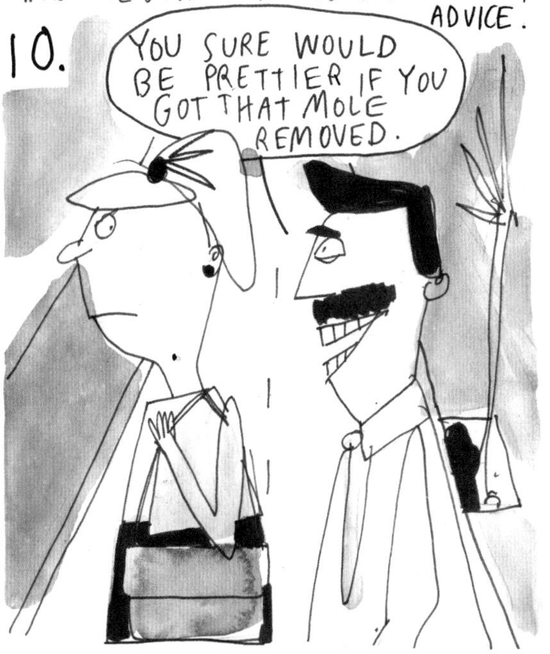
10.
YOU SURE WOULD BE PRETTIER IF YOU GOT THAT MOLE REMOVED.

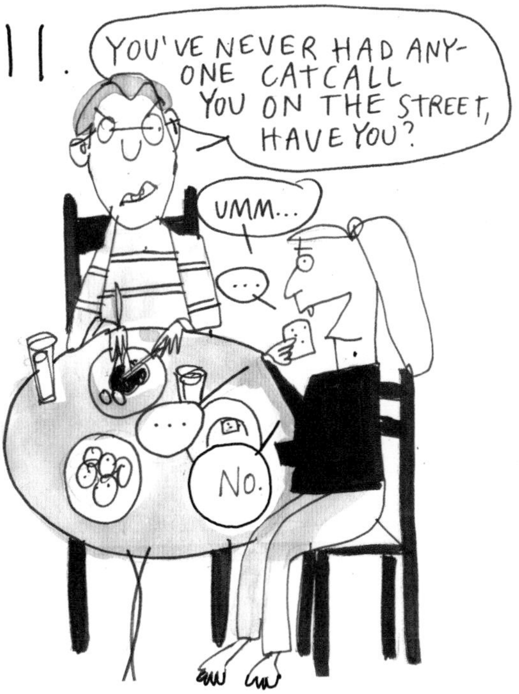
11.
YOU'VE NEVER HAD ANYONE CATCALL YOU ON THE STREET, HAVE YOU?
UMM...
...
...
NO.

MY DAD DECIDES TO CHECK IN AT DINNER.

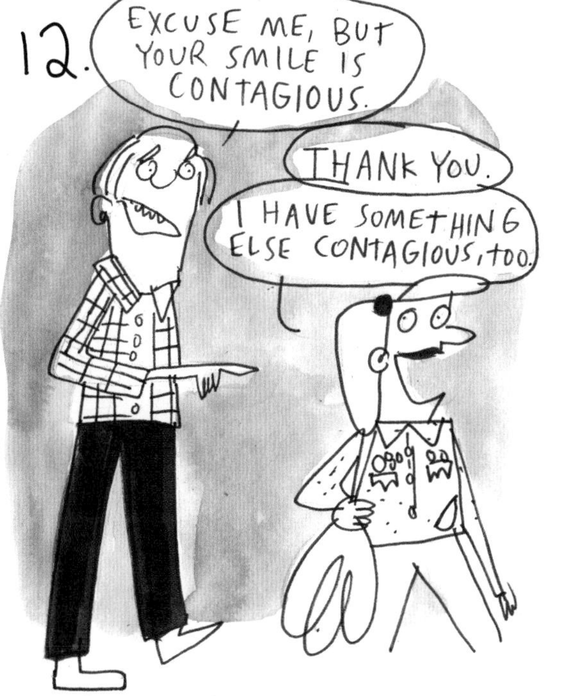
12.
EXCUSE ME, BUT YOUR SMILE IS CONTAGIOUS.
THANK YOU.
I HAVE SOMETHING ELSE CONTAGIOUS, TOO.

I TRY OUT SOME COMEDY ON A STRANGER.

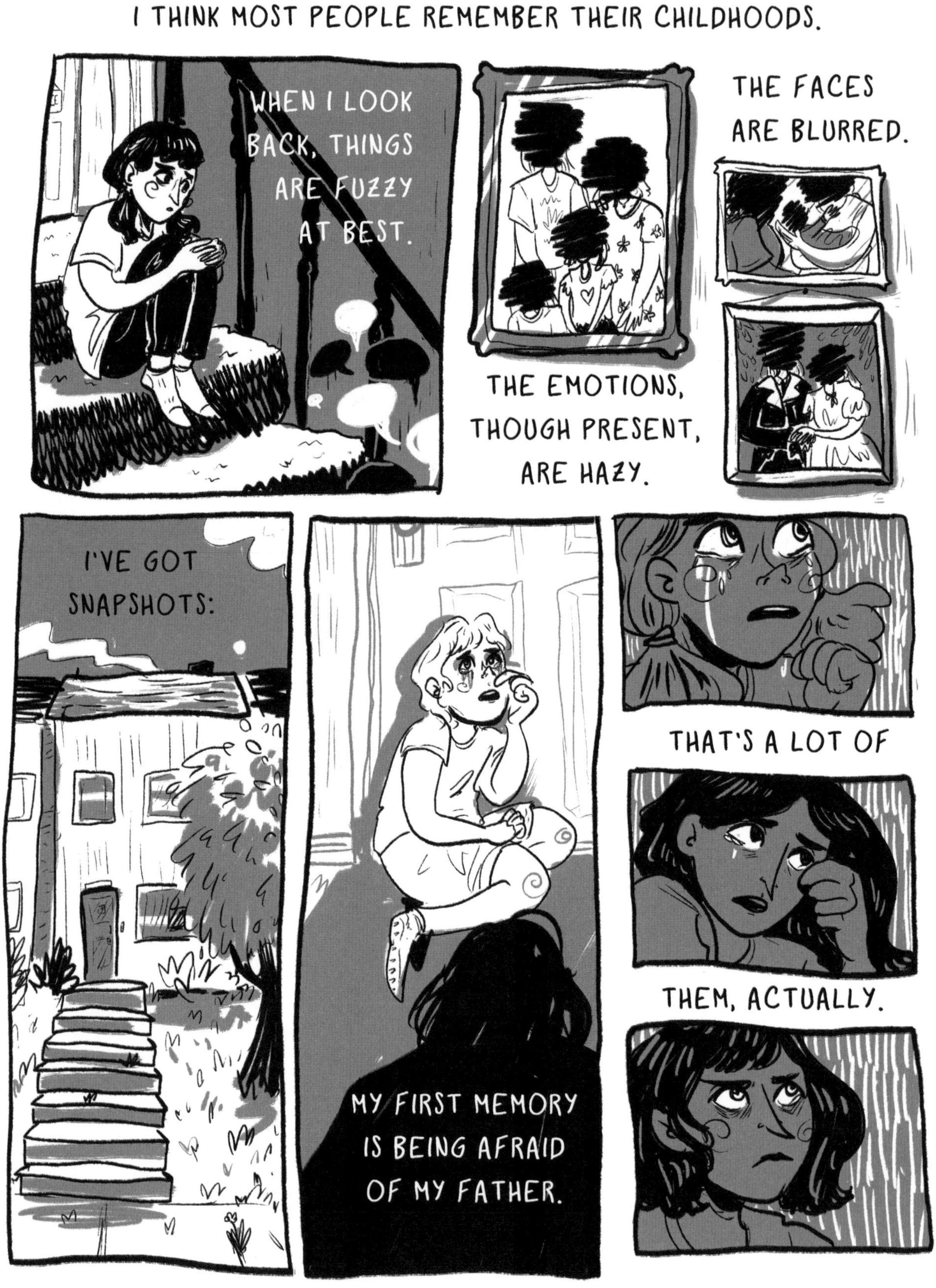
I THINK MOST PEOPLE REMEMBER THEIR CHILDHOODS.
WHEN I LOOK BACK, THINGS ARE FUZZY AT BEST.
THE FACES ARE BLURRED.
THE EMOTIONS, THOUGH PRESENT, ARE HAZY.
I'VE GOT SNAPSHOTS:
MY FIRST MEMORY IS BEING AFRAID OF MY FATHER.
THAT'S A LOT OF
THEM, ACTUALLY.

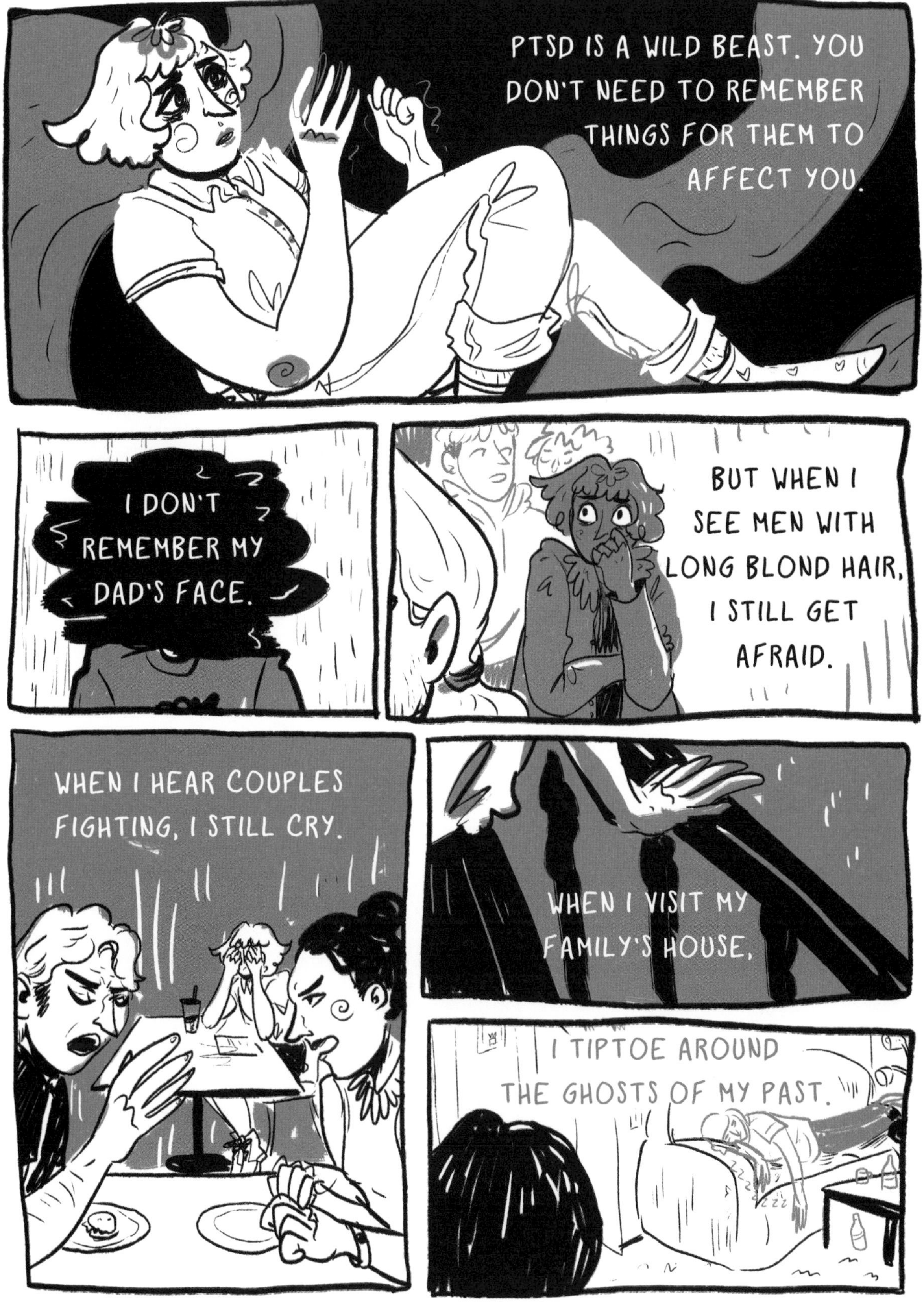
PTSD IS A WILD BEAST. YOU DON'T NEED TO REMEMBER THINGS FOR THEM TO AFFECT YOU.
I DON'T REMEMBER MY DAD'S FACE.
BUT WHEN I SEE MEN WITH LONG BLOND HAIR, I STILL GET AFRAID.
WHEN I HEAR COUPLES FIGHTING, I STILL CRY.
WHEN I VISIT MY FAMILY'S HOUSE,
I TIPTOE AROUND THE GHOSTS OF MY PAST.

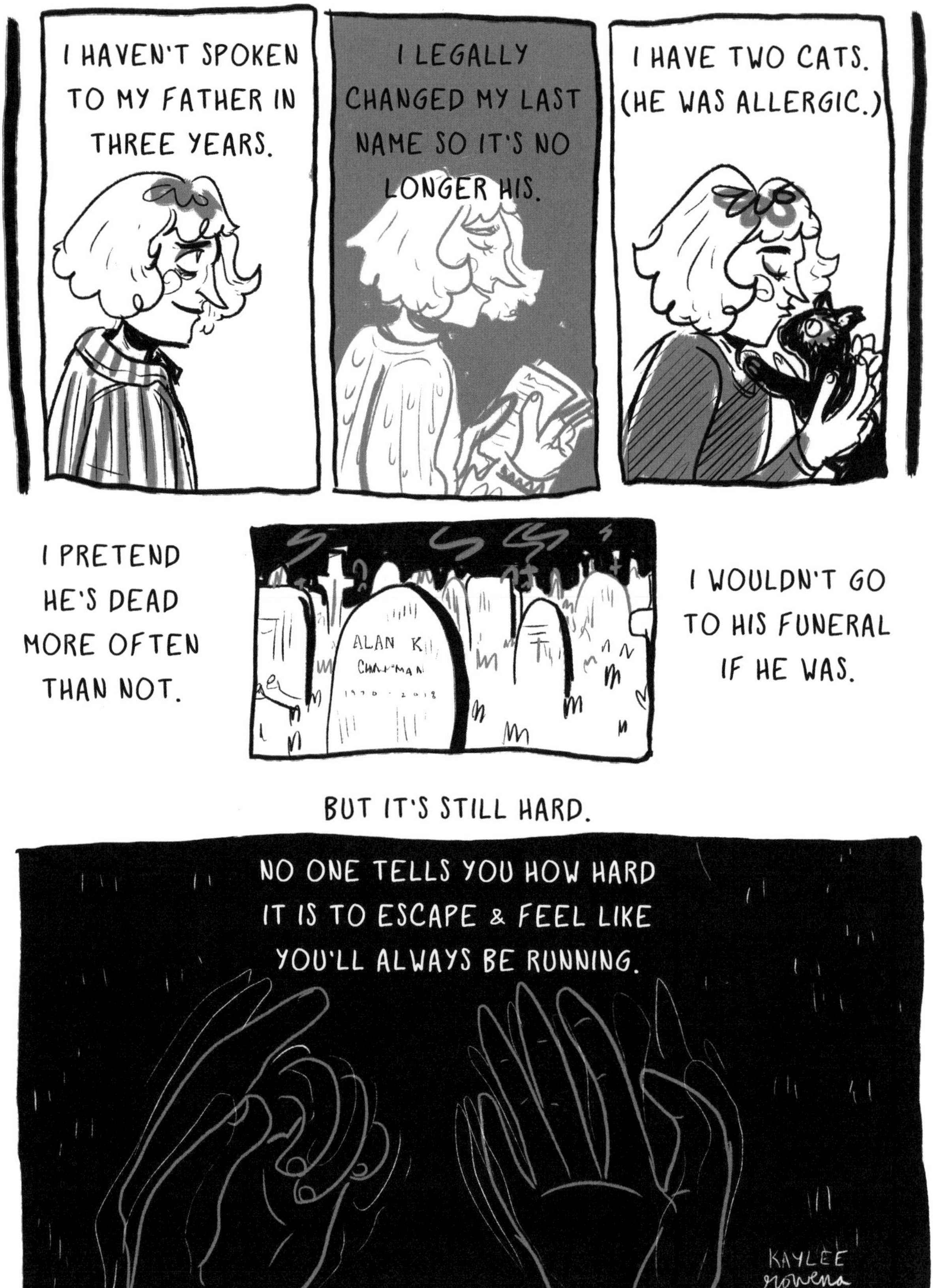
I HAVEN'T SPOKEN TO MY FATHER IN THREE YEARS.
I LEGALLY CHANGED MY LAST NAME SO IT'S NO LONGER HIS.
I HAVE TWO CATS. (HE WAS ALLERGIC.)
I PRETEND HE'S DEAD MORE OFTEN THAN NOT.
ALAN K
I WOULDN'T GO TO HIS FUNERAL IF HE WAS.
BUT IT'S STILL HARD.
NO ONE TELLS YOU HOW HARD IT IS TO ESCAPE & FEEL LIKE YOU'LL ALWAYS BE RUNNING.
KAYLEE rowena

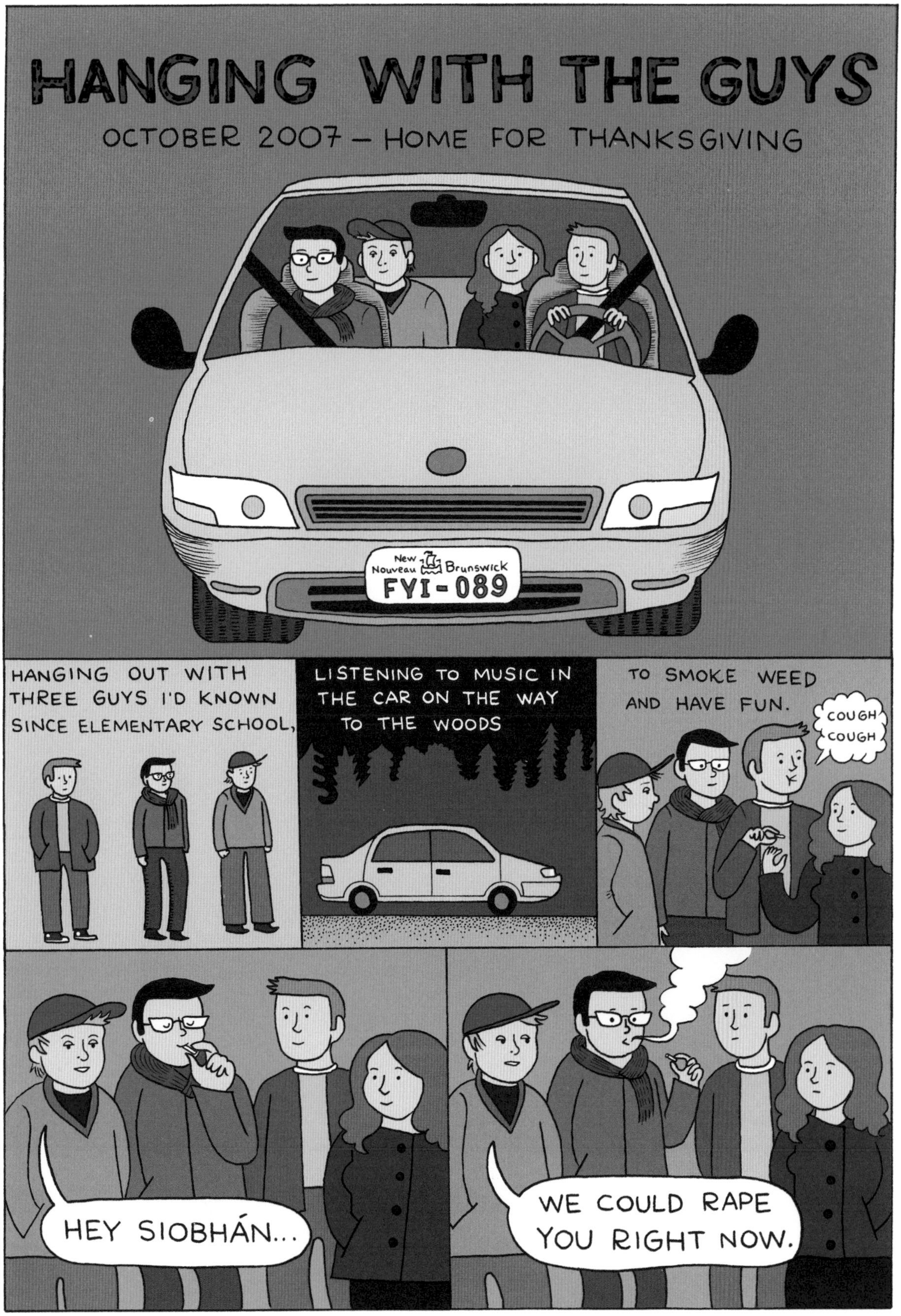
HANGING WITH THE GUYS
OCTOBER 2007 – HOME FOR THANKSGIVING
New Nouveau Brunswick
FYI-089
HANGING OUT WITH THREE GUYS I'D KNOWN SINCE ELEMENTARY SCHOOL,
LISTENING TO MUSIC IN THE CAR ON THE WAY TO THE WOODS
TO SMOKE WEED AND HAVE FUN.
COUGH COUGH
HEY SIOBHÁN...
WE COULD RAPE YOU RIGHT NOW.

ON THE ROAD

HILA NOAM

When my mother turned 18 she decided to become a nurse

Every few weeks she would go home for a weekend off with her family

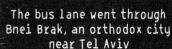

The bus lane went through Bnei Brak, an orthodox city near Tel Aviv

Every once in a while, some random guy who happened to sit beside her would try to "get to know her better"

It's not like she wasn't familiar with the orthodox world – her father, a Holocaust survivor, studied in Poland in a yeshiva, but then he left and cut off his payot* and beard

It's possible of course that guys on that particular bus were somehow usually very sleepy

In any case, it made me kinda grateful I didn't inherit her glorious bosom

*Side curls

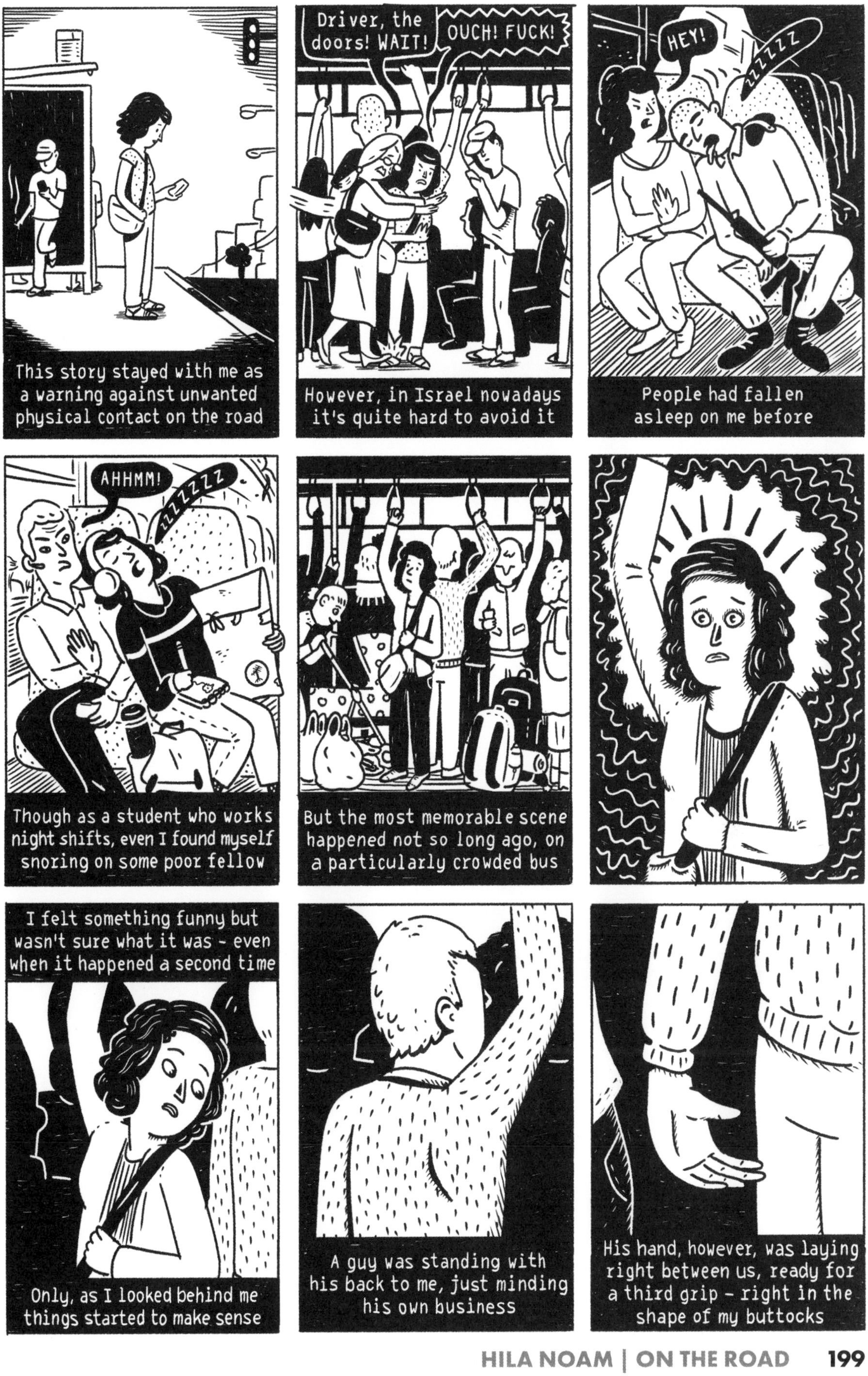
This story stayed with me as a warning against unwanted physical contact on the road
Driver, the doors! WAIT!
OUCH! FUCK!
However, in Israel nowadays it's quite hard to avoid it
HEY!
ZZZZZZ
People had fallen asleep on me before
AHHMM!
ZZZZZZZ
Though as a student who works night shifts, even I found myself snoring on some poor fellow
But the most memorable scene happened not so long ago, on a particularly crowded bus
I felt something funny but wasn't sure what it was - even when it happened a second time
Only, as I looked behind me things started to make sense
A guy was standing with his back to me, just minding his own business
His hand, however, was laying right between us, ready for a third grip - right in the shape of my buttocks

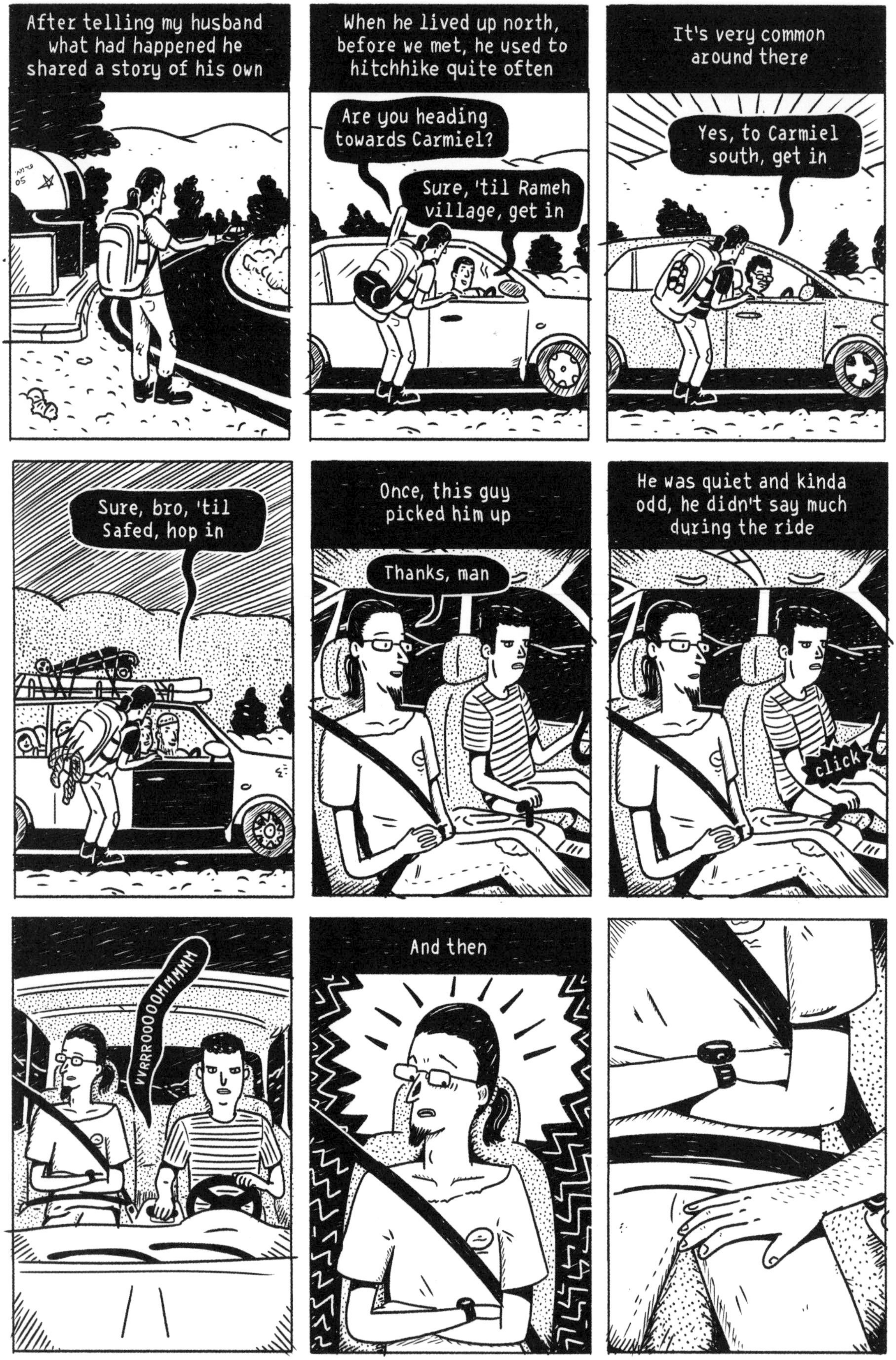
After telling my husband what had happened he shared a story of his own
When he lived up north, before we met, he used to hitchhike quite often
Are you heading towards Carmiel?
Sure, 'til Rameh village, get in
It's very common around there
Yes, to Carmiel south, get in
Sure, bro, 'til Safed, hop in
Once, this guy picked him up
Thanks, man
He was quiet and kinda odd, he didn't say much during the ride
click
VVRRROOOOOMMMMM
And then

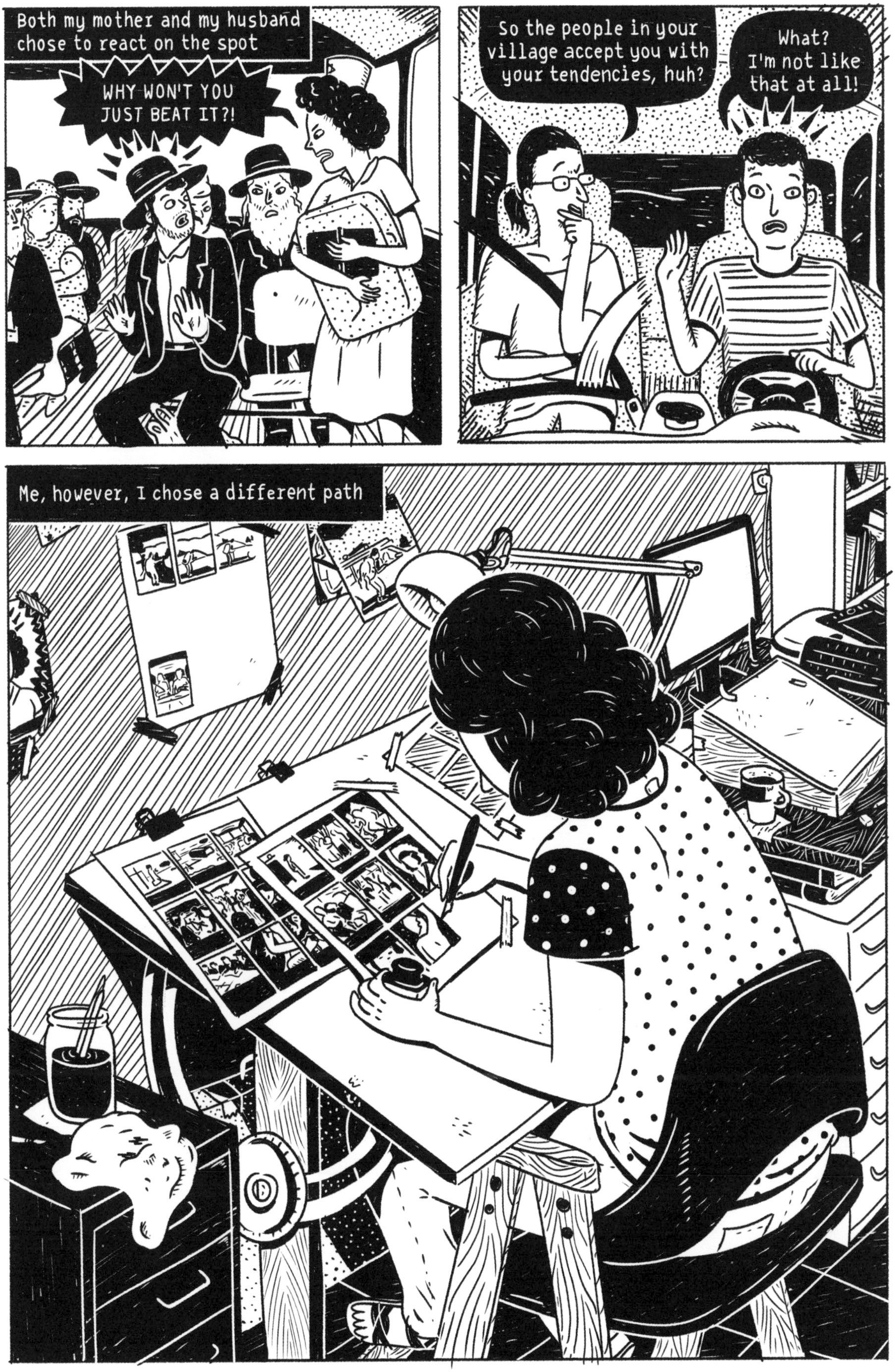
Both my mother and my husband chose to react on the spot
WHY WON'T YOU JUST BEAT IT?!
So the people in your village accept you with your tendencies, huh?
What? I'm not like that at all!
Me, however, I chose a different path

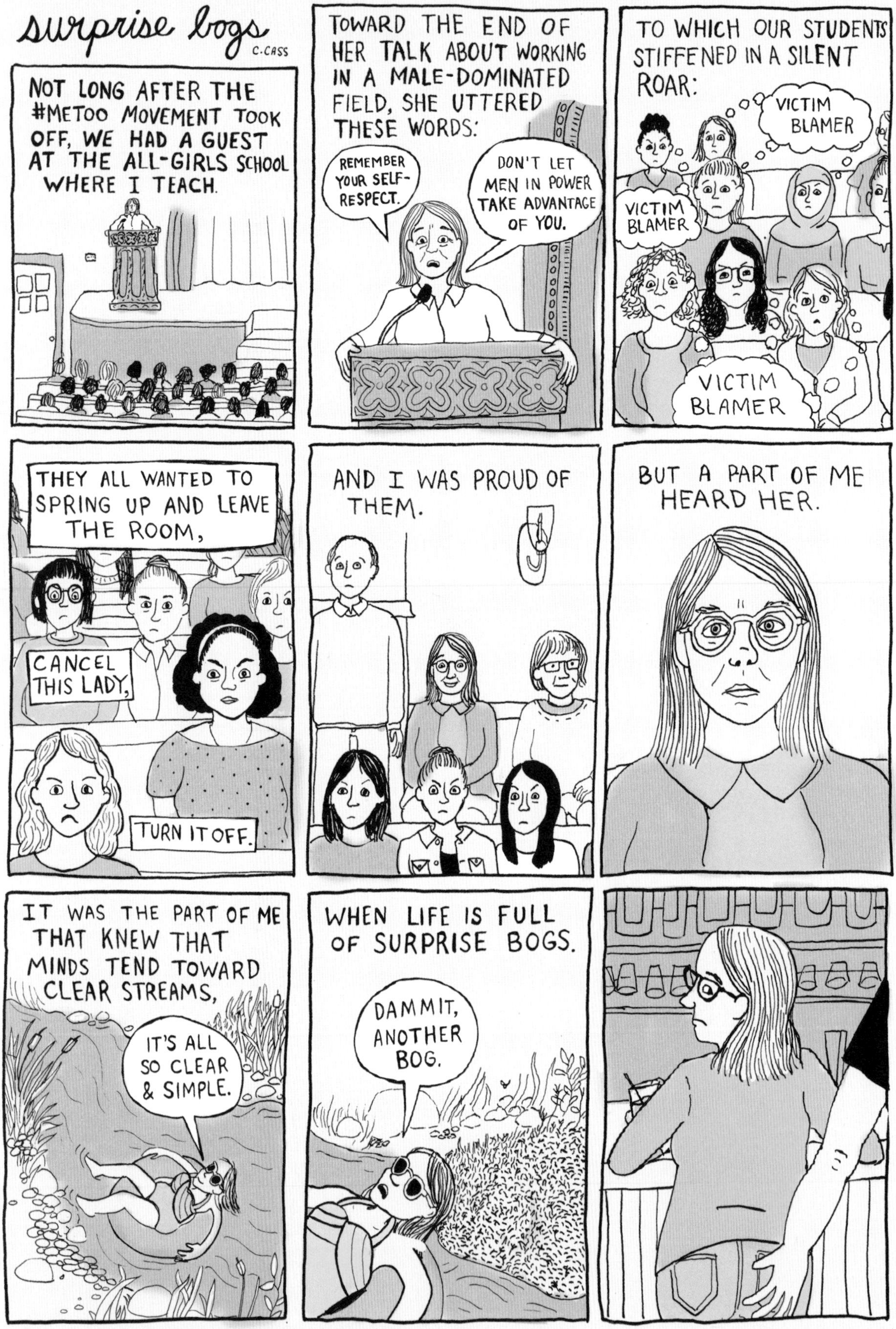
surprise bogs
C.CASS
NOT LONG AFTER THE #METOO MOVEMENT TOOK OFF, WE HAD A GUEST AT THE ALL-GIRLS SCHOOL WHERE I TEACH.
TOWARD THE END OF HER TALK ABOUT WORKING IN A MALE-DOMINATED FIELD, SHE UTTERED THESE WORDS:
REMEMBER YOUR SELF-RESPECT.
DON'T LET MEN IN POWER TAKE ADVANTAGE OF YOU.
TO WHICH OUR STUDENTS STIFFENED IN A SILENT ROAR:
VICTIM BLAMER
VICTIM BLAMER
VICTIM BLAMER
THEY ALL WANTED TO SPRING UP AND LEAVE THE ROOM,
CANCEL THIS LADY,
TURN IT OFF.
AND I WAS PROUD OF THEM.
BUT A PART OF ME HEARD HER.
IT WAS THE PART OF ME THAT KNEW THAT MINDS TEND TOWARD CLEAR STREAMS,
IT'S ALL SO CLEAR & SIMPLE.
WHEN LIFE IS FULL OF SURPRISE BOGS.
DAMMIT, ANOTHER BOG.

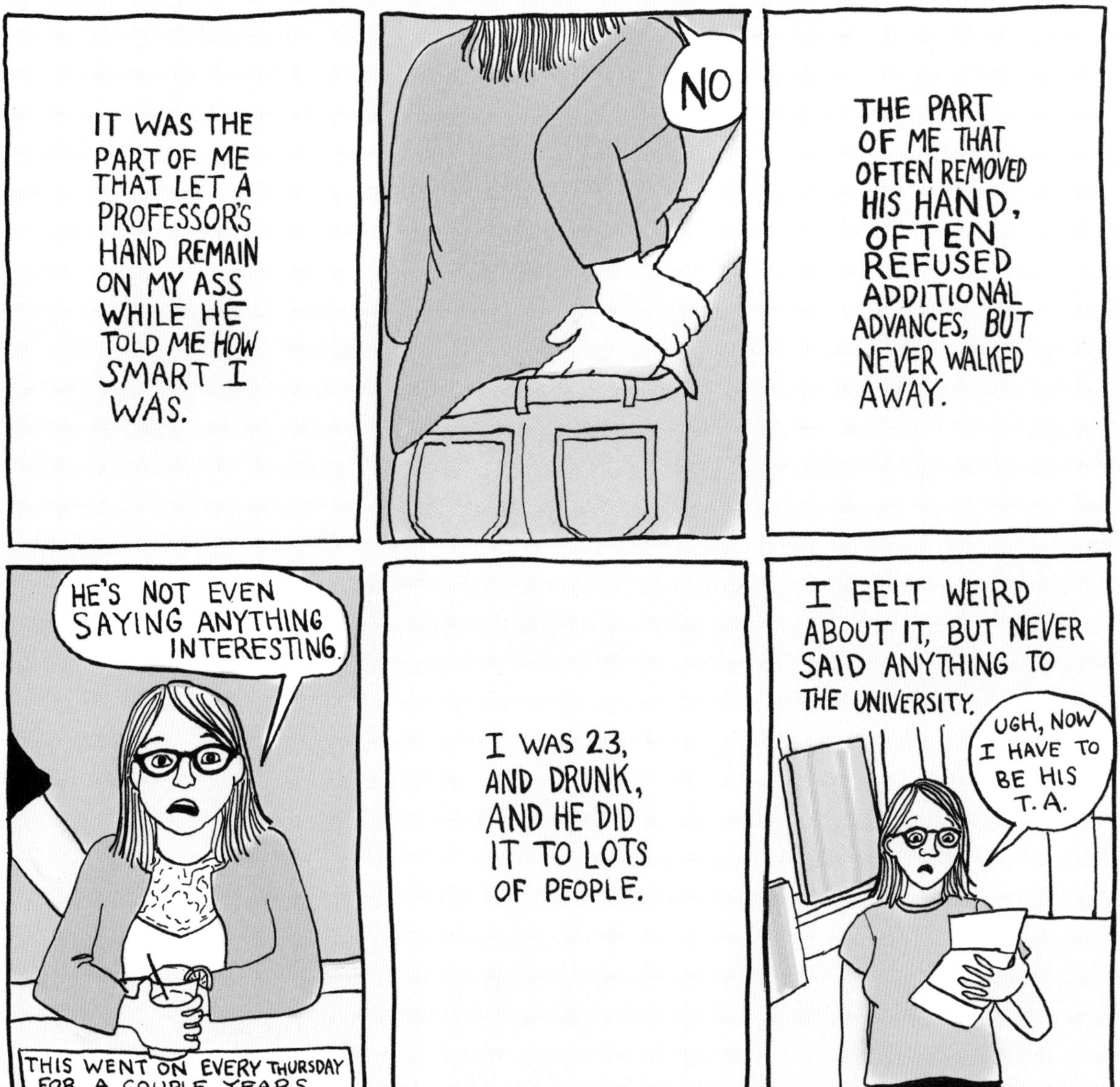
IT WAS THE PART OF ME THAT LET A PROFESSOR'S HAND REMAIN ON MY ASS WHILE HE TOLD ME HOW SMART I WAS.
NO
THE PART OF ME THAT OFTEN REMOVED HIS HAND, OFTEN REFUSED ADDITIONAL ADVANCES, BUT NEVER WALKED AWAY.
HE'S NOT EVEN SAYING ANYTHING INTERESTING.
THIS WENT ON EVERY THURSDAY FOR A COUPLE YEARS.
I WAS 23, AND DRUNK, AND HE DID IT TO LOTS OF PEOPLE.
I FELT WEIRD ABOUT IT, BUT NEVER SAID ANYTHING TO THE UNIVERSITY.
UGH, NOW I HAVE TO BE HIS T.A.
SEVERAL YEARS LATER HE LEFT HIS JOB. THERE WERE RUMORS IT WAS BECAUSE OF SEXUAL HARASSMENT, BUT HIS COLLEAGUES WERE VAGUE.
HE LEFT BECAUSE HE'S SICK.
RIGHT.
NOW HERE, SURROUNDED BY STUDENTS, I KNEW THIS GROPING WASN'T MY FAULT,
BUT I ALSO KNEW THAT I COULD HAVE ACTED DIFFERENTLY.
AT LEAST HE'S NOT TEACHING ANYMORE.

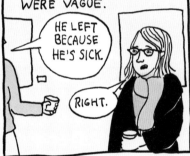

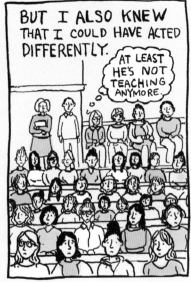

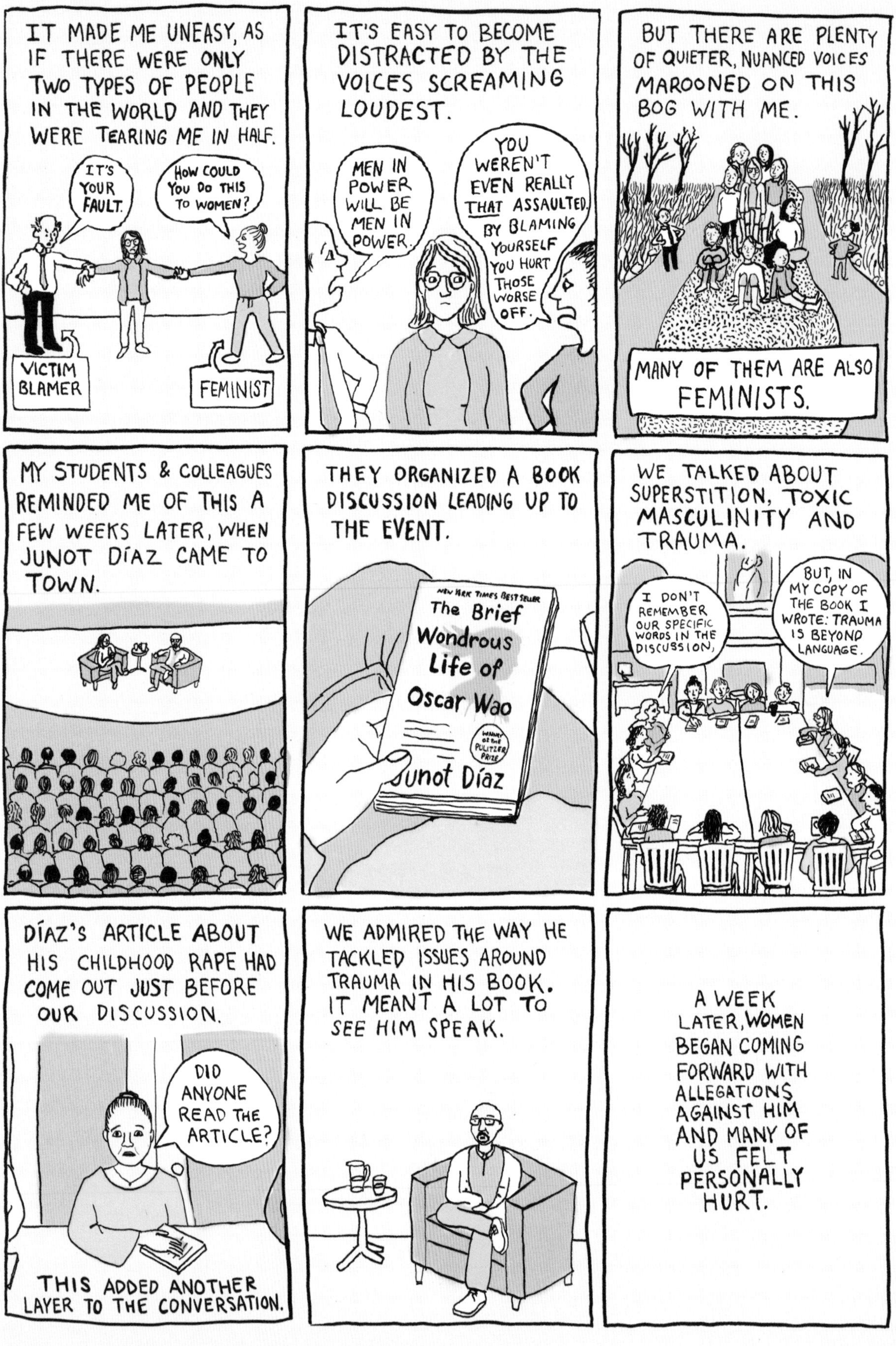
IT MADE ME UNEASY, AS IF THERE WERE ONLY TWO TYPES OF PEOPLE IN THE WORLD AND THEY WERE TEARING ME IN HALF.
IT'S YOUR FAULT.
HOW COULD YOU DO THIS TO WOMEN?
VICTIM BLAMER
FEMINIST
IT'S EASY TO BECOME DISTRACTED BY THE VOICES SCREAMING LOUDEST.
MEN IN POWER WILL BE MEN IN POWER.
YOU WEREN'T EVEN REALLY THAT ASSAULTED. BY BLAMING YOURSELF YOU HURT THOSE WORSE OFF.
BUT THERE ARE PLENTY OF QUIETER, NUANCED VOICES MAROONED ON THIS BOG WITH ME.
MANY OF THEM ARE ALSO FEMINISTS.
MY STUDENTS & COLLEAGUES REMINDED ME OF THIS A FEW WEEKS LATER, WHEN JUNOT DÍAZ CAME TO TOWN.
THEY ORGANIZED A BOOK DISCUSSION LEADING UP TO THE EVENT.
NEW YORK TIMES BESTSELLER
The Brief Wondrous Life of Oscar Wao
WINNER OF THE PULITZER PRIZE
Junot Díaz
WE TALKED ABOUT SUPERSTITION, TOXIC MASCULINITY AND TRAUMA.
I DON'T REMEMBER OUR SPECIFIC WORDS IN THE DISCUSSION,
BUT, IN MY COPY OF THE BOOK I WROTE: TRAUMA IS BEYOND LANGUAGE.
DÍAZ'S ARTICLE ABOUT HIS CHILDHOOD RAPE HAD COME OUT JUST BEFORE OUR DISCUSSION.
DID ANYONE READ THE ARTICLE?
THIS ADDED ANOTHER LAYER TO THE CONVERSATION.
WE ADMIRED THE WAY HE TACKLED ISSUES AROUND TRAUMA IN HIS BOOK. IT MEANT A LOT TO SEE HIM SPEAK.
A WEEK LATER, WOMEN BEGAN COMING FORWARD WITH ALLEGATIONS AGAINST HIM AND MANY OF US FELT PERSONALLY HURT.

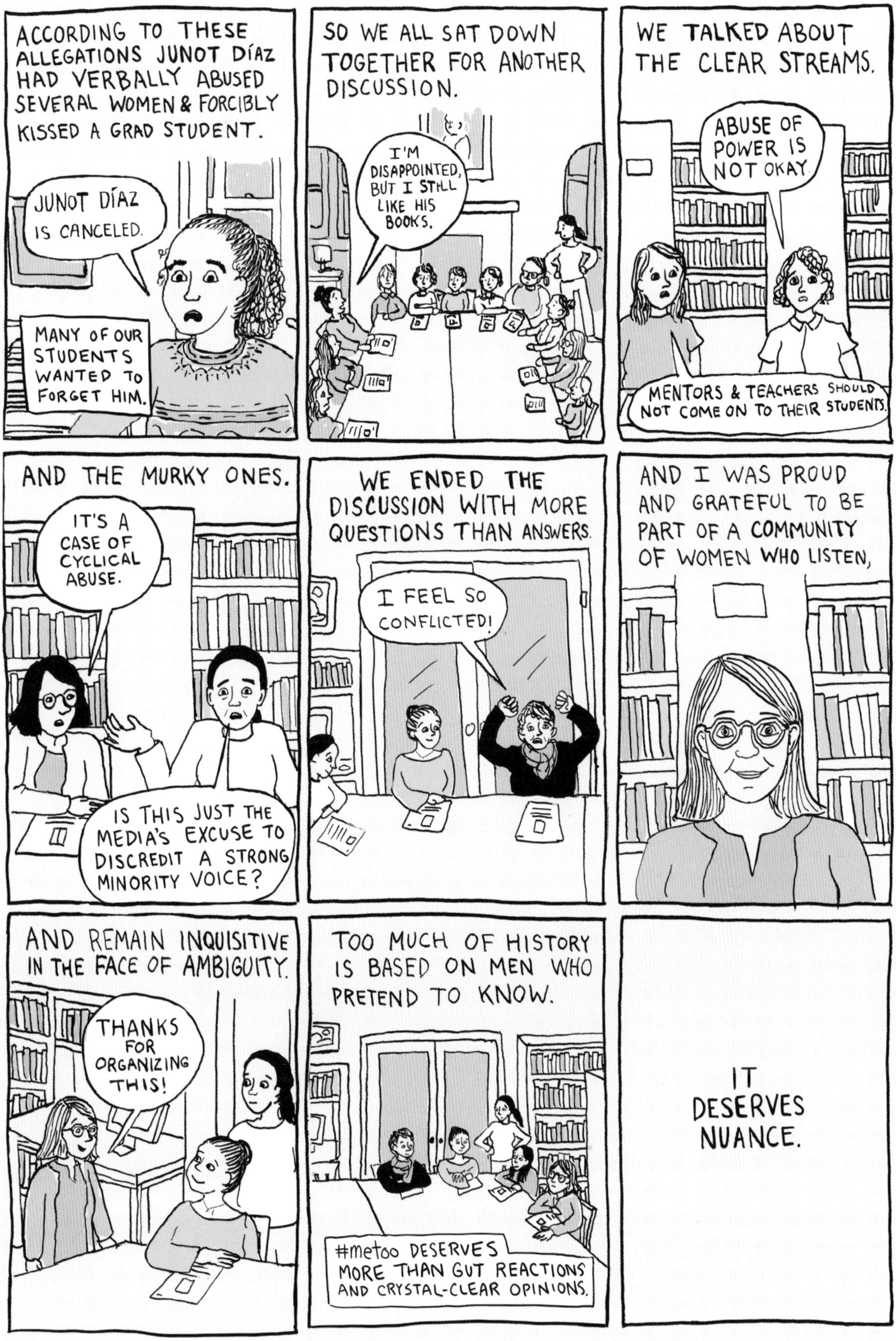
ACCORDING TO THESE ALLEGATIONS JUNOT DÍAZ HAD VERBALLY ABUSED SEVERAL WOMEN & FORCIBLY KISSED A GRAD STUDENT.
JUNOT DÍAZ IS CANCELED.
MANY OF OUR STUDENTS WANTED TO FORGET HIM.
SO WE ALL SAT DOWN TOGETHER FOR ANOTHER DISCUSSION.
I'M DISAPPOINTED, BUT I STILL LIKE HIS BOOKS.
WE TALKED ABOUT THE CLEAR STREAMS.
ABUSE OF POWER IS NOT OKAY.
MENTORS & TEACHERS SHOULD NOT COME ON TO THEIR STUDENTS.
AND THE MURKY ONES.
IT'S A CASE OF CYCLICAL ABUSE.
IS THIS JUST THE MEDIA'S EXCUSE TO DISCREDIT A STRONG MINORITY VOICE?
WE ENDED THE DISCUSSION WITH MORE QUESTIONS THAN ANSWERS.
I FEEL SO CONFLICTED!
AND I WAS PROUD AND GRATEFUL TO BE PART OF A COMMUNITY OF WOMEN WHO LISTEN,
AND REMAIN INQUISITIVE IN THE FACE OF AMBIGUITY.
THANKS FOR ORGANIZING THIS!
TOO MUCH OF HISTORY IS BASED ON MEN WHO PRETEND TO KNOW.
#metoo DESERVES MORE THAN GUT REACTIONS AND CRYSTAL-CLEAR OPINIONS.
IT DESERVES NUANCE.

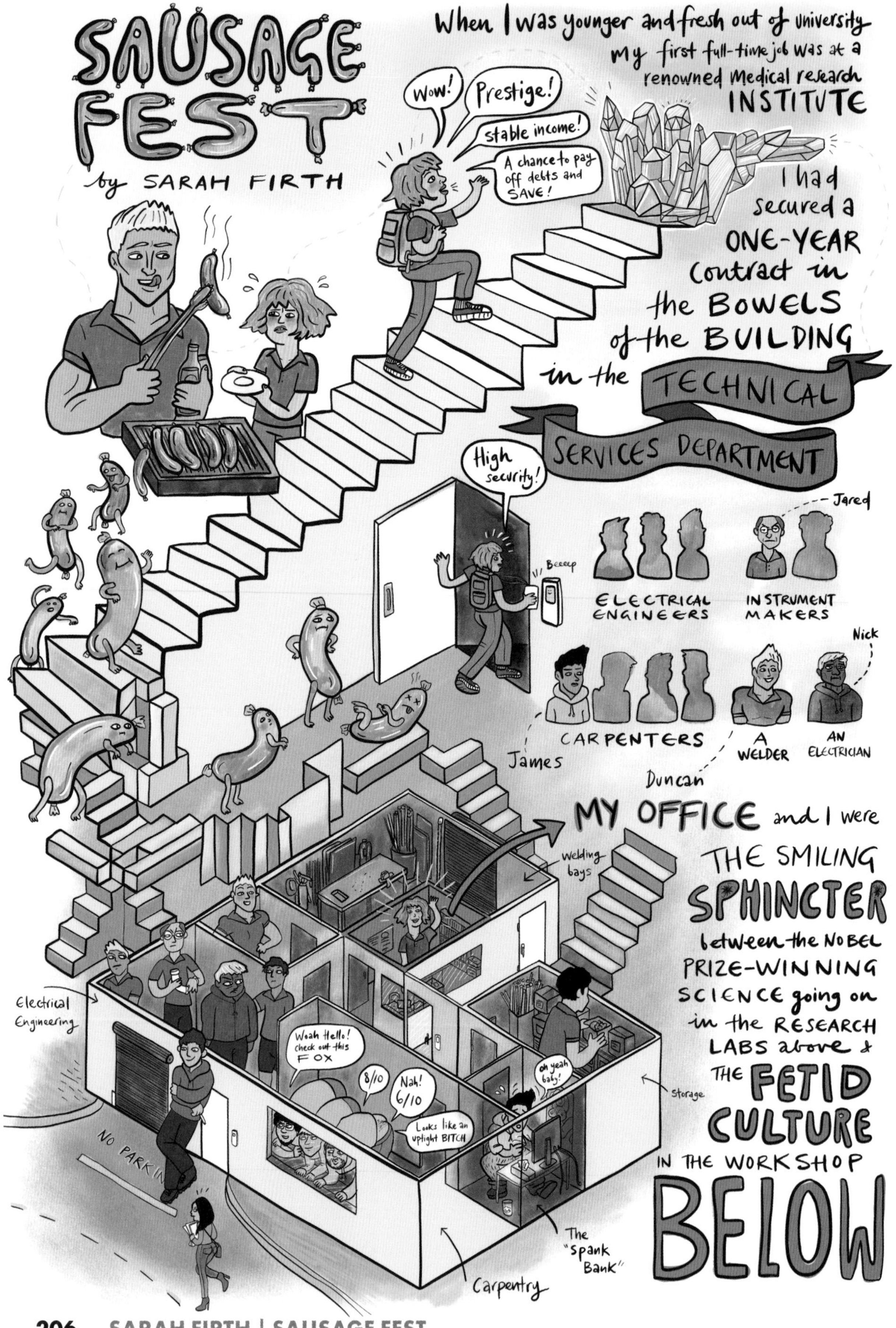
SAUSAGE FEST
by SARAH FIRTH
When I was younger and fresh out of university my first full-time job was at a renowned medical research INSTITUTE
Wow!
Prestige!
stable income!
A chance to pay off debts and SAVE!
I had secured a ONE-YEAR contract in the BOWELS of the BUILDING in the TECHNICAL SERVICES DEPARTMENT
High security!
Beeeep
Jared
ELECTRICAL ENGINEERS
INSTRUMENT MAKERS
Nick
CARPENTERS
James
A WELDER
Duncan
AN ELECTRICIAN
MY OFFICE and I were THE SMILING SPHINCTER between the NOBEL PRIZE-WINNING SCIENCE going on in the RESEARCH LABS above & THE FETID CULTURE IN THE WORKSHOP BELOW
Welding bays
Electrical Engineering
Woah Hello! check out this FOX
8/10
Nah! 6/10
Looks like an uptight BITCH
oh yeah baby!
Storage
NO PARKIN
The "spank Bank"
Carpentry

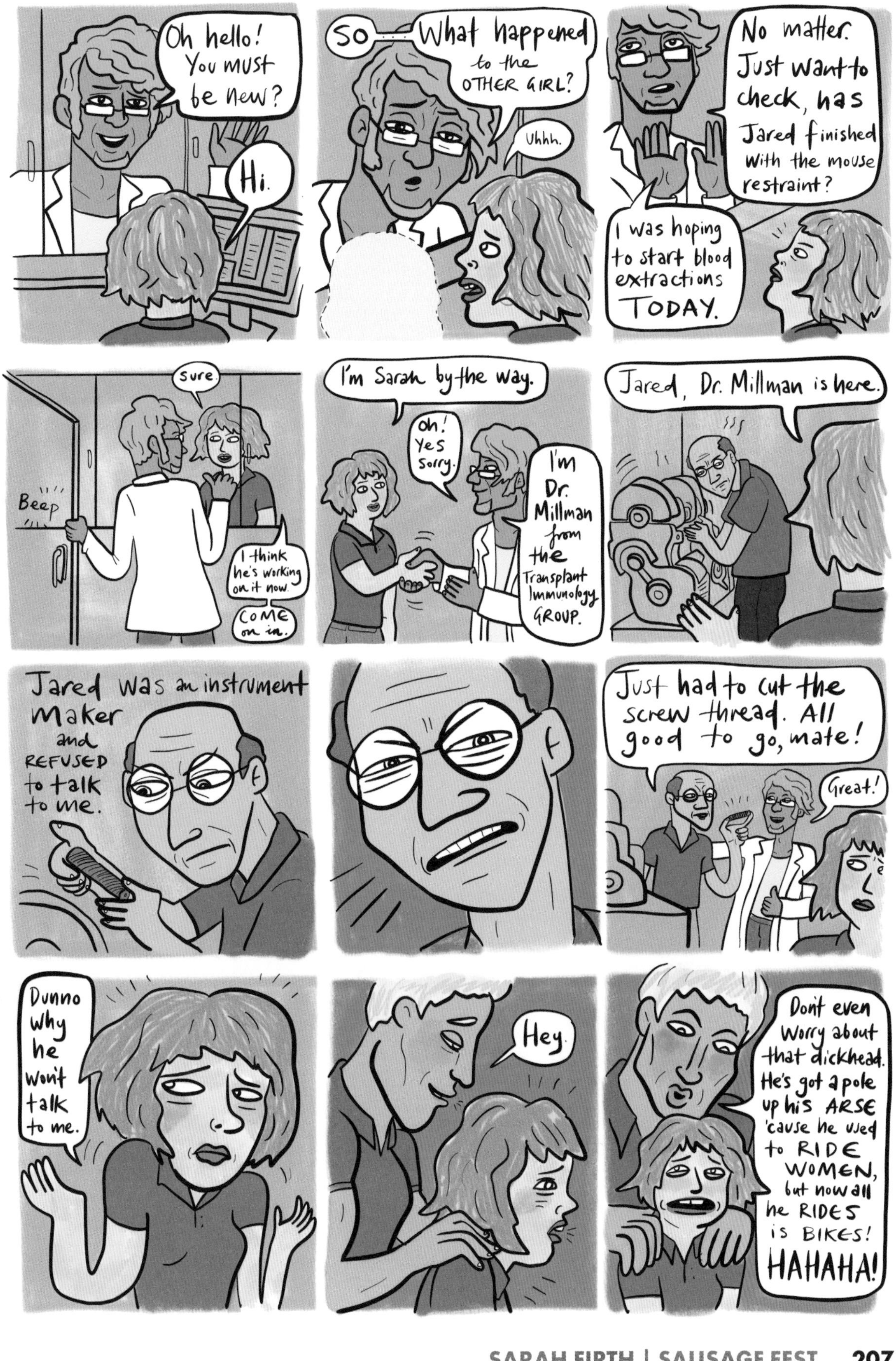
Oh hello! You MUST be new?
Hi.
SO... What happened to the OTHER GIRL?
Uhhh.
No matter. Just want to check, has Jared finished with the mouse restraint?
I was hoping to start blood extractions TODAY.
Sure.
Beep
I think he's working on it now.
COME on in.
I'm Sarah by the way.
Oh! Yes sorry.
I'm Dr. Millman from the Transplant Immunology GROUP.
Jared, Dr. Millman is here.
Jared was an instrument maker and REFUSED to talk to me.
Just had to cut the screw thread. All good to go, mate!
Great!
Dunno why he won't talk to me.
Hey.
Don't even worry about that dickhead. He's got a pole up his ARSE 'cause he used to RIDE WOMEN, but now all he RIDES is BIKES! HAHAHA!

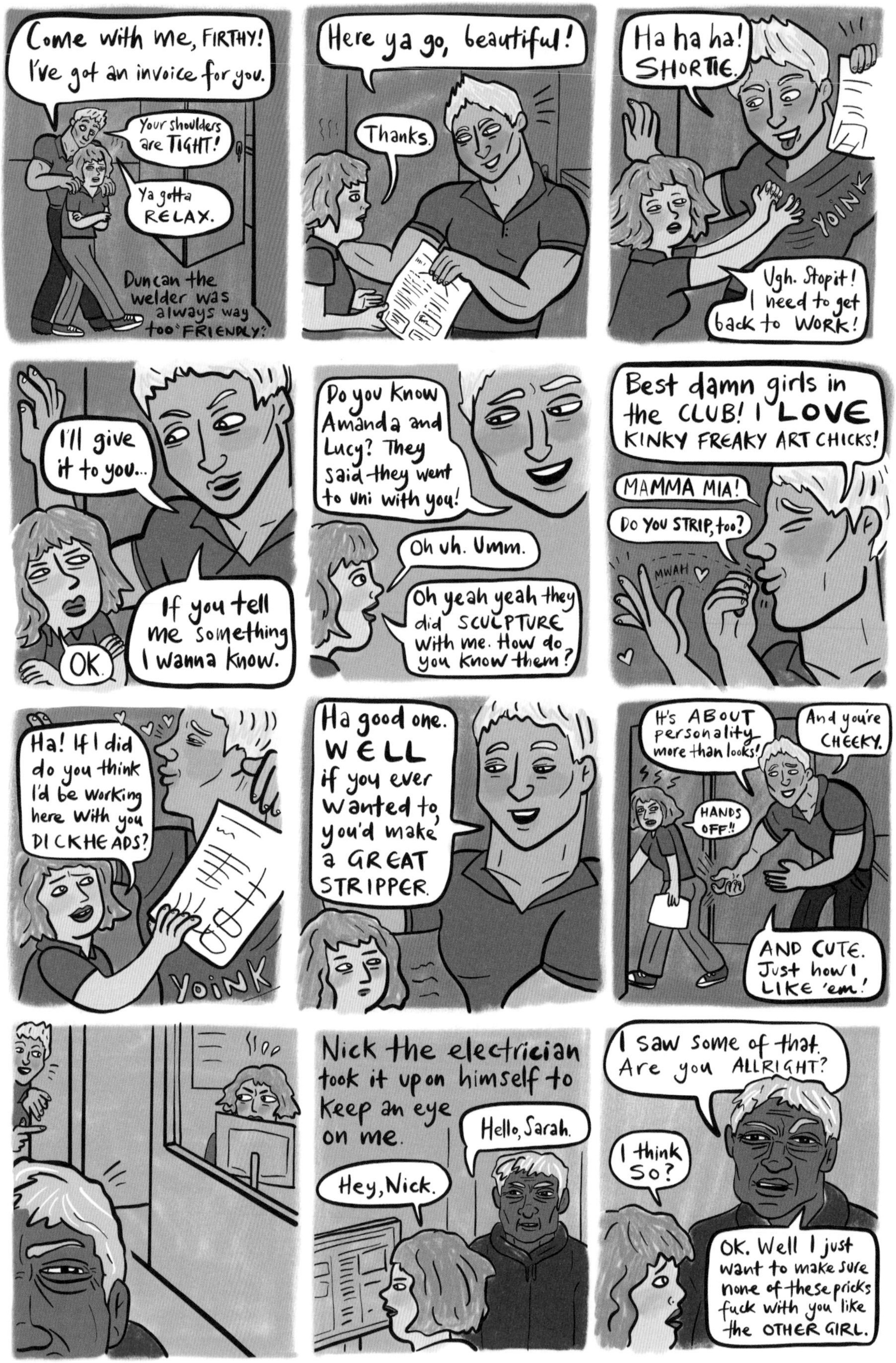
Come with me, FIRTHY! I've got an invoice for you.
Your shoulders are TIGHT!
Ya gotta RELAX.
Duncan the welder was always way too "FRIENDLY."
Here ya go, beautiful!
Thanks.
Ha ha ha! SHORTIE.
YOINK
Ugh. Stopit! I need to get back to WORK!
I'll give it to you...
If you tell me something I wanna know.
OK.
Do you know Amanda and Lucy? They said they went to uni with you!
Oh uh. Umm.
Oh yeah yeah they did SCULPTURE with me. How do you know them?
Best damn girls in the CLUB! I LOVE KINKY FREAKY ART CHICKS!
MAMMA MIA!
Do YOU STRIP, too?
MWAH
Ha! If I did do you think I'd be working here with you DICKHEADS?
YOINK
Ha good one. WELL if you ever wanted to, you'd make a GREAT STRIPPER.
It's ABOUT personality more than looks!
And you're CHEEKY.
HANDS OFF!!
AND CUTE. Just how I LIKE 'em!
Nick the electrician took it upon himself to keep an eye on me.
Hello, Sarah.
Hey, Nick.
I saw some of that. Are you ALLRIGHT?
I think so?
OK. Well I just want to make sure none of these pricks fuck with you like the OTHER GIRL.

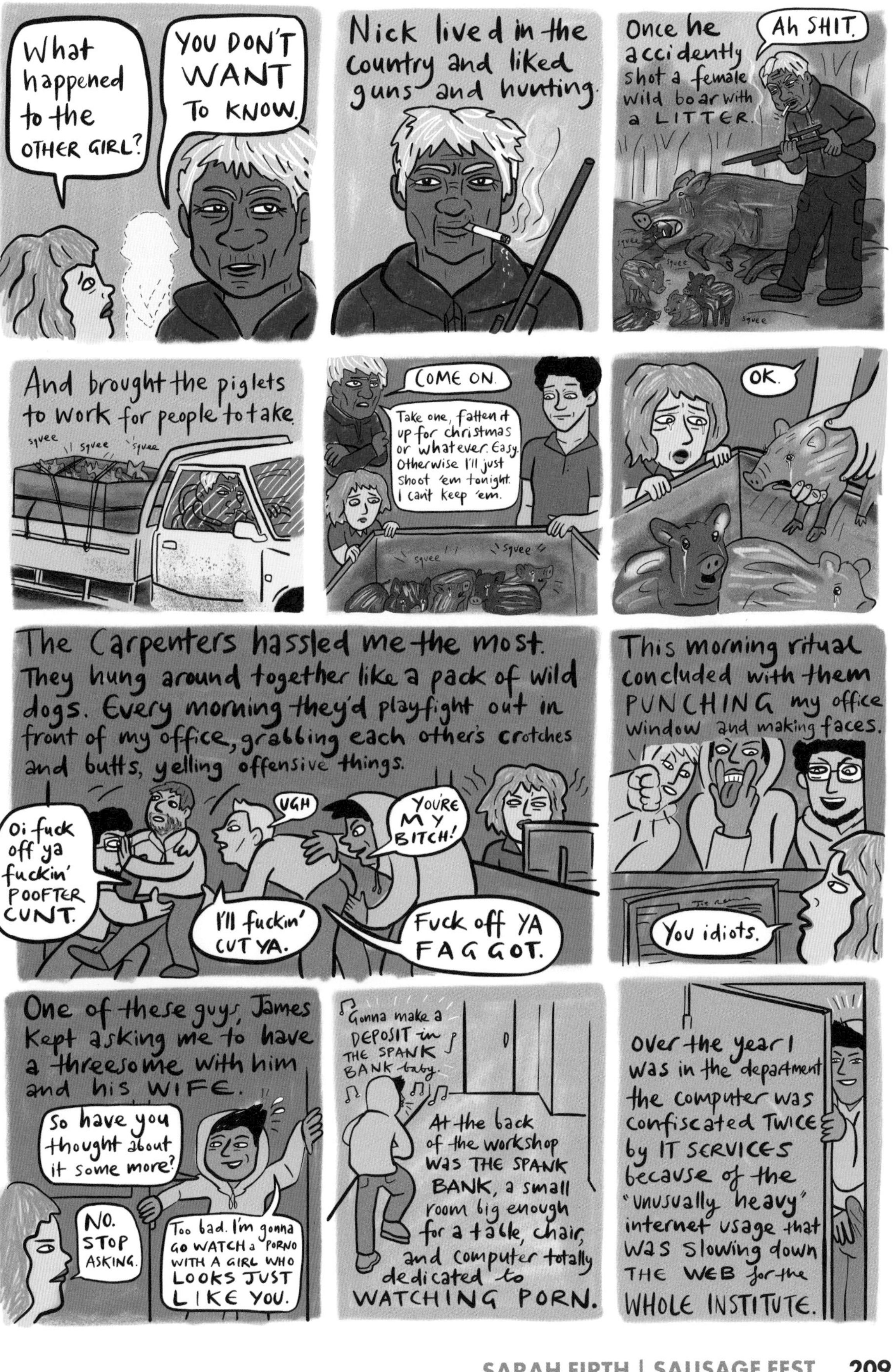

What happened to the OTHER GIRL?
YOU DON'T WANT TO KNOW.
Nick lived in the country and liked guns and hunting.
Once he accidently shot a female wild boar with a LITTER.
Ah SHIT.
squee
squee
squee
And brought the piglets to work for people to take.
squee squee squee
COME ON.
Take one, fatten it up for christmas or whatever. Easy. Otherwise I'll just shoot 'em tonight. I can't keep 'em.
squee
squee
OK.
The Carpenters hassled me the most. They hung around together like a pack of wild dogs. Every morning they'd playfight out in front of my office, grabbing each other's crotches and butts, yelling offensive things.
Oi fuck off ya fuckin' POOFTER CUNT.
UGH
YOU'RE MY BITCH!
I'll fuckin' CUT YA.
Fuck off YA FAGGOT.
This morning ritual concluded with them PUNCHING my office window and making faces.
You idiots.
One of these guys, James kept asking me to have a threesome with him and his WIFE.
So have you thought about it some more?
NO. STOP ASKING.
Too bad. I'm gonna GO WATCH a PORNO WITH A GIRL WHO LOOKS JUST LIKE YOU.
Gonna make a DEPOSIT in THE SPANK BANK baby.
At the back of the workshop was THE SPANK BANK, a small room big enough for a table, chair, and computer totally dedicated to WATCHING PORN.
Over the year I was in the department the computer was confiscated TWICE by IT SERVICES because of the "unusually heavy" internet usage that was slowing down THE WEB for the WHOLE INSTITUTE.

Despite the OPPRESSIVE hyper-masculine culture of the workshop, I did enjoy our regular Thursday pub lunches. Duncan always bought a stack of raffle tickets, so each of us had two chances in the meat raffle.

Because there were so many of us someone inevitably won a meat tray, which we used for our Friday BBQ.

I got it!

The BBQ is on me BOYS!

Once I won two meat trays in a row with my tickets. I was briefly a hero.

Things quickly went down hill the next day when James brought his wife along to the BBQ. He just wouldn't give up on trying to arrange a threesome experience.

Julia, this is Sarah.

James has told me all about you.

WTF? Oh. Hello.

SO BABES HOW 'BOUT IT?

SO HOT.

NO

James grow up.

The next day phallic OBJECTS started to appear on my chair EACH MORNING.

??

FIRST it was a COPPER PIPE.

Then a carrot,

a rasp,

a cucumber,

a broken light,

then a hammer.

I mentioned to Nick that I was starting to feel quite threatened.

I THINK it's James, but of course he denies it.

I'll find out and tell 'em to STOP.

The next day it was a vandalised printout of my STAFF PHOTO.

The next day a STANLEY KNIFE.

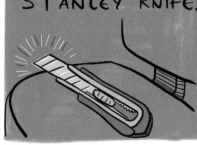

Nick, it's still fucking happening. Who is it?!

Definitely one of the boys from Carpentry. But no one will admit it. Fuckers.

I'd done my best to hide how stressed I was feeling but I couldn't pretend anymore.

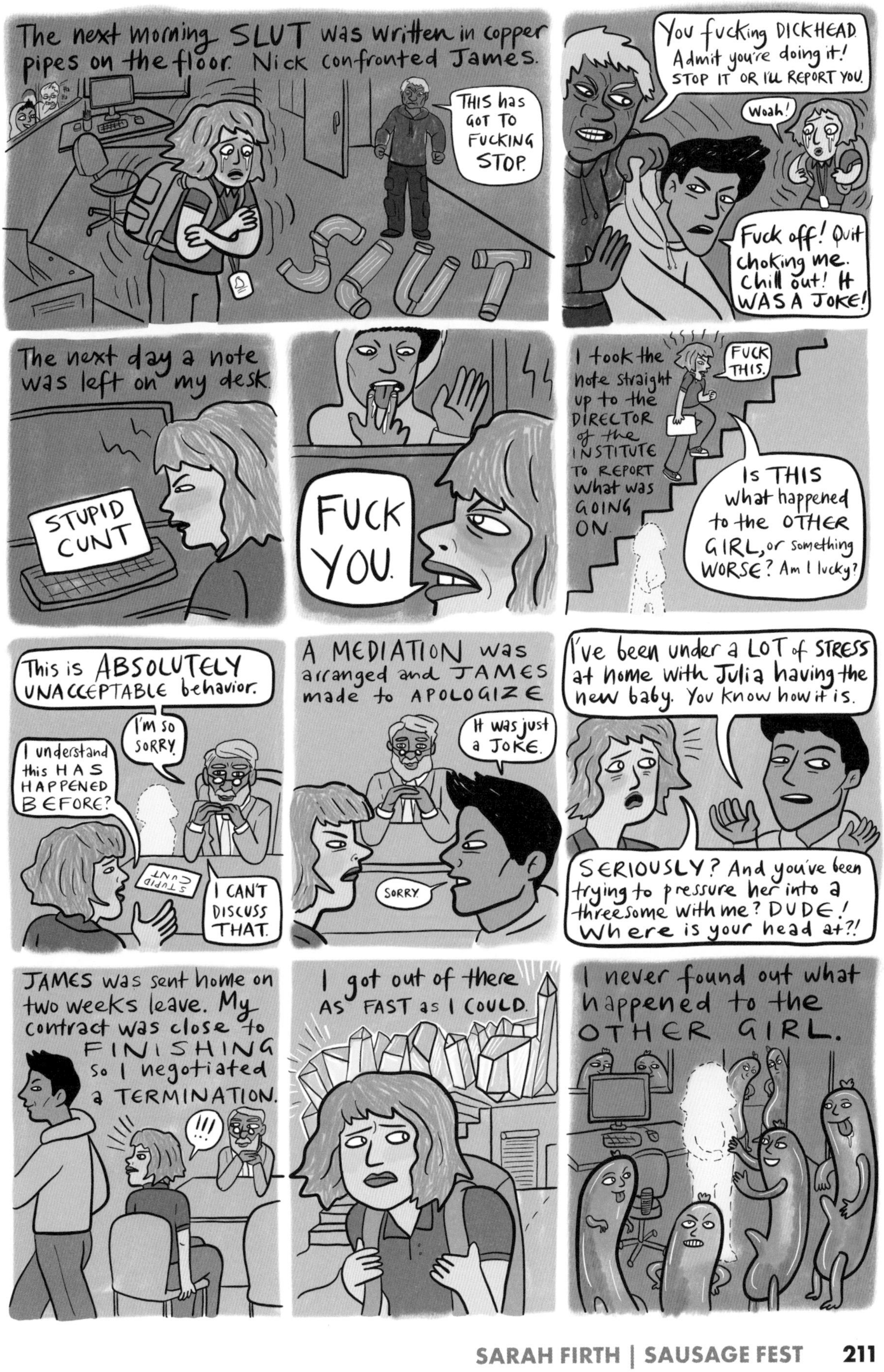
The next morning SLUT was written in copper pipes on the floor. Nick confronted James.
THIS has GOT TO FUCKING STOP.
SLUT
You fucking DICKHEAD. Admit you're doing it! STOP IT OR I'LL REPORT YOU.
Woah!
Fuck off! Quit choking me. Chill out! It WAS A JOKE!
The next day a note was left on my desk.
STUPID CUNT
FUCK YOU.
I took the note straight up to the DIRECTOR of the INSTITUTE to REPORT what was GOING ON.
FUCK THIS.
Is THIS what happened to the OTHER GIRL, or something WORSE? Am I lucky?
This is ABSOLUTELY UNACCEPTABLE behavior.
I'm so SORRY.
I understand this HAS HAPPENED BEFORE?
STUPID CUNT
I CAN'T DISCUSS THAT.
A MEDIATION was arranged and JAMES made to APOLOGIZE
It was just a JOKE.
SORRY.
I've been under a LOT of STRESS at home with Julia having the new baby. You know how it is.
SERIOUSLY? And you've been trying to pressure her into a threesome with me? DUDE! Where is your head at?!
JAMES was sent home on two weeks leave. My contract was close to FINISHING so I negotiated a TERMINATION.
!!!
I got out of there AS FAST as I COULD.
I never found out what happened to the OTHER GIRL.

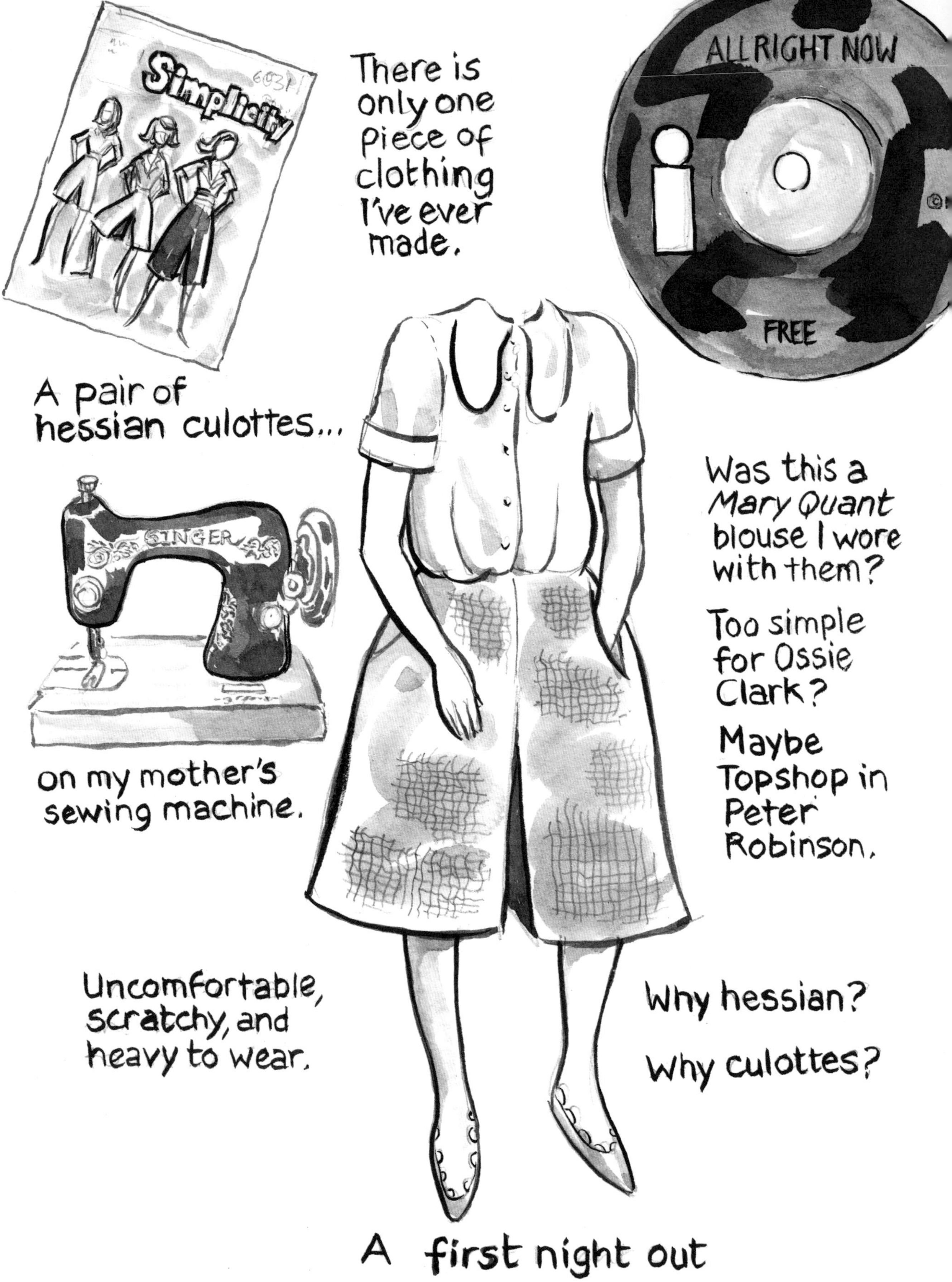
Simplicity
There is only one piece of clothing I've ever made.
ALL RIGHT NOW
FREE
A pair of hessian culottes...
SINGER
on my mother's sewing machine.
Was this a *Mary Quant* blouse I wore with them?
Too simple for Ossie Clark?
Maybe Topshop in Peter Robinson.
Uncomfortable, scratchy, and heavy to wear.
Why hessian?
Why culottes?
A first night out

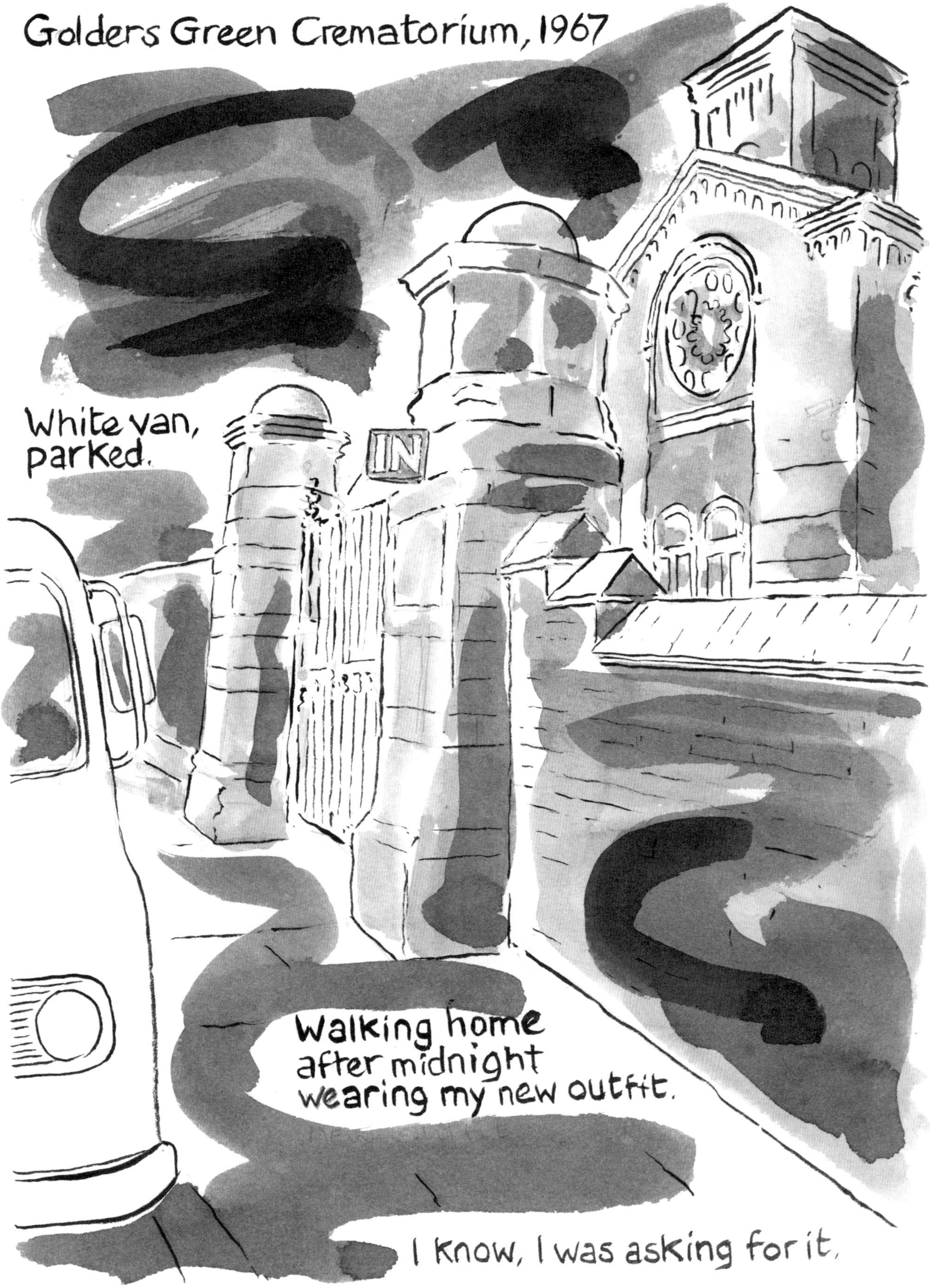
Golders Green Crematorium, 1967
White van, parked.
IN
Walking home after midnight wearing my new outfit.
I know, I was asking for it.

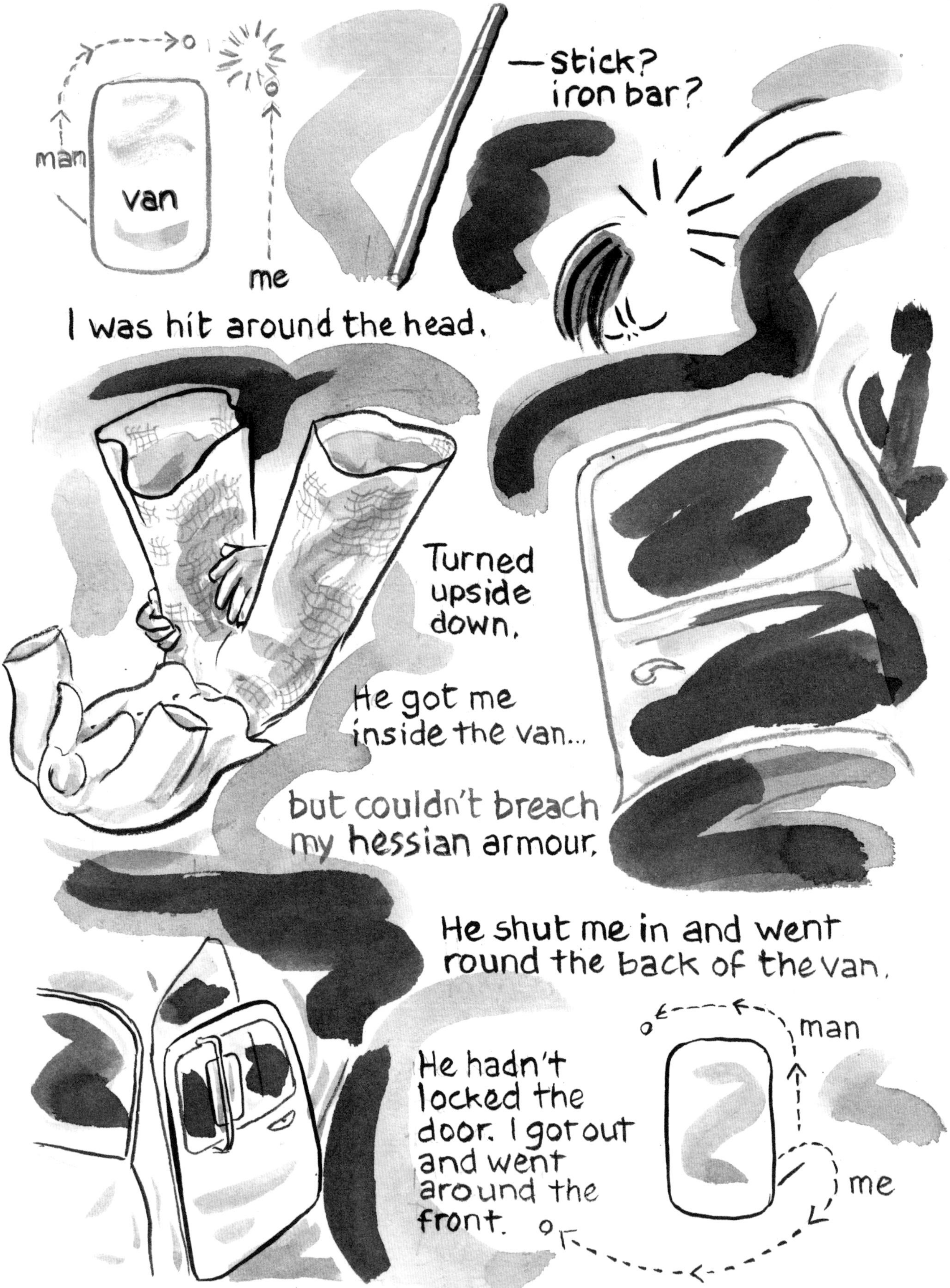
man
van
me
—stick?
iron bar?
I was hit around the head.
Turned
upside
down.
He got me
inside the van...
but couldn't breach
my hessian armour.
He shut me in and went
round the back of the van.
man
He hadn't
locked the
door. I got out
and went
around the
front.
me

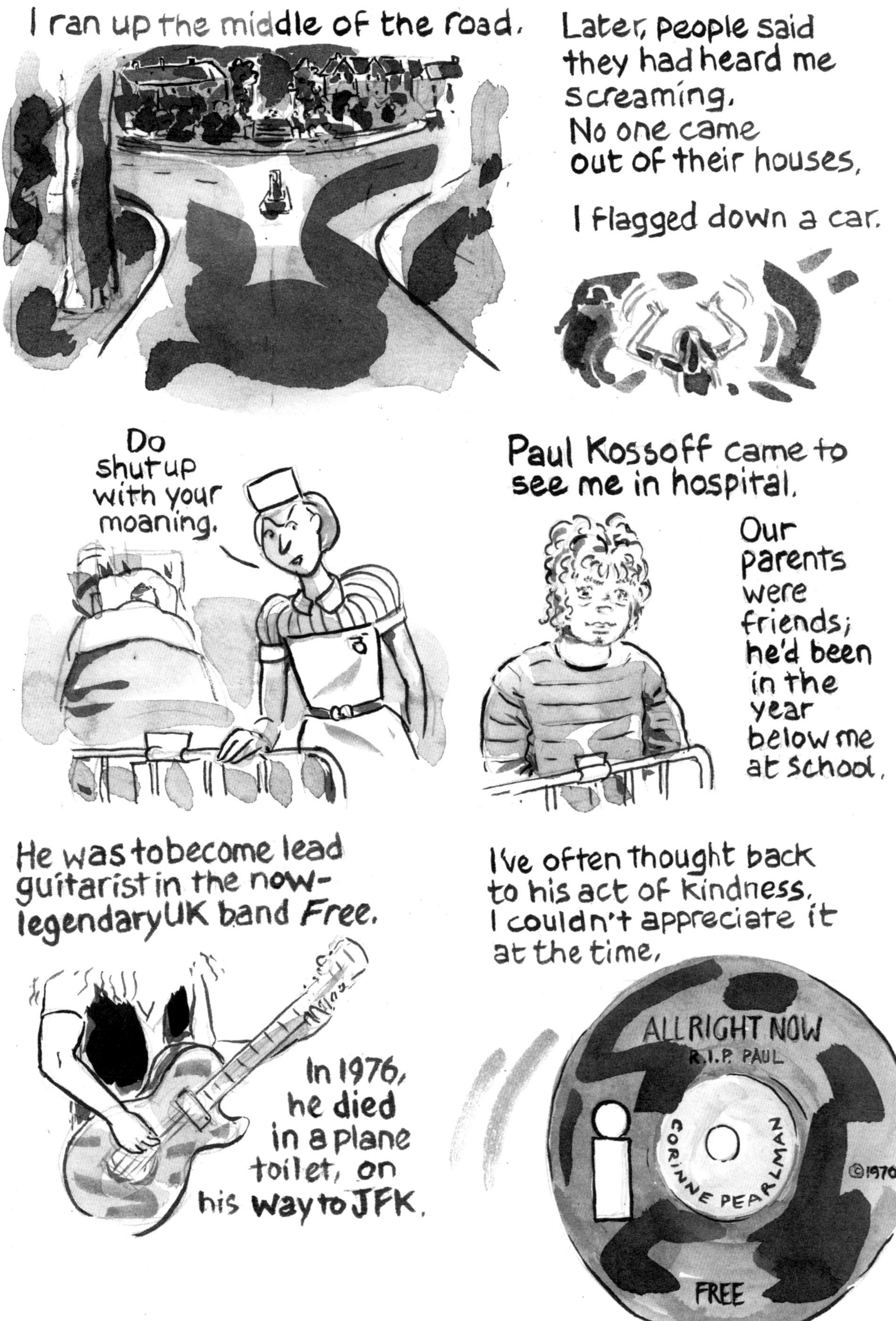
I ran up the middle of the road.
Later, people said they had heard me screaming. No one came out of their houses.
I flagged down a car.
Do shutup with your moaning.
Paul Kossoff came to see me in hospital.
Our parents were friends; he'd been in the year below me at school.
He was to become lead guitarist in the now-legendary UK band *Free*.
In 1976, he died in a plane toilet, on his way to JFK.
I've often thought back to his act of kindness. I couldn't appreciate it at the time.
ALLRIGHT NOW
R.I.P. PAUL
CORINNE PEARLMAN
©1970
FREE

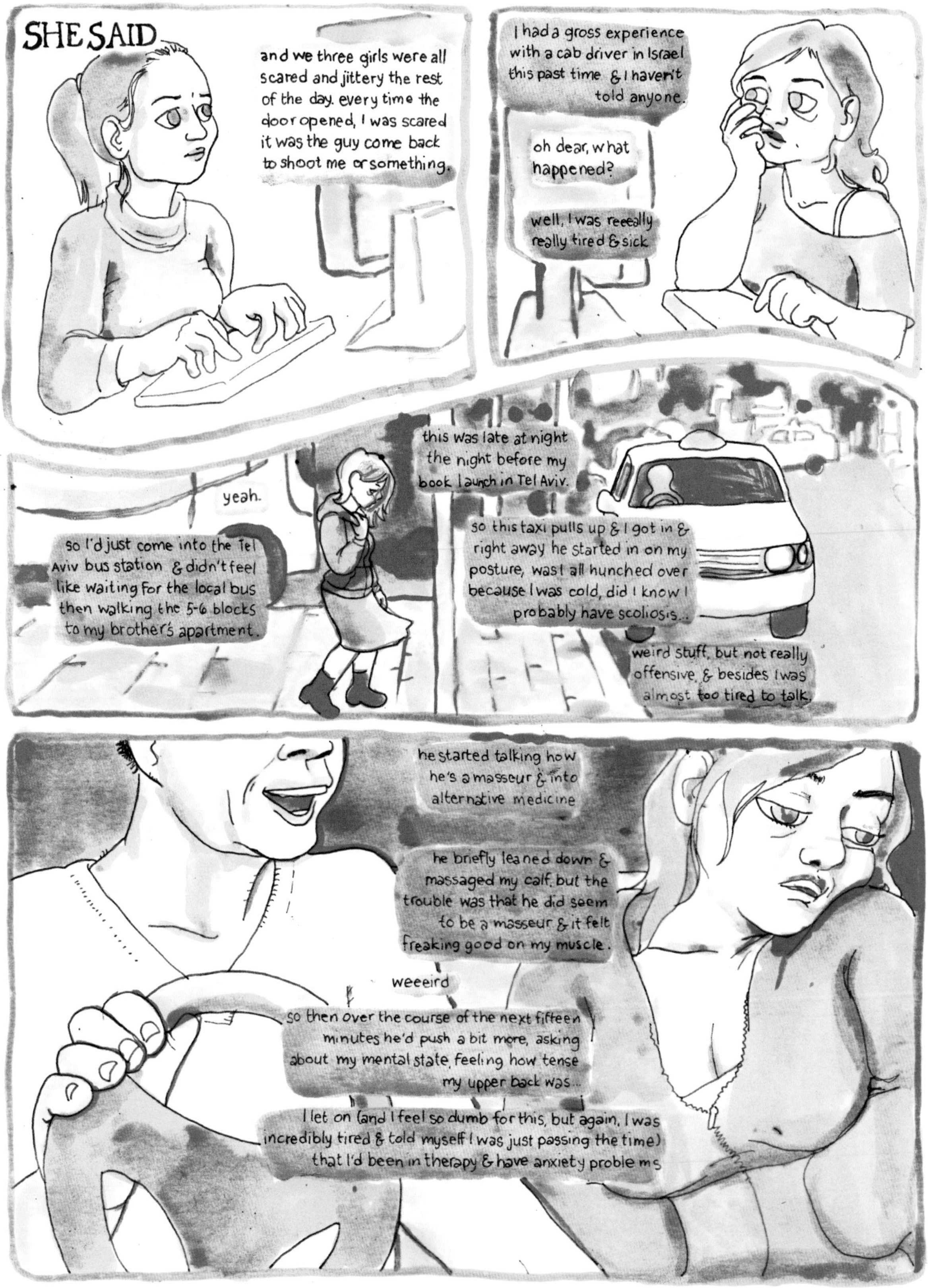
SHE SAID
and we three girls were all scared and jittery the rest of the day. every time the door opened, I was scared it was the guy come back to shoot me or something.
I had a gross experience with a cab driver in Israel this past time & I haven't told anyone.
oh dear, what happened?
well, I was reeeally really tired & sick
yeah.
so I'd just come into the Tel Aviv bus station & didn't feel like waiting for the local bus then walking the 5-6 blocks to my brother's apartment.
this was late at night the night before my book launch in Tel Aviv.
so this taxi pulls up & I got in & right away he started in on my posture, was I all hunched over because I was cold, did I know I probably have scoliosis...
weird stuff, but not really offensive, & besides I was almost too tired to talk.
he started talking how he's a masseur & into alternative medicine
he briefly leaned down & massaged my calf. but the trouble was that he did seem to be a masseur & it felt freaking good on my muscle.
weeeird
so then over the course of the next fifteen minutes he'd push a bit more, asking about my mental state, feeling how tense my upper back was...
I let on (and I feel so dumb for this, but again, I was incredibly tired & told myself I was just passing the time) that I'd been in therapy & have anxiety problems

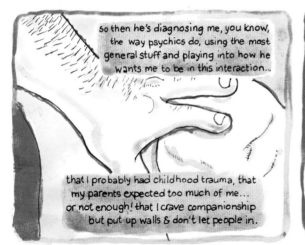

so then he's diagnosing me, you know, the way psychics do, using the most general stuff and playing into how he wants me to be in this interaction...

that I probably had childhood trauma, that my parents expected too much of me... or not enough! that I crave companionship but put up walls & don't let people in.

at this point, I began to feel offended at how dumb he must think I am, but I didn't have the energy (or the Hebrew words) to push back.

yeah, that's so horrid to feel vulnerable

if I argued, would he kick me out of the cab? We were like on the back streets of Yafo in the middle of the night! I had no idea where we were. I just wanted to get home.

& then, of course, to demonstrate how I crave the gentle touch of another, he started stroking my face, & decided he needed to feel the muscle, like, right above my breast

oh no! and he's DRIVING poor you

& if I smack him, that's just me pushing people away because I hate myself, right?

by then we were just about at my brother's building, & he's like

let me ask you, you don't have a boyfriend, right?

(because I can't keep men because of my frigidity)

I do, as it happens.

he looked deeply and skeptically into my eyes

but is it good for you?

EW
EW
EW
EW to the max

I think I scowled, 'cause he's like "of course, I'd never want to make you uncomfortable." I said, "I am uncomfortable now."

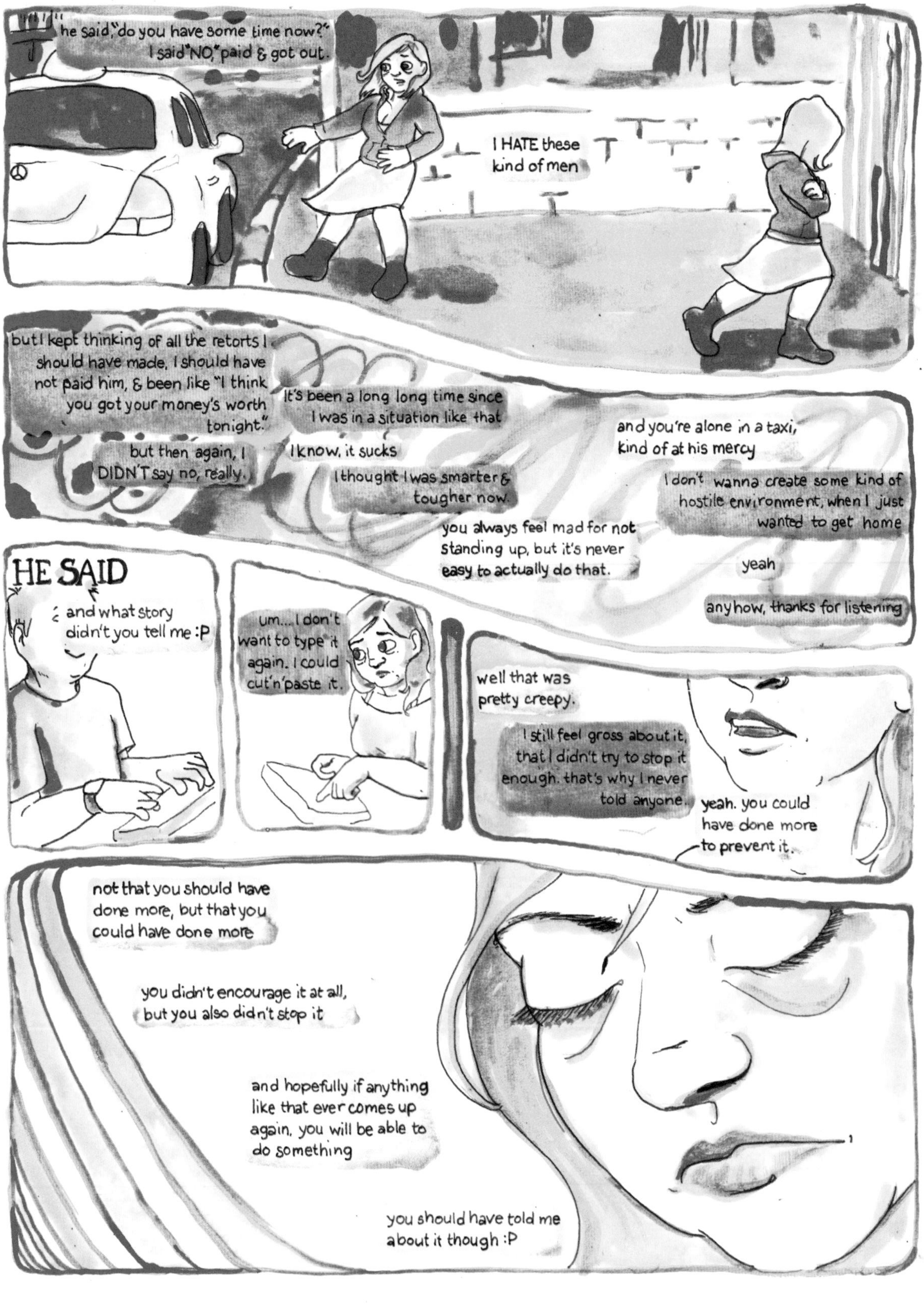
"he said, "do you have some time now?"
I said "NO," paid & got out.
I HATE these kind of men
but I kept thinking of all the retorts I should have made. I should have not paid him, & been like "I think you got your money's worth tonight."
but then again, I DIDN'T say no, really.
It's been a long long time since I was in a situation like that
I know, it sucks
I thought I was smarter & tougher now.
and you're alone in a taxi, kind of at his mercy
I don't wanna create some kind of hostile environment, when I just wanted to get home
you always feel mad for not standing up, but it's never easy to actually do that.
yeah
anyhow, thanks for listening
HE SAID
and what story didn't you tell me :P
um... I don't want to type it again. I could cut'n'paste it.
well that was pretty creepy.
I still feel gross about it, that I didn't try to stop it enough. that's why I never told anyone.
yeah. you could have done more to prevent it.
not that you should have done more, but that you could have done more
you didn't encourage it at all, but you also didn't stop it
and hopefully if anything like that ever comes up again, you will be able to do something
you should have told me about it though :P

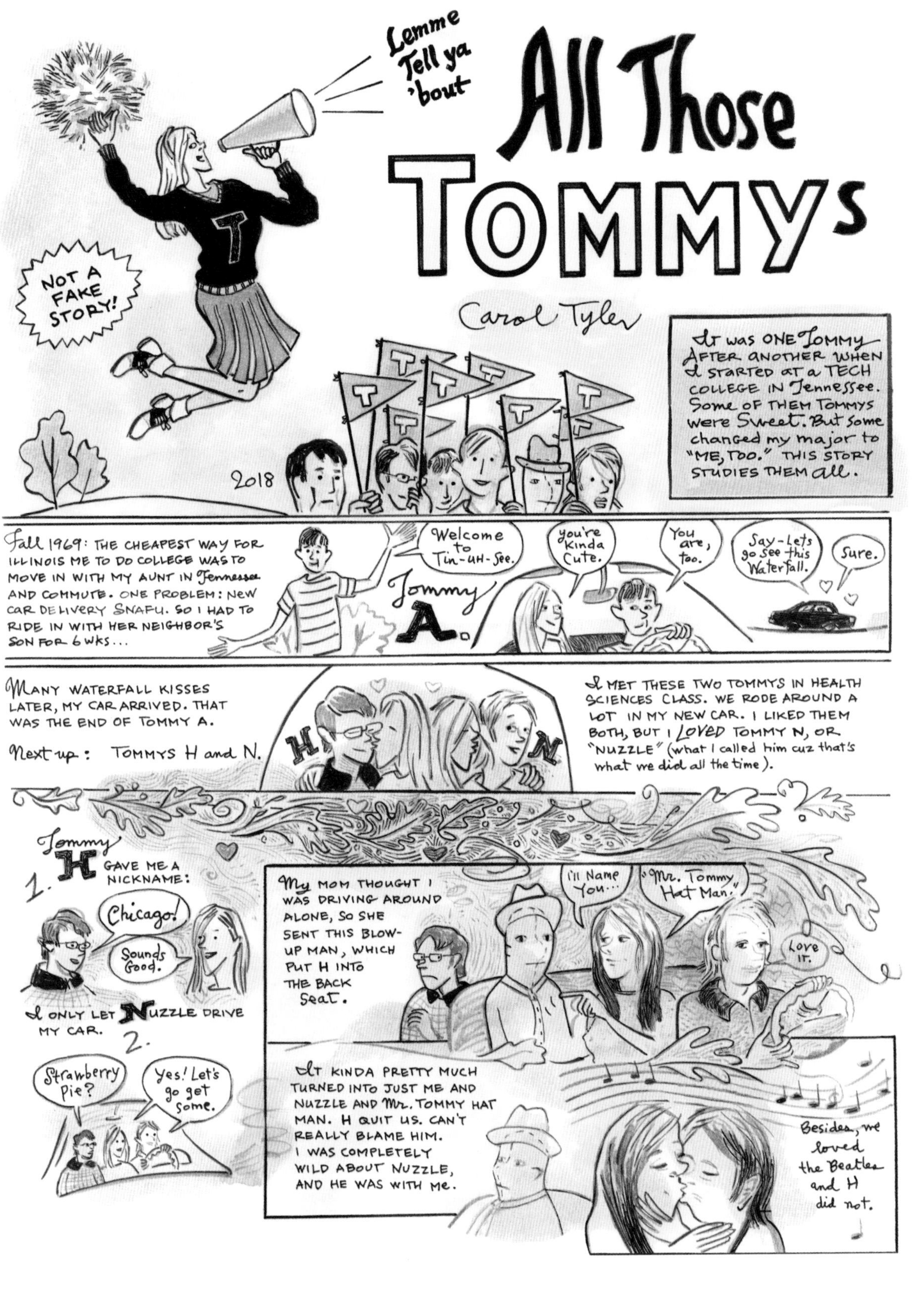
Lemme Tell ya 'bout
All Those TOMMYs
NOT A FAKE STORY!
Carol Tyler
It was ONE Tommy After another when I started at a TECH college in Tennessee. Some of them Tommys were Sweet. But some changed my major to "ME, TOO." This story studies them all.
2018
Fall 1969: The cheapest way for Illinois me to do college was to move in with my aunt in Tennessee and commute. One problem: new car delivery snafu. So I had to ride in with her neighbor's son for 6 wks...
Welcome to Tin-uh-See.
Tommy A.
you're kinda cute.
You are, too.
Say-Lets go see this Waterfall.
Sure.
Many waterfall kisses later, my car arrived. That was the end of Tommy A.
Next up: Tommys H and N.
I met these two Tommys in health sciences class. We rode around a lot in my new car. I liked them both, but I LOVED Tommy N, or "Nuzzle" (what I called him cuz that's what we did all the time).
1. Tommy H gave me a nickname:
Chicago!
Sounds Good.
I only let Nuzzle drive my car.
2.
Strawberry Pie?
Yes! Let's go get some.
My mom thought I was driving around alone, so she sent this blow-up man, which put H into the back seat.
I'll Name You...
"Mr. Tommy Hat Man."
Love it.
It kinda pretty much turned into just me and Nuzzle and Mr. Tommy Hat Man. H quit us. Can't really blame him. I was completely wild about Nuzzle, and he was with me.
Besides, we loved the Beatles and H did not.

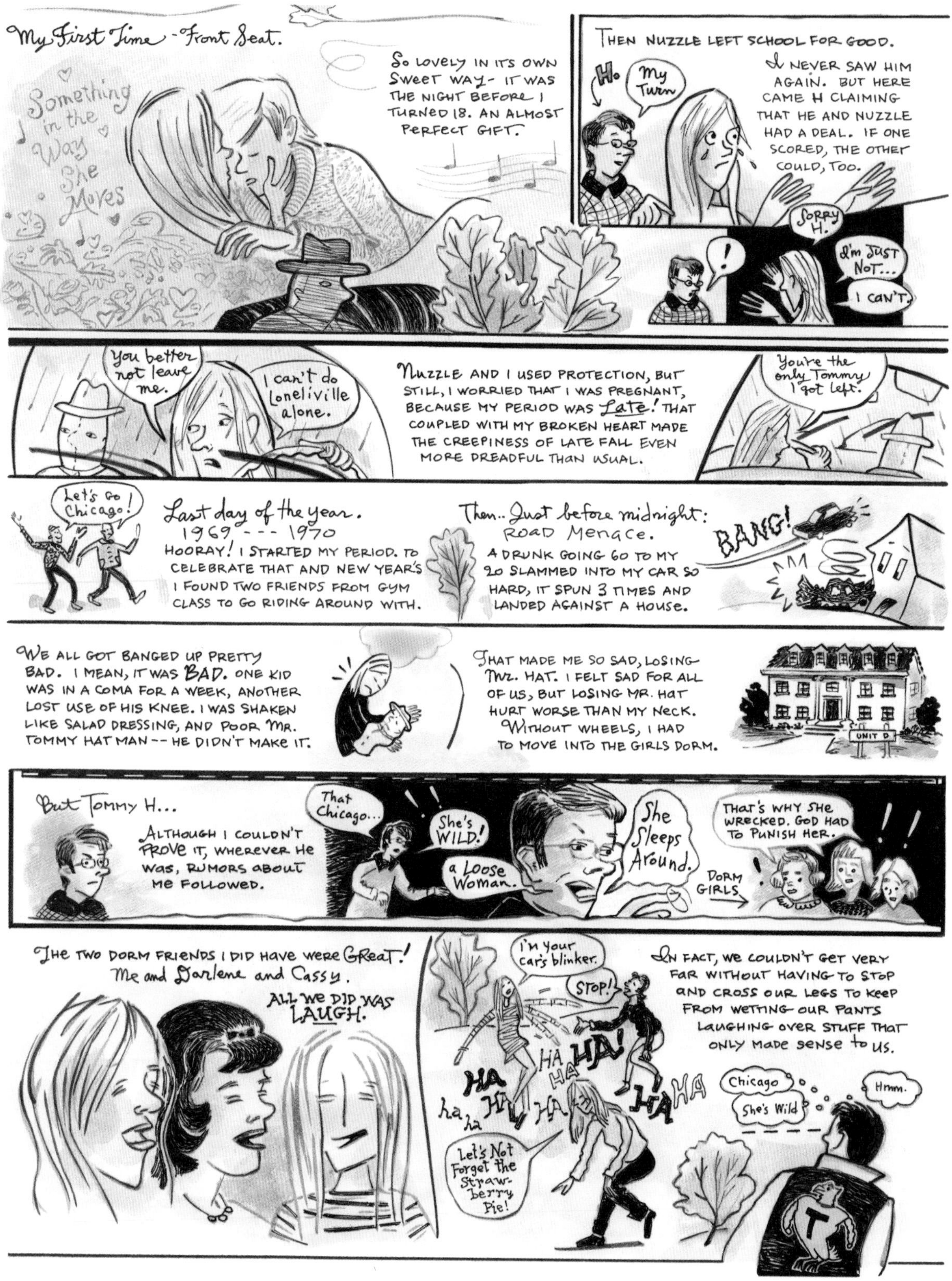
My First Time - Front Seat.
Something in the Way She Moves
So lovely in its own sweet way- it was the night before I turned 18. An almost perfect gift.
Then Nuzzle left school for good.
H.
My Turn
I never saw him again. But here came H claiming that he and Nuzzle had a deal. If one scored, the other could, too.
Sorry H.
!
I'm just not...
I can't.
You better not leave me.
I can't do Loneliville alone.
Nuzzle and I used protection, but still, I worried that I was pregnant, because my period was Late! That coupled with my broken heart made the creepiness of late fall even more dreadful than usual.
You're the only Tommy I got left.
Let's go Chicago!
Last day of the year. 1969 - - - 1970
Hooray! I started my period. To celebrate that and New Year's I found two friends from gym class to go riding around with.
Then.. Just before midnight: Road Menace.
A drunk going 60 to my 20 slammed into my car so hard, it spun 3 times and landed against a house.
BANG!
We all got banged up pretty bad. I mean, it was BAD. One kid was in a coma for a week, another lost use of his knee. I was shaken like salad dressing, and poor Mr. Tommy Hat Man -- he didn't make it.
That made me so sad, losing Mr. Hat. I felt sad for all of us, but losing Mr. Hat hurt worse than my neck. Without wheels, I had to move into the girls dorm.
UNIT D
But Tommy H...
Although I couldn't prove it, wherever he was, rumors about me followed.
That Chicago...
She's WILD!
a Loose Woman.
She Sleeps Around.
That's why she wrecked. God had to punish her.
Dorm Girls
The two dorm friends I did have were Great! Me and Darlene and Cassy.
All we did was LAUGH.
I'm your car's blinker.
Stop!
HA HA HA HA ha ha HA HA HA HA HA
Let's Not Forget the Strawberry Pie!
In fact, we couldn't get very far without having to stop and cross our legs to keep from wetting our pants laughing over stuff that only made sense to us.
Chicago
She's Wild
Hmm.
T

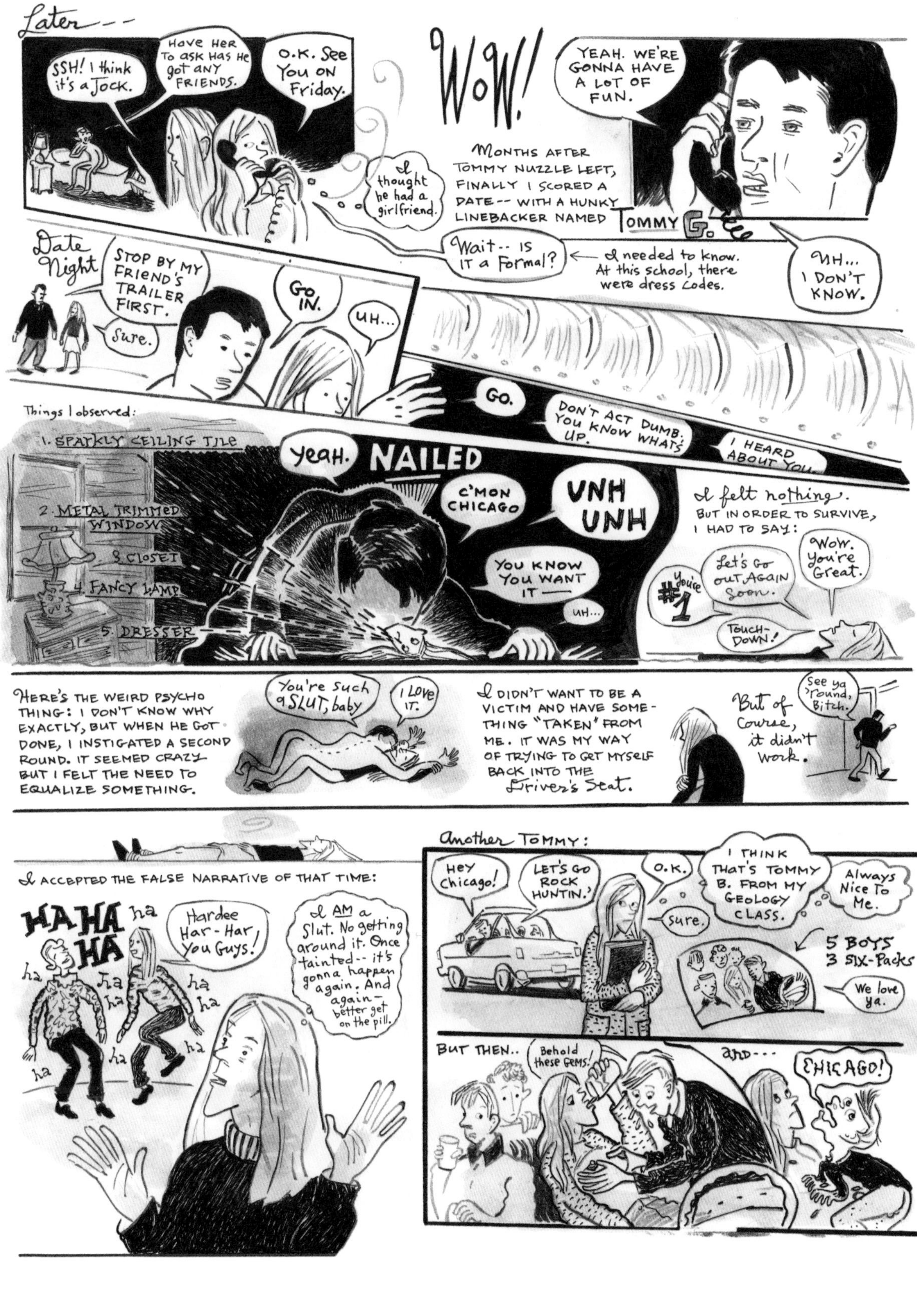
Later---
SSH! I think it's a Jock.
Have her to ask has he got any friends.
O.K. See You on Friday.
WoW!
I thought he had a girlfriend.
Months after Tommy Nuzzle left, finally I scored a date-- with a hunky linebacker named Tommy G.
Yeah. We're gonna have a lot of fun.
Wait-- is it a Formal?
I needed to know. At this school, there were dress codes.
Uh... I don't know.
Date Night
Stop by my friend's trailer first.
Sure.
Go in.
Uh...
Go.
Don't act dumb. You know whats up.
I heard about you.
Things I observed:
1. Sparkly ceiling tile
2. Metal trimmed window
3. Closet
4. Fancy lamp
5. Dresser
Yeah.
NAILED
C'mon Chicago
UNH UNH
You know you want it —
uh...
I felt nothing. But in order to survive, I had to say:
You're #1
Let's go out again soon.
Wow. You're Great.
Touch-down!
Here's the weird psycho thing: I don't know why exactly, but when he got done, I instigated a second round. It seemed crazy but I felt the need to equalize something.
You're such a SLUT, baby
I love it.
I didn't want to be a victim and have something "taken" from me. It was my way of trying to get myself back into the Driver's Seat.
But of course, it didn't work.
See ya 'round, Bitch.
I accepted the false narrative of that time:
HA HA HA HA
ha ha ha ha ha ha ha ha
Hardee Har-Har You Guys!
I AM a Slut. No getting around it. Once tainted-- it's gonna happen again. And again- better get on the pill.
Another Tommy:
Hey Chicago!
Let's go rock huntin.'
O.K.
Sure.
I think that's Tommy B. from my geology class.
Always nice to me.
5 Boys 3 Six-Packs
We love ya.
But then..
Behold these gems!
and---
Chicago!

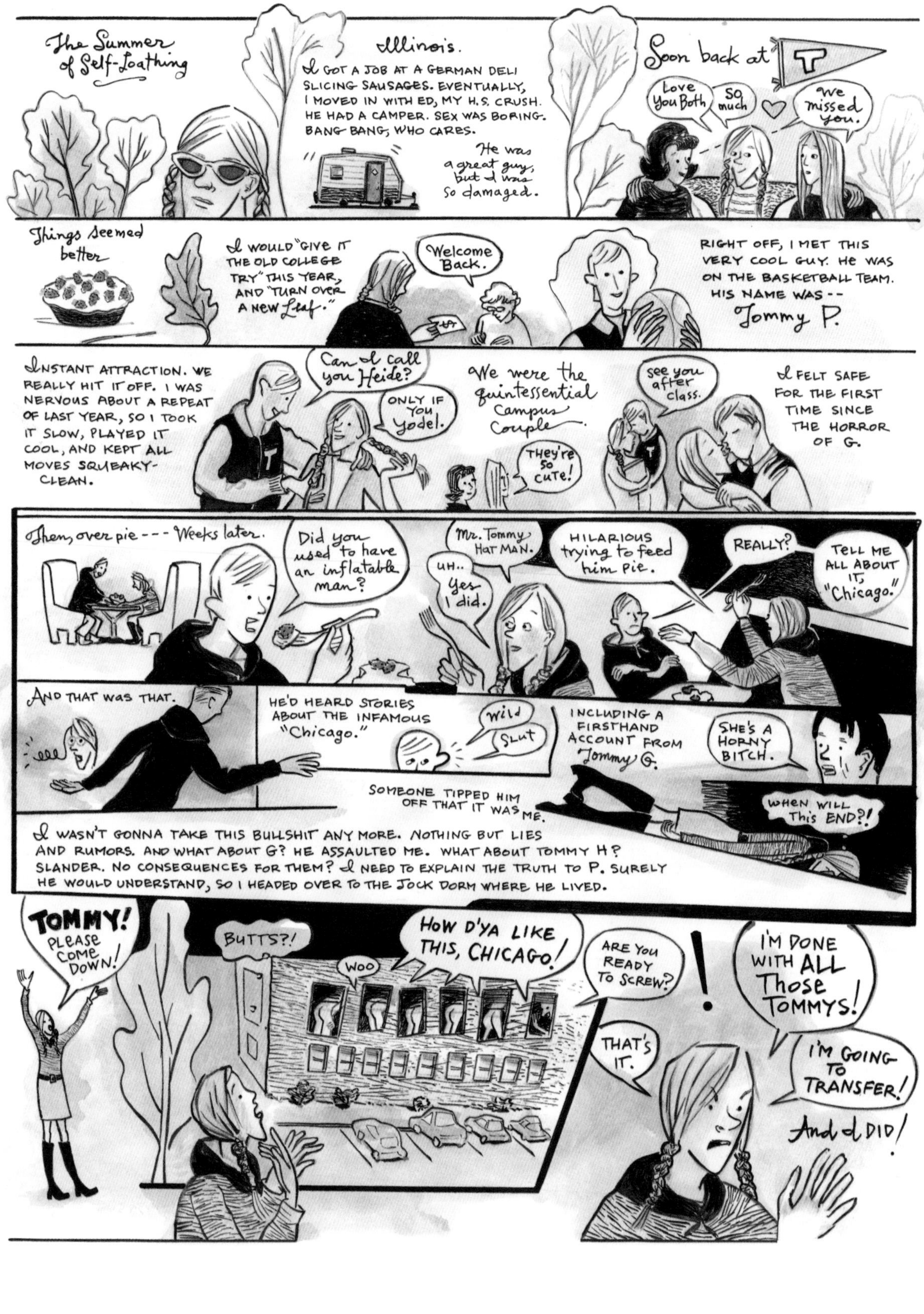
The Summer of Self-Loathing
Illinois.
I GOT A JOB AT A GERMAN DELI SLICING SAUSAGES. EVENTUALLY, I MOVED IN WITH ED, MY H.S. CRUSH. HE HAD A CAMPER. SEX WAS BORING. BANG BANG, WHO CARES.
He was a great guy, but I was so damaged.
Soon back at
T
Love You Both
So much
We missed you.
Things seemed better
I WOULD "GIVE IT THE OLD COLLEGE TRY" THIS YEAR, AND "TURN OVER A NEW Leaf."
Welcome Back.
RIGHT OFF, I MET THIS VERY COOL GUY. HE WAS ON THE BASKETBALL TEAM. HIS NAME WAS -- Tommy P.
INSTANT ATTRACTION. WE REALLY HIT IT OFF. I WAS NERVOUS ABOUT A REPEAT OF LAST YEAR, SO I TOOK IT SLOW, PLAYED IT COOL, AND KEPT ALL MOVES SQUEAKY-CLEAN.
Can I call you Heide?
ONLY IF YOU Yodel.
We were the quintessential Campus Couple.
They're so cute!
See you after class.
I FELT SAFE FOR THE FIRST TIME SINCE THE HORROR OF G.
Then, over pie --- Weeks later.
Did you used to have an inflatable man?
Mr. Tommy HAT MAN.
UH.. Yes I did.
HILARIOUS trying to feed him pie.
REALLY?
TELL ME ALL ABOUT IT, "Chicago."
AND THAT WAS THAT.
HE'D HEARD STORIES ABOUT THE INFAMOUS "Chicago."
Wild
SLUT
INCLUDING A FIRSTHAND ACCOUNT FROM Tommy G.
SHE'S A HORNY BITCH.
SOMEONE TIPPED HIM OFF THAT IT WAS ME.
WHEN WILL THIS END?!
I WASN'T GONNA TAKE THIS BULLSHIT ANY MORE. NOTHING BUT LIES AND RUMORS. AND WHAT ABOUT G? HE ASSAULTED ME. WHAT ABOUT TOMMY H? SLANDER. NO CONSEQUENCES FOR THEM? I NEED TO EXPLAIN THE TRUTH TO P. SURELY HE WOULD UNDERSTAND, SO I HEADED OVER TO THE JOCK DORM WHERE HE LIVED.
TOMMY! PLEASE COME DOWN!
BUTTS?!
WOO
HOW D'YA LIKE THIS, CHICAGO!
ARE YOU READY TO SCREW?
!
THAT'S IT.
I'M DONE WITH ALL Those TOMMYS!
I'M GOING TO TRANSFER!
And I DID!

I don't even like sunflowers

MARIA STOIAN

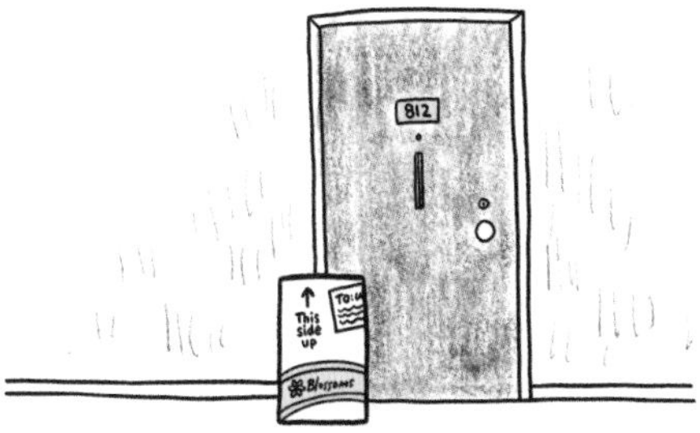
812

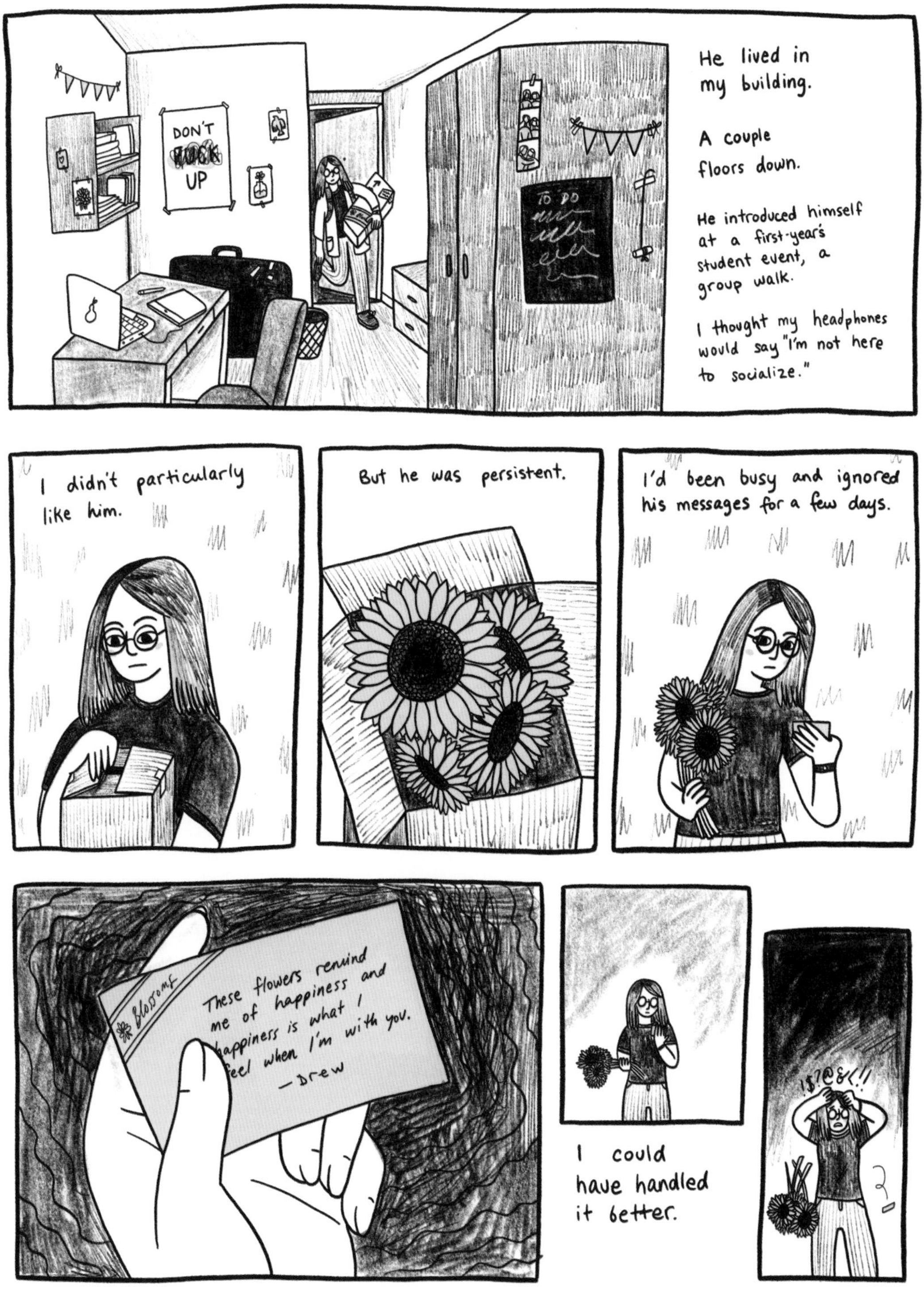
DON'T
UP
TO DO
He lived in my building.
A couple floors down.
He introduced himself at a first-year's student event, a group walk.
I thought my headphones would say "I'm not here to socialize."
I didn't particularly like him.
But he was persistent.
I'd been busy and ignored his messages for a few days.
Blossoms
These flowers remind me of happiness and happiness is what I feel when I'm with you.
—Drew
I could have handled it better.
!$?@&!!!

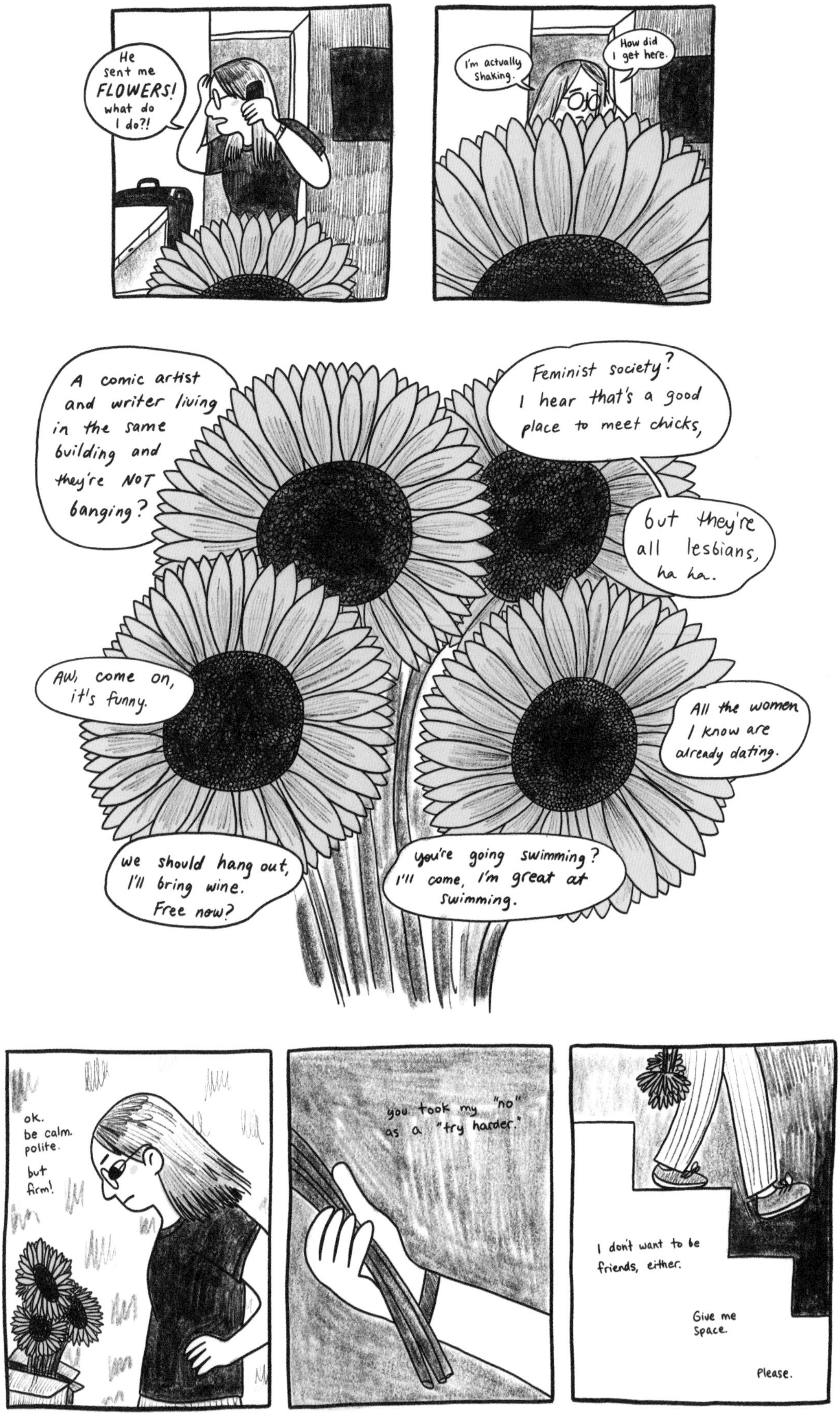
He sent me FLOWERS! what do I do?!
I'm actually shaking.
How did I get here.
A comic artist and writer living in the same building and they're NOT banging?
Feminist society? I hear that's a good place to meet chicks,
but they're all lesbians, ha ha.
Aw, come on, it's funny.
All the women I know are already dating.
we should hang out, I'll bring wine. Free now?
you're going swimming? I'll come, I'm great at swimming.
ok. be calm. polite.
but firm!
you took my "no" as a "try harder."
I don't want to be friends, either.
Give me space.
Please.

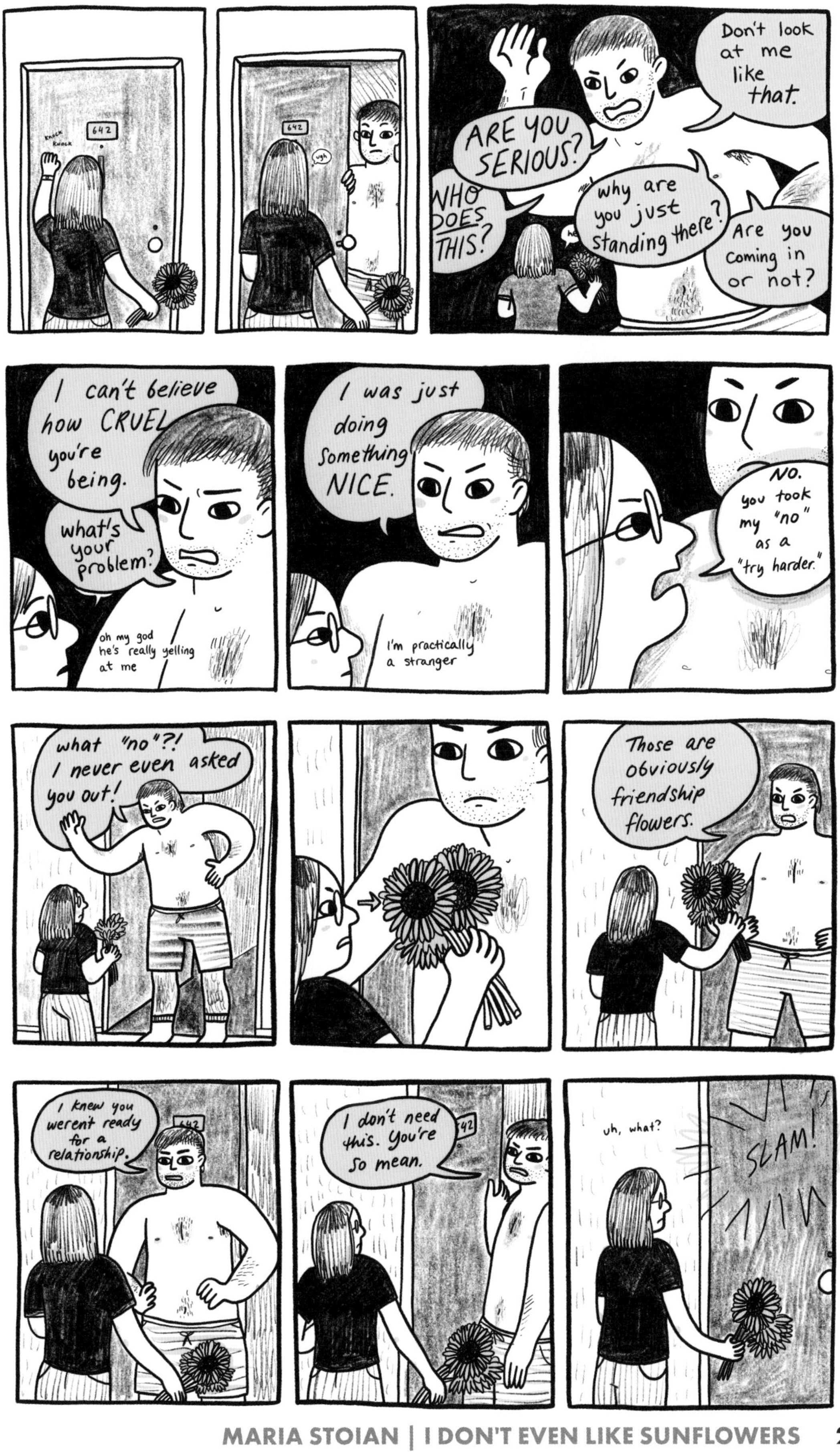
knock knock
642
642
ugh
Don't look at me like that.
ARE YOU SERIOUS?
WHO DOES THIS?
why are you just standing there?
Are you coming in or not?
I can't believe how CRUEL you're being.
what's your problem?
oh my god he's really yelling at me
I was just doing something NICE.
I'm practically a stranger
NO. you took my "no" as a "try harder."
what "no"?! I never even asked you out!
Those are obviously friendship flowers.
I knew you weren't ready for a relationship.
I don't need this. You're so mean.
uh, what?
SLAM!

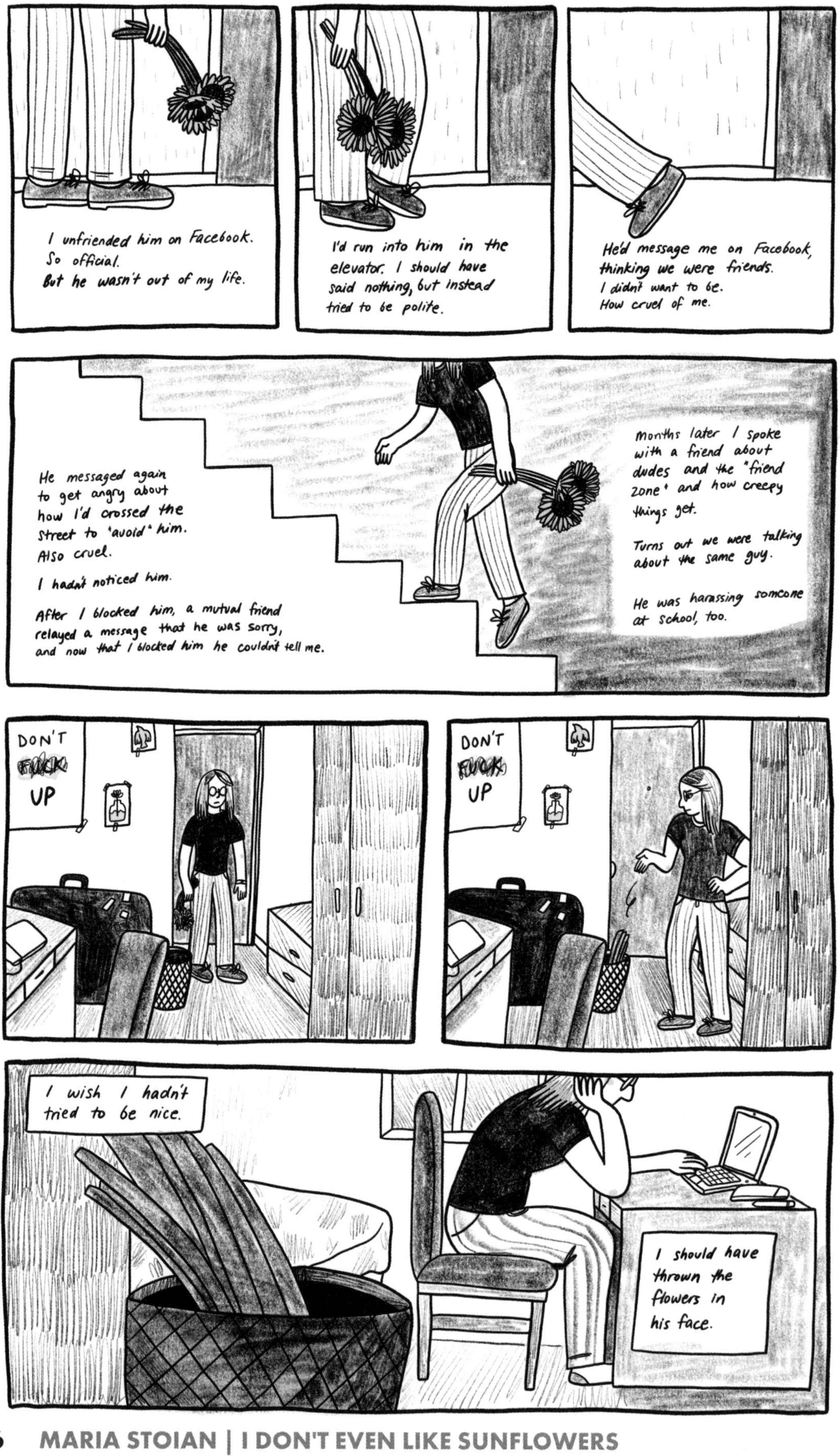

I unfriended him on Facebook.
So official.
But he wasn't out of my life.
I'd run into him in the elevator. I should have said nothing, but instead tried to be polite.
He'd message me on Facebook, thinking we were friends.
I didn't want to be.
How cruel of me.
He messaged again to get angry about how I'd crossed the street to "avoid" him.
Also cruel.
I hadn't noticed him.
After I blocked him, a mutual friend relayed a message that he was sorry, and now that I blocked him he couldn't tell me.
Months later I spoke with a friend about dudes and the "friend zone" and how creepy things get.
Turns out we were talking about the same guy.
He was harassing someone at school, too.
DON'T [redacted] UP
DON'T [redacted] UP
I wish I hadn't tried to be nice.
I should have thrown the flowers in his face.

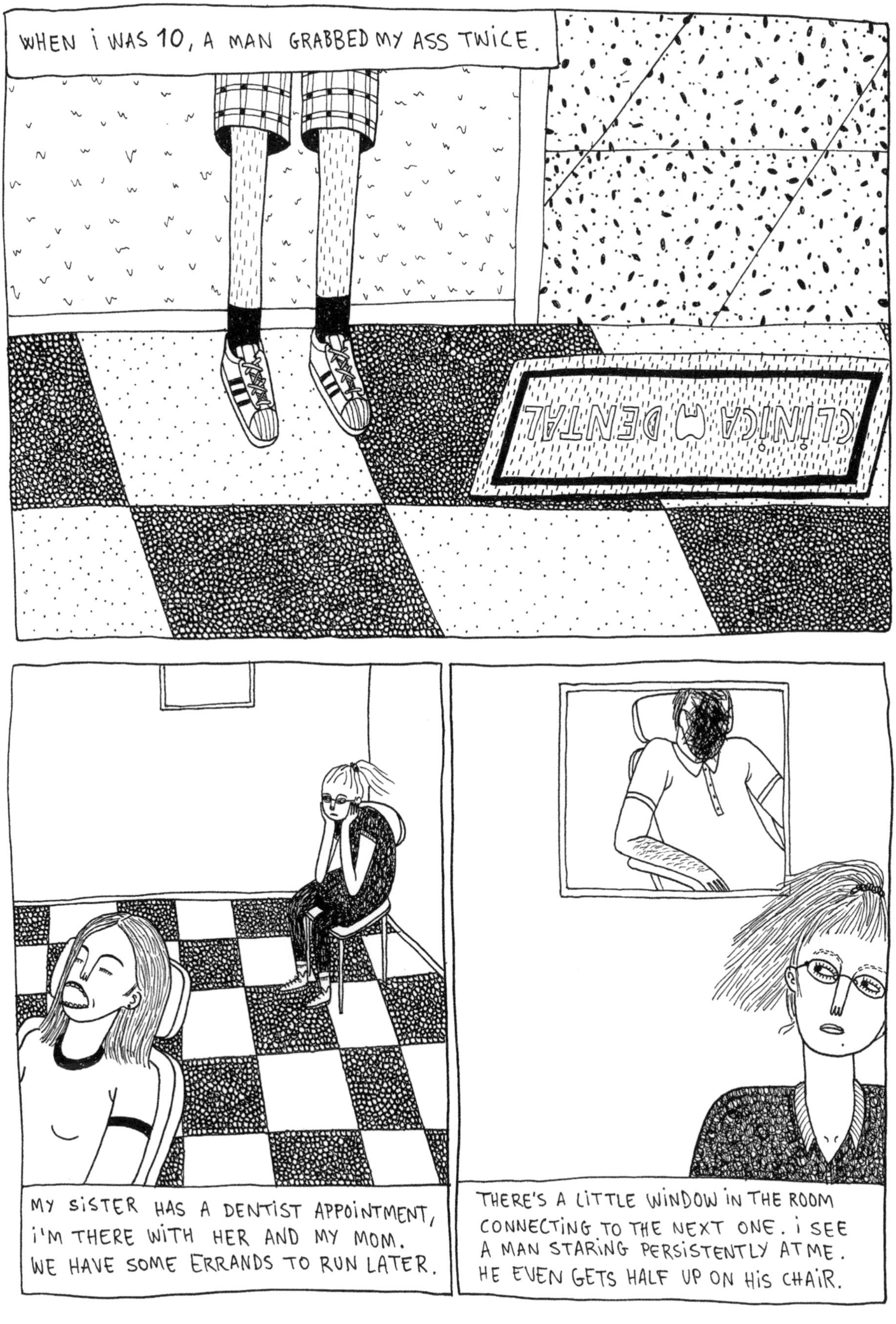
WHEN i WAS 10, A MAN GRABBED MY ASS TWICE.
CLÍNICA DENTAL
MY SiSTER HAS A DENTIST APPOiNTMENT, i'M THERE WITH HER AND MY MOM. WE HAVE SOME ERRANDS TO RUN LATER.
THERE'S A LiTTLE WiNDOW iN THE ROOM CONNECTiNG TO THE NEXT ONE. i SEE A MAN STARiNG PERSiSTENTLY AT ME. HE EVEN GETS HALF UP ON HiS CHAiR.

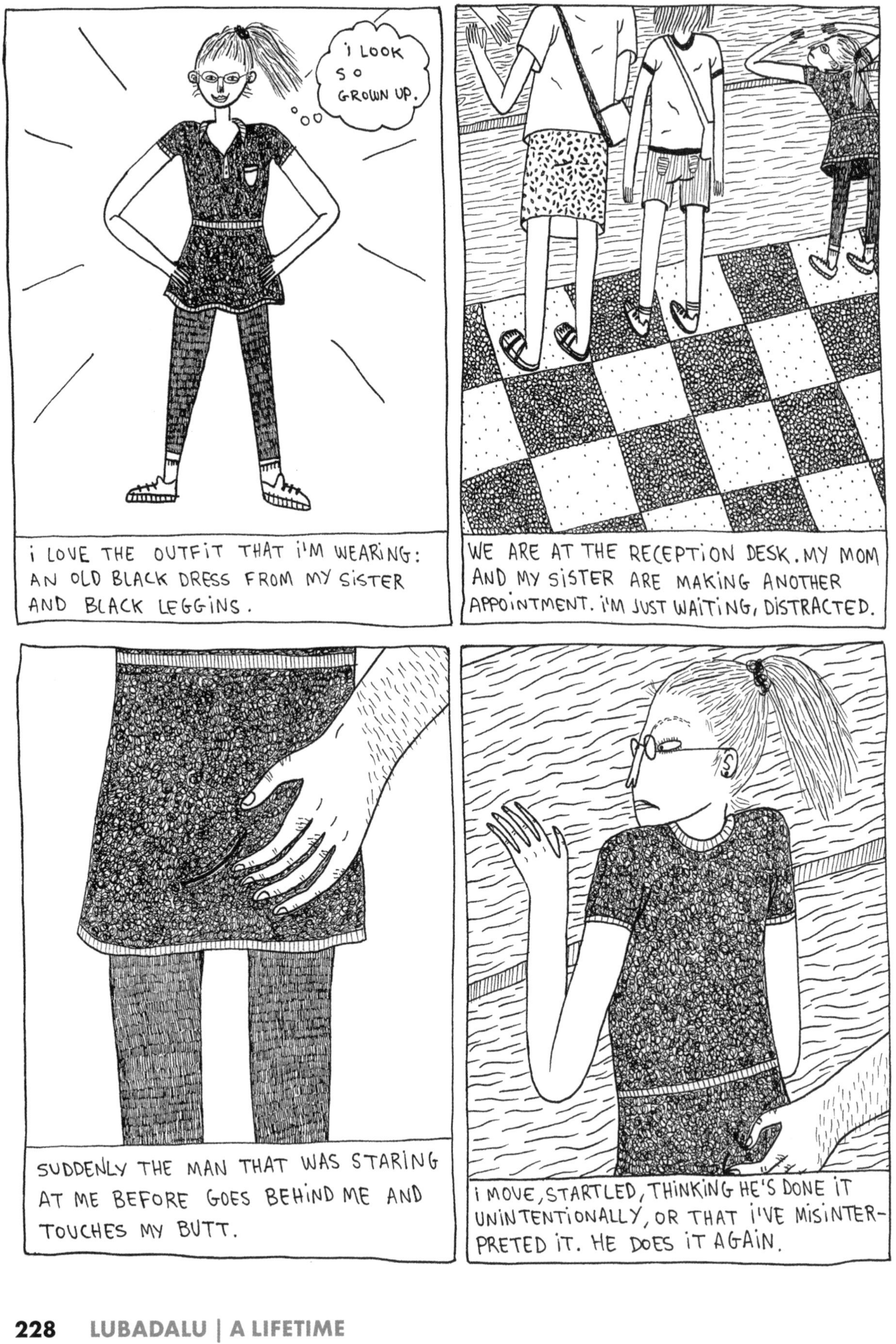
i LOOK SO GROWN UP.
i LOVE THE OUTFIT THAT i'M WEARING: AN OLD BLACK DRESS FROM MY SiSTER AND BLACK LEGGiNS.
WE ARE AT THE RECEPTiON DESK. MY MOM AND MY SiSTER ARE MAKiNG ANOTHER APPOiNTMENT. i'M JUST WAiTiNG, DiSTRACTED.
SUDDENLY THE MAN THAT WAS STARiNG AT ME BEFORE GOES BEHiND ME AND TOUCHES MY BUTT.
i MOVE, STARTLED, THiNKiNG HE'S DONE iT UNiNTENTiONALLY, OR THAT i'VE MiSiNTERPRETED iT. HE DOES iT AGAiN.

i TURN AROUND AND WATCH HiM AS HE QUICKLY LEAVES. i DON'T KNOW WHAT TO DO. i DON'T UNDERSTAND WHAT JUST HAPPENED. i'M ONLY 10.

THERE'S A BOY, A BiT OLDER THAN ME, BESiDE THE DOOR. HE'S ALSO LOOKiNG AT THE MAN. i GUESS HE DOESN'T KNOW WHAT TO DO EiTHER.

MY MOM AND SiSTER HAVEN'T SEEN ANYTHiNG. AT FiRST i DON'T WANT TO TELL MY MOM. i'M SO FUCKiNG ASHAMED AND ANGRY. i TELL HER ONCE WE LEAVE THE BUiLDiNG, iN A FURIOUS MUMBLE. i FEEL POWERLESS. i KEEP THiNKiNG THAT i SHOULD HAVE DONE SOMETHiNG. i SHOULD HAVE KiCKED HiM. i DON'T WANT TO WEAR THiS DRESS AGAiN.

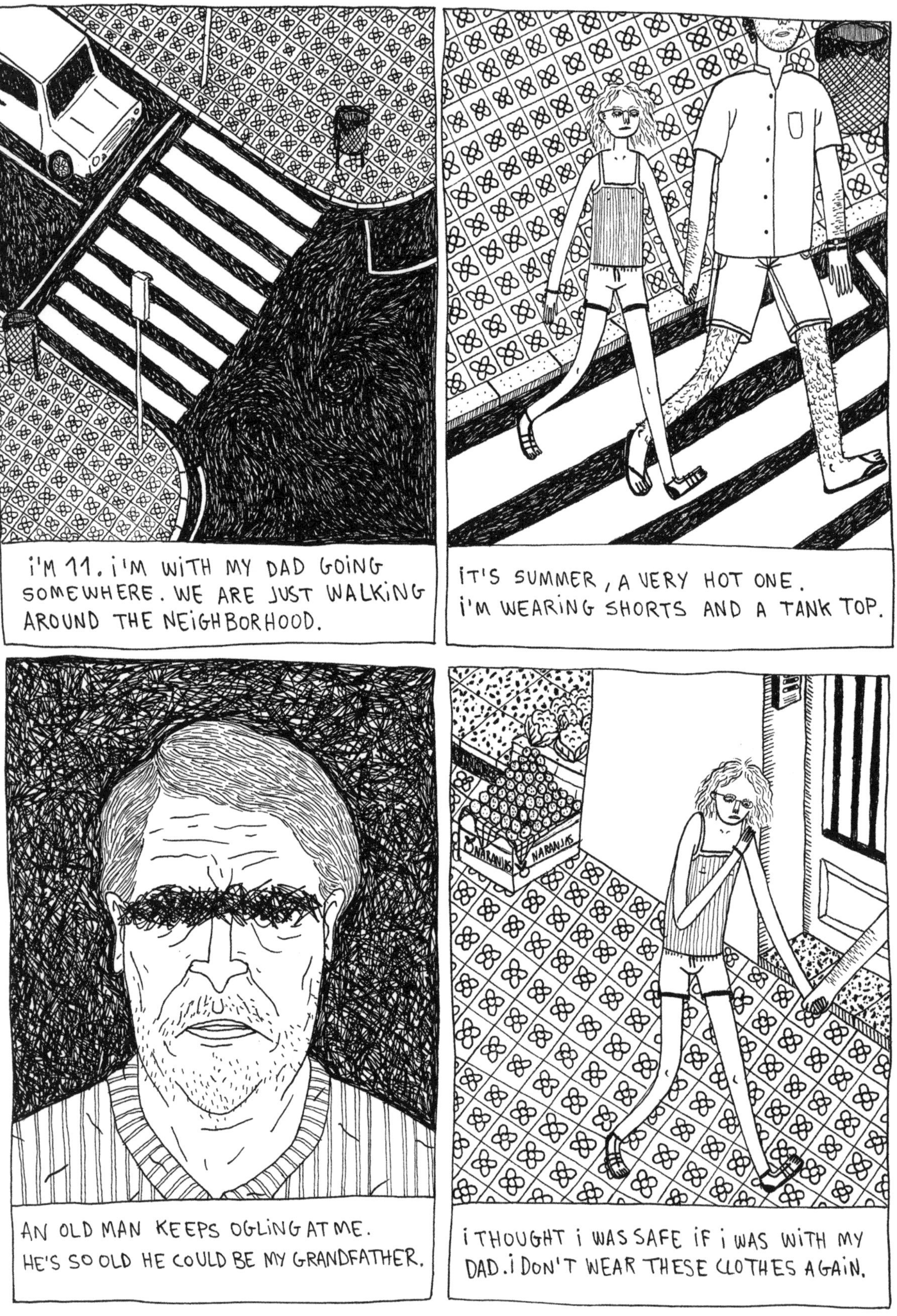
I'M 11. I'M WITH MY DAD GOING SOMEWHERE. WE ARE JUST WALKING AROUND THE NEIGHBORHOOD.
IT'S SUMMER, A VERY HOT ONE. I'M WEARING SHORTS AND A TANK TOP.
AN OLD MAN KEEPS OGLING AT ME. HE'S SO OLD HE COULD BE MY GRANDFATHER.
I THOUGHT I WAS SAFE IF I WAS WITH MY DAD. I DON'T WEAR THESE CLOTHES AGAIN.
NARANJAS
NARANJAS

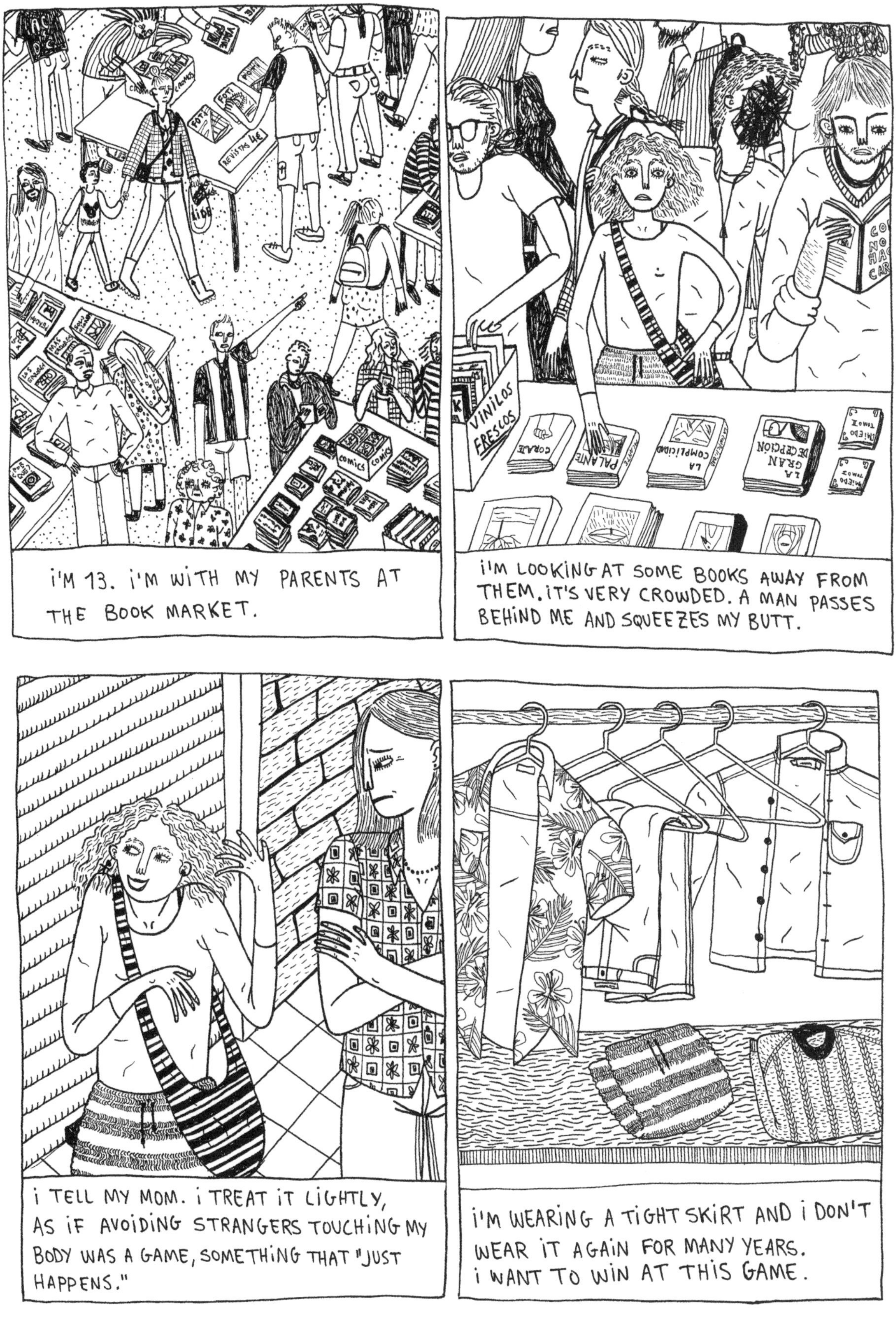
I'M 13. I'M WITH MY PARENTS AT THE BOOK MARKET.
VINILOS FRESCOS
I'M LOOKING AT SOME BOOKS AWAY FROM THEM. IT'S VERY CROWDED. A MAN PASSES BEHIND ME AND SQUEEZES MY BUTT.
I TELL MY MOM. I TREAT IT LIGHTLY, AS IF AVOIDING STRANGERS TOUCHING MY BODY WAS A GAME, SOMETHING THAT "JUST HAPPENS."
I'M WEARING A TIGHT SKIRT AND I DON'T WEAR IT AGAIN FOR MANY YEARS. I WANT TO WIN AT THIS GAME.

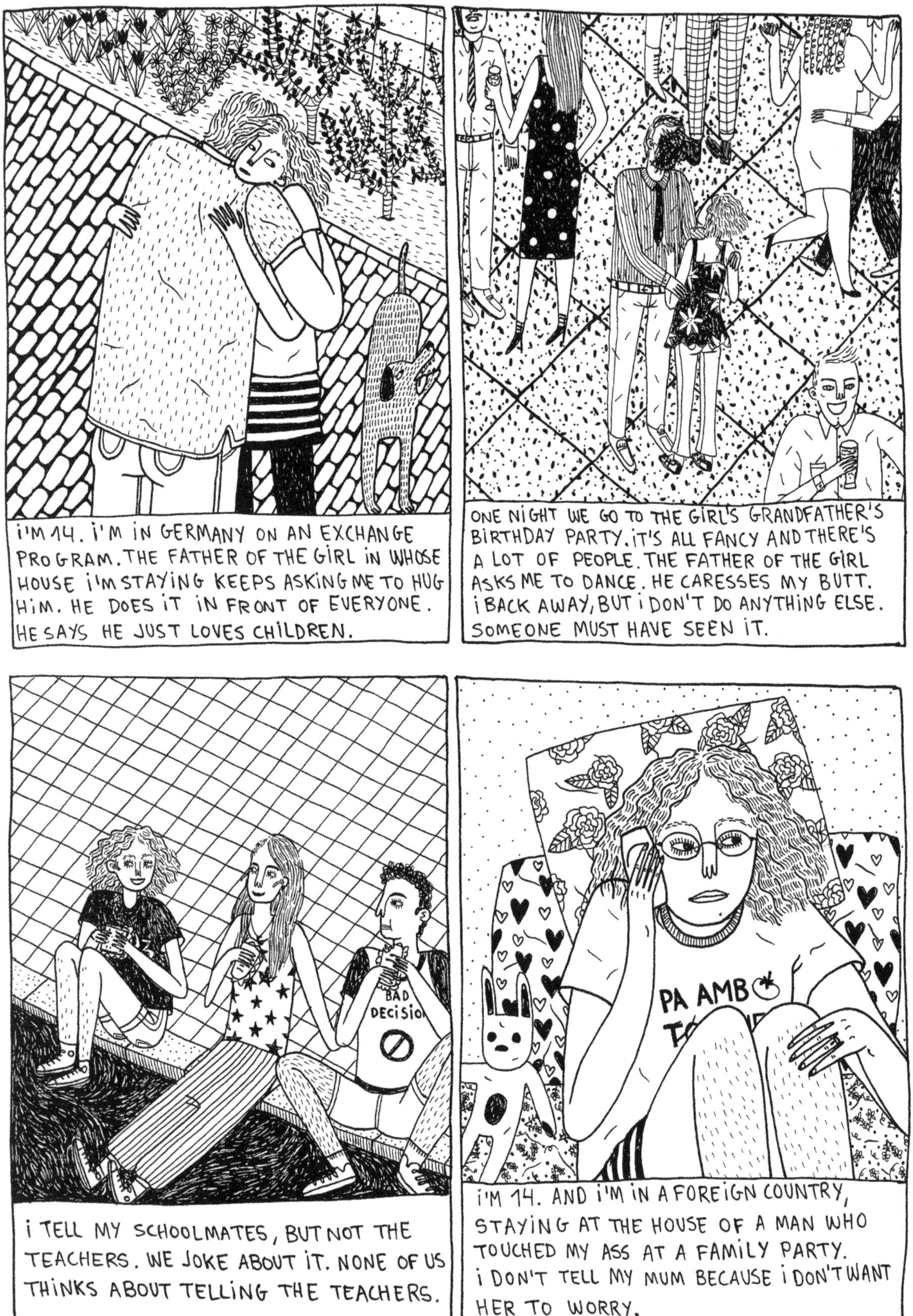
I'M 14. I'M IN GERMANY ON AN EXCHANGE PROGRAM. THE FATHER OF THE GIRL IN WHOSE HOUSE I'M STAYING KEEPS ASKING ME TO HUG HIM. HE DOES IT IN FRONT OF EVERYONE. HE SAYS HE JUST LOVES CHILDREN.
ONE NIGHT WE GO TO THE GIRL'S GRANDFATHER'S BIRTHDAY PARTY. IT'S ALL FANCY AND THERE'S A LOT OF PEOPLE. THE FATHER OF THE GIRL ASKS ME TO DANCE. HE CARESSES MY BUTT. I BACK AWAY, BUT I DON'T DO ANYTHING ELSE. SOMEONE MUST HAVE SEEN IT.
BAD
I TELL MY SCHOOLMATES, BUT NOT THE TEACHERS. WE JOKE ABOUT IT. NONE OF US THINKS ABOUT TELLING THE TEACHERS.
I'M 14. AND I'M IN A FOREIGN COUNTRY, STAYING AT THE HOUSE OF A MAN WHO TOUCHED MY ASS AT A FAMILY PARTY. I DON'T TELL MY MUM BECAUSE I DON'T WANT HER TO WORRY.

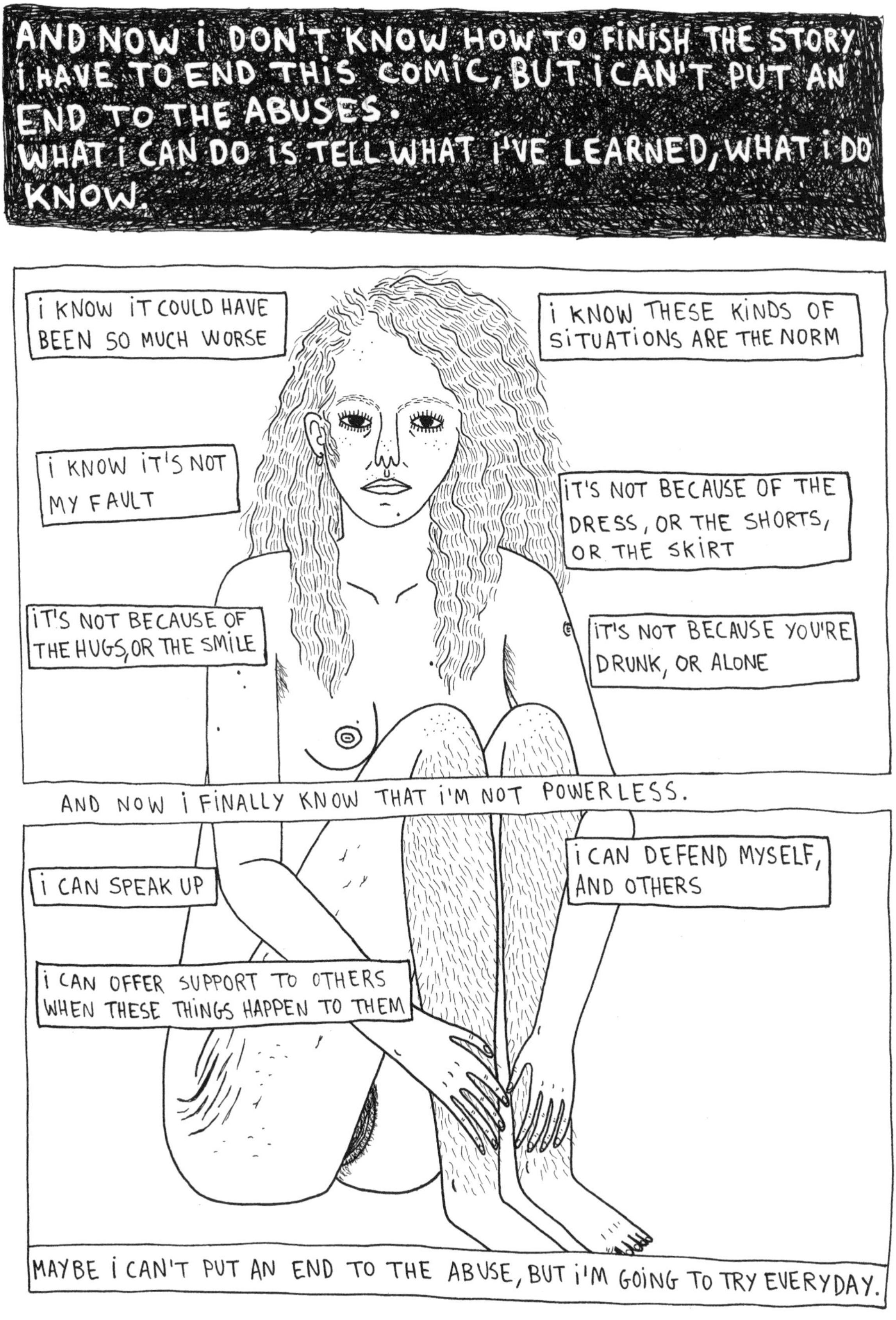
AND NOW I DON'T KNOW HOW TO FINISH THE STORY. I HAVE TO END THIS COMIC, BUT I CAN'T PUT AN END TO THE ABUSES.
WHAT I CAN DO IS TELL WHAT I'VE LEARNED, WHAT I DO KNOW.
I KNOW IT COULD HAVE BEEN SO MUCH WORSE
I KNOW THESE KINDS OF SITUATIONS ARE THE NORM
I KNOW IT'S NOT MY FAULT
IT'S NOT BECAUSE OF THE DRESS, OR THE SHORTS, OR THE SKIRT
IT'S NOT BECAUSE OF THE HUGS, OR THE SMILE
IT'S NOT BECAUSE YOU'RE DRUNK, OR ALONE
AND NOW I FINALLY KNOW THAT I'M NOT POWERLESS.
I CAN SPEAK UP
I CAN DEFEND MYSELF, AND OTHERS
I CAN OFFER SUPPORT TO OTHERS WHEN THESE THINGS HAPPEN TO THEM
MAYBE I CAN'T PUT AN END TO THE ABUSE, BUT I'M GOING TO TRY EVERYDAY.

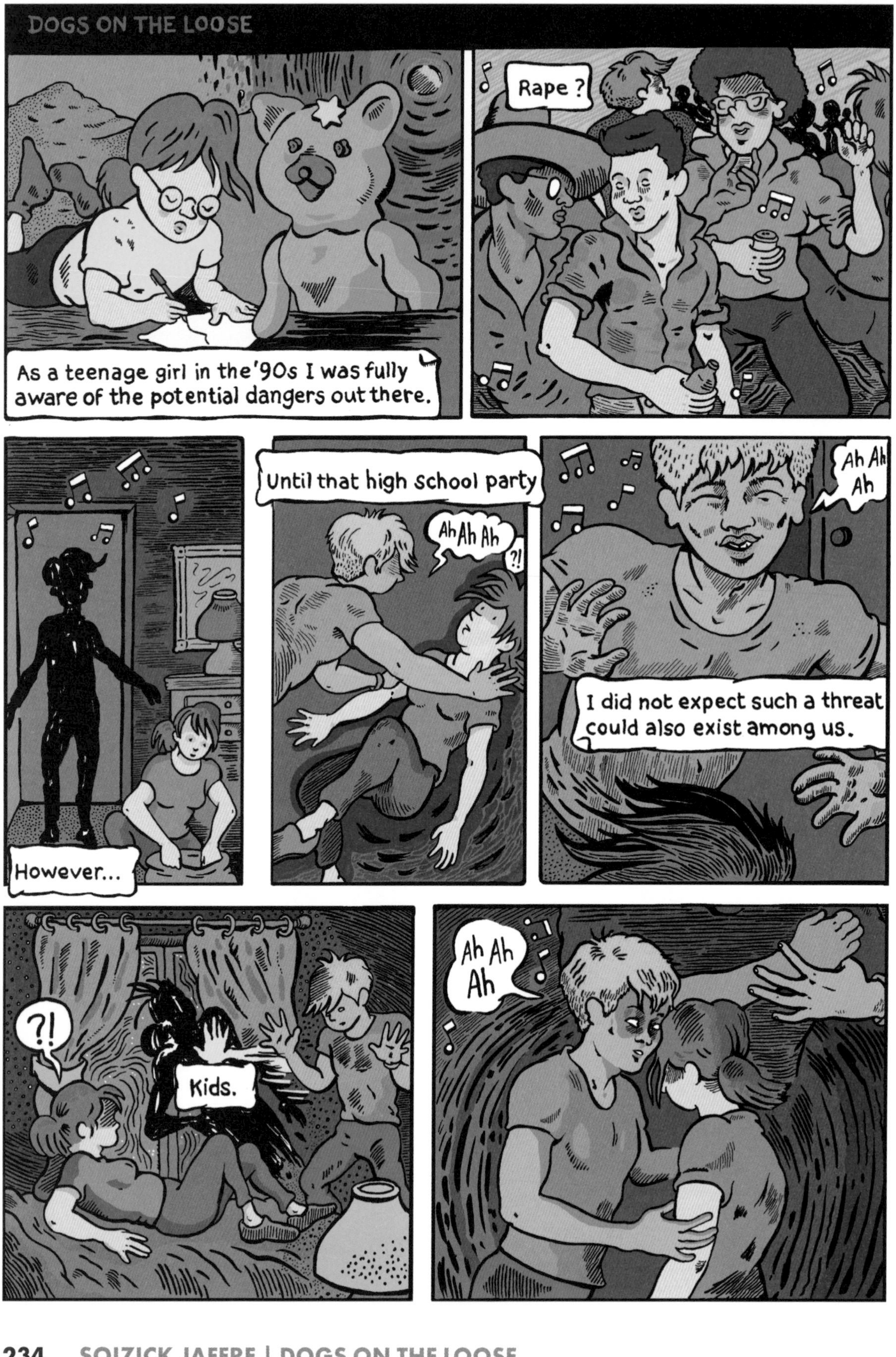
DOGS ON THE LOOSE
As a teenage girl in the '90s I was fully aware of the potential dangers out there.
Rape ?
However...
Until that high school party
Ah Ah Ah
?!
Ah Ah Ah
I did not expect such a threat could also exist among us.
?!
Kids.
Ah Ah Ah

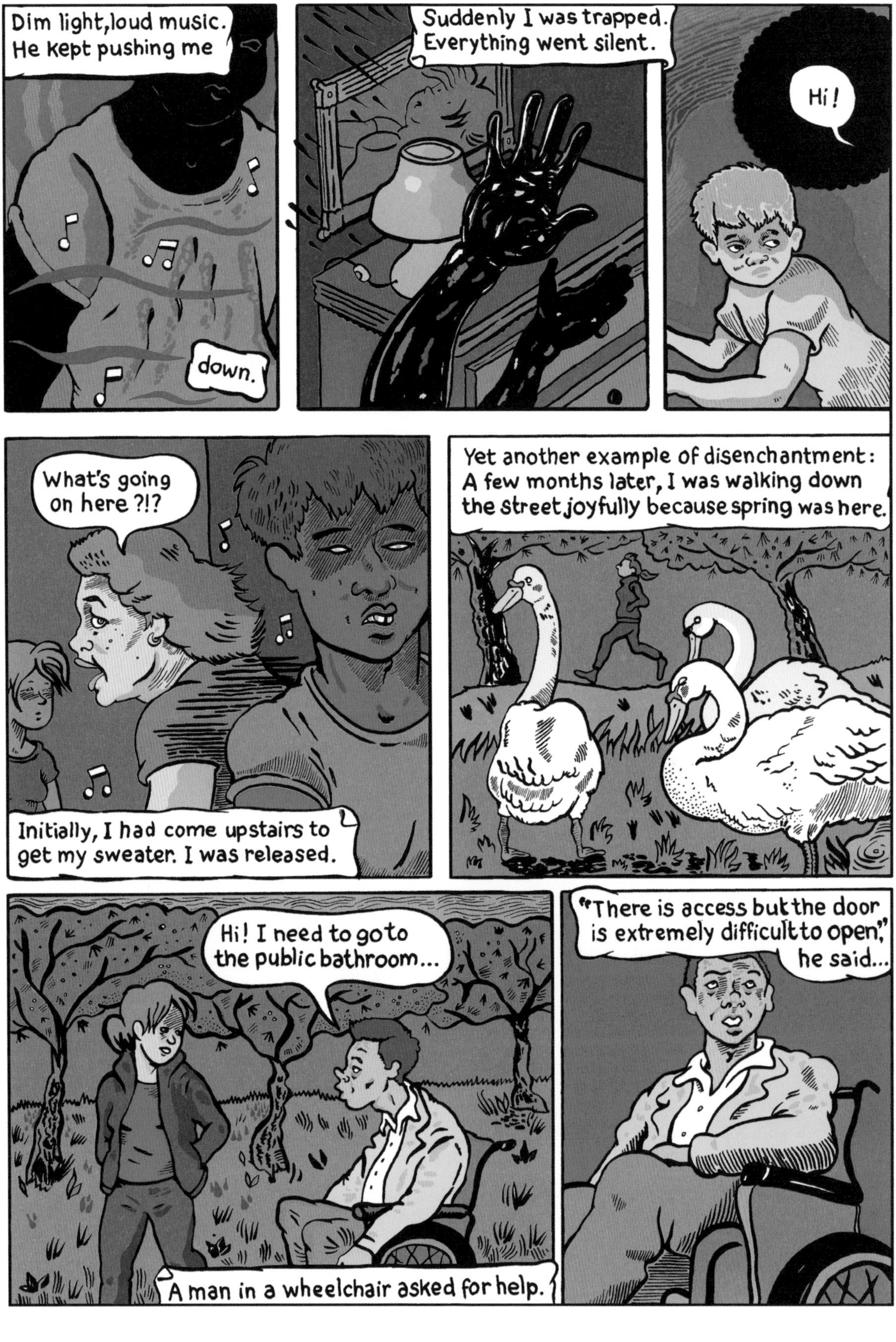
Dim light, loud music.
He kept pushing me
down.
Suddenly I was trapped.
Everything went silent.
Hi!
What's going on here ?!?
Initially, I had come upstairs to get my sweater. I was released.
Yet another example of disenchantment:
A few months later, I was walking down the street joyfully because spring was here.
Hi! I need to go to the public bathroom...
A man in a wheelchair asked for help.
"There is access but the door is extremely difficult to open,"
he said...

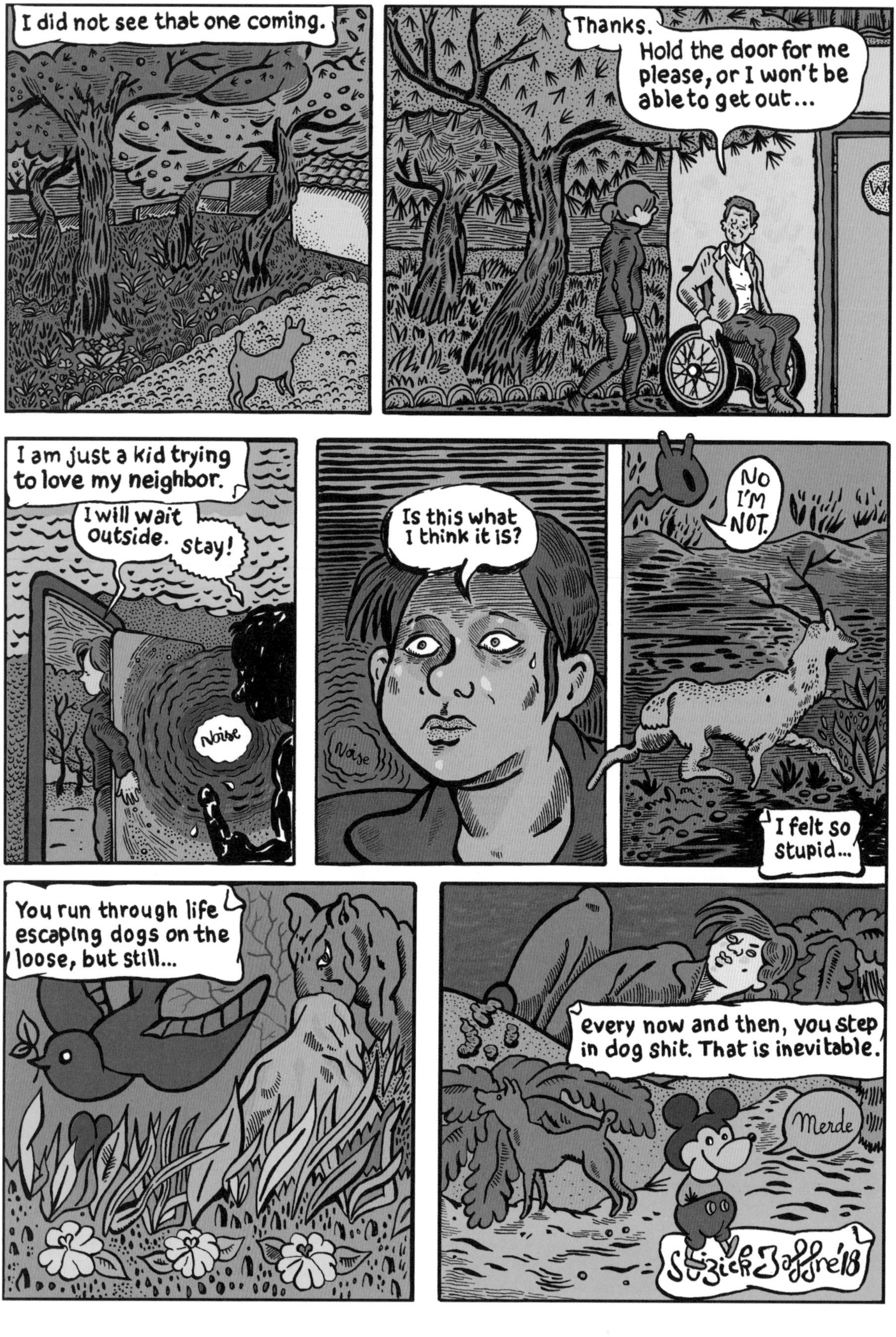
I did not see that one coming.
Thanks.
Hold the door for me please, or I won't be able to get out...
I am just a kid trying to love my neighbor.
I will wait outside.
stay!
Noise
Is this what I think it is?
Noise
NO I'M NOT.
I felt so stupid...
You run through life escaping dogs on the loose, but still...
every now and then, you step in dog shit. That is inevitable.
Merde
Soizick Jaffre'18

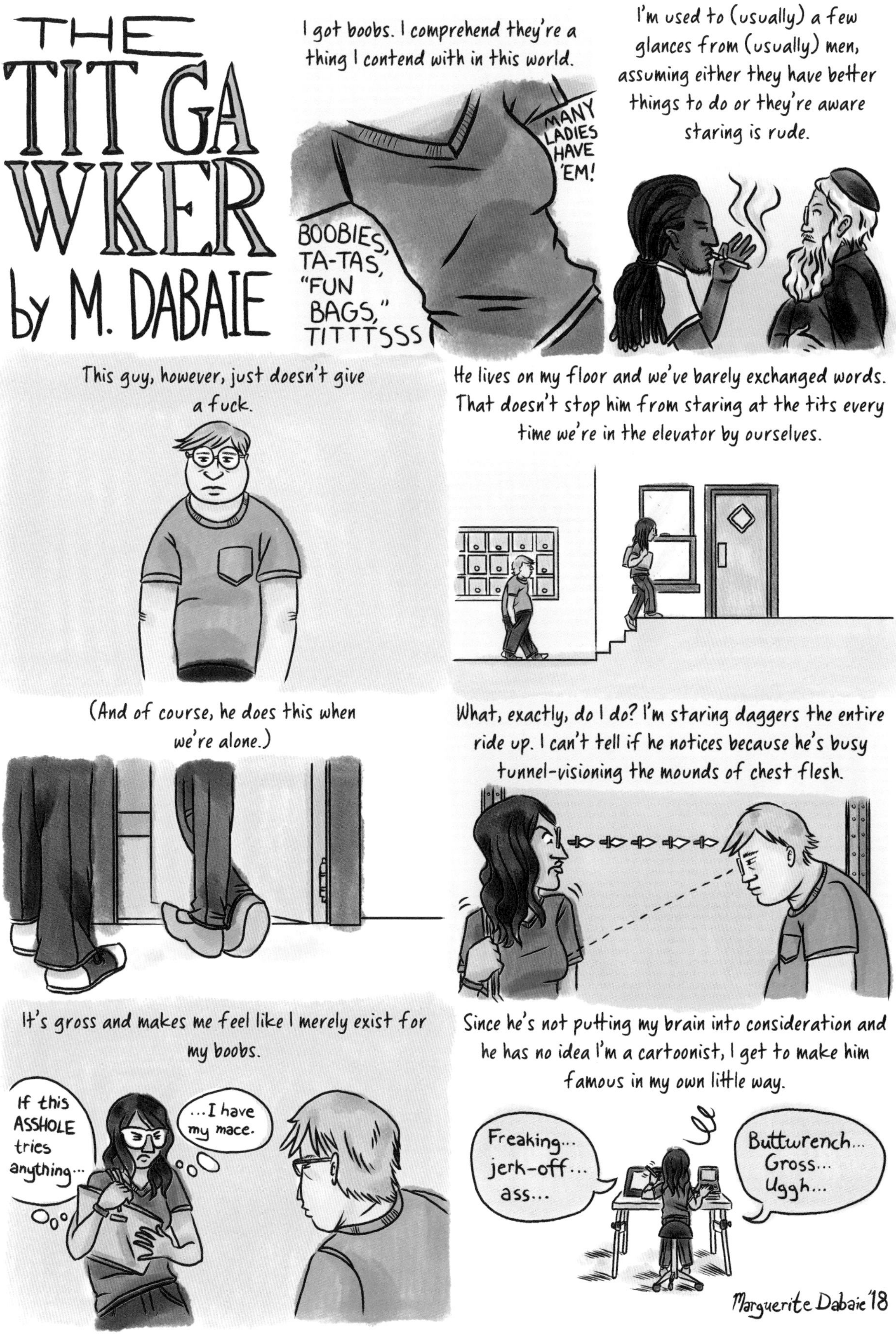
THE TIT GAWKER
by M. DABAIE
I got boobs. I comprehend they're a thing I contend with in this world.
MANY LADIES HAVE 'EM!
BOOBIES, TA-TAS, "FUN BAGS," TITTTSSS
I'm used to (usually) a few glances from (usually) men, assuming either they have better things to do or they're aware staring is rude.
This guy, however, just doesn't give a fuck.
He lives on my floor and we've barely exchanged words. That doesn't stop him from staring at the tits every time we're in the elevator by ourselves.
(And of course, he does this when we're alone.)
What, exactly, do I do? I'm staring daggers the entire ride up. I can't tell if he notices because he's busy tunnel-visioning the mounds of chest flesh.
It's gross and makes me feel like I merely exist for my boobs.
If this ASSHOLE tries anything...
...I have my mace.
Since he's not putting my brain into consideration and he has no idea I'm a cartoonist, I get to make him famous in my own little way.
Freaking... jerk-off... ass...
Buttwrench... Gross... Uggh...
Marguerite Dabaie '18

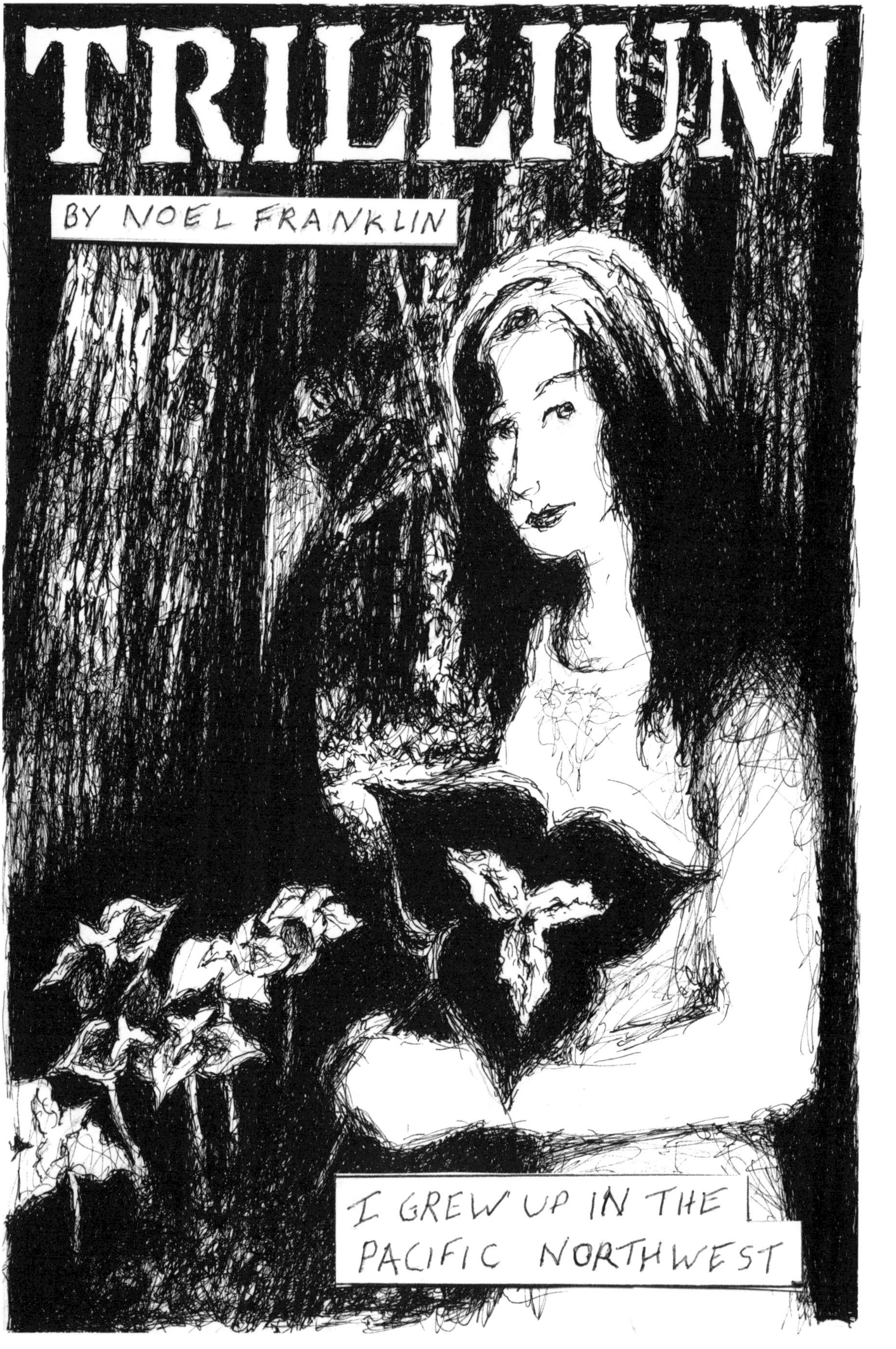
TRILLIUM
BY NOEL FRANKLIN
I GREW UP IN THE PACIFIC NORTHWEST

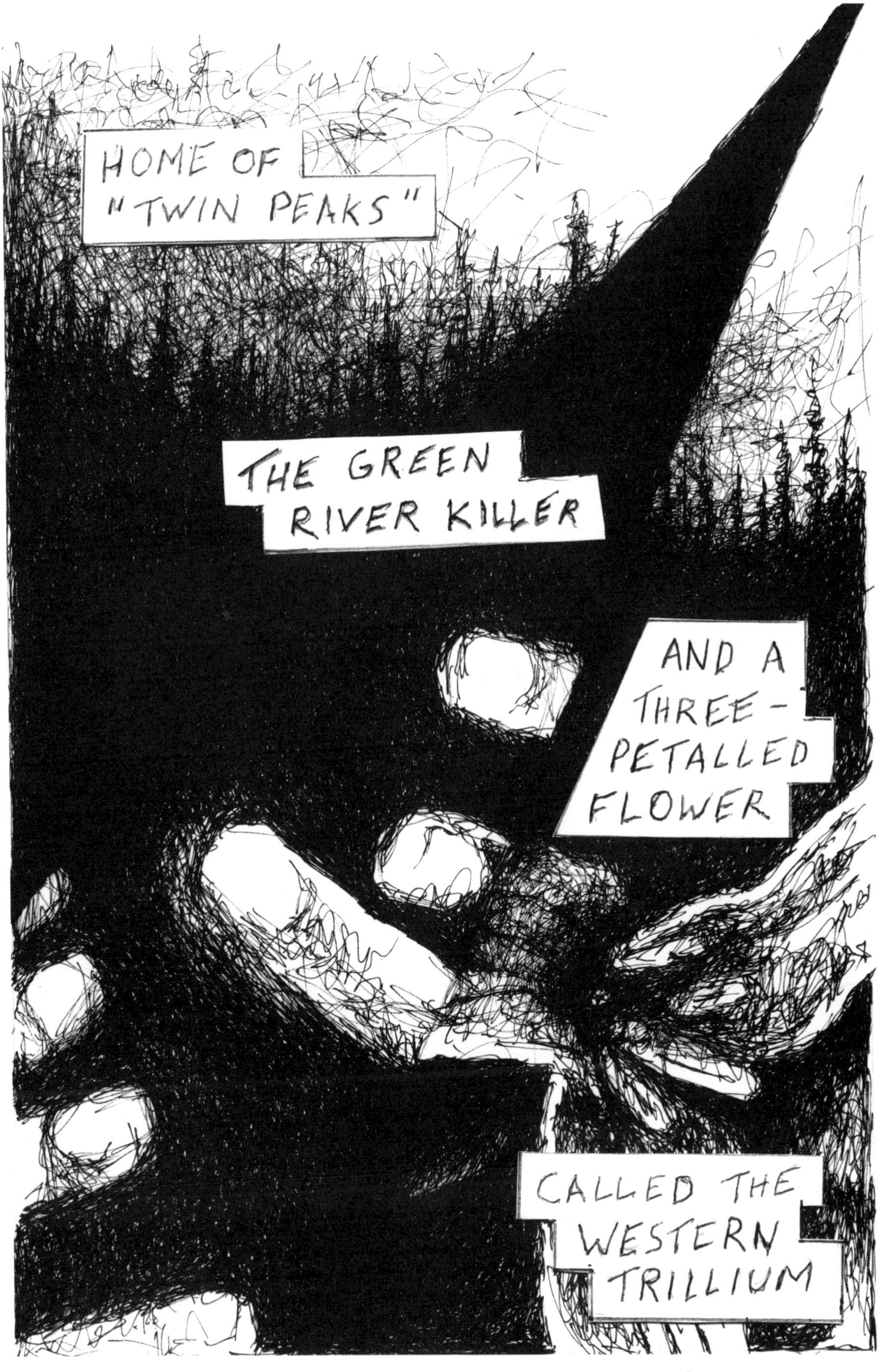
HOME OF "TWIN PEAKS"
THE GREEN RIVER KILLER
AND A THREE-PETALLED FLOWER
CALLED THE WESTERN TRILLIUM

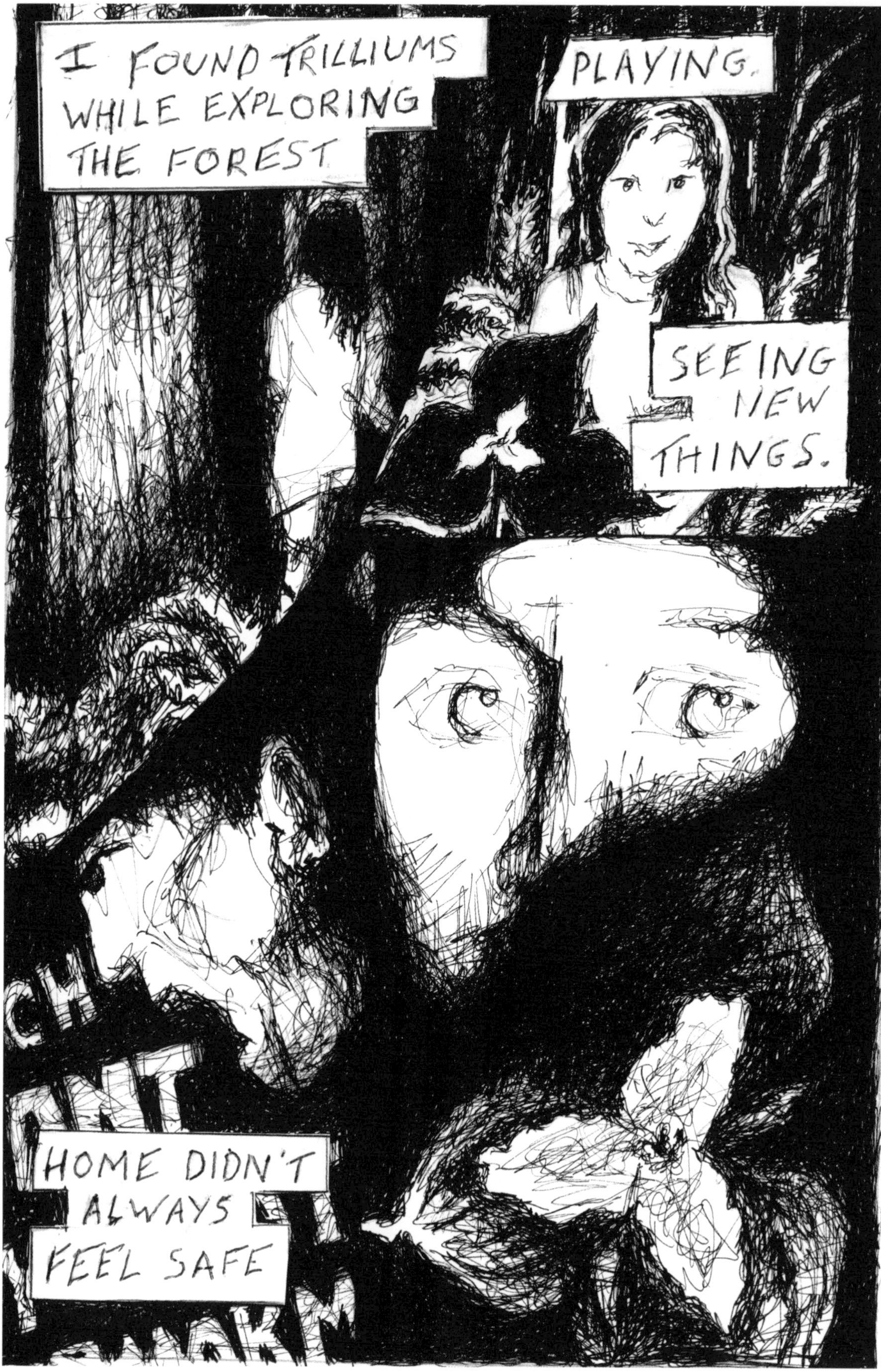
I FOUND TRILLIUMS WHILE EXPLORING THE FOREST
PLAYING.
SEEING NEW THINGS.
HOME DIDN'T ALWAYS FEEL SAFE

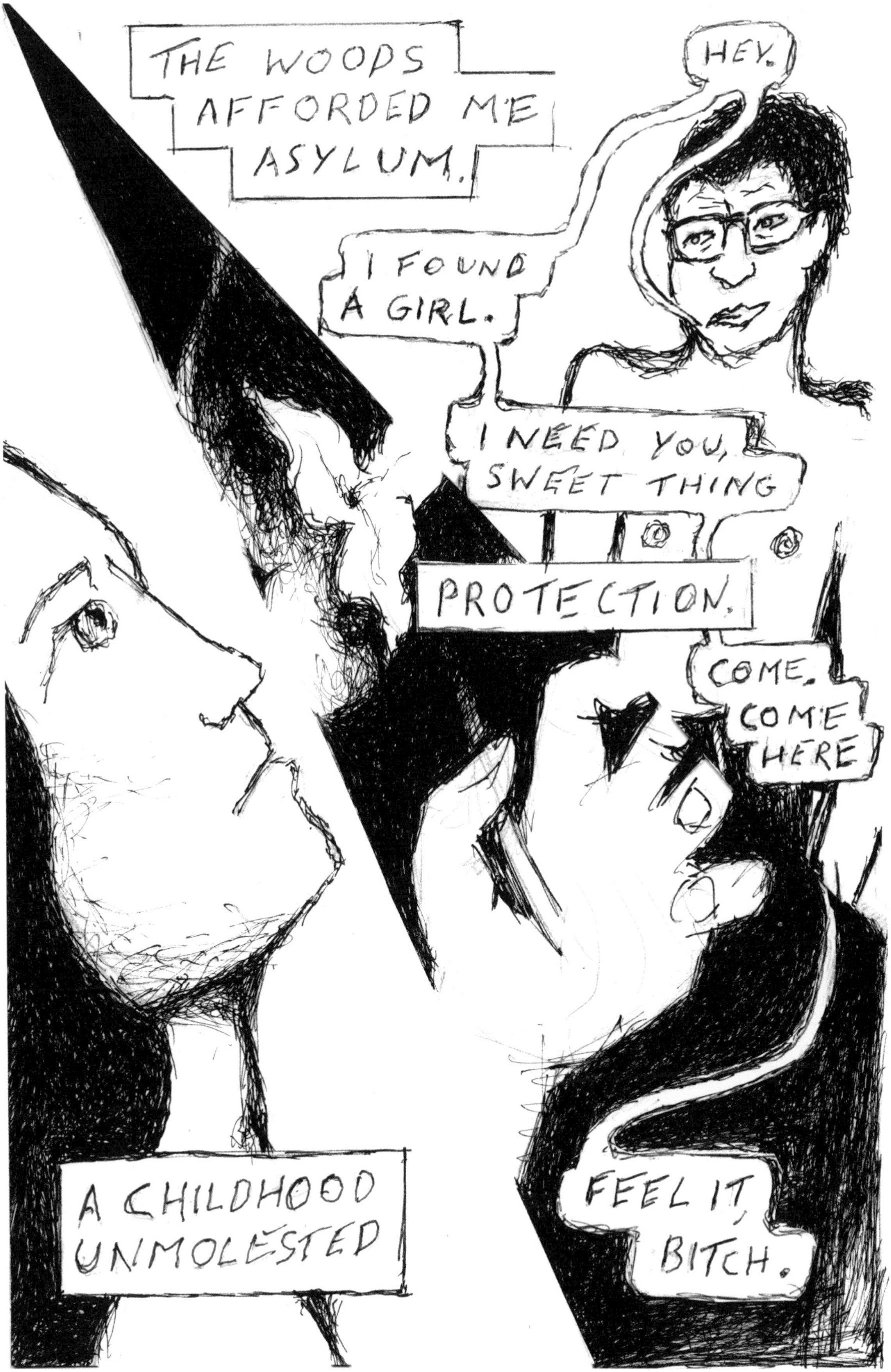
THE WOODS AFFORDED ME ASYLUM.
HEY.
I FOUND A GIRL.
I NEED YOU, SWEET THING
PROTECTION.
COME. COME HERE
A CHILDHOOD UNMOLESTED
FEEL IT, BITCH.

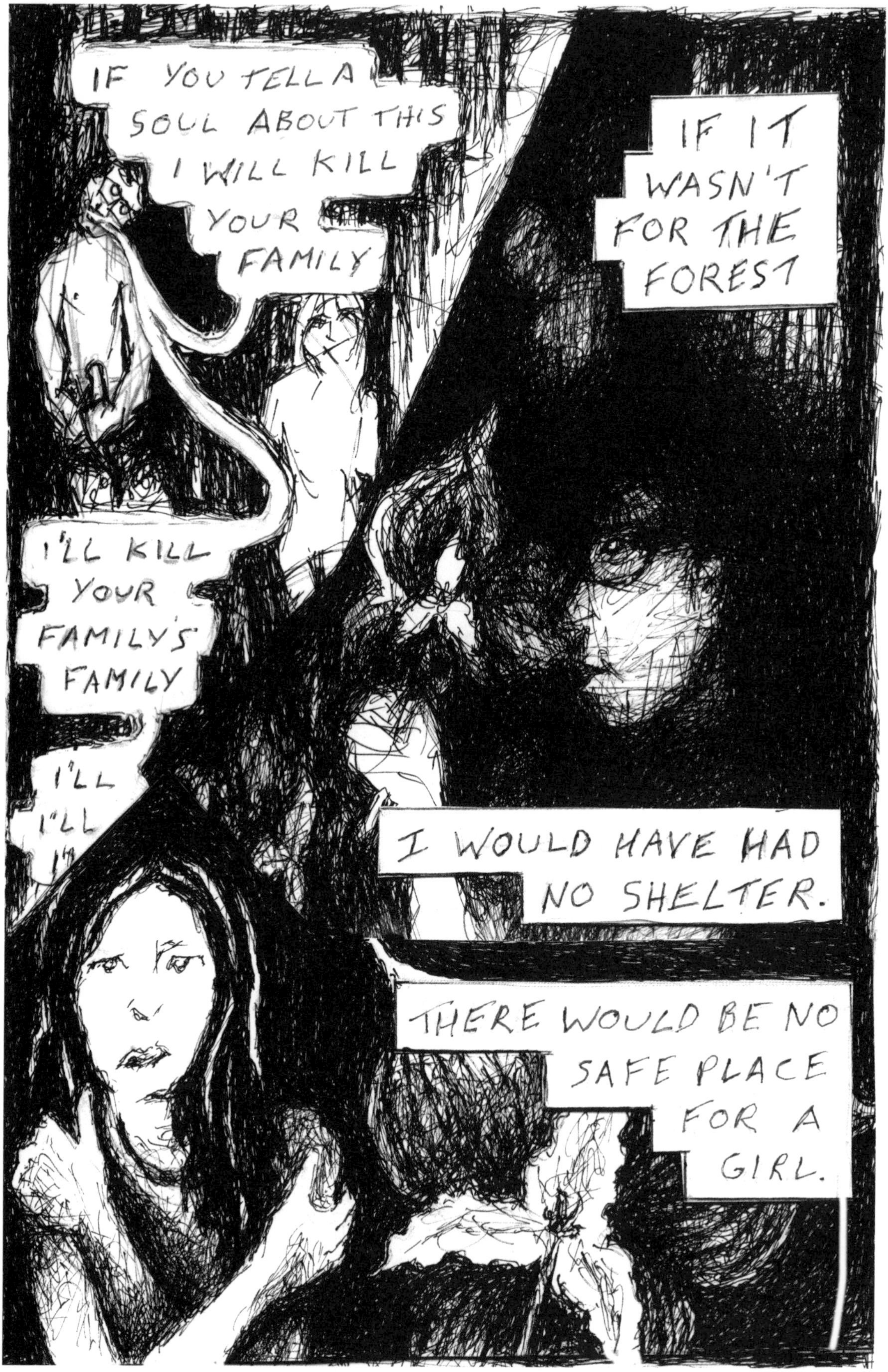
IF YOU TELL A SOUL ABOUT THIS I WILL KILL YOUR FAMILY
IF IT WASN'T FOR THE FOREST
I'LL KILL YOUR FAMILY'S FAMILY
I'LL
I'LL
I WOULD HAVE HAD NO SHELTER.
THERE WOULD BE NO SAFE PLACE FOR A GIRL.

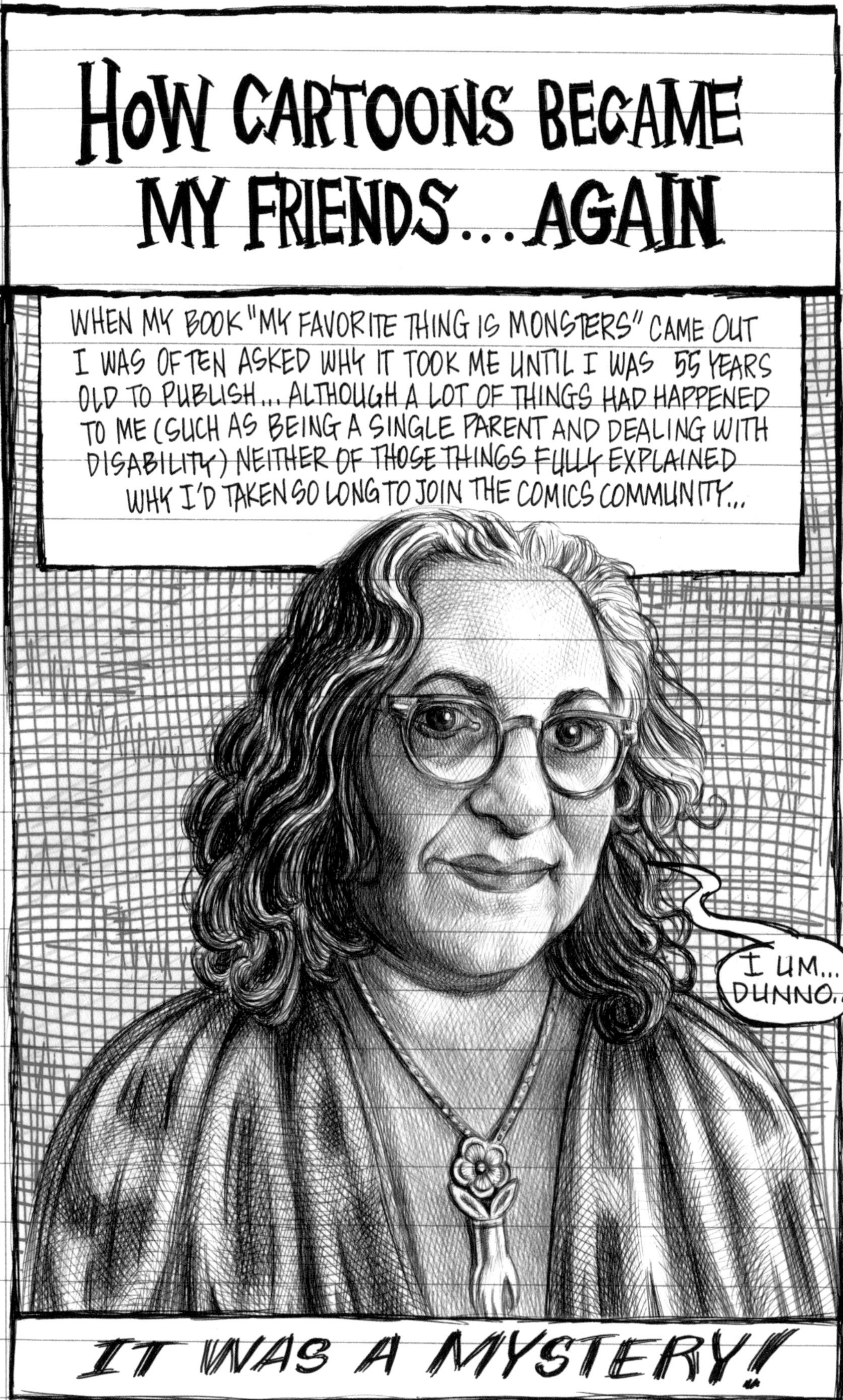
HOW CARTOONS BECAME MY FRIENDS... AGAIN
WHEN MY BOOK "MY FAVORITE THING IS MONSTERS" CAME OUT I WAS OFTEN ASKED WHY IT TOOK ME UNTIL I WAS 55 YEARS OLD TO PUBLISH... ALTHOUGH A LOT OF THINGS HAD HAPPENED TO ME (SUCH AS BEING A SINGLE PARENT AND DEALING WITH DISABILITY) NEITHER OF THOSE THINGS FULLY EXPLAINED WHY I'D TAKEN SO LONG TO JOIN THE COMICS COMMUNITY...
I UM... DUNNO...
IT WAS A MYSTERY!

I WAS VERY PROUD OF MY SHARP TEETH.

AS A KID I'D DRAWN CARTOONS BECAUSE I LOVED THEM. I'D BEEN NUTS ABOUT MONSTERS, HORROR COMICS AND MAD MAGAZINE... I'D STARTED WITH BABAR, DONALD DUCK'S BIG LITTLE BOOKS, AND TINTIN. EVENTUALLY I WAS FEASTING ON BATMAN, SPIDERMAN & FANTASTIC FOUR, AS WELL AS DRINKING UP NEW YORKER AND PUNCH CARTOONS, AUBREY BEARDSLEY AND CHARLES ADDAMS AND GOYA'S 'LOS CAPRICHOS.'... I HAD ADORED EVERYTHING TO DO WITH COMICS AND ANYTHING CARTOONY...

... BUT THAT LOVE HAD CHANGED AND I DID NOT KNOW WHY ...

SO AS I STOOD IN MY KITCHEN CONSIDERING THE 'WHY' OF IT... I SAW - IN MY MIND'S EYE - A FOLDING DOOR CLOSING....

... AND AS I THOUGHT ABOUT IT, I REMEMBERED ...

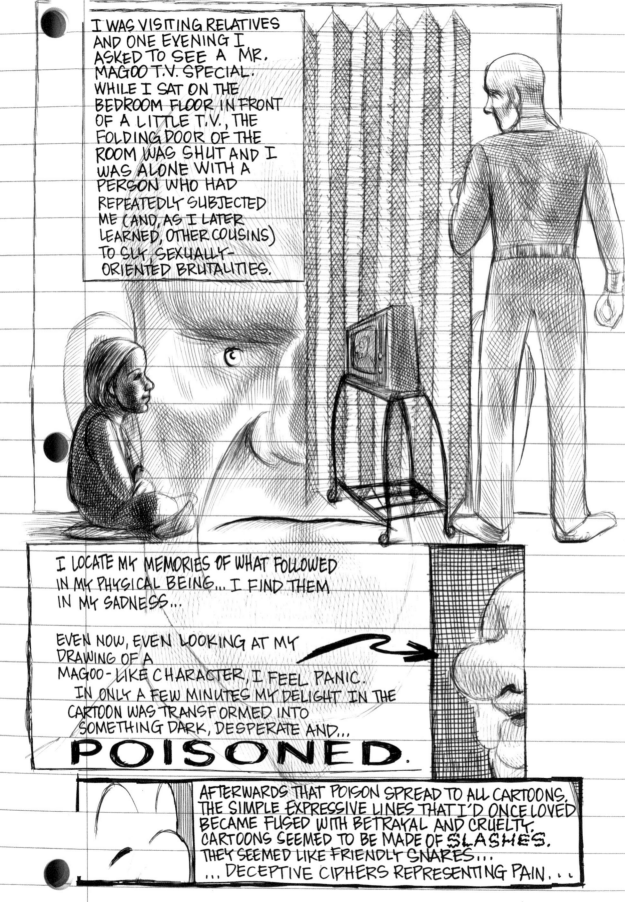

I WAS VISITING RELATIVES AND ONE EVENING I ASKED TO SEE A MR. MAGOO T.V. SPECIAL. WHILE I SAT ON THE BEDROOM FLOOR IN FRONT OF A LITTLE T.V., THE FOLDING DOOR OF THE ROOM WAS SHUT AND I WAS ALONE WITH A PERSON WHO HAD REPEATEDLY SUBJECTED ME (AND, AS I LATER LEARNED, OTHER COUSINS) TO SLY, SEXUALLY-ORIENTED BRUTALITIES.

I LOCATE MY MEMORIES OF WHAT FOLLOWED IN MY PHYSICAL BEING... I FIND THEM IN MY SADNESS...

EVEN NOW, EVEN LOOKING AT MY DRAWING OF A MAGOO-LIKE CHARACTER, I FEEL PANIC. IN ONLY A FEW MINUTES MY DELIGHT IN THE CARTOON WAS TRANSFORMED INTO SOMETHING DARK, DESPERATE AND...

POISONED.

AFTERWARDS THAT POISON SPREAD TO ALL CARTOONS. THE SIMPLE EXPRESSIVE LINES THAT I'D ONCE LOVED BECAME FUSED WITH BETRAYAL AND CRUELTY. CARTOONS SEEMED TO BE MADE OF SLASHES. THEY SEEMED LIKE FRIENDLY SNARES...
... DECEPTIVE CIPHERS REPRESENTING PAIN...

I SPENT YEARS IN THE FINE ART WORLD AS WELL AS FREELANCE ILLUSTRATING. YET I WAS ALWAYS PERPLEXED BY MY SADNESS WHEN MY ILLUSTRATION JOBS REQUIRED ME TO EMPLOY A CARTOONY STYLE. IT FELT TO ME AS THOUGH CARTOONS WERE AT THE OTHER END OF A LONG BRIDGE THAT I COULDN'T QUITE CROSS... UNTIL...

CLAUDE MONET 'WATER LILY POND' 1900

AT 40 YEARS OLD, AFTER BECOMING PARALYZED FROM THE WAIST DOWN AND IN MY RIGHT HAND, I DECIDED TO RETURN TO COLLEGE. WHILE THERE I WAS EXPOSED TO THE GREAT CARTOONISTS OF OUR TIME.

UPON GRADUATION (AFTER MUCH PHYSICAL RECOVERY) I DECIDED TO FINISH A STORY ABOUT A KID WHO LOVES MONSTERS.

I BEGAN TO REPRISE MY NOTEBOOKS OF THAT PAST TIME WHEN I'D UNRESERVEDLY LOVED COMICS. STRANGELY AS I PROGRESSED WITH THE PROJECT I FOUND MYSELF USING A CARTOONIER STYLE WHEN I NEEDED TO TALK ABOUT DIFFICULT THINGS... ESPECIALLY THOSE REVELATORY MOMENTS WHEN A CHARACTER CONFRONTS ABUSE, FEAR AND SHAME...

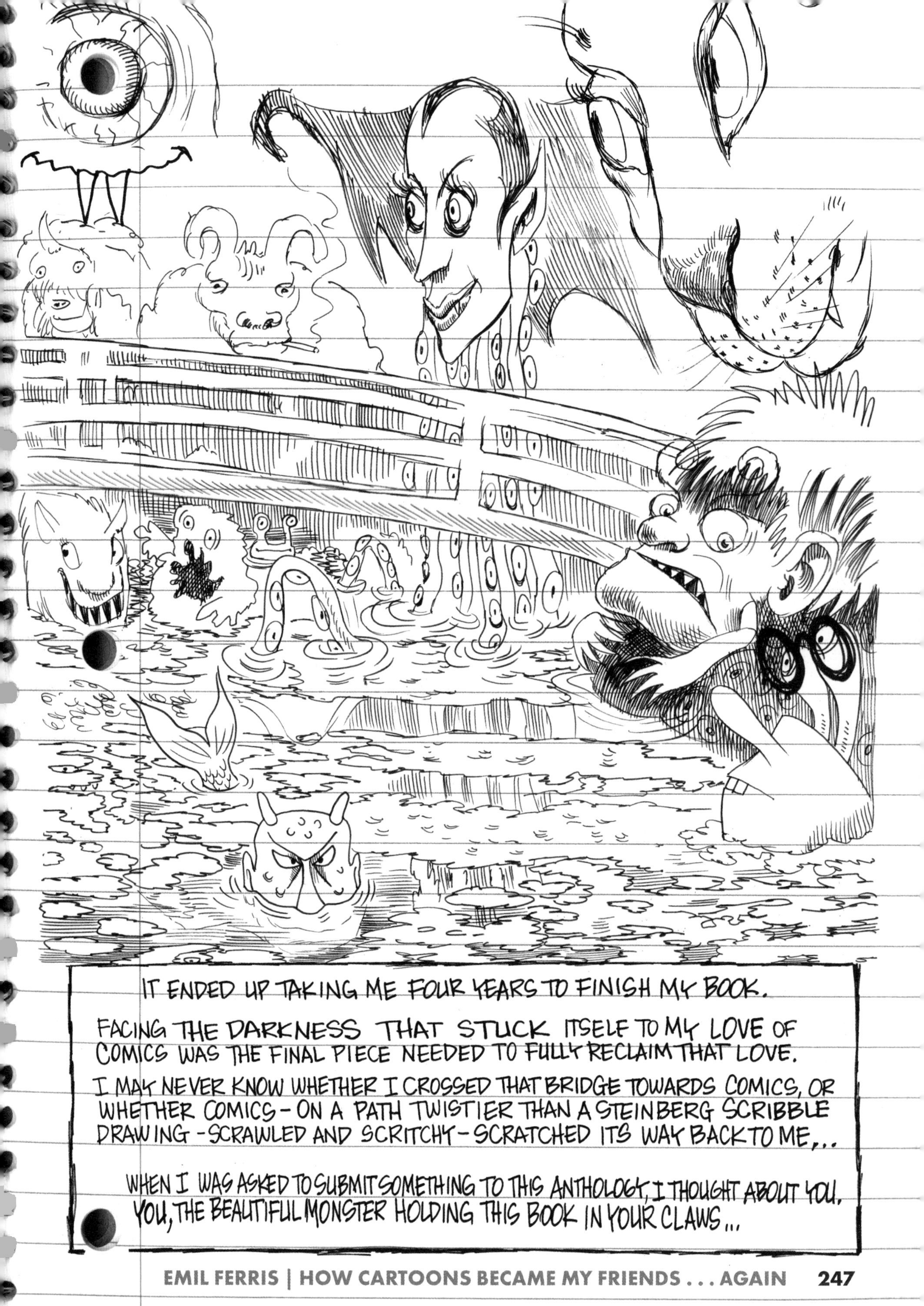

IT ENDED UP TAKING ME FOUR YEARS TO FINISH MY BOOK.

FACING THE DARKNESS THAT STUCK ITSELF TO MY LOVE OF COMICS WAS THE FINAL PIECE NEEDED TO FULLY RECLAIM THAT LOVE.

I MAY NEVER KNOW WHETHER I CROSSED THAT BRIDGE TOWARDS COMICS, OR WHETHER COMICS – ON A PATH TWISTIER THAN A STEINBERG SCRIBBLE DRAWING – SCRAWLED AND SCRITCHY – SCRATCHED ITS WAY BACK TO ME...

WHEN I WAS ASKED TO SUBMIT SOMETHING TO THIS ANTHOLOGY, I THOUGHT ABOUT YOU. YOU, THE BEAUTIFUL MONSTER HOLDING THIS BOOK IN YOUR CLAWS...

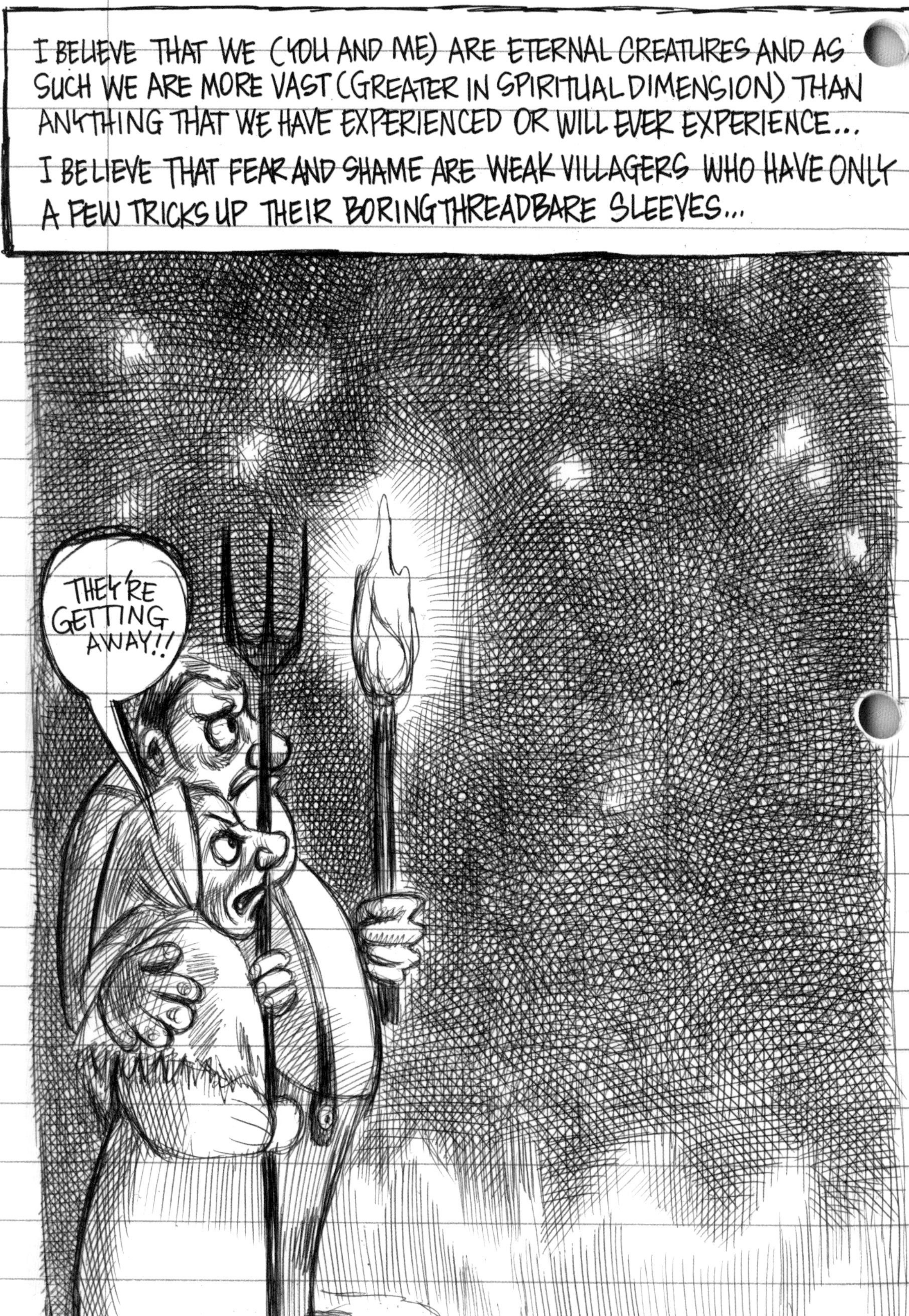
I BELIEVE THAT WE (YOU AND ME) ARE ETERNAL CREATURES AND AS SUCH WE ARE MORE VAST (GREATER IN SPIRITUAL DIMENSION) THAN ANYTHING THAT WE HAVE EXPERIENCED OR WILL EVER EXPERIENCE...
I BELIEVE THAT FEAR AND SHAME ARE WEAK VILLAGERS WHO HAVE ONLY A FEW TRICKS UP THEIR BORING THREADBARE SLEEVES...
THEY'RE GETTING AWAY!!
I ALSO BELIEVE THAT...

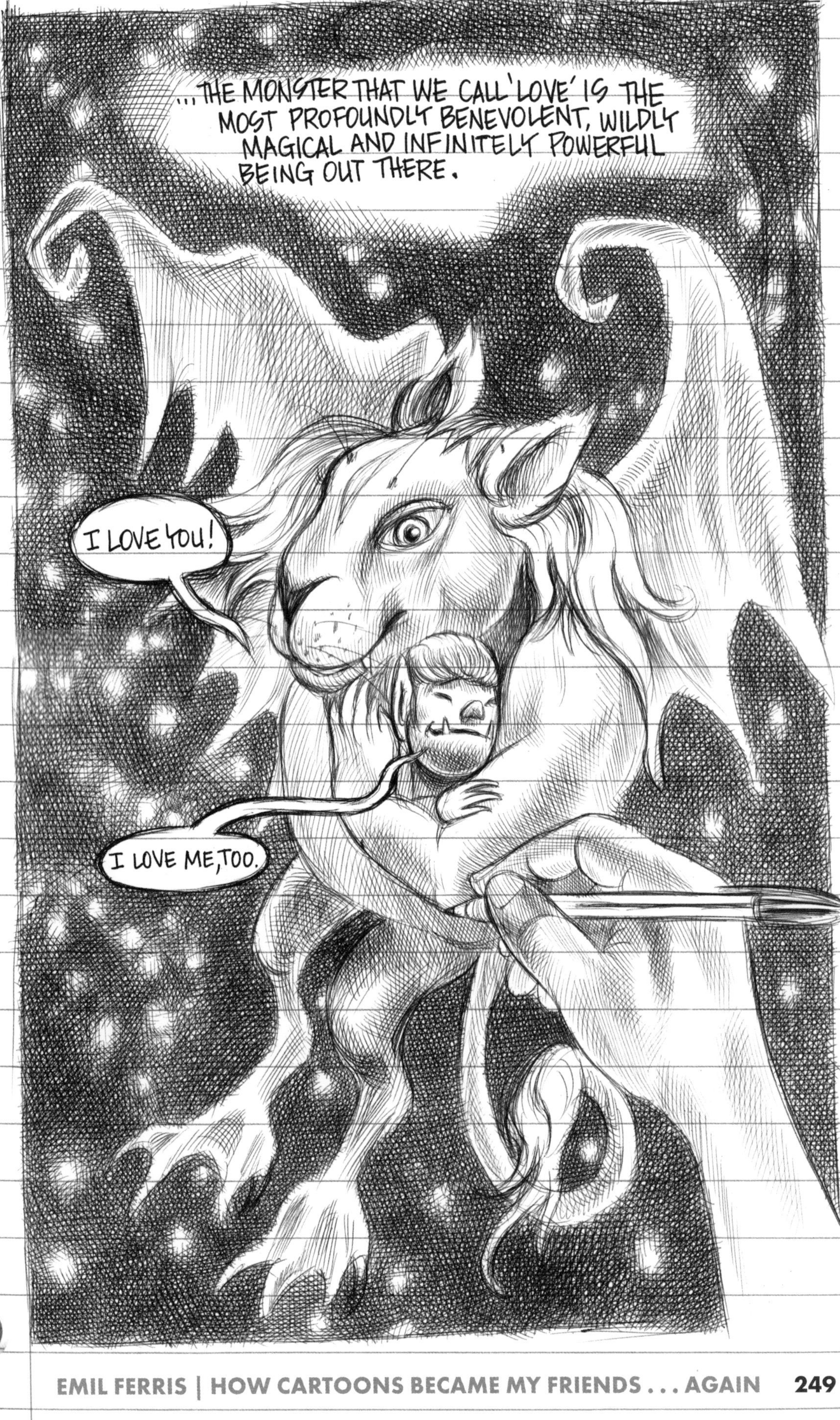
...THE MONSTER THAT WE CALL 'LOVE' IS THE MOST PROFOUNDLY BENEVOLENT, WILDLY MAGICAL AND INFINITELY POWERFUL BEING OUT THERE.
I LOVE YOU!
I LOVE ME, TOO.

Editor
Diane Noomin

is the creator of the comics character DiDi Glitz, editor of both *Twisted Sisters* anthologies, and was one of the early contributors to *Wimmen's Comix*. She has been nominated for Harvey and Eisner Awards and received an Inkpot Award. *Glitz-2-Go*, a collection of Noomin's art throughout her career, was published in 2013. Her work is included in the Library of Congress Prints and Photographs collection.

Rachel Ang

is a comics artist from Melbourne, Australia. Her first book, *Swimsuit*, was published by Glom Press in 2018. She holds a master's degree in architecture from RMIT University.

Zoe Belsinger

was born in Belgium's dullest town, in 1990. Unfortunately, she still lives there with her cat, Sasha. She has self-published a few zines and is currently working on her first stop-motion movie. She also dedicates her life to kitsch and bad taste.

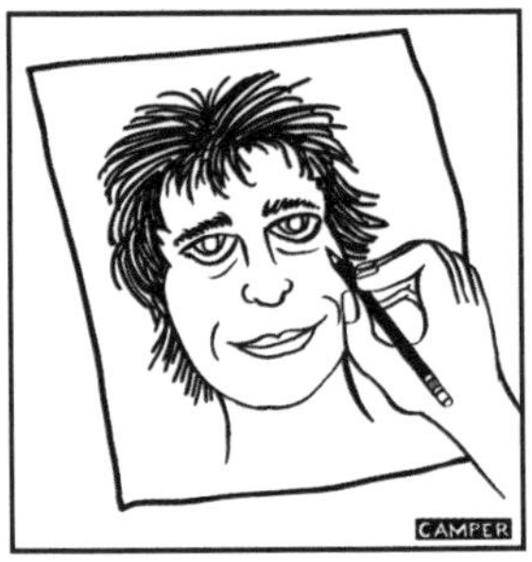
CAMPER

Jennifer Camper

is the author of several books, including *Rude Girls and Dangerous Women* and *subGURLZ*, and the editor of two *Juicy Mother* comics anthologies. Her work has appeared in numerous publications, comic books, and anthologies, and has been exhibited internationally. She is the founding director of the biennial Queers & Comics Conference.

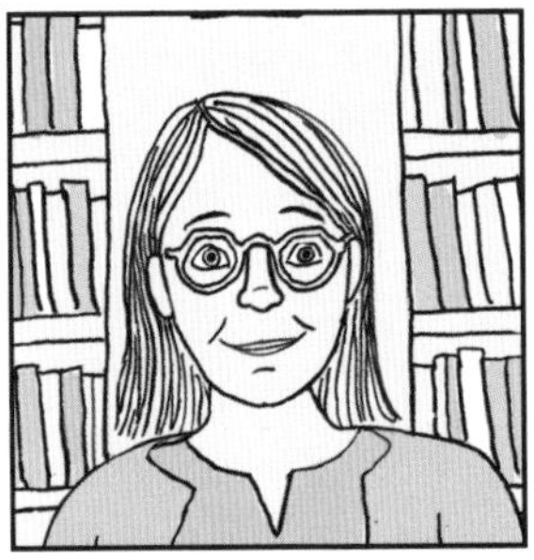

Caitlin Cass

makes comics, drawings, and museums that folklorize historic failure and foretell grim futures. She publishes a bimonthly comics periodical called *The Great Moments in Western Civilization Postal Constituent*. Her work has also appeared in the *New Yorker* and online at *The Nib*. In 2018 she received a NYSCA/NYFA Artist Fellowship in Fiction for her comics.

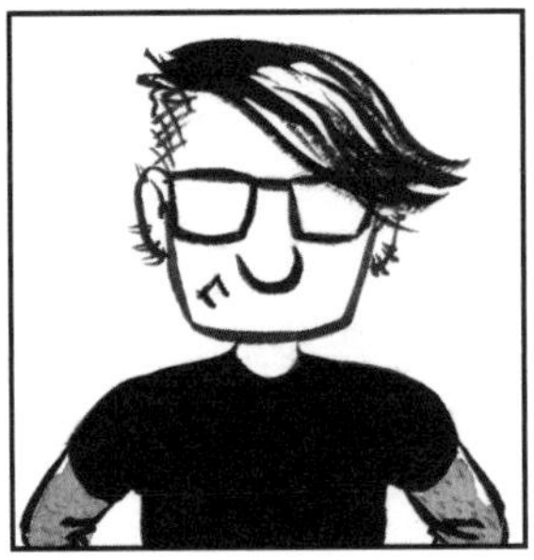

Tyler Cohen

is a cartoonist who uses autobiography and surrealism to explore gender, parenthood, race, and female experience. Her book *Primahood: Magenta* won the 2017 Bisexual Book Award for Graphic Memoir. Her work has appeared online in *Illustrated PEN* and *Mutha Magazine* and in print in numerous anthologies. See primazonia.com for more.

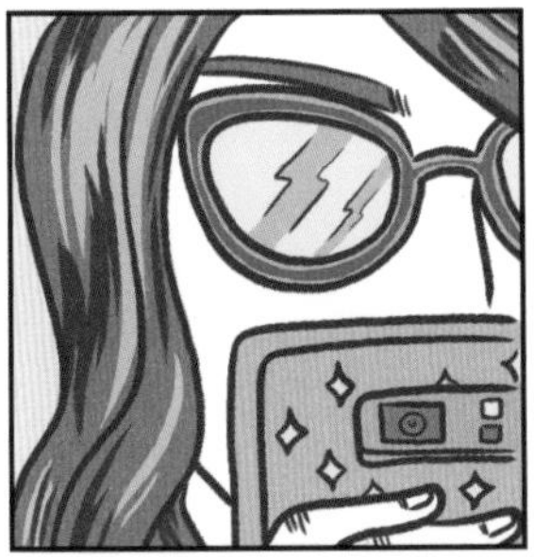

Marguerite Dabaie

is the author of the graphic novel *The Hookah Girl and Other True Stories* (Rosarium, 2018). She draws autobio, sociopolitical, and historical-fictional comics with a decorative flair. Once a year, Marguerite also cohosts Pete's Mini Zine Fest, the fest-in-a-bar, in Brooklyn. See mdabaie.com for more.

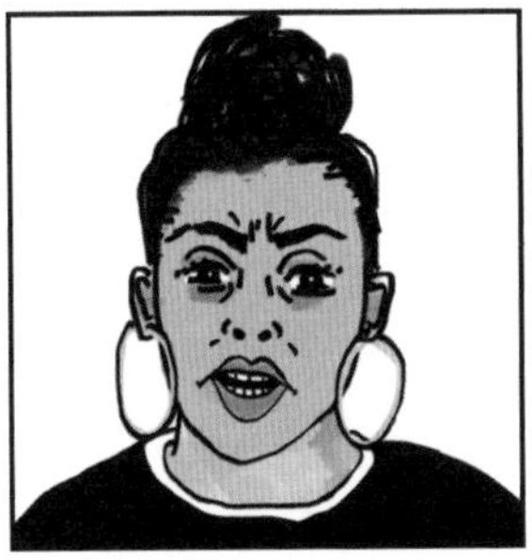

Soumya Dhulekar

was born in Mumbai and raised in New Jersey. She makes comics and animations about her family, Hinduism, immigration, and sex. Her work has been published in *Catapult* magazine and in various comics anthologies. She is also a member of Bigmouth Press & Comix.

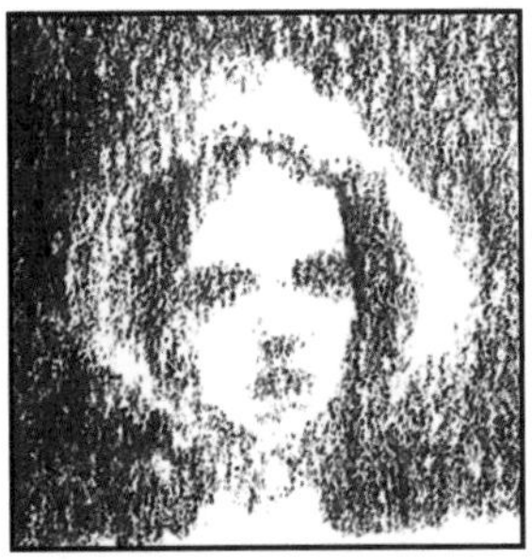

Wallis Eates

is an autobiographical comics creator who also makes comics with and about community groups to raise social awareness. These have included prisons, brain injury survivors, and her local boxing club. She is a London coordinator for the UK's leading graphic novel forum, Laydeez do Comics.

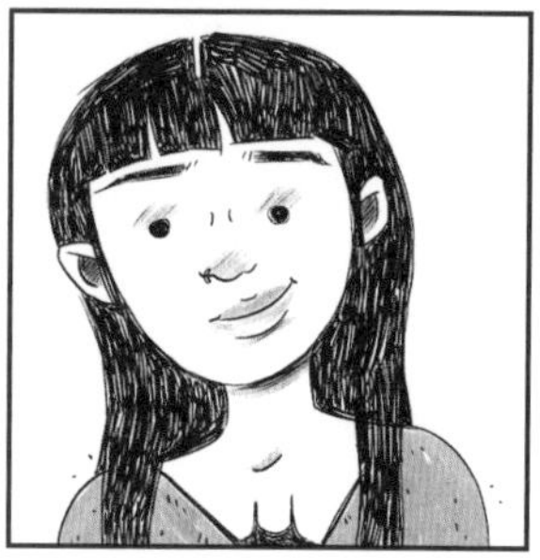

Trinidad Escobar

is an alumnus of the Jack Kerouac School of Disembodied Poetics as well as the MFA in Comics program at California College of the Arts. Her graphic novel *Of Sea and Venom* will be published by Farrar, Straus and Giroux in 2021. She lives in Oakland, California, with her son, Kalayo.

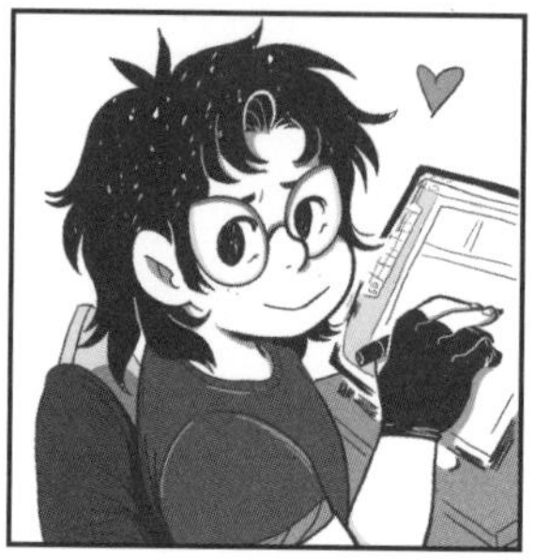

Kat Fajardo

is an award-winning comics artist and illustrator based in New York City. She's created work for Disney-Hyperion, Penguin Random House, *CollegeHumor*, and several comics anthologies. She enjoys creating playful and colorful work about self-acceptance and Latinx culture.

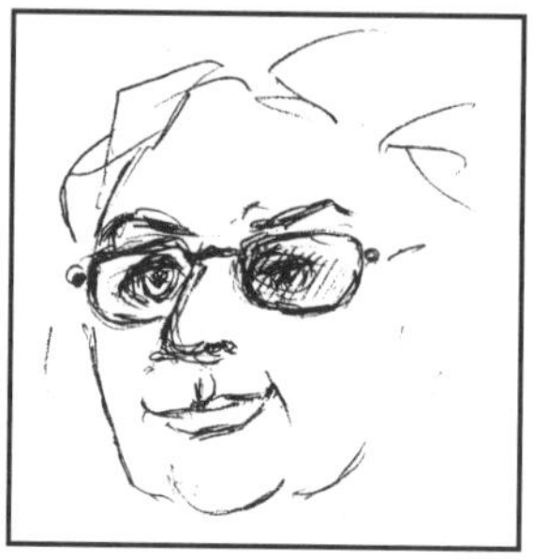

Joyce Farmer

has been a cartoonist since the series *Tits & Clits* (1972–1987). Controversial at first, she is now considered a pioneer of underground comix. Her graphic memoir, *Special Exits* (2010), won the Reuben and was nominated for the Eisner. The book has been translated into five languages.

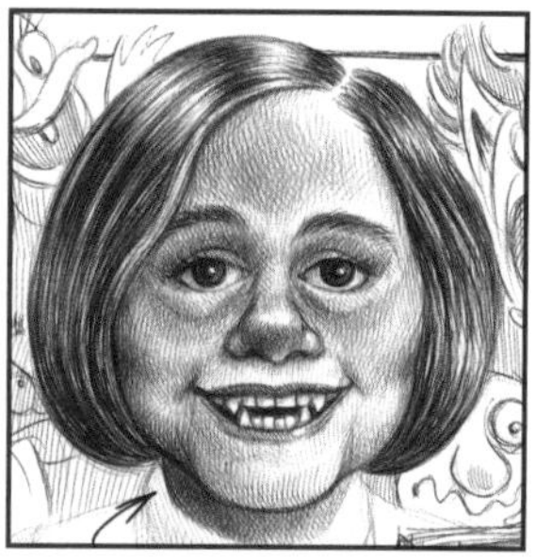

Emil Ferris

is a Chicago-born artist and writer. Her career as a painter was sidetracked when she became afflicted with West Nile virus, partially paralyzing her. Ferris regained much of her mobility while working on her graphic novel *My Favorite Thing Is Monsters* (Fantagraphics, 2017), which won three Eisner awards, two Ignatzes, the Fauve d'Or, and more. She is currently working on its sequel.

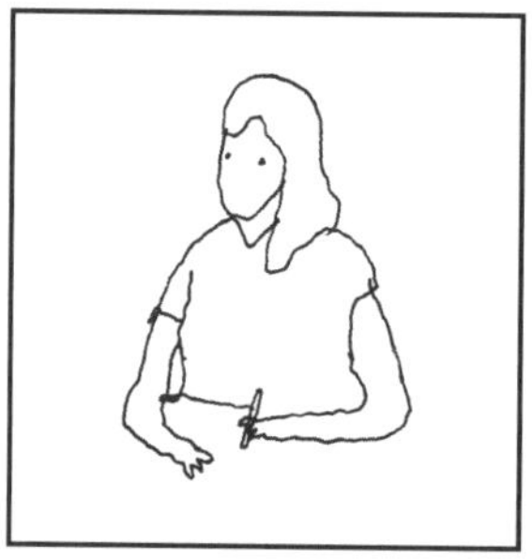

Liana Finck

is a cartoonist whose work appears regularly in *The New Yorker* and on her Instagram feed. Her most recent graphic novel is called *Passing for Human* (Random House, 2018).

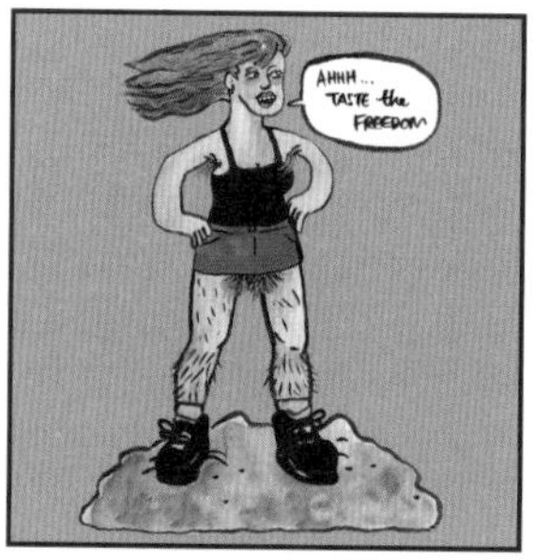
AHHH... TASTE the FREEDOM

Sarah Firth

is an award-winning comics artist, writer, and animator based in Melbourne. Her recent graphic essay on complexity was listed in the ten best literary comics in Australia. She has a fat stack of self-published comics and is about to have work in anthologies with Picador, Allen & Unwin, and Affirm Press. She is currently working on her debut graphic novel.

Mary Fleener

started self-publishing her own mini comics in 1984, and her work has appeared in many anthologies such as *Weirdo* and Twisted *Sisters*. Her solo title, *Slutburger*, was autobiographical stories that were later collected as the book *Life of the Party*. She's just finished her first graphic novel, *Billie the Bee* (Fantagraphics, 2019).

Ebony Flowers

holds a PhD in Curriculum and Instruction from the University of Wisconsin–Madison, where she wrote her dissertation as a comic. She is a 2017 Rona Jaffe Award recipient. Her debut graphic novel is called *Hot Comb*. You can find more of her work at ebonydrawsflowers.com.

Claire Folkman

is an artist living and working in the Fishtown neighborhood of Philadelphia, Pennsylvania. She creates out of Mercer Street Studios, where she works on her nationally exhibited collages, comics, and costume projects. She is coeditor/publisher of *Dirty Diamonds: An All-Girl Comic Anthology*, which has been archived in the Library of Congress.

Noel Franklin

is a formerly Seattle-based cartoonist currently living in Arizona. Her work has been published in many anthologies including *Outré* (Norway), *Skulptura* (Serbia), *Strumpet* (U.K.), and *Rock Is Not Dead* (Canada). Noel is the recipient of grants from the Seattle Arts Commission, 4Culture, and Artist Trust, and is working on her first graphic novel *Girl on the Road*. Learn more at noelfranklinart.com.

Katie Fricas

is a cartoonist in New York City. Her nonfiction essay comics have appeared in the *Guardian*, *Illustrated PEN*, and the *New Yorker*. She is the creator of *Checked Out*, a comic about working at NYC's oldest library, that runs regularly on Medium.com/Spiralbound.

Siobhán Gallagher

is a Canadian illustrator and book designer living in New York City. Her illustrations have been featured in publications such as the *New York Times*, Penguin Classics, *Elle* Canada, and *US Weekly*. She self-publishes multiple zines per year, draws every day, and is the author of *In a Daze Work: A Pick-Your-Path Journey Through the Daily Grind* (TarcherPerigee, 2017).

Joamette Gil

is a (gender)queer Afro-Cuban cartoonist who makes comics about race, disability, magic, and queers of color. She's also the one-man operation known as Power & Magic Press, publisher of such titles as *Power & Magic: The Queer Witch Comics Anthology* and *Heartwood: Non-binary Tales of Sylvan Fantasy*.

J. Gonzalez-Blitz

is a multi-disciplined artist who does comics, drawing, painting, music, and is studying butoh dance. She lives in New York City with her husband and sometime collaborator, the percussionist Eric Blitz. More at jennydevildoll. wordpress.com.

Georgiana Goodwin

was born in New York City in 1958 and has always drawn, although she makes her living as a graphic designer. Her favorite kind of work has been book jacket design because it is a way to express emotions quickly through an image, which is what drawing is to her. Visit georgianagoodwin.com for more.

Roberta Gregory

has been making comics since forever. Her first stories appeared in *Wimmen's Comix* and *Tits & Clits* in the 1970s, as did her self-published comic book, *Dynamite Damsels*. She is best known for her Bitchy Bitch character in the forty-issue series *Naughty Bits*. Her later books include *Follow Your Art* and *True Cat Toons*, and she's still keeping busy.

Marian Henley

is a cartoonist and author of the graphic novel *Maxine* and the graphic memoir *The Shiniest Jewel*, which *Publishers Weekly* described as "a near-perfect book" ("near" being better than "far from"). She lives in Austin, Texas.

Soizick Jaffre

is a teacher and comics artist based in France. She has published fiction, poetry comics, and autobiographical stories in various independent comic strip publications in Europe and North America. Her typical style combines strong colors and surrealistic details. She can be found on social networking sites. Her website is soizickjaffrecomics.com.

Avy Jetter

writes, draws, and self-publishes the comic book *Nuthin' Good Ever Happens at 4 a.m.* and is an avid horror and gore movie fan. She currently lives and works in Oakland, California, and spends her time organizing community events and zine fests. You may also find her in a local café debating the merits of the latest B horror flick or sci-fi action thriller with friends.

Sabba Khan

is an architectural designer and graphic novelist. She lives and works in London. She is currently working on a full-length graphic novel that explores identity, memory, and belonging through her lived experience as a second-generation Pakistani Muslim immigrant. It is set to be published in 2021 by Myriad Editions.

Kendra Josie Kirkpatrick

enjoys large amounts of black on both her comics pages as well as her clothes, and has a passion for music that features people screaming. BFA Cartooning, SVA, 2016.

Aline Kominsky-Crumb

is an underground comics artist who began her career in 1971 with *Wimmen's Comix*. Her work includes *Love That Bunch* (Drawn & Quarterly, 2018), and *Drawn Together* (W. W. Norton, 2012), a collaborative collection with her husband, Robert Crumb. The Crumbs live in Southern France, where Aline makes comics, paints, and teaches yoga.

Nina Laden

is a bestselling award-winning children's book author and illustrator. She graduated with a BFA in illustration from Syracuse University's College of Visual and Performing Arts a million years ago. She grew up in the New York City area, but now lives on a little island in the Pacific Northwest with her husband and cat.

Miss Lasko-Gross

is the author and illustrator of *Henni* (honored by ALA's Amelia Bloomer List and YALSA's 2016 Great Graphic Novels for Teens), *A Mess of Everything* (Fantagraphics Books), and the YALSA-nominated *Escape from "Special."* She is the creator/writer of Z2 Comics' sci-fi series *The Sweetness*. She's also contributed to the *New Yorker*'s "Daily Shouts."

Carol Lay

has created comics, short stories, and illustrations for many publications including Ahoy Comics, Bongo, *LA Weekly*, the *Wall Street Journal*, and the *New Yorker*. Her current comic strip, *Lay Lines*, can be seen on GoComics.com and carollay.com.

Miriam Libicki

is the creator of the Israeli Army memoir *jobnik!* and the book of drawn essays *Toward a Hot Jew* (recipient of the 2017 Vine Award for Canadian Jewish Literature). She lives in Vancouver and teaches illustration at Emily Carr University of Art and Design.

Dr. Sarah Lightman

is the editor of *Graphic Details: Jewish Women's Confessional Comics in Essays and Interviews* (McFarland, 2014), which was awarded an Eisner Award (2015), the Susan Koppelman Award (2015), and a Jordan Schnitzer Award (2016). She cofounded Laydeez do Comics, and her graphic novel, *The Book of Sarah* (Myriad Editions, 2019), is forthcoming.

LubaDalu

draws things that happen, some to her, some not, that she thinks need to be in pencil and ink. A feminist based in Barcelona, she shares a living room with proto-people and a rabbit. There, and anywhere, she captures with sharp lines stories about love, violence, sorority, bodies.

Ajuan Mance

is a professor of African American literature at Mills College and a lifelong artist and writer. Ajuan's work has appeared in a number of online and print publications. Her art and comics use humor and color to explore the complexities of race and gender in the United States.

MariNaomi

is the author/illustrator of four graphic memoirs and a graphic novel trilogy. Her work has been featured in *Bitch* magazine, the *Smithsonian*, at the Cartoon Art Museum, and many other publications and institutions She created the Cartoonists of Color and Queer Cartoonists databases and is cohost of the Ask Bi Grlz podcast. Visit MariNaomi.com for more.

Lee Marrs

is the first woman to work for DC Comics *and* Marvel simultaneously. She was also one of the founders of *Wimmen's Comix*. An Emmy and Inkpot Award winner and 2016 Eisner Award nominee, Lee is best known for her *Pudge, Girl Blimp* series, now a book. Her other work includes Batman, Wonder Woman, Indiana Jones, and Gay Comics. Lee is the retired multimedia arts chair of Berkeley City College.

Liz Mayorga

is a cartoonist from California. Her work combines folklore and popular culture with feminist theory. When she's not teaching or creating something new, she enjoys playing with animals and riding her bike. Liz is a DIY artist who is also proud of being a working-class Xicana.

Lena Merhej

is an award-winning visual artist from Beirut. She illustrated more than thirty Arabic children's books. She did animation films such as the award-winning *Drawing the War* (2002). She authored several acclaimed books such as *Yogurt and Jam, or How My Mother Became Lebanese* (2011) and cofounded Samandal.

Bridget Meyne

is a comics maker and illustrator based in the UK. She writes stories about life, teenage angst, and the digital age. Her work is inspired by horror stories, the supernatural, real-life magazines, romance comics, and B-movie special effects.

Carta Monir

lives in Ann Arbor, Michigan. Her work is largely focused on family, transness, trauma, and memory. Her upcoming book, *I Want to Be Evil*, will be published by Youth in Decline. You can find her work online at cartamonir.com, and if you feel inclined to send her money you can do that at PayPal. me/cartamonir.

Hila Noam

is an Israeli comic book artist and illustrator based in Tel Aviv. Her work has been published in magazines, anthologies, and children's books worldwide and has been displayed in solo and group exhibitions around the globe. Hila is a lecturer at the Bezalel Academy of Arts and Design in Jerusalem.

Breena Nuñez

is an Afro-Salvadoran/
Guatemalan cartoonist and
zinester from the Bay Area of
Northern California. She creates
a series of semi-humorous
autobiographical comics
that explore her complicated
experiences as an awkward
Central American from the
United States.

Meg O'Shea

is an Ignatz Award–nominated
maker of pictures, pictures
arranged into narratives, and
occasionally pictures that move.
She lives in Sydney, Australia.

Corinne Pearlman

has been a freelance designer and
cartoonist for many years, editing
and contributing to anthologies
and commissioning a list of
highly acclaimed graphic novels
for Myriad Editions in the UK.
She cofounded Comic Company,
specializing in comics for health
information, and created a
regular comic strip for the *Jewish
Quarterly*.

Cathrin Peterslund

(born in 1991) is a Danish
cartoonist and illustrator based
in Copenhagen. In 2017 she
graduated with a BA in graphic
storytelling from the Animation
Workshop and is now working
as a freelance artist. Visit
cathrinpeterslund.com for more.

Minnie Phan

is an illustrator and cartoonist
living in Oakland, California. She
focuses on themes of cultural
heritage, diversity, personal
stories, and the invisible things
that shape who we are. Clients
include NPR, Live Nation,
Starbucks, and *Colorlines*.
See more of her work at
minniephan.com.

Kelly Phillips

is a cartoonist living in
Philadelphia. She's the creator of
Weird Me about her teenage years
as the moderately successful
webmaster of a "Weird Al"
Yankovic fan site, and she is the
coeditor and publisher of the
award-winning all-girl comic
anthology *Dirty Diamonds*.
Comics interests include: cats,
space, real life.

Powerpaola

is the daughter of a psychic and an ex-priest. She draws, paints, and writes. She splits her time between Bogotá and Buenos Aires.

Sarah Allen Reed

is the author of the underground comix series *Tabula Rosetta* and the face of the mysterious organization known as Blackwork. You can read a good deal of the series she's most known for at tabularosetta.com, purchase her books via blackwork.org, or find her on Instagram @sketchreed.

Kaylee Rowena

is a Brooklyn-based cartoonist and illustrator. When she isn't drawing comics about ghosts and LGBT history, she can be found playing Dungeons & Dragons or hanging out with her cats. Find her on the web at kayleerowena.com or @ kayleerowena on social media.

Ariel Schrag

is the author of the graphic memoirs *Part of It*, *Likewise*, *Potential*, *Definition*, and *Awkward*, and the novel *Adam*. She has written for television series on HBO and Showtime. She lives in Brooklyn, New York.

M. Louise Stanley

makes paintings that juxtapose myth and allegory in order to poke fun at contemporary politics and mores with a deadly serious brush. Stanley teaches painting and drawing at Berkeley City College and resides in Emeryville, California. She is a recent recipient of both the Pollock-Krasner Foundation and John Simon Guggenheim Fellowships.

Maria Stoian

is a Romanian Canadian illustrator based in Scotland. Her first graphic novel, *Take It as a Compliment*, is a collection of real-life stories of sexual violence. She likes to make zines and is probably checking the news right now.

Dr. Nicola Streeten

(born 1963) is an anthropologist-turned-illustrator and author of the award-winning graphic memoir *Billy, Me & You* (Myriad Editions, 2011). She was coeditor of *The Inking Woman* (Myriad Editions, 2018), a picture-led history of 250 years of women's cartoons in Britain. She cofounded the forum Laydeez do Comics in 2009. Visit streetenillustration.com and laydeezdocomics for more.

Marcela Trujillo

(b. 1969) is a cartoonist and painter from Chile. She studied art at the University of Chile, as well as the Art Students League of New York and the School of Visual Arts in New York City, where she lived for seven years. Trujillo has published six autobiographical comic books and her work has been mounted at several art shows. She teaches graphic narrative and has two daughters.

Carol Tyler

is the writer/artist of *Fab4 Mania* (2018); *Soldier's Heart* (2015); *Late Bloomer* (2005); and *The Job Thing* (1993). She has been featured in numerous anthologies and has received eleven Eisner nominations. She was named a Master Cartoonist at the 2016 Cartoon Crossroads Festival and has won the SOI Gold Medal and the OAC Excellence Award.

Una

is the author of *Becoming/Unbecoming* (2015), a graphic novel that has been widely translated and was featured on BBC Radio 4's *Woman's Hour* and Oprah.com, as well as in *Elle*, the *New York Times*, and *Newsweek*. She is also the author of *On Sanity: One Day in Two Lives* (2016) and *Cree* (2018). Una is currently working on a graphic novel for Virago titled *Eve*.

Lenora Yerkes

is an artist and writer based in Washington, DC. She is interested in scotch, coffee, natural bodies of water, disasters, and drawing every day, and is currently at work on a long-form visual narrative about the Sacramento–San Joaquin Delta in California's Central Valley.

Ilana Zeffren

is an Israeli comics artist from Tel Aviv. She has published two graphic novels (*Pink Story* and *Rishumon*), as well as comics and stories in newspapers and literature anthologies, and has illustrated three children's books. For the past several years, her cartoon "Petting Corner," starring her cats, has been published weekly in *Haaretz* magazine.